TERRORISTS, ANARCHISTS, AND REPUBLICANS

Terrorists, Anarchists, and Republicans

THE GENEVANS AND THE IRISH IN TIME OF REVOLUTION

Richard Whatmore

PRINCETON UNIVERSITY PRESS
PRINCETON & OXFORD

Published by Princeton University Press
41 William Street, Princeton, New Jersey 08540
6 Oxford Street, Woodstock, Oxfordshire OX20 1TR

press.princeton.edu

Library of Congress Control Number 2019938815
First paperback printing, 2021
Paper ISBN 978-0-691-20664-6
Cloth ISBN 978-0-691-16877-7

British Library Cataloging-in-Publication Data is available

Editorial: Ben Tate and Charlie Allen
Production Editorial: Jill Harris
Jacket/Cover Design: Carmina Alvarez
Production: Merli Guerra
Publicity: Alyssa Sanford and Katie Lewis

Jacket/Cover art: "Geography Bewitched! or, A Droll Caricature Map of Ireland." Published by Bowles & Carver, London, 1797. 1950,0808.4 © The Trustees of the British Museum

This book has been composed in Miller

For Donald Winch (1935–2017)

[S]i Dieu n'est pas moins admirable dans les petits ouvrages de la nature, que dans les grands, où la matiere suit ses mains, il ne l'est pas aussi moins dans la conduite des petits Etats, que dans celle des grands Royaumes: de mesme qu'un Pilote ne fait pas moins paroître son adresse à resister avec une petite Barque aux flots d'une mer agitée par la tempête, qu'à preserver du naufrage un grand Vaisseau contre qui les vagues ne sont souvent que des efforts inutiles.

—JACOB SPON, *HISTOIRE DE LA VILLE ET DE L'ESTAT DE GENÈVE* (LYON: THOMAS AMAULRY, 1780), 2 VOLS, I, 2 (ORIGINAL PUNCTUATION)

CONTENTS

ILLUSTRATIONS

PREFACE

THIS BOOK IS about two divided societies, Geneva and Ireland, whose political antagonisms resulted in civil war, and whose histories became intertwined for a short period of time at the end of the eighteenth century, at a place called New Geneva near Waterford. A remarkable experiment took place in moving republicans from a city state in mainland Europe into the kingdom of Ireland. Ireland was sometimes described as an English colony, having seen the establishment of Protestant plantations, both Anglican and Presbyterian, on land confiscated from the Irish inhabitants in the sixteenth and seventeenth centuries. Ireland had its own parliament, but the major population group of Catholics, and the substantial body of Presbyterians in Ulster, were excluded from political life and enjoyed limited civil liberties. Many people within Ireland and across Britain felt that Ireland was ready for rapid economic development, being endowed with splendid harbours, fertile soil, cheap labour and adequate transport networks. By contrast, Geneva was a republic suffering an acute political crisis. Popular rebellion in April 1782 was crushed by foreign invasion at the end of June 1782. This resulted in the total domination of the republic by France, the neighbouring superpower, and the allies who had contributed troops to the invading force, Savoy and Bern. The victors in the short-lived civil war within the city, the rich Genevan magistrates and bankers who resumed their offices after the revolution, paid lip-service to national independence and sovereignty. Both had in fact been lost to France. References to Geneva as a free and sovereign republic became altogether fake. This was why so many Genevans fled, in the hope of finding liberty in another country. The rebels took the difficult step of abandoning their homeland only because they could see no way of countering French dominion. Liberty had been lost. At Geneva, it could not be recovered. Asylum was sought in the hope both of enjoying liberty anew, and of taking the industrious and liberty-loving citizens away from an old and degraded place. For some optimists among the Genevan exiles, the asylum might itself be transformed into a utopia. New Geneva at Waterford was for a time described as the first step in the process of creating a better world.

The perception that Ireland was ripe for peaceful improvement was altogether mistaken. As at Geneva, popular rebellion culminated in the armed insurrection of 1798, which was brutally put down by British troops and the

Irish militia. New Geneva, the key to the Waterford experiment, played a significant role in the story of the attempt to turn Ireland into a republic in 1798. For the British, victorious through the might of their arms, the solution to the problem of further Irish unrest, against a background of international war against revolutionary France, was to incorporate Ireland within the greater union of Britain.[1] The union between Britain and Ireland was itself accompanied by anticipations of economic transformation, especially in Ireland, amounting to an additional utopian moment following that of New Geneva. The price of union, the loss of political liberty in the form of an independent Irish parliament, was deemed to be worthwhile in consequence. The promise was that through union Ireland would follow what was held up as the successful story of Scotland since 1707. Such a verdict was contested, with critics asserting that Scotland remained divided and poor.

Significantly for Irish parliamentarians, a positive image of Scotland was projected in a revealing print made by the Scots caricaturist Isaac Cruikshank, 'A Flight Across the Herring Pool', dated 20 June 1800. The print showed prime minister William Pitt and his friend the war secretary Henry Dundas, 1st Viscount Melville, encouraging Irish members of parliament to leave the rotunda building across the Irish Channel, and enter the 'imperial pouch', promising places and honours, signified by ribbons and stars. Pitt, opening the pouch, says, 'Come on my little Fellows—theres [*sic*] plenty of room for you all—the Budget is not half full'. Dundas himself represents the likely future of Ireland's legislators, saying, 'If you've ony [any] Conscience at a[ll], heres [*sic*] enugh [*sic*] to satisfy ye a[ll]'. Dundas is corpulent, well dressed and ruddy-faced, sitting on a large package which lists his own offices, ranging from 'Elder Brother of the Trinity House' (the naval charity), 'A Secretary [of State for War]', 'Govr [*sic*] of the Bank in Scotland', 'A Commissioner for India affair [*sic*]', 'A Commissioner of Chelsea Hospital', 'A Governor of Greenwich Hospl', 'Treasurer of the Navy', 'Custos Rotulorum for Middlesex', 'Patent Printer of the Bible in Scotland.', 'Chancellor of the University St Andrew's [*sic*]' and 'Joint Keeper of the Signet in Scotland', to 'Govr [*sic*] of the Charter House'. The Irish parliamentarians could expect to become rich and prominent; the darker message was that the Irish people would be less fortunate. In Cruikshank's image the people are represented by two men, one in rags, who kneel alongside a woman with open arms, beside a dog and naked child, begging the flying men, '[D]o not leave us'. They would be abandoning 'your Old House', which 'will look like a big Walnut shell—without a Kernel'.

FIGURE 0.1. Isaac Cruikshank, 'A Flight Across the Herring Pool', 20 June 1800. British Museum Collection, no. 1868,0808.6899. Copyright © The Trustees of the British Museum

Ireland did not follow the Scottish example and enjoy an economic boom. Part of the reason was the association between Britishness and Protestantism, and the resulting refusal of George III to grant Catholic emancipation at the time of the Union.[2] Ireland remained a country apart, something exemplified by the Great Hunger of 1845 to 1849. The Irish Question continued to bedevil British politics.[3] In the 1790s the Irish rebels and republicans believed they might well be able to go their own way, and create an alternative and happier future. By reconstructing the history of the Waterford experiment, this book seeks to explain why for a time they had confidence, and why their dreams were ultimately shattered.

II

In the case of Geneva and of Ireland, larger and more powerful states, France and Britain, intervened in the affairs of smaller and weaker countries. In both instances, they justified their actions on the grounds that they were putting an end to the anarchy and terrorism of dreadful rebels who, if they succeeded, would destroy society and government. In Geneva and in Ireland, many of the rebels called themselves republicans. As republicans they were opposed to monarchy and heirs to a tradition of small-state independence, often deemed to rest upon ancient notions of virtue, and a willingness to sacrifice the self to the public good.[4] Republicans tended to be as critical of democracy, in the sense of the direct rule of the people, as were the advocates of monarchy.[5] In the 1780s and 1790s, however, republicans in Geneva and in Ireland often called themselves democrats, meaning that they saw the people as a sovereign body distinct from the government, and necessary as an agent in the formulation of law, either directly or through representatives.[6] Democrats in Geneva and in Ireland continued to argue that democracy could only work in conditions of adherence to a severe moral code; democracy was a form of government primarily for men of property, and had at all costs to be distinguished from licence. In addition to calling themselves republicans and democrats, the rebels in Geneva and in Ireland perceived themselves to be willing martyrs to liberty and rights; some of them had visions of a cosmopolitan future characterised by civil and political liberty. In the Irish case alone, certain rebels articulated a future for humanity across the globe living in societies without ranks, without war and sometimes without property.

The crushing of the revolutionary forces in Geneva and in Ireland marked the collapse of an old Europe characterised by diverse political forms and cultures. Corsica and Poland had already failed to maintain their status, and the Dutch Republic, suffering profound internal division, was soon to be invaded by Prussia. The experience of the smaller states underlined the increasing prevalence of a process by which large states seeking empire and markets became the norm. States became more homogeneous, fractious and ideologically divided than ever before.[7] Small states in turn became endangered species, lacking the capacity to maintain themselves, especially militarily. There was an end to enlightenment, the great achievement of which had been to terminate the religious divisions that had torn the European continent apart since the Reformation. The end of enlightenment at the close of the eighteenth century saw justifications of political massacre and extremism being translated from religion into politics. Many contemporaries recognised that polarised camps were reintroducing species of enthusiasm into politics that recalled historic bloody battles between Protestants and Catholics.[8] Images of fire were everywhere, signifying the return of violence, massacre and atrocity, with those who condemned and those who justified revolution each portraying themselves as moderates and peacemakers. Nowhere is this better illustrated than in Thomas Rowlandson's print of December 1792, 'Philosophy run mad or a stupendous monument of human wisdom', which contrasted the claims of the revolutionaries to stand for law, liberty, equality, plenty, peace, the abolition of offensive war and universal benevolence with the reality of butchery, famine, murder, impoverishment, the rule of the thugs and civil war. The revolutionaries were accused of being empire builders, themselves invading Geneva, using their avowed pacific intentions to mask the truth. At the time Rowlandson drew the print, a French army was at the gates of the city of Geneva; the entrance once more of French soldiers was expected, although it did not in fact occur until 1798, when Geneva did lose its sovereignty forever. The central image of Rowlandson's print is a hideous portly man with wild hair, who rises from a falling gilded armchair atop a pile of broken pieces of columns labelled 'Humanity', 'Social Happiness', 'Tranquiliy' [*sic*], 'Security', 'Domestic Peace', 'Laws', 'Urbanity', 'Order', and 'Religion'. The man is seen to be saying 'Ca ira', underlining his support for the Revolution. Key, however, is that he has in his hands a print entitled 'Religious Indifference'. In this image a bishop and a monk are being burned at the stake. Revolutionary enthusiasm has rekindled forms of fanaticism last seen centuries before in times of religious conflict. Political ideologies now legitimised the burning of opponents, whose death by any means is suddenly justified. In Rowlandson's view, the French Revolution amounted to a new kind of politics, in which aspirations to be free might well turn into the fostering of terror; cosmopolitanism or the love of rights could easily be transformed into nationalism and the oppression of civil liberties. Rowlandson believed that the British, in part through their constitution, had prevented the growth of enthusiasm, fanaticism and extremism. A large number of contemporaries disagreed with him, setting the scene for political antagonisms that have lasted into the present.

III

As noted at the beginning of this preface, the key moment in the story of the Genevan and Irish rebels occurred in April 1782, when the leading magistrates of the city republic of Geneva, being the majority of the members of the governing Council of Twenty-Five, were faced by critics who dominated the other councils of the state, including the sovereign General Council of all citizens and bourgeois. The critics of the governing magistrates, members of a party calling themselves the *représentants*, were convinced that the rulers of the state, rather than pursuing the good of the republic, were in thrall to France. For the most part devout Calvinists, the *représentants* asserted that the magistrates had become traitors, threatening the sovereignty of the republic, introducing luxury goods deadly to the austere mores of the people of Geneva, and selling the Protestant Rome to a Catholic power. Taking control of the city during a night of violence, the *représentants* locked up the magistrates, proclaimed an era of reform and renewal within the city and, to popular acclamation, began to redraw the constitution of the state.

Many of the *représentants*, describing themselves as democrats, worked through clubs of citizens meeting to discuss the affairs of the city each night; they perceived themselves to be proud inheritors of traditions of republican argument seeking to make states both popular and free. Some *représentants* believed themselves to be following the philosopher Jean-Jacques Rousseau, the great Genevan rebel who had renounced his own citizenship in 1765, on the grounds of having been persecuted by magistrates who had taken offence at his justification of the *représentants*, the *Lettres écrites de la montagne* (1764). Rousseau had been damned as a heresiarch and anarchist in a concerted campaign involving magistrates from across Switzerland and philosophers across Europe, led by Rousseau's arch-enemy Voltaire. In 1782 the accusations levelled against Rousseau were directed against the *représentants*; they were called advocates of terror for locking up the magistrates, and rumours circulated that the magistrates were being tortured within the city. In initiating popular

FIGURE 0.2. Thomas Rowlandson, 'Philosophy run mad, or a stupendous monument of human wisdom', December 1792. British Museum Collection, no. 1851,0901.626. Copyright © The Trustees of the British Museum

revolution, the *représentants* were libelled as annihilators of property and exterminators of government. France, under the leadership of the foreign minister Charles Gravier, comte de Vergennes, who was concerned about the possible effects of a popular republic on his borders, gathered together an invasion force. This included substantial detachments from Savoy and, significantly, the powerful Swiss canton of Bern, traditionally the protector of Geneva's independence.

Arriving at the gates of the city on 29 June, the invaders set up cannon and prepared to bombard Geneva and restore what they declared to be the legitimate government of the state. The *représentants*, having worked with the people of the republic, including women and children, to repair the city walls, prepared for republican martyrdom. They knew that the mortars and cannon employed on elevated ground outside the city walls would spark fire in the wooden buildings of the city. The defenders were equally aware that however great their valour and patriotic zeal, they had no chance against the twelve thousand professional soldiers at their gates. Accordingly, they filled the great icon of Calvinist Geneva, the Saint-Pierre Cathedral, in addition to several of the houses of their enemies the magistrates, with mounds of gunpowder. The anticipated conflagration would bring fire and death, but was expected to be a warning to the world of the danger of treachery against republicans, of the effects of luxury upon republics and of the danger accompanying an over-powerful and militant Catholic France.

In the early hours of the morning prior to the attack, the leaders of the *représentants* decided that their cause was not worth the destruction of the city they loved. Many of them fled, setting themselves up initially in the adjacent principality of Neuchâtel, then governed from Prussia. During the period of their rule at Geneva, between April and the end of June, the *représentants* had sought to take advantage of long-established connections between their party at Geneva and foreign powers. The *représentants* in particular aspired to take advantage of Protestant antagonism towards Catholicism, and more especially Europe-wide concerns about the overweening power of France. Such links did not lead to the *représentants* receiving direct aid from abroad, or even much indirect or verbal support from foreign politicians. After they abandoned Geneva, however, many states were interested in attracting the *représentants* to their lands, because they were seen to be part of the most industrious part of Geneva, responsible for much of the domestic trade of the city, and especially watch-making. Observers were well aware of the effects from the mid-1680s of the French expulsion of the Huguenots on the economies of the states where

FIGURE 0.2. Thomas Rowlandson, 'Philosophy run mad, or a stupendous monument of human wisdom', December 1792. British Museum Collection, no. 1851,0901.626. Copyright © The Trustees of the British Museum

revolution, the *représentants* were libelled as annihilators of property and exterminators of government. France, under the leadership of the foreign minister Charles Gravier, comte de Vergennes, who was concerned about the possible effects of a popular republic on his borders, gathered together an invasion force. This included substantial detachments from Savoy and, significantly, the powerful Swiss canton of Bern, traditionally the protector of Geneva's independence.

Arriving at the gates of the city on 29 June, the invaders set up cannon and prepared to bombard Geneva and restore what they declared to be the legitimate government of the state. The *représentants*, having worked with the people of the republic, including women and children, to repair the city walls, prepared for republican martyrdom. They knew that the mortars and cannon employed on elevated ground outside the city walls would spark fire in the wooden buildings of the city. The defenders were equally aware that however great their valour and patriotic zeal, they had no chance against the twelve thousand professional soldiers at their gates. Accordingly, they filled the great icon of Calvinist Geneva, the Saint-Pierre Cathedral, in addition to several of the houses of their enemies the magistrates, with mounds of gunpowder. The anticipated conflagration would bring fire and death, but was expected to be a warning to the world of the danger of treachery against republicans, of the effects of luxury upon republics and of the danger accompanying an over-powerful and militant Catholic France.

In the early hours of the morning prior to the attack, the leaders of the *représentants* decided that their cause was not worth the destruction of the city they loved. Many of them fled, setting themselves up initially in the adjacent principality of Neuchâtel, then governed from Prussia. During the period of their rule at Geneva, between April and the end of June, the *représentants* had sought to take advantage of long-established connections between their party at Geneva and foreign powers. The *représentants* in particular aspired to take advantage of Protestant antagonism towards Catholicism, and more especially Europe-wide concerns about the overweening power of France. Such links did not lead to the *représentants* receiving direct aid from abroad, or even much indirect or verbal support from foreign politicians. After they abandoned Geneva, however, many states were interested in attracting the *représentants* to their lands, because they were seen to be part of the most industrious part of Geneva, responsible for much of the domestic trade of the city, and especially watchmaking. Observers were well aware of the effects from the mid-1680s of the French expulsion of the Huguenots on the economies of the states where

FIGURE 0.2. Thomas Rowlandson, 'Philosophy run mad, or a stupendous monument of human wisdom', December 1792. British Museum Collection, no. 1851,0901.626. Copyright © The Trustees of the British Museum

revolution, the *représentants* were libelled as annihilators of property and exterminators of government. France, under the leadership of the foreign minister Charles Gravier, comte de Vergennes, who was concerned about the possible effects of a popular republic on his borders, gathered together an invasion force. This included substantial detachments from Savoy and, significantly, the powerful Swiss canton of Bern, traditionally the protector of Geneva's independence.

Arriving at the gates of the city on 29 June, the invaders set up cannon and prepared to bombard Geneva and restore what they declared to be the legitimate government of the state. The *représentants*, having worked with the people of the republic, including women and children, to repair the city walls, prepared for republican martyrdom. They knew that the mortars and cannon employed on elevated ground outside the city walls would spark fire in the wooden buildings of the city. The defenders were equally aware that however great their valour and patriotic zeal, they had no chance against the twelve thousand professional soldiers at their gates. Accordingly, they filled the great icon of Calvinist Geneva, the Saint-Pierre Cathedral, in addition to several of the houses of their enemies the magistrates, with mounds of gunpowder. The anticipated conflagration would bring fire and death, but was expected to be a warning to the world of the danger of treachery against republicans, of the effects of luxury upon republics and of the danger accompanying an over-powerful and militant Catholic France.

In the early hours of the morning prior to the attack, the leaders of the *représentants* decided that their cause was not worth the destruction of the city they loved. Many of them fled, setting themselves up initially in the adjacent principality of Neuchâtel, then governed from Prussia. During the period of their rule at Geneva, between April and the end of June, the *représentants* had sought to take advantage of long-established connections between their party at Geneva and foreign powers. The *représentants* in particular aspired to take advantage of Protestant antagonism towards Catholicism, and more especially Europe-wide concerns about the overweening power of France. Such links did not lead to the *représentants* receiving direct aid from abroad, or even much indirect or verbal support from foreign politicians. After they abandoned Geneva, however, many states were interested in attracting the *représentants* to their lands, because they were seen to be part of the most industrious part of Geneva, responsible for much of the domestic trade of the city, and especially watchmaking. Observers were well aware of the effects from the mid-1680s of the French expulsion of the Huguenots on the economies of the states where they ultimately established communities. Possible Genevan exodus was anticipated as having similar consequences, and potentially as having the capacity to facilitate the growth of commerce in states which held themselves to be backward or in need of action to catch up in the race for wealth generated by trade. As a result, despite their association with democracy, terror and anarchy, the *représentants* received numerous offers of support; the question was whether they could organise the mass abandonment of the old city, now under French control, where the leaders of the *représentants* were outlawed, and where dissent was forbidden.

IV

The unexpected outcome of the negotiations entered into by the *représentants* was that they chose Waterford in Ireland to create a New Geneva. Their decision was contested, but they believed that they would be safe in a country that was protected by the armed might of the greatest enemy of France. They were also optimistic about prospects of Irish economic development, just as they thought Britain was likely to decline as a military and economic power. This book tells the remarkable story of the decision by republicans to abandon their republic and seek liberty in a country they believed to be a free monarchy. The Genevan republicans were attacked as democrats, anarchists and terrorists. While many of their number were happy to accept the first description, they held that claims that they were anarchists and terrorists made no sense, because they were the persecuted and the oppressed, rather than themselves being a threat to property, government and society. The *représentants* found themselves, on reaching Ireland, in a country drawing anew upon established traditions of rebellion. Rebellion in Ireland was demanded to combat the oppression of the Catholic majority, to end the dominion of rich Protestant landowners and to end the governance of the Irish economy for the benefit not of Ireland itself but of the England-dominated mainland. Some Irish patriots, as noted above, planned to make Ireland into a republic, following the model of the French after 1789. Where the Genevans had turned away from France in the hope of maintaining republican values, the Irish turned towards that state, once more at war with Britain from 1 February 1793. Irish republicans were also attacked as democratic demagogues, masters of an unruly mob which was ignorant, brutal and cruel. They were persecuted by soldiers and spies, sought aid from France and were accused of being anarchists and terrorists, just as the Genevan republicans had been before them. New Geneva had by this time failed as a community of republican exiles. It was turned into a barracks, and then became a prison for Irish republicans. Many of them died there after the failure of the attempted republican revolution in Ireland in 1798. Accordingly, this book relates the history of the Genevan republicans in Ireland, and of the fate of Irish republicans at New Geneva. The ease with which critics of government were branded anarchists and terrorists is worthy of note. Controversies about politics, religion and the economy began to divide eighteenth-century societies, and led to violence both domestically and internationally. Political languages formed in their world continue to define our own. Imagined communities as fantastic as those conceived of by the Genevans and the Irish still have a powerful impact upon political argument.

One of the claims of the book is that we can only understand what happened at New Geneva if we understand both the history of Geneva, and especially its relationship with France, and the history of Ireland, and especially its relationship with Britain. Two introductory chapters outline the story of the prison of New Geneva in Ireland, and why the Genevan republicans ended up trying to create a new community at Waterford. The histories of small states or communities, and their relationships with larger powers, tend to be complicated, and the first two chapters have been designed to help the reader navigate what comes after. The story of rebellion in Geneva and in Ireland involved a great many individuals, drawing in those who are well remembered historically and those who left the smallest of footprints. In order to do justice to the story overall, there is some moving backwards and forwards chronologically. This may cause dismay to particular readers used to straightforward narratives, but it is intentional in this instance because of the diversity of the cast, because of the cultural and physical distance between Geneva and Ireland, and because it was felt to be the only way of conveying the fullest possible sense of what happened at the end of the eighteenth century and why. Accordingly, the book turns after the initial introductory chapters to the history of Geneva. This is in order to explain the nature of the rebellion of 1782 and its tragic outcome. Furthermore, it explains the decision of the leaders of the rebellion to abandon their home and to reaffirm their republican values in another place. It equally reveals the complicated set of factors that led the Genevans to choose Waterford in Ireland as the location of New Geneva. The book then considers Ireland itself, providing in the seventh chapter a brief history of the country and its situation in 1782, to show what the Genevans found when they arrived. A chapter also explains the role of William Petty, then known as Lord Shelburne, and amongst the least known of prime ministers in British history. Without Shelburne's action to support and to fund the project, New Geneva would never have been initiated; without his putting an end to the war in North America, a full-scale Irish rebellion might well have occurred much sooner than 1798. The final part of the book deals with the failure of New Geneva as a republican community, and its transformation into a prison for republicans. Some readers will find the extensive citation from primary sources disturbing of the narrative. A decision has been taken to include these, because so few are familiar, and because so many of them are significant in explaining what happened during these years of turbulence and revolution. Readers who want to move past the documentation can be assured that the message and the story are also conveyed in the main text. The broader claim is that those involved with New Geneva experienced an end of enlightenment, presaging the incorporation of the old republic of Geneva, and the old colony of Ireland, into larger political units, in a Europe altogether transformed.

ACKNOWLEDGEMENTS

THIS BOOK IS dedicated to Donald Winch, who appointed me to a lectureship in intellectual history at the University of Sussex in 1993, and then acted as mentor and friend for the following twenty-four years. This is the first book of mine over which his critical eye has not passed; I miss him greatly. Others whom I relied upon have died since my last book appeared, including Istvan Hont, Nicholas Phillipson and my close friend at St Andrews, Nick Rengger. I'm happy to have been involved, or to be involved, either with the publication of books in their honour, or with the acquisition of their papers for St Andrews Special Collections and the Institute of Intellectual History.

A large number of people have helped me to complete this work. Special thanks go, as they always do, to Knud Haakonssen, Béla Kapossy and Michael Sonenscher. I'm grateful for the advice and comments of Richard Bourke, James Harris, John Pocock, Martyn Powell, Gabriel Sabbagh, Louise Seaward, Quentin Skinner, Max Skjönsberg, James Stafford, Koen Stapelbroek, Lina Weber and Amy Westwell, all of whom read some or all of the book in draft form. Martyn Powell was singularly generous in guiding me towards sources I was unaware of, in helping me to get the facts right about Ireland and in sharing his own work. Large thanks go too to all of the people who, through conversation or through their own work, have helped me in formulating the arguments to be found herein, whether they were aware of this or not, including Thomas Ahrnert, Manuela Albertone, Ali Ansari, David Armitage, Toby Barnard, Cyprian Blamires, Annabel Brett, Clarissa Campbell Orr, Dario Castiglione, Emmanuelle de Champs, Greg Claeys, J.C.D. Clark, David Coates, Stefan Collini, Aurelian Craiutu, Cesare Cuttica, Michael Drolet, John Dunn, Colin Kidd, Cailean Gallagher, Graham Gargett, Jamie Gianoutsos, Mark Goldie, Peter Ghosh, Rachel Hammersley, Emma Hart, Boyd Hilton, Tim Hochstrasser, Julian Hoppit, Anthony Howe, Ian Hunter, Joanna Innes, Maurizio Isabella, Sue James, Jeremy Jennings, Tom Jones, Duncan Kelley, Minchul Kim, Linda Kirk, Paschalis Kitromilides, Laszlo Kontler, Jim Livesey, Avi Lifschitz, Luke Long, Rosario Lopez, John Marshall, Christian Maurer, Ian McBride, Iain McDaniel, Jim Moore, Paul Moorhouse, Martin Mulsow, Isaac Nakhimovsky, Eric Nelson, William O'Reilly, Mark Philp, Maria-Cristina Pitassi, Anna Plassart, Peter Price, Janet Polasky, Maxine Pollock, Michel Porret,

Jennifer Powell-McNutt, François Quastana, Isabel Rivers, Jean-Marc Rivier, Emma Rothschild, John Robertson, Helena Rosenblatt, Philip Schofield, Hamish Scott, Ruth Scurr, Michael Seidler, Gabriella Silvestrini, Céline Spector, Gareth Stedman Jones, Philippe Steiner, Christopher Storrs, Ann Thomson, Edoardo Tortarollo, Keith Tribe, Richard Tuck, Kate Tunstall, Georgios Varouxakis, Katia Visconti, Ryan Walter, Paul Wood, Blair Worden, Brian Young and Simone Zurbuchen.

I would also like to thank colleagues and friends involved with the St Andrews Institute of Intellectual History, in addition to those mentioned above, and at St Andrews and beyond more generally, including David Allan, Lasse Andersen, Frances Andrews, Clémentine Ann, Damiano Bardelli, Riccardo Bavaj, John Clark, Sarah Easterby-Smith, Aileen Fyfe, Cailean Gallagher, Giovanni Gellera, Ken Goodwin, Kris Grint, Lorna Harris, Anna Hont, John Hudson, Caroline Humfress, Bill Jenkins, Elsie Johnstone, Lucy Kidd, Tony Lang, Felicity Loughlin, Donald MacEwan, Roger Mason, Steve Murdoch, Paul Myles, Synne Myreboe, Frances Nethercott, Jesse Norman, Lucy Ragosy, Nayeli Riano, Katrin Redfern, Louise Richardson, Jacqueline Rose, Katie Stephenson, Bernhard Struck, Garry Taylor, Mara van der Lugt, Emma Veitch, Sam Walton and Dolly Winch.

Librarians at the British Library, British Museum, National Archives, National Library of Ireland, Bibliothèque nationale de France, Bibliothèque de Genève, Public Record Office of Northern Ireland and St Andrews Special Collections and University Library all deserve thanks for ceaseless bibliographic services. Staff at the Bibliothèque de Genève were extremely generous in allowing me to use images derived from their collections. I would also like to thank Ben Tate, who has been a wonderful editor, Francis Eaves, who did a masterful job at the copy-editing stage, Jill Harris, Charlie Allen and the staff of Princeton University Press, for seeing the book through the production process, and two anonymous referees for useful comments on the original manuscript. I would also like to thank The Leverhulme Trust, the Institute of Intellectual History and the University of St Andrews for financial support. Without my wife Ruth Woodfield, and our sons Jess, Kim and Davy Whatmore, I would not be able to write anything, and as always the greatest debt goes to them.

NOTE ON THE TEXT

MUCH OF THE contents of this book has been derived from English and French manuscript sources, and especially epistolary exchanges. In the case of transcriptions from the French, I have provided my own translation rather than the original in order to help contemporary readers. When a somewhat free translation has been employed, in the hope of better conveying the contemporary meaning of a text, the French original has been included. I would like to acknowledge, along with all scholars of this period, reliance upon Ralph Leigh's magisterial edition of Rousseau's correspondence. When transcribing from manuscripts and in citing contemporary books, I have expanded contractions and modernised spelling and occasionally punctuation, except in cases where this made the original meaning unclear. Some sections of chapter 3 are derived from the article 'Geneva and Scotland: The Calvinist Legacy and After', *Intellectual History Review*, 26/3 (2016), 391–410. A brief overview of the story here related can be found in 'Saving Republics by Moving Republicans. Britain, Ireland and "New Geneva" in the Age of Revolutions', *History. The Journal of the Historical Association*, 102/3 (2017), 386–413.

ABBREVIATIONS

BdG Bibliothèque de Genève

BL British Library

BN Bibliothèque Nationale de France

CC *Correspondance complète de Jean-Jacques Rousseau*, ed. R. A. Leigh et al. (Oxford: The Voltaire Foundation, 1965–1998), 52 vols

CEB *The Correspondence of Edmund Burke*, ed. Thomas W. Copeland et al. (Chicago: University of Chicago Press, 1958–78), 10 vols

DIB *Dictionary of Irish Biography from the Earliest Times to the Year 2010*, ed. James McGuire and James Quinn (Cambridge: Cambridge University Press, 2009), 11 vols

MP Member of Parliament

NA National Archives, UK

NLI National Library of Ireland

KCRO Kent County Record Office

PRONI Public Record Office of Northern Ireland

OC Jean-Jacques Rousseau, *Œuvres complètes*, ed. Bernard Gagnebin and Marcel Raymond (Paris: Gallimard, 1959–95), 5 vols

ODNB *Oxford Dictionary of National Biography*, ed. Colin Matthew, Brian Harrison et al. (Oxford: Oxford University Press, 2004)

PART I

Rebellion

PART I

Rebellion

CHAPTER ONE

The Power of Place

THE OLD AND ramshackle walls in a large field in Crook parish in the village of Passage East, on a hill beyond the city of Waterford on the southern coast of Ireland, have been overtaken by grass, broken down over the years and form part of a ruin. It is a ruin with a peculiar and largely forgotten history. When the local historian Patrick Egan walked around the site in the 1890s, he was informed by a local farmer that foreign folk had once lived there, but their attempt to establish a silk industry had failed because of the weather:

> You see, sir, these people that came here were great silk waivers [*sic*], and they expected, of course, to go on well at their trade. Myself doesn't know, but as I hears. They set a lot of mulberry trees to feed the silkworms, but sure you know they wouldn't grow, the climate was too damp, so they gave up the place and went back again to their own country.[1]

Events that are better remembered are recalled by the plaque that can be found at the site today, stating that here in 1798 republicans were martyred at 'New Geneva Barracks', a dirty and foul prison:

> NEW GENEVA BARRACKS 1798. Thousands of United Irishmen were held here under inhumane conditions, many awaiting transportation. Described by Col. Thomas Cloney, a prisoner himself, . . . as the filthiest most damp and loathsome prison devoid of any comfort . . . Remember all who died here, Liberty, Equality, Fraternity.

An earlier plaque stated, incorrectly, that the buildings dated from 1786 and correctly that New Geneva was 'associated with many dark deeds against the United Irishmen'.[2]

The Society of United Irishmen, whose original proposed name had been the Irish Brotherhood, for the promotion of 'the rights of man in Ireland', was founded in Belfast on 14 October 1791.[3] It was inspired by William Drennan, the poet and physician, who in 1784, unhappy with the lack of progress in the Volunteer movement in achieving reform, had begun to speculate about the necessity of Irish independence. In the same year Drennan had published, anonymously, the *Letters of Orellana, an Irish helot*, boldly declaring that the Irish were slaves; the national unity that was required for economic and political progress could only come by means of a union between Catholics, Anglicans and dissenters.[4] By 1791 Drennan had become a republican, and proposed that men gather together in a secret society, contracting solemnly, wearing a symbol next to the heart, and communicating with 'leading men in France, in England and in America' in the hope of cementing 'the scattered and shifting sand of republicanism into a body'. Drennan's idea was for a 'benevolent conspiracy—a plot for the people' aimed at securing in society the 'rights of men and the greatest happiness of the greatest number'. Rights and happiness could only be secured by 'real independence to Ireland' and the creation of a republic. Drennan told his friend Samuel McTier that 'such schemes' should not 'be laughed at as romantic', because 'without enthusiasm nothing great was done, or will be done'.[5] Theobald Wolfe Tone, a fellow-founder of the United Irishmen, wrote in a pamphlet of 1791 that Ireland was blessed as no other country in Europe with regard to natural resources, which were 'necessary materials for unlimited commerce'. Ireland had an 'evil government' rather than a 'national government', so that 'religious intolerance and political bigotry, like the tyrant Mezentius, bind the living Protestant to the dead and half corrupted Catholic'.[6] James Napper Tandy, acting as secretary for the Dublin branch of the Society of United Irishmen, declared on 9 November 1791 that as Ireland was in a 'state of abject slavery', a 'sincere and hearty union of all the people' must be established, seeking a 'radical reform of parliament' and 'the removal of absurd and ruinous distinctions', and 'promoting a complete coalition of the people.'[7]

William Drennan was in the chair when the Society reached out to Scottish republicans like Thomas Muir. Scotland was described as 'the land where Buchannan wrote, and Fletcher spoke, and Wallace fought', the fear being that it was in the process of being 'merged and melted down into another country' (that is, England).[8] In the London parliament, it was noted that the United Irishmen were linked to the Constitutional Society, 'which had long existed, but about this time [1792] assumed a new character', the Corresponding Society, 'which was instituted in the Spring of 1792', and The Friends of the People. These groups embraced 'all the extravagant and violent Principles of the French Revolution' and laboured with 'bigotry and enthusiasm', to propagate 'among the lower classes of the community, a spirit of hatred and contempt for the existing laws and government of the country'.[9] The rebels responded to what they perceived to be libel by themselves shaming the 'sanguinary system of terror' of the government, and the 'infernal system of terror, slavery and oppression, with all their attendant evils of poverty and famine'.[10] The United Irishmen had embraced Thomas Paine's philosophy espoused in parts one and two of his *Rights of Man* in 1791 and 1792, that the end of every political association was the establishment of the rights of man, that all men were born free and equal, and that sovereignty lay in the body of the nation.[11] Such views were fostered in the newspaper *Northern Star*, which was launched by United Irishmen in Belfast in January 1792.

Views that smacked of republicanism were branded treacherous in 1793. Theobald McKenna, the pamphleteer and campaigner for an end to penal laws against Catholics in Ireland, warned in February 1792 that 'the dangers of this age seem to impend rather from the people than the monarch'. McKenna praised the English constitution as 'highly estimable', having 'all eminent writers on its side', and asserted that 'a double experience justifies it; that of England, in which it has produced great good; that of every other form of government, none of which have ever procured permanent and radical happiness'. For McKenna, 'the oppressions of absolute monarchy [and] the convulsions of democracy, constitute alike the panegyric of the English Constitution'.[12] McKenna attempted to prove that republicanism was incompatible with commercial society, which needed inequality to promote the desire for improvement. It was a fact that all historic republics were factious, which meant that republics tended to collapse, and were incompatible with what he termed 'the social arts':

> In fact, as nations have improved in the social arts, they have declined from the forms of Republicanism, they found them incompatible with tranquility. Carthage was ruined by the factions which arose from the want of a presiding influence. Rome abandoned her liberties in despair, after the most sanguinary contests ever known in the world. Holland, which was much more adapted by its size than Ireland for a Republic, has subsided into an aristocracy, or rather into a limited monarchy. Inequality of condition is inevitable in society, and the controlled pre-eminence of one [figure in the person of the monarch] remedies

> the evils arising from this inequality. From all these reasons, from the experience of other nations, and the experience of our own, we are led to conclude in favour of a limited monarchy; but it is not alone necessary to have a king; he should be invested with power and influence sufficient to keep him so.[13]

Advocates of republicanism such as Paine had to be refuted to prevent the collapse of any state. For McKenna, 'The example of America, and the small expense of the Republican system, are the principal arguments of Mr. Paine and his adherents.' In fact, the circumstances of North America were entirely different from those to be found across Europe. As McKenna put it, there were particular reasons for the initial success of republican ideas across the Atlantic, which could never be replicated in Europe, and were likely in any case, sooner or later, to be become problematic in North America too:

> Paine, having America constantly in view, reasons uniformly wrong, for he supposes uniformly, that every other country is in the same circumstances. Six words refute him completely, *There is no mob in America.* There are yet in that country but two classes, those which correspond to the middle gentry, and to the yeomanry of England. The population of the States not affording such a number of hands, that some find it necessary to minister to the indolence of others, every man is occupied, and there is not leisure for the speculations or the contentious passions which distract Europe. Thus the casualty of the moment renders America the most easily governed country, and guarantees her from the imperfections of Republicanism. She has few sufficiently idle to pursue ambition, sufficiently rich to bribe, or poor to be corrupted. But the series of cause and effect which lead to the dissolution of the American Democracy, or at least to alter it materially, may be easily traced by any man of discernment.[14]

McKenna concluded that 'There can be very little of Republican design in Ireland', because 'the wretched speculations which involved France in calamity, can have few admirers'. The true risk was that the prerogative was weakened so as to allow republicanism, the 'inconvenient [and] boisterous form of government' to become an option in Ireland.[15] McKenna was entirely incorrect about the attractiveness of republican ideas in Ireland. Once it was accepted that the Irish were not free, and that the British were unwilling to grant further reforms that promised future liberty, especially after the Roman Catholic Relief Act of 1791 failed to emancipate

Catholics in Ireland fully, republican ideas became more attractive. To many observers, creating a republic in Ireland presented an opportunity to create a nation in a unified sense, overcoming through shared commitment to republican ideas of equality the divisions that were responsible for the political corruption and economic backwardness of the country. This was what had happened in France, where a diverse and divided nation was becoming a unified, and singularly powerful, republican *patrie*. Paine himself recognised this;[16] the links between the United Irishmen and French republicans were especially strong from 1792, with many prominent figures in the movement spending time in Paris.[17]

II

When, on December 14 1793, the United Irish Society issued an address to the volunteer companies of Ireland, calling upon them to take up arms as citizens, to force the government to undertake parliamentary reform and Catholic emancipation, a Rubicon was perceived by the authorities to have been crossed. Already dealing with widespread Catholic Defender insurrections, what became a war against the United Irishmen was commenced by government. The proprietors of the *Northern Star* and John Rabb its printer, were prosecuted for seditious libel in January 1793. On February 22 1793, an act was passed that prevented the importation or movement of arms without a licence. On April 9 in the same year a Catholic Relief Act extended the franchise to propertied Catholics and allowed them to take a university degree, while the Militia Act established a fifteen thousand-strong force, which was increased to over twenty-one thousand in 1795. On August 16 1793, the government forbade assemblies in the name of the people from preparing petitions to George III or to parliament. By this time French agents such as Eleazer Oswald and the Reverend William Jackson were active in Ireland. The popular barrister and landowner Archibald Hamilton Rowan was found guilty of distributing the seditious proclamation of the United Irish Society of December 14 1792, and on January 29 1794 he was fined the large sum of £500 and imprisoned for two years. He escaped on May 2 and fled to France. The Reverend William Jackson was arrested in Dublin and charged with high treason on April 28 1794, committing suicide in prison almost exactly a year later. William Drennan was prosecuted for seditious libel but acquitted by a jury on June 25. This was a rare victory, as on May 23 the United Irishmen were declared an illegal society, and through the informer Thomas Collins their Dublin premises at Tailors Hall were raided and all their documents seized. The Society went underground and established close links with other clandestine organisations, and especially the Defenders.[18]

Throughout 1796 a large number of United Irishmen were arrested, and others fled to North America or to France, the latter in the hope of promoting the invasion of Ireland. On March 24 1796 the Insurrection Act promised the death penalty for the taking of illegal oaths, legitimised searches for armaments and impositions of curfew and gave magistrates the authority to imprison any person found in an unlawful assembly. Thomas Russell, named as 'an United Irishman', published his *A Letter to the people of Ireland, on the present situation of the country* in September 1796, calling the Protestant landlords of Ireland agents of England and a vile aristocracy. Russell attacked the Whigs as false friends of the people for having betrayed the Irish since the failure of the volunteer movements in the early 1780s, and for failing to create a nation:

> No persons reviled the Rights of Man or the French Revolution, or gabbled more about anarchy, and confusion, and mobs, and United Irishmen, and Defenders, and Volunteers, or coincided more heartily in strengthening the hands of that government which they had opposed, and riveting the chains of the people, or to sum up all, plunged this unfortunate country into all the guilt and calamity of the present war, with more alacrity than the gentlemen of the opposition.[19]

Russell called the Irish slaves, but argued that Britain was weak, and that if the Irish followed the Dutch, Swiss and North Americans in seeking to restore their lost liberty, nothing would be able to stop them. His work was a call to arms, in the name of an envisaged country-wide coming together and union across religious divides, following the example of the French, which would see the end of aristocracy, the giving of land, called the source of all wealth, to the poor and the creation of a soon-to-be-great nation.[20] In the days following Russell's publication the offices of *Northern Star* were once again raided, on 16 September, and Russell and a number of United Irishmen or members of the Jacobin Club were accused of high treason. The Antrim farmer William Orr was also arrested in September 1796, for administering the oath of the United Irishmen, and was hanged in October the following year.

In December 1796 the Bantry Bay expedition to liberate Ireland with French troops failed, but across Ireland societies of United Irishmen continued to organise themselves. In May 1797 the presses of the *Northern Star* were destroyed by militia and further arrests were made. By March 1798, government informers were warning that Lord Edward

FitzGerald had plans for the use of pike-men and riflemen against militias. Revolution was perceived to be imminent and action was taken by the authorities to crush it. Informers such as Edward John Newell and Thomas Reynolds facilitated the removal of the leaders of the United Irishmen, with the Leinster executive taken at Oliver Bond's house in Dublin on 12 March 1798. Ireland was declared by the Privy Council to be in a state of open rebellion and martial law was proclaimed. On 19 May, FitzGerald was arrested, dying of wounds inflicted during the process on 4 June. The arrest of the brothers John Sheares and Harry Sheares followed on 26 May; they were executed on 14 July. Unrest commenced in Meath, Leinster and Wexford at the end of the May. Despite ad hoc victories of the insurrectionists, government and loyalist forces triumphed, and more leaders were hanged, including Henry Joy McCracken and Henry Munro in the north, and Beauchamp Bagenal Harvey and John Hay in the south. Tone, captured on a French frigate, committed suicide in prison.

The great hope of the United Irishmen had been armed support from the First French Republic. The secret committee of war secretary Henry Dundas that amassed documentation concerning rebellion in the 1790s made the point that the French invading forces anticipated aid from the domestic population, and especially members of the 'militia' and 'Irish sailors', in addition to the 'people and the rabble of the country'. Such individuals were not to be incorporated into French formations, but were rather to be formed into new corps of troops under French officers, so that 'no native of the country may become acquainted with the state of our force'. Such views were propagated by General Jean-Joseph-Amable Humbert, the commander of the invading forces that landed at Killala on 23 August 1798. Humbert was instructed to inform the Irish that the French were going to grant them liberty and break their chains:

> Bear in mind that all Europe, the eyes of which are now upon you, will judge whether you deserve that your chains should be broken. Nothing is more easy, if you engage in it with determined courage. Rise at once in a mass at every point of your Island. My brave brethren in arms and myself, will be the centre for you to rally round. A force so considerable ensures to you, without striking a Blow, a speedy and complete victory; and in the same manner as the vivifying rays of the sun purify the earth from pestilential vapours, and destroy the insects which they nourished, so from the ardour of your patriotism shall issue that splendour which will banish tyranny, and annihilate its satellites amidst the

> unanimous shouts of the Irish and the French, exclaiming Liberty and Equality for ever![21]

Humbert had only a thousand men, as although he had successfully sailed from Rochefort, a larger force from Brest had delayed its departure. Confident that a greater force was on its way, he was told to declare to the soldiers of Ireland that they ought to join the French to vanquish tyrants, and that they would soon be governed by laws made by their own representatives rather than by their English oppressors:

> Be Irishmen Be free! Come and join our ranks! We will shew you the path of honour. In a word, you will learn how men love and serve their Country. Come, and speedily our common enemy will be annihilated. We know that you have long sighed for our arrival. A thousand times have you shewn yourselves free by your heroism, and by your virtues. Let us instantly unite, and let your tyrants disappear. You ought to recognise no masters but the Laws, which, very soon, you will receive from your faithful representatives.[22]

Humbert was too late. Although he defeated Irish militia forces at Castlebar in Mayo, and proclaimed the Republic of Connaught at the end of August and planned to take Dublin, things came to naught. Humbert lacked reinforcements, because a British squadron under Admiral Sir John Berlase Warren prevented Admiral Bompart from landing off the coast of Donegal, and captured the leading ship, and Theobald Wolfe Tone with it. Humbert surrendered on 8 September after defeat at Ballinamuck, being faced by overwhelming numbers of loyalists. French troops and rebels added to the numbers imprisoned, including at New Geneva Barracks.

III

That Irish republicans were imprisoned on lands within the fishing village of Passage was portentous. Henry II, the English king who first invaded Ireland, had landed on the beach below what was to be New Geneva in 1171. Oliver Cromwell, whilst laying siege to the city of Waterford, also took Passage in November 1649, killing two hundred of the garrison in the process. Almost a hundred and fifty years on, New Geneva Barracks encompassed a vast open square surrounded by buildings and a high wall. It had been a place where soldiers readied themselves to fight Irish republicans and to maintain British power in Ireland. Afterwards, as the memorial plaque indicated, it became a location for the death of republicans, by either disease or execution. It was called 'a monster prison', where men 'suspected of treason, or a creed or political opinion to justify the appearance of suspicion' were 'cast into gaol without the intervention of judge or jury'.[23] There was enormous irony in this, the site having been called New Geneva because it was supposed to herald the rebirth of the old republic of Geneva. Genevan republicans had once populated the place, with the intention of transforming Waterford, and helping to bring wealth and republican and industrious Protestant mores to Ireland. Planned as an asylum for republicans, it ended up a republican graveyard.

The precise date at which New Geneva was turned into a barracks has been lost. There is a report in *The Times* dated 14 July 1786 stating that New Geneva was being examined as a possible location for a barracks:

> Last Tuesday morning the Right Hon. The Lord of Tyrone [George Beresford, 2nd Earl of Tyrone], the Right Hon. Wm. Augustus Pitt, Commander in Chief of his Majesty's forces in this kingdom, and Major-General [Charles] O'Hara, arrived from Curraghmore, his Lordship's seat. After viewing Mr Allen's concerns at Ballytruckle, they visited New Geneva, and on their return Mr Wm Penrose's ground, for the purpose of fixing on the most eligible situation for building barracks.[24]

By the outbreak of the French Revolution it had become a place where troops were stationed before departure for foreign climes, especially the Mediterranean and the North Atlantic.[25] In August 1793 it was reported that the 64th Regiment of Foot, called the 2nd Staffordshire Regiment, which had seen active service in North America, and in Jamaica after the end of the American wars, was 'now quartered at New Geneva, to hold themselves in readiness for immediate imbarcation [*sic*].'[26] The 64th had been at New Geneva a year earlier, as three soldiers found guilty of leading a mutiny at Limerick were brought in front of the regiment on 1 September 1792, in order to be shot, receive a thousand lashes and receive five hundred lashes respectively. Having been berated by their commanding officer for their 'criminal and ruinous tendency', and after a further pause of a minute, the mutineers were informed that the Lord Lieutenant had pardoned them, because of their contrition.[27] In September 1793, the 56th Regiment, called the West Essex Regiment, also left New Geneva for Waterford and then Cork, en route to serve abroad. Prior to leaving, it had been involved in crushing a riot in Wexford, on 11 June, and a Major Valloton had been killed with a scythe while advancing on the protesters, leading his troops to fire on the crowd.[28] In September of the same year, the 31st Regiment quartered at Wexford was reported to have marched 'to New Geneva, there to join the other troops, destined for foreign service'.[29]

In 1798, New Geneva was quickly transformed into a prison for between four and five thousand United Irishmen. It was reported by an anonymous British officer who found himself at New Geneva, that Ireland had experienced 'mobs of poor infatuated creatures armed with pikes and guns everywhere prowling about'. United Irishmen were burning, pillaging and destroying property, and 'madly threatened to rescue their country from the hands of a government which wicked and designing demagogues had industriously represented as hostile to the very name of Ireland'.[30] In other words, by the summer of 1798 Ireland was filled with would-be revolutionaries, dedicated to making Ireland into a free state. The first step was to expel the British, and this could only be achieved by violence. The British officer recalled that in his opinion few of the United Irishmen truly knew what they were doing, but had been seduced by cunning ringleaders with promises of liberty once the tyrants were vanquished:

> Some had been sworn into it—others drawn into it. It was an endemial [*sic*] mania evidently excited, kept up, and blown into action, by crafty and discontented ringleaders, who, whilst they put the reckless rabblement in motion, had generally cowardice and cunning enough cautiously to keep in the back ground. The machine was in fearful operation, but the springs that set it at work were artfully concealed. The number here incarcerated amounted at this time to between four and five thousand men, in the prime of life generally, full of health and vigour, and who had been urged from their allegiance and their home by the most virulent misrepresentations.[31]

The prisoners were guarded by soldiers of the 5th battalion of the 60th Regiment of Foot, many of them Swiss and Germans who had served in the wars in North America. It was also manned by the Dumbarton Fencibles, a Scottish loyalist regiment.[32] The Dumbarton Fencibles had been raised by Colonel Campbell of Stonefield in October 1794, had first been stationed in Guernsey, and then moved to Ireland in 1797. They remained in Ireland until 1802.[33] Irish loyalist volunteers were also stationed in the locality of Waterford. The British officer present at New Geneva whose testimony has survived claimed that the 5th battalion of the 60th Regiment of Foot consisted 'almost entirely of Germans', and that the Dumbarton Fencibles were 'a fine, well-behaved, and steady regiment' commanded by a man named Colonel Scott, said to be 'a most humane and intelligent officer'. It was alleged in consequence that initially the prisoners 'were properly fed, and, under the circumstances, the most laudable attention was paid to their health'. Such humanity meant nothing, it was reported, because the Irish revolutionaries, being 'like the entrapped hyena', were 'bound, not tamed'. Wild behaviour was the result, which could only be repressed by force:

> [T]he indulgence which had been humanely granted, was shamefully abused. Spirits were clandestinely introduced by the visiting relatives, as was very clearly evidenced by the scenes of riot and drunkenness which every day prevailed. To repress these irregularities, orders upon orders were issued; but all common methods of prevention were tried, and failed; and it was at last discovered that the wives and sisters of the prisoners brought whiskey so secreted as to elude the vigilance of the sentries. Various attempts were also made to bribe the soldiers, and to break out of confinement. Scarcely a day passed without uproar.[34]

The portrait of low humanity bamboozled by demagogues, addled by drink, and deranged by a false cause was commonplace in loyalist accounts of the United Irishmen. Yet no other account stated that conditions at New Geneva were at any time acceptable, or that any consideration was given to the welfare of the prisoners: rather, the opposite. Indeed, the treatment of those who found themselves forced to live within the walls of New Geneva Barracks passed into folklore. New Geneva was a prison of choice and a place where prisoners could be assembled prior to transportation. *The Times*, for example, reported the arrival of thirty-six prisoners on 13 October 1798, to be transported.[35] In November, the Athlone cavalry conducted to the barracks the rebel Colonel Maguire and seventeen associates, prior to their court martial, with sixty-eight arriving from Waterford soon after.[36] Rebels were still being sent to New Geneva a year later.[37] In September 1799, a man named Harris was brought from Waterford to New Geneva for transportation, having been court-martialled for 'administering the United Oath in the county of Kilkenny'. It was reported that 'in the county of Cork many have been taken up for a similar offence'.[38] The Dumbarton Fencibles stationed at New Geneva were still looking for hidden caches of arms across Waterford in the spring of 1799, although they only found 'a few old guns'.[39]

IV

Visiting the site of New Geneva Barracks in the 1890s, Patrick Egan called the remains of the barracks 'a strange enclosure' of eight acres surrounded by a wall between nine and twelve feet in height, with a visible former parade ground and barracks buildings still standing, with room for approximately sixty officers and just under two thousand infantry. Local peasants regaled Egan with lurid stories of events at the prison. These included tales of the torture of women and the hunting down and murdering of any who attempted escape. Egan called it a place of 'loathsome horrors', noting the assertions by the inhabitants that dried blood could still be traced on the stones that formed the ruin, having dripped from the many heads that had been stuck upon the walls.[40] A similar story was related in the 1930s, when, during an investigation into Waterford memories, it was attested that it was at New Geneva Barracks that the 'Croppy Boy famed in song and story met his death'. The term 'croppy' derived from the tendency of the rebels to have their hair cropped or shaved, in the manner of the French *sans-culottes*. A man named John Colfer, interviewed in the 1930s, gave an account handed down to him by members of the Walsh family, who had lived in the area since the eighteenth century, concerning the killing of United Irishmen, and of their heads being placed on spikes at the gates of New Geneva Barracks. Householders were invited to view the scene as a warning and deterrent:

> Beside Geneva Barracks is a small house owned by William Walsh. The Walshes have lived here for many generations. The present man's grandfather occupied the house in 1798 and witnessed many a heart rending sight of cruelty to the poor peasants. William Walsh gives this incident as related by his grandfather. One night there was a loud knock at the door. Walsh asked 'who's there?' The answer was 'open in the King's name'. In fear Tom Walsh opened the door and saw standing there a British officer. Instinctively Walsh lifted his hands above his head but the officer told him he need not fear as he did not mean to harm him. He asked Tom Walsh to accompany him to the gates of Geneva Barracks for he comprehended that the sight of the Croppies' heads spiked upon the gates made him nervous. Tom Walsh did so.[41]

The origin of what Egan termed the 'the most notorious case of all' was recalled as a story of a well-bred young prisoner who asked his guard when he might leave the prison for his trial. The guard told him to scale the wall and to go. The young man naively did so and was shot down. (For the story in greater detail, see chapter 10 below.) It was his blood that was said to have seeped into the walls and still to be visible decades later. This rebel was employed as a character in James Joyce's *Ulysses* (1922), in which he said, 'I bear no hate to a living thing. But I love my country beyond a king.' Joyce also referred to the song 'The Croppy Boy', written by William B. McBurney under the pseudonym Caroll Malone in 1845, which ended 'At

Geneva Barrack that young man died, / And at Passage they have his body laid. / Good people who live in peace and joy / Breathe a pray'r and a tear for the Croppy Boy.'[42]

Another story goes that a mother named Mrs O'Neil travelled a hundred and fifty miles from Antrim, in the hope of visiting her son, who was held at New Geneva Barracks and selected for service in the Prussian army; prior to the rebellion he had been destined for the Catholic priesthood. After she was accused of bribing an officer in order to see her son, she was stripped 'almost naked' by the soldiers guarding the place, held down on a blanket whilst men held each of the corners, and repeatedly thrown into the air, as a prelude to being further tortured. Whether shame or injury led to her death is not known, but she expired the following day.[43] An account of 1814 from someone who conversed with those involved on the military side was the probable source of the story of Mrs O'Neil. It portrayed Colonel Scott, the commander of the Fencibles, as a 'ruffian monster' and 'infamous brute' who enjoyed torturing prisoners and stripping naked female visitors; this was said to be 'to the disgrace of Britain', compounded by the fact that his wife 'was always present at these exhibitions, and took particular delight in their infliction on Irish rebels'.[44]

In total several hundred were executed in the aftermath of the 1798 rebellion. Dozens were killed at New Geneva Barracks. Some of the executions occurred by firing squad within its walls. Many of those who claimed that they had been wrongly accused of being rebels remained at New Geneva for twenty months, and had to find two men willing to stand bail in lieu of good behaviour, for the large sum of £200, before being released.[45] Others were there for a shorter time. Such men confirmed the ghastliness of the place. Thomas Cloney, whose name appears on the modern plaque at the site, wrote a memoir of his life as a rebel, including the days he spent at New Geneva. Cloney claimed he was not a United Irishman. Rather, he was an opponent of the 'general system of tyranny which was then established in Ireland', whereby 'an Eastern Bashaw never exercised more ruthless and despotic sway in his Pachalic than did many of the county Wexford magistrates'.

Cloney took up arms at Wexford, and was appointed colonel in the movement, only, he said, because the Irish were so persecuted by a corrupt class of Protestant landlords, whom he termed 'the Ascendancy faction', governing Ireland for themselves rather than for the people:

> I beheld my country in chains and bleeding at every pore under the whip of the executioner and the bayonet of the mercenary. The best,

> the most useful, and the most patriotic of her citizens [were] either transported, or obliged to fly from the country of their fathers, to wander on the banks of the St. Lawrence and Mississippi, or to wear the degrading slave cap and the costume of the felon in New South Wales. The functions of the Civil Magistrate [were] superseded by those of the drill sergeant, and the tribunals of justice desecrated by drunkards, profligates, and horsejockies.[46]

Cloney held that he had been set up and falsely imprisoned at Wexford gaol in violation of a promise that in return for giving up his arms he could emigrate to North America. Instead he was transferred to New Geneva, recalling that 'the very name of the place had something horrible in it, it having been the depot for so many unfortunate people, whom the severity of the Ascendancy faction had exposed to torture, privations of every sort, and perpetual banishment'.[47] Cloney then described New Geneva as 'a most damp and loathsome prison', which 'really exceeded any description I could give of it for filthiness and a want of every sort of comfort'. The prisoners, Cloney said, were all wretched. Only the letters Cloney had on his person from prominent Irish friends enabled him to avoid inspection by the garrison surgeon, and allowed him to purchase his own meals from the officers' mess, rather than putting up with the sustenance provided for normal prisoners. Despite such privileges, Cloney stated that 'the filth everywhere around us, and the intolerable smell in our sleeping place baffles description, so that it was impossible to eat of the best fare with any degree of satisfaction'. Cloney also reported the negative treatment of Irish priests. One of them, 'Gannon, from the county Mayo', ultimately found his way to Spain, where Lucien Bonaparte, then his brother's ambassador at Madrid, gave him funds to travel to Paris, after which he was given a living near Versailles.[48]

New Geneva was mentioned in the Irish House of Commons by the attorney-general John Toler, 1st Earl of Norbury, on February 20 1799. Toler presented a bill for 'Suppressing the Rebellion at present existing in this country', by giving the Lord Lieutenant a power to punish rebels by military law, and to prevent civil powers from interfering with decision of Courts Martial. In response to arguments that his bill was an attack on the liberties of every person living in Ireland, and amounted to the establishment of a military despotism, Toler replied that if the rebels were punished only through the civil law, the right of Habeas Corpus could only be met with difficulty, because there were so many accused revolutionaries whose persons had to be brought forward for trial. Even if the persons were carried to trial in accordance with Habeas Corpus, there were not enough juries, or persons willing to serve the law, to process the civil law. This was why military justice had to be relied upon:

> In the present state of the country, however, it was impossible to go on—destruction must follow, if the civil and military jurisdictions of the country were continually suffered to clash with each other. The benefit of the Habeas Corpus Act was constantly applied for in the Court of King's Bench to bring up the bodies of persons convicted before different military tribunals of treasonable crimes, on the clearest evidence, and sentenced to transportation instead of being hanged; and General Johnston, the man who saved Ireland, was at this moment under attachment of that Court for not instantly bringing up from New Geneva a mob of convicts of this kind, who only waited there an opportunity of transportation. The Court of King's Bench, so long as the law stood as it now does, could neither refuse the motion for Habeas Corpus or attachment; and in disturbed districts where rebellion, or the unequivocal symptoms of it appeared, it would be absolutely for the safety of the country that the military power should be employed to act with promptitude, without the control of the civil law. In many counties, the Judges could not go to the circuit, particularly Wexford and Wicklow; Jurors could not be found to do their duty; and without this strong measure, justice must be at an end.[49]

General Henry Johnston, referred to by Toler, had two thousand troops fighting rebels across the south-eastern counties of Ireland in 1798. Wexford county was said to be full of United Irishmen, being 'a terrible example of their fury and licentiousness'. John Jeffreys Pratt, Earl of Camden, then lord lieutenant of Ireland, informed his chief secretary at Dublin Castle, Thomas Pelham, that he expected British rule in Ireland to collapse because the Irish rebels were so numerous, and loyalist forces so weak. Camden confessed to having written to the prime minister, William Pitt, to ask him to send large numbers of troops under a general such as Charles Cornwallis, of North American fame, and offered to give up his own office to a military man, as the crisis in Ireland was so great. Camden wrote that if the French invaded, everything would quickly be lost for the British in Ireland: 'a landing, even of a small body of French, will set the country in a blaze, and I think neither our force nor our staff equal to the very difficult circumstances they will have to encounter'.[50]

Robert Stewart, Viscount Castlereagh, then lord of the treasury in Ireland, a member of the Irish Privy Council, and a lieutenant-colonel in the militia, confirmed that the Wexford area was a hotbed of revolutionary activity:

> The rebellion seems to have taken serious root in Wexford. Their force is very great, the body in question exceeding ten thousand men, a considerable proportion of fire-arms, and conducted with an attention to military principles. Wexford is still in their hands, and a very large force said to be assembled in that side of the county.[51]

Castlereagh reported that large numbers of rebels were moving towards Waterford via Ross, that crown forces were meagre by comparison with those they were facing, that further action by the United Irishmen was anticipated across Ireland and that if French help came, as was likely, the mainland itself was under real threat:

> You know how fully prepared every part of Ireland is for revolt. Nothing but a speedy suppression of the mischief can prevent its becoming general. Your information where you now are will enable you to judge whether an invasion of England is likely to happen. Unless it is inevitable and immediate, Great Britain cannot better employ her force than in sending a large force, were it only for a few weeks, into Ireland. Everything depends on the first successes. It will cost much exertion to reconquer the island should the rebellion establish itself in the four provinces. We want officers much; pray press the sending over our brigadiers.[52]

Castlereagh went on to assert that 'the rebellion in Wexford has assumed a more serious shape than was to be apprehended from a peasantry, however well organized', because of the dedication of the Irish revolutionaries and their large numbers, with 'their enthusiasm excited by their priests'.[53] Camden was speedily convinced that the force at Wexford was so great 'that it is not thought proper to advance against them', and that 'a rising within the city' of Dublin was imminent.[54] So grim were the circumstances faced by the British that Castlereagh asked Pelham to beg Pitt to make 'the militia of both countries what it ought to be, an imperial force, for the defence of the empire at home'. One of the positives of the Irish rebellion in Castlereagh's view was the loyalty to Britain of the Irish militia, who 'completely dispelled all our apprehensions as to their fidelity and must remove every jealousy on the part of England in employing them in Great Britain'. The condition of Britain was so bad that Castlereagh foresaw a time when loyal Irish militiamen would be needed on the mainland: 'the day may come when the plague may have spent itself here, and when England may experience the same struggle'.[55]

V

That New Geneva Barracks became infamous as a prison, a place of tragedy and hurt, of oppression and open brutality, was due in part to the acknowledgement on the part of the British loyalists that they were fighting not only for their own lives but for the very survival of the British state. In the aftermath of the rebellion of the United Irishmen it was asserted that even the local militia were not to be trusted. A report was received by William Wickham, then under-secretary of state for the Home Department, serving the home secretary William Cavendish-Bentinck, 3rd Duke of Portland, from a government spy at Waterford, and passed on to Robert Stewart, Viscount Castlereagh, now the acting chief secretary for Ireland. It advised against the continued employment of a loyalist militia in Ireland on the grounds that 'friends and foes are all the same to them'. At Waterford, among the militiamen, 'drunkenness is prevalent beyond anything that I ever witnessed before' in part because 'every other house in the town is a whiskey-shop'. This went against Castlereagh's earlier assessment of the Irish militia as worthy of service across Britain. The spy further advised of the dangers of sending those convicted of treason against the crown into the armed forces. As the anonymous informer put it,

> [M]ost of these rascals, it is to be feared [rather than remaining in foreign parts], will find their way to Chatham [the naval docks in Kent]: many of them are uncommon fine fellows, and our regiments will be finally filled with them; if precautions, and the strictest precautions, are not taken on this head, what are we to expect? In my opinion, wherever we send them, we send emissaries. The mode of disposing of them is a dangerous one, and their admission into the navy or army is likely to be attended with consequences equally fatal.[56]

In other words, the United Irishmen were so dangerous that they could never be trusted to be British soldiers, and were likely to foment rebellion wherever they found themselves across the British Empire.

In practice, the destinies of those imprisoned differed. Some were fortunate. It was later claimed that Waterford itself had few United Irishmen, that those who were involved were not 'persons of education or fortune', and that 'the Roman Catholic gentlemen of the county remained loyal to the last'. In the city of Waterford, however, spies uncovered a conspiracy to kill members of the yeomanry. The United Irishmen included a publican named Sargent and a man named Quinn, who was servant of the Dean of Waterford. These men were found guilty but 'through the intercession of friends, they were only sentenced to be transported'. Whilst at New Geneva awaiting the arrival of their ship, they were 'permitted to effect their escape'.[57] The outcome for the majority of the prisoners housed at New Geneva Barracks was initially uncertain. Conditions were cramped in the extreme. It was reported that the 64th Regiment, at the beginning of 1799, 'marched from hence to New Geneva, there they are to remain till transports arrive to convey the prisoners from thence'.[58] It was also claimed that the ranks of the prisoners were swelled by a thousand peasants, rounded up for being rebels after the battles had ended; an accusation was made that many of them were there not because they had taken part in any violent action but 'for keeping late hours in public houses'. After the king of Prussia expressed a need for additional troops, a thousand of those accused of being United Irishmen were shipped to join his service.[59] The under-secretary of state for the Home Department, William Wickham, at one point thought that the Prussians were going to reject the proposal, and worried Castlereagh in Ireland that they would have to think of solutions of the problem of what to do with those they termed 'our convicts'.[60] In August 1799, *The Times* reported that '12 privates of the Kildare regiment, charged with seditious practices, were marched from Limerick to New Geneva, preparatory to their being sent to the Prussian service'.[61] Ironically, one of the men sent to Prussia, who spent nine months at New Geneva, died fighting in Portugal as a lancer in De Berg's French unit against Wellington's infantry; he was mentioned in the latter's dispatches, as reported in the *Dublin Evening Herald* of 28 October 1811, where he was said to have fought gallantly against the British, refused quarter, and before being cut down to have called out, 'Remember I am an Irishman, and my name is O'Finn.' The story then emerged that Edward Finn at the age of nineteen in 1798 had been arrested by British mercenaries looking for arms, for saying that there were no rebels, but that the actions of the soldiers were inciting the people. He was transported to New Geneva, despite protestations by his family of his innocence, and then with two hundred others 'sold like an African slave' to Prussia. Finn was then sent to Emden, forced to serve in the army, and was among those defeated at Jena, at which point he and his associates joined the French army.[62]

Forced transportation and enlistment was also undertaken to support British regiments stationed in the West Indies. One of the officers sent to organise the transportation recalled at New Geneva Barracks the 'ragged, destitute condition of the prisoners, their filthy habits, and the necessarily crowded state of the rooms'. He also remembered that several hundred rebels attempted to escape and were shot down, and that female relatives

of the prisoners, who were smuggling in spirits hidden in bladders under their clothing, were brutally disciplined for doing so. One morning all of the prisoners were brought out and made to listen to the reading of a Royal proclamation. The proclamation offered a free pardon to any rebel willing to volunteer to serve in the British Army abroad. In the square of New Geneva Barracks the colours of two regiments were placed in corners. The rebels were requested to join either standard, whilst a band played 'God Save the King'. Not a single rebel went forward, all remaining 'sullen and scowling'. The commanding officer then selected a thousand of the healthiest men and asked the first in line if he would agree to enlist. On refusing with 'an horrid oath' against the king, the man was brought before a drumhead court martial, which was legal because the entire country was under martial law. Once more, on being asked if he would agree to serve in the army of the King, he replied that 'he would rather live on grass like a beast than go soldiering'. The man was then whipped:

> Scarcely had the lash crossed his shoulders, when all his ranting and hectoring vanished, and with an effort of loyalty that seemed magically to spring up from under the drummer's cat, he loudly vociferated, 'take me down, your honour—now, I'll serve the King, long life to him.' He was cut down [from the frame holding him still].

All of the other selected men agreed to serve and in due course were marched to the vessel waiting to take them to Martinique, a captured Dutch seventy-four gun ship named the *Admiral de Vries*.

Attempts to free the rebels before they embarked were anticipated, so as they marched slowly towards the ship, before the entire local population, the waistbands of their breeches were let out, so that each of them had to hold up their own trousers and could only run with difficulty. The British officer recalling this time served with many of these rebels-turned-government troops over the following two decades. He stated that, although only one in fifty survived, 'nothing could exceed the propriety of their behaviour. They became good and valuable soldiers'.[63] Other prisoners were transported in chains to Australia, reputedly without any papers or official notices having been filed.[64] A report in *The Times* of May 1799 did report that two armed transports bound for New South Wales put into Passage, and eighty prisoners from New Geneva were put on board.[65] The inhumane conditions at the Barracks were described as the cause of the sickness of prisoners sent from Cork in a ship full of Irish rebels destined for New South Wales; there were so many deaths that the prisoners were removed and the entire ship was whitewashed and fumigated.[66] An army surgeon, commenting in 1803 on some of the Irish soldiers who became his charges in a British hospital, noted that the men who arrived from New Geneva Barracks 'generally brought with them a contagious fever'.[67]

Once the last of the United Irishmen had been killed, transported or released, the prison was turned once again into a barracks. This took some years. As late as February 1803, the Reverend John Roberts, who was acting as clergyman to the convicts in the prison, was asking for remuneration for his services.[68] Soldiers were then garrisoned at New Geneva for many years. New Geneva in July 1801 was the location for a duel between an assistant staff surgeon and a lieutenant of the Devon and Cornwall Fencibles.[69] There is evidence of the desertion of a man 'from the Dunbartonshire Fensible Infantry, quartered at New Geneva . . . under a forged pass' called Peter Bain, said to be a 'private soldier in the above regiments, 5 feet 8 inches tall, 34 years of age, fair complexion, born in Glenorchy'.[70] Other soldiers found the barracks commodious. An ensign named James Mill wrote letters to his father from October 1810 stating that conditions at New Geneva were so good that his 'chief wish is that we may remain here the winter'. Mill reported that 'provisions in general in Ireland are much lower in price than you would suppose', which meant that the troops ate extremely well, with 'poultry and fish . . . very cheap; and meat is but 5d. per lb. Pat geese are sold in Waterford at 2s. a-piece, and chickens at 1s. 6d. per pair'. On the other hand, 'butter and groceries are exorbitantly dear'.[71] Mill argued that the site of New Geneva was excellent, but that the lack of contact with the outside world presented a problem, with the absence of newspapers a particular shortcoming:

> In this place, which is an extremely stupid one, one cannot get any news except what comes from the London and Dublin papers. Our barracks are good and commodious. From two of my windows at present I command a very pleasant prospect of the sea, in my sitting-room and a side window to the barrack-yard, besides having a bedroom within.[72]

Although Mill was especially concerned with the progress of the war in Spain and Portugal, and anticipated being transported into battle under Wellington, troops stationed at New Geneva continued to be used for domestic purposes. Mill related that 'the only thing in agitation and of real importance here in Ireland seems to be the unanimity and earnestness with which the petitions for the dissolution of the Union are being carried on'. Opposition to the Union of 1801, which united Britain and Ireland, meant that 'the houses of several gentlemen in this county have been forcibly entered by great numbers of disguised persons, and robbed of their fire-arms and other means of protection'. What Mill termed 'marauding' he disclosed 'is not confined to Waterford, but, in fact, is practised all over Ireland'. It was not a surprise that his regiment was moved to Clonmel in February 1811, due to the 'well-organised and regular nocturnal meetings [of rebels], for the purpose of drilling and manoeuvring', which resulted in the hanging of eight rebels and fifty men being sentenced to be whipped. The latter, Mill stated 'have the option of that infliction or of enlisting in any Regiment they think proper, I suppose West India Regiments'. He also underlined the brutality of the use of the whip: 'the floggings that soldiers receive, though at times very severe, are as mere flea-bites compared to the floggings these poor wretches have received'. Mill considered flogging to be vital in the army because 'the service is composed of so large a portion of the worst and most unprincipled members of the lowest grades'.[73]

Further records of the barracks give information about regiments on the move, courts martial and crimes, births and odd deaths and all the stuff of a normal military life. In 1810 one Lieutenant Lawson Huddlestone, of the 2nd battalion of the 40th Regiment of Foot, was arraigned at Kilkenny on 27 December 1810 for having, between 3 and 21 December, had a fight with privates of his regiment in 'a petty pot house' [tavern] outside New Geneva barracks. It was claimed that Huddlestone had associated with 'women of bad character', whom he had brought into the barracks, refused orders, abandoned his post, 'induced a private soldier, of the regiment, to quit his guard for the purpose of going to his room, at New Geneva barracks, to dance and drink with him' and promised 'to run any man through the body, that should oppose him' whilst 'using highly disrespectful and abusive language' towards his commanding officer.[74] Huddlestone was cashiered early in 1811. In 1817, New Geneva barracks was stated as having space for sixty-two officers and 1,728 private soldiers; it was also stated that it might be disposed of, being surplus to current military requirements. This was the verdict of the deputy barrackmaster of the forces in Ireland, Lieutenant-General Quin John Freeman, who made the proposition to Sir Robert Peel, then Irish chief secretary, on 12 September. It was reported that the barracks was now devoid of troops, and part of the complex had been turned into a coal store. Pilfering of material on a nightly basis became so great that the buildings began to deteriorate rapidly. A man named George Ivie offered £3,000 to purchase the site in 1819, but refused to pay when he realised the extent of the destruction, with sashes, window frames, flags and shutters all having been stolen. A general advertisement for sale, along with several other Irish barracks, was issued in 1821.[75] In the end, Henry de La Poer Beresford, 2nd Marquess of Waterford, paid £1,500 for New Geneva. (Another report states that he actually paid £800.) The fact that a Beresford, a scion of one of the families of the Protestant Ascendancy, ended up paying a pittance for New Geneva was of profound significance. Yet Beresford did not have a plan for the site. Rather, walls were dismantled and bricks reused in other places. Beresford sold the houses 'to a Mr. Galway, for almost a nominal price, who disposed of some of the materials on the spot with considerable profit, and conveyed part of the remainder to Dungarvan, where he used them in erecting cabins for his tenantry'.[76] Oddly, as late as 1833, a fee of £159 was listed as being paid by the British army for the 'annual expense of garrisons at home and abroad' for New Geneva.[77] By this time, however, history had abandoned the place. The following chapters of this book reconstruct, from a multitude of contemporary sources, the story of New Geneva, and the Genevan and Irish histories that led to the erection of a new town, which then became a barracks and a prison. As is always the case, to make any sense of what happened, we have to start by going backwards.

CHAPTER TWO

The Waterford Experiment

FOR MUCH OF THE eighteenth century Britain and its empire were widely perceived to be falling apart. Despite surviving the initially uncertain Hanoverian succession, and Jacobite challenges to it in the first half of the century, enormous problems were perceived to remain. Everything came to a head in the early 1780s. The national debt had reached a level that was inducing fears of bankruptcy. French, Dutch and Spanish forces, fighting in conjunction with the rebels in the thirteen American colonies, were challenging British trading interests and political authority across the globe, from New South Wales to Nova Scotia. The creation of the United States of America signalled to many that Britain was on the edge of ruin. During these years, the Gordon riots of June 1780 saw mob violence in London and widespread attacks on Catholics, which had to be put down by the army. Cornwallis surrendered his army of six thousand men at Yorktown to the Americans in October 1781.

In Asia, the ruler of Mysore, Hyder Ali, was seeking to chase the British out of southern India, descending on the Carnatic and threatening Madras (Chennai) on the Bay of Bengal. Gibraltar was under siege and Minorca had been lost by early 1782, and the French had taken all of the West Indies bar Jamaica, Barbados and Antigua. This was to be expected, many observers believed, because Britain was a corrupt commercial empire. With policy dominated by a crooked nexus of merchants and politicians, the pursuit of profit had muddied any sense of the national interest or the public good. As a contemporary poem had it

Behold then Laws unlawful made
Tribunals, which by gold are sway'd
State-Ministers, whose bungling brains

Would make us think our losses gains
A Senate, a mad bedlam-house
Elections, scenes of low abuse
Cities where wants with taxes vie
And Borough-Towns, in slavery
Base Statesmen who their country rob
Nobility a very mob
Bishops an hireling, useless race
A Clergy with a borrow'd face
Directors of the war for spoil
And Generals unfit for toil
A War—our weakness to betray
And Battles fought to run away.[1]

The Scottish philosopher Adam Smith's great book, *An Inquiry into the Nature and Causes of the Wealth of Nations* (1776), was widely perceived to have identified the central problem facing the British Empire, in having become what Smith famously called a 'mercantile system'. Smith described the reduction of wealth caused by the bounties, drawbacks and duties levied upon imported and exported goods that were intended to maintain the trade of Britain at the expense of the trade of its rivals. Smith also described the corruption that accompanied the system, in the form of the excessive wealth, and sometimes the excessive political influence, of its beneficiaries. The result was that the mercantile system operated in the interest of the few rather than the many, and for the rich rather than for the poor. As Smith put it, 'It is the industry which is carried on for the benefit of the rich and the powerful that is principally encouraged by our mercantile system. That which is carried on for the benefit of the poor and the indigent is too often either neglected or oppressed.'[2] Britain was losing resources and the British state was wasting them.

A sense of decline and possible collapse was becoming pervasive. Voltaire, once the most Anglophile of writers, declared as early as 1752 that 'the time of Newton, Locke, Pope, Addison, Steele, Swift, is gone. It seems all the world is degenerated'.[3] Voltaire considered himself to have been 'an Englishman' but now announced, 'I am one no longer since they have been assassinating our officers in America and are pirates on the seas and I wish a fitting punishment to those who trouble the peace of the world.'[4] The association of Britain with war, debt and commercial corruption was reiterated in Voltaire's subsequent work.[5] Between 1689 and 1815 France and Britain were officially at war for sixty-two years. Johann Zimmermann,

physician to George III at Hanover, noted that 'no people upon earth both despise and hate each other, more than the English despise and hate the French'.[6] The outcome of this second hundred years' war appeared clear. French influence was being asserted across Europe in consequence.

II

Such a political environment led those living in the multitude of small states across Europe to feel as uncertain as the British about their future. In the past, such states had developed a variety of strategies for self-preservation, including the payment of tributes, diplomatic manoeuvre, the balance of power, alliances, investment in the debts of larger states, city walls and the construction of federal leagues for defence. Above all else, however, they relied upon the valour and patriotism of their citizens to defend themselves against larger powers in times of crisis. The Swiss and the Dutch were seen to have done exactly this through the early modern period, and publicly commemorated their remarkable historic victories against more powerful foes. In the Swiss case, the Old Confederacy (*Alte Eidgenossenschaft*) had been victorious against Duke Leopold I of Austria's Imperial troops at Morgarten in 1315, against Duke Leopold III's larger forces at Sempach in 1386 and, in 1474 and 1476, against Charles the Bold, Duke of Burgundy, at Grandson and Murten. The latter victories, together with their exploits in the Great Italian Wars between 1494 and 1559, supplied the Swiss with a reputation for invincibility. As the humanist Francesco Guicciardini put it, writing of the wars in Italy in 1511,

> This great and unpolished nation has gained great renown through its union and glorious exploits in war. For the Swiss, by their natural ferocity and orderly discipline, have not just constantly defended their own country with great valour, but greatly underlined their martial abilities in foreign service.[7]

The question was whether the republican self-sacrifice that had allowed small states to establish themselves, and to survive in the face of the overwhelming power of larger monarchies, whilst still in mind, was very much a phenomenon of the past.

Edward Gibbon, the historian of Rome who spent a substantial portion of his life living in the Pays de Vaud, then ruled by the most powerful Swiss canton of Bern, on visiting the battle site of Grandson noted that the castle walls still held some of the cannonballs. He called the event 'as honourable in Swiss annals as Marathon, Salamis, Platea and Mycale is for the Greeks'.[8] According to the prolific author John Campbell, the Swiss had 'defended themselves at different times against most of the great powers in Europe, and never [been] beaten, or reduced to demand peace by any power whatever; so that they may be justly considered . . . the most unconquerable people in Europe'.[9] The view that Switzerland remained the archetypal example of a successful republican confederation was reiterated by Voltaire.[10] The claim was in turn repeated by an English visitor to Switzerland, William Coxe, in letters of 1779:

> [W]ith such wisdom was the Helvetic union composed, and so little have the Swiss, of late years, been actuated with the spirit of conquest, that since the firm and complete establishment of their general confederacy, they have scarcely ever had occasion to employ their arms against a foreign enemy; and have had no hostile commotions among themselves, that were not very soon happily terminated. Perhaps there is not a similar instance in ancient or modern history, of a warlike people, divided into little independent republics, closely bordering upon each other, and of course having occasionally interfering interests, having continued, in an almost uninterrupted state of tranquillity. The youth are diligently trained to all the martial exercises . . . a considerable number of Swiss troops are always employed in foreign services; and the whole people are enrolled, and regularly exercised in their respective militia. By these means they are capable, in case it should be necessary, of collecting a very respectable body of forces, which could not fail of proving formidable to any enemy who should invade their country, or attack their liberties. Thus, while most of the other states upon the continent are tending more and more towards a military government, Switzerland alone has no standing armies; and yet, from the nature of its situation, from its particular alliances, and from the policy of its internal government, is more secure from invasion than any other European power, and full as able to withstand the greatest force that can be brought against it.[11]

Despite such testimony, by the mid-eighteenth century it was increasingly recognised that the public virtue, courage and patriotism of the citizenry was no longer sufficient to maintain a state. As the English envoy to the cantons Abraham Stanyan reported in 1714, 'a disuse of war, during so long a tract of time, has given rise to an opinion, that the Switzers are much fallen from their ancient valour'.[12] As all states began to chase commerce, the size of the market available to a state was accepted as a measure of national power. Small states, lacking large markets or the capacity to create a market through the pursuit of empire, could no longer afford the military technology available to large states, and their militias could no longer stand against the vast armies of the larger European monarchies. The barrister and pamphleteer John Lind, who was acting as tutor to the young Prince Stanisław Poniatowski in Warsaw, wrote in 1773—the year following the first partition of the Polish-Lithuanian Commonwealth by Russia, Prussia and Austria)—that weak states like Poland, when faced by armed monarchies seeking empire, could only be saved by equally strong monarchies.[13] Otherwise they would be eaten up or threatened with being parcelled up by the great.

Another example commented upon by contemporaries of the decline of a once-great power was Genoa, from which France secretly purchased Corsica in 1764. French troops then began to put down the rebellion of Pasquale Paoli, who had proclaimed Corsica an independent republic in 1755, created a constitution and founded a university. James Boswell, who visited Corsica in the mid-1760s, wrote that he 'saw with enthusiasm a brave People who have vindicated their liberty with as much real spirit as was ever found in antiquity'.[14] Guerrilla warfare between the republicans and the French continued until 1769, when Paoli was finally defeated and forced into an English exile. No matter how great the commitment of the Corsican patriots, they had no chance of victory against overwhelming French numbers. Although the independence of Corsica became a *cause célèbre* across Europe, no state was willing to arm the Corsicans or fight a war with France for liberty. The impotence of rebels and the gulf in power between France and other states was underscored. The Corsican experience seemed to many to prove Britain's decline and diplomatic weakness. The anonymous 'Junius', in a third letter to the *Public Advertiser* on 7 February 1769, stated that the colonies had been alienated and 'Corsica shamefully abandoned', while commerce languished and the national debt increased.[15] Battles for liberty continued to be lauded; but, however prevalent neo-Roman concerns about the excessive prerogative powers of executive bodies might be across Europe, and especially in Britain, advocates of liberty faced challenging times and were increasingly on the defensive, because of the success of oppressive measures.[16] Battles for liberty had always been about the nature and location of sovereignty, but new questions were being asked about whether sovereign states dedicated to the pursuit of the public good could be created at all. Foreign forces and sinister financial interests were perceived to be interfering in politics and subverting the public good.

France arranged for the funding of Gustav III's *coup d'état* of 1772 that put an end to the 'age of liberty' in Sweden by curtailing the powers of the gathered estates or Riksdag (*Riksens ständer*). After the French diplomat who orchestrated the coup, Charles Gravier de Vergennes, became foreign minister in 1774, a more aggressive stance was taken by France against Britain, especially in support of the North American insurgents from 1777. During these years, France became still more imperially minded, especially as Britain began to lose the American war. A case in point was the invasion of the republic of Geneva in 1782, with France at the head of a coalition. A popular and democratically elected government at Geneva was put down with the very troops who had been fighting for liberty in North America. The Genevan rebels fortified the city, took hostages from among the French-supporting magistrates and filled the Cathedral of Saint-Pierre with gunpowder.[17] Their goal was to become republican martyrs, underlining for the world the fact that French imperialism was again on the march, and that small republics were no longer safe in the continent they had done so much to define in terms of culture and politics. Adam Ferguson's view of the existing republics, articulated in his *An Essay on the History of Civil Society* (1767), was being confirmed: the republics were no longer masters of their own destiny. However much they fought to maintain their liberty, it was altogether precarious and dependent upon the whim of great monarchs:

> The small republics of Greece, indeed, by their subdivisions, and the balance of their power, found almost in every village the object of nations. Every little district was a nursery of excellent men, and what is now the wretched corner of a great empire, was the field on which mankind have reaped their principal honours. But in modern Europe, republics of a similar extent, are like shrubs, under the shade of a taller wood, choked by the neighbourhood of more powerful states. In their case, a certain disproportion of force frustrates, in a great measure, the advantage of separation. They are like the trader in Poland, who is the more despicable, and the less secure, that he is neither master nor slave.
>
> Independent communities, in the meantime, however weak, are averse to a coalition, not only where it comes with an air of imposition, or unequal treaty, but even where it implies no more than the admission of new members to an equal share of the consideration with the old. The citizen has no interest in the annexation of kingdoms; he must find his importance diminished, as the state is enlarged: but ambitious men, under the enlargement of territory, find a more plentiful harvest of power, and of wealth, while government itself is an easier task. Hence the ruinous progress of empire; and hence free nations, under

> the shew of acquiring dominion, suffer themselves, in the end, to be yoked with the slaves they had conquered.[18]

Ferguson was obsessed by the history of Rome; it was the contemporary parallel to Roman decline that he perceived all around him.

III

Geneva had survived as an independent republic since the Reformation. It had become famous as a 'Rome for Protestants', as a place of Calvinist devotion and piety and as a centre of learning, on account of the Genevan Academy, and was also renowned for trade.[19] Geneva considered itself a free state and the government there was popular. Many outsiders, and some Genevan citizens, called their government a democracy, 'the most wise and the most happy'.[20] Bordered by Catholic territories, jealous Savoy and the great monarchy of France, in addition to tiny Neuchâtel, then governed by Prussia, and the Swiss cantons of Bern and Zurich, Genevans fiercely maintained their independence. In times of crisis, as had occurred when Savoy sent invaders to quell the city in 1602, Genevans relied on their valour, the courage to resist whatever force was sent against them; their virtue was proven when the Savoyard invaders were routed.

The world changed between 1602 and 1782 for Genevans. The republic faced a crisis because of the relative decline of the Swiss in terms of international influence, and because of the corresponding increase in French involvement in the city. Many of the leading families at Geneva, whose members were repeatedly elected to the highest magisterial offices in the republic, welcomed closer links between Geneva and France. A growing number of citizens, however, abhorred French power as a threat to Calvinism and to the independence of the republic. Violence broke out between the parties in the 1730s and 1760s. During the civil strife, negotiators from France were involved in the pacification process. By the 1760s, the most renowned Genevan, Jean-Jacques Rousseau, was widely accused of being the inspiration of the anti-French party. The public condemnation by the magistrates at Geneva of Rousseau's *Contrat social* and of *Émile* in June 1762, as books destructive of religion and government, led to serious domestic unrest at Geneva.[21]

Such events facilitated longstanding calls for republican reform. Rousseau was portrayed as a spokesperson for the party called the *représentants*, who advocated democratic and economic reform in addition to the restoration of a form of Calvinism that encouraged popular adherence to moral virtue. As such, Rousseau was bitterly attacked by all of those who favoured the status quo. It was said that Rousseau 'attacks government, the kings are idiots, the priests little knaves. He condemns revealed religion with an unequalled liberty and passion.'[22] The Genevan magistrates' decision to condemn Rousseau's books was justified in *procureur-général* Jean-Robert Tronchin's *Lettres écrites de la campagne*, which appeared in September 1763. Tronchin had initially reported on Rousseau's work for the governing councils and had concluded that he was a sceptic, an advocate of 'extreme liberty', of 'periodic assemblies', and of making constitutional law 'always revocable'.[23]

The most brutal attack was that of Voltaire, who in the *Sentiment des citoyens*, published at the end of 1764 (dated 1765), revealed to the world that Rousseau had abandoned his own children on the steps of a foundling hospital at Paris.[24] Rousseau was identified as an archetypal hypocrite. This was an especially serious accusation against a person who was renowned for his own moral standing, and whose writings had become popular because they recommended the living of a life in accordance with the natural passions, and especially those associated with parenthood. Rousseau renounced his status as *citoyen de Genève* in 1765 and declared that he would no longer involve himself in the politics of the city of his birth.[25] Afterwards, in many letters, he reiterated this self-imposed injunction. He did not in practice adhere to it, however; in part because his Genevan friends would not let him.

Many of Rousseau's followers said that he was never the same again after Voltaire's public besmirching. A rift opened between the *représentants* because Rousseau wrongly identified one of their leaders, the pastor Jacob Vernes, as the author of the *Sentiment*. Yet Rousseau continued to be asked to provide advice to the republican reformers at Geneva, some of whom continued to see him as a latter-day Calvin, and the only person in Europe equipped to work out how republics could maintain themselves in a world dominated by commercial monarchies with an eye to empire. One such person was François-Henri d'Ivernois, whose letters to Rousseau ensured that the latter was always up to date with regard to *représentant* policy. As the impasse between the *représentants* and the magistrates over reform led to violence across the city in 1766 and 1767, Rousseau was called upon by d'Ivernois, and by other Genevan friends, to give his verdict.

What the *représentants* wanted to know was how France would respond to the creation of a free republic on its borders. In other words, to what extent could the international limits to domestic republican reform be delineated? Rousseau's response was characteristically blunt. There

was no point, he wrote in private letters, in establishing a democratic republic at Geneva. Such a move did not fit with what he had advocated in his *Lettres écrites de la montagne* of 1764. The fundamental point, in any case, was that France would never stand for it.[26] The consequence of republican reform would be war, the likely destruction of Geneva and the need for an exodus of the reform-minded. Rousseau's argument was so abhorrent to some of the *représentants* that François d'Ivernois, the son of François-Henri, attacked Rousseau as a man who foolishly loved peace more than liberty.[27]

What Rousseau said would happen in the case of Geneva came to pass four years after his own death, in the aftermath of the revolution there in 1782. The *représentants* took control of the city in April of that year. Republican reform was instituted, with proposals for the establishment of a more democratic constitution, the reformation of manners and measures to put an end to political and commercial corruption. The French foreign minister Vergennes refused to sanction the reforms, citing the French guarantee of what he identified as Geneva's ancient constitution to legitimise his intervention. He then established a coalition with Bern, traditionally also a guaranteeing power, and Savoy, traditionally the enemy of Geneva, and invaded with twelve thousand troops. The *représentants* appeared then to be faced with the choice of fighting or dying. They planned for both, fortifying the walls, filling the cathedral and the houses of chief magistrates with gunpowder and imploring the mass of the people to embrace republican martyrdom, which they seemed ready and willing to do. A third option emerged, however, when the foreign troops reached the city and were on the verge of using their guns against Geneva's walls.

As the French mounted their guns on specially constructed ramparts outside the city, and aimed them into its heart, the people of Geneva were ready to fight just as they had done 180 years before against the Savoyard invaders. But seeing the force of the arms raised against them, the leaders of the republican rebels or *représentants* decided that an alternative future could be discerned. Rather than turn Geneva into a ruin, they decided to run away, and create a new Geneva in another place. Accordingly, they opened the gates of the city during the night, and fled to Neuchâtel. They claimed not to be acting as cowards, but rather as saviours of the republic. Their ultimate aim was to move all of their supporters, mainly drawn from the industrious artisans of the city, and a number of the professors at the Genevan Academy, to somewhere where France would no longer be a threat, and where republican virtues might flourish.[28] Putting an end to the once great republic of Geneva would do nothing for the cause of republics more generally, they decided, because republics were too small to fend for themselves. Republican martyrdom might underline for Europeans the state of the republics, the fact of their decline and present status as an endangered species, but it would do nothing to facilitate future reform. Rousseau's final piece of advice to the Genevans had been to abandon the city and create a new Geneva elsewhere. The chiefs among the *représentants* had glimpsed an alternative future for their city. They thought they could save their own lives and those of their compatriots, restore their lost liberty and make the name of Geneva great again.

Attacked as anarchists and democrats by the French, the rebels were invited to come to Britain. William Petty, then 2nd Earl of Shelburne (from 1786 1st Marquess of Lansdowne), and prime minister, promised to use the resources of the British state to help to create a New Geneva, proving that Britain remained supportive of liberty, whatever the republicans in America might declare.[29] Shelburne, his government and the circle of intellectuals who surrounded him had ulterior motives. They wanted to use the Genevans to address the problems of Ireland, introducing entrepreneurial Protestants into areas perceived to be economically backward, a condition that was often blamed on the Catholicism of the Irish peasantry. This was why Shelburne and his government gave the rebel *représentants* £50,000 to erect a city, to be called 'New Geneva', at Waterford. The greatest British supporter of New Geneva, Charles Stanhope, then Lord Mahon (from 1786 3rd Earl Stanhope), was similarly motivated, in part because he had been brought up at Geneva and was a longstanding member of the rebels' party. Shelburne and Stanhope shared hopes that the Genevans would introduce cultures capable of combating the excessive corruption they saw in modern commercial society, and which was evident across Britain. New Geneva was part of a broader plan for international reform that encompassed saving the republics, but was more focused upon Britain in particular. The new settlement would help to counter the economic corruption of the 'mercantile system', which was destroying the morals and liberties that the free British state rested upon. Britain was seen by Shelburne and by Stanhope to be in the midst of an acute crisis that might very well destroy the state. Shelburne was a practical politician, and this was reflected in many of the decisions he took, some of which antagonised more principled but less influential contemporaries. Nevertheless, he saw New Geneva for a brief period as one of several sources of change, potentially capable of transforming the political world from a state of corruption to a state of moral and economic health.

The Genevan republicans were welcomed with open arms by everyone from George III, to Shelburne, to George Nugent-Temple-Grenville (later 1st Marquess of Buckingham), the lord lieutenant in Ireland, to members of the landed aristocracy and to the local dignitaries of Dublin and the people of Ireland themselves. The plan, of course, was not simply to abandon an old city and to found a new one. The move was accompanied by great expectations, for the transformation of Ireland, for the growth of wealth and of virtue and for the reform of the empire of Britain itself. In short, the transfer of republicans from Geneva was expected to inaugurate an era of radical reform and reformation. The result was a remarkable experiment at the ancient city and significant port of Waterford in southern Ireland. New Geneva was established at the site of a village called Passage, near the confluence of the 'Three Sisters' rivers, the Barrow, the Nore and the Suir, just outside Waterford, on the west bank opposite the promontory of Duncannon Fort. The settlement was to be peopled by rebels. It was said by contemporaries that these rebels, after the invasion of Geneva by foreign armies, became 'fugitives in the mountains' and 'victims of the most profound and odious machinations that a people has ever been subjected to', and were seeking 'a new country' that would 'save old Geneva'. They wished to find asylum 'in a great monarchy, in an empire where the rights of man are respected'. They believed that their success would punish tyrants and the states whose politics were motivated only by ambition: for the Genevans, this meant France, Savoy and the Swiss cantons.[30] It was written that as a 'great national occurrence . . . the emigration of the Genevans has called forth those splendid virtues, the amiableness of which is sufficient, in some measure, to redeem the fallen dignity of human nature'.[31] Historians, and especially historians writing today, have neglected the story and its implications for our understanding of the turbulent final decades of the eighteenth century.[32]

Several prominent Genevan rebels became Irish subjects at Dublin. As noted above, it was agreed that £50,000 would be sufficient to establish the new city. The prominent architect James Gandon drew up plans and the buildings began to be erected. Families were transferred on British ships and a community was gradually established. Across Europe the view was expressed that the future of republics might lie within monarchies with republican histories themselves, or where the political culture was well disposed towards republics. Parallels were drawn between the Genevan experience and that of Scotland. Just as Scotland had retained its

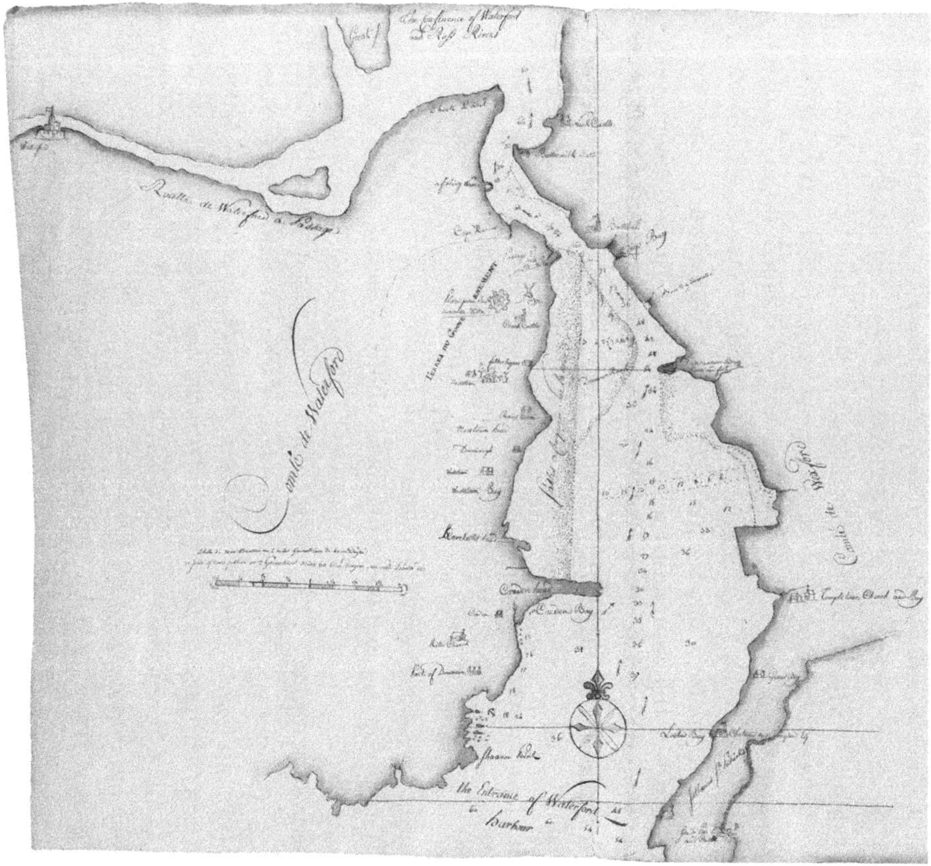

FIGURE 2.1. 'Map of New Geneva in Waterford'. Papiers H. A. Gosse, Département des manuscrits, Bibliothèque de Genève

separate law, religion and culture since the Union of 1707, so the Genevans anticipated much the same. Just as Scotland had seen extensive economic development since the Union, so the presence of the Genevans promised similar economic development in southern Ireland.[33] As a propaganda tool the experiment was equally important, being a response to the extension of French power on the European mainland. As old Geneva was expected to sink under the weight of French despotism and Catholicism, so New Geneva, as it thrived, was anticipated to underscore the greatness of Britain, and the constancy of its opposition to the tyranny of France.

New Geneva failed for a variety of reasons, from the weather, to the use of the money, to a change of ministry in London. The leaders of the experiment continued to seek means of maintaining small states, and of defending their republican heritage. They still had hopes of turning Britain into a cosmopolitan empire, premised on Britain being a friend to the cause of liberty across Europe. They were convinced of the direct relationship between political liberty, civil liberty and free trade. When the French Revolution erupted, many of the Genevan republicans, having returned to their own country early in 1789, then went directly to Paris, hoping that a new age of peace between the British and French leviathans was imminent. The ideal envisaged future was that both superpowers would underwrite the sovereignty of the existing republics, and sign commercial treaties for the development of free commerce globally. For those who continued to argue that Britain was a mercantile system, it was of fundamental importance that means be sought to distance the country from political and economic corruption; free trade with France was seen to be one such means, being a solvent to the sinister interests that were held to be dominating trade and weakening the British polity.

IV

From the traditional republican perspective, and that of the British friends of French liberty, many of whom had involved themselves with New Geneva, the French Revolution gradually created a different kind of republicanism. The policy of turning large states with monarchical manners into large republics was heralded. Rousseau, whose works are so often described as the ideological inspiration for the French Revolution, had entirely opposed the conversion of large corrupt monarchies into large republics. He had written, in a letter to the Paris bookseller Duchesne, that his *Contrat social* 'was not a book made for France'. Rather, he described the *Contrat social* as having been 'quoted several times, and even summarised in the treatise on education [*Émile*]', as needing to be 'regarded as a kind of appendix . . . the two together mak[ing] a complete whole'.[34] The new idea of the French revolutionaries was that of a republic founded upon the legal destruction of aristocratic ranks, which were blamed for political tyranny and for economic stagnation.[35] Instead of political society being comprised of a set of orders or ranks, with differing interests that needed to be balanced by the legislator who represented the state, the nation itself was the sole source of sovereignty. As the Abbé Sieyès put it, 'The nation exists before everything, it is the object of everything. Its will is always legal, it is the law itself.'[36] The nation did not include unproductive aristocrats. Rather, it was comprised of the unified body of the labouring people. Unifying the people meant making them more homogeneous; it is no surprise that Sieyès was involved in defining what it was to be French, and in the departmentalisation of the country, at the outset of the Revolution.

Edmund Burke, in his *Reflections on the Revolution in France*, appearing in multiple editions from November 1790, declared that the revolution was weakening France and could not be sustained. Sieyès's vision of a unified nation went against what Burke saw as the actual nature of society, necessarily diverse and hierarchical. In seeking the establishment of a new form of the sovereign nation, France was, for Burke, in the process of returning to barbarism, destroying property, losing liberty and breaking itself up into 'a republican system of eighty-three independent municipalities'. The future could be discerned in the events of 6 October 1789, when the mob attacked Versailles, forcing the royal family to flee a palace 'swimming in blood, polluted by massacre, and strewed with scattered limbs and mutilated carcasses'.[37] Burke was elevated into a seer in politics over the following four years, as every prediction he had made seemed to come true. Most pertinently, he asserted that the French Revolution would result in civil and in international war, and in the outbreak of astonishing civil violence, called by contemporaries, when it came, 'the Terror'.

Burke himself did not share the widespread view that he could see into the future. Rather, he warned increasingly that 'the times are so deplorable, that I do not know how to write about them'.[38] He was convinced up to his death in 1797 that the difference between the French Republic and all historical states lay in its superiority at making war. By the beginning of 1793, France had defeated Prussia, conquered Savoy, pillaged Germany, invaded the Dutch Republic and was threatening Spain and all of the states of Italy. In Burke's opinion, something new had been created in politics. Revolutionary republicanism was deadly because it amounted to a new form of imperialism. In the name of liberty, the existing states of Europe were being eaten up, restructured and turned into republics or democracies, and annexed to or forcibly allied to France. The French Republic needed war, because the Revolution had near-destroyed the state and the economy. The states of Europe were the victims, and their rulers had failed to fight France and to recognise the threat that it posed to traditional politics, understood as the seeking of peace and security. As Burke put it in a memorable paragraph, the First French Republic had reversed traditional political logic in turning a weak state into a military Behemoth:

> The Republic of Regicide with an annihilated revenue, with defaced manufactures, with a ruined commerce, with an uncultivated and half depopulated country, with a discontented, distressed, enslaved, and famished people, passing with a rapid, eccentric, incalculable course, from the wildest anarchy to the sternest despotism, has actually conquered the finest parts of Europe, has distressed, disunited, deranged, and broke to pieces all the rest; and so subdued the minds of the rulers in every nation, that hardly any resource presents itself to them, except that of entitling themselves to a contemptuous mercy by a display of their imbecility and meanness.[39]

Burke observed a French Republic that he feared because its ambitions were unlimited. Furthermore, revolutionary philosophy seduced the people living in the very states it was seeking to invade and overthrow. When sailors of the Royal Navy mutinied at Spithead in April 1797, Burke saw it as 'the first nidus and hot-bed of their [French] infection'. He claimed that he 'should not be surprised at seeing a French [invading force] convoyed by a British Navy to an attack upon this kingdom'.[40] Burke's only hope, believing that 'the heart of the citizen is a perennial spring of energy to the state', was that the British would fight the French to the death. John Brown's *Estimate of the Manners and Principles of the Times*, despite being treated as a work of Pythagorean certainty, had in 1757 wrongly predicted defeat in war against France because of the growth of a frivolous effeminacy in Britain; Burke felt that revolutionary France likewise might yet fall before British arms.[41]

Edward Gibbon was equally certain that French republicanism was distinctive in history. For Gibbon too, it spelled death for all of the existing republics that he held so dear. Britain was at war with revolutionary France from 1st February 1793. One of the key issues for supporters of the British state was whether French-style democratic republican ideas would take root across the Channel. The revolutionary disease appeared to be spreading across Europe with the progress of French arms. Gibbon concluded that 'the whole horizon is so black, that I begin to feel some anxiety for England, the last refuge of liberty and law'. As 'the Gallic dogs' were enjoying the 'most insolent prosperity', Gibbon became fearful that the British would succumb to the revolutionary ardour and 'eat the Apple of false freedom'.[42]

It was evident to every observer that a likely place for French republicanism to attract popular support was Ireland. Ireland was seen to be both Britain's shame and point of weakness: the place where civil and political liberties were forbidden to a Catholic majority, where economic activity had been curtailed to prevent competition with industries on the mainland and where Protestant landlords were accused of behaving like tyrannical aristocrats of the most atrocious kind. In other words, Ireland was a product of the mercantile system at its worst, just as the experience of Scotland provided arguments supportive of the positive and productive effects upon small states of the imperial economy. As mentioned in the first chapter it was at Belfast in 1791, with eleven other Protestants, that the lawyer, self-styled 'Northern Whig' and advocate of Catholic emancipation Theobald Wolfe Tone created the Society of United Irishmen, devoted to making Ireland independent and to putting an end to the civil, political and religious divisions within the country.[43] In 1798, the Society boasted more than a quarter of a million members. Although the French had failed in an attempt to invade Ireland in 1796, it was still anticipated in 1798 that French military force would protect popular revolution by the people of Ireland. The way would be open to realise Thomas Paine's vision, articulated in the second part of his *Rights of Man* (1792), of a global republic free from the corrupting forces of monarchy and nobility, and characterised in consequence by perpetual peace and an end to poverty.[44]

By the time of the Irish rebellion in 1798, the supporters of the British state had for many years readied themselves to respond both in military terms and through counter-claims against the anarchist and terrorist nature of French republicanism. The English Statute of Treasons of 1351 (25 Edward III) contained a clause defining treason as 'when a man doth compass or imagine the death of our Lord the King, of our Lady his Queen, or of their eldest son and heir'. Legal authorities across the centuries had interpreted this clause as signifying the attempted murder of monarchs or plots with such an outcome as their aim. In the early years of the French Revolution, however, crown lawyers in Britain began to employ a much broader definition of treason, as any kind of challenge to the monarchical polity. Calls for assemblies to discuss reform and the advocacy of republican ideas came to be deemed treasonable acts, since by *mens rea* they presumed the death of the monarch.[45] An illustration of this is the case of John Frost, the solicitor and founder member of the Society for Constitutional Information, who was involved in trips to France with Paine and in the movement for reform carried on by the London Corresponding Society. Frost was overheard to say in the Percy coffee-house, just north of Oxford Street, on 6 November 1792, that he was 'for equality and no kings'. He was indicted in December for sedition, tried in May 1793, and imprisoned for six months with an hour in the pillory. Mainland Britain was meanwhile becoming increasingly divided, with images of Paine burned in effigy across the country.[46]

Thomas Erskine, the great Whig lawyer and Westminster member of Charles James Fox's opposition to William Pitt and to war with France, defended Frost with the argument that coffee-house conversation was private and accordingly privileged. He also condemned the men who complained about Frost—a hosier's son, an upholsterer and 'an apothecary passing for a gentleman'—for ignoring such etiquette: these 'coffee-house politicians' were too low to recognise the rights of Englishmen and the necessity of defending the popular liberty of private conversation.[47] Nevertheless, in 1794–95 the government initiated what became a series of prosecutions against political radicals in London and in Edinburgh, including the Scottish 'Friends of the People' Robert Watt and David Downie, and members of the London Corresponding Society such as John Horne Tooke, John Thelwall and Thomas Hardy. While the latter three were acquitted, others were found guilty and sentenced to be transported.[48]

In 1795 the Treasonable Practices Act replaced the 1351 Act and redefined treason; the Seditious Meetings Act of the same year then confirmed an era of repression in which all critics of the government and its war were presented as republicans, atheists, cosmopolitans, Francophiles and revolutionaries, terrorists and traitors. Their writings were burned and advocates of republican democracy were identified, put on trial and in numerous cases transported. Loyalist and anti-Jacobin societies were established in every part of the British Isles. Britain was presented as a cosmopolitan empire, a defender of order and liberty against French anarchy and atrocity. In Isaac Cruikshank's print of January 1793, 'French Happiness, English Misery', French *sans-culottes* are portrayed as bedraggled and famished, pulling on the legs of a frog, while in an empty fireplace a pan named 'Tree of Liberty' lacks any food. The dreadful nature of revolutionary society is signified by a corpse hanging from a lamp-post, while a child, evidently the son of an aristocrat, is impaled on a spike and a soldier carries a severed head on his bayonet. A reference is made to the French victory at Jemappes, the point being that the revolutionaries did not care about numbers being killed, calling a victory a battle where they had lost so many dead. A contrast is drawn with the fat Englishmen enjoying meat and ale and warmth, thanks to the king, the constitution and Christianity.

Britain was portrayed as the protector of all that was precious in European history against the terrorist republican advocacy of a utopia founded on the abolition of everything that had gone before. Proof that Britain was superior to France, it was claimed, lay in its treatment of small states. French revolutionaries were condemned for tearing up old Europe: by 1798, the Dutch Republic, the Swiss cantons, Venice, Genoa and Geneva had ceased to be independent states. As one British observer put it, 'Thus did the MONSTROUS REPUBLIC, fascinate and fix the little Republics, of Holland, Venice, Switzerland, &c. till they were swallowed up in succession.'[49] When France became a republican empire seeking to develop its trade and to spread liberty, this translated into traditional reason-of-state politics, as noted by small-state republicans such as the journalist Jacques Mallet du Pan, writing about the invasion of Switzerland by the French Directory in 1798:

> This Directory punishes the Swiss for their neutrality . . . proclaims its respect for their independence, whilst with the fire of the canon it deprives them of their laws and their ancient Constitution . . . institutes republics against the will of republicans . . . which, in its destructive rage overturns all states, throws republics upon monarchies, neutral countries on belligerent ones, and manifestly demonstrates to all countries, that the worst of all conditions is to be at peace with it, and to remain secure under the faith of treatises.'[50]

Significantly, Mallet du Pan ended his work with the statement, 'Now all Europe is concentrated in England. Its salvation depends upon the fate of that power!'[51] Of all of Europe's republics, only the tiny Republic of San Marino remained, because one of its ministers enjoyed a personal connection to Napoleon Bonaparte.

Against French imperialism, the benefits of civil liberty and trade were extolled as accompanying British dominion. The case of Scotland was everywhere cited in support of British rule, providing evidence that Britain was not subject to a mercantile system whereby policy was ultimately determined by short-sighted merchants and bankers. Scotland was associated with a vibrant intellectual life and the creation of a philosophical

FIGURE 2.2. Isaac Cruikshank, 'French Happiness, English Misery', 3 January 1793 British Museum Collection, no. J,4.91. Copyright © The Trustees of the British Museum

school so great as to rival ancient authority. Negativity about the future was not the lesson to be derived from Scotland. It was a success story of commercial progress and the resolution of inveterate conflicts, whether between Highlanders and Lowlanders, Jacobites and Hanoverians or Presbyterians and Episcopalians. The Reverend Thomas Brooke Clarke, who had livings in Ireland, conveyed this view in numerous publications at the turn of the century. Clarke was an indefatigable supporter of a union between Britain and Ireland, and he employed the history of eighteenth-century Scotland to support an argument that Britain had resolved the rich country–poor country problem. Scotland, once desperately impoverished and suffering economic decline, had thrived since 1707. Clarke quoted Henry Dundas, 1st Viscount Melville, the war secretary, to the effect that the union had not only established liberty for Scotland, but had 'broken asunder the bands of feudal vassalage'. Britain was a unique state, because poor nations that were united with it experienced economic growth far greater than that of England.[52] The kinds of faction that were rife in poor states, which Clarke called in Scotland's case 'distractions, divisions and clanship', ceased with the Union, and 'the industry of the inhabitants was awakened'. The result had been an explosion of the population, the formation of great cities and the growth of the kinds of 'politeness' and civility that characterised cosmopolitan commercial societies.[53] Ireland, to a multitude of observers, was troubled because it had seen, by comparison with Scotland, so little economic improvement.

PART II

Divided Geneva

CHAPTER THREE

Religion and Enlightenment

IN ORDER TO explain why a group of republicans calling themselves democrats sought sanctuary in Ireland, we have to revisit the crisis at Geneva which came to a head in 1782. Many were shocked at events within the city, because, as Calvin's adopted home and a centre of enlightened learning, civil war was not supposed to break out. Yet between the 1750s and the 1780s republicans at Geneva began to be branded as democrats, certain citizens were labelled anarchists and the magistrates were increasingly attacked as tyrants, running the state with their own interests to the fore, rather than the public good. This was certainly a new departure. During the political crises of the first decade of the century, and during those of the 1730s, political abuse had been commonplace, with accusations of treachery and corruption abounding.[1] The accusation was not levelled, however, that Geneva would be destroyed if a particular group continued to hold power, or that particular positions were so far beyond the pale that violence was required to put things right. The extremist language that developed, clearly in evidence by the mid-1760s, was a return to the kinds of polarity that marked the era of the Reformation.

This is important. So many political actors in the eighteenth century believed that the great achievement of their forebears had been to put an end to the obsession with heresy and its accompanying brutality that so marred European life between the 1520s and the Peace of Westphalia in 1648. Fear of the return of religious antagonism, and its translation once again into political affairs, remained a contemporary obsession in the war-scarred eighteenth century. Although many historians have seen the politics of the later eighteenth century in secular terms, religion continued to set the tone, not least because fear in politics was defined by religious imagery. This meant that both sides in political argument saw their opponents as reigniting the religious warfare of the past.

That extremist language began to mark Genevan politics struck many as remarkable. Geneva had been so stable since Calvin's time, with reputed levels of equality and undoubted levels of civic order that could be contrasted with the tempestuous lives of other states: there was no general crisis in seventeenth-century Geneva. The city had avoided being embroiled in European wars, had repelled invasion, was singularly prosperous and appeared to have managed to combine religious devotion with the pursuit of wealth. More especially, the French-inspired mediation of the 1730s had largely united opposed parties. Geneva had been stable throughout the War of the Austrian Succession. The future looked bright, with Savoy acknowledging the sovereignty of the city in 1754. By the end of 1764, however, relations between the citizens and their magistrates had altogether broken down. What went wrong?

Answering this question means we have to examine perceptions of life at Geneva in the eighteenth century. David Mallet, the poet and dramatist, in 1735 sent a revealing description of the city of Geneva to his friend Alexander Pope. Like most visitors, he noted that Geneva was pretty, built on rising ground in the middle of a plain full of vineyards, meadows and small villas, with the great Lac Leman before it, and the still greater Jura mountains framing the city. As with all new travellers, he further commented that Geneva was 'of no great extent'.[2] Thomas Gray, another poet who visited the city in the 1730s, wrote that 'perhaps Geneva, and all that belongs to it, are not of equal extent with Windsor and its two parks'.[3] The population, except in times of refugee crisis, such as that which followed Louis XIV's persecution of Huguenots after the revocation of the Edict of Nantes in 1685, was no higher than twenty-five thousand persons.[4] One English visitor stated that there was 'no place in the world better served with provisions than this', as the Genevans enjoyed 'good wine, and cheap, excellent wild fowl, and incomparable fish, particularly trout'. The church of Saint-Pierre was said to be remarkable for two very large bells, the larger of which required ten men to toll it. The bells were required in case of alarm, which was anticipated because Geneva was 'in the midst of enemies'.[5] Every visitor raised a question over the capacity of the city to defend itself, being at a crossroads sharing borders with France, Savoy, the Pays de Vaud, governed by the canton of Bern, and Neuchâtel, a part of Prussia since 1707. Geneva was garrisoned by seven hundred troops, Mallet said, who would surely 'be found not near sufficient to man the walls'. As such, 'the little republic depends chiefly for its security on the mutual jealousy of the French king and the Duke of Savoy'. Geneva subsisted, as another visitor put it, 'like a bone 'twixt three mastiffs, the Emperor, the French King, and the Dukes of Savoy', maintaining its independence only because no power dared to 'touch it singly, for fear that the other two would fly upon him'.[6] The implication was that if the antagonism between surrounding states were ever to be overcome, the independence of Geneva would immediately be jeopardised. Precisely this happened in 1782.

Mallet's portrait of life within Geneva echoed the findings of a thousand tourists. Geneva was an astonishingly well-regulated commercial town, with tall buildings, narrow streets and ample market places, surrounded by a three-mile wall, the gates of which were locked every evening.[7] Mary Shelley later noted that while bribery in France would have opened the doors into the night, this would never be the case at Geneva. The people were far too much 'inclined to puritanism'.[8] Similar lives appeared to be lived by all the residents. The influence of Calvin was dominant. In the eighteenth century, fornication was punishable by death, imprisonment, whipping or banishment. Church attendance was monitored. Catholic images were forbidden. Catholics could remain in the city beyond three days only with permission from the magistrates. Rules governed the ages of brides and of grooms. Sons were held responsible for the debts of their fathers, under threat of losing their own right to hold political office. Sumptuary laws governed dress, with silver and gold lace prohibited, and limits placed upon numbers of carriages, horses and servants.[9]

Religious belief established common forms of life. There was little display or evidence of luxury, and next to no libertinism or opportunities to act the rake.[10] Mallet praised the order and good conduct of the inhabitants of Geneva, but his account, with its implied contrast with life in London, was ultimately melancholic and bleak:

> As all public spectacles are forbidden, our amusements are few. These honest burghers lead a plain, uniform life, which, if it is not enlivened by many pleasures, is not ruffled by strong passions; a little commerce, a little love, and a very little gallantry, make up the business and ambition of the place. The whole town dines regularly at half an hour after twelve. About two they form themselves into parties, which they call societies, for cards, where, if a man is in an ill run of fortune, he may lose three or four shillings. This continues till six; and then all the little *beau monde* of Geneva appears either on the bastions of their fortifications or in a public walk which they call the *Treille*. The women simper at the men, and the men say silly things to the women,

till half an hour after seven, when everyone returns to his own home to supper and to bed.

Dancing in public or in private, and secular public music, could not be found. Charles Burney, visiting at the beginning of the 1770s, noted 'there is but little music to be heard in this place, as there is no play-house allowed; nor are there organs in the churches, except two, which are used for psalmody only'.[11] For the prominent Genevan theologian Jacob Vernet, the key to Geneva's success was that 'everything is connected'. Stability relied entirely upon the 'moral and religious regime'. Genevans needed 'sumptuary laws, ecclesiastical discipline, simple customs and a regular domestic and social life, military exercises and such like, no theatre, dances or masques, the play of commerce but no gambling'.[12] George Keate held in 1760 that the result was 'a republic founded in wisdom and virtue . . . a people happy and free, yet who have defended themselves with bravery on every occasion'.[13]

Voltaire, having left Geneva for the French border town of Ferney in 1759, continuously bemoaned the contrast between the singular location of the city and the dispiriting existence within its walls. He blamed Calvin, 'that vile interpreter of holy Paul'. Geneva's Calvinist pastors were 'a rigid, melancholy race', who 'stamped austerity on every face'. Voltaire accused the Consistory of Pastors of failing to encourage people to do good to one another, because of the Calvinist doctrine 'that God does all, and man has nought to do'.[14] In 1762, Voltaire wrote to his close friend Jean d'Alembert, whose scandalous article 'Genève' in the *Encyclopédie* of 1757 was itself part of Voltaire's war against Calvinism, 'I promise you, my friend, not to go to Geneva, because only small fools and petty tyrants dwell there.'[15] The counter-argument was that Geneva merited attention because of three distinguishing features, which together made it the most significant city on earth relative to its size: it was a free state, a commercial state and a 'Rome for all Protestants'.

II

Geneva considered itself to have been a free city since medieval times. The Dominican friar and bishop Adhémar Fabri, in a document named 'les Franchises' of 1387, had asserted the authority of the commune to defend the city and to elect councillors annually to govern alongside the bishop.[16] For reasons of the protection of trade, Geneva was initially allied to Fribourg, the Swiss canton to the north, and followed Fribourg in establishing a Council of Two Hundred to work with the elected magistrates to govern the state in the early sixteenth century. As Fribourg remained Catholic, closer ties were established in the 1530s with Bern, which ruled the Pays de Vaud and nearby Lausanne. During the wars of religion, Geneva was included in alliances between the cantons and France, allowing mercenaries to enter the French army. The Treaty of Soleure (1579) confirmed French support for the protection of Geneva by the cantons. In 1584, the canton of Zurich made a perpetual alliance with Geneva, and the triple alliance between Bern, Zurich and Geneva was renewed in 1642. The rulers of Savoy, who had become kings of Sardinia under Victor Amadeus II (1666–1732), only renounced their claim to be the legitimate sovereigns of Geneva in 1754. Into the eighteenth century, the city was, it was said, 'acknowledged as a free, sovereign State by all the Princes of Europe, even the greatest, as the King of France, Louis XIV . . . hath sometimes used the expression, *We desire and pray the Republick of Geneva*'.[17]

That Geneva was a free state was widely seen to explain why the attempt by Savoy to take it on 11 December 1602—the 'Escalade'—had failed. Charles Emmanuel, the son of Philibert, Duke of Savoy, invaded Geneva at night with over a thousand troops, many of whom used ladders (*escalades*) to scale the walls.[18] The citizens managed to repel the attackers, killing over two hundred of them. Prisoners were executed and the heads of all the dead invaders placed on the ramparts, with their bodies being cast into the Rhône. The historian Maximillien Misson noted, 'Some body at that time happily enough found out the Word VENGÉE [reveng'd] in that of Genève.'[19] All citizens and burghers were armed henceforth, and Bern agreed to supply up to forty thousand troops to defend the city at short notice in time of crisis.[20] Improvements to its defences commenced in the 1660s, and continued into the eighteenth century. It was never altogether safe, however. Crisis points included Louis XIV's invasion of the Franche-Comté in 1684, generating fears of an imminent attack, and during the War of the Austrian Succession (1740–48), when reports circulated that France had agreed to let Savoy take Geneva.[21] Whenever war engulfed mainland Europe, as it did for so much of the eighteenth century, a state of emergency was proclaimed within the city, and preparations were made to repel invaders once again.

In what did liberty consist? Jean Bodin, in his *Six livres de la republique*, wrote that Geneva became a free state when it ceased to be governed by dukes or bishops. It was in 1528 that Geneva's 'pontifical monarchy' became 'a Popular state, governed in the manner of an Aristocracy'. Sovereignty lay in the Council of Two Hundred, but the ultimate authority was shared in practice with the general assembly of all citizens, which could censure magistrates, challenge laws and had to consent to war.[22] Its distinctive division of sovereignty, between magistrates who held their offices for long periods of time and citizens who could in principle remove them, was for Bodin the key to the stability of the city. Liberty was linked too to Protestantism. It was no accident, Bodin wrote, that religion and the state were re-made at the same point in time. A direct relationship between Protestantism and liberty was presumed by all of the commentators who praised Geneva.

Liberty was seen to be maintained because of an explicit social hierarchy. Equality was a threat to liberty. The equality associated with modern republics was altogether foreign to republicans at Geneva. The gradation of ranks was essential to the proper functioning of politics. There were five social orders, each of whose members had to express their support for the Protestant faith: 'citizens' (*citoyens*), 'burgesses' (*bourgeois*), 'natives' (*natifs*), 'inhabitants' (*habitants*) and 'subjects' (*sujets*). Citizens alone could serve as magistrates; they had to be born in the city to a father who was either bourgeois or citoyen. Bourgeois could practice commerce within the city; they were either granted or, more commonly, had to purchase their status. Numbers were restricted because the price of being bourgeois rose in the eighteenth century, to a figure that meant only very wealthy persons could afford the fee. The *habitants* were foreigners who had purchased a right to live in the city but had no political rights, and restricted rights to engage in commerce. With their children, the *natifs*, they formed the largest social group in the state, being approximately twice in number to the body of citizens and bourgeois. The *natifs*, as the children of *habitants*, were likewise not allowed to enter politics. Like their parents, they paid a fee each year to enable them to be involved in commerce, in addition to a tax in case they became reliant upon the state through destitution. The *sujets* lived within or beyond the city and lacked commercial or political rights, being simply 'Protestants who have no other benefit than that of living under a mild government'.[23]

Geneva was governed by several councils. The notionally sovereign Council of Two Hundred (*Conseil des deux cent* or *Grand conseil*) delegated the governance of the state to the executive Council of Twenty-Five, also known as the *Petit conseil*.[24] The magistracy, who were elected on the first Sunday in the new year, were led by four syndics, elected from the Council of Twenty-Five, who presided over the councils, held their office for a year, and could not be re-elected for a further four years. In addition, there was a *lieutenant de police* responsible for policing the city, also from the Council of Twenty-Five, and six *auditeurs du droit* from the Council of Two Hundred, who aided the *lieutenant* and served for three years, with two of the six losing their posts annually. Finally, there was the *procureur-général*, who served for three years and could be re-elected for a further term, and whose role was to observe and superintend the rights and laws of the state and to identify abuses, crucially not *ex officio* but by order of the Council of Twenty-Five.

Tension existed on occasion between the Council of Two Hundred and the Council of Twenty-Five. As the eighteenth century wore on, however, friction was to be found more regularly between the General Council of all citizens, called the *Conseil général*, and the Council of Twenty-Five. The General Council, of approximately fifteen hundred citizens and bourgeois, which met at the Saint-Pierre Cathedral twice a year, could not summon itself or debate matters of state. Its function in politics was to consent to or to reject propositions put to it by the smaller executive councils concerning domestic or international affairs, and to set the wine tax.[25] Constitutional revisions were made in edicts of 1543, 1568 and 1570, limiting the power of the General Council. In the 1530s the Council of Two Hundred and the Council of Twenty-Five began to elect each other's members annually. After 1543, they determined the issues brought to the General Council for assent or rejection, taking this right away from individual citizens. Furthermore, the four syndics, elected annually by the General Council every January, had to be chosen from eight candidates presented by the smaller councils. Following the election, the syndics would summon the Council of Two Hundred and confirm in their offices or reject the members of the Council of Twenty-Five, a process called *le grabeau*. Those who had lost their offices would be replaced from a list of candidates submitted for selection to the Council of Two Hundred by the Council of Twenty-Five. Once the Council of Twenty-Five was reconstituted, it would similarly confirm or replace the members of the Council of Two Hundred.

The system of dividing sovereignty and government, between the Council of Two Hundred and the Council of Twenty-Five, was undoubtedly successful. Many considered the Council of Two Hundred to be the supreme court of justice, having the power to pardon, and also to be the source of deliberation about propositions for the General Council. The Council of Two Hundred met on the first Monday of each month. The Council of Twenty-Five also claimed rights to judge criminal cases, dealt with civil disputes, had the right to summon the Council of Two Hundred, to grant individuals bourgeois status and to administer national finances.

FIGURE 3.1. A meeting of the General Council at Geneva, 10 February 1789, Christian Gottfried Geissler (1770–1844). AKG Images/De Agostini Picture Library

It functioned as the executive government of the state. Regular meetings made decisions by majority vote.

While the outside world in the seventeenth century faced what has recently been termed a global crisis, Geneva was calm and prosperous.[26] Part of the reason was the acknowledged link between liberty and Calvinism. In the General Council, each elector every year declared an oath, promising to use his power to promote the best person for each office, this being the most godly act, and most likely to maintain the liberties of the city:

> We promise and swear before God and before all of the community, to elect and nominate to the office of Syndic, those who we believe to be proper and suited to the office, in order to maintain the honour of God and the honour of the Christian Religion in this town, and to guide and govern the people in good order, and to conserve the liberty of the town.[27]

Before any election, a sermon was preached by the most senior member of the consistory. Before electors retired to a closet each to put a mark against a desired candidate, they placed their hands upon a large open Bible.

Express devotion to a discernible common good, derived from shared religious beliefs, failed to maintain peace at Geneva in the eighteenth century, however. At the beginning of the century Pierre Fatio, a member of a prominent family, accused the magistrates of creating a corrupt oligarchy. In January 1707, proposals were introduced to reduce family membership within the executive councils, to publish a constitutional code through a specially convened general council and to introduce secret ballot for elections.[28] Fatio was declared in turn to be seeking to subvert the government of the state. Found guilty, he was condemned to public decapitation. Prior to his execution, Fatio read the first verse of the 58th Psalm: 'Are your minds set upon righteousness, O ye congregation, and do ye judge the things that are right, O ye sons of men?' He professed his innocence, his devotion to Christ and to the city.[29] Fatio, for subsequent generations, was a national martyr. To the revolutionaries who took control of the city in 1782, he was Geneva's first Gracchus.[30]

The brutal control of dissent worked when the city was threatened by Europe-wide war, lasting until the Peace of Utrecht in 1714. Trouble flared up again in the 1730s, however, when pastor Michel Léger claimed in print that the magistrates and the Council of Twenty-Five were taking away the power of the General Council, and were introducing mercenaries into the city for the defence of the magistrates themselves, rather than relying upon a citizen milita. Léger's *Représentations des citoyens et bourgeois de Genève* were submitted to the executive councils in 1734.[31] Over the following three years, an uneasy truce held between magistrates and citizens, until violence exploded on 21 August 1737, when the militia attacked the mercenary garrison, leading to eleven deaths. By this date, Louis XV had decided to intervene. Mediators were called from France, Zurich and Bern, an action stated to be in accordance with the Treaty of Soleure. The leading mediator was the comte de Lautrec, then *lieutenant-général* of the French province of Guyenne, who arrived in the city in October 1737.[32] In 1738, he imposed a compromise called the *Reglèment* or *Médiation*.[33] Geneva was becoming renowned for its turbulent politics. As one observer wrote, the battle for political dominion between over-powerful families and their opponents made Geneva 'unfortunate' and 'afflicted'.[34]

III

After widespread agitation by Protestant preachers visiting Geneva, the populace had rejected the bishop and Catholic Mass on 21 May 1535. In August of that year, Guillaume Farel, the most active Protestant proselytiser, persuaded Jean Calvin from Noyon in northern France, who had recently published his *Institutio Christianae religionis*, to remain at Geneva, where he had stopped on his way to Strasbourg, his place of asylum since 1529. Calvin became a minister at Geneva in September 1536, and with Farel formulated a plan for a new church government in January 1537. When the syndics of Geneva opted to follow the Bernese policy of strictly separating the duties of religious ministers from politics in the spring of 1738, Calvin and Farel left the city. Calvin returned in September 1541 and drafted new 'ecclesiastical ordinances'. These ordinances defined four categories of ministry within the reformed faith: the first was the doctors responsible for determining and conveying the message derived from the Bible; the second was ministers who preached and administered the sacraments; the third was deacons dedicated to relieving the lot of the poor; and the fourth was elders who maintained morals among the populace. The deacons, like the elders, were annually elected. All pastors were paid a modest salary by the state. The twelve lay elders derived from the magisterial councils. In 1542, Calvin established a Consistory or ecclesiastical court, comprised of the pastors and elders. By the end of the 1540s, he had himself become 'Patriarch of Geneva, and Architect that framed all their state and discipline'.[35] Calvin's doctrine became orthodoxy, a fact exemplified by the beheading of Jacques Gruet for libertinism in 1547 and the burning of Michel Servet for heresy in October 1553. Calvin was, however, never a citizen. A foreign resident at Geneva, or *habitant*, he was declared *bourgeois* in 1559, which gave him second-order civic privileges. Calvin could never serve as a magistrate.

The famous 'church discipline at Geneva' entailed the doctors and pastors forming the 'Company of Pastors' or 'Venerable Company' that met quarterly to consider the organisation of the church and the religious health of the republic. The Consistory or 'standing ecclesiastical court' was given the role of 'the cure of men's manners, power of determining all kinds of ecclesiastical causes, and authority to convent [call before a judge], to control, to punish as far as with excommunication, whomsoever they should think worthy, none excepted'.[36] While the Company of Pastors governed the church, the Consistory held itself responsible for popular morals; both bodies liaised with the members of the magisterial Council of Twenty-Five, and especially the four syndics, with regard to matters of morality and religion. The rationale for the existence of the free city was stated to be 'that the doctrine of the Holy Gospel of our Lord God be conserved well in purity, and a Christian Church maintained accordingly', with laws fitting for 'an ecclesiastical policy, which is taken out of the gospel of Jesus Christ'.

To maintain such a lofty aspiration, it was vital that 'the Christian religion be purely observed'.[37] Many members of the population appeared before the Consistory for acts of immorality.[38] Prayers and sermons were held every day, beginning in the early hours for servants and workmen, children were regularly catechised and each family was visited at least four times a year for moral evaluation.[39] By the 1760s, when the fornicator Robert Covelle refused to bow before the pastors to request forgiveness, and was supported by a large body of the populace in consequence, it was reported that 'the Consistory has become a useless tribunal'.[40] Despite such challenges the Consistory remained conjoined with Genevan life and politics.

Calvinism generated patriotism. The aged Theodore Beza had slept through the agitation of the Escalade in 1602, but returned to the pulpit on 12 December, and preached a sermon during which the 124th Psalm was sung. The psalm became the quintessential expression of popular patriotism, with its plain message that Genevans had thrown back the invaders because of 'the Lord who was on our side'. There could be no more direct example of the beneficial relationship between Calvinism, republicanism and liberty. The austere morals guaranteed by the Consistory underlined the capacity of Geneva to defend itself.

A further connection between Calvinism and the stability of Geneva lay in its reputation for Protestant learning. Theodore Beza established the Genevan Academy in 1558 to train pastors. Initially there were professors of divinity, Greek, Hebrew and philosophy. The education available was later broadened to include church history, civil history, eloquence, geography, law and oriental languages; in the 1720s, chairs of natural and civil law and of the law of nations were added.[41] Eleven professors could be found in the 1760s and after, in theology and ecclesiastical history (3), oriental languages, natural and civil law (2), German law, philosophy (2), mathematics and belles-lettres.[42] Each year ended in June with an oration by the rector, in which he reflected on the mission of the city in relation to God's higher plan.

Academy professors such as François Turrettini (1623–87) had been in the forefront of the orthodox response to Arminianism, in putting into practice the tenets of the Helvetic Formula Consensus of 1675. Turrettini, alongside Lucas Gernler and Johann Heinrich Heidegger, rejected Moses Amyraut's 'hypothetical universalism', which held that Christ had died for the sins of the entire human race and not solely of the elect, although only the latter would benefit from the Atonement.[43] François Turrettini's son and successor Jean-Alphonse Turrettini (1671–1737), who became professor of church history at the Genevan Academy in 1697, rector in 1701 and professor of theology in 1705, followed a different path.[44] He abrogated the Helvetic Formula Consensus in 1706 and embraced a tolerant and ecumenical form of Calvinism, inspired by Louis Tronchin, the professor of theology at the Academy and himself the student of Amyraut at the Saumur Academy.[45] Along with figures such as the Anglican archbishop of Canterbury John Tillotson, Jean-Alphonse Turrettini was at the forefront of the syncretic movement in the first decades of the eighteenth century.[46] He expressed genuine hopes for uniting the Reformed Churches through agreement over fundamental issues of doctrine while sidestepping points of controversy such as the presence of Christ in the Eucharist, and predestination.[47] Turrettini saw 'the coat of Christ torn to pieces' through war and poverty, causing 'the waters of the deluge' to be fast about all Christians. This view was shared by more prominent Protestant theologians such as Samuel Werenfels and Jean-Frédéric Ostervald, for whom 'our age is more unhappy than the precedent' because the looseness of manners, popular ignorance of the gospel and growth of 'heathenism' was 'authorised by laws and supported by force'.[48]

Neo-Augustinianism and neo-Epicureanism had to be combated, and arguments formulated in doing so against the widespread religious scepticism of the age. Turrettini, Werenfels and Ostervald advocated a primitive Christianity, largely derived from the New Testament, in conjunction with virulent opposition to non-Christians and the severe control of public and private mores. Part of the solution, for Turrettini, lay in politics, and it is significant that he especially praised the union of England and Scotland as exemplifying one means of ending the global war he perceived all around him:

> If we turn our eyes upon the present state of affairs in Europe, in what juncture of time, in what age, as far as the memoirs of history reach, was there observed a greater convulsion of the whole world, more revolutions and changes in almost all kingdoms and commonwealths; in a word, have there been more surprising miracles than in this age, which everywhere brings them forth? We see the world engaged in a cruel war of many years continuance, kingdoms exhausted, countries laid waste, one king set up against another, and this though so rare an instance, has happened in several nations; most numerous armies on either side both by sea and at land. Nor has the controversy been, as for the most part formerly it was, concerning some punctilios of honour; not for the advantage of trade, nor whether the sea was free or shut up; not concerning the enlarging or contracting the bounds of provinces, but

> they have fought for empire, and this over the largest kingdoms, so that a principal part, not only of America, but of Europe likewise, has been a long while in suspense and doubt to whose government she must at last fall. And if we cast our minds upon that fortunate island, and princess of all others, Great Britain, what more happy, what more to be wished for, what more to be praised, what better adapted to the security of the kingdom and religion, could happen, than that the union of England and Scotland, a thing so often desired and attempted, should be reserved to the happy and glorious times of Queen Anne?[49]

William Coxe wrote that, in the eighteenth century, Geneva had become the most tolerant of reformed states in Switzerland, being the only one that allowed the public exercise of Lutheranism: 'in this respect the clergy, no less wisely than suitably to the spirit as well as the letter of the Christian revelation, have renounced the principles of their great patriarch, Calvin'.[50] This was in line with the infamous claim of Jean d'Alembert that Genevan Calvinism had, by the 1750s, transformed itself into 'the perfect Socinianism'. D'Alembert claimed that 'Most of [the pastors] do not believe in the divinity of Christ, of which Calvin, their chief, was so zealous a defender, and on which account he had Servet burned to death.' The pastors had ceased to believe in a vengeful God and in consequence rejected hell and replaced belief in revelation with a believe in utility, supportive of whatever was conducive to the happiness of the community. D'Alembert stated that only a 'reverence for Christ' prevented the pastors from becoming deists.[51] D'Alembert's view was met with national outrage and a campaign of refutation.[52] He did not realise that the pastors saw the world outside as characterised by sin and catastrophe; the pastors continued to be wedded to the view that politics could not be practised without religious commitment. The seal of the city read *post tenebras lux* ('after the darkness, light'), derived from the Vulgate version of the Book of Job 17:12: 'after the darkness I hope for light' (*post tenebras spero lucem*). Calvin had provided the city with stability and godliness, but the light that emerged was in no sense compatible with Voltaire's enlightenment. This too was to be underlined as the political crisis of the second half of the eighteenth century deepened.

IV

Geneva had always been a commercial centre because of its geographical situation, being the main thoroughfare into Switzerland from southern Europe, and enjoying famous fairs throughout the Middle Ages. It was at

Geneva that the major trade routes crossed from Marseille to Lyon and to southern Germany, and from Milan to St Bernard and to Paris. This continued into early modern times, with the city acting as a hub for the exchange of goods between Italy, the Swiss cantons, France and the German states, having particularly good road and commercial connections with Lyon, Strasbourg and Frankfurt.[53]

Genevans were renowned merchants and manufacturers. Writing in 1714, Abraham Stanyan, who had served for nine years as British envoy to the Swiss cantons, wrote that the people of Geneva were 'naturally industrious, and do not only encourage all sorts of trade in their city, but readily receive good workmen from any other'.[54] Established trade in linens and velvet, dyeing and painting was followed in the eighteenth century by jewellery and watchmaking, making Genevans 'the best merchants in Europe, after the Dutch'.[55] Another visitor found industries in 'silks, gold and silver lace, thread-lace, pistols, shammy leather, watches, and printing of books'.[56] William Coxe wrote that the flourishing nature of the city was due to the 'great industry and activity of its inhabitants; to its more extensive commerce; to the facility of purchasing the burghership; and to the privileges which government allows to all foreigners'.[57] National revenues were largely supplied by trade. The sale of property was taxed at ten per cent, as were bequests from non-family members and from foreigners. Such funds, in addition to a tax upon each inhabitant in proportion to the person's wealth, paid for the garrison of 750 men.[58]

Genevan trade was further stimulated in the eighteenth century because of the influx of French Protestants, who 'supplied Geneva with excellent workmen and artificers in almost every branch of trade, so that at present there are reckoned upwards of three hundred employed in the watch-trade and its several branches'.[59] The sometime Venetian ambassador to the cantons Vendramino Bianchi reckoned that half of the population were Huguenots 'expelled out of France'; they were responsible for the re-fortification of the city, the introduction of 'a great quantity of manufactures of all sorts' and the growth within it of 'the manners and customs of the French'.[60] That Geneva had become 'the most flourishing town of all Switzerland' was due in large part, Abraham Stanyan contended, to the large number of Huguenot refugees who had settled there. Such was the impact of the refugees upon trade that the city began to supply all of Switzerland 'with their best commodities, even to the furniture of their houses, because workmen are reckoned the most fashionable'.[61]

Genevans were also noted for seeking out opportunities for trade.[62] One example was Genevan investment in the national debts and commercial companies of Europe's monarchies, as banking became more prominent, initially with the Lullins, Gallatins and Boissiers, the latter family having fled from Louis XIV's religious persecution, and subsequently with the Detournes, de la Rives, Lullins, Rilliets, Mallets, Neckers, Thellusons and Vernets, among others.[63] Abraham Stanyan noticed in 1714 that the Genevans 'have several bankers of note, who have dealings in most of the trading towns of Europe', and who had negotiated, during the War of the Spanish Succession, 'great sums of money, both for France and the Allies'.[64] The wealth generated from banking in particular gained singular notoriety. It was said of Isaac Thelluson that 'though living somewhat expensively, he had happened to accumulate such a stock of property as is seldom collected together by one individual'. Thelluson became Genevan *résident* at Paris and lived in the French capital from 1740 to 1754; he was rewarded for his work with presents of money not only from the French court but also from the government of Geneva. On his death in 1754, he left an enormous fortune to his children. One of the most famous Genevan bankers of the second half of the eighteenth century, Jacques Necker, started his career as a clerk in Thelluson's bank.[65]

Another important development, especially marked after 1750, was the growth of the jewellery industry, to the detriment of Paris; this was significant because of Geneva's loss of British markets for the sale of watches. For many statesmen it was self-evident that Genevan commerce was increasingly dependent upon a policy of free trade for Genevan goods in France. One of the ways of ensuring the continuance of this policy was to help to supply revenues to the French state by investment in the French national debt. It was equally recognised that such a strategy threatened the independence of the republic, either by tempting French ministers to direct Geneva's trade, or by tying the interests of Geneva too closely to those of France.[66] Meanwhile, the fact that increasing numbers of families were dependent for their income on French life annuities was of considerable concern to those opposed to French influence at Geneva. This was exemplified in the person of Jacques Necker, who served as Genevan ambassador or *résident* to Paris, headed the French *Compagnie des Indes* and represented the interests of the Genevan banking families living at Paris, including the Thellussons, Vernets, Rilliets and Boissiers.[67]

How far was the pursuit of wealth compatible with Calvinism? Many observers emphasised this tension. Calvin had been contemptuous of riches, leaving a meagre sum at his death and living with the utmost frugality.[68] All of the Protestant divines of the early eighteenth century, concerned about the worldly forces that appeared to be ushering faith away, condemned luxury and lives devoted to the pursuit of wealth.[69] Geneva had, however, altered. One observer noted that at the Reformation there had been little commerce, but that since this time 'Geneva has truly changed its face'.[70] The antiquarian and traveller Pierre-Jean Grosley held that 'nowhere is the thirst of gain more predominant'. Although the people were sober and industrious, religion no longer dictated national manners. Rather, Geneva 'has more of the school of the Portico or Lyceum, than of any kind of worship'.[71]

The compatibility of wealth and virtue continued to be questioned at Geneva. As the Anglican bishop and historian Gilbert Burnet noted, eminent pastors such as François Turrettini, who were extremely rich, avoided any hint of their wealth in their dress and their conduct.[72] It was in order to maintain manliness and godliness that luxury was forbidden, manners monitored and supervised and estates divided between children equally at death in order to prevent the growth of excessive riches. Joseph Addison, another early eighteenth-century visitor, noted that the latter policy was essential to prevent rich merchants 'heaping up vast sums from year and year' and becoming 'formidable to the rest of their fellow-citizens', ruining the equality 'which is so necessary in these kinds of governments'. Addison reckoned that some merchants at Geneva were worth twenty thousand crowns, but the key fact was that 'there is not one of them that spend to the value of five hundred pounds a year'.[73]

A central strategy to limit the clash between wealth and virtue was the maintenance of public grain stores. Officials purchased grain of the highest quality from beyond twelve miles out of Geneva, in order not to interfere directly with local markets, and stored supplies reputed to be capable of sustaining the republic for two years. This was vital when the price of wheat rose, as it did repeatedly between 1709 and 1789, reaching crisis levels in 1733–34 and 1778–79, and then again throughout the 1790s.[74] Officials were also able to intervene in the local corn market if prices rose too high, and acquired revenues from the rule that local inns and public houses were obliged to purchase grain directly from the stores, in order to ensure its freshness, at an above-market price. Such a policy, when combined with the sumptuary laws of the city, refuted the view 'of enlightened persons who hold that the ills of the state arise from excessive fortunes occasioned by commerce, which creates too great an inequality between families'.[75] The policy of the *Chambre des bleds* (responsible for regulating grain price and supply to the city) was praised as vital to Genevan survival, and a model institution for republics.[76]

V

Geneva faced two profound difficulties in the eighteenth century. The first was how to accommodate the continued existence of an independent republic to the ever-rising power of France, whose diplomats were active in making the governors of the republic aware of the disparity in strength.[77] The commonplace solution, advocated by leading magistrates such as the natural jurist Jean-Jacques Burlamaqui, was to accept Geneva's place in a French sphere of influence, entailing increasing French involvement in Genevan politics. The price was recognised as being Geneva's role in promoting Protestantism internationally; the awesome power of France within the region translated into the necessary renunciation of the traditional identity of Genevans as being in the vanguard of the Calvinist mission. The French 'guarantee' of the constitution was advanced in justification of close involvement in the affairs of the city, especially in the 1730s. It seemed natural by this time for the French *résident* to take the lead in mediating between its opposing parties.[78] The French guarantee was used again to endorse intervention in the 1760s and in 1782. Additional forms of French influence over Geneva were by then being established, in part through attempts to censor controversial books that were being published in the city.[79]

Taking Geneva closer to France in politics and in culture was never going to receive the support of the people of the city, whose Protestantism remained strong. Critics of magisterial policy were convinced that independence was being lost, just as national identity was being undermined. It became necessary for pro-French magistrates to limit the powers of the General Council of citizens, and to deter actively those bourgeois and citizens who sought to combat Francophilia. This became the great split in Genevan politics in the eighteenth century. It was tied up with the issue of the formal structure of the citizenry, because widening access to citizenship was expected to generate further Francophobia. It was equally tied to the question of whether the form of government at Geneva was now the major impediment to national survival, as the accusation was levelled increasingly, as the eighteenth century wore on, that the existing structure of government had allowed the magistrates to transfer sovereignty to France.

The second problem faced by Geneva in the eighteenth century was that the executive councils were increasingly dominated by members of a small number Geneva's leading families, such as the Pictets, Lullins, du Pans, Trembleys and Rilliets, and the rich families of Italian origin, the

Callandrini, Turrettini, Gallatini, Sartoris's, Bonnets, Legers, Diodati and Minotali.[80] Laws of consanguinity were established in the first decade of the eighteenth century because of Fatio's actions, allowing only a father and two sons, three brothers or six members of the same name and family to serve in the Council of Two Hundred, while in the Council of Twenty-Five fathers and sons or two brothers could not be members conjointly. George Keate praised such laws for preventing 'particular families from becoming too considerable in the state . . . that proved destructive to Florence, and which has occasioned the ruin of so many flourishing commonwealths'.[81] He was altogether mistaken about the operation of the policy in practice, however. By the 1760s, accusations of aristocratic tyranny were rife. The magistrates had by this time identified their opponents as rebels and anarchists, rather than sober defenders of the citizenry. In turn, the supporters of the rights of the General Council called the magistrates tyrants, dictators and advocates of the dominion of Geneva by France. Part of the reason for this development was that the split in Genevan politics became a veritable chasm on account of responses to the city's most famous citizen in the eighteenth century, Jean-Jacques Rousseau.

CHAPTER FOUR

Extremism

JEAN-JACQUES ROUSSEAU WAS identified during the 1760s and forever after as the overwhelming cause of the polarisation of Genevan politics. It was claimed at Geneva and across Europe that Rousseau wanted to replace Christianity with a new religion, purged of the corruption and fakery that he perceived all around him. As one aghast correspondent told Rousseau around 1762, he should either respect 'the errors of the peoples among whom you live' or 'raise the standard of Reformation, and become an Apostle'.[1] The term 'combustible' cropped up all the time in discussions of Rousseau, and was applied to his ideas about politics as well as to his view of religion. Rousseau was increasingly accused of seeking to foment a war between aristocrats and democrats. This was widely held to be the end point of his political theory, the necessary prelude to the reformation of commercial societies that he imagined, through the defeat of luxury and the establishment of the sovereignty of the people, as the vital principle of political legitimacy, and as the foundation of a prosperous household economy within an agrarian republic.[2]

Accordingly, it was widely argued by contemporaries that Rousseau had primed the muskets and loaded the cannon, by supplying the critics of magistrates and mores with the language of resistance and revolution. Geneva fell first, and France was to follow. As Germaine de Staël put it, Rousseau 'was consumed by a fire that devoured him . . . dominated by innumerable ideas' that took hold of him each in their turn, and spread from Rousseau to his readers.[3] For Alexis de Tocqueville, he was 'the sole teacher of the [French] Revolution in its youth.'[4] This was why R. R. Palmer, in *The Age of the Democratic Revolution*, gave a prominent place to events at Geneva, and why Franco Venturi made the same decision in the third volume of his *Settecento riformatore* series.[5] Historians have tended to follow the verdict of Rousseau's contemporary critics, that it was the Genevan philosopher who inspired revolutionary fanaticism.[6] The brilliant engineer Achille-Nicolas Isnard published as early as October 1789 a book which stated that Rousseau's *Contrat social* contained the 'dangerous principle' that had produced revolution in Geneva, France and North America.[7] For Marie-Joseph Bardel, an opponent of the Terror in France who was attempting in 1794 to christianise the Declaration of the Rights of Man, Rousseau was *the* arch anarchist; the most important task of any person was 'to refute the anarchic doctrine of Jean-Jacques Rousseau', because he was the 'master and oracle' of all revolutionaries.[8] This chapter addresses the question of the accuracy of such a judgement. Was Rousseau responsible for the escalation of extremist language, and indeed for the accumulation of justifications of reform by violence?

The view of Rousseau's great rival Voltaire, outlined in a letter of January 1765, was clear-cut. Rousseau was altogether responsible for the 'violent combustion' at Geneva. Democrats had brought war to the town. Envy was everywhere, and the democrats were beginning to demand the equality of fortunes. As Voltaire put it, 'Rousseau is the source of this uproar. He finds it pleasant, at the top of his mountain, to collapse a city, like the trumpet of the Lord that toppled the walls of Jericho.'[9] It was precisely this verdict that was replicated with regard to the French Revolution by those who traced the source of Jacobinism to Rousseau's 'anti-Christian conspiracy', with events at Geneva in 1782 constituting a significant stage in the story of the offensive against throne and altar.[10]

II

The well-known Genevan pastor Jacob Vernet, who in the past had considered himself to be a friend of Rousseau's, was asked in February 1763 to analyse the contents of the latter's work, for Geneva's magistrates, because of the controversy his latest books had generated. The storm had started after a decision was taken to burn Rousseau's recently published *Émile* and *Contrat social*, on 18 June 1762 at Geneva, for fostering anarchy and heresy; it was also decided that should Rousseau return he would be brought bodily before the magistrates.[11] The *Contrat social* had been published at the end of April 1762 and was quickly banned in France; the same decision was taken regarding *Émile* when it appeared on 24 May. On 9 June, the Paris *parlement* censored *Émile* for impiety, ordered all copies to be destroyed and issued an arrest warrant for Rousseau. Rousseau fled from France into Bernese territory, but was soon hounded out; the magistrates expelled him from the canton on 1 July. On 10 July, he found refuge at Môtiers in Neuchâtel, governed by the Scottish former Jacobite George Keith, the tenth Earl Marischal, for Frederick II of Prussia.[12]

With the decision at Geneva to follow France and censor Rousseau's books, it is possible that only a minimal amount of opposition was anticipated within the city, because the savage attacks of prominent commentators were so widespread. Rousseau was seen to have attacked Calvinism, and the sentiments of the populace might therefore have been expected to be antagonistic towards him. The distinguished physician Théodore Tronchin wrote in June 1762 that he wished Rousseau dead, because he believed him to be proclaiming himself a deist and seeking to extirpate established Christianity.[13] The natural philosopher Charles Bonnet, also writing in June, condemned Rousseau for trying to establish a secular republic.[14] For another leading magistrate at Geneva, Jean-Louis Dupan, Rousseau had assaulted government, law and religion.[15] Geneva's *procureur-général* Jean-Robert Tronchin, in his response to Rousseau's books of 19 June 1762, concluded that he was an advocate of 'extreme liberty' and a sceptic, who would allow the people to rewrite the laws and invoke regular popular assemblies, leading to mob rule and political ruination.[16]

By the time Tronchin published his culminating assault on Rousseau's works, the *Lettres écrites de la campagne*, in the autumn of 1763, the philosopher was being depicted as the chief of every opposition group, and the inspiration for every act of defiance against civil magistracy. Yet Rousseau had many supporters within Geneva. A close friend wrote to him to underline that he had 'very few enemies at Geneva', except among the followers of Voltaire; the latter group unfortunately included numerous leading magistrates, who wanted to justify their own luxury and excess, and condemn anyone who had the temerity to oppose them.[17] Support for Rousseau was especially strong among those who called themselves *représentants*, who demanded reform by means of written 'representations' to the magistrates, presenting lists of their grievances and asserting that the ancient constitution was being violated.[18] Rousseau had not asked to become a member of the reform party at Geneva; his association with the critics of magistracy was largely due to Jacques-François Deluc, a master-watchmaker resident in the lower town.[19]

In the 1750s, Deluc was concerned about declining trade, through competition from immigrants to Geneva, about likely high taxes to pay for refortification and about the loss of religious belief and good manners.[20] He was undoubtedly attracted to Rousseau because he believed him to be a staunch moralist and advocate of the benefits of the virtuous life. Deluc's relationship with Rousseau was established during a six-day boat trip around Lac Leman in September 1754.[21] In letters, Deluc then sought to persuade Rousseau that he was a *représentant*.[22] This was also the line taken by fellow *représentants* who became friends with Rousseau, including Pastor Jacob Vernes and the merchant François-Henri d'Ivernois. These men considered themselves to be devout Calvinists, and were critical of Rousseau's stance on revelation in *Émile*. Most *représentants* were, however, convinced that Rousseau was a Protestant, and had not intended either in *Émile* or the *Contrat social* to demand religious reformation. It was reported to Rousseau that 'Deluc loves you with a passion', and that the watchmaker was convinced he could return Rousseau to orthodox Calvinism through argument.[23] By September 1762, Deluc was circulating Rousseau's letters, making hundreds of copies, treating him like an oracle and a latter-day Calvin for Genevans seeking reform.[24] The *représentants* were using Rousseau. They cast him in the role of their intellectual inspiration, whilst the grievances they presented to the magistrates centred on the abuse of him. They believed that his books had been condemned both unjustly and without due process. In particular, they asserted that the magistrates had no authority to demand the arrest of Rousseau himself, since the ecclesiastical ordinances at Geneva forbade such an action.

The claim of the *représentants* was that practices with regard to books accused of heresy had been confirmed by the experience of Jean Morelli, whose *De la discipline ecclésiastique* had been burned by Calvin in 1562, without any bodily arrest.[25] In other words, the magistrates had violated the constitution in burning Rousseau's books at the same time as they continued to demand the physical arrest of his person, and representations were launched against the magistrates detailing extensive legal infraction. When the Council of Twenty-Five vetoed proposals put to it by the *représentants*, refusing to bring their grievances before the General Council of all citizens, the process was identified as an exercise of a veto power called the *droit négatif*. The magistrates were sanguine that the use of the *droit négatif* had been sanctioned by the authority of the *Médiation* of 1738, because article six of the *Médiation* asserted that every proposal considered by the General Council had to be 'considered and approved [*traité & aprouvé*]' by the Council of Two Hundred. The greatest supporter of the *droit négatif*, Jean-Robert Tronchin, was re-elected *procureur-général* of the Republic on 19 November 1762. The *représentants* held, by contrast, that the balance of the constitution was being destroyed by the *droit négatif*, which was a deadly constitutional innovation because it gave the magistrates means to control the General Council and thereby usurp sovereign authority for themselves.[26] Two parties formed, and their opposition to each other became intense, employing ever more vitriolic language, between 1762 and 1765.

III

It was against such a background that leading magistrates and pastors sought to determine the truth, beginning with whether it had been fair to indict Rousseau as a heresiarch. The claim by Rousseau's opponents was that if the threat he posed to society was confirmed, the actions of the magistrates would be seen to have been just. One report sought to bring peace to the city by dealing with Jacques-François Deluc directly. Jean Cramer, a leading magistrate and one of the four syndics in 1763, was approached by Deluc, who repeated his opinion that Rousseau was a Protestant who had been illegally dealt with by the state. Cramer's reply was unequivocal. Rousseau had failed to meet the obligation incumbent upon him as a citizen of Geneva to live in accordance with the Holy Gospel. Furthermore, he had questioned 'the truth of the Holy Scripture and the Prophets', in addition to seeking 'to destroy the certainty of miracles'. Cramer's conclusion was that Rousseau was a sceptic, and the likely effects on his audience, 'fathers and mothers, governesses and teachers', did not bear consideration. His *Émile* had 'scandalised all of Christian Europe'. Rousseau was dripping poison. He was dealing Christianity 'a deadly blow'.[27]

Jacob Vernet's response was more careful. Rousseau's friends were initially delighted that Vernet was involved in the controversy. Vernet shared the suspicision, it was reported, that prominent Genevans had influenced the Bernese when they expelled Rousseau. Rousseau was informed that Vernet 'likes you and has infinite admiration for you', and 'hates Voltaire'.[28] Mention of Voltaire was significant, because all of Rousseau's associates felt that in the burning of his books, and not those of Voltaire, double standards were at play. One pastor wrote to Rousseau in August 1762 that he had just read Voltaire's *Sermon des cinquante*: 'a horrible thing, never has Christianity been assaulted so openly, with such bad faith, and in such a degrading fashion. It presents a parody of the Old and New Testaments.' The point was that while Rousseau's books were forbidden, Voltaire's were being printed at Geneva.[29] The hope of Rousseau's supporters was that Vernet would confirm that Rousseau was a Christian and a Protestant. The Consistory at Geneva would then be justified in employing their influence over the magistrates to allow Rousseau to return home. Hopes were high in the early days after Rousseau's condemnation. One of his followers wrote that in the affair, 'I have been charmed by the moderation shown by our Company [of Pastors]'.[30]

In his response, rather than damning Rousseau in general terms, Vernet was more specific about the texts in question, and tried to work out Rousseau's intentions in writing. He also provided more background. The key issue, he agreed with Cramer, was whether Rousseau could be said to have violated his civic oath. Rousseau had converted to Catholicism in his youth, having left Geneva for Italy at the age of sixteen, in 1728. He had then lived with heretics in Paris, Vernet recalled. In July 1754, Rousseau had requested to return to the Reformed Church at Geneva, had reasserted his Protestant faith, and had been granted the status of citizen, attending the General Council in July and paying his civic *taxe des gardes*.[31] The *dédicace* to the *Discours sur l'origine et les fondements de l'inégalité parmi les hommes* was dated 12 June 1754—just before his appeal to return to the city—and lauded the city and its magistrates. Rousseau, unlike many heretics returning to the fold, avoided public scrutiny.[32] It was crucial for Vernet that Rousseau's publications up to 1754 'did not contain anything to render [his actions] suspect.' He stated the opinion that Rousseau's *Discours sur l'origine et les fondements de l'inégalité parmi les hommes* (1755) and *La Nouvelle Héloïse* (1761) did contain reprehensible arguments, but, crucially, nothing 'that openly wounds religion'. The opposite was the case, however, with 'the pretended Discourse of the Savoyard Vicar' in the third book of *Émile*, and the final chapter of the *Contrat social*. In *Émile* Rousseau had questioned divine revelation, doubting the existence of the miraculous and the prophetic on the basis that such faith was unnecessary, 'because God has provided everyone with natural means to knowledge of the truth'.[33]

Vernet indicted Rousseau for attacking areas of the Old Testament that depicted a cruel God, for identifying absurdities in scripture and for presenting elements of scripture that portrayed men 'full of pride and cruel'. His fundamental error, in Vernet's view, was in claiming that all divine revelation was in truth the product of human testimony. Rousseau was accused by Vernet of ridiculing Holy Scripture, implying that God was born in Judea and died in Jerusalem. Vernet also asserted that Rousseau had mistaken Protestant doctrine by claiming that all Christians believed that those who did not accept the divinity of Jesus were eternally damned. Furthermore, he was said to have no confidence in the capacity of the Christian religion to foster the duties that sustained social life. In the last chapter of the *Contrat social*, in addition to 'many false ideas about theocracy', Rousseau had composed a satirical portrait of the Hebrew monarchy, in which the civil and the religious elements of the state were separated ('separant le Systême theologique du Systême politique'), leading to 'profound divisions that have never ceased to agitate Christian peoples'. Vernet acknowledged that Rousseau had praised Protestantism as 'sacred, sublime, true, where men who are children of the same God recognise one another to be brothers'. Yet he had gone on to say that Christians lacked patriotism and the virtues necessary to defend the state: 'nothing is more contrary to the social spirit [*l'esprit social*] than such a religion'.[34]

Vernet concluded that Rousseau had injured Christianity in his books, by collecting standard critical arguments and presenting them with 'éclat and vivacity'. Rousseau had also praised the scriptures, Jesus Christ and the effects of Christianity, in both *Émile* and the *Contrat social*. Vernet himself praised Rousseau's defence of natural religion as an antidote to the heretics who pushed their deism as far as atheism. This meant that each book could be read in different ways. Rousseau's intentions in writing were obscured by a style that was enigmatic and refined. Vernet was sure, however, that Rousseau's real message, conveyed by the Savoyard Vicar, was to reject revealed religion, accept whatever creed you were born into, to live discreetly, and not to trouble those whose faith was firmer. In other words, Rousseau was a sceptic rather than a deist. Such views allowed the Vicar himself, in Rousseau's book, to remain in holy office without believing in the mysteries of the Mass. Nevertheless, there could be no doubt that Rousseau was encouraging deism in his readers, because of his assault upon revelation and scripture. He was 'closing the book of Holy Scripture' in favour of natural theology or 'the book of Nature'. The claim that Rousseau was only attacking the kinds of intolerance associated with the Roman church did not hold water, because he was attacking the scriptural basis of both Catholicism and Protestantism.

Vernet argued that if Rousseau was himself 'more Christian than his book [*Émile*]', as had been alleged, then he needed to assert his real opinions immediately, and at the very least repeat the process initiated in 1754, when he had returned to the Reformed faith. This aside, Vernet was of the opinion after his investigation that Rousseau deserved to be deprecated and proscribed. On the basis of his most recent books, he could not be said to be a 'sincere Christian' and had done real damage to the Creed and the Commandments.[35] It was Vernet's analysis that became the basis of the response of the magistrates at Geneva to Deluc's representations in defence of Rousseau. On 25 June 1763, the *Petit conseil* proclaimed that Rousseau's books 'tend to weaken, undermine and destroy the main foundations of the revealed Christian Religion, and in so doing inspire the most deadly opinions, as far as to say that we [at Geneva] are mistaken in saying "a Christian Republic", as each of these words [according to Rousseau] excludes the other'.[36] In other words, the logical end-point of Rousseau's writing was the ruination of Geneva as a Calvinist republic.

Throughout 1763 and 1764, the *représenants* launched successive assaults on the authority of the magistrates, on the grounds that they had moved beyond their legitimate powers in dealing with Rousseau, and were behaving like tyrants. The magistrates responded by defaming Rousseau, reiterating Vernet's point that Rousseau was a genuine threat to the survival of the republic; the *représentants* were acting as enemies of the state and had to be dealt with as such.[37] The imputation was that the *représentants* had been seduced by Rousseau and wanted to put his ideas into practice by dechristianising and democratising the polity. Rousseau responded to such accusations in March 1763, with his *Lettre à Christophe de Beaumont*, and at the end of December 1764 with the publication of the *Lettres écrites de la montagne*. By this time many were seeing Rousseau's period of constant involvement with Geneva as forshadowing moral and political apocalypse. As one of his closest friends wrote in February 1763, 'As God is my witness, I am disgusted since your unfortunate affair, and if I had to choose a homeland, it would not be Geneva that I selected. Your people like only cabals and gambling dens, and are without force and without vigour.'[38]

IV

The writer who was disgusted with Geneva was Paul-Claude Moultou, from a wealthy Huguenot merchant family, who had been trained for the ministry at Geneva, was ordained in 1753 and both married into the prominent Cayla family and purchased bourgeois civil status in 1755.[39] Although he described himself as an outsider, referring to the Genevans in letters to Rousseau as 'your people', Moultou was heavily involved in the political and religious life of the city; he also enjoyed corresponding with friends across Europe. He became close to Rousseau at the end of the 1750s, through letters exchanged between the two men. Rousseau recognised Moultou as someone who understood his books, and each confided in the other until a break, inevitable in almost all of Rousseau's relationships, came in 1766. By this time, Moultou was the custodian of numerous Rousseau manuscripts, and with other associates he was involved in the publication after the philosopher's death in 1778 of his collected works, including the controversial *Confessions*. Moultou's correspondence with Rousseau merits close scrutiny, because it charts the transition from hope to fear, from optimism about the future to pessimism and from anticipated toleration to violence. What Moultou went through in engaging with Rousseau was replicated by innumerable readers.

Moultou first wrote to Rousseau after the appearance of the *Lettre à d'Alembert sur les spectacles* in August 1758, and the purpose of the letter was to explain what Rousseau's book had done to him. It was, Moultou said, a rallying call to 'all good citizens, and condemned and frightened the bad'. The key for the survival of a republic like Geneva was 'to conserve its ancient manners or to recover them'; d'Alembert, in claiming to have found evidence of new, anti-Calvinist manners in the city, in his article 'Genève' in the *Encyclopédie*, was 'conducting the republic to its ruin'. If Rousseau had exaggerated the levels of virtue among the Genevans, he was revealing what levels of virtue were necessary to maintain the republic. The problem was commerce and luxury. According to Moultou, the rich had long been corrupted, and they were now ruining the manners of the poor at Geneva. Rousseau was combating this corruption by kindling 'the Republican fire that burns in all your writings'.[40] He had summarised 'political science and morals' in stating that 'Nature has made man good, but society depraves him ['La nature a fait l'homme bon, la Société le déprave'].' In so doing, he had gone beyond Montesquieu, by proving to the world 'so concisely that Monarchies can sustain themselves only by false and corrupt principles, and that virtue can only be found in small Republics, because they are formed from associations of men rather than from what would be termed societies'.[41] Rousseau was the decided defender of small states and of republicanism in the modern world. He was also the arch-critic of corrupt monarchy, and of every state seduced by commerce and by luxury.

Over the following years, Moultou described himself as 'an enthusiast for Rousseau' and 'fanatic for liberty'. When he read *La Nouvelle Héloïse*, Moultou commented on 'what an astonishing book' it was, with each page exalting 'decency and honesty [*honneteté*], but the decency of virtue, rather than that to be found in the world'. It was 'necessary to die having made this book, and to live after having read it'.[42] Moultou called Rousseau 'Nature's avenger' and 'our angel instructor', and called upon him to write a treatise for Genevans on the corruption of republics, revealing to moderns how to delay such decline and ruin.[43] Both men were independently minded when it came to religion, but also recognised the dangers posed by atheism and deism; as Moultou put it, each accepted the necessity of '[religious] dogmas essential to moral order'.[44]

When Moultou was sent the confession of faith of the Savoyard Vicar, before *Émile* was published, he reported to Rousseau, 'No one has ever written so forcefully, profoundly and truthfully concerning natural religion, and you yourself have written nothing that approaches this piece.' Against Rousseau, Moultou admitted the utility of the belief in miracles in persuading the people to be moral. Moultou's argument was that existing society was corrupt, with even what he termed the 'enlightened part of the people' being only 'half-enlightened', pulled either towards the depravities of fanatical priests or the impieties of philosophers lacking a clear vision of what needed to be done. Rousseau's work was important in restoring religion and morals to their pure foundation. Although Moultou thought that the majority of people at Geneva would support Rousseau's position, he anticipated opposition, and feared that the philosopher's enemies would want to deal with him as the Athenians had dealt with Socrates.[45]

Moultou was convinced that Rousseau *was* a Christian and not a heretic. In a significant passage, in a letter of March 1762, he gave Rousseau his own opinion that *Émile*, and indeed all of the philosopher's works, translated into nothing other than support for the Christian religion:

> Your Natural religion is nothing other than Christianity properly understood, the difference being that you prove what the Gospel teaches by its authority alone. You differ from the true Christian only in that what he believes comes from heaven you define from the light of your own reason. A reasonable Christian who accepted the miracles of Jesus Christ would not refuse you the title of being a Christian.[46]

The problem was that 'this enlightened Christian, this Christian philosopher, is not the people, who only believe in Christianity because they believe in its miracles'. Rousseau's attack on revelation would enable his enemies to libel him an unbeliever, and reverse the positive effects at Geneva of his dedication to the *Discours sur l'inégalité* and the *Lettre sur les spectacles*. Equally, Moultou recognised that those he termed 'bad citizens', and their supporters among the French *philosophes* led by Voltaire, would use any apparently unorthodox statement to impugn Rousseau. This meant that Rousseau was truly vulnerable.[47] As Moultou put it, the tragedy was that 'true Philosophers are as rare as good Kings'.[48] Such anxieties were initially vanquished when Moultou read the *Contrat social*, which made him suddenly optimistic about the future.

About the *Contrat social*, Moultou wrote to a friend from childhood, Élie Salomon François Reverdil, a professor of mathematics in Copenhagen and tutor to the Danish king Christian VII, that 'it is a book that Montesquieu would not have disavowed', being 'profound, luminous [and] full of useful truths'. The only part that needed to be set aside was the chapter on civil religion, which Moultou disapproved of. The question was how the *Contrat social* would be received at Geneva, 'where liberty still exists'.[49] Moultou soon reported to Rousseau that the book was being welcomed within the city, appealing to all those who supported aristocratic government, but with clear limits upon the use of executive authority.[50]

Ironically, many of the *représentants* were critical. As Moultou noted to Rousseau, 'The men to whom you are so dear feel they are conflicted, because they are not content with what you have written concerning religion in the *Contrat social*.' At the same time, the bourgeois in general, Moultou avowed, were reading the work as a clarion call for reform,

> saying no less than that the *Contrat social* is the arsenal of liberty, and while a small number throw fire and flames, the multitude triumph. They almost pardon your [view of] religion in the light of your patriotism.[51]

Moultou was even more buoyed-up in a further letter of 18 June, in which he divulged that the *Contrat social* 'is being consumed greedily', and that Rousseau's greatest work to date was likely to have profound consequences:

> [E]ven your enemies are forced to avow that it is in this book, of all your work, that your genius is employed to the greatest effect. What force! What profundity. You are superior even to Montesquieu. Your book will strike fear into every tyrant now and into the future. It will inspire liberty in every heart.[52]

Moultou informed Rousseau that within the *Petit conseil*, his book was being defended by the first syndic, Pierre Mussard, and by another leading magistrate, Jean Jallabert. He expected both *Émile* and the *Contrat social* to be openly sold at Geneva until the Consistory had examined them. In order to pacify all parties, Moultou advised Rousseau to confirm that he was a Protestant and altogether at home with religion at Geneva. In so doing, he would be following Montesquieu's defence of *De l'esprit des loix* of January 1750, in which he combated accusations of heresy levelled by articles in the *Nouvelles ecclésiastiques*:

> [Show that] your principles of religion are not different from those of all true Christians, that you accept precisely the same doctrines that they accept, and that in rejecting the Roman Church . . . you do not reject revelation which could be true, but that you cannot be as certain as you would wish to be, and it is very far from such doubt to unbelief [*l'incredulité absoluë*], and that with your principles it is possible to be as honest [*honnête*] a man as the Christian most persuaded of the divine revelation.

Moultou's further advice reiterated that Rousseau should emphasise in any writing 'the superiority of the Religion of Geneva above all other religions'. He added a note that the chief of the *représentants*, Jacques-François Deluc, had been shocked by the *Contrat social* because 'he saw there a Citizen and not a Christian'; Moultou warned Rousseau that Deluc would be visiting him, because he was convinced that if Rousseau read Deluc's own book refuting heresy, the *Observations sur les Savans Incrédules, et sur quelques-uns de leurs ecrits* (1762), he would be converted to orthodoxy. Neither man had faith in Deluc's capacity for argument, and found the watchmaker's misplaced self-confidence altogether amusing.[53]

Disaster struck, and Geneva changed in Moultou's eyes, when the magistrates censored *Émile* and the *Contrat social*, then called for Rousseau's arrest. It is significant that the decision, entirely unexpected by Moultou, was perceived as a return to the kinds of violence associated with the religious bigotry of previous centuries. Presenting Rousseau as a challenge to Calvinism, and as an oath-breaker, was precisely the kind of persecution that had marred Geneva's religious history in the sixteenth century. The burning of Michel Servet by Calvin came immediately into Moultou's mind: 'What shocking fanaticism! What are we preparing? The flames that are burning your books seem to me to be rekindling the bonfire around Servet.'[54] He repeated this opinion to friends:

> [The condemnation of Rousseau is] without parallel . . . d'Alembert was mistaken, we are worse than the intolerant. We go against our own enlightenment, we want at all cost to continue to be accused of having burned Servet. I saw this in the flames that burned the books and that even time cannot destroy.[55]

In the following days, Moultou was able to report that his friends among the *représentants* had reversed their position. While they were not happy with Rousseau's description of Christianity, by 2 July Moultou was informing Rousseau that the *représentants* were petitioning the magistrates not to sanction him. Through Moultou, they requested that Rousseau not return to Geneva before September. When Rousseau did return, he would be examined by four syndics, who would press him on his view of Christianity, in the hope of extracting a promise that he would not in future write against religion at Geneva.[56] During this period, Moultou was trying to arrange asylum for his hero at Zurich, described as 'the wise republic'.[57]

Any residual hopes Moultou entertained came to naught with what he saw as the further betrayal of Rousseau by Geneva's pastors. These fell into two categories. Among the first was Antoine-Jacques Roustan, who attacked Rousseau's view of Christianity but felt that the magistrates had violated the law in condemning Rousseau, and continued to act hypocritically in favouring infinitely more dangerous critics of religion like Voltaire. Roustan, Moultou argued, misunderstood Rousseau, for whom existing society was corrupt, and Christianity had socially positive effects, 'seeing men and women as brothers' and encouraging 'cosmopolitanism rather than patriotism'. The second group comprised those pastors who accepted the verdict of the magistrates and indeed justified it. Pastors, such as Jacob Vernes and Jacob Vernet, were dangerous fools. This verdict on Vernet may have been seconded by Moultou's other hero, Montesquieu himself, who had faced problems with the man during the publication of his great *De l'esprit des loix*.[58] Moultou called Vernes a 'cockroach' and Vernet an 'idiot'.[59] His own explanation for events in the city was straightforwardly the corruption of manners. Genevans had become too fond of wealth and luxury, and politics and religion had become aligned with self-interest rather than the public good in consequence.[60]

V

In 1763 and 1764 Moultou became more devoted to Rousseau as a person and more of a disciple with regard to Rousseau's philosophy. He considered the philosopher's letter to the archbishop of Paris, Christophe de Beaumont, to mirror exactly Montesquieu's defence of *De l'esprit*; in other words, it was the ideal vindication. Rousseau's letter, in Moultou's view, underscored the fact that he *was* a Christian, entirely refuting Voltaire and the irreligious party, and proving that the Genevan magistrates, and the pastors who had attacked *Émile* and the *Contrat social*, were fools behaving like tyrants. Moultou considered it to be a magnificent justification of Genevan Calvinism, 'la religion de Genève':

> O my dear, my dear fellow citizen, what a book! What soul! What candour! What sublimity! Philosophers will blush when comparisons are made with you. Leave the fanatics and the tribunals to hurl abuse. They burn your books, you have burned the minds of your readers. The Genevans will tremble while reading your book, and if they do not amend their opinions after having read it, forsake them to their depraved ideas, dedicated to longstanding errors.[61]

Deluc was equally reported to have been 'transported' by reading Rousseau's work.[62] Moultou stated that even Vernet had admitted that 'there is not a wise man at Geneva who could deny that [Rousseau] is a Christian'.[63] Additional support was clear among the magistrates, Moultou believed, and for a short time after the appearance of the *Lettre à Christophe de Beaumont* he evidently thought that the *représentants* would be victorious and that Rousseau could return to Geneva. All hopes were quickly dashed as the letter had in fact been 'a triumph for Rousseau's enemies'.[64] Moultou wrote to the Jansenist Pierre Quesnel that the vitriol of Voltaire and those who 'teach materialism at Geneva' had become so overwhelming, and that Rousseau was so exposed to the 'particular hatreds' that now governed Genevan manners, that the philosopher was renouncing his citizenship.[65]

Rousseau was then accused of fomenting revolution at Geneva, through writing the letter to Marc Chappuis of 26 May 1763 that was being called 'the tocsin [alarm bell] of sedition'.[66] Chappuis was a salt merchant and *représentant*, who since July 1762 had been avowing his devotion to Rousseau; at this time he had asked Rousseau to come back to Geneva, despite the threat of arrest, because 'the times of Servet are over'.[67] Rousseau abdicated his citizenship on 12 May 1763, after the *Petit conseil* censored the *Lettre à Christophe de Beaumont*, under pressure from the French *résident*, Étienne-Jean de Guimard des Rocheretz, baron de Montpéroux. After this, Chappuis was convinced that the government was acting against the people, because there ought to have been a reconciliation after Rousseau made his Protestantism clear in the *Lettre*.[68] If the state continued to attack Rousseau, the greatest Genevan of the age, then the state was at fault and needed to be challenged. This had to be done in order to save the state itself, which had outlawed someone who remained a dedicated patriot, who had desired only to live in his homeland.[69] Chappuis had written to Rousseau arguing that his status as a citizen would be restored when the government came to its senses.

Rousseau responded to Chappuis with a letter that declared how incensed he was that his so-called supporters at Geneva, the *représentants*, had done so little in the aftermath of this public humiliation by the magistrates. Five or six of them together could have made representations to the magistrates, as was their right, when they were certain that the laws had been violated or that the magistrates were behaving improperly. Given that they had not done so, Rousseau, abandoned by his government and seemingly without vocal support among the people, had followed the advice of Grotius and the jurists, renouncing his citizenship because his rights as a citizen were not being upheld.[70] This letter was interpreted as a clarion call to the *représentants* to take action. It was quickly published in the *Journal encyclopédique ou universel*.[71]

Chappuis in particular began to write in an apocalyptic mode, on the basis that the issues in hand presented a choice between liberty and death:

> The nation (*Patrie*) must not accept what has been done to your books . . . The nation has sacred rights, which come immediately after God, and if our Fathers . . . had acted [like the magistrates], my God, what would have become of us? Our Fathers sacrificed their blood and their lives in order to pass [liberty] on to us.[72]

For Chappuis, Geneva was not yet like Athens; Socrates had refused the offer of escape because he felt that the laws of his country were altogether corrupt and unjust. Chappuis was, however, certain that the key historical parallel was with events in ancient Greece, and that the message was that a Calvin figure had to arise to purge the abuses. He admitted to Rousseau that 'I know little of Grotius and the natural jurists [*jurisconsultes*] you refer me to'. The *représentants* began to argue that violence in defence of the constitution might be necessary in order to restore virtue to the state and vanquish the corrupt magistrates. The first of a series of representations critical of the magistrates was issued on 18 June 1763.

In such circumstances, because he abhorred bloodshed, Moultou appealed to Rousseau to write letters to restore peace between the parties, as if Rousseau had such authority. Moultou was correct, however, in sensing that Rousseau was always an advocate of moderation, and had no faith in extreme measures, considering them altogether self-defeating.[73] Rousseau followed Moultou's advice, noting that 'the interpretation of my letter to Chappuis has been so inaccurate that when I have said "no", the verdict has been that I said "yes"'.[74] Rousseau wrote to Deluc to underline that he was not a *représentant*, and considered the policy of challenging the magistrates to be dangerous, both to the citizens and to the state itself:

> I fear, my dear friend, that your patriotic zeal has gone a little too far on this occasion, and that your love for the laws might threaten what is more important than anything else, the safety of the state [*le salut de l'État*]. I have been informed that you and your dignified Citizens are planning new representations, and the certainty of their failure makes me fear that they will only increase antagonism between the Bourgeois and the Magistrates . . . I know that your intention is to challenge the injustices that, although they concern individual citizens, in turn do damage to our public liberty [*blessent la liberté publique*]. Yet whether I considered this course of action relative to myself or to the Bourgeois as a group, I find it to be both useless and dangerous.[75]

Rousseau did not think that the *représentants* could be victorious in any clash with the magistrates. The outcome would be stalemate, resulting either in the loss of the very sovereignty of the General Council that Deluc and his friends saw themselves to be fighting for, or, alternatively, the anarchic government of the people. As Rousseau put it, 'success is either impossible or deadly'.

Despite Rousseau's intervention in the debate, it was a simple task for the opponents of the *représentants* to present him as the leader of the movement for reform at Geneva. His reputation had been so tarnished that the *représentants* in turn would be branded heretics and anarchists. From all sides—the magistrates, Voltaire, and the pastors—new assaults were launched against Rousseau, culminating in Tronchin's *Lettres écrites de la campagne*, which appeared in August 1763. Tronchin portrayed the *représentants* as mad sophists, violators of a constitution that had brought stability and prosperity by their opposition to the lynchpin of the political wheel, the *droit négatif*.[76] Rousseau was once more identified as the arch-enemy of religion and government, impugning the Gospel, the efficacy of prayer, the existence of miracles and the association of Christianity with liberty. He had attacked Genevan Calvinism and citizenship, violating the oath he had taken in 1754.[77]

For Moultou, the sense of being under siege was manifest, at the same time as his sense of a general malaise intensified. He was increasingly pessimistic about the future. The language he used to describe those involved in the Rousseau controversy became more extreme. Moultou called the 'miserable' book Vernes had recently published against Rousseau, the *Lettres sur le Christianisme de Mr. J.J. Rousseau*, 'insolent', 'beastly' and 'wicked', labelling Vernes himself 'worse than an inquisitor'. Vernes had garbled the meaning of *Émile* by extracting random passages, and put them together to form an anti-Christian message. In truth, he had 'not understood a word'.[78]

By October 1763, Moultou was proclaiming that he had become equally despairing of the *représentants*; they had foolishly moved beyond the defence of Rousseau to consider remaking the constitution from its foundations. Significantly, Moultou stated that some among the *représentants* risked establishing an anarchic democracy: '[They] wish that the People had the right to carry to the General Council all of the concerns that agitate them, without thinking about the anarchy into which we would fall.' For Moultou, the exercise of the *droit négatif* was a vital part of government, being a bulwark against popular passion.[79] To his friend Léonhard Usteri, he reported that he was considering leaving Geneva, because his view of the future was so bleak. Moultou knew that the *représentants* were not Rousseauists. Rousseau, far from being a cause of the turbulence in the city, was rather its victim. This was clear when the gap between Rousseau's politics and those of the *représentants* was considered.[80]

Moultou reiterated his view in a letter to another friend, Élie-Salomon-François Reverdil. The hypocrisy of the magistrates was inexcusable, attacking the books of a Protestant while the works of Catholics and *philosophes* like Voltaire were welcomed in Geneva. Rousseau was unorthodox and a reformer, demanding the reformation of manners, but he was not a heretic. Few of his critics read his books. Far more were willing to condemn him without any knowledge of what he was saying. The Genevan people had been duped. As Moultou put it, '[O]ur people is wise, it is educated, but when it acts in the interests of God, it is like all peoples, very easily mislead.' Events in Paris had been worse, and the condemnation of Rousseau by the *parlement* had been 'all the more atrocious because of the enlightened century in which we live'.

It was easy to attack Rousseau by selecting passages from his works ad hoc. As he was so productive, more material was available each year, and more enemies, including the Jansenists criticised in *La Nouvelle Héloïse*, joined the fray. Moultou considered the *Contrat social* to have been an attack on the *philosophes*, because it asserted as a principle that religion was vital for a good constitution. There was nothing in the justification of the sovereignty of the people, or the declaration of the superiority of aristocratic government, to trouble anyone at Geneva. But the book had been burned by the torch directed at *Émile*. Moultou came to two conclusions. The first was that Rousseau was a 'monster who has been invented', although one who tended to provoke others to move to extreme points he himself did not share. The second was that the *représentants* were mad in seeking to defend Rousseau by repeated representations.[81]

Moultou explained what the problem was. The *Petit conseil* claimed the right to bring new laws, or to interpret old laws, before the General Council. This power, called the *droit négatif*, rested upon the document of the *Médiation* of 1738, and specifically articles five and six.[82] In bringing representations, the *représentants* were asking the *Petit conseil* to bring issues to the General Council against itself, or to confirm, as it was doing in Rousseau's case, that the laws were clear, and no miscarriage of justice had taken place. Moultou's fear was that if the *Petit conseil* lost the *droit négatif*, allowing the people to bring any issues they wanted to the General Council, anarchy would result:

> It seems to be that the Mediation of 1738 [*Règlement de la médiation*] attributes the *droit négatif* to the *Petit conseil*. This right, in the hands of the people, would give to our Constitution an instability that would precipitate us sooner or later into the most dreadful Anarchy. Under the specious pretext of not understanding the sense of a law, the people would make new laws everyday. It is certain that every people who joined to the legislative power the *droit négatif*, would change their government without cease, as it is nothing less than the combination of the legislative and executive powers, making the passing of any legislation impossible.[83]

Moultou left Geneva, disgusted by the conduct of all parties, and especially the Consistory, in openly favouring the magistrates and Voltaire during their assaults upon Rousseau. Vernes received particular criticism, because he had written to Rousseau stating his morality to be sublime, at the same time as he attacked it in public. In his correspondence with Rousseau, Moultou made the point that the times were so corrupt that it might take a century for people to recognise that Rousseau was 'altogether an innovator, a Socrates', and would be venerated everywhere once 'religion is better understood'.[84] When Rousseau's final defence of his relationship with the Genevan republic, the *Lettres écrites de la montagne*, appeared at the end of 1764, Moultou declared, '[I]f the government of Geneva is ever perfected, it will be your plan that will be followed.' He also asked Rousseau to send a copy to David Hume, who was 'entirely of your opinion concerning miracles and politics, and is a sensation at Paris'. How things would end between the *représentants* and the magistrates, Moultou had no idea, but he sensed that 'this is the epoch of our own true liberty, or of our enslavement'.[85]

Moultou was of the opinion that Rousseau had been consistent in the *Lettres écrites de la montagne*, expressing the view that while the magistrates had behaved like tyrants, the *représentants* had no solutions to the problems of the state. The core argument of the *Lettres sur les spectacles* and of the *Discours sur l'origine de l'inégalité* still pertained. Commercial societies were corrupt, governments, trading and religious corporations were ever more powerful and dangerous, and few appeared to be aware of what was happening to the societies they belonged to. Cultures were being bankrupted at the same time as states, and domestic and international war was the likely outcome. Was Moultou right about Rousseau's views? As noted above, there can be no doubt that Rousseau perceived Moultou to be one of the few readers who saw precisely what he was about. Moultou's summary descriptions of Rousseau flattered the philosopher, but they entirely accorded with Rousseau's self-perception, that his was a moderate voice. The world was in turmoil. Many apologists who benefited from commercial society, or desired the wealth that accrued to those who praised the powerful, denied that societies were in trouble. Rousseau, by contrast, saw himself to be seeing through the veil that the corruption of language, itself the product of luxury and inequality, set up to maintain the status quo. War, poverty and loss lay ahead, and civil war within and between states was being institutionalised, turned into a norm of political life.

The solution of renouncing commerce, of embracing the Fénelonian injunction that the towns be abandoned in favour of the countryside, by force if necessary, was to Rousseau worse than the social disease that accompanied the ubiquitous selfishness of lives devoted to *amour propre*. As Istvan Hont revealed, in a posthumous publication, Rousseau believed that turning back the clock was impossible, and wanted to develop solutions to the problems of commercial society that were practical and subtle.[86] He believed himself to be an enemy to projects demanding speedy and radical change, on the grounds that they would always maintain the established and corrupt cultures of the past, that could only ever gradually be altered by a legislator of genius. As such, the last thing he saw himself as being was an 'enthusiast', because enthusiasts promised everything and always made things worse. As he wrote to the bookseller Nicolas-Bonaventure Duchesne, he was ready to avow that there was nothing in the *Lettre à Christophe de Beaumont* to displease 'Catholics, the French, or your [French] government'. Rather, Rousseau stated, '[I]f I had been treated equitably this book would have been encouraged and welcomed in your country.'[87]

The magnificent irony was that Rousseau was perceived in so many places to be the greatest projector and enthusiast of a century when such personae became commonplace. Rousseau would have had a ready answer as to why: the false interactions of commercial society were accompanied by commodification, and Rousseau himself was packaged as a revolutionary and dissident voice, the political correlative of the economic topsy-turvyism of commercial society itself. The proof that Rousseau was a moderate, an advocate of peace and gradual reform, lay in his relations with Geneva. This was why he was so careful in composing his *Lettres écrites de la montagne.*

VI

Rousseau's *Lettres écrites de la montagne* was written in secret. He received documents concerning the history of Geneva from *représentants* within the city, using a code in messages that referred to the book as 'les airs de mandoline'.[88] The fact that the *représentants* helped Rousseau with material did not make the *Lettres* a *représentant* tract. Deluc, François-Henri d'Ivernois and other leading *représentants* were by now fully aware that Rousseau would go his own way. This was why it was vital for them to produce their own manifesto, to be published quickly after Rousseau's *Lettres*, straightforwardly entitled *Réponse aux Lettres écrites de la campagne.* The expectation was that this book, carefully respectful of *la religion de Genève*, could be compared with Rousseau's heterodoxy; precisely this came to pass. What the *représentants* wanted from Rousseau was an onslaught upon the rulers of Geneva, a majestic refutation of the magistrates' claims to have acted always for the good of the republic, in accordance with the ancient constitution and the *Médiation* of 1738. In other words, they were relying upon Rousseau's singular capacity for iconoclasm and self-defence.

As Moultou realised, Rousseau was being manipulated. Hence the *représentants* flattered the philosopher when the *Lettres* appeared, while not engaging with any of Rousseau's arguments. Deluc's son Jean-André Deluc informed Rousseau that the *Lettres* were written by 'a Christian who deserves to be happy and who will be because his soul is disposed to enjoy celestial benefits and is waiting for them'.[89] François-Henri d'Ivernois called Rousseau the saviour of his homeland.[90] In reality, Rousseau had provided ammunition for the *représentants.* His major service to them, by writing directly about Geneva, was to make the magistrates infamous across Europe, and to make the defence of liberty at Geneva a *cause célèbre*. Rousseau was paving the way for the *représentants*, whose own *Réponse aux Lettres écrites de la campagne*, written by Jean-André Deluc and Jean-Jacques Vieusseux, presented themselves as defenders of the traditional Genevan liberties identified in the *Lettres*. Their strategy was risky, because they knew that Rousseau would be vilified and that they would be defamed along with him. Again, this was why the near-simultaneous appearance of the *Réponse* in January 1765 was crucial, in order to stake the claim that the *représentants*' position was distinctive. There was a further reason for using Rousseau. The *représentants* were fearful of French interference in internal Genevan politics, in part through the medium of Voltaire. Only Rousseau could shame the magistrates, it was believed, to the extent that French ministers would be wary of getting directly involved.

Rousseau did indeed profess that the magistrates at Geneva had become tyrants. In so doing, he fell into the trap set for him by the *représentants*, who had ceaselessly encouraged him to attack the magistrates, knowing that Rousseau's language would be more brilliant, and more than likely more acidic, than their own. As was always the case, Moultou, despite his praise for the *Lettres*, recognised the problem. Writing to a friend he admitted, 'Yes, I admire Rousseau, and his last book must conserve our liberty, it must return the reformation of things to their true foundations.' Yet he denigrated the humour, bitterness and irony directed against religion. Such a tone misdirected readers, who would end up by becoming sophists.[91] Rousseau had stated that the magistrates had become a corrupt oligarchy destroying the constitution. The consequence might well be a disastrous popular revolution.

Rousseau was as critical of the *représentants* as he was of the magistrates, defending the *droit négatif* and arguing that the policy of endless representations was futile; it would inevitably lead to a new mediation, in which the *représentants* would be weak because of French support for the magistrates.[92] Increasingly, Rousseau felt that the *représentants* wilfully failed to understand his politics. When François-Henri d'Ivernois, in a letter of 1767, referred to Rousseau's project 'to reverse the constitution [of Geneva] and establish a pure democracy', Rousseau asked whether d'Ivernois was aware of his assault on democratic government in the *Contrat social*.[93]

Over the next three years, Rousseau refused to get involved in what had become in effect a civil war at Geneva, except to reiterate the need for moderation and compromise, in addition to reminding all Genevans of the overwhelming benefit of peace.[94] In letters of early 1768, once again written to d'Ivernois, he warned that the evils at Geneva were being caused by the tendency of the magistrates to tyranny, which was only equalled by the *représentants*' tendency towards democracy. Each was an unstable form of state. Rousseau identified a solution in revising the relationship between the three ruling councils at Geneva, and creating a means whereby *représentants* could become magistrates themselves, while ceasing to be a party. Astonishingly—from a *représentant* perspective—Rousseau stated that the right to make representations needed to be abolished, and that the magistrates had to continue to employ the *droit négatif* against policies derived from popular ignorance. Intermediate powers had to be established that allowed the people to be free but without allowing them to be masters.[95] When the new mediation established peace once again within the city, Rousseau wrote happily that 'subordination and confidence' had been re-established. Magistrates were once again rightly being venerated.[96] To his great friend Moultou, he confessed how saddened he was at being used by the *représentants*, how little faith he had in their politics and how much more important peace was than anything else.[97] When Rousseau's admirers wrote that 'I love in [you] the virtuous Author, the zealous Republican devoted to liberty', it was an entirely moderate and ordered republican liberty that was being defended, incompatible with civil violence and revolution.[98]

VII

Whatever Rousseau published, and however many letters he sent in order to make his position clear, he was berated as an advocate of revolution in politics, reformation in society and anarchy everywhere. The rationale was evidently that, if Rousseau was associated with extreme politics, or indeed the destruction of all political order, his friends among the *représentants* would be tarnished. Within Geneva, as a result, he was presented as the epitome of evil. Jacob Vernet was no longer cautious, or careful to cite the text in question. Rather, he announced that Rousseau's *Lettres* were Medea's farewell, a means by which the philosopher could identify Geneva's magistrates as monsters, in the hope of casting them out.[99] Théodore Tronchin went beyond his earlier insults, in stating that Rousseau's book had been written 'for Milton's demons by the most demonic demon of all'.[100] Rousseau was portrayed as trying to challenge existing forms of Protestantism, and in so doing re-stoking the fires last kindled against heresy in Europe in the seventeenth century.

Some parties may have been convinced that Rousseau *was* plotting discord. The French *résident* at Geneva, the baron de Montpéroux, representing the crown, informed the foreign minister Choiseul that Rousseau's *Lettres écrites de la montagne* had began to circulate on 18 December 1764. The magistrates had not been able to consider the book because of the Christmas festival, but when they did, Montpéroux was convinced that they would recognise the *Lettres* as singularly dangerous to the state: 'These letters, that [Rousseau] has caused to circulate widely among the Bourgeois, whose movements he directs, are likely to lead to a great deal of unrest.'[101] Rousseau's intention was, Montpéroux declared, a mediation that could raise the issues he wanted and remove the magistrates, taking away the established sovereignty of the state and transferring it to the people. Montpéroux was altogether ignorant of Rousseau's true intentions.

Geneva's magistrates appeared to be so apprehensive about the consequences of Rousseau's *Lettres écrites de la montagne* that they took the decision to blacken his name irredeemably. Documents were given to Voltaire revealing that Rousseau had abandoned his own children in Paris. Voltaire published, anonymously, a pamphlet revealing this to the world, declaring, 'Here are the feelings of the city; we have taken pity upon a madman, but when dementia turns into fury, he has to be challenged.' Voltaire accused Rousseau of being a buffoon, a hypocrite and a debauchee, who attacked honourable pastors and virtuous men, and whose private life was lived entirely against nature. As such, Rousseau was the enemy of pure manners, having published novels that corrupted the reader, and a danger to religion, magistracy and government, seeking the end of any civil power.[102] Why did Voltaire do all he could to crush Rousseau? From one angle, the men had much in common, being rejectors of traditional forms of Calvinism as impediments to necessary reform. Voltaire himself, alongside his pupil d'Alembert, believed that Geneva, by internal cultural change, was moving towards their 'enlightened' position on liberty, politics and morality.

Rousseau had entirely repudiated such a view of Geneva, and Voltaire's approach to religion and politics, in his *Lettre sur les spectacles*. Since that time, Voltaire had attacked Rousseau in any way he could, and after his move to Ferney in 1759 had become friends with many magistrates who also abhorred Rousseau. Voltaire professed the view in further publications that Rousseau wanted to dissolve governments and churches; he was an unrelenting libertine and malcontent.[103] Such connections were evident after the appearance of Rousseau's *Lettres écrites de la montagne*.

One magistrate, Voltaire reported in a letter to his close friend the French diplomat Charles-Augustin de Ferriol, comte d'Argental, had asked if he minded if one of his own works was burned, in order to confute Rousseau's accusation that the Frenchman, despite being a true enemy to Christianity, had avoided public censure. Voltaire replied he did not mind as long as his person remained inviolate.

In the same letter, Voltaire noted that Rousseau's *Lettres écrites de la montagne* had been accused of fomenting civil war, but Voltaire was sceptical that this was going to be the likely effect. Rousseau's book, he wrote, 'will not make a dangerous noise'.[104] Voltaire further wrote that Rousseau 'had begun by being mad, and finished by becoming a bad [*malhonnête*] man'. Once again referring to the *Lettres*, Voltaire said that Rousseau had 'unleashed the people against the magistrates', and stated that he hoped that French troops would not be needed, as they had been in Corsica to put down Paoli's popular uprising.[105] Voltaire evidently did not think they would be necessary. Why then was he willing to present Rousseau and his book as capable of destroying the world? Voltaire was close to French officials at Paris involved in foreign policy; d'Argental himself had served both as an *intendant* and as an ambassador. The mention of Corsica is significant, because these years, after the end of the Seven Years' War, saw France assert its power internationally, and especially within Europe, in a bid to reverse the defeat at the hands of Britain and Prussia, or at least to prove that France remained a singular power on the continent. That Voltaire was actively abetting French policy by sowing discord at Geneva—since troubled magistrates were sure to turn to France—or combating the *représentants* because they opposed French involvement in Geneva politics, is a real possibility. The assumption that Voltaire was somehow a republican, or an advocate of republican ideas about liberty, is altogether nonsense.[106] Voltaire saw Geneva as naturally a French satellite. Geneva could not be allowed to look elsewhere for allies, either to the cantons independently of France or to Britain. If this end had to be achieved by befouling Rousseau's reputation, so be it.

As Rousseau had recognised in the *Lettres écrites de la montagne*, what had gone from Genevan politics was willingness to compromise, itself in Rousseau's view a key element of any stable regime. Politics was so often about disagreement, and Rousseau was obsessed with means of preventing verbal argument from turning into physical war. As is well known, he had very little faith in groups coming together and talking issues out until agreement was reached: discussion was much more likely to result in adding to tension than in reconciliation.[107] This was why the distinction between sovereignty and government was so important to Rousseau, representing a mechanism by which compromise was built into political life, because the sovereign and the government simply had to accept their relative powers if war and the collapse of the state was to be avoided. At Geneva, from Rousseau's perspective, the sovereign, in the form of the General Council, was being called upon by the *représentants* to assert itself and redefine government, so that the people would always be involved in the day-to-day running of the state, or at the very least in overseeing and checking what magistrates were doing. Equally the government, in the form of the *Petit conseil*, was seeking to reduce the functions and authority of the sovereign General Council, such that it could never act as a check upon the magistrates. In other words, the stage was set for civil war. Rousseau believed that the final preventative check upon such an outcome, the mediation of external powers—Bern, Zurich and above all France—was all that was going to stop the Genevans from fighting one another. Geneva was fortunate in being able to call upon external parties, although the natural risk was that France, being so much more powerful than the cantons, would either take Geneva for itself, or reduce its independence to nothing.

The process of getting to the point of having to call upon external mediators required both parties, the *représentants* and the magistrates, to lose all faith in each other as trustworthy agents in politics. This was definitely the case by early 1765. In a declaration dated 12 February, the magistrates called the accusations levelled against them 'shocking':

> The country has been portrayed as suffering from oppression. The Council [*Petit conseil*] is depicted as a mass of tyrants seeking supreme power since the beginning of the Republic . . . [and] exercising the harshest despotism, destroying the liberty that they were supposed to be defending, creating a fearful Inquisition within the state, and rendering against the citizens unjust and atrocious judgements.[108]

The Council claimed it was not concerned with the attacks upon itself, but rather the corresponding assaults upon all of the institutions of the state. As the declaration put it, Rousseau was part of a process by which 'our religion is identified and destroyed, our ministers defamed and traduced as persecuting hypocrites, and Magnificent Council of 200 presented as a vile accomplice of tyranny, the Constitution of the State recalled and torn up, the Mediation of 1738 . . . subverted . . . seeds of discord sown for our misery and to end our prosperity'. Furthermore, Rousseau's 'monstrous production' had been followed by another book, the *Réponse aux Lettres écrites de la campagne*, which 'reverses the constitution established by law', would lead to division and 'finally dig the tomb of liberty'. Rousseau had made the people into zealous fantatics who no longer respected social hierarchy. As such, they were rejecting the principles of the Reformation itself. The effects of Rousseau upon the people could be seen by the fact that back in 1763 they had, in their representations, honoured the magistrates as being 'worthy of their esteem, all their respect and their entire confidence'. They no longer did so.

The declaration stated that, henceforth, critiques of magistracy would be combated with ordinary procedures of justice 'entirely disproportionate with the enormity [of the accusations]'. The evidence presented against Rousseau's claims was significant. Geneva was, the magistrates stated, singularly prosperous. Prosperity was a good 'which disappears before tyranny and is only the fruit of an equitable and moderate government'. In other words, because Geneva was thriving commercially, the government had to be good. If the government had been tyrannical, the economy would have collapsed. The strategy chosen by the magistrates in response to the ongoing Rousseau affair was not only to blacken his name. They demanded that the 'children of the country declare before the Syndics if they regard the Council an assembly of good and faithful magistrates'. Every citizen was expected to accept that the magistrates, far from being tyrants, were indeed the fathers of the nation, and worthy of political trust. The view of the magistrates was that the people had been duped by a militant enthusiast who was intent on wrecking religion and the social order at Geneva. As carnage would be the outcome, any measures were justified against Rousseau and the *représentants.*

The great advantage enjoyed by the magistrates was the support of France. As noted above, after the Seven Years' War, France was more concerned than ever about maintaining its sphere of influence on mainland Europe. Both César-Gabriel de Choiseul, duc de Praslin, foreign minister between 1761 and 1766, and his cousin Étienne-François, duc de Choiseul, a key minister until 1770, were dedicated to the policy of using any means necessary, including military force, to defend French interests internationally. The *résident* Montpéroux died in 1765; Pierre-Michel Hennin followed him, becoming even more closely involved with the magistrates. Hennin hated Rousseau, calling him 'the apple of discord' and 'professor of democracy'. In Hennin's view, the *Contrat social* seduced the *représentants* and was entirely responsible for their extremist views.[109] Geneva was described by Hennin as being in a state of crisis, with political trust between the magistrates and the people having broken down completely. French intervention was vital to prevent civil war.[110]

On the other side, a sense of Rousseau's impact, especially upon the young, can be seen from a letter he received from Paul Chappuis, the nephew of Marc Chappuis and the son of a member of the Council of Two Hundred, who at twenty-eight professed the impact Rousseau had had upon him in the aftermath of the appearance of the *Lettres écrties de la montagne*. Chappuis stated in his letter what he believed to be Rousseau's philosophy, that 'prejudice naturally conducts us to error, and this is the cause of all our problems, and the source of all the disorders that proliferate in society'. An example of prejudice was that 'when the term king has been invented, that of subject automatically follows'. Fortunately, Rousseau had traced the plan 'to restore things to their natural state' and revealed what was good for humanity in general. Opposition to Rousseau was explicable because 'corruption is so great, prejudice so deep-rooted, the kings obsessed with their glory and their power, priests too attached to their income and to the selfish pleasure of directing consciences, the rich are too in love with their money'. Significantly, Chappuis found hope in 'happy revolutions' led by 'great men' not corrupted by their environment, and who had the 'vision and force' to realise change. At the same time, as the existing generation was too befouled, and as established religion was a tool employed to make sure change did not occur, Rousseau would have to wait for the future to have his intentions appreciated.[111]

VIII

A narrative can certainly be formulated, on the basis of such evidence, that it was Rousseau's work that transformed the critics of the ruling magistrates at Geneva into violent revolutionaries, who plied their trade in 1782, and then again in 1789. This is a mistake. Those who studied Rousseau's writings without prejudice, those who corresponded with him or who discussed politics with him, came to the conclusion that as regards Geneva, Rousseau was a moderate. If he favoured any party in terms of his political theory, it was that of the magistrates. This was confirmed by his stance on the *droit négatif*, and his view that when the government was democratic it was likely to be prey to tumult and civil turmoil. The problem was that the magistrates were not behaving like the moderate concilitators they were meant to be. Charles Bonnet called Rousseau 'a black and diabolical soul', delighting that Hume had come to a similar verdict upon his former friend.[112]

During the quarrel that developed, Rousseau was certainly implicated in the advance of extremist accusations, because of the manner in which he was read by people like Bonnet; but his role was indirect. Voltaire was more to blame than Rousseau, fanning the flames through correspondence from Ferney. Politics became ever more confrontational at Geneva from the winter of 1765, with the *représentants* vetoing all of the proposed candidates for magistracy in seven successive general councils. When the same strategy was employed in January 1766, the magistrates took action. Having consulted with France, Bern and Zurich, they announced a new mediation. Offers were made of bringing French troops to the border in order to make the people aware that military strength was on the side of the magistrates rather than the *représentants*.[113] Hennin's secret policy was to make Geneva more Francophile and to tie the states together economically, prior to making the Genevans 'subjects of the King of France'.[114] Voltaire was altogether in support of this policy, and called Hennin 'the angel of peace'.[115] Pierre de Buisson, chevalier de Beauteville, was appointed lead mediator, and by July 1766 had drawn up a peace plan with officials from the cantons. Beauteville wrote to Rousseau and blamed him directly for Geneva's troubles; the draft plan itself condemned the attack on the magistrates in the *Lettres écrites de la montagne*.[116] The belief had become widespread that apocalyptic times in politics were imminent, requiring extreme measures by those who wanted to prevent Armaggedon.

CHAPTER FIVE

Civil War

THE REVOLUTION OF 1782 at Geneva was not inevitable. It had been anticipated in the 1760s, however, because of the extent of the antagonism between the parties in Genevan politics, and the accusations levelled against one another. Many of the magistrates involved in the events of the 1760s believed that they had suffered a defeat with the compromise or pacification of 1768. They were also sure that the lesson was learned that France needed to intervene militarily to crush the anarchists and democrats among the *représentants*. Certainly the magistrates were prepared for civil war in 1782, in a manner that they had not been in the 1760s. This became evident after the events of 15 December 1766, when, at a gathering of the General Council of all bourgeois and citizens, the *représentants* rejected Pierre de Buisson, chevalier de Beauteville's peace plan, the November 'Règlement de pacification'. For the *représentants*, the right to petition the magistrates was 'annihilated', the chains of the people 'were not even covered with velvet' and the 'abominable' plan brought Geneva 'close to being a tyranny'.[1] French authorities were furious. Beauteville had already concluded that anti-French, pro-Rousseau, and therefore pro-*représentant* factions were spreading unrest from Geneva across the cantons.[2] Zurich especially was held to have become infected. The anticipated first stage of the illness was the rejection of current political authority; as such, many commentators saw the actions of the *représentants* to be entirely in keeping with Rousseau's philosophy, and to be confirming his impact upon the culture of the city. Equally dangerous, to the magistrates and to the French, was a perception that the British ambassador to the Protestant cantons, William Norton, was taking advantage of the situation by encouraging opposition to France.[3] Beauteville was aware that more British visitors were travelling to Geneva as part of their grand tour, that some were taking the decision to live there for a period of time, and that they were becoming more interested in Genevan politics and pushing the British government to do the same.

On this score Beauteville was absolutely right. The most prominent example was Philip, 2nd Earl Stanhope (1714–86), who lived with his wife Grizel Hamilton (1719–1811), at Geneva from July 1764 until 1774, for the health of their delicate son and heir Charles Stanhope. Their elder son Philip had been brought to Geneva to be treated by Théodore Tronchin for tuberculosis; this failed and Philip had died in the city. Philip Stanhope, a patron of the Royal Society, was known for his independence of mind, for his interest in mathematics and for his friendships, notably with Joseph Priestley, Benjamin Franklin and his own cousin William Pitt the Elder. In 1767, Stanhope decided that the troubles at Geneva might be resolved by turning the city into a canton. He pressed Pitt to adopt this policy, the added benefit of which was that it would combat French influence.[4] Whether Beauteville was aware of the full extent of such counsel is unclear. The sense of a fight to the death, between anti-French Rousseauists and Francophile magistrates, was certainly palpable in Beauteville's correspondence:

> [At Bern] feelings are running high. Rousseau and the *représentants* have dedicated supporters, Zurich has declared for them . . . the British minister Norton fans the flames and is openly at the head of the party, accusing us of having designs on [independent] Geneva, among other sordid accusations . . . On our side [at Bern] there is all the Senate and the secret council [*Geheim rat*] which, despite the opposition of Zurich, has consistently and unanimously approved our own declaration [regarding the future of Geneva].[5]

In such circumstances, French troops were sent to the Genevan border. Pierre Lenieps, the ageing critic of Geneva's magistrates and friend both of Rousseau and of the *représentants*, was imprisoned in the Bastille. The twenty-four *représentant* commissioners involved in the negotiations were threatened with arrest.[6] It was later said that the duc de Choiseuil wanted to bring these twenty-four commissaries to Paris in manacles to be executed.[7] The party opposing the *représentants* was termed the *négatifs* for saying 'no' to representations. Like the French, the *négatifs* adhered to the view that what was happening at Geneva, and in the cantons, could be traced to Rousseau, the anarchist and conspirator who was inspiring rebellion in the expectation of introducing 'equality and pure democracy'.[8] In other words, a populist and extremist movement, dedicated to the destruction of existing politics and society, was fighting to take power and implement its designs. Some *négatifs* began to leave the city, being afraid of assassination and murder. Such reactions were ridiculed by those such as the leading *natif* Jean-Pierre Bérenger. Bérenger continued to present current affairs as normal politics, and believed that ongoing negotiation towards a peaceful solution remained worthwhile:

> The project of conciliation has just been rejected, and the anger of a powerful king is directed against us, his ambassador has abandoned us, rich citizens and even magistrates have abandoned their country, as if daggers were being used against them, as if enemy soldiers were advancing to destroy us, astonishment is on their faces, fear in their heart, timidity and weakness yield bloody and awful pictures, and the courageous man is silent.[9]

A number of the more perceptive *négatifs* realised that circumstances had changed. The *représentants* had evolved from Jacques-François Deluc's inarticulate complaints of the early 1760s. As one anonymous work had it, the magistrates were now faced by 'the principles of anarchic democracy contained in the *Réponse aux Lettres écrites de la campagne*'. It was this text, rather than any by Rousseau, that justified war between a popular party favouring democracy and the magisterial party of aristocracy and order.[10] As the natural philosopher Charles Bonnet put it, the *représentants* might still be said to be inspired by 'the Apostle Rousseau', but their stance opposing the magistrates was distinctive. For Bonnet—one of those convinced that Geneva was on the eve of apocalypse—the *représentants* had gone beyond the position ascribed to Rousseau, to an extent that would 'make Machiavelli himself blush'.[11] Voltaire too realised that the *représentants* had shifted their stance, to a position 'more evil and more insane than that of Rousseau himself'.[12]

As tended to be the case, both Bonnet and Voltaire had a point. The *représentants* had indeed travelled beyond anything Rousseau would have found to be acceptable. Rousseau had stated many times that the likely outcome of the battle between *représentants* and magistrates was going to be a new mediation. He realised that trust might well break down at Geneva when the institutionalised forces for moderation and compromise between the politically divided ceased to function. This happened when, in Rousseau's terminology, the distinction between sovereignty and government became unclear, and when the respect for magistrates that was vital to the proper functioning of any polity began to be lost.[13] In Rousseau's view, it was fortunate for Geneva that a final force existed to bring the parties together in order to re-establish a constitutional settlement; here he was thinking of the guarantee of the constitution by France, Bern and Zurich, which had operated so successfully in the 1730s, and which justified further mediation. When mediators were called upon from these states, Rousseau advised the *représentants* both to embrace the process and to come to an agreement. If they did not, they would either see Geneva fall to France, or experience civil war within the city.[14] The alternatives were stark, but in Rousseau's eyes no other options existed, other than to seek an alternative homeland. The latter eventuality would mean becoming subjects rather than citizens. Rousseau made these points in January 1768, in a letter to François-Henri d'Ivernois that was to become famous. There he stated that, while he was 'persuaded that nothing is worth a price paid in human blood, and that there is no greater liberty on this earth than in the heart of a just man', he was willing to acknowledge that 'it is natural for men of courage who have lived free to prefer an honourable death to the heaviest servitude'. As there was no way Rousseau could see of overcoming the powers ranged against the *représentants*, there remained the one further honourable option, of exodus:

> Instead of defiling your hands in the blood of your compatriots, abandon [to your enemies] those walls which were intended to protect liberty, and which will become no more than a lair of tyrants. You can leave, all together, in broad daylight, with your wives and children in the midst of you, and since you must wear irons, carry at least those of some great prince, and not the unbearable and odious yoke imposed by your equals. And do not imagine that in such a case you would remain without asylum; you do not know what esteem and respect your courage, your moderation and your wisdom have inspired throughout Europe. I do not imagine that there is any sovereign on the continent, excepting none, who would not receive with honour, and I dare say with respect, this emigrant colony of men too virtuous not to know how to be subjects as faithful as they were zealous citizens.[15]

Rousseau also recognised that the new *représentants* who began to lead the party from 1766, elected from among the gatherings called 'circles' (*cercles*) that had formed since 1762 to discuss politics and to socialise, were certainly not his disciples. Those elected formed the twenty-four commissioners appointed to contribute to the mediation. Five younger men in particular began to lead the *représentants*: Gédéon Flournoy, Jacques Vieusseux, Théodore Rilliet, Étienne Clavière and Jean-André Deluc. Of Flournoy, little is known. Vieusseux, a devout Calvinist, had been a *représentant* and friend to Rousseau since the early 1760s; he was related to Jean-André Deluc, Clavière and Rilliet by marriage.[16] Rilliet was a scion of the prominent Rilliet and Saussure families, studied at the Genevan Academy and in 1751 became a lawyer. He composed one of the classic *représentant* tracts, the *Solution générale ou lettres à Monsieur Covelle le fils, citoyen de Genève* (1765), which supplied a history of the usurpation of the sovereignty of the General Council by Francophile magistrates dedicated to self-aggrandisement.[17] Clavière was a merchant, whose father had been a French Huguenot exile; he was a 'bourgeois' rather than a 'citizen', because his father had purchased bourgeois status after his son's birth. Clavière could thus become a member of the Council of Two Hundred, but he could never become a magistrate. Jean-André Deluc, the son of Jacques-François, was a merchant like his father, but had a passion for natural philosophy, the exploration of the Alps and the invention of implements to study and to measure the fossil record. He was equally devoted to politics.

It was Jean-André Deluc and Clavière together who were responsible for the brilliant *représentant* strategy of presenting themselves as moderates ever willing to compromise.[18] This at least was in accordance with Rousseau's counsel, the difference being that the *représentants* rejected the view that they were necessarily weak, and that they ought to accept French proposals for peace. Rather, the strategy was to portray the magistrates as tyrants at the same time as an appeal was made to any party friendly either towards Geneva particularly or to republics in general, in the hope that external powers could be persuaded to pressurise the mediators from the cantons and from France to accept a *représentant* peace. The *représentants* also presented themselves as the party of industry and trade. The interconnectedness between Genevan commerce and that of mainland Europe, and especially of France and the cantons, was expected to provide leverage. What was at risk, the *représentants* claimed, was the Genevan economy. If this collapsed because of a civil war, all of the bordering states would suffer. Asserting the argument that the *représentants* were offering compromise, peace and prosperity was the central strategy, and pursued with vigour.

Jean-André Deluc, sometimes with Rilliet in tow, did much of the heavy lifting to this end, in terms of seeking to implement *représentant* policy across the cantons and in the courts of France and Savoy. He corresponded with Jacques Necker in the hope of getting access to French authorities and as a means of influencing Geneva's magistrates. Both men were devout, and Deluc appealed to Necker as an advocate of the public good, in addition to being someone who could be convinced that the *représentants* were willing to compromise.[19] Deluc visited Paris in consequence, and accepted failure, although he remained on excellent terms with Necker. He also led diplomatic missions to the cantons that succeeded in persuading Bern and Zurich to deter armed French intervention and to continue with the mediation, despite the rejection of Beauteville's plan.[20] Clavière had much stronger connections with Britain, and disappointingly reported that the magisterial party's wooing of British ministers was succeeding, with the news that a member of the Tronchin family was dining with Lord Shelburne.[21]

Jean-André Deluc's solution to the political impasse, outlined in his 'Projet de conciliation pour la République de Genève', was to remove the *grabeau*, which prevented candidates being put forward to the Council of Twenty-Five, but to keep the *droit négatif*, restoring the Council of Sixty as a body to make sure laws were being adhered to, and balance the powers of the magistrates by having half the Council of Sixty elected by the General Council.[22] This amounted to a compromise with the magistrates, and was intended to operate through a power-sharing arrangement. Despite going beyond Rousseau in terms of his willingness to combat France, Jean-André Deluc's was ultimately a Rousseauian proposal for peace, entailing the restoration of the distinction between sovereignty and government in addition to popular respect for the magistrates reinstated as the fathers of the people. Some *représentants* were critical, arguing that because the magistrates *were* tyrants, it would be better to replace them by the *représentants* in the government of the state. How the French could ever have accepted this more radical proposal was never explained.

In fact, Deluc's compromise was close to the actual agreement secured between the magistrates and the *représentants*, under Beauteville's gaze, on 11 March 1768. Constitutional changes were agreed that were to be implemented over five years: the bourgeois lost the *grabeau* but gained the power to elect, as members of the General Council, half of the members of the Council of Two Hundred, and to remove each year four members of the Council of Twenty-Five. The Council of Twenty-Five retained the right to convoke the other Councils, to elect half the Council of Two Hundred and to make proposals to the General Council.[23] Both parties united in the churches of Geneva to give thanks for the restoration of unity, as the bells rang around them. A new era of concord appeared to have commenced. Many magistrates were soon to rue the failure of Beauteville to crush the *représentants* by force.

II

Over the following years, the leaders of the *représentants* began to contribute to the governance of the republic of Geneva through election to the Council of Two Hundred. Jean-André Deluc entered the Council of Two Hundred in 1770, but was already concocting plans to leave Geneva: the unexpected death of his wife since 1752, Françoise Vieusseux, provoked a crisis, and he had no desire to remain a merchant. Significantly, the destination he proposed was Britain, where he hoped to obtain a position teaching the children of Swiss bankers.[24] Contacts such as Charles Stanhope, who had joined the *représentant* party by the late 1760s and had been granted bourgeois status, were expected to help. So were Deluc's publications, such as *Recherches sur les modifications de l'atmosphère, contenant l'histoire critique du Baromètre & du Thermomètre*, originally published in 1772. It was this writing that facilitated his becoming a Fellow of the Royal Society in 1773. Remarkably, and underlining the growing links between Geneva and Britain, he was also appointed reader to Queen Charlotte in 1774. He lived at Windsor and continued his research into natural philosophy, with a series of notable further works.[25] His departure from Geneva, meanwhile, had left Clavière as leader of the *représentants*.

Jean-André Deluc's departure was crucial to subsequent events in the city. During the negotiations that led to the compromise of March 1768, Jean-André Deluc had learned to appreciate the position of the magistrates. He was greatly impressed by individuals such as Jacques Necker, and was pleased when Necker was named the Genevan *résident* at Paris in 1768. Deluc's position is significant, because he was sure that Geneva, at one point on the brink of revolution, could be returned to a state of peace. Despite the *représentants* having been branded anarchists by the magistrates, it was possible to establish a new union, by accepting the compromise of 1768 and working with the magistrates to govern the state. Deluc's father Jacques-François believed, with many *représentants*, that the magistrates could never be trusted after the Rousseau affair in 1762: Jean-André wrote his father a stinging rebuke in November 1768, in which he gave grounds for his personal optimism.[26]

For Deluc *fils* it was often the case that 'injustice triumphs and liberty is oppressed'. This was just, because Providence decreed all, and governed all men to a higher end. If 'secondary causes' were considered in the case of Geneva, however, it became clear that Providence was acting differently. He told his father that 'we have produced a happy revolution'.

Men had been bitterly divided; it was now clear that it was the interest of the citizens/bourgeois and the magistrates to live in harmony. If they failed to do so, the *natifs*, who were already petitioning to obtain full civic rights, would turn Geneva into a democracy. At the same time, some of those Jean-André Deluc termed 'violent *négatifs*' were involving themselves in the plan of Voltaire and the French authorities to limit Geneva's trade by establishing a free port at nearby Versoix, the idea being to attract industrious *natifs*. In short, Geneva was facing economic ruin; trade had declined, Deluc said, because of the political troubles, and he himself had direct experience of the loss of commerce.

Jean-André Deluc was convinced that the magistrates' attempt 'to turn Geneva into an aristocratic republic three times in the last century' had failed and could not now be renewed; the power-sharing with the *représentants* determined upon in March 1768 ensured this. Accordingly, he wrote, 'things have altogether altered'; a new political world could be formed by magistrates and citizens working together, aware of the threat posed by the *natifs*, and of the greater threat posed by a France now seeking to lessen the wealth of Geneva through economic competition. Deluc claimed that his strategy of friendship and compromise had led to the end of domestic unrest. The duc de Choiseul, he informed his father in confidence, had no designs upon the sovereignty of Geneva, considering the magistrates to be fools and the *représentants* to be wicked. This too was a reason for all parties interested in the public good, in peace and in economic wellbeing, to pull together. The *représentants* and the magistrates were both seeking 'a government sufficiently popular for liberty, but not too popular for instability and for license'. Directed by reason, conscience and prudence, it was vital, Deluc stated, to foster concord in the hearts of all the people, and put the period of turmoil, antagonism and intermittent civil war behind them.

Jean-André Deluc might himself have been able to succeed in the difficult task of governing Geneva alongside *négatif* magistrates who had been at war with the *représentants* through the 1760s. Clinging to the position he had articulated in 1768, he continued to be involved in Genevan affairs while serving the British court. While the *représentants* and the magistrates began to form new camps in the 1770s, Deluc made trips to Paris and to the cantons in the hope of enforcing the 1768 settlement, his own recipe for peace and moderation. In a revealing letter of 1777, to his brother-in-law Jacques Vieusseux, he stated that he was following Rousseau in explaining what 'union' meant in politics.[27] It did not entail a homogeneous political culture. Nor did it entail endless debate and division. Rather, union in politics for Jean-André Deluc was whatever established peace, and in Geneva's case this was by having magistrates who were respected and citizens who loved the constitution and were not plotting violent revolution. In other words, union entailed abiding by Rousseau's distinction between sovereignty and government. There was nothing sacred about a republican constitution, because 'constitutions are like the climate, men can be happy living in every kind'. It now seemed to Deluc that, unfortunately, the *représentants*, having achieved power in 1768, were seeking to dominate the governing councils, replace the magistrates and set themselves up as a unified political authority.

Deluc thus declared himself to be of the view that the greatest threat to Geneva was popular revolution, and that the path being walked by the *représentants* was that of so many other historical republics, towards ruination and death:

> I am now in agreement with what has been said for a long time, that the victorious parties are always oppressive, and among the different kinds of oppression, that of the multitude is the most insupportable. This is why republics have always collapsed, through too much of what is termed liberty.[28]

He went further, stating that Geneva was likely to end because of the *représentants* rather than the magistrates, that a demagogue had become the leader of the *représentants*, who did not realise what the good of the state entailed, and that Geneva was in a position like Corsica and Poland, being weak and divided. Jean-André Deluc had ceased to be a *représentant*. He now felt far more sympathy with the position of the magistrates. In his view, the *représentants* had transformed themselves into a movement seeking to change the state. The result would be violence and anarchy. Any steps to combat such a threat were justified. The person Deluc identified as a dangerous leader of the people was Jacques-Antoine Du Roveray, the young *procureur-général* of the republic and a close associate of Deluc's own great friend and sometime ally, Étienne Clavière.

III

Clavière was different from Deluc. One difference was his wealth. His father was Jean-Jacques Clavière, a merchant born in Serres in 1704, who entered Geneva as a Protestant refugee from persecution in 1724, and acquired bourgeois status in 1735. It was noted in the registers of the council that Jean-Jacques Clavière was intelligent and industrious, but

FIGURE 5.1. Étienne Clavière, painted by François Bonneville. Bibliothèque de Genève

that because his fortune was above the norm it was to be hoped that his actions would be compatible with the mores of the city.[29] Clavière followed his father into trade, but also embraced city politics. In the period up to 1768, Clavière had been less willing to compromise than Jean-André Deluc, seeing the magistrates as the servants of the people according to natural law. For Clavière, both the right of election and the right of resistance justified the cause of the *représentants*, being derived from the law of nature.[30] He was more pessimistic than Deluc about the capacity of the magistrates to rule Geneva alongside the *représentants*, and more optimistic that the *représentants* could rule the city alone, when and if the magistrates were replaced or ended their stranglehold over Genevan politics. Despite increasingly open disagreement, each man remained devoted to the other into the late 1770s, as is clear from the letters that have survived between them. In the early 1770s, Clavière offered to lend Jean-André Deluc money, to stave off an imminent bankruptcy due to a debt owed to the d'Ivernois family. He advised Deluc on finance more generally, and was heavily involved in the attempt to arrange employment for him as a tutor to the children of the banker Étienne Delessert, and in securing apprenticeships for Deluc's own children. In return, Clavière used Deluc's connections with Necker to find out about the condition of the French economy, with a view to investing 'my own small fortune' in the French national debt.[31] As André Gür has explained, Clavière was at this time shifting his commercial interests away from the cloth trade and into *rentes viagères*, the loans to the French government the profit upon which was determined by the continued life and health of thirty young Genevan women.[32]

Clavière often wrote to Jean-André Deluc from London or from Paris, provided him with homilies about the sins of humanity and was remarkably well informed about events in the great courts and about day-to-day politics. He had no faith in what for him were spurious unions of people and magistrates. Individuals were motivated by interest, and this was the core fact behind every political rumination. Such a perspective on the world led Clavière to realise from the outset, as against his friend Deluc, that the agreement of 1768 was an armistice rather than a peace settlement, and as such a prelude to the renewal of hostilities. As he wrote to Deluc in 1774, '[T]he republic is very much as you left it, governed in my view as if it were about destroy itself.'[33]

Clavière was open in his belief that conciliation at Geneva would fail, and that in this respect Jean-André Deluc's judgement had been poor. Deluc did not fully comprehend the nature of contemporary commercial society and the malaise within it. Societies were becoming ever more decadent. Morals, the foundation of healthy politics, were in jeopardy because of the march of commerce, which brought with it luxury and extensive corruption. Corruption manifested itself in different ways, but one of the indisputable consequences of commerce, in Clavière's eyes, was growing inequality. Inequality was not measured only by relative income levels and economic disparities between social groups. Rather, it was evident in the power of the rich by comparison with the seeming incapacity of the poor to stand against them. The great political challenge of the modern world, for Clavière, was to prevent 'the cruel war carried on by the rich against the poor'. He declared himself a defender of property rights, but held that they were more often than not deployed to exploit the poor. He portrayed the rich as devouring the poor, ever seeking their own gain at the expense of the less well-off, and controlling public opinion through their power and influence, to ensure their own happiness and leave in misery of the vast majority of humankind. Clavière's conclusion was that if the rich were ever banished from a state, the people would soon find themselves forming new opinions and becoming happy. The rich themselves, once corrupted, were largely beyond salvation. Jean-André Deluc, he declared, was far too soft on them.[34]

The additional difficulty for Geneva was its size, being too small to defend itself against the armies of France or of Savoy. Diplomatic exertions were necessary to prevent such states from dominating Geneva. The threat derived not solely from the possibility of invasion, but also regarded the security of food supplies and the capacity of the city to obtain grain to feed its inhabitants. Furthermore, large states seeking empire, which in the modern world tended to mean commercial empire through economic dominion, had to be countered. Fortunately, all of the great powers, in lusting after commerce, could be persuaded that a strong economic relationship with Geneva would be of benefit. Clavière was expounding the view that Genevan trade was a bargaining chip in possible political alliances. This was evident from a letter by James Hutton sent in 1767 to Lord Shelburne, then secretary of state for the Southern Department, and responsible for British relations with southern Europe. Hutton stated that the French, through their blockade of Geneva, were preventing merchants from purchasing vast amounts of cotton cloth that was normally sold in France. The solution was to break the blockade and facilitate the transfer of the goods to Britain. Hutton noted that one of the merchants who purchased the large quantities of muslin was one of the 'rabble' *représentants*, Clavière himself, who was clearly keen on developing an economic relationship with Britain:

> [T]here are ten or twelve Merchants, wholesale men who purchase together I may fairly compute made up the rest of the £200000, all of which the French dealers buy at Geneva, but are now hindered from any sort of intercourse with Geneva, I say it is the palpable interest of England to finish if possible the blockade, & prevent the stopping so considerable an article of trade. I can argue for the fact being intimate with the Merchants. He who bought above £3500 worth of other kinds, one of the men whom the French and their party at Geneva call rabble, and is one of the 24 Commissaries of the Citizens, his name is Clavière (entre nous).[35]

Hutton's identification of Clavière as a rich merchant at Geneva underlined the fact that the latter, to many, epitomised the very thing he himself despised: a deluded, wealthy hypocrite. This was Jean-Paul Marat's view, expressed several times in later years.[36]

Clavière has always been a difficult figure to pin down, for historians. Rather than writing manifestos, his preference was to work through others, either directly or indirectly. Jacques-Pierre Brissot came to know Clavière through François d'Ivernois, whose works defending the *représentants* he had read, and this brought him to Geneva after sending a letter in February 1782. Brissot, in a letter to d'Ivernois, confessed that although he did not consider himself to have been born a republican, he aspired to be one:

> I was not born Republican, but I recognised the energy of those who have the happiness to be born as such. I have sometimes aspired to imitate this, but have never managed to vanquish the [opposite] impressions imposed by my education. I will always revere, however, all the souls who, like your own, are dedicated to the public good, and willing to sacrifice even life itself to it.[37]

When Brissot met Clavière in 1782 he was quickly overwhelmed by a man who was so inspirational that he made Brissot's own political philosophy seem parochial and wrong-headed. Clavière was honest and virtuous, with cosmopolitan inclinations. He had a fault, however, which was that he needed others to write up his ideas and turn them into a systematic philosophy. Brissot was delighted to have found a great mentor in politics, capable of seeing behind the veil of political machination, and wanted himself to act as the 'craftsman', capable of transforming Clavière's genius into reforms bringing both happiness and liberty to the people:

> [Clavière] had an inexhaustible stock of new ideas, of great ideas capable of captivating minds; but he lacked the ability to express them. He

> ignored the art of analysis; there was no order in his ideas, no clarity in his style. His thought was superior but it was necessary for another to write for him. His [mind] was a limitless mine of brute diamonds: it required a craftsman to fashion them.[38]

When the young Samuel Romilly was contemplating the writing of a history of the Genevan revolution of 1782, his brother-in-law Jean Roget provided him with accounts of the personalities of the principal actors. Jean-Pierre Bérenger, the prominent *natif*, informed Roget that, in his view, Clavière was the deepest political thinker among the *représentants*. For the pastor Ésaïe Gasc, a *natif* who purchased bourgeois status in 1774 for 1,500 *écus*, Clavière's 'love of liberty for the sake of liberty' was underlined by the fact that he could have abandoned politics in 1768, being both rich and happy, but instead continued to fight the magistrates over the following twelve years.[39]

Clavière lived a full life, with business interests spanning Europe, and was devoted to his wife and daughter. His hero was not Rousseau. Rather, it was Adam Smith, who had travelled to Geneva for two months in the autumn of 1765 while serving as tutor to the Duke of Buccleuch; he visited the Stanhope family and later corresponded with the 2nd Earl Stanhope. Smith was an eccentric figure. There is no evidence that he met with Clavière at this time or had any sympathy for the *représentants*.[40] Indeed, it is likely that Smith was more supportive of the magistrates. At Glasgow, in 1761, Smith had tutored the physician Théodore Tronchin's son François-Louis. Later, in a letter to David Hume, he praised Charles Bonnet, the enemy of the *représentants*, as 'one of the worthiest and best hearted men in Geneva or indeed in the world, notwithstanding he is one of the most religious'.[41] Smith fascinated Clavière, nevertheless, because they shared the view that the modern world had altered irredeemably with the growth of commerce. Clavière believed that Smith had provided the tools through which the nature of commerce, and the politics and international relations commerce generated, could be understood. For Clavière, the lesson was that the crisis of commercial society in Europe was best dealt with by popular revolution, initially in small republics like Geneva. That Adam Smith, the eccentric sage of Kirkcaldy and absolute enemy to revolution as the worst species of enthusiasm, inspired such a man as Clavière, is one of the nicer ironies of the later eighteenth century.

Why did Clavière come to the conclusion that civil war with the magistrates was inevitable? He believed in the power of communities characterised by a relatively homogeneous culture, dedicated to industry and enjoying relative equality between social groups. In his vision of a successful society, he was greatly influenced by his mother, Jeanne-Elisabeth Rapillard, the daughter of a citizen at Geneva. Jeanne-Elisabeth was a member of the Pietist Moravian Brethren, or *Unitas Fratrum*, the 'unity of the brothers' as depicted in the 133rd Psalm. She may well have joined the sect in 1741, as it was in this year that Nikolaus Ludwig von Zinzendorf, then leader of the Moravian Brethren, arrived at Geneva. Zinzendorf had been brought up as a Pietist, and joined the tiny sect of Brethren in 1722, when a group that had been living in northern Moravia arrived at his Berthelsdorf estate in south-eastern Saxony.

Over the following years, Zinzendorf and the Brethren converted many inhabitants of the nearby town of Herrnhut, who agreed on 12 May 1727 to live in conformity with a written 'Brotherly Agreement'. The Brethren lived godly lives devoted to good works and universal love, entailing constant prayer, the study of selected passages from the Old Testament (the 'Daily Watchwords'), the confession of sin and mutual support to promote lives dedicated to serving God. The direct revelation of the Holy Spirit was anticipated and the making of oaths forbidden, in accordance with biblical injunction. Industry was encouraged, not only to meet the physical needs of the community, but also to facilitate connections with the outside world. Zinzendorf, now a bishop of what was termed 'the Renewed Unity', recognised that the first step to conversion was often social interaction through trade.

From the first, the Moravians were missionaries, and the successful model of Herrnhut, soon a thriving community, in commercial terms, and characterised by relative equality and social harmony, began to be exported across Germany and further afield. Zinzendorf was devoted to spreading the Gospel, which was the reason for his stay at Geneva between March and May 1741 with forty or fifty fellow Brethren. The Moravians showed there how to live infused by the Holy Spirit, with singing, ceaseless prayer and direct communication with God: all of this to remove the sins of the world. Although they were stoned on their way out of the city, Zinzendorf had established relations with leading pastors, and especially Jacob Vernet.[42] He returned to Geneva in 1757 to visit some of those he had converted, probably including Jeanne-Elisabeth Rapillard.[43]

Clavière was not a devout man or a Moravian himself, but his description of the ideal life lived within a community was remarkably similar to that of the Brethren, whose practices he had seen at first hand. His continued closeness to Moravians across Europe was revealed by James Hutton's letter to Shelburne of 1767. Hutton was an English bookseller who had been 'awakened' by the Wesley brothers in 1735, established the Moravian Fetter Lane Society in London at the end of the decade and travelled to Heernhut in 1739, where he married the Swiss Moravian Louise Brandt in an arranged marriage.[44] Afterwards, he was involved with Zinzendorf in proselytising trips across Switzerland and in England. He established links with Geneva and with Clavière more particularly. In *Memoirs* published in the nineteenth century, it was reported that Hutton considered himself to be capable of bringing peace to Geneva. He corresponded with Shelburne with a view to bringing the *représentants* to England, because of the tyranny of the magistrates. He also sought to prevent France from intervening and thereby increasing the 'danger and distress of so many thousands whom I loved'. Hutton also sent Clavière a letter, which he felt had been inspired 'directly from the Lord', and the magistrates a further letter, in which he expressed the view that peace could be established between the parties within an hour if they followed its contents.[45] Hutton was reprimanded for interfering, but links with Clavière were probably maintained over the following years, because he ended up living with Jean-André Deluc in the later 1770s in Pimlico; Hutton and Deluc were by that time favourites of George III and of Queen Charlotte.[46]

It was important that Clavière, in addition to his having knowledge of the Moravian Brethren, was apprenticed as a young man to a company in Christian-Erlangen, the town established in 1686 by Margrave Christian Ernst of Brandenburg-Bayreuth, for Huguenot refugees fleeing French persecution. Erlangen was renowned for the godliness and industriousness of its inhabitants, for its straight streets and ordered living, and for the number of manufacturing companies it housed.[47] Clavière then entered the family trading company established in 1744, 'Jean et David Cazenove et Clavière'; on his joining it was renamed 'Cazenove, Clavière et fils'. This company lasted until 1769, when it became 'Clavière père, fils et Gros', as his nephew François Gros also joined it. One of his tasks was frequently to travel to Frankfurt to exchange imperial money for French, and in consequence he learned German. During this period too, he often lived with his father in Amsterdam and in Paris, where he was treated for deafness he had contracted whilst in Erlingen. Visits to London were also necessary, because of the extent of the company's interests, particularly in the trade of cloths to and from the Indies.[48]

Clavière's links with Britain became ever more extensive in the following decade, through men such as Hutton and through the Stanhope family. Britain was described by Clavière in his letters to Jean-André Deluc as the key to the survival of the republic, being the only power capable of preventing France from giving the magistrates *carte blanche* in governing the city. In the same letter of 1774, he identified corruption and decadence as the great evils of the modern world, gradually destroying states just as they brought men to premature death.[49] Clavière's great goal at Geneva in the 1770s was the restoration of republican virtue, the living of an austere life of industry and of devotion to the community. In so aspiring, he was translating many of the practices of evangelical Protestant communities into a secular form, with the objective being the survival, prosperity and power of the state, rather than the religious life ending in salvation. The irony was that the Clavière family was becoming extremely wealthy, and purchased a large property outside the city in the mid-1760s, next to that of the Tronchins. Clavière himself entered the Council of Two Hundred in 1770, and in the following years increased his fortune still further with the movement of his funds into government debt speculation. In 1776, he became one of the directors of Geneva's hospital, and also a member of the exclusive *Société des Arts*, which allowed him to associate with the very richest in the state.[50]

The corruption of Geneva's magistrates, and confirmation that they could not be trusted to rule, appeared to Clavière to be confirmed by their raising of public revenues by indirect taxes that tended to fall upon the poor; this appeared to underline the selfishness of the magistrates and their rejection of the public good.[51] The key issue signifying the sorry state of politics at Geneva, however, was the reform of the city's law code, one of the provisions agreed upon in 1768, as Article XII of the edict of pacification. The magistrates, in Clavière's view, refused to countenance the confirmation of the legal edicts that defined the state and the powers of each of its branches, preferring to rely upon an unwritten set of practices that facilitated their own rule.[52] A new code was the last hope for reform, because corruption was 'attacking and destroying that which must be conserved', and more especially the manners that lay behind stable politics. The Council of Twenty-Five in 1774 brought the legal reform project before the Council of Two Hundred, to be discussed article by article. The process proved laborious and contentious, so at the end of 1776 a new commission was established, to collect the acts of the General Council and then to revise them, with the work to be concluded by August 1779. By 1779, only a third of the work had been done, and the Council of Two Hundred then put an end to the process, on the grounds that so much of the debate was pointless. A smaller committee was created instead, to expedite matters. The Council of Twenty-Five refused to accept this, and in the stalemate that followed called upon Bern and Zurich, in September 1779, to negotiate between the parties. For Clavière and his associates, the actions of the Council of Twenty-Five was a ruse to maintain aristocracy and reverse the settlement of 1768, ideally returning to that of 1738. For the magistrates and *négatifs*, the thirty years after 1738 began to appear as as a golden age, during which the aristocratic authorities had been secure in their rule. From the perspective of the *représentants*, this period had in fact seen a growing decadence and the related demise of devotion to the public good. On 7 April 1779, the magistrates published their version of the new code. On 1 September, the Council of Two Hundred, with Clavière a leading member, rejected it entirely. A civil war was beginning.

IV

Three factors prevented the kind of peace settlement that had succeeded in 1768 from being agreed anew ten years later. The first was the confidence of the magistrates that they could defeat the *représentants*. Those formerly called *négatifs* were now led by Joseph Des Arts and Jean-Jacques Chapeaurouge, and identified themselves as *constitutionnaires*, upholding established laws and practices against dangerous projects for change. Organised as a committee, in imitation of the *représentants* in the 1760s, they included large numbers of members of the Council of Two Hundred, former magistrates and professors at the Genevan Academy, in addition to some two hundred bourgeois and citizens, making a total of around 450 men.[53] They launched an unremitting barrage of abuse against the *représentants*. The *représentants* were presented as power-hungry revolutionaries plotting to turn themselves into presidents and demagogues by means of the revisions to the law code. They were accused of seeking to rule through the secret government of the *cercles*, itself behind the planned unlimited sovereignty of the General Council.[54] If the *représentants* were successful, government at Geneva would become akin to that of the Ottomans. As schismatics violating natural ideas about politics, the *représentants* were reversing the established constitution that had secured peace and prosperity for centuries.[55] Rousseau was regularly blamed in the *constitutionnaire* brochures as the source of the malaise, having erected his own 'temple of discord' within the city. As one pamphlet of November 1780 had it, Genevan politics showed how far human nature had degenerated: 'how far we have travelled from the noble simplicity of our ancestors . . . in our decadent days we make Philippics . . . without being inspired, while the ancients admired Diogenes in his barrel, and today we reproach artisans for their simplicity and modesty'.[56]

Politically naive and addicted to 'pride and dominion', the *représentants* would, it was said, recreate all of the atrocities experienced by ancient Athens. The people were 'the most ungracious, the most capricious, and the most unjust of all masters'. In writing their own law code anew, and in erecting the General Council as sovereign over all, the *représentants* were also challenging Christianity at Geneva:

> The Republic of Geneva has no other sovereign than the Supreme Being, and no other rule of conduct and manners than the good language that is contained in the canonical books of the Old and New Testaments, and no other laws than those which [these books] would sanction.[57]

As 1780 wore on, the *constitutionnaire* attacks upon the *représentants* became more intense, in part through a long series of declarations. These reiterated the need for peace, the necessary restoration of the ancient constitution and the avoidance of enthusiastic innovation. By November and December 1780, intervention was being demanded to stop the *représentant* plot to take over the state.[58] The *représentants* were accused of creating a war between the propertied and non-propertied because of Rousseau; the *cercles* were presented as recreating the plebiscites of ancient Rome. The result was predicted as being a social war that would turn Geneva into a despotism.[59]

The second factor preventing agreement was Isaac Cornuaud. Cornuaud was a *natif* who hated the *représentants* and derided them in a series of brilliant pamphlets labelling them extremists, levellers, fanatics and anarchists, self-serving demagogues and lovers of luxury, lusting after power and riches. Cornuaud's first works, the *Lettre d'un natif à un bourgeois de ses amis* (1777), *La famille divisée* (1777) and the *Examen politico-patriotique des questions suivantes* (1777) were laments for the *natifs*, identifying them as living beyond the body politic and demanding greater liberties. As such, the *Lettre* and the *Examen* were burned by the public executioner on 18 April and 12 May respectively.[60] By 1779, however, Cornuaud's pamphlets moved beyond the demand that the *natifs* sever relations with the *représentants* and remain neutral. Rather, he painted a picture of a city with loose manners and declining commerce, if the revolutionary *représentants* took power, advocating instead the rule of what he termed 'the elites', who were moderate and wise.[61] In a veritable deluge of pamphlets throughout 1781, Cornuaud ridiculed the 'mad and delirious' *représentants* for crying against aristocracy, tyranny and 'the arbitrary power of the councils', claiming that there was no conspiracy by the magistrates but rather one from the people, and that the intervention of the guaranteeing powers was vital to restore peace at Geneva.[62] Cornuaud argued that the *représentants* founded their ideas upon Rousseau's *Lettres écrites de la montagne*, but were moving far beyond this text, for Rousseau had never justified democracy. Inspired by a hatred of the rich, the *représentants* were pushing for complete equality and a democratic constitution. Their strategy would ruin the state, and was historically unjustifiable, because democracy was suited to the first and most basic societies alone, where passions were limited. Geneva was more aristocratic than democratic in structure, following model republics such as Bern. To be otherwise was madness.[63] Des Arts paid for Cornuaud's allegiance with large sums from 1780. The *natifs* were promised civil equality, and with the magistrates formed a secret committee for war, modelled on those of the *représentants* of the 1760s.[64]

If Cornuaud was a placeman, articulating the view of his masters, it was also the case that he was honest in not trusting the *représentants*' alternative vision of a revivified Genevan politics. The source of his critique of the *représentants* as deluded utopians was Jacques Mallet du Pan. Mallet du Pan was by this time putting forward a sophisticated assessment of the options for republicans in modern times in *Idées soumises à l'examen de tous les conciliateurs, par un médiateur sans consequence*—a final attempt to bring the warring factions at Geneva together. Mallet du Pan must have been aware that his plan, completed on 16 November 1780, was going to fail, and it was thus above all a warning to the *représentants* not to be so sure about their assault on magistrates and aristocrats. The greatest danger for republicans, in Mallet du Pan's view, was the false hope that accompanied projects promising an ideal future on the basis of popular sovereignty. Geneva was 'infected', he wrote, by such reasoning, relying on spurious assumptions about the possibility of applying historic republican ideas to the present. The emulation of ancient states was not practicable:

> If there is a species of quackery to avoid, in the crises of small states, it is that of enthusiasts dreaming of projects. Within monarchies such men are mocked. In republics, they ought to be dreaded . . . [D]o not look for wisdom among the ancient republics, as the ideas that have come down to us concerning them are too confused and imperfect. It is not, moreover, in the perpetual movement from the most oppressive oligarchy to the most turbulent democracy, which characterise [ancient history] that we should select our models. By the aid of moral

> institutions which we are only permitted to admire, or circumstances peculiar to their situation, these states reached a state of dazzling brilliance, which we cannot emulate.[65]

If an eye was cast over the republics that might serve as models to Geneva, the most obvious had to be the United Provinces, where there was a government 'which links together liberty and authority, and where jealousy between the two renders everyone vigilant, without causing domestic instability'. The form of government in the Dutch Republic was aristocracy rather than democracy wisely tempered (*démocratie tempérée*), but Mallet du Pan drew a direct parallel with Geneva, where there was 'an aristocracy of two thousand Genevans . . . which is no different to the position of the bourgeois at Amsterdam'.[66] For the Dutch and the Genevans, Mallet du Pan argued, the key to politics was to prevent aristocracy from becoming oligarchic, in the form of rule by patrician families over the generations. An instance of oligarchy was Genoa, which Mallet du Pan called 'the hardest, most despotic and most powerful of governments, whose history is only a list of crime and faction among the nobility, and misery among the people'. Other Italian republics were wiser, he said, in preventing oligarchy by making sure that offices were moveable. Lucca, Ragusa and Venice, for example, had enjoyed peace domestically and internationally because magistrates could be removed. In the case of Venice, three million subjects had to be protected from the rule of two thousand nobles, and this was achieved in part by an inquisition, which the magistrates could use when necessary against the nobility and against the people: 'the terror that it inspires gives confidence to the people and ensures everyone's security. It is in the dungeons of ten despots that the foundations of liberty are to be found.' Only the doge and the procurators served for life, with most offices being renewed annually, and this explained why, when Europe had seen so much turbulence, the government of Venice 'remains stable across four centuries'.[67]

Equally, free cities such as Hamburg could be said to enjoy liberty because their senate, *burgermeister* and syndics could be replaced, as guaranteed by the Holy Roman Emperor. In other imperial cities, things were different, with patrician families at Frankfurt, Nuremburg and Ratisbon dominating the senate and turning the state into an oligarchy. Mallet du Pan held that Hamburg too was akin to Geneva, because they shared a form of government whereby the senate proposed legislation and the people in council decided whether to accept it. Mallet du Pan advised Genevans to avoid 'speculative visionaries', and to listen instead to historians. Livy had shown that the despotism of Carthaginian magistrates was due to corruption generated by the perpetuity of their offices. Tacitus and Montesquieu had come to identical conclusions, while Harrington's *Oceana*, 'alone among the utopias in containing judgement and practical suggestions', justified Genevan practice in advocating a senate that discussed legislation and a people that assented or declined. Hume too, who, Mallet du Pan claimed, had adapted Harrington to English circumstances, retained the movement of judges, representatives and senators in his imagined republic: '[W]hat he says on this subject is a truth for all times, and good for all places.' Finally, the marquis d'Argenson found the movement of offices to be key to preventing excessive authority and acting as a source of confidence for the people.

Applying these truths to Geneva, Mallet du Pan concluded that the magistrates had to be regularly replaced, ideally with the election of the Council of Twenty-Five by the General Council from nominees chosen by the Council of Two Hundred, staggering departure from office and allowing magistrates to serve for four years.[68] While patrician wealth was a real threat to the stability of any republic, and to popular liberty more particularly, the greater threat was new wealth, the kind associated with speculation on shares, which could quickly generate greater wealth than a person could earn in a lifetime of labour. The argument was evidently that Genevans needed to be circumspect about leading figures among the *représentants*, and especially Clavière, who lived from investment in shares and public debts: 'Riches that come from money, new money, the wealth of financiers, who are called to govern, and thereby extend their influence, this is a thousand times more insupportable and more dangerous [than an established aristocracy].'[69] The danger was that such men became corrupt, encouraging forms of jealousy destructive of public mores, and formed 'a battalion so united', of similarly rich men, that the people submitted to them and said farewell to their liberty. As manners were more important than laws, and as agrarian laws to redistribute property or sumptuary laws to control manners always failed, it was vital that trust between magistrates and people at Geneva be re-established, by the existing magistrates embracing the removal and election of those in public office as speedily as possible.[70]

The third and overwhelming factor that prevented conciliation was that the new French foreign minister, Vergennes, decided that the *représentants* were dangerous anarchists and democrats; the power of France had to be deployed to crush them.[71] Vergennes had imbibed the claims of the crown's representative at Geneva, Hennin, that the *représentants* were growing in power and threatening to destroy Geneva:

> [T]he increase in the number of the Bourgeois makes the popular party everyday more powerful. It has been estimated that for the last five years, three hundred and twenty persons have been entered into the Bourgeoisie, almost all devoted to the Demagogues, and enemies to the Council.[72]

Hennin was of real significance. Having served as *résident* at Geneva between 1765 and 1778, he moved to Paris, becoming *premier commis* to the Department for Foreign Affairs from 1779 until 1783, and greatly influencing Vergennes. In addition to Hennin, the key link in the chain was Horace-Bénédict Perrinet des Franches, who, since the late 1770s especially, had enjoyed close links with Vergennes; Vergennes had written to the Council of Twenty-Five to praise the singular contribution of des Franches in negotiating the Treaty of Soleure between the cantons and France in 1779, and arranged for des Franches's son Bossey to obtain the position of *aide-de-camp* in the French army at Brest.[73] Des Franches, it was later said by d'Ivernois, had abandoned Geneva for Paris in 1768, on the grounds that the city had become too much dominated by the people, and anticipating 'the degradation of aristocratic families' such as his own.[74] Des Franches had interests in the St Gobain glassworks and, when Necker was called to the post of *directeur général des finances* at the French court in 1777, was approached to become the new ambassador for the republic at Paris. He took the position only as *ministre sans caractère* in order to maintain his independence, which meant in practice that he could more easily continue working for the *constitutionnaires*, and issue vitriolic criticisms of the *représentants*. Des Franches can be presumed to have facilitated the connection between the French authorities and Cornuaud's *natif* faction. Cornuaud, who enjoyed direct contact with Paris from 1780, was informed, among other things, that Clavière, 'the demagogue par excellence', was being watched and having his correspondence both intercepted and copied, with a view to public shaming.[75] Voltaire was another link between the *natifs* and the French government, having been shocked by the perpetual banishment, on 22 February 1770, of eight *natifs* who had demonstrated on 15 February in favour of equal civil and political rights.[76] France recognised the benefits of drawing skilled artisans away from Geneva. Versoix and Ferney became places of asylum, with Voltaire and Hennin directly involved, encouraging the population to abandon Geneva to work for France.[77] Meanwhile the city's citizens and bourgeois came together to condemn and burn what was termed 'the bible of the *natifs*', written by Jacques Mallet du Pan in 1771, with an epigraph drawn from Voltaire: 'Today our tyrants but hitherto our equals'.[78] Mallet du Pan was encouraged to leave Geneva by Voltaire, who arranged for him to become professor of history and belles-lettres at the Academy of the Landgrave of Hesse-Cassel in 1772.[79]

V

Clavière initially employed the strategy of 1768, following Jean-André Deluc's advice to look to the cantons and to France itself. Yet he was sceptical from the outset, writing to his old friend, 'Where today can one find the good Swiss? They furnish mercenaries to foreign powers, and sell their country to any who would command them.'[80] Clavière was abetted by Jacques-Antoine Du Roveray and increasingly by François d'Ivernois. Du Roveray's father François Du Roveray had been a *représentant* commissioner in 1768. Jacques-Antoine Du Roveray was educated in law at the Collège de Genève, qualified as an advocate in 1771, joined the committee to revise the law code, entered the Council of Two Hundred in 1775 and was elected to the position of *procureur-général* on 19 December 1779. He was renowned for his bravery and devotion to the cause: as one delighted resident wrote, 'he has become a magistrate, but remains a citizen'.[81] He was also recognised as being 'obstinate, hot-tempered and violent'.[82] François d'Ivernois also studied law at the Collège de Genève, graduating in 1777 and becoming an advocate in 1781. At the same time he took advantage of his father's relationship with Rousseau, and his links with those who held Rousseau's manuscripts: Thérèse Levasseur, René-Louis Girardin, Paul-Claude Moultou and Pierre-Alexandre Du Peyrou. Between 1778 and 1784, d'Ivernois created, with his two friends Pierre Boin and Jean-François Bassompierre, the *Société typographique de Boin, d'Ivernois et Bassompierre*. Their intention was to create a complete edition of Rousseau's works, which would become known as the 'Geneva' edition.[83] Among their problems was that in presenting works that everyone knew alongside hitherto unknown ones, including the *Confessions*, they obtained fewer subscriptions than anticipated.[84] Rather than being a publishing success, d'Ivernois generated money worries. In politics he was termed 'the seditious subaltern' by the magistrates.[85]

By 1780, it was clear that support for the *représentants* was not going to come from Bern. Clavière and Du Roveray travelled to Paris in January

1780 in the hope of changing Vergennes's mind. When this failed, Clavière published, in February 1780, a letter he had composed and sent to Vergennes. The letter is fascinating, revealing the strategy Clavière and Du Roveray had determined to pursue in order to prevent a *négatif* victory. The sense of being under siege, and of being on the back foot, could not be hidden. Despite this, as always, the *représentants* presented themselves as the true voice of the people of Geneva, speaking for a union of the vast majority of the populace. Much of the letter read as deadly dull, going through the articles of the Edict of 1738 that was acknowledged to have brought peace and be worthy of great praise, and the decisions being taken by the law commission to revise or to accept the provisions of the Edict. The conclusion, however, was that the commission for revising the laws at Geneva was acting in accordance with the spirit of the Edict of 1738. This was of profound importance. It enabled Clavière to refute accusations that the *représentants* were seeking to overturn the existing constitution, were seeking a 'pure democracy' or were planning revolution by means of a syndic who would turn himself into a demagogue on the basis of *représentant* support. Rather, the *représentants* were the true *constitutionnaires*.

Clavière, again following the strategy from 1765, presented the *représentants* as moderates and as patriots, always seeking the public good and willing to compromise; their enemies, the *négatifs*—Clavière refused to call them *constitutionnaires*—were the source of disorder in the state. The battles of the 1760s were being refought, in exactly the same fashion as a decade before. Just as the Delucs *père* and *fils* had done in times past, Clavière presented himself as a simple republican, 'little versed in the art of speaking to the great', and frightened by 'the letters which have come from the office of your excellency, against the citizens, who have been abandoned until now to the attacks of their adversaries'.[86] Clavière appealed to Vergennes as having been misinformed and misled by a mischievous faction. This faction presented itself as the true government but was in fact seeking to dominate the sovereign General Council. Refusal to allow the law commission to get on with its work was proof that the *négatifs* wanted to maintain the current state of civil strife, whereby the small council, relying on a particular interpretation of the Edict of 1738, controlled the business of the General Council. The *représentants*, being moderates, acknowledged the need for bridles on both democracy and aristocracy, while asserting the sovereignty of the General Council and its role as the legislative power within the state. Readers involved in earlier fights at Geneva must have had a strong sense of *déjà-vu*.

FIGURE 5.2. Jacques-Antoine Du Roveray, by an unknown artist. Bibliothèque de Genève

Clavière ended the letter with a set of statements intended, like the letter as a whole, for a Genevan audience and for interested parties abroad rather than for Vergennes specifically. Indeed, although he was its recipient, the last person the letter was actually meant to convince was Vergennes. Clavière and Du Roveray were well aware that the minister was their enemy, and that nothing at all was going to persuade him of the validity of their cause. It is possible that the letter was intended for Vergennes's replacement: Clavière and the *représentants* always appeared to be well versed in events at Versailles, and it may be that they were anticipating the fall of Vergennes; at this time, the *représentants* still had faith in Necker, and Necker had possibly informed them that Vergennes's *disgrâce* was imminent; such was the view of Cornuaud.[87] In fact this was all madness, because after the death of Louis XVI's mentor Maurepas in 1781,

Vergennes's position at the court was unassailable. Whatever the expectation, however, Clavière presented in stark terms the predicament of the *représentants*. They were at risk of destruction by a foreign power, having seen a minister of a great state meddling in the affairs of an independent republic. Vergennes was threatening the religion of Geneva and its very existence. The first counter-strategy was to praise Vergennes and France. The minister was wise and just, and therefore to be trusted not to accept the word of the enemies of the *représentants* alone. Such an assertion was, of course, pure rhetoric:

> And what conduct can be expected from citizens, if the judgement of their conscience, supported by a right evidently good, cries out to them that they do not deserve this interference from your excellency? Should they submit themselves to the will of those who, in declaring what the law is, might be tempted to suspend their religion? What would virtue counsel them to do? Your hand directs a force that, undoubtedly, can dissolve our little republic. What makes us confident is that this hand is directed itself by a justice and a wisdom that is recognised.[88]

A second strategy was more convincing. It was to remind Geneva's neighbours that it had long been a free state, had managed to overcome civil turbulence in the past and above all that the liberty enjoyed by the citizens had been the foundation for the growth of commerce that directly benefited all of the states in the region and beyond:

> And how could the liberty that we defend, this good belonging to us, and that we know how to contain within wise limits, be destructive, in some manner, to those states that surround us? The Genevan people have for a long time been honoured for their wisdom. This virtue among us is a need; and if we lose sight of it, we are soon led back to it through the natural and deadly effects of its loss. But we are far from such a danger. Our neighbours, it is true, are pleased always to see prosper on the banks of Lake Leman a small republic jealous of its liberty. And they [our neighbours] are only the more interested because of the industrious activity [*activité industrieuse*] which is the result [of our liberty].[89]

Clavière then reminded his readers that, from one perspective, nothing of particular significance was happening at Geneva, because unrest was a fact of politics everywhere, and did not require foreign interference, or need to cause worry about dissention spreading abroad. As he put it, 'There is no state where discussion of public affairs does not from time to time excite unrest.'

The most powerful argument Clavière put forward was that if France stopped involving itself in Genevan politics, the turbulence would speedily cease. The law commission would continue with its work, and normal politics would gradually be resumed. In other words, it was the minister himself who was causing the so-called unrest that he was so eager to condemn and suppress. As Clavière wrote, where would the independence, sovereignty and liberty of Geneva be 'if, when unrest occurred, or even appeared to be beginning, there arose in their midst [i.e., from the citizen body or magistrates] men who encouraged the dominion of a foreign neighbour, in order to have their opinions adopted by their fellow citizens?'[90] Vergennes was the dupe of a faction, and was being played for a fool. Again, Clavière expressed optimism because 'HIS VERY CHRISTIAN MAJESTY is pleased to support our independence' and 'recalls on all occasions, the engagements contracted together with their excellencies of Zurich and of Bern' to maintain this independence.[91]

The actual point being made was that France was violating its own treaties with the cantons by interfering in Genevan affairs. The singular irony was that Vergennes, who presented himself as the greatest defender of the Edict of 1738, was breaking that very edict through the actions of his government.[92] This was strong stuff. Clavière must have known that it was going to provoke Vergennes's ire. The verbal war on Vergennes was always wrapped in an appeal to the good king Louis XVI and to the historic justice of the French state towards independent republics. There was an expectation that other ministers, including Necker, might be convinced that it was better to leave Geneva be, and that their counsel would lead to pressure upon Vergennes to cease his interference. As Marc-Théodore Bourrit wrote to Clavière in August 1781, other members of the court at Versailles, including senior ministers such as Maurepas, felt that Vergennes's obsession with Geneva was folly. Vergennes was, however, entirely immovable in his opinions.[93] As he had written to Zurich in 1780, the *représentants* were in his view a seditious faction in need of extermination, carrying on a 'great revolution' at Geneva that would continue to disturb the peace by creating a new constitution, unless it was crushed.[94] Cornuaud made the same point in numerous pamphlets. The *représentants* were obsessed with aristocratic perfidy, which did not exist, in order to dominate the people. They had become demagogues, and the consequences would be pestilential.[95]

VI

The *représentants* were gambling that anti-French feeling at Geneva could be harnessed to unite the populace, presenting a virtuous front against would-be invaders. An added benefit was that the *constitutionnaires* could be identified as agents of a foreign power. Another hope associated with the strategy was that the cantons would be shamed into taking action in the case of what would amount to a gross violation of historic Swiss liberties, if French interference at Geneva continued. Antagonism towards France was undoubtedly growing. One issue of concern was that French government bonds were reputed to have made so many at Geneva rich beyond the norms of republican life that the republic was being destabilised. Assertions in apocalyptic mode, redolent of Moultou's pessimism about the future outlined in letters to Rousseau of the 1760s, continued to be commonplace. A typical example came from the pastor Jean Roget, writing in 1780 to his brother-in-law Samuel Romilly in London, to the effect that manners were entirely corrupted at Geneva because of the progress of commerce; people were rich but miserable in consequence:

> [E]quality, the foundation of the happiness of our republic, has been destroyed absolutely . . . luxury increases ceaselessly and idleness accompanies it, vanity, excess, the love of pleasure, the collapse of the soul all come to the rich, and the poor seek only to imitate them.[96]

Evidence from the period indicates that prominent families were indeed generating wealth comparable almost to the rich tax farmers of France. Sumptuary laws were ignored, with luxury being defended as being compatible with moral practice and a devout mind.[97] Simultaneously, the same families dominated the magisterial positions within the state.[98] Fears of French dominion were ever more present in the minds of the populace. It was reported, for example, that the pastor Pierre-Gédéon Dentand had died prematurely because 'the sovereignty of this country has been sold to France'.[99] Clavière was certain that the real cause of the *représentant's* death was Cornuaud, who had refused to return a letter by Dentand damning France, which brought shame on the pastor. The event illustrated for Clavière both Cornuaud's bad intentions and 'the darkness of his soul'.[100]

Standing against France, which Rousseau had considered a policy of insanity, was also seen as mad by leading *représentants* of the 1760s, including Théodore Rilliet.[101] Clavière and Du Roveray were well aware that they were taking a huge risk. France, as Clavière himself had said, was on the rise, paying off its debts, defeating Britain in war, and enjoying the rule of a patriot king, the young Louis XVI. Britain, by contrast, was plagued by the economic corruption associated with the mercantile system, and by rebellion in its colonies.[102] At the same time, as Vergennes appeared only to have ears for the magistrates, and perhaps as it became clear that money was flowing from France and the magistrates towards Cornuaud, opposition appeared the best course of action. Du Roveray, from his office of *procureur-général*, on 20 October 1780, accepted a representation declaring that France was plotting to take away Geneva's sovereignty.[103] This was followed by another representation, on 15 November, which questioned the use of the French 'guarantee' of Geneva's constitution to prevent the reform of Geneva's laws. It also identified a plot involving Hennin and Vergennes to overturn the 1768 settlement and frustrate the will of the General Council. Action by France was violating the republican maxim that the the greater the number of people involved in political life, the more stable the regime would be. Equally, the magistrates were behaving like Roman patricians battling the plebs.[104]

On 23 November a further declaration denounced the *constitutionnaires*, declaring the republic to be on a knife's edge in terms of public order, denying the accusation of *représentant* conspiracy, and asserting that intervention by foreign powers would lead to the end of independence at Geneva.[105] D'Ivernois began to make similar points against Vergennes and the *constitutionnaires* during November.[106] From the party of *natifs* supporting the *représentants*, arguments became commonplace in 1780 that the citizens were fighting for liberty and patriotism against an illegitimate restriction of liberties. The *natifs* were 'condemned by a barbarous constitution to exist sadly under an arbitrary power', living in consequence like helots among Spartans. At the same time the aristocracy of the wealthy was drawing more power to itself, this being, as Montesquieu and Rousseau had pointed out, the gravest threat to modern republics.[107] The key document attacking French policy under Vergennes was, however, Du Roveray's speech of 11 December 1780, which became known as the *Fameuse remonstrance*.

Du Roveray's *remonstrance* was a brilliant piece of rhetoric, revealing to the world a French plot to destroy Genevan independence by bringing in mediators from France, who were in fact pawns of Vergennes. Du Roveray stated that conclusive evidence had been brought to him by patriotic citizens who could not stand by and watch while their fellow citizens, prominent *constitutionnaires* and *natifs*, became de facto agents of France. Du Roveray presented a letter from the French *résident* Gabard de Vaux to a set of Genevans, dated 29 November 1780, revealing, in Du Roveray's view, a direct violation of the *droit des gens*, because it instructed the *constitutionnaires* and *natifs* how to behave as events played out. Du Roveray claimed that he had immediately taken the letter to the first syndic. As no reply came after a day of waiting, he made the decision to go to the people, so grave was the plot he had uncovered to undermine 'the integrity, independence and sovereignty of the republic'.[108]

Vergennes was identified as the Machiavellian figure behind Gabard de Vaux. Du Roveray stated that Vergennes was violating Geneva's existing treaties with France, because mediation was never called for by an external power. With evident relish he cited a memorandum of the duc de Choiseul of June 1767, addressed to the cantons of Bern and of Zurich, stating that if their 'guarantee' was able to be exercised on a regular basis, and called for by foreign powers, then Genevan independence would cease, and Geneva itself would no longer be a republic.[109] Du Roveray accused those who were in cahoots with Vergennes of treachery. He argued that the magistrates who favoured such a course of action were destroying the social union that had maintained the state for centuries. By 'a happy transmigration, the interests of different orders of persons were mixed together at Geneva', because every member of the community had faith in the magistrates and their capacity to act for the benefit of all. This was now being lost, because a foreign power was seeking to turn certain *natifs* and *constitutionnaires* at Geneva into rebels acting for France. Du Roveray argued that if such conduct by magistrates was contrasted with Rousseau's description of the rulers of Geneva in his dedication to the *Discours sur l'inégalité* of 1755, a genuine sense of decline and crisis would be evident. The situation was terrible, because the people, including the *représentants*, trusted the magistrates. The magistrates had, however, ceased to trust the people, to the point that they were conspiring with Vergennes to destroy the *représentants*.[110]

Du Roveray proclaimed that he was naming the beast, and refuting altogether the accusation that the *représentants* were the rebel party. In fact it was the *constitutionnaires* and Vergennes who were reversing traditional policy, as specified in the Edict of 1738 and the settlement of 1768. All of these documents had described Geneva as an independent state first and foremost. Each forbade independent action by any of the three guaranteeing parties, France, Zurich and Bern: France was thus violating treaties with the cantons as much as with Geneva itself. The root of the problem was that Vergennes had been misled by Hennin, among others, and was becoming convinced that Geneva was a pariah state where there was no justice, especially for individuals put on trial from abroad, because of the power of the *représentants* since the settlement of 1768. Du Roveray stated that when he and Clavière had personally met with Vergennes they had refuted such accusations, as well as the claim that a democratic Geneva was a threat to its neighbours.[111]

More particularly, Vergennes was under the impression that the process of creating a new law code at Geneva was establishing a wild democracy. Du Roveray portrayed the process as an entirely peaceful restatement of the fundamental laws of the polity. Overall, Vergennes and the French party at Geneva had things entirely upside down. They were the true danger to the republic, and more particularly to republican manners. Once trust was destroyed, people began to behave badly in every walk of life. Seriousness, dedication to duty and pride were replaced by servility, machination, frivolity and excess: 'in the place of simple and republican manners, and the rigid and careful education exemplified by the practices of so many families, one soon sees a taste for dissipation, idleness and all of the vices forming a shameful cortege, establishing their empire in our midst'.[112] Commerce, especially. relied on frugality, industry and other simple manners. In consequence, once trust collapsed, the economy would follow.

Du Roveray ended, however, by shifting his focus. He addressed directly the magistrates at Geneva, making clear his opinion that all of the magistrates were part of the French party, and underlining the depth of the cancer in the body politic. He warned the magistrates that if they proceeded along the path they had chosen, violence would be the result. The people of Geneva would not stand by while their state was lost to an external power. Virtuous men would resist 'when they have their liberty and their independence to defend'.[113] Surely, the independence of the republic was more important than the issues currently causing internal strife, and that fact would always unite Geneva. The *représentants* were the true *constitutionnaires*, and were patriots who wanted to unite all of the members of the state, using the new law code to extend the rights of the *natifs*.

In his peroration, Du Roveray praised Bern, 'our faithful ally', and asked this state not to support a mediation that would result in French dominion. His was a call to arms, a warning to France that further interference would be met with violent republican resistance. Otherwise, the Geneva that had existed since the Reformation would be lost. On the same day, a representation was issued to the magistrates, claiming that peace remained an option, but only if it was recognised that 'the independence of our country is the very basis of our happiness'.[114]

Vergennes's response to Du Roveray was brutal. He first wrote to the cantons informing them of the shocking behaviour of the *représentants* in violating established treaties. Gabard de Vaux was informed that Du Roveray had to be punished for defamation. A letter to the magistrates from

Gabard de Vaux at the beginning of January 1781 demanded that Du Roveray be removed from his position as *procureur-général*. Du Roveray was cast out on 17 January, exiled also from the Council of Two Hundred, and the *Fameuse remonstrance* was publicly burned. The 'revolution' that the *représentants* were instigating could not be allowed to be 'for them a bed of roses'.[115] Jean Roget wrote that hundreds of 'true patriots' were ready to 'die for liberty' because of the actions of France.[116] Roget accepted that the pressure on the Swiss to conform to Vergennes's will was such that the historic guarantee of the constitution could not survive. In other words, Geneva was alone. Even Frederick the Great of Prussia wrote to the cantons, on 30 January 1781, that anarchy within Geneva was leading the republic to its ruin. He demanded that action be taken to restore the 'ancient and legitimate constitution'.[117] Within the city, leading magistrates seconded such counsel, demanding foreign intervention to crush the rebels.[118]

The *représentants* then took action to consolidate their reputation among the population as the defenders of the people. This occurred after demonstrations against France and the magistrates, undoubtedly coordinated by the *représentants*, were led by *natifs* on 5 February 1781. Taking control of the city, the *représentants* ameliorated the condition of the *natifs* with an edict on 10 February. This brought back those exiled for resistance in 1770. The edict also added a hundred *natifs* to the *représentants* by giving them bourgeois status, and promised the same for eight more per year and for every third-generation *natif*. Furthermore, the February edict allowed all *natifs* to serve in the militia, and gave them full commercial privileges. Bern and Zurich condemned the edict as illegal, violating the constitutional principles established in 1738, and stated that action would have to be taken to restore order.[119] On 14 February 1781, Jacob Vernet, on behalf of the Consistory of Pastors, appealed to Bern to act as a mediator. Vernet wrote that for two centuries that canton had been the instrument of divine providence in procuring for the Genevans temporal and spiritual liberty. In asking for help in establishing peace, Vernet made it clear that a Swiss solution would be better than one involving France.[120] This may have been why in private correspondence with the magistrates and Vergennes, Bern and Zurich expressed the view that they would rather restore peace without military intervention, by returning all parties to the agreements of 1738 and 1768. Vergennes accepted, provided that, as a result, the *représentants* were crushed in the aftermath.[121] He showed no sign of backing down. Rather the opposite: he made his support for the *constititionnaires* clear in a public response to the magistrates at Geneva in April 1781. Military intervention, he declared, was a genuine option.[122] This response had been engineered by Perrinet des Franches: in a revealing letter to his fellow *constitutionnaire* Marc Cramer dated 22 April 1781, des Franches stated that he informed Versailles of everything that went on at Geneva, working all day to ensure that 'peace and good order will be re-established'. Vergennes had recognised, des Franches reported, the mistakes that had been made in the 1760s in coming to a compromise with the *représentants*. This was the source of the current problems within the city. For the past three years, des Franches said, Vergennes and Hennin had been working with him against *représentants* who wished 'to reverse the laws, make them anew, and oppress us all, with the bayonet at the end of a rifle'. One of the key moves had been to ensure that the cantons supported the French position.[123] When Necker was dismissed, on 19 May 1781, the impression of the *représentants* appeared to be confirmed that they had no friends at Paris. Throughout the year, Vergennes sought to craft a league of states that would support his action against Geneva. Within the city, Cornuaud was accusing the *représentants* of carrying on a civil war entailing endless acts of violence against their enemies among the community of *natifs* allied to the *constitutionnaires*. In so doing, he supplied the magistrates with evidence for Vergennes that bloody revolution was imminent.[124]

A further step Vergennes took was to shame the *représentants*. He did this by making clear the support of their former leader, Jean-André Deluc, for his own stance. Vergennes met Deluc at Versailles in September 1781, October 1781 and February 1782. Deluc allowed his views to be made public, articulating the view that his former friends were now members of a dangerous faction, and that their control over Geneva was such that only French intervention could save the state from turning into a wild democracy.[125] A decision was taken by Clavière and his associates to embarrass Jean-André Deluc, in turn making public his personal account of 1768. Somehow a copy of the manuscript of this document had been acquired. It revealed Deluc to have condemned France in the later 1760s, and to have argued that the cantons alone could sustain Geneva. Thus Jean-André Deluc emerged as turncoat and a hypocrite.[126] The magistrates also attacked Deluc through Cornuaud, who wrote a pamphlet stating that Deluc's proposals would result in the rule of the *représentants*.[127]

Vergennes now accused the *représentants* of having allowed a civil war to break out at Geneva. In October 1781, he informed the magistrates that he was now defending the constitution, that the guarantee of the constitution no longer existed and that he was willing to use military force against the 'tumultuous democracy'.[128] French troops entered the Pays de Gex on Geneva's border. Vergennes then gave orders to summon the leading *représentants* to the home of the latest French *résident*, Jean-Baptiste Castelnau. Through his ambassador, Vergennes warned them that they would be held personally responsible for violence or unrest. Castelnau informed Vergennes especially against the pastors Étienne-Salomon Reybaz and Jacob Vernes, in addition to Du Roveray, while Clavière was identified as the most evil rebel of all.[129] While this was happening, the magistrates, through their spokesperson Cornuaud, were calling for French intervention against the traitors and terrorists.[130] Vergennes was also seeking to persuade foreign powers to understand that what was happening at Geneva was a civil war against the established constitution; he succeeded.

VII

At some point in the summer of 1781, the magistrates at Geneva decided that they could not retain their power unless the *représentants* were extirpated. The message to France was to do precisely this with as much alacrity as possible. As tended to be the case, the person who arranged for the visit of a leading *constitutionnaire* to Versailles was Perrinet des Franches, stating that 'the Patron', Vergennes, wanted information from the coal-face, so as to make a decision about the future of Geneva. The leading *constitutionnaire* Antoine Saladin de Crans travelled to Paris on 30 August 1781 and remained for three weeks.[131] Jean-André Deluc arrived soon after and, in a further letter, des Franches noted Deluc's failure to bring the parties together; Deluc was indeed clearly working with full knowledge of the *constitutionnaires* rather than of the *représentants*.[132] Vergennes and Hennin were by now convinced that they alone could save Geneva from the forces of democracy, demagoguery and disorder. Des Franches had written to his friend Marc Cramer, on 30 September, that he was working ceaselessly on the basis that 'our unfortunate country will only find tranquillity once again through good government'. The latter had to be imposed on a resentful populace by the French. As the cantons could not be relied upon, Cramer in his reply acknowledged that 'if France abandons us, we are lost'. Des Franches, in a letter of 4 November 1781, reassured his friend that the French would never 'leave us at the mercy of Clavière and company'.[133] The first consequence of the decision to facilitate direct French interference was that the magistrates refused to acknowledge the Edict of 10 February, or to reinstate Du Roveray. The assumption may well have been that once the head was cut off the *représentant* hydra, the populace would gradually return to obedience. Alternatively, the brutal experience of French power would persuade the people in general of their impotence, and they would turn away from the *représentants* because of the futility of resistance. Anticipating this, the magistrates, calling themselves true patriots and defenders of the ancient constitution, announced that they were rejecting the settlement of 1768. Their argument was that 1768 had been a titanic mistake, and entirely incompatible with the true source of peace in the polity, the settlement of 1738.[134] Such an argument was made despite the same magistrates having negotiated in 1768, and having expressed support for the agreement until 29 October 1781, the date of their declaration that a new constitutional settlement was necessary.[135] The magistrates' central claim was that sovereignty had always been shared at Geneva, with law emanating from the combined and harmonious wills of the Council of Twenty-Five, which proposed law, the Council of Two Hundred, which discussed and refined the law, and the General Council, which gave the final seal of approval, yes or no. There was no single legislator but rather a union, only existing in combination with other, equally significant, political bodies. The fundamental point was that it was a heresy to assert that the General Council was sovereign alone and above the other bodies of state. Precisely this had been implied, or could be mistakenly understood, from the settlement of 1768. The latter had in any case been the product of insult and menace. As mischief was being done to the republic by the new democratic perspective on the constitution, a return had to be made to the union of orders which had been the basis of 1738.[136] The magistrates had a plan and were confident of French support. As Jean-Marie Roland wrote to his Genevan friend Henri-Albert Gosse in November 1781, it was said in France that Geneva's aristocrats 'are very satisfied with the disposition of spirits and affairs.'[137]

On the other side, the *représentants* continued to present themselves as moderates. Towards the end of September, they responded as a body to the recent accusations against them, professing the sovereignty of the General Council as the basis of the settlement of 1768, which had been agreed upon by all parties, including France and the cantons, and lamenting the fifth column of magistrates who were acting for France rather than for Geneva.[138] As late as 24 October the *représentants* were appealing to Louis XVI to take action against his minister, because peace and conciliation was possible once Vergennes had been removed. Vergennes and the magistrates were the alarming innovators.[139] By this point such self-presentation was entirely false. The leading *représentants* had already decided that Geneva had to become a *représentant* state.[140] The magistrates were tyrants and had to be replaced. This was vital if Geneva was to remain sovereign. For some of the *représentants* it was essential too if Geneva was to continue to be Calvinist. The core belief, however, was that small republics survived only because they formed moral communities, expressive of a particular set of values that the population adhered to in their daily lives. Excessive wealth and immigration by groups opposed to the common culture were dangers; immigration was defined as the granting of civic rights not solely to foreigners, but to those living at Geneva who had not proven themselves yet to be capable of embracing Genevan traditions. It was such concerns that led the *représentants* to be so careful about giving full rights to the *natifs*. The danger that the *représentants* perceived themselves to be facing was effectively a *coup d'état* whereby magistrates took power who had already rejected the virtues that embodied Genevan life. That they had done so was a tragedy, because traditionally the magistrates were the most important disseminators and protectors of those very virtues. Accusations of treachery, deceit and tyranny could legitimately be levelled against the magistrates because they had presided over the cultural decline of Geneva. As Clavière put it, the *constitutionnaires* were usurpers of the popular authority that lay at the core of the constitution. The *représentants* were the only true republicans at Geneva.[141]

The *représentants* expected their predictions about the future to be confirmed if the magistrates were allowed to continue to rule, providing empirical proof of the veracity of their own claims. The first step would be the gradual abandonment of the virtues that were central to Geneva's economic wellbeing: sobriety, frugality and industry. Economic collapse would then occur. Finally, as the resources of the state diminished, its capacity to defend itself would be reduced. One power or another, and undoubtedly France if Vergennes remained minister, would put an end to the republic. Such arguments were expressed in François d'Ivernois's *Offrande à la liberté et à la paix*, a *représentant* manifesto published towards the close of 1781. As always, the work was couched as a conciliatory document. The writing was ferocious, however, in damning Jean-André Deluc, Vergennes and the current magistrates, all of whom were described as living in a fantasy land, while the republic of Geneva teetered on the brink of disaster. D'Ivernois refuted accusations that the *représentants* were anarchists, arguing instead that they were proposing the kind of 'wisely tempered democracy' established in 1768. The magistrates could be replaced by the people gathered in General Council, creating a check that made republics stable, and allowed them to maintain themselves over time against the threat of tyranny.[142] This line of argument, emphasising the need to institutionalise forms of resistance against magistrates in the form of checking powers, was reiterated by Du Roveray and Clavière, who supported similar moves against the magistrates within the canton of Fribourg.[143] The Bernese smashed the rebels at Fribourg in May 1781. In representations at the end of 1781, submitted to the magistrates at Geneva, material was drawn together proving that all parties had hitherto accepted the 1768 settlement and the sovereignty of the General Council. It was asserted that a base cabal was now being orchestrated by France to put an end to Geneva as an independent republic.[144]

Such arguments were supported by the *natif* leader Jean-Pierre Bérenger, who issued a call to Genevans to stop France and the magistrates. Bérenger had been exiled in 1770 and in 1773 had his *Histoire de Genève* publicly burned by the authorities. In 1780, he was hoping that times were changing, in accordance with the prescriptions of those he considered to be the greatest republican philosophers, and especially Montesquieu. Montesquieu had taught, Bérenger stated, that virtue was the foundation of a healthy republic and the basis for the spirit of patriotism that brought the inhabitants together. Virtue was being challenged by luxury, because citizens had embraced 'mercantile greed', had become selfish and were increasingly addicted to 'the destructive luxury which makes ever more progress'. Such forms of luxury led to crises within families, a lack of incomes sufficient to cover the cost of living and ultimately to depopulation. The threat was all the greater at Geneva because the economy depended upon low prices, quality products and cheap labour, in order to make products suitable for export. What Bérenger called a 'mercantile aristocracy' addicted to luxury was subverting the state; the people who could be trusted, because they were merchants and artisans, had to take action against those who wanted to turn Geneva into France. It was a mistake to associate the defence of the people with anarchy and 'shameful democracy', or the tyranny of the countryside over the town. Rather, a new society was being created, that had the potential to bring all groups together, reversing depopulation and establishing a 'national spirit' that would lead to a flourishing commercial republic.[145] The passing of the February Edict of 1781 was the key to everything for Bérenger, defining as it did a new republic.

The *représentants* and their friends among the *natifs*, however, increasingly saw themselves as battling a world unsuited to their kind, destructive of republics and of liberty. By their deeds they were reminding Europe of the greatness of republics and of their cultural value. Rather than waiting for the decline of Geneva and its loss of sovereignty, they were willing to fight. In the Council of Two Hundred, on 1 April 1782, the pastor David Chauvet and Guillaume Ringler declared that they would battle to the last drop of blood rather than give in to any foreign plan to take away the sovereignty of the General Council.[146] Revolution was imminent.

CHAPTER SIX

Revolution and Exodus

THE *REPRÉSENTANTS* INTENDED gradually to take power at Geneva by means of a new law code. Law would place limits upon the powers of the magistrates by establishing a clear distinction between sovereignty and government. As the General Council was comprised of a majority of *représentants*, it would support new magistrates deputed to check that laws were being followed by the governing Council of Twenty-Five. It was also anticipated that over time the families currently dominating the magistracy, with their dual lives, often at Paris and at Geneva, their large holdings of land beyond the city, and their love of luxury, would ultimately give way to the *représentants* themselves. In the short term, however, the extreme inequality between most bourgeois and citizens and the magisterial families of the upper town—the Tronchins, Cramers, Calandrini, Thellussons, Navilles, Pictets, Galiffes, Gallatins, Rilliets, Lullins, Diotati, Turrettini, Fabri, de Tournes's, Fatios and de la Rives, among others—was held responsible for the refusal of the magistrates to compromise. The magistrates were accused of forming an increasingly corrupt aristocracy of the rich, who ran the state in such a way that it translated into material benefits for their dynasties over time. That the magistrates would do anything to maintain their position at the apex of society was clear in the contrast between their own historic support for the sovereignty of the General Council, articulated in Jean-Robert Tronchin's *Lettres écrites de la campagne* in the 1760s, and their very different stance in 1782. The *représentants* perceived themselves to be on the side of law and tradition, and their opponents to be the dangerous projectors.[1]

Certainly, the contrast between the lives lived by the richest and the rest was self-evident. When J.B.G. Galiffe in the 1870s collected eighteenth-century correspondence, including that of his own family, he identified what he called a patriciate at Geneva, and made the point that while politics obsessed women and men among the *représentants*, fun and frivolity divorced from civil strife marked the letters of those born into the elite.[2] Whether the magistrates were predominantly malign or simply misguided, for the *représentants* the point had been reached at which they could not be trusted to pursue the public interest. Constitutional change, in the form of the new law code, was justified especially when the magistrates wanted to involve the French in day-to-day politics, seemingly handing over Genevan sovereignty to the foreign power. At the same time, the argument was reiterated that the *représentants* were protecting independence and the established constitution. It was the magistrates who had once been the fathers of the state, living honourable lives of simplicity and frugality, but who had turned to luxury and selfishness. This was the view of the well-known pastor Jacob Vernes, who since he had been ordained in 1751 had been combating what he termed 'royal luxury'. Vernes linked together luxury, irreligion and idleness.[3] His unpublished history of Geneva, drafted with his fellow pastor Jean-Jacques Roustan, related the gradual corruption of magistracy, and the decline of the magistrates themselves as moral persons.[4] In catechisms published through the 1770s, and again in 1781, Vernes reiterated his opinion that luxury lay behind all the ills of Geneva. Luxury was the source of pride, and contrary to biblical injunction.[5] In light of this, the *représentants* presented themselves as old magistrates in new times, being dedicated to Calvinism and the welfare of the people. They declared that they were not democrats in any dangerous sense of the term.[6]

The *représentants* asserted that if Vergennes imposed a new settlement, the gains of 1768 would be lost, effectively turning Geneva into a protectorate run from Paris. The magistrates appeared happy with such an outcome, because France wanted to reverse the recently acquired *représentant* dominion in the General Council and Council of Two Hundred. The *représentants* were well aware that Vergennes talked more and more of the Edict of 1738 as the foundation stone of the legitimate constitution; he was making the point that the 1768 settlement had failed. A return to the calm that lasted from the late 1730s to the early 1760s was vital, to be established if necessary by French arms. A different threat came from the other side, the *natifs*, who were ratcheting up their demands for the promulgation of the Edict of 5 February 1781. This placed the *natifs* in direct conflict with the Council of Twenty-Five. The fear of many *représentants* was that if violence was initiated, the magistrates would use it as an excuse for direct French intervention. In such times preparations needed to be

PRÉCIS HISTORIQUE

DE

LA DERNIERE REVOLUTION DE GENEVE;

Et en particulier de la Réforme que le SOUVERAIN de cette REPUBLIQUE *a faite dans les Conseils Administrateurs.*

SEroit-ce dans ce siècle de justice & d'humanité, qu'on verroit périr une petite République, que ses Habitans ont rendue jusques ici si intéressante? Genève, agitée par des contestations inséparables de l'esprit de liberté auquel elle doit son lustre, perdra-t-elle sa qualité d'Etat libre, indépendant & souverain? Et le coup qui la feroit décheoir de cette précieuse prérogative, lui seroit-il porté par des voisins à qui elle ne sauroit jamais causer aucun ombrage? Enfin, une dispute qui se réduit à savoir, si les Genevois seront gouvernés par le ressort précieux de la confiance, causera-t-elle la perte de cette peuplade industrieuse & éclairée?

Pour rendre compte des événemens qui exposent Genève à ces dangers, nous sommes obligés de remonter jusqu'au commencement de ce siecle, & de suivre le Gouvernement dans la marche de ses usurpations successives. On y verra l'ambition lutter contre les Loix; & les Citoyens, toujours attaqués ou opprimés, réduits enfin, pour se défendre, à réformer des Conseils qui fouloient aux pieds les principes de toute Administration républicaine.

Geneve repose sur un sol ingrat: mais là, *Comme il appartient en une bonne Police & République, tous doivent être contens en degré de Citoyens & Bourgeois, sans se vouloir préférer & s'attribuer quelque autorité & Seigneurie par-dessus les autres, sinon en tant qu'Office de Justice portera (a). Nul ne doit être en Office qui ne soit agréable au Peuple (b).* C'est à ces principes que l'Etat de Genève, ce coin de terre à peine connu des Géographes, doit une population dont la sixième partie n'y trouveroit pas sa subsistance, sans l'attrait de la liberté.

Il n'existe donc point de patriciat à Genève; on y connoit encore moins les distinctions de noblesse & de roture; mais l'inégalité dans les fortunes, effet nécessaire des ressources de cette Ville, y tend, depuis le commencement de ce siècle, à dénaturer la Constitution. Les Loix qui établissent l'égalité politique, & les mœurs qui la font respecter, ont eu jusques ici besoin de toute la vigilance des Citoyens, pour résister à l'ascendant de la ligue des riches; ligue puissante, dont l'empire s'exerce naturellement sur ceux qui ont le maniement des affaires publiques, & d'autant plus dangereuse, que les Citoyens, occupés journellement du commerce & des arts dont leur subsistance dépend, lui ont laissé trop souvent le champ libre.

Une Législation imparfaite, que cette ligue n'a jamais voulu laisser compléter, a servi d'aliment aux entreprises de la puissance exécutive; une multitude d'usages non écrits, incertains, souvent contraires aux Loix, & qui règlent cependant des affaires de la plus grande importance, mettent dans les mains du Conseil des Vingt-Cinq le pouvoir arbitraire, le plus commode des pouvoirs pour ceux qui gouvernent, mais le plus terrible pour ceux qui sont gouvernés. Cet état de choses découle de ce que les Petit & Grand Conseils s'étoient insensiblement accoutumés à ne plus consulter sur rien l'Assemblée Générale (c), & à pourvoir d'eux-mêmes, par des Réglemens ou des Usages, aux objets de Législation.

LES premières réclamations des Citoyens datent du commencement du siècle: pour en arrêter l'effet, les Conseils se permirent l'abus le plus criant du pouvoir. A l'aide d'un secours qui n'avoit été envoyé à la République que pour la défendre contre des troupes étrangères, & au mépris d'une amnistie & d'un Edit de pacification, dans lequel les principaux griefs des Citoyens avoient été redressés, quatre-vingt d'entr'eux furent, les uns flétris, les autres privés de leur Patrie, de leur liberté, de la vie même. Cette époque mérite d'être observée, parce que la barbarie des Conseils, lorsqu'ils ont eu la force en main, fait le contraste le plus frappant avec la modération qui a distingué les Citoyens dans les occasions où la Providence & la justice de leur cause leur obtinrent la supériorité.

Quoique ces scènes odieuses, & le système qu'elles manifestoient, eussent forcé les Citoyens à se réunir, les Conseils n'en poursuivirent pas moins leurs projets d'usurpation; ils allèrent jusqu'à imposer le peuple sans l'aveu du Conseil Général, & jusqu'à vouloir soutenir par la force, le refus de consulter sur cet objet le SOUVERAIN de la République. On découvrit même à cette époque une conspiration, dont les auteurs, membres des Conseils, se proposoient d'intimider le peuple par le supplice des principaux Citoyens. A une pareille découverte, la Généralité auroit pu retirer à elle les pouvoirs & dissoudre des Conseils qui avoient trahi tous leurs devoirs; cependant elle se contenta de se plaindre & de demander le bannissement d'un Magistrat & la démission

(a) Edit de 1555.
(b) Edit de 1568.

(c) Le Conseil Général est composé de tous les Citoyens & Bourgeois, âgés de 25 ans.

A

FIGURE 6.1. Anon., *Précis historique de la dernière révolution de Genève; Et en particulier de la Réforme que le Souverain de cette République a faite dans les Conseils Administrateurs* (Geneva: n. p., 1782). Author's collection

made for the defence of the position being taken by the *représentants.* In October 1781, Clavière gave François d'Ivernois a note to be shown to any person holding documents concerning the history of Geneva, asking that these be entrusted to him.[7] The evident purpose was to write a history of the city from the perspective of the *représentants.* The task was to take d'Ivernois until after the revolution at Geneva. He rarely completed any project on time, and his failure to produce the goods ultimately led Clavière to look to other propagandists, including Jacques-Pierre Brissot and Honoré-Gabriel Riqueti, comte de Mirabeau.

II

Clavière, being clear-eyed about the likelihood of disasters in politics, was also particularly worried that revolution would be the product of a Franco-magisterial plot. As a *représentant,* he wanted a legal and gradual transfer of power away from the existing magistrates, rather than a shift by means of popular upheaval and public violence. Cornuaud, who remained prominent among the *natifs*, was expected to push them to extreme measures on behalf of his paymasters, who would then take advantage of political instability in the city, and any atrocities that might accompany it, to call openly for French intervention. Such concerns were reflected in a letter Clavière sent to Marc-Théodore Bourrit, the Alpine artist and *natif*, who had strong connections with the French court, in early February 1782. Clavière noted that a group of pastors had attempted to bring the warring parties within Geneva together, but that the *constitutionnaires* were refusing because they were waiting for a plan from Versailles, which they anticipated would crush the *représentants*. Vergennes remained intransigent, reiterating the argument that without intervention Geneva would never be pacified. Rumours abounded too that Pierre-Michel Hennin had written a new constitution for Geneva, which France would seek to impose by force. The only option, Clavière said, was 'to join with my fellow citizens in hope that God and the legality [of our cause] will save us'.

At the same time, those Clavière termed the 'Cornualistes' were encouraging disaffection on the grounds that the Edict of February 1781 had yet to be ratified. This might cause 'disorders that will lead to the taking up of arms'. As Clavière put it, it was always the case that 'defiance is so easy to facilitate', and he wanted to avoid it if at all possible. While the *représentants* supported the Edict of February 1781, and wanted to see it ratified, they were in a quandary because of the stalemate created by the magistrates' refusal to come to an agreement with them. Clavière was candid in demanding to know 'how [the February Edict] can be executed other than by violence, and where would that take us?' If brute force was used once against the magistrates, even if it succeeded in the enactment of edits legally ratified, a precedent would have been established that would justify more savagery, going on into the future. In other words, the great danger of revolutions was that the extreme measures they necessitated might become part of normal politics, destroying liberty in the process.[8]

Clavière felt that patience was the best response to the crisis. He perceived an additional problem to be that so few men were 'enlightened and calm'. Clavière ended his letter to Bourrit by noting that 'for the rest, the city is peaceful, and I cannot recall a time when this was so much the case'. In other words, continued peace would help their cause, more than anything else.[9] The *représentants* had nothing to gain from bloodshed or revolution. They lacked external support, especially the crucial backing of Bern. Although the *représentants* were anticipating crisis points, sending their ambassadors across Europe in the hope that some power might be willing to stand against Vergennes, these precautions had come to nothing by early 1782. The *représentants*' two domestic strategies, of presenting themselves as moderates and of extending their support among the Genevan populace, were succeeding. These were not going to be sufficient, however, because France was increasingly the dominant power in mainland Europe, united with Spain and the Dutch Republic against the British in North America, and on the verge of victory against its historic foe. The timing was wrong for successful resistance, given Vergennes's evident fascination with Geneva. Without foreign friends, resistance was likely to be futile. The *représentants* did not, therefore, take up arms. Rather, it was recognised even by their enemies that they had 'a great interest in restoring calm'.[10]

Clavière was so agitated by the prospect of revolution that he sent a further anguished letter to Bourrit in mid-February, identifying a secret French plan that was about to destabilise Geneva. Vergennes, it was reported, had informed his ministers at Vienna, Berlin and Hesse-Cassel that his 'plan for the pacification of Geneva will be put into action soon'. Clavière had noticed that the *constitutionnaires* were menacing the *représentants* daily and 'mark the victims upon whom they will unleash their vengeance'. Accordingly, he wrote to Bourrit that there was 'no time to lose', meaning that if anything could be done at Paris to protect the *représentants*, it had to be done immediately. The *constitutionnaires* had forgotten the 'republican maxim' that bloodshed in politics was always to be avoided. Fortunately, Clavière wrote, the *natifs* were aware that 'acts of violence will ensure that we plunge into a situation far more grave and uncertain'. The wise counsel was accepted to be moderation. Yet Clavière was perturbed, because '[n]ever have the citizens been in need of more unity and more prudence'. There were many young men among the disaffected at Geneva who might be tempted into fighting, while the magistrates, mainly older men who should have known better, were effectively baiting them. Clavière bluntly admitted that the *représentants* 'are in need of powerful friends . . . to counterbalance the force that acts against us, and to preserve the republic from the external challenges that it faces'. Even Jean-André Deluc, Clavière advised Bourrit, might be drawn into helping his former colleagues. Clavière informed Bourrit that he should not be angry with Deluc for having criticised the *représentants*. For Clavière, Deluc remained 'at heart a citizen', and could be expected to challenge any threat to the independence of Geneva.[11]

For the magistrates, by contrast, a sense of security pervaded, because of the extent of their contacts with Versailles. The four syndics for 1782, André-Jacques Baraban, François Sarasin, Claude-Philippe Claparède and Pierre Lullin, enjoyed close connections with their friends at Paris. Hennin, then a secretary working for Vergennes, had by this time married into the Mallet family, and had written to the magistrates stating that he had become 'almost a citizen [of Geneva]'. Antoine Saladin de Crans was also in Paris once again, and had four meetings with Vergennes in November 1781.[12] The former syndic Jacob de Chapeaurouge was at Paris too, pressing the cause of the *constitutionnaires*. Leading Genevan men of letters across Europe detested the *représentants*. One such was Paul-Henri Mallet, royal professor of belles-lettres at Copenhagen in the 1750s, who had returned to Geneva as professor of civil history in the 1760s, and who served on the Council of Two Hundred. Another was Pierre Prévost, who since 1780 had been professor of philosophy at Berlin, and was entirely opposed to the *représentants*. Mallet had been present in Paris in 1780 when Clavière and Du Roveray were seeking French support; the latter were termed 'the pilgrims' because of the travels they undertook. The fundamental point was that the *constitutionnaires* felt threatened by the *représentants*. The *constitutionnaires* were leading figures in Genevan society, and saw themselves to be part of a civilised Europe altogether defined by its prominent elite. Jacob Tronchin wrote to his friend Antoine Saladin de Crans, on 4 March 1782, that the *représentants* had long pursued a strategy that combined menace, silence, apparent moderation and intimidation. They were, he wrote, 'like a harlequin wearing the skin of the fox and the wolf'.[13]

All of the *constitutionnaires* believed that Rousseau had sown dragon's teeth at Geneva in the 1760s. As Charles Bonnet put it, Rousseau had started a fire in the manner of Herostratus, who had burned the temple of Diana at Ephesus in order to bring himself renown. The magistrates, for Bonnet, were generous and moderate in their response to the failure of the people to recognise their true interests. The result had been the mad settlement of 1768, which had given far too much to Rousseau's disciples.[14] This was a point Bonnet made time after time. Historic Geneva had been a peaceful place. The strife of Europe had largely been forgotten behind its walls. Good relations were enjoyed with Catholic powers externally.

When domestic disputes occurred, they were resolved by drawing on foreign parties from France and the cantons who could be trusted to be neutral between the rival groups at Geneva. Precisely this had happened in the 1730s, and the peace had lasted until Rousseau emerged as a social solvent. The tragic consequences were all the more shocking for the fact that, when compared with the natural jurists to whom Rousseau likened himself, his work was altogether inferior. As Bonnet put it, concerning Rousseau considered as a philosopher,

> [R]egarding the *Contrat social*[:] What stability will a government have which the people dismiss each year? What can one think of a book where the principle is asserted that Christianity can only make slaves? Compare this work with those of Grotius, Burlamaqui, Montesquieu, &c., and tell me if you prefer it to them? Be warned, obscurity can be presented as profundity and sentences which are often epigrammatic do not make principles. Montesquieu has such sentences, but what principles and true principles he does offer to us![15]

Bonnet could not understand the *représentants*, because for him it was obvious that civilisation and civilised values were on his side. Natural jurisprudence taught first and foremost that unleashing the people would lead to political turmoil. The people as a force were irrational. Politics that pandered to the people became fake, being founded upon deceit and false promises, the necessary currency of popular trust, however fleeting it might ultimately prove to be. The fact that Rousseau wanted to topple authority, and replace it with a political will derived from the people, made him insane. As Bonnet wrote, 'Why when Rousseau grants to the populace such a large dose of pity, do they reply with such greed to see the wretch expiring on the wheel?'[16] Rousseau was all the more crazed because it was evident that great strides had been taken in the study of politics and morals in the eighteenth century, not least at Geneva, with the great jurist Jean-Jacques Burlamaqui as professor of natural and civil law between 1723 and 1739, and member of the Council of Twenty-Five between 1742 and his death in 1748. Burlamaqui's posthumously published *Principes du droit politique* of 1751 underlined the inconstancy of popular rule, asserting that the people did not have a right to resist except in cases of dire tyranny and massacre, and certainly not in cases of concern about luxury and taxes.[17] Burlamaqui's stance on the would-be rebels at Geneva of the 1730s, witnessed at first hand, was clear: their challenge to the magistrates was illegitimate. Burlamaqui's great work, reissued in a corrected edition in 1763, with its emphasis upon the duties associated with the various offices of life, was perceived to be a direct refutation of the *représentants* and of the *Contrat social*, which had appeared the year before.[18]

For Jacob Vernet, it was equally Rousseau's *Contrat social* that had given the *représentants* the notion that they were sovereign, and could erect a perfect community devoid of strife on the foundation of the goodness of the people. The outcome was that the balanced constitution that had supplied peace at Geneva for centuries had been destroyed. Geneva was for Vernet, writing in 1769, reaping Rousseau's and Voltaire's harvest of dissidence and impiety, in the form of ceaseless unrest.[19] Between the late 1760s and the 1780s, the magistrates and their friends had simply developed successful measures to deal with Rousseau's children, the basis of which was force. As they could not generate force themselves, they relied entirely upon France. This was acknowledged in a letter from a *constitutionnaire* captain in the service of Savoy, which Perrinet des Franches received early in 1782: 'All our eyes are turned towards Versailles, as it is the sun from which we draw both light and life.'[20] It was with a sense of relief that des Franches could write to his friends that the French *résident* Castelnau was furious at the manner by which he was addressed by the *représentant* 'demagogues'; the view from Versailles was that the prosperity of France required the prevention of 'a turbulent faction destroying the Republic, and turning a well-ordered government into a democracy'.[21] Another supporter of the magistrates wrote to des Franches that as nothing could be expected from the Swiss in their cause, they were entirely at the mercy of the French, who had thankfully offered 'extraordinary and extra-judicial' support. This was justified, because 'the spirit of representatism [*représentatisme*] or revolt' was equivalent to being placed 'between the hands of the Devil himself'.[22]

III

The immediate cause of the revolution at Geneva was the refusal of the magistrates to ratify the edict of 5 February 1781. After repeated representations, including a major demonstration on 18 March 1782, a decision was taken once more in the Council of Twenty-Five, on 7 April, to reject the edict. Gatherings of the people commenced that same night. Leading *représentants* and *natifs* met at the house of the lawyer Jacques Grenus, including Du Roveray, Clavière, David Chauvet and Jean-Pierre Marat, the brother of Jean-Paul Marat, from among the *natifs*. Clavière reportedly preached non-violence once again, and the conclusion of the gathering was that the parties opposed to the magistrates must avoid upheaval.

By evening on 8 April, however, arms were being amassed, magistrates harassed and large groups seen outside the house of the French *résident* Jean-Baptiste Castelnau. With accusations that spies were about and attacks upon the populace imminent, the cry 'Aux armes!' was issued. Mobs took control of the gates of the city. When the syndics emerged with their batons of office, intending to put an end to the affray, they were jostled, abused and in some cases physically attacked.[23] The first victim of the affair was the eighty-two-year-old Madame Saladin-Grenus, who was called to move away from her window; being deaf, she failed to do so, and was shot, dying instantly.[24] Up to thirty-five deaths were reported, although the actual figure was much lower. The *représentants* took control of the city, calling to action the members of their *cercles*, in part to stop the rampage.

On the morning of 10 April, at 5.30 AM, Castelnau left Geneva. The General Council appointed committees to select new magistrates, and the city became calm. Twelve *constitutionnaires* were taken hostage and imprisoned, including Antoine Saladin de Crans and his son Antoine-Charles-Benjamin Saladin-Egerton, Joseph Des Arts, Ami Lullin and François-André Naville Des Arts. Individuals among the magistrates who were ill stayed under house arrest. They were all charged for their meals. On 12 April, a committee of security (*comité de sûreté*) was established under the former syndic and lawyer Julien Dentand, who had been a member of the Council of Two Hundred since 1770 and heavily involved in revising the law code.[25] The eleven members were Guillaume Ringler, Jacques Grenus, Jean-Charles Achard, Bernard Soret, Jacques Vieusseux, Jean-Marc Chappuis, Jean Flournoy, M.-F. Joannin, Jean Brusse and Étienne Clavière. Chauvet and Du Roveray were appointed secretaries to the committee. Perrinet des Franches reported that 'total anarchy reigns in our city'; the 'factious' had become the masters, and were violating 'the law of nations [*droit des nations*]'. His correspondent stated that 'the spirit of conspiracy against authority is the spirit of this century'.[26]

On 17 April Castelnau arrived at Versailles, supplying a first-hand report of the vile *coup* and his ejection. Louis XVI was said by this time to have become incensed, demanding action by France to put down the rebels. Bern too severed all relations with Geneva. The Bernese appointed two plenipotentiaries to coordinate their response, Niklaus Friedrich Steiger and David-Salomon de Watteville, baron de Belp. Vergennes returned all messages to Paris from the new government, stamped 'refused'.[27] The existing guarantee of the constitution was cited as a justification for intervention, because government was being conducted at Geneva 'by an armed faction'. Such a justification did not last. Vergennes made manifest that the terrorist regime had to be put down for violating all of the norms of international law and for assaulting the legitimate members of its own government, who had to be restored. A new settlement was going to be established, without reference to that of 1768, which had failed to keep the peace. A new guarantee was also going to be created. One *constitutionnaire* wrote that 'the republic has been dissolved'; everything now depended upon 'the balance of physical force'.[28]

Vergennes had long been advising his minister at Turin, Filippo Maria Giuseppe Ottone Ponte di Scarnafigi, that the demagogues who followed Rousseau at Geneva, and who proclaimed the sovereignty of the people, needed to be crushed; they posed a threat to surrounding states. King Victor Amadeus III had agreed, as early as the end of January 1782 to join France in putting an end to disorder. For Savoy, a new relationship with Geneva, and real influence in the city, was singularly attractive, at the same time as it was undesirable to allow France to impose a new constitution alone. A secret message was sent from Victor Amadeus III to Philippe-François Ferrero, comte de La Marmora, appointed to lead the Savoyard part of the invading force. This stated that while 'the government that we must eliminate is an unlimited and tumultuous democracy', it was vital not to alienate the people of Geneva or to create a hated aristocracy. The latter was likely, given the attitude of Vergennes. The inclusion of Savoy caused consternation, even among the *constitutionaires*, because the traditional enemy of all Genevans was moving to put an end to a popular rebellion.[29]

At the beginning of May, a member of the Council of Twenty-Five, Jean-Louis Micheli du Crest, who had served in the French military, wrote to the French court. He demanded that the 'criminal conspiracy' of malign anarchists, violating by their actions the right of the peoples (*droit des gens*) and humanity by putting into place martial law at Geneva, be crushed.[30] Hennin, acting for Vergennes, arranged support from all of the interested powers in the region. On 5 May he wrote to Friedrich von Sinner, the *avoyer* (chief magistrate) at Bern, underlining the importance of working together to defeat the rebels at Geneva, and giving instructions about how things should proceed. He finished his letter by telling Sinner to inform Johann Heinrich Ott, the *burgermeister* at Zurich, of details of the plan:

> [I]t is of the greatest importance that your canton continues to show opposition towards all that goes on at Geneva, to demand the liberation

> of the hostages and especially that no desire is shown to wish to pacify the republic without the intervention of the King. Ms. the comte de Vergennes is absolutely counting upon your patriotism, in order to prevent this affair from inciting through its effects particular opinions and passions . . . I am authorised to say to [your excellency] that the King has decided absolutely this time to put Geneva beyond insurrection and to establish there a solid government based on the rules of 1738. His Majesty is convinced that making a lesson and an example of the *représentants* at Geneva will be valuable for the Swiss, and will gain support from your own subjects, and that it is time to extinguish this germ. Nothing will deter him from this project. There is no need, of course, to say to your excellency that in no respect does the King wish to question the liberty and independence of Geneva.[31]

At a meeting at Soleure in April with the French ambassador to the cantons, it was agreed that France could take the lead in forming plans, having abandoned the guarantee, and having a monarch devoted to restoring order.[32] Prussia too was advised that military action would be forthcoming, and Savoy had already been primed. All the attempts of the roving ambassador of the *représentants*, the former syndic Augustin de Candolle, to separate the cantons from France and gain time for the new government to prove its legitimacy, were blocked; he was treated as a pariah and as a representative of an illegal regime.[33] The Consistory of Pastors, led by Jacob Vernet, appealed to the Bernese on 18 April, and to Bern and Zurich on 29 April, not to break with Geneva, and offered to have the hostages taken out of the city. Vernet disliked the *représentants*, but did not want Geneva to be dominated by the Catholic powers of France and Savoy. All such entreaties failed.[34]

By 21 April it was clear to the new authorities at Geneva that they were going to be invaded by France and probably also by other powers. A guard was formed to protect the city. By 28 April five hundred people were working to restore the city walls under the direction of Charles de Chastel, appointed captain of the garrison. Pastor Isaac Salomon Anspach inspired the labourers, which included large numbers of women and children, claiming that it would take an army of sixty thousand to capture the city.[35] One Genevan wrote that 'the true patriots among the men, women and children are resolved to defend their liberty to the last drop of their blood'.[36] To this end, women too were trained in arms, in readiness for the defence of their homeland: in times of crisis, women were deemed to be just as capable as men of acting as republican patriots willing to sacrifice themselves for the survival of the state.[37] Jean Roget, who visited Geneva from his residence at Lausanne, was delighted that the Consistory was returning to its ancient role of police of manners, and in a more rigorous fashion than in recent times. Sumptuary laws were being enforced, and the excessively rich encouraged to leave the city: 'equality is being reborn, and with equality there is less luxury, less corruption and less pride'.[38] Republicanism as understood of old, in Roget's view, had been reinvigorated. Of an evening, the *cercles* met constantly to discuss events, creating a sense of community and social cohesion among the people. All of the leading *représentants* were involved in guard duty. Clavière was reported to have said that through such labour true equality was being established; as he put it, 'Equality with my fellow citizens, that is what I desire.'[39] Declarations were made that everyone would be happy to die facing the invaders.

On 5 May, news spread that six thousand French troops under Charles-Léopold, marquis de Jaucourt, were joining two thousand Bernese under Robert Scipion de Lentulus, baron de Redekin, and four thousand soldiers from Savoy under the comte de La Marmora. Many individuals then began to leave the city, sometimes escaping under women's skirts. Mallet du Pan reported that everyone at Geneva was armed and preparing for battle.[40] It was claimed that d'Ivernois, Anspach, Sautier and Ami Melly anticipated another Saguntum, where every adult had been put to death by Hannibal after eight months of siege in 219 BC.[41] Henri-Albert Gosse wrote to Jean-Marie Roland de la Platière, at the beginning of May, that everyone felt the troubles of Geneva would be over if the Genevans were left alone. Violence was inevitable, however, because of the intimate links between the city's 'aristocratic party', Vergennes and the cantons. The only option was to spill blood in the hope of ending such outside control over the city. Roland replied that it was recognised that Gosse's party were moderate lovers of peace, liberty and humanity, defending a 'poor refugee liberty in a corner of the world'.[42]

Attempts continued to be made externally to restore peace. In early May, Jacob Vernes was one of the authors of a document intended to bring the factions together. Entitled *Lettres d'un ami de la paix; Réponses d'un Citoyen de Geneve*, it came to nothing. In Britain, Philip Stanhope, 2nd Earl Stanhope, asked Charles James Fox, minister of foreign affairs in the Rockingham ministry, to intervene in the Genevan conflict, on the grounds that it might boost opposition to France on mainland Europe. When Admiral Rodney defeated the combined French and Spanish navies under Admiral de Grasse, at the battle of the Saintes on 12 April 1782, thereby preventing an invasion of Jamaica and the collapse of Britain's sugar trade, British interest in Geneva waned, however.[43] Fox did meet Du Roveray in May 1782. He informed the Genevan that the only contribution Britain could make was to pressure Savoy not to become involved. This was an outcome that could hardly be delivered, as Du Roveray well knew.[44]

Isaac Pictet, one of the *représentants*, acted as an official diplomat linking Geneva and Britain. Pictet had in 1781 petitioned John Stuart, known as Lord Mount Stuart, the British ambassador at Turin, to pay for Swiss mercenaries to invade Alsace, bringing the American war to France. Pressure on Geneva would thereby be reduced.[45] Mount Stuart was the son of Mary Wortley Montagu and John Stuart, 3rd Earl of Bute, George III's favourite and prime minister from 1762 to 1763. As a member of the House of Commons in 1775 and 1776, Mount Stuart had introduced a bill for the creation of a Scottish militia, which was defeated. At Turin, possibly through Stanhope, Mount Stuart made contact with the *représentants* and became concerned by their plight. D'Ivernois sent an impassioned letter to Mount Stuart, dated 14 May 1782, noting that the Bernese were opposed to the *représentants*, and that, inspired by a desire to protect Geneva's existing constitution and independence, he was forced to appeal for 'the protection of the power in Europe that knows best the advantages of a wise and honest liberty, the rights of free peoples [*droits des peuples libres*], and the value of public confidence'.[46] D'Ivernois enclosed a copy of a letter sent by the *représentants* to Charles James Fox on 11 May, which similarly asked, in desperate language, for British support. He identified Fox as someone who had shown a zeal 'for the maintenance of republican governments ['pour le maintien des gouvernemens républicains']'. He also tried to make clear to Fox that the *représentants* were honest brokers, appealing for intercession, and that France was browbeating the cantons, historically allied to Geneva, into accepting the invasion of the republic[47] On the same day, 14 May 1782, it was later reported that Mount Stuart went so far as to put forward his own peace plan, stating that compromise was vital to save the republic from destruction; this too was ignored. It was recognised, as Jean Roget put it, that 'Britain, humiliated and defeated, has already experienced so many reverses of her own, that she could never even consider preventing ours'.[48] D'Ivernois continued to petition Mount Stuart, sending copies of letters from Vergennes to the cantons, in an attempt to reveal the extent of French action in the region.[49] On 11 June, d'Ivernois declared that Geneva was victim to 'the most profound and odious scheme that any people has suffered', seeing 'depraved magistrates' oppress the people for eighty years, before betraying the republic to France. An appeal was made to Mount Stuart's 'English soul', which 'loves a wise and honest liberty, detesting [both] the misrule of those in power [*dérèglements de l'autorité*] and popular license [*la licence des peuples*]'.[50] A final attempt to involve the British was made on 10 June 1782. Willoughby Bertie, 4th Earl of Abingdon and an associate of the rebels, informed the *représentants* that Britain was too weak to help, being 'rent by divisions at home, and surrounded by enemies abroad'.[51] In November 1782, when d'Ivernois came to publish his history of the *représentants* up to 1768, he condemned Britain, which ought to have 'declared that she would watch over that independence, and cover the liberty of this small state with her powerful protection'. In 1782, he claimed, Britain could have 'rescued Geneva from the interposition of France'.[52]

At Paris, Clavière's emissary Marc-Théodore Bourrit submitted a memoir to Vergennes on 23 May, stating that France would lose out economically if Geneva collapsed; there was no justification for intervention, because government had not ceased to function. He warned Vergennes that 'the prosperity of this small state is due only to the liberty of its citizens', and that the people were willing to die for liberty. Vergennes had Bourrit sent away from Paris.[53] The *représentants* were making further overtures to prevent battle, especially towards the Swiss. On 9 May, an open letter to Bern and Zurich declared that the will of the people was being carried out at Geneva. The so-called rebels were men devoted to independence and to preventing a conspiracy by the magistrates. The revolution had been carried out for liberty and in defence of the law.[54] Such appeals were near pointless, however. Bern replied the following day that only the restoration of the legitimate government would save the republic.[55] On 18 May, Sinner informed Hennin that Bern was entirely dedicated to putting an end to the 'fanatics who persist in their false principles'. The Bernese view was that the *représentants* had been inspired by Rousseau and other 'false philosophers' who spread 'fanaticism and enthusiasm'. Sinner added that 'the amnesty so carefully sought by Clavière and his consorts, proves that they are afraid, above all for their offices'. Zurich, being 'very *représentant*', had refused to be involved in military action. All of the other parties were collaborating with France, to an extent that the *représentants* at Geneva had not anticipated. On 31 May, the citizens at Geneva signed a declaration stating that, 'If Providence wills that we should perish, it will be as free men and as virtuous citizens.' The Committee of Security was given permission by the General Council on 13 June to continue in its work for a further four months. By this time Lentulus was at Coppet, La Marmora had reached Château-Blanc and Jaucourt was at Ferney.[56] On a trip to Lausanne, where he was hoping to negotiate with the Bernese, the pastor Jacob Vernes was arrested for several hours for declaring 'there will be carnage'.[57]

IV

By the time that the invasion force reached the city, Cornuaud, Paul-Henri Mallet and Jean-Louis Micheli du Crest had been busy drafting what they termed a history 'of the conspiracy against the government'. This circulated widely in manuscript from May. It affirmed that foreign intervention was the only possible response to the anarchy and terrorism that now characterised life at Geneva. In the text they asserted that sovereignty there had always been shared between orders, and that the democratic experiment being undertaken was in violation of everything legally accepted since time immemorial.[58] The *représentants* responded with public letters stating that they were dedicated to peace and prosperity, having established a sanctuary for all those who loved Geneva and wished to see the republic remain prosperous and independent.[59] Cornuaud then replied with an account of the events of the revolution based on eyewitness testimony. This detailed wild behaviour by mobs and brutal attacks upon the innocent. The magistrates were portrayed as being peace lovers, who had seen everything fall apart because of the disastrous experiment in direct democracy established in 1768.[60] Already voices within the community of *représentants* were arguing that it would be better to abandon Geneva than to fight and die. Rousseau's executor Pierre-Alexandre Du Peyrou made this point to d'Ivernois's friend and fellow lawyer, and the publisher of the Geneva edition of the works of Rousseau, Pierre Boin:

> Are the citizens so frenzied as to prefer their animosity, and their pretensions, to the salvation of the country and to the voices of nature and of blood? Are all these claims equally well founded, or equally important to merit this odious preference? The surface of the globe offers no other corner than Geneva to live and die as free men? . . . The most efficacious defence of the citizens would have been, through a unanimous resolution of great clarity, to renounce a country which their physical strength could not defend, the moment that this country ceased to be the asylum of liberty.[61]

To d'Ivernois himself, Du Peyrou wrote that Geneva was likely to become 'the theatre of new dissensions, or the dungeon of slaves'. He advised that

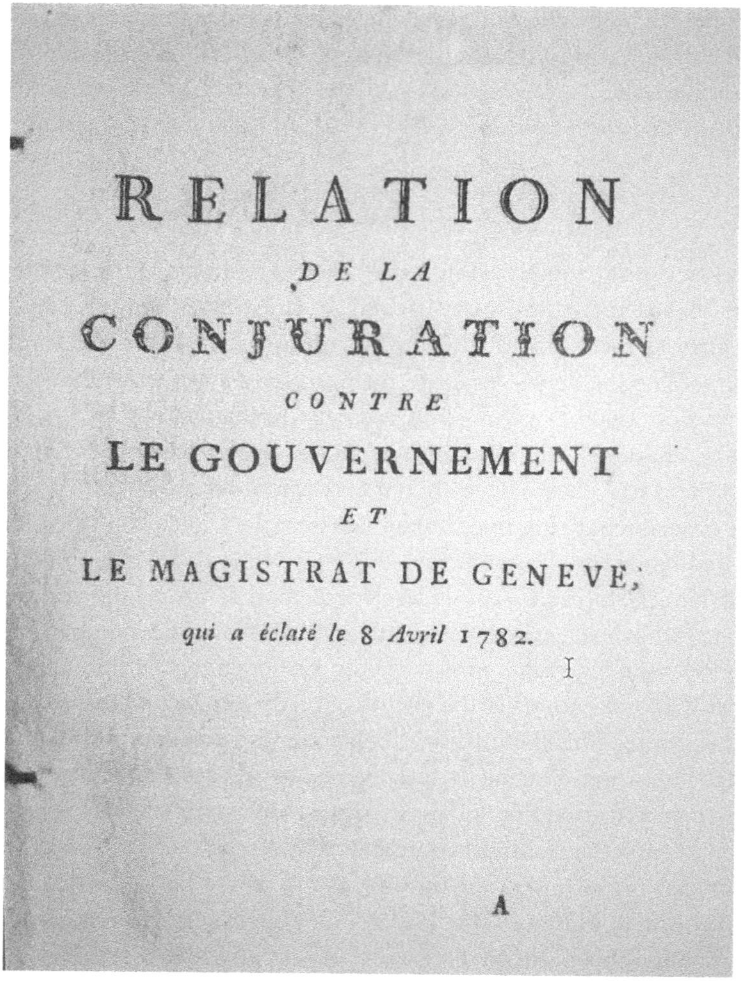

RELATION

DE LA

CONJURATION

CONTRE

LE GOUVERNEMENT

ET

LE MAGISTRAT DE GENEVE;

qui a éclaté le 8 Avril 1782.

A

FIGURE 6.2. [Isaac Cornuaud, Paul-Henri Mallet and Jean-Louis Micheli du Crest], *Rélation de la conjuration contre le gouvernement et le magistrat de Genève; qui a éclaté le 8 Avril 1782* (Geneva: n. p., 1782). Author's collection

FIGURE 6.3. 'Entreé des troupes suisses et françoises dans Genève, le 2 juillet 1782', by an unknown artist. Bibliothèque de Genève, VG 1027

'the truly free men, the men who deserve to be free, will take steps to move elsewhere'. The only hope was that the Savoyards had an interest in the prosperity of Geneva, rather than in its destruction.[62] D'Ivernois himself was keeping Mount Stuart informed in Turin, underlining the peril being faced by the Genevans, and the stoicism felt by more than five thousand citizens under arms.[63]

Foreign soldiers had surrounded Geneva by 15 June. Bread had become scarce within the city and rationing was in place by this point, a circumstance the generals were aware of through the use of spies. In addition to isolation, the city was shown what it was up against, with cannon being raised at Les Délices, Voltaire's residence between 1755 and 1760, on the hill of St Jean, just beyond the city gates. The armies had six twenty-four-pound cannon, two sixteen-pounders and twenty-two smaller howitzers, in addition to mortars. Within Geneva, injunctions were made to behave as the Protestants had against the bishop of Saint-Gallen in the war of 1712, uniting to defeat Swiss Catholics. Geneva's two bridges linking the Rhône and Bel-Air were severed, cartridges for rifles were manufactured, and the Saint-Pierre Cathedral became home to large quantities of gunpowder; it was reported that gunpowder was also placed in the houses of the hostages, including the Tronchin residence on the rue des Granges.[64]

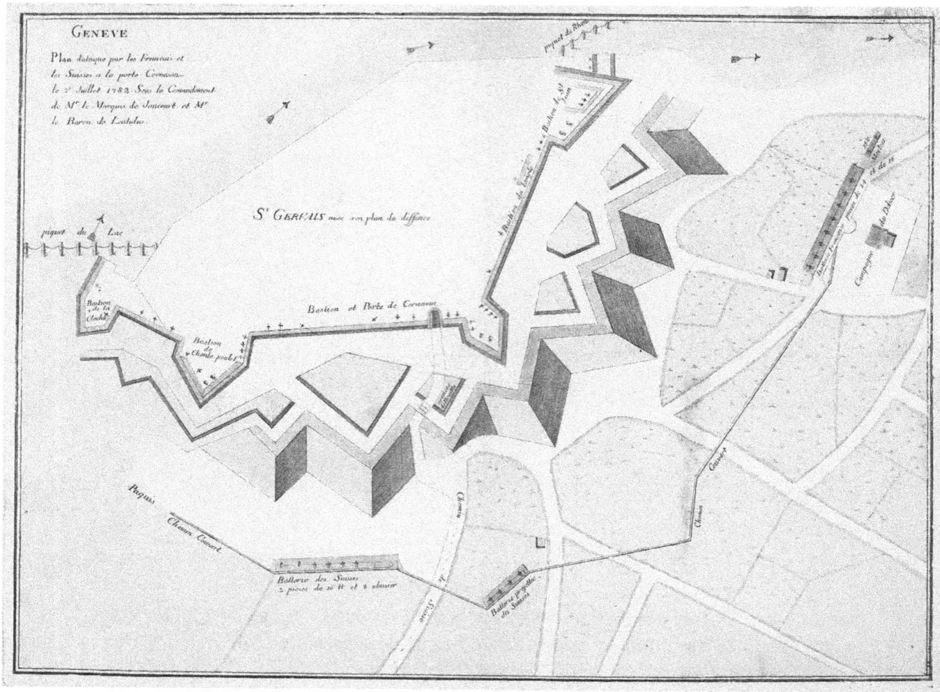

FIGURE 6.4. 'Genève, Plan d'attaque par les Francais et les Suisses . . . le 2 Juillet 1782. Sous le Commandement du Mr le Marquis de Jaucourt et Mr le Baron de Lentulus', by an unknown artist. Bibliothèque de Genève

On 28 June, the invaders issued a proclamation demanding the liberation of the prisoners and the banishment of twenty-one leading *représentants*. Those proscribed offered to give themselves up, declaring that they would be content to leave the city for ever if their action brought security and happiness. Deputies from the *cercles* rejected this proposition, asserting that foreign troops at Geneva *had* to be combated.[65] On Saturday 29 June, the marquis de Jaucourt then opened trenches around the walls, raised his cannon on to batteries and prepared to give the order for thousands of troops from three nations to attack. After visits from leading pastors, he granted a delay to the defenders of two days. The *cercles* announced that 'the Genevans of 1782 are worthy of those of 1602'.[66] In short, the people were ready for self-sacrifice.

It was at this point that the nerves of leading *représentants* broke. Clavière and Gasc, supported by Chastel, the commander of the defence of the city, announced that they had changed their minds about resistance.

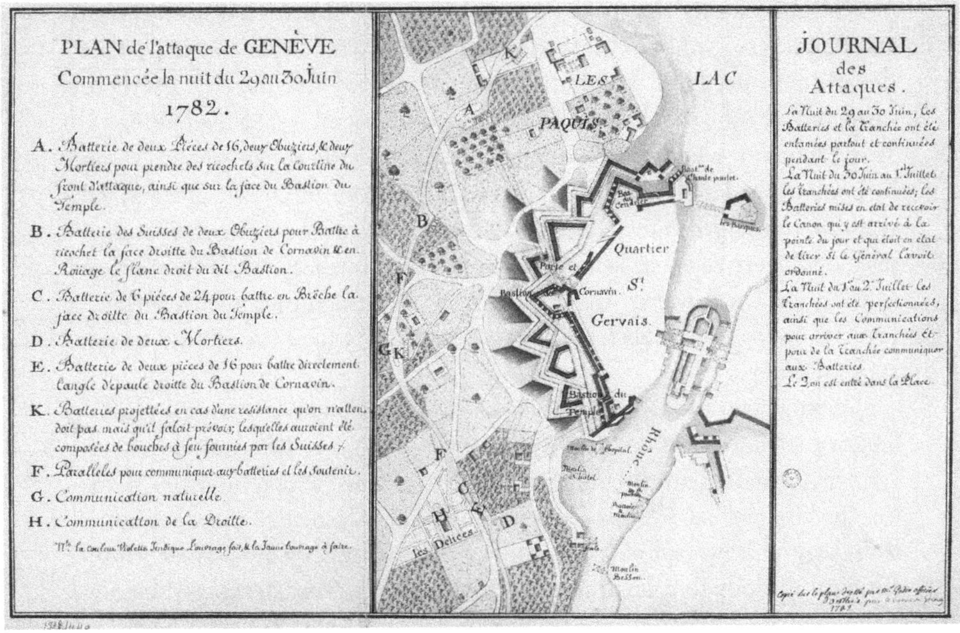

FIGURE 6.5. 'Plan de l'attaque de Genève commencée la nuit du 29 au 30 Juin 1782', a copy by the artillery officer Godin, 1782. Bibliothèque de Genève

For them, there was no point in embracing death if the result was bound to be the end of the city of Geneva. It was madness to turn the place into a ruin, no doubt a shrine for republican martyrs, but no longer a viable residence for citizens. Seeing the vast array before them, fractious discussions took place on the evening of 1 July and beyond midnight. At 1 AM on 2 July, a decision was then taken by the combined *cercles* to give up, carried by only thirty votes. British newspapers reported an even closer figure, stating that when an earlier vote was taken by the *cercles*, on the evening of 30 June, only four out of two hundred wanted to surrender. After argument, however, one hundred and eight voted 'not to surrender but to give way to force on condition of leaving the city'. The remaining ninety-two were horrified by the outcome.[67] During the discussion, Jacques Grenus reportedly threatened those who wanted to abandon the city with his sword. However divided they had become, the *représentants* then acted with rapidity on the basis of the decision, informing the imprisoned chief syndic that the town was now his, and disbanding the Committee of Security. Cannon were emptied of powder and hostages were liberated. At two o'clock on the morning of 2 July, Jaucourt received a letter from the magistrates stating that they were once more in control and that the city was open to the soldiers. Within Geneva, guns were broken and fired into the air in desperation. Two individuals committed suicide. At 5 AM on the same day, 2 July, the leading *représentants* determined to flee, except for Jean Flournoy, who decided to remain whatever the consequences. Going by boat across Lac Leman, a French bark followed the *représentants*, who were forced to swim for shore.[68] They were fired on by the city itself, so disgusted were the people at their apparent cowardice. When they arrived at Cologny, Du Roveray was attacked and wounded by a sword thrust.[69] From Cologny the rebels travelled to Neuchâtel, where they found temporary sanctuary.

Having seen the leading rebels escape, La Marmora's troops entered Geneva without fanfare. The Swiss entered from a different gate at the same time, with drums beating. Jaucourt and the French followed, securing the city and having his sappers move the gunpowder from the cathedral, several houses and some underground stores into the river Rhône. Enough gunpowder was discovered to have entirely destroyed Geneva as soon as the first mortar bomb caused a fire. Eight hundred barrels of powder were reported to have been poured into the rivers, and with the proclamation of martial law fourteen thousand rifles were collected from the populace. The city was said to be 'tranquil and sad', with regular movements of dragoons through the streets in order to ensure that no further disorder occurred.[70] The Bernese held the Rive gate, the Savoyards the Neuve gate, and the French the Cornavin gate. Troops bivouacked in the streets. On 4 July, a proclamation was issued erasing all actions of government since 7 April. On the same day, all of the 194 *natifs* who had been granted bourgeois status with the revolution saw their social ascent annulled.[71] The reassembled Council of Twenty-Five asked the Venerable Company to pray for the king of Savoy, after their prayer for the king of Britain, and before their prayers for the kings of Germany and of Scandanavia. By 5 July, some individuals were leaving Geneva. The emigrants declared that they could no longer describe as their own country a city whose best citizens were forced to flee, where foreign troops controlled daily life, and where laws no longer came from the citizens themselves. Numbers departing were reported to be as high as six hundred.[72] Numerous *représentants* remained in the city, including leading members of the Council of Two Hundred, such as Jacques-Antoine Odier, Jacob Meynadier, Jean-Jacques Choisy and Jean Johannot. There was a recognition, however, that such councils were now impotent. It was reported that a Genevan woman went to the French general Jaucourt with a problem;

when he advised her to seek out her own magistrates, she replied, 'I would never address servants when I can speak to the master.'[73]

Writing from Paris, Jacob Tronchin informed his friend Antoine Saladin de Crans, the former hostage, that Hennin was ecstatic about the course of events and Vergennes delighted. The prominent *constitutionnaire* Jacques de Chapeaurouge wrote to des Franches calling him 'the saviour of my country', for having done so much to ensure the French invasion; Vergennes was identified as 'our great and generous liberator'.[74] Chapeaurouge stated that he hoped the people would be persuaded of their mistake in supporting popular government over time, but would only do so once the perpetrators of the revolution were brutally punished and banished. External observers were convinced that Vergennes had been the author of Geneva's demise as a free state:

> You must, Sir, attribute the enslavement of your country principally to M. de Vergennes, [as] this man carries despotism in his head and in his heart, and wishes to banish freedom from all of Europe; he has destroyed the constitution of Sweden, that required correction but not annihilation; he has destroyed your republic and you have indeed committed two crimes against him; the first is to be free, the second of seeking in the neighbourhood of France a legal government, since France is the mortal enemy of such government . . . [Vergennes feared] that some spark of liberty [at Geneva] might lead the despicable mass of slaves [he governs] to revolt.[75]

Vergennes had, however, enjoyed an entire victory. In 1783, Hennin was to be rewarded for his labours by being promoted *secrétaire de la Chambre et du Cabinet du Roi*. Tronchin continued to be worried, despite the defeat of the *représentants*. He remained convinced that Rousseau was the source of all of the ills of the city, and that Rousseau's views continued to be widely accepted: 'You cannot believe what is said here about the sovereignty of the people, that the will of the greatest number is the supreme law in a republic, & c. It is absolutely from Rousseau, [who] inspired the hateful and envious elements of the rebellion.'[76] Rousseau had supplied the *représentants* with the ideas that turned them into democrats, which led them in turn to become anarchists.[77] Rousseau may have envisaged popular sovereignty in describing the foundation of a community, but to apply his idea to an existing people was 'to open the door to anarchy, and to ease the path for tyrants'.[78] Vergennes's actions were justified for having put an end to anarchy and grotesque violence.[79] One question was how to combat such opinions, and more especially to prevent them from leading to further unrest. For the Bernese *avoyer* Sinner, writing on 22 May, measures had to be taken to deter individuals from embracing Rousseau's philosophy: '[I]f the demagogues at Geneva remain unpunished,' he stated, 'Geneva will never become peaceful.'[80]

Such sentiments, in the midst of a climate where further insurrection was anticipated, led to the passing of what the *représentants* termed the 'Code noir', the edict of pacification, which was unanimously accepted by the Council of Twenty-Five on 4 November and signed by Jaucourt, La Marmora, Steiger and Watteville. When it was ratified by the General Council on 21 November, only 580 members were present, accepting the edict by 411 to 130 votes. The edict included an act of guarantee of the constitution by France, Bern and Savoy, a treatise of neutrality between these powers, and the confirmation of 'liberty, peace and happiness' at Geneva. The edict was equally pronounced to be 'fundamental and perpetual law'.[81] It announced the closing of the *cercles*, the return of an absolute veto by the Council of Twenty-Five on proposals from the General Council (the *droit négatif*) the disbanding of the militia and an end to any discussion in the General Council. In short, the settlement of 1768 was entirely reversed. Henceforth, foreigners were to command the garrison, rebellion was punishable by death and martial law was to be invoked whenever the public peace was disturbed. Over one thousand foreign troops remained in the city.[82] A general amnesty was then granted, with the exception of the twenty-one leaders of the *représentants* and *natifs* deemed responsible for the rebellion. Jaucourt stated that these men could not be pardoned, because lenity 'would prove detrimental to the republic, and would exceed the limits of what every free state owes to itself, and the rights of all sovereigns'. It was therefore 'indispensably necessary' that pastors such as Jacob Vernes and Isaac Salomon Anspach, merchants such as Étienne Clavière and lawyers including Jacques-Antoine Du Roveray and François d'Ivernois be banished for life.[83] Hennin received a letter from a magistrate avowing that his gratitude for the routing of the *représentants* was limitless; the letter also sent congratulations that 'your political masterpiece has reached the level of perfection'.[84]

Evidence of altered times appeared immediately in the acceptance by the Council of Twenty-Five of the erection of a theatre at Geneva, for the pleasure of the visiting generals and their troops. This was demanded by the invaders on 2 July, with Jaucourt, remarkably, ensuring that performances were allowed even on the Sabbath. Requests from the pastors that the theatre be made of wood, for easy demolition at a time in future, were rejected. The theatre was stone-built. It continued to be controversial, with particular upheaval following comedic portrayals of biblical stories, such as that of Samson on 19 March 1784. It was this performance that infuriated the young pastor Étienne Dumont, ordained on 2 December 1783. Dumont preached, at Temple-Neuf on 28 March 1784, a sermon on the psalm, 'J'ai fait le compte de mes voies et je ne diffère point d'observer tes commandements', attacking theatrical frivolity and the enslaving corruption that followed lives devoted to pleasure. Dumont, like all pastors who became involved in politics during these years, had to hand over the text of his sermon to the magistrates, excise certain offending passages, and acquiesce in censorship by the Consistory.[85]

A request from Savoy for a permanent ambassador in the city was accepted on 30 October 1782. Following this decision, it was decided that the Escalade would not be celebrated at Geneva on 11–12 December 1782, or during the years following, for fear of insulting Savoy. The cannon that were captured during the Escalade in 1602, hitherto considered sacred, were given to La Marmora and to Jaucourt. The Genevan state gave presents and medals to the leaders of the invasion, and commissioned portraits to hang in the public councils, on the grounds that they had 'delivered the republic' and 'secured peace, happiness and liberty into the future'.[86] Prayers were said for the glorious pacification that was held to have saved the republic. Three hundred copies of the ancient edicts describing the constitution of the state were disseminated, claiming to present incontrovertible proof that the *constitutionnaires* had had the ancient constitution on their side.[87]

A campaign was initiated to ridicule further the *représentants*. In one placard, entitled *Le Colporteur Genevois*, a bookseller was portrayed selling incendiary texts by Clavière, Grenus, Du Roveray, d'Ivernois, Chauvet and Vieusseux, four hundred volumes of representations and an empty volume called 'the Code', teaching people 'how best to govern men and women, with an appendix for children and animals'. The *colporteur* also sold tracts, including an 'Easy method for encouraging the people to riot by a society of men of letters', 'The art of avoiding the effects of bombs, bullets and other incendiaries, published by order of the Noble Commission of Security' and, above all, a pamphlet concerned with 'Courage, how it comes and how it goes, an allegory'.[88] While such writing was circulating, it was rumoured that two thousand passports had been issued to *représentants* who wanted to leave Geneva.[89]

Du Peyrou warned d'Ivernois that spies and oppression abounded at Geneva, and that the post was monitored and intercepted. He was able to

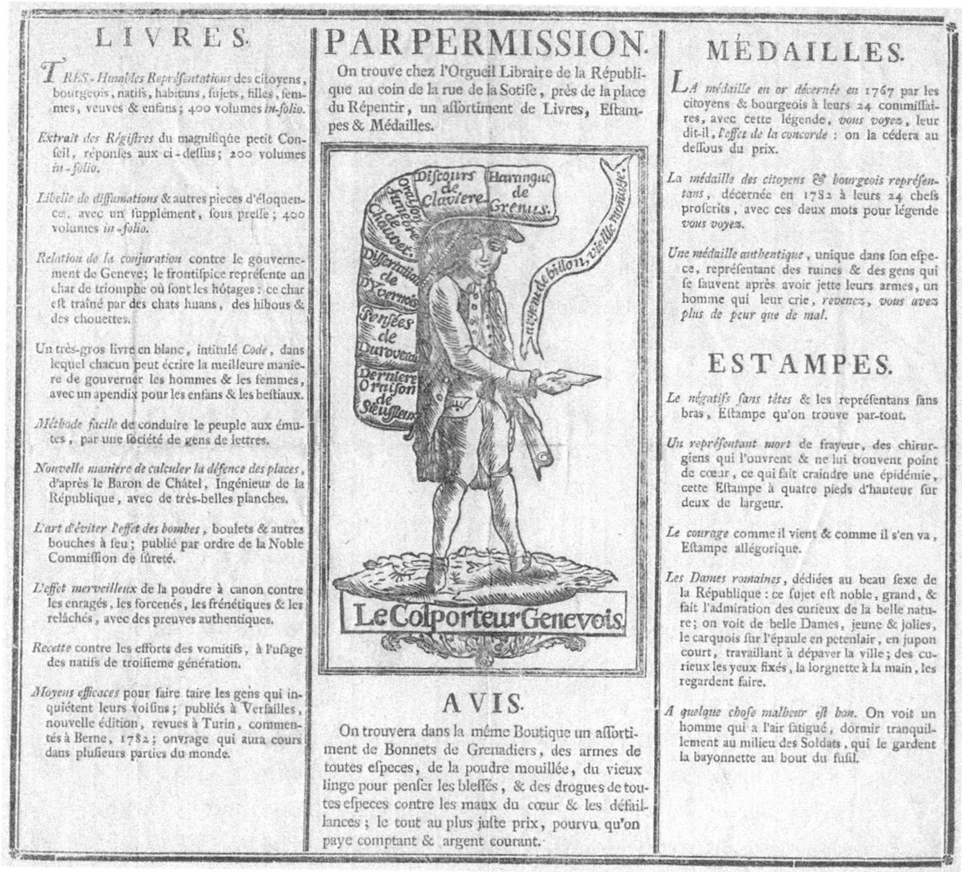

LIVRES.

TRES-Humbles Repréſentations des citoyens, bourgeois, natifs, habitans, ſujets, filles, femmes, veuves & enfans; 400 volumes *in-folio.*

Extrait des Régiſtres du magnifiqûe petit Conſeil, réponſes aux ci-deſſus; 200 volumes *in-folio.*

Libelle de diffamations & autres pieces d'éloquence, avec un ſupplément, ſous preſſe; 400 volumes *in-folio.*

Relation de la conjuration contre le gouvernement de Geneve; le frontiſpice repréſente un char de triomphe où ſont les hôtages: ce char eſt traîné par des chats huans, des hibous & des chouettes.

Un très-gros livre en blanc, intitulé *Code*, dans lequel chacun peut écrire la meilleure maniere de gouverner les hommes & les femmes, avec un apendix pour les enfans & les beſtiaux.

Méthode facile de conduire le peuple aux émutes, par une ſociété de gens de lettres.

Nouvelle maniere de calculer la défence des places, d'après le Baron de Châtel, Ingénieur de la République, avec de très-belles planches.

L'art d'éviter l'effet des bombes, boulets & autres bouches à feu; publié par ordre de la Noble Commiſſion de ſûreté.

L'effet merveilleux de la poudre à canon contre les enragés, les forcenés, les frénétiques & les relâchés, avec des preuves authentiques.

Recette contre les efforts des vomitifs, à l'uſage des natifs de troiſieme génération.

Moyens efficaces pour faire taire les gens qui inquiétent leurs voiſins; publiés à Verſailles, nouvelle édition, revues à Turin, commentés à Berne, 1782; ouvrage qui aura cours dans pluſieurs parties du monde.

PAR PERMISSION.

On trouve chez l'Orgueil Libraire de la République au coin de la rue de la Sotiſe, près de la place du Répentir, un aſſortiment de Livres, Eſtampes & Médailles.

AVIS.

On trouvera dans la même Boutique un aſſortiment de Bonnets de Grenadiers, des armes de toutes eſpeces, de la poudre mouillée, du vieux linge pour penſer les bleſſés, & des drogues de toutes eſpeces contre les maux du cœur & les défaillances; le tout au plus juſte prix, pourvu qu'on paye comptant & argent courant.

MÉDAILLES.

LA médaille en or décernée en 1767 par les citoyens & bourgeois à leurs 24 commiſſaires, avec cette légende, *vous voyez*, leur dit-il, *l'effet de la concorde*: on la cédera au deſſous du prix.

La médaille des citoyens & bourgeois repréſentans, décernée en 1782 à leurs 24 chefs proſcrits, avec ces deux mots pour légende *vous voyez.*

Une médaille authentique, unique dans ſon eſpece, repréſentant des ruines & des gens qui ſe ſauvent après avoir jette leurs armes, un homme qui leur crie, *revenez, vous avez plus de peur que de mal.*

ESTAMPES.

Le négatifs ſans têtes & les repréſentans ſans bras, Eſtampe qu'on trouve par-tout.

Un repréſentant mort de frayeur, des chirurgiens qui l'ouvrent & ne lui trouvent point de cœur, ce qui fait craindre une épidémie, cette Eſtampe à quatre pieds d'hauteur ſur deux de largeur.

Le courage comme il vient & comme il s'en va, Eſtampe allégorique.

Les Dames romaines, dédiées au beau ſexe de la République: ce ſujet eſt noble, grand, & fait l'admiration des curieux de la belle nature; on voit de belle Dames, jeune & jolies, le carquois ſur l'épaule en petenlair, en jupon court, travaillant à dépaver la ville; des curieux les yeux fixés, la lorgnette à la main, les regardent faire.

A quelque choſe malheur eſt bon. On voit un homme qui a l'air fatigué, dormir tranquillement au milieu des Soldats, qui le gardent la bayonnette au bout du fuſil.

FIGURE 6.6. Anon., 'Le Colporteur Genevois', 1782, by an unknown artist. Bibliothèque de Genève

be frank in his own letter, as it was sent via an associate of Charles Stanhope.[90] When Marie-Jeanne Phlippon, Madame Roland, visited Geneva in 1787, she described a city under military control, where virtue had been lost and where the people were the servants of a tyrannical aristocracy wallowing in luxury. Decadence had replaced liberty:

> Voltaire said that the city of Calvin had become that of Socrates, so wise were the inhabitants. This has changed. An active and industrious people are now simply labourers and merchants . . . their chiefs have become aristocrats, today masters and tomorrow tyrants, they increase corruption and employ it to oppress their fellow citizens.[91]

For Madame Roland, the fact was that commerce was incompatible with republican virtue, and the *représentants*, in seeking a commercial republic, had acted out their own demise in believing otherwise:

> The commerce that vivifies and enriches Geneva militates constantly against republican authority, and must contribute to its destruction. It [commerce] can be seen as the first cause of the last revolution [at Geneva]. A democratic state, that is also commercial, is a moral contradiction, and such a state cannot be maintained for long. The essence of democracy is incompatible with commerce. They necessarily destroy one another.[92]

In the English translation of his history of Geneva, d'Ivernois declared that in 1782 'Geneva has ceased to be a republic'. The result was going to be that the 'aristocratic faction' would 'plunge their fellow citizens still deeper into luxury and corruption'. Geneva had been destroyed by foreign invaders, rendered desolate, and was no longer a place for those who loved liberty:

> Ye jealous Americans, and ye patriots of Ireland, survey the ruins of the constitution of Geneva, and interrogate her dispersed citizens; they all will inform you that the interference of foreigners in the internal divisions of an independent state is death to public liberty, and that the assistance of a despotic power must be ever attended with perfidy and danger. Believe the words of a citizen, banished from a country that he idolized, by three foreign sovereigns, who, whilst they destroy her vitals, call themselves her benefactors. Believe the words of a citizen, who daily sheds the tears of bitterness over the iniquity of those who subverted the constitution of his country, and reproaches them, not so much for having deprived him of the right to inhabit there, as for having rendered it unworthy to be inhabited.[93]

D'Ivernois concluded that, for those who still lived in Geneva, there was no future: '[T]here are disorders for which no remedy is left but opium.'[94]

V

The immediate response to the Genevan revolution was despair. As noted above, when the fleeing leaders of the *représentants* landed at nearby Cologny they were attacked. Jean Roget wrote to Samuel Romilly that he considered Clavière to be a coward. The *représentants* ought to have fought and died.[95] A similar sentiment was expressed by Henri-Albert Gosse, who wrote to his father that he had left the city, that all Genevans were now slaves and that he felt he ought to be dead. Feeling depressed, he reported that Clavière and Du Roveray were being accused of treachery. His father Jean Gosse replied that he was happy that the outcome had been peaceful, despite the failure of their cause.[96] In a further letter, this time to Madame Roland, Henri-Albert Gosse stated that, with six thousand defenders, the rebels should have fought the invading troops, but were let down by 'cowardly leaders'. The result was that Geneva had become 'entirely subject to France' and every Genevan 'has become a slave'. For Gosse, it was the end of an era, because hopes of establishing a world based upon equality and virtue were now gone:

> [T]he attempt at creating an equality of conditions has gone for ever; libertinism and the complete corruption of manners have replaced it, and Geneva contains only men of pride and cowardice. A stone theatre is being built at the Bourgeois bastion, in order to quickly extinguish any virtue that is left.[97]

Clavière, assaulted on all sides, wrote to Jacques-Pierre Brissot that abandoning Geneva had been right, because although his own death would not have mattered, that of the women and children was too much to contemplate.[98]

At the same time, the association of the *représentants* with industry led to significant offers being made to them. Charles Theodore, elector of Bavaria, was reported to have offered the Genevan exiles money, land and housing, their own criminal code and other liberties if they settled in Mannheim in the Palatinate. Bavaria was linked to the Palatinate through the inheritance of the Sulzbach branch of the Wittelsbach dynasty after the Bavarian line failed in 1777. With Catholic Bavaria being linked to the predominantly Calvinist Palatinate, there was a need for religious toleration and economic development. Elector Charles Theodore was determined 'to have the glory of opening a refuge to an enlightened, industrious and oppressed people'.[99] The Genevans had other options. Invitations had been received from the Landgrave of Hess-Homburg, from the Countess of Neustadt at Dresden, from the Grand Duke of Tuscany (Leopold) and from his brother the Holy Roman Emperor Joseph II, who wanted the exiles to settle in the imperial city of Konstanz or at Brussels.[100] They were also invited by Frederick II of Prussia to remain at Neuchâtel, in the area called Wavre, which it was predicted would become 'one of the most flourishing commercial entrepôts on earth, and lead [the exiles] to forget Old Geneva'.[101]

Another choice had to be made. A week after his flight from Geneva, on 7 July 1782, d'Ivernois had written to Mount Stuart stating his desire 'to transplant into England the Republic [of Geneva], or at least the most advantageous part of the Republic'. By this he meant the watchmaking part of Geneva, which he estimated at 'half of the city'.[102] D'Ivernois must have received encouragement, or had a plan in place, because he travelled to London as soon as he could, staying with his old friend Charles Stanhope, at Chevening in Kent, by 28 July. He requested that Mount Stuart address correspondence to him via Stanhope at Harley Street. Stanhope and Mount Stuart promoted the Genevan cause before the new ministry of Lord Shelburne; having been secretary of state for home, colonial and Irish affairs under Rockingham, after the latter's death Shelburne served as first lord of the treasury from July 1782 to April 1783. D'Ivernois presumably remained with Stanhope in August, as Stanhope appealed to Shelburne at this time, reporting that d'Ivernois would be returning to Neuchâtel at the end of that month. Stanhope wrote that d'Ivernois was likely to be threatened with violence, either from the French or the Bernese, in territories he might have to pass through, or from authorities in Neuchâtel itself, in the latter case because the government in the Prussian territory would not want their own watchmakers to follow the Genevans in emigrating. Stanhope suggested that the British government or even George III as elector of Hanover give d'Ivernois a diplomatic office or other status as a British envoy, in order to ensure his own safety, but also to give the Genevans the sure knowledge that the British were now on their side.[103] Whether this was granted is not known, but d'Ivernois was not interfered with when travelling on the continent, and on his return to Britain submitted a memorandum to the government, on 27 September 1782. The fact that the newspapers were informing readers of the favourable response of the ministry only days later underscores the high level of support that d'Ivernois's initiative received. Charles Stanhope's father, Philip Stanhope, immediately offered the Genevans substantial lands in Derbyshire.[104]

That Charles Stanhope was in close contact with *représentants* like d'Ivernois was unsurprising. Stanhope had become a *représentant* as early as 1771, when he was given bourgeois status, elected to the Council of Two Hundred, and made commander of the *Tir de l'Arc* or company of archers.[105] Stanhope's entrance into this office, in July 1771, was accompanied by extensive public celebrations, affirming the liberty of the citizens, their fidelity to republican manners, and the military readiness of the state. The accompanying report of the event went into remarkable detail, praising the moderation and simplicity of Genevans living in 'this century of vanity', and delighting in the fact that citizens could be found 'even within the courts of monarchs'.[106] In *représentant* fashion, Stanhope was concerned about the decline of morals within the city, arguing that 'the simplicity of ancient manners is absolutely necessary for the preservation of the republican spirit'.[107] He opposed Genevans visiting the theatre, and established a Society of Arts to improve political debate and to foster commercial innovation.[108] Seeing Geneva as a popular government in which the citizens and bourgeois were sovereign, he always defended the General Council. Before 1782, Stanhope had contributed to the development of the political thought of the *représentants*; he always referred to Geneva as 'his second country', a point made in his *Discours prononcé au Pré-l'Evêque le 9 août 1773*, when he resigned as commander of the archers:

> I was brought up at Geneva and I love this city as my second country. I will love it forever, so long as virtue and liberty rule within its walls, and please God let this be for always.[109]

During the 1770s, he proposed an alternative voting system for elections at Geneva, intended to prevent aristocratic dominion at the same time as it facilitated efficient political decision-making.[110]

Stanhope was particularly close to Du Roveray; it was to him that he offered copies of Blackstone's *Commentaries on the Laws of England* (1765–69) in order to facilitate the construction of a new law code at Geneva.[111] Stanhope condemned the magistrates' refusal to agree to a new code, and attacked the growth of aristocracy caused by inequality of wealth. The latter, he felt, would ruin Geneva. Religion and manners were tied together, and if religion became corrupted by luxury or aristocratic manners, the result would be the speedy loss of liberty. One route to disaster was to tax the poor rather than the superfluous wealth of the rich, which had happened at Rome with terrible consequences:

> The great inequality of fortunes was one of the first causes of the loss of the liberty, and of the decadence of the Roman Republic. We feel greatly the dreadful consequences of the treasures that come to us from the Indes. Hope that one can inure the self against such sources of ruin at Geneva.[112]

Stanhope recommended a return to the fundamental principles of the state, a refounding that was possible in small states but more difficult, though equally necessary, in large empires like Britain.[113] After his return to England in 1774, he was in many respects seeking in Britain exactly the constitutional refounding that he had been promoting at Geneva. Although he failed to be elected to the Westminster constituency on a

Wilkesite platform in 1774, he made links with reformers around the Earl of Chatham and Shelburne, becoming a particular friend of Christopher Wyvill. His connections with the Pitt family were strengthened when he married Hester Pitt in the same year.

Among Stanhope's first speeches in the Commons, after he was elected member for Chipping Wycombe in 1780, was a condemnation of the government, 'whose baleful measures had loaded their country with disgrace and distress'. This was followed by numerous speeches advocating peace with North America, and proposals for greater parliamentary control over the army and the civil list.[114] In the following year, he defended Wilkes's status as a member of parliament and introduced a bill for the reduction of bribery and expenses during elections.[115] Stanhope supported a militia in Scotland, like his friend Mount Stuart, and the right of the people to petition the crown, in the manner of the *représentants* at Geneva; he became a member of the Society for Constitutional Information, and an advocate of parliamentary reform and religious toleration.[116] One of Stanhope's critics noted, '[W]hat a pity it is that the wards of Bedlam are unrepresented.'[117] On Stanhope's death in 1816, the author Nathaniel Wraxall remembered him as a man who, had he lived a century before, would have been in the vanguard of the regicides, being a latter-day republican and leveller:

> This eccentric nobleman, who, as Earl Stanhope, has acted a conspicuous as well as a very useful part in the discussions of the House of Peers during a long period of time, and whose recent death may, in my opinion, be considered as a public misfortune, was brought up by his father principally at Geneva. He had there imbibed very strong republican, or rather levelling principles, ill adapted to a man whose high birth and prospects should naturally have inspired him with sentiments more favourable to monarchy. If he had flourished a century and a half earlier, under Charles I instead of under George III, he would unquestionably have rivalled Ludlow or Algernon Sidney in their attachment to a commonwealth.[118]

Stanhope was probably the person who stymied his father's offer to the Genevans of family lands in Derbyshire. In 1781, he had tried, from the House of Lords, to have the quality of British gold used in manufacturing watches reduced from twenty-two to eighteen carats, in the hope of allowing the British to compete with states like Geneva, where a higher proportion of alloy was added to the base metal. In this he failed, but his attempt underlined the worries English goldsmiths and watchmakers would have with regard to New Geneva: Ireland was chosen in part to avoid direct competition with English trades.[119] Such concerns explain why, in August 1782, Stanhope was writing to the *représentant* Gédéon Flournoy that Ireland was 'at present the most free country in Europe, without any doubt whatsoever, and [the place] where one senses most strongly the immense importance of liberty'.[120]

VI

It was through Mount Stuart and Stanhope that d'Ivernois found Shelburne.[121] On 28 July, d'Ivernois wrote a letter to Shelburne stating that 'Geneva is no more our country [*patrie*]' because the only law prevailing was that of necessity, a vile tyranny had been created and the decision had been taken 'to seek under another sky the pure air of liberty and live there in peace'. D'Ivernois was to use this phrase again in subsequent documents, but to Shelburne he said that the 'advantageous situation of England for commerce and its free constitution [*sa constitution libre*]' greatly attracted the Genevans.[122] A more detailed letter was sent on 2 August from London, where d'Ivernois was staying at Isaac Du Roveray's merchant house on Bishopsgate Street in Great St Helens. The letter confidently asserted that great riches would accrue from any establishment of Genevan watchmakers in England; for the first time mention was made of Ireland by d'Ivernois, as a place where watchmakers might also settle, but as a watchmaking centre subsidiary to the primary English location. D'Ivernois also made mention of the £50,000 that he believed would be required to ease the transfer of the emigrants.[123] By the end of August, Shelburne was convinced of the plan and throwing the weight of the government behind it. Indeed, he initially agreed to give d'Ivernois everything that the Genevan rebels desired. The response of the British government was then remarkably swift. A decision was taken immediately to find permanent shelter for the Genevans in Ireland, rather than in England. This is clear from a letter from Stanhope thanking Shelburne for his support for the grand project:

> I can scarce sufficiently express how strongly I feel the whole of your Lordship's conduct, relative to the people of Geneva, and the proposed establishment in Ireland; it will, to your immortal honour, be made known, in due time, to the public. A more noble commercial project was never attempted to be carried into execution.[124]

Shelburne himself introduced d'Ivernois to the new lord lieutenant of Ireland, George Nugent-Temple-Grenville, Earl Temple (created Marquess of Buckingham in 1784). D'Ivernois dined with Shelburne and Temple in London in September.

It was to Temple that d'Ivernois addressed his remarkable memorandum of 27 September 1782. Temple had requested the document, undoubtedly to use it to drum up support within Ireland. D'Ivernois's text commenced by stating that he had explained first to Shelburne the predicament of the exiles, and gave a brief overview of what had happened to d'Ivernois himself and to his friends. He declared that the Genevans had faced foreign invasion and recognised that resistance, in the form of self-sacrifice, would be pointless, particularly because it would have done nothing for Geneva itself other than lead to the deaths of innocents and to destruction. Honour dictated that Geneva had to be abandoned. D'Ivernois included in his memorandum to Temple a document that he claimed had been sent to the three invading generals, and which explained what had happened on the fateful night of 1–2 July 1782. Having reflected upon 'the impracticality [*inutilité*] of resistance' and the nature of the 'the awful catastrophe that [invasion] brings to our city', and 'wishing to avoid the effusion of the blood of so many virtuous men who would die among the ruins of their country', the *représentants* decided not to die. Rather, they had accepted the constraints upon them. The first fact was that they could no longer consider Geneva their homeland. The city was now a place 'where the best citizens are forced to flee', under foreign dominion, and where 'the laws are no longer derived from the free wills of the majority of the citizens'. The magistrates at Geneva were men of such ill repute, and the future for the city was so bleak, that the *représentants* had no option other than to decide that they must 'go to seek under another sky a land where we can breathe in peace the pure air of liberty'. The document transmitted to the generals begged that the three military powers should allow the *représentants* to leave, proclaiming that to prevent them from departing would be to 'violate the sacred rights of humanity'. The text was dated 2 July, and two hours after midnight.[125]

The memorandum then underlined the certainty and sanctity of the *représentants*' decision to 'abandon for ever a country that they could no longer defend, and to leave to depraved aristocrats the governance of a deserted city'. The task then became one of finding a place where they could live in peace, and restore the prosperity and wealth that they were losing along with their homeland. Britain was stated as being attractive because of 'the advantageous situation of England and Ireland for commerce, their free constitution' and the clear benefits of being 'incorporated into the British Nation [*la Nation Britannique*]'. D'Ivernois reported that this was why he had contacted Mount Stuart and Shelburne. He said that emigration to Britain was his idea rather than being the product of collective deliberation, the latter being impossible because the *représentants* were either dispersed or living at Geneva 'under the yoke'. Having praised Britain and provided a background history of his initiative, d'Ivernois began to make demands, based on 'the benefits that watchmaking had brought to Geneva' and which could easily be transferred to Britain. He asserted that 'the more extensive the support offered to the emigrants, the more [Britain] will be the beneficiary'. If the incentives offered to the Genevans were meagre, the immigration would be partial and costly. By contrast, 'if support was sufficient to establish a considerable colony [of watchmakers], once formed it would increase in size every day; the well-being of the first emigrants determines the number of the patriots who will follow'.[126]

D'Ivernois argued that the ministers he had spoken to had been convinced that large benefits were sure to accrue from 'such an industrious class of men'. Shelburne had asked him to identify a minimum sum that would be necessary to realise the project. D'Ivernois reported to Temple that he had taken advice from members of the exile community in London, and that the sum of fifty thousand English pounds had been accepted as being the minimum amount, the plan being to distribute the sum to the first thousand emigrants, to cover the costs of transport and of buildings for permanent residence. A note was appended that this sum had been proposed for a community in England, because Philip Stanhope had offered the Genevans £50,000-worth of lands in Derbyshire; costs, d'Ivernois admitted, were likely to be higher in terms of transport to Ireland. The question was anticipated that the Genevans should pay for themselves because they were already rich, having 'between them such considerable property, and . . . in their commerce and their industry such extensive resources'. To this, d'Ivernois answered that the Genevans who were rich had given up houses and property, had been forced to monetise assets at short notice and at a loss, that the price of maintaining their independence had been high and that they would have to establish from scratch workshops in a place that was new to them, in addition to having to furnish houses and everything necessary to start lives afresh. On the other hand, d'Ivernois advised Temple that watchmaking was the mainstay of Geneva's wealth, allowing individuals to live in ease and independently, through their individual enterprises. So great had Geneva's wealth become that a global commerce had been established, with branches in every part of Europe and further afield. This in turn was the basis of

Genevan banking and money-lending, so extensive that 'they furnish sums so prodigious to France that the interest on the debt amounts to more than 500,000 English pounds each year'. Other countries similarly benefited from economic investment derived from such profits. D'Ivernois reminded Temple that the Genevans had received a number of offers from across Europe, and that this was unsurprising: educated men, and 'enlightened spirits' recognised that 'the wealth of a country derives from the numbers of men, and more especially from the active industry that employs them'.[127] This project was therefore a rare, indeed unique, opportunity to develop the barren soil of Ireland. D'Ivernois stated that because Temple had been so encouraging, he would return to Switzerland to discuss the matter with the eminent leaders of the community of *représentants*, who would likely want to return to discuss where the community would be established, and the practicalities of turning it into a reality. The memorandum ended with a comment on what d'Ivernois termed the 'privileges' that were to be accorded to the Genevans when they settled in Ireland. These were said to include

> the power to elect our own municipal magistrates, to be responsible for the internal police of the new colony, and to maintain our rules of industry and commerce, in addition to our sumptuary laws.[128]

D'Ivernois wrote that it would be evident to Temple how important such privileges were to men who wanted to maintain their morals and their manners, and how far the guarantee of such laws being within the control of the Genevans would persuade emigrants to make the arduous journey, for the ultimate benefit of Ireland and of Britain. He had his memorandum printed alongside the responses of the Irish, entitled *Pièces relatives à l'asyle ouvert en Irlande aux Genevois opprimés*. This collection of documents may have been used by d'Ivernois on his return to Switzerland, to persuade his compatriots to follow his scheme rather than to emigrate elsewhere. An introduction gave thanks to the benefactors of the Genevans, from George III and his ministers to the Irish Privy Council. Their actions, in supporting the emigration, 'enable Europe as a whole to know the greatness of British character'. It was the case that 'a virtuous people' had been called to repair 'the evils that despotism has done to us'. D'Ivernois declared the *représentants* to be 'an honest people, victims of their attachment to the laws of their country'.[129] Vergennes, meanwhile, was seeking to have the *représentants* hounded out of their asylum at Neuchâtel, and observed every move towards emigration further afield.[130]

VII

Earl Temple, like Shelburne and the Stanhopes, was positively disposed towards the Genevans. Within days of the receipt of d'Ivernois's memorandum, he was writing to an unknown person, expressing the view that he was dedicated to bringing the Genevans to Ireland:

> From the first moment of my arrival in this kingdom I have endeavoured to inform myself with every possible attention upon the subject of the emigration of many of the citizens and manufacturers of Geneva, as proposed to me by the Sieur d'Ivernois, who by Lord Shelburne's directions and my wishes has followed me into Ireland. The importance which I annexed to this object from the moment in which it was first mentioned to me, and with particular recommendation of it in his Majesty's Instruction, have made me avail myself of all opportunities of informing myself in what manner I could turn these objects most to the advantage of this Kingdom.[131]

Temple discussed d'Ivernois's memorandum with his brother, the chief secretary of Ireland William Wyndham Grenville (from 1790 1st Baron Grenville). Grenville took it in turn to the Irish Privy Council, which included John Ponsonby, John Beresford, John Blaquiere and John Hely-Hutchinson. The urgency of the matter was signified by the fact that the Genevans were discussed on the date of the memorandum, and that the Privy Council came to the conclusion that the project of moving to Ireland 'a considerable body of artists in the watch manufacture' merited their complete support:

> His Excellency and their Lordships are fully sensible of the importance of the object and the advantages to be secured to this Kingdom by the considerable accession of a body of respectable citizens and to its commerce by the introduction of a manufacture so extensive and beneficial and by the immediate acquisition of a very material addition to the national wealth, and being convinced of the necessity of coming to an immediate decision in a case, the circumstances of which admit of no delay. Request his Excellency to transmit to his Majesty the said Memorial accompanied with their humble advice that every proper encouragement shall be held out for so desirable a purpose, and for inducing the said citizens of Geneva to settle in this country. They therefore unanimously request that his Majesty will be graciously pleased to take the same into his Royal Consideration and to adopt such measures in this case as to his Majesty's great wisdom shall seem to meet.[132]

The response of the Irish Privy Council was the first time that religion was mentioned in d'Ivernois's dealing with the British. Temple replied to d'Ivernois on the same day that, with regard to the Privy Council of Ireland, he could not 'sufficiently do justice to the zeal with which they received a proposition, which is to conciliate to them so respectable a body of religious and enlightened citizens, whose principles they admire, and for whose situation they truly feel'. Temple confirmed that he was taking steps to secure the £50,000 and reassured d'Ivernois of 'the King's disposition of holding out to you every attention and assistance, which this Kingdom can afford'. Temple said that he would be ready to meet with Genevan commissioners, and to grant a charter of incorporation, 'which will settle to them the election of their magistrates, and the power of making regulations for their interior government, not inconsistent with the laws of this country'. His only caveat was that the money 'shall be appropriated to one thousand emigrants who shall be merchants, watch manufacturers, or persons recommended from particular circumstances, amongst whom shall not be more than 200 children or servants not employed in the manufactory'.[133] The scale of this investment becomes evident when the cost of pulling down and rebuilding the cathedral church at Waterford, between 1773 and 1779, is considered for comparison: expenditure in this case amounted to '£5397, defrayed by the Corporation, by the tithes of Cahir, the sale of pews, and by private subscriptions'.[134] At ten times that amount, the grandeur of the Waterford experiment becomes clear.

A report in the *Morning Herald and Daily Advertiser* on Tuesday 8 October 1782 announced that the Genevan *représentants* were being encouraged by the British government to settle in Ireland. They were to establish a colony and bring with them the skills that had made Genevan manufactures renowned:

> We are happy to inform the public that an order yesterday was made by the Privy Council, to encourage a colony from Geneva to settle in this country. Some most respectable citizens of that oppressed republic have been soliciting an asylum in this rising land of liberty, for a number of their inhabitants give the preference to Ireland, and propose to bring with them the arts and manufactures that have long rendered that city the envy of Europe and the continued object of the jealousy of France.[135]

A large sum of money was reported to have been offered 'to a number of unfortunate but virtuous citizens of Geneva' as an inducement. In addition, William Robert FitzGerald, 2nd Duke of Leinster, a leader of the

Volunteers made knight of the Order of St Patrick in 1783, had offered 'two thousand acres in excellent cultivation' to the asylum seekers in addition to 'convenient houses'. He intended 'an absolute gift of the whole of this territory to the Genevan emigrants forever, without referring to [him]self a quit-rent or any rights of seigniority'. The land was 'two miles from Athy and Castle Dermot, and six miles from Carlow'. Leinster stated that his motivation was that of a 'friend of virtue', desirous of providing 'an asylum in which [the Genevans] may experience that liberty, enjoyed by this in preference to any other nation in the universe'. Leinster's motivation was the economic development of Ireland, which he saw to be the vital corollary to Catholic emancipation. Henry Loftus, 1st Earl of Ely, who as a member of the Privy Council had first-hand knowledge of the issue, also offered a settlement of land on his estate in the county of Wexford 'where it shall be my constant study to make your people a more rich, free and happy colony, than ever the city of Geneva could boast'. Confessing that he was 'abundantly rich', his motivation was to erect 'a more durable monument to my memory than marble can boast, or the most skilful artist devise'. This would be realised by acting as 'the protector of a body of men whom I regard with the greatest reverence'.[136] Ely had earlier written to Shelburne wishing 'joy to every good Whig', and asking him in government 'to pay every attention to subdue the turbulent spirit of the present time in this Kingdom [Ireland]'.[137] The French original of Leinster's letter of 30 September was included in d'Ivernois's *Pièces relatives à l'asyle ouvert en Irlande aux Genevois opprimés*, describing the road and canal system linking Athy to Dublin and to Waterford, the excellence of the land, and the duke's offering of his own mansion, Leinster Lodge. Leinster asserted that his sole motive in bringing the Genevans to Ireland, which he called 'today the most free country in the universe', was to 'counteract the sacrifices which the love of liberty had caused our unfortunate compatriots to make'.[138] The *Pièces* also included Ely's letter, in French and in English, stating that his lands in Wexford were ideal for the task, and that he would devote everything he could to establishing 'the first Protestant colony on earth':

> As to your future tranquillity; your ease and your enrichment, there certainly is no situation in Ireland so beneficial, so pleasurable or where so certain tranquillity is to be found as upon my lands in the County of Wexford where tumult or rift never was known; and where a profussion of the necessaries of life abound, upon the most reasonable terms and where it shall be the study of my life to make yours if possible a happier,

> a freer and a richer people than even Geneva could ever boast of . . . I am called upon by the most sincere impulse of my heart, to protect, to accommodate, and to make you happy, as the first Protestant colony upon the earth . . . [you Genevans] prove by [your] conduct that that corner of the world only is their country where law is liberty and honesty the highest honour.[139]

The haste with which such arrangements were made, and the fact that d'Ivernois was soon armed with translations of the letters and documents confirming British support, underlined the fact that d'Ivernois and Temple had already arranged everything with Shelburne, and that Shelburne had already obtained the support of George III. With such singular backing secured, d'Ivernois then returned to Neuchâtel to promote the emigration with eight commissioners representing the Genevans. The news soon reached Geneva, where Ami Dunant transcribed articles in the 31st, 32nd and 34th issues of the *Courier de l'Europe*, commencing 24 October, reproducing letters from Dublin that revealed the extent of British support. Ireland was described as a country underpopulated and without manufactures, and therefore ideal for Genevans who prefered 'to live under a free government than the constitution of their republic ['un gouvernement libre à la constitution de leur république'].' Many thousands were expected to move, it was reported.[140] Each commissioner was one of the individuals banished from Geneva by the French: d'Ivernois himself, Clavière, Du Roveray, the pastor Gasc, the watchmaker Melly, the lawyer Jacques Grenus and the *représentants* Guillaume Ringler and Baumier. D'Ivernois then returned to London with Du Roveray. Clavière left Neuchâtel in December 1782. He travelled to Basle, taking a boat down the Rhine to Ostend, and stopping en route at Düsseldorf and at Mannheim in order to evaluate the prospecets for a New Geneva in Germany. Nothing appealing was to be found:

> It is reported that Clavière and his travelling companions stopped at Dusseldorf but saw nothing there to attract the attention of our compatriots. The locale is beautiful, it is true, with cheap food and excellent prospects for trade. There is not, however, among the principal figures in the place, the same eagerness to welcome us that was demonstrated by the Regent of Mannheim, but rather the opposite. And then these [small] states with which it would be necessary to negotiate . . . are composed of people infatuated with their sixteen degrees of nobility, and are consequently very little motivated to favour the principles of equality and openness [*popularité*] which must be the foundation of

> a colony of artisans. Madame Clavière and others therefore prepared to continue their journey and intended to be on 16 January in Brussels and 18 January in Ostend.[141]

Clavière was indeed in Brussels on 16 January and had reached Ostend by the 18th. He then travelled to Dover and on to London on 20 January, where he met members of the Genevan merchant community, and also Jacques-Pierre Brissot, who began to work for him. With Gasc, Grenus, Melly and Ringler, Clavière then travelled to Dublin, where they met Earl Temple at Dublin Castle on 14 February 1783.[142] The next step was to complete the negitations with regard to the establishment of the new settlement with British and Irish negotitators.

Clavière's arrival in Ireland coincided with the final weeks of Shelburne's ministry, which fell on 26 March 1783. The change of ministry meant that by May there was a new lord lieutenant of Ireland, Robert Henley, 2nd Earl of Northington, and a new chief secretary, William Windham, who served only from May to July, when he was replaced by Thomas Pelham. The Irish contingent charged with negotiating with the Genevans was more stable. It included George de la Poer Beresford, 2nd Earl of Tyrone (created Marquess of Waterford in 1789), who had been governor of Waterford since 1766, and his brother John Beresford, the MP for Waterford, a member of the Irish Privy Council from 1768 and a revenue commissioner from 1770. John Blaquiere also served as a member of the negotiating party; formerly a colonel in the light dragoons, he had been Lord Harcourt's secretary when ambassador at Paris and chief secretary of Ireland between 1772 and 1779. Other members included Colonel Henry Theophilus Clements MP, who held offices in the Irish treasury, John Foster, a prominent MP and acting chancellor of the Irish exchequer, James Cuffe MP, David La Touche MP, a Dublin banker, Andrew Caldwell MP, a Dublin barrister who had been involved in projects to widen the streets of the capital, Travers Hartley, a Dublin merchant and MP for the city and Alexander Jaffray, another Dublin merchant and banker.[143]

Those charged with finalising arrangements for the new city on the British/Irish and on the Genevan side had every reason to be optimistic in the first half of 1783. Post-invasion Geneva was reported as being near collapse. As noted above, the magistrates had already consented to the building of a theatre for the entertainment of foreign troops, which was said to be 'a sure means of corrupting the manners of the people'. Ever greater numbers of bourgeois and citizens were seeking to leave, being fearful for the future.[144] In the following weeks, further details emerged.

The opportunity to emigrate to the new city was being offered to any who would go. It was later reported that ten thousand inhabitants were willing to leave the city because of the 'league that was entered into by France, Sardinia [Savoy], and Bern, to destroy the independence of Geneva'.[145] Other estimates went as high as twenty thousand.[146] The newspapers were being made aware that a decision had been taken by the British government to 'secure a favourable reception for such families as were determined to quit Geneva, and not only a favourable reception but such positive encouragement & support as might reimburse their expenses, & lay the foundation of an establishment in this country'.[147]

Samuel Romilly, then a young lawyer and of Huguenot descent, informed his brother-in-law Jean Roget, still living at Lausanne, that the government had offered £50,000 to the Genevans. The funds were to pay for the establishment of a colony of a thousand watchmakers who were 'to have a charter of incorporation, by which they will be enabled to elect their own magistrates, and to regulate entirely their own internal police'. The location of the settlement had yet to be decided. Romilly confirmed that the Duke of Leinster had made a remarkably generous offer:

> The Duke of Leinster, by letter, invites the colony to settle upon his estate in the county of Wexford, in the province of Leinster. He offers to give them, by a pure and perpetual donation, a very large tract of ground -which he now lets (though much below its value) for 600l a-year; he engages to procure them places of abode, and particularly offers his own house, Leinster Lodge, a mansion capable of lodging one hundred persons, till they can build houses for themselves. The spot of ground where he proposes that they should build their little city is, he says, in one of the most fertile and temperate parts of Ireland, at the confluence of two rivers, at a convenient vicinity to the sea, and distant about thirty miles from Dublin. All this news you may depend on, for I have seen the order of the Irish Council, and the letters of Lord Temple and the Duke of Leinster. Other noblemen have invited the colony to settle upon their estates, but none offer terms so advantageous and so noble as the Duke of Leinster.[148]

Two issues had been determined, Romilly reported. The city was to be called New Geneva. Furthermore, it was 'to resemble the old Geneva in everything, except in having an upper and a lower town'. In other words, New Geneva was not to allow a caste of magistrates or aristocrats to develop through living apart from ordinary people. Romilly likened the settlement to a second Troy. He added that there were also plans to move the Genevan Academy to Ireland.[149] The reinstated magistrates at Geneva were furious about the actions of the British government, and complained to both George III and the home secretary, Thomas Townshend.[150] In some minds a parallel was clearly being drawn between the likely Genevan emigration and the exodus of French Huguenots after the revocation of the Edict of Nantes (1685). Almost a hundred years after that event, similar plans were afoot for a further Protestant diaspora.[151] The historian John Angel, dedicating his book to the Duke of Leinster, reminded his readers that 'the English were indebted to foreigners both for their woollen and silken manufactures', and had given Huguenot refugees 'a reception as is scarcely to be paralleled in history'. Ireland was ready to reap similar rewards, by tempting 'those at present groaning under foreign arbitrary governments, to fly from their oppressions and reside in this kingdom'.[152]

That the British ministers pushed the Genevans towards Ireland was unsurprising. The history of early modern Ireland was replete with attempts to alter the nature of the colony by immigration. Making Ireland British through colonisation and plantation was expected to turn a Catholic society widely seen to be barbarous and rebellious into one more loyal, industrious and peaceable, and as such amounted to a Protestant rejoinder to comparable Spanish activities in the New World.[153] Foreign Protestants were increasingly welcomed in such projects, as migration from Britain tailed off, as Irish Protestants themselves left for North America and as economic conditions in Ireland failed to improve.[154] The scheme to bring Genevans to Ireland was in many respects characteristic of what had gone before, being an extension of the 'Protestant International' that had seen Huguenot and Vaudois refugees establish safe havens in Britain and North America during Louis XIV's wars.[155] In tune with the motivation behind former schemes, some of those involved considered New Geneva a brilliant means of turning Ireland's backward peasants into industrious artisans. Significantly, equally commonplace was the statement that the new city would be accompanied by large-scale Protestant conversion.

Why did the Genevans themselves opt for Ireland? D'Ivernois was candid in a letter to Mount Stuart in which he stated that it was impossible to settle in England because of the debts of the state, the need to provide succour to refugees from North America rather than Geneva, and concerns about the antagonism of English watchmakers and jewellers fearful of competition and well supported in Parliament. The contrast with an exhausted England embroiled in war was Ireland, which d'Ivernois called 'a new country, newly free' and ripe for commercial development. Mount Stuart's support was for d'Ivernois 'the first cause of my success'.[156] Clavière wrote that it was through the foundation of new cities that 'we will give to men of all countries the courage to resist despotism'.[157] Dumont predicted that 'the colony will rise, and will allow our people, who have been corrupted in our native soil, to re-establish their vigour on foreign soil'.[158] One of the paid agents of the *représentants*, Honoré-Gabriel Riqueti, comte de Mirabeau, who was working for Clavière, warned Vergennes in October 1782 that Britain, 'the rich and calculating nation', was pushing the Genevans towards Ireland, 'the least cultivated and most savage [state] in Europe'. It was also 'one of the most fertile and ideally situated for commerce'. As the British were offering full political rights, few laws, free trade and minimal taxes to the Genevans, Mirabeau anticipated the transformation of Ireland. Indeed, he stated that Ireland might become 'the most free country on earth and the most desirable abode for men who know the value of liberty'.[159] Such letters were intended to remind Vergennes of the terrible consequences of his policy towards Geneva. Others were similarly enthused, including the Bordeaux lawyer and republican Guillaume-Joseph Saige:

> I hope you will excuse me for my enthusiasm, which has been inspired by your business and the keen interest I take in the permanent happiness of New Geneva. Since fate has denied me the opportunity of seeing the old free Geneva and of living with its walls, I dare to hope, Sir, that if I decided to leave my country and to transport my patrimony out of the Kingdom [of France] to enjoy the joys of liberty, and to get away from the persecutions which the publication of some political works might excite against me, you would allow me to become an inhabitant of your new city.[160]

Saige wrote a further letter stating that he had Irish relatives on his mother's side, knew English and was willing to join in the work of establishing an asylum for the oppressed. He said that there should only be one Geneva on the earth, and that the appellation 'New Geneva' was not necessary in consequence, because only a free state could carry the name.[161]

Jacques-Pierre Brissot, by early 1783 one of Clavière's propagandists, summarised the perspective of the exiles. In their last public declaration within Geneva the *représentants* had announced their collective decision to find a new abode, on the grounds that their country 'had been reduced to slavery'. Geneva had ceased to be independent. It was under French dominion. According to Brissot, the *représentants* took as their model Aristomenes after the brutal defeat by Sparta of his kingdom of Messenia. Seeing 'the destruction of liberty they fled their country and went to found a new colony in Sicily, which has since become very eminent'. Geneva would wither within a century and 'be likely to have been removed from the list of political states'. The Swiss, the Bavarians and Frederick the Great through his territory at Neuchâtel had offered land and resources to the exiles. But the preference had to be a 'new country'.

Brissot described the new country of Ireland as 'perhaps the only asylum of liberty at present [in Europe], the only place where remarkable enterprises could fruitfully be taken forward'. Ireland was attracting exiles from other states because it offered civil and political liberty, easy naturalisation, the protection of a free parliament and few laws. Furthermore, it was rich in natural resources and ripe for commercial development.[162] Finally, it was fortunate, because 'the terrible burden of [the British] national debt did not touch Ireland'. The plan of the Genevans was to 'bring life to a savage place by their industry'. A charter had been signed, with the British promising that the refugees would govern themselves in accordance with their own laws and customs.[163] The British newspapers also reported the view of the *représentants* that investment in the public debts of states across Europe had made too many Genevans far wealthier than their compatriots. Excessive inequality had corrupted Genevan politics. Reports in the press explained the internal civil war between magistrates seeking to turn themselves into aristocrats and their enemies. The remedy had to be that 'the bell must be melted down and cast again'. This was what the Genevans were doing at New Geneva. They were willing 'to drop [their] sweat upon its foundations'.[164]

PART III

Disunited Ireland

CHAPTER SEVEN

Ireland: Oppression and Opportunity

THE GENEVANS PRESENTED Ireland as a new and stable state, pregnant with possibility for enlightened living and commercial development. Numerous Irish observers must have rolled their eyes. Yet Ireland was undergoing constitutional and economic upheaval. The first Catholic Relief Act was passed in 1778, allowing Catholics in Ireland to bequeath land to a single heir, thereby reversing one of the penal laws introduced from 1695.[1] Between the mid-1770s and 1782 a part-time military force of self-styled Volunteers was formed to protect against invasion from France or Spain, compensating for professional troops normally stationed in Ireland but transferred for service in North America. Numbers rose from approximately twelve thousand in 1779 to sixty thousand by May 1782. Approximately fifteen hundred individual corps were raised independently, with distinctive uniforms but enjoying a shared patriotic iconography.[2] The Volunteers included prominent members of parliament and the aristocracy, and were involved in the campaign for the removal of restrictions upon Irish trade. In a *Letter to the people of Ireland* justifying the Volunteers in 1779, the Patriot or Protestant nationalist MP Henry Flood declared that Ireland was 'losing her trade, impairing her liberty, and reducing her people to want'. The cause was English mercantile dominion, the 'jealousy, monopoly and pride, combining in the soul of a commercial empire'.

In Flood's view, Ireland's condition was worse than being exposed to the whims of an absolute monarch. This was because the country was governed by tyrannical merchants from England. Where an absolute monarch 'takes from the tree too much of its fruit', the English merchant 'starves the root and prevents the bearing. The one is a moral evil, the other a tyranny, amounting to physical interdict.' English merchants cared only for the 'industry, punctuality and that species of probity which is necessary for credit'. Drawing a parallel with the American rebellion, Flood argued that the time was right for the Irish to recover their liberties. The English were unlikely to crush them militarily, being 'involved in a civil war with America . . . in another war with France . . . [and] in apprehension of being involved in another war with Spain'. England had learned 'by experience the misery of attempts to coerce nations by starving them'. What the Irish wanted was self-rule and never union, because the latter would intensify and perpetuate England's tyranny.[3] Flood's view was echoed by the Presbyterian minister James Crombie, who justified the establishment of volunteer companies for national defence. Britain was said to be in decline, with an empire that 'seems to totter', because of the rise of luxury and the collapse of public virtue, and in such circumstances Ireland might well have to defend itself against inevitable foreign invaders.[4]

Ireland was seen to be in crisis in part because of the effects of events in North America upon trade. As one anonymous pamphlet put it, Ireland had been prosperous before the accession of George III, with new trades such as linen, 'sprung up like some flourishing oak', and a surplus of national revenue. All this changed because of the rapacity of English ministers, who filled their own purses rather than attending to the public good:

> The kingdom of Ireland has struggled for near a century, under the iron rod of commercial oppression. The narrow illiberal temper of the trader, seemed to have reached and subdued the wisdom of the state. Instead of beholding Ireland in the light of a partner and friend, the ruin of that kingdom, in the eye of mercantile avarice, appears to have been considered as the destruction of a dangerous rival . . . Since the last peace, this unhappy country has been the melancholy subject of a boundless rapacity and extravagance, which cannot be beheld without concern and indignation. Viceroys have been sent over, as to another Roman Sicily, to repair their ruined fortunes, and gratify their partisans with the choicest spoils of the kingdom.[5]

The conclusion was that '[t]he situation of Britain presents, at this period, an awful spectacle to the world' and that Ireland was being dragged down by English policy. Benjamin Franklin's point would also have been born in mind, that having failed 'to preserve from breaking that fine and noble china vase, the British Empire', the likelihood was that 'being once broken, the separate parts could not retain even their shares of the strength and value that existed in the whole, and that a perfect reunion of those parts could scarce ever be hoped for'.[6] In other words, Britain could expect further turmoil and likely dismemberment.

Inspired by such analyses, boycotts of British goods in Ireland were initiated in 1779. The campaign intensified at an armed gathering of the Volunteers at the statue of William of Orange at College Green in Dublin on 4 November. On 15 November, a crowd of thousands rallied outside parliament. Thomas Allan, an English MP and Irish revenue commissioner, admitted to his friend John Beresford that he was fearful for the present situation of Ireland ('I lament the times') particularly because of uncertainty about the meaning of free trade: 'You say a free trade, without defining what you want; we say, we shall give a free trade, without specifying what we mean to give.'[7] On 13 December, the prime minister, Frederick North, 2nd Earl of Guilford, granted Ireland the right to trade directly with the colonies, and to export wool and glass. He had come around to the opinion that if 'something very effectual' was not done to appease the Patriots, 'this kingdom is forever lost to Great Britain or you . . . have a civil war'.[8] What North granted was termed 'free trade', but in fact meant that Ireland gained membership of Britain's mercantile system, and enjoyed the protections and privileges that this entailed.[9] Such privileges had been withheld from the colony since the seventeenth century.[10]

Such a victory gave further impetus to the reform movement. At Dungannon in Ulster, on 15 February 1782, the Volunteers gathered and resolved in favour of Irish legislative independence, Irish parliamentary control of the army, and security of tenure for judges. Patriot politicians who were prominent in the Volunteer movement, led by the lawyer and MP Henry Grattan, were demanding that the Irish parliament at College Green be given the right to make its own laws: as British subjects, they were entitled to live under a free constitution, rather than being subjects of an Irish executive at Dublin Castle, in turn selected in London.[11] Frederick Howard, 5th Earl of Carlisle, serving as lord lieutenant from 1780–82, and William Eden, 1st Baron Auckland, the Irish chief secretary for the same period, serving under Lord North, supported the Irish MP Barry Yelverton's bill of December 1781, which took away the right of the Privy Councils in London and Dublin to initiate or amend legislation. Eden had earlier published his correspondence with Carlisle, acknowledging that the 'distresses' of Ireland, while they might have resulted from 'temporary causes', including the American rebellion, were 'founded in real sufferings'. The mystery was why Ireland, possessing 'nearly all the natural advantages of Great Britain, and having, besides, in point of commerce, some others peculiar to her situation . . . has yet in all ages been comparatively poor and distressed'. In his own explanation, Eden admitted that 'in all these reasonings, the commercial and the political interests are inseparably blended'.[12] He also described governing Ireland as 'teasing and ticklish work. The jealousies of individuals, and of the people, are innumerable, incessant, and unaccountable.'[13]

With the replacement of Lord North as prime minister by Charles Watson-Wentworth, 2nd Marquess of Rockingham, in March 1782, the Irish case for reform was still more positively received. The Declaratory Act of 1719, known as the Sixth of George I, restricting the powers of the Irish parliament, was repealed on 21 June 1782 and Yelverton's Act became law on 27 July, modifying Poynings' Law of 1494 that asserted the royal prerogative over Ireland. Irish bills could still be vetoed by the British Privy Council, and the government of the country continued to be accountable to the British cabinet; but despite such limitations, in 1782 longstanding grievances were being addressed, and Irish politicians felt that they had been granted new powers to determine the future of the country. The Patriot leader Henry Grattan passed through massed ranks of Volunteers into parliament on 16 April 1782, and made a speech that began, 'I am now to address a free people.' A new Ireland, he announced, had been created. Ireland was, for the first time, 'a nation':

> I found Ireland on her knees, I watched over her with a paternal solicitude; I have traced her progress from injuries to arms, and from arms to liberty. Spirit of Swift, spirit of Molyneux, your genius has prevailed! Ireland is now a nation! In that new character I hail her; and bowing to her august presence, I say, *Esto perpetua.* She is no longer a wretched colony, returning thanks to her Governor for his rapine, and to her King for his oppression; nor is she now a fretful, squabbling sectary, perplexing her little wits, and firing her furious statutes with bigotry, sophistry, disabilities, and death, to transmit to posterity insignificance and war. Look to the rest of Europe. Holland lives on the memory of past achievement. Sweden has lost her liberty. England has sullied her great name by an attempt to enslave her colonies! You are the only people, you, of the nations in Europe, are now the only people, who excite admiration; and in your present conduct, you not only exceed the present generation, but you equal the past. I am not afraid to turn back and look antiquity in the face.[14]

Grattan called the Revolution of 1688 'that great event', but said it was 'tarnished with bigotry' because 'the great deliverer', William of Orange, ruled 'by oppression'. William had been 'forced to assent to acts which deprived the Catholics of religious liberty, and all the Irish of civil and commercial rights, though the Irish were the only subjects in these islands who had fought in his defence'. In the present, however, religious differences were disappearing. As Grattan put it, 'See the Presbyterians of Bangor petition for the Catholics of the south.' He concluded that 'A flame has descended from Heaven on the intellect of Ireland, and plays round her head with a concentrated glory.'[15] Ireland did, however, remain Protestant and a British colony, with an Anglican established church. Thus the events of the late 1770s and early 1780s were a response to the new Ireland that had been created in the sixteenth and seventeenth centuries.[16]

II

Since the Norman invasions of the twelfth century, Ireland had been an ecclesiastical fiefdom of the Catholic church, governed as a lordship from England. It was divided between longstanding and originally Anglo-Norman settlers—some of whom remained loyal to the English crown, controlling directly only the relatively small Pale, from Dundalk in the north to the Wicklow mountains—and the native Irish, governed under a clan system, with their distinct language, customs and laws. Governance was notionally delegated to aristocratic chiefs, and often their leading representative, the lord deputy of Ireland, from the FitzGerald clan. This state was torn asunder after the crushing in 1534 of the rebellion of 'Silken Thomas'. Thomas FitzGerald, 10th Earl of Kildare, took up arms against Henry VIII on the mistaken grounds that his father had been executed in London. Ireland soon ceased to be a lordship and was proclaimed a kingdom in 1541. Such a status was accompanied by a policy of 'surrender and regrant', whereby Irish lords gave their lands to the crown, proclaimed their loyalty and received them back with English titles. An era of tension, because of the loss of Irish authority, was inaugurated, characterised by a series of bloody rebellions.

The further divisive factor was the Reformation. When England turned Protestant, Ireland became a battleground for godly conversion, pitting native Irish and Old English residents against new Protestant settlers. English dominion was established in part by the introduction of a centralised administration, and the imposition of English Common Law. The main measure, however, was the expropriation of land. The granting of land to immigrants from the mainland, termed 'plantation', was initiated in the 1550s. The policy was accelerated after the destruction of the rebellious

Desmond dynasty, who lost their land in Munster in the final decades of the sixteenth century. Plantation proceeded apace again after the Nine Years' War in Ulster, between 1593 and 1603, when the O'Neills and O'Donnells were defeated, ultimately fleeing to the continent in 1607 in the hope of a return to power by means of Spanish invasion. James VI and I then broke up the land of the Irish Catholic aristocracy across Ulster into two-thousand acre plots, which were granted to immigrant Protestants. The planting of Protestants occurred in six colonies, Derry, Donegal, Fermanagh, Tyrone, Cavan and Armagh, after which the native Irish were left with only a quarter of the land. Plantation was sold to the English as a commercial opportunity. It also attracted large numbers of Scottish Calvinists, themselves fleeing religious persecution, and self-identifying as an elect nation, experiencing persecution, lamentation, exodus and deliverance.

The assault on established Gaelic culture, and the deep division between Catholic and Protestant, led to further turmoil in the seventeenth century. Rebellion occurred when the possibility arose of attracting support from abroad for Irish Catholics, and more still when England itself experienced crisis. In part because of the widespread perception that the Irish had become slaves and victims of a brutal tyranny, and also because conflict could be justified by the prospect of saving souls, rebellion tended to be accompanied by singular brutality on both sides. In November 1641, an Irish force took the castle of Obins in Portadown and forced one hundred English and Scottish settlers off the bridge into the river Bann, where they were drowned or shot. Those involved in the rebellion were reported to have said, 'We have been your slaves all this time, now you shall be ours.'[17] A Gaelic poem of 1650, *An Síogaí Rómhánach* ('The Roman Vision') portrayed armed Gaels setting Ireland free from the 'Saxon' and 'the bare-faced Scot', triumphing with their priests over 'the crafty, thieving, false sect of Calvin'.[18] On the English side, Oliver Cromwell, after breaching the walls of Drogheda, massacred around three thousand royalist troops and civilians, including many who had surrendered. Priests were murdered and the commander of the garrison, Sir Arthur Aston, was clubbed to death with his own wooden leg. Others were burned while hiding in churches. Cromwell justified the deaths by calling them 'a righteous judgment of God upon these barbarous wretches'.[19] The Rump Parliament, on 12 August 1652, passed an Act of Settlement for Ireland. This took away the estates of all of the rebels of 1641, and removed two thirds of the estates of the Irish leaders of the armies of 1642–49 and one third of the land of any Catholic who had not supported the English Commonwealth between 1649 and 1650.[20] By the 1650s, approximately one fifth only of the land of Ireland was owned by Catholics, because of the Cromwellian confiscations.[21] Investigations were launched into why Ireland was 'not more increasing in trade and wealth from the first conquest till now' and by which 'wealth-wasting enormities' it was 'kept poor and low'.[22]

The process of rebellion, suppression and dispossession was repeated after the 'Glorious Revolution' of 1688. James VII and II, the ousted Stuart king, landed at Kinsale in Cork on 12 March 1689, supported by troops and arms supplied by Louis XIV. The invaders were joined by Catholics desirous of religious liberty, and those seeking the restoration of lost land. In April, siege was laid to Derry, home to a Protestant garrison and refugees, which lasted for 105 days, during which thousands died of starvation and disease, until food was supplied by merchant ships breaking through the boom on the river Foyle. In June 1690, William III landed at Carrickfergus, and by the beginning of July, with an army of thirty-six thousand troops, was facing a Jacobite army of twenty-five thousand at Oldbridge on the river Boyne. Although the engagement was not decisive, King James, claiming that his Irish army had 'basely fled', himself left Dublin for France. With Jacobites controlling much of the south-west of Ireland, and the counties west of the river Shannon, the war continued until 3 October 1691, when the Treaty of Limerick brought peace. This offered a pardon, and the opportunity to retain land and arms, in return for an oath of fealty to William III and Mary II. Those who refused the oath were punished by a series of penal laws, enacted after the Pope declared James II the rightful king in 1693. These penal laws, inspired by fears of further Catholic rebellion, comprised a series of acts passed between 1695 and 1727. Catholics were forbidden from entering public office, from holding arms, from entering the Irish parliament, the legal profession or the military, from matriculating at Trinity College Dublin, from marrying a Protestant or inheriting land from a Protestant, from passing on undivided estates to a son, from buying land or purchasing a lease for longer than thirty-one years, from enjoying a foreign education, from owning a horse to the value of over £5 and from voting (this last from 1728).[23]

The penal laws also applied to dissenters, the majority of whom were Presbyterians. In England, dissenters were excluded by the Corporation Act of 1661 from public office, and by the Test Acts of 1673 and 1678 from voting and from entering university. At the same time, with the passing of the Toleration Act of 1689, nonconformists who pledged loyalty to the English crown and rejected the doctrine of transubstantiation were allowed to gather and worship, as long as they registered their meetings and licensed their preachers. The Toleration Acts were not applied to

Ireland. Rather, although Presbyterians retained the ability to vote and to enter the Irish parliament, the Sacramental Test Act of 1704 forced them to follow the rites of the Church of Ireland with regard to the Eucharist if they wished to hold civil or military office. Such a demand led to the resignation of many burgesses, including in the commercial centres of Belfast and Derry.[24] Meanwhile poor harvests in Scotland in the later 1690s caused a further wave of immigration into Ulster. This intensified the fears of the members of the Anglican communion, who after 1691 had observed a gathering of leading Presbyterians annually at the Synod of Ulster. Presbyterians saw their right to declare members of their congregations married questioned, and were forced to pay taxes to support the established church. In such circumstances, many Catholics and dissenters converted, keen to enjoy the privileges of the ruling Anglo-Irish Protestants. Others, both Catholic and Presbyterian, emigrated to North America.

With the establishment of what became known later in the century as the Protestant Ascendancy—the union of supporters of the established Church of Ireland with a land-owning aristocracy—Ireland saw a long period of relative peace.[25] Remarkably, the country was quiet during the Jacobite rebellions initiated in Scotland in 1715 and 1745, though it was still said that 'the Pretender runs in the heads of most of the people of Ireland'.[26] Roads and canals were built, and economic growth was marked, especially in the major cities. Rather than being stagnant, population growth was buoyant, and trade, other than in years of famine, developed apace.[27] At the same time, Ireland's dependent status had significant consequences. The Irish parliament remained subservient to London through Poynings' Law of 1494 and the Declaratory Act of 1719, stating that Irish legislation had to be approved by the Irish Privy Council and was subject both to the royal prerogative and to the British parliament; in practice, the need for compromise over bills to raise revenue gave members of the Irish parliament a greater say from 1692. The secondary status of the Irish parliament led to tension, however. As Joseph Addison, then secretary to Thomas Wharton, the lord lieutenant of Ireland, put it,

> There is indeed a great reluctancy in all sorts of people here to the having it thought that they are a conquered and dependent Kingdom, and that even acts of parliament in England may not be superseded by those in Ireland as to what relates purely to the affairs of their own country.[28]

Addison further noted, in addition to a complicated relationship with London, the extent to which anti-Catholic feeling coloured political life for 'the Gentlemen of Ireland'. It was also clear to him that private interest often favoured the exclusion of Catholics 'from purchases, mortgages and merchandize'.[29] William King, archbishop of Dublin, writing around the same time, observed that when dealing with English politicians, 'the good of Ireland has no weight at all'.[30] A popish plot was identified, involving secret work to foster French invasion.[31] The Irish people, being 'Papistical' and rebellious, were being encouraged by Jesuit emissaries to call for freedom of conscience and other popular liberties.[32] With England, later Britain, so much at war with France, the fear that Ireland would be the locus of rebellion was widespread.[33]

III

The Irish parliament lacked above all else authority in matters of trade. As the physician and political arithmetician William Petty noted in his *Political Anatomy*, posthumously published in 1691, Ireland was 'by nature fit for trade', being rich in the natural resources of wood, stone and salt. More particularly, it 'lieth commodiously for the trade of the new American world, which we see every day to grow and to flourish'.[34] Petty had been arguing since the 1660s, however, that opportunities for the increase of trade were limited by a number of factors. One was the Catholicism of four fifths of the population of Ireland, corrupted as they were, according to Petty, by doctrines imparted by their priests, who served the separate interests of the Church of Rome:

> Their preaching seems rather bugbearing of their flocks with dreadful stories, than persuading them by reason or the scriptures. They have an incredible opinion of the Pope and his sanctity, of the happiness of those who can obtain his blessing at the third or fourth hand. Only some few, who have lately been abroad, have gotten so far, as to talk of a difference between the interest of the court of Rome, and the doctrine of the Church.[35]

Petty was particularly concerned that the priests taught that lives lived in poverty were altogether acceptable, being 'like the Patriarchs of old, and the saints of later times, by whose prayers and merits they are to be relieved, and whose examples they are therefore to follow'. Labour was discouraged, in consequence, by the dominant Catholic culture of Ireland.

Another significant factor, however, was the policy of the English in preventing the Irish from enjoying improvement.[36] Petty was writing in the context of widespread demands for the prevention of the export of Irish cattle, which led to an act being passed to this end in 1674, in order to maintain English prices and trade. He was also aware of the effects of the series of English Navigation acts. The first was passed in 1651, stipulating that English ships alone could carry goods to England and its colonies, in addition to ships from the state where the goods were originally produced. This meant that the ships of the United Provinces, whose trade the Act was intended to deter, could carry butter and cheese into English ports, but were prevented from carrying fish oil or salted fish. At the Restoration, a further Act, of 13 September 1660, demanded that domestic ships be crewed at least three quarters by English sailors, and stated that products not produced in England, including cotton, tobacco and sugar, were to be shipped from the colonies only to England or to other English colonies. A further Navigation Act of 27 July 1663 asserted that all goods bound for England's colonies had to be shipped via an English port, with particular products, including sugar, rice and tobacco, paying a levy when they landed. This Act prohibited exports from Ireland to the colonies, a provision made permanent in 1666.

To an observer such as Petty, the effects of English policy in prohibiting and fettering Irish commerce were manifest in the general poverty of the population, the extent of beggary and a propensity he identified to theft and to crime. If an Irish person embraced trade, there was little to obtain in exchange, because merchants could either not be found or could supply only a limited range of goods. Again, the fundamental cause was English policy. As the Irish parliament was entirely dependent upon London, laws supportive of the interests of Ireland were not likely to be forthcoming. More worryingly, property was not secure in Ireland, being dependent on the whim of politicians and selfish landowners, and likely to be usurped. Petty concluded that trade could not exist 'where tricks and words destroy natural right and property':

> And why should they breed more cattle, since it is penal to import them into England? Why should they raise more commodities, since there are not merchants sufficiently stocked to take them of them, nor provided with other more pleasing foreign commodities, to give in exchange for them? And how should merchants have stock, since trade is prohibited and fettered by the statutes of England? And why should men endeavour to get estates, where the legislative power is not agreed upon; and where tricks and words destroy natural right and property?[37]

Despite their devotion to Catholicism, Petty did not blame the native Irish themselves for their predicament. Rather, the land was so fecund that 'the labour of one man can feed forty'. A house could be erected 'in three days' and limited prospects made individuals satisfied with eating potatoes and 'cockles, oysters, mussels [and] crabs'. Petty concluded that the apparent lack of industry of the Irish was due to their circumstances: 'Their lazing seems to me to proceed rather from their want of employment and encouragement to work, than the abundance of phlegm in their bowels and blood.'[38]

Petty's solution was a union between England and Ireland. This policy was expected to generate English practices with regard to trade on Irish soil, gradually realising the goal of the Irish being 'transmuted into English'. Once this process was initiated, the Gaelic language would decline, property rights would be respected and a mutual sense of interest between landlord and tenant would be established, favouring again the union of the peoples:

> As for the interest of these poorer Irish, it is manifestly to be transmuted into English, so to reform and qualify their housing, as that English women may be content to be their wives, to decline their language, which continues a sensible distinction, being not now necessary; which makes those who do not understand it, suspect, that what is spoken in it, is to their prejudice. It is their interest to deal with the English, for leases, for time, and upon clear conditions, which being performed they are absolute freemen, rather than to stand always liable to the humour and caprice of their landlords, and to have everything taken from them, which he pleases to fancy. It is their interest, that he is well-pleased with their obedience to them, when they see and know upon whose care and conduct their well-being depends, who have power over their lands and estates.[39]

Petty's strategy for Ireland was not merely an ideal project for an anticipated future. Rather, he held it to be urgent, an element of a broader policy of making the British Isles safe from France. France was not only the dominant state in Europe, but was in a vibrant condition both militarily and commercially. France was likely to defeat England, possibly by taking action in Ireland:

> [T]heir fleet is such, that it ought to breed jealousy and fears of encroachments upon the right of our sovereignty on these seas, on our plantations, sea-port towns, and our inward and outward trade and commerce, on the rights and privileges of our neighbours, who for these many ages stood as our bulwarks and banks against the swellings of this ambitious and active nation, never so powerful as now.[40]

Petty demanded union as a means to securing property across Ireland and to establishing free trade between the states, in order to counter French ambition. An impoverished Ireland would be prey to French designs. By contrast, an Irish populace who shared the commercial manners of the English, and who were similarly wealthy in consequence, were likely to be patriots, and natural enemies to France. Petty was neo-Machiavellian in accepting that states had first to be secure in order to maintain themselves, and that security depended upon greatness. He differed from contemporaries, not in his correlation of greatness with trade, but in arguing that it was possible for an empire to encourage the commerce of its peripheries in the same manner as it defended that of the metropole.

Petty's proposal for union fell on deaf ears. In instances where Irish trade fell into competition with that of England to any significant extent, it continued to be suppressed. After cattle, came wool. Irish wool had traditionally supplied the English market, but the production of higher-quality cloths from the 1660s, termed the 'new drapery', for domestic consumption became marked, in part because of the immigration of skilled artisans from Europe. Export abroad of wool or woollen cloth was pronounced a felony in an act of 1662. As fears grew that English production might be inferior to that of Ireland, demands from mainland merchants were made that the trade of the colony be prevented from competing with that of England and Wales. Against Petty, the argument was made that this was entirely natural. The diplomat and statesman Sir William Temple warned the Irish in an essay of 1673 that as a 'subordinate' state, they should accept that their own trade had to be 'declined or moderated' so as to ensure the 'health and vigour' of English trade, because this in turn secured Ireland from external attack and domestic upheaval.[41] In 1697, when he was discussing the issue as a member of the Board of Trade, John Locke came to the same opinion, that it was dangerous for Ireland to compete with English wool production.[42] In December of that same year, Exeter merchants petitioned parliament, claiming that Irish woollens were destroying their industry, and a campaign was initiated to restrict Irish wool production. One solution lay in the development of Irish linen, an idea that Locke owed to his friend William Molyneux, the prominent Dublin writer and member of the Irish parliament:

> England most certainly will never let us thrive by the woollen trade. This is their darling mistress, and they are jealous of any rival. But I see not, that we interfere with them in the least by the linen trade, so that is yet left open to us to grow rich by, if it were well established

> and managed. . . . There is no country [that] has better land or water for flax and hemp; and I do verily believe the navy may be provided here with sailing and cordage cheaper by far than in England. Our land is cheaper, victuals for workmen are cheaper, and labour is cheaper, together with the other necessaries for artificers.[43]

This opinion was reflected in the final report of the Board of Trade in 1697. Locke was doubtful, however, that the linen trade would thrive in Ireland, because, as he wrote to Molyneux, 'Private knavery, I perceive, does [in Ireland] as well as here destroy all public good works, and forbid the hope of any advantages by them.' Locke acknowledged himself to be pleased to be stepping down from the Board of Trade, since 'The corruption of the age gives me so ill a prospect of any success in design of this kind, never so well laid, that I am not sorry my ill health gives me so just a reason to desire to be eased of the employment I am in.'[44]

For Molyneux, Locke's response was inadequate. In his pamphlet *The Case of Ireland's Being Bound by Acts of Parliament in England Stated* (1698), Molyneux held that Ireland had a right to develop its commerce in the same manner as any other state. The solution to Ireland's troubles lay not, however, in legislation for trade passed by England, but rather in the establishment of legislative independence for Ireland.[45] This would ensure that a domestic trade policy could be developed in the interests of Ireland, something that became much more problematic in the period 1779–83. Molyneux justified his argument with reference to the history of the English and Irish parliaments, and the authority of 'the civilians', Grotius, Pufendorf and Locke. He declared that his cause 'is the cause of the whole race of Adam that I argue: liberty seems the inherent right of all mankind'.[46] Ireland after the Glorious Revolution needed to be seen as a separate society from the English, with distinct privileges, although with a shared monarch dedicated to the rights and liberties of his subjects everywhere.[47] This was why *The Case of Ireland* was confidently dedicated to William III. Molyneux's position attracted support.[48] England would gain, it was argued, if Ireland was treated not as a colony for trade, altogether dependent upon the mother country, but rather as a colony for empire. The distinction was explained by the Irish judge Richard Cox, in 1698:

> I would distinguish between Colonies for Trade, and Colonies for Empire. The first is when a small number of your people are sent forth to plant commodities which your native country does not produce, as in the West-Indies, or else when they are sent to negotiate a trade with the natives, and build forts for their security, as in Africa and the East

> Indies. In both these cases it hath been usual to restrain their whole trade to their mother kingdom; for there can be no other reason for their establishment, and their number being small, they will have sufficient encouragement for all their charge, industry, and hazard.

Colonies for empire, by contrast, were 'planted to keep great countries in subjection, and prevent the charge and hazard of constant standing armies'. Colonies for empire, Cox declared, 'have always received the utmost encouragement, much less been restrained from making the best advantage of their natural product, and having their whole trade restrained to their mother-kingdom'. Encouragement of the trade of colonies for empire, such as Ireland, was necessary to strengthen imperial bonds and raise wealth for all.[49] The goal was shared with Petty, that the Irish would be turned into patriots and merchants. The difference was that Petty, against Molyneux and his acolytes, could never conceive of such cultural transmutation without formal union between England and Ireland.

IV

Molyneux's pamphlet was condemned unanimously by the English House of Commons as being 'of dangerous consequence'.[50] A campaign of refutation was initiated. From one side the argument was launched against Molyneux that the English parliament was supreme. As one observer put it, 'the authority of England is wove[n] into the very constitution, and the Parliaments of Ireland own that authority by their very sitting and enacting'.[51] For the Bristol merchant John Cary, it was acceptable for assemblies in the plantations to make private law, but these 'ought still to be in submission to the superior power of the Parliament of England'.[52] From another angle, Molyneux's view of the trade of Ireland was rejected. All of those who refuted Molyneux accepted that Irish economic development could only take place once England's trade was secure.[53] England's trade, both foreign and domestic, was seen by many to be in a dire condition between the mid-1690s and the early 1700s. In the case of the plantation of colonies, the particular danger was that England would 'split upon the same rock Spain hath done' by moving people and resources to the colonies at the expense of the mother country:

> Spain is a lively instance and proof of this, who from the greatest monarchy in Europe, is declined to what it now is, and who have commenced their declension gradually from the time they dispeopled Spain to plant in the West-Indies; and the treasure of the Indies which they

> have in their power, and fetch yearly to Spain, not being able to recompense the loss of their people; and this instance may serve to confirm the truth of a position that is already agreed on by all, as far as I know at least, as unobjectionable. *That all kingdoms or governments are strong or weak, rich or poor, according to the plenty or paucity of the people of that government.*[54]

A chorus of voices, demanding restrictions upon trade in the 1690s, focused on the danger of foreign trade, 'because we draw from thence nothing of solid use, materials to support luxury, perishable commodities, and send thither gold and silver, which is there buried and never returns'.[55] Again, John Cary's view was clearly asserted. The 'gentry of England' had to be made 'more in love with our own manufactures, and to encourage the wearing of them by their examples, and not of choice to give employment to the poor of another nation whilst ours starve at home'.[56] Irish trade had been 'injurious' and 'destructive' to that of England, risking the movement of people towards Ireland and the loss of English wealth. Given these facts, in defining the 'true interest' of Ireland, it became evident that 'husbandry, trade and manufactures stand diametrically opposite thereto'.[57] Ireland needed to remain an agricultural nation, with trade geared to meeting domestic needs alone.

Even those who were sympathetic to Ireland's predicament moved away from Petty's optimistic view of union, towards a starker acceptance that security trumped trade. Ireland was England's point of vulnerability. If England was weakened, Ireland would become more of a threat. France was always looking to invade, either directly through Ireland, or in the aftermath of a rebellion in Ireland that tied up English troops and ships. If England faced crisis and civil war once again, Ireland might well be the cause of England's demise as a state: 'It might be remembered, that twice or thrice in forty years, there hath been revolutions, in which Ireland might have been fatal to England, had they taken the wrong side.'[58] Alternatively, if Irish trade was allowed to develop at the expense of that of England, the decline in England's wealth would once more operate as an invitation to the French to take military action.[59] In 1699 an act was passed forbidding Irish export of wool.[60] Queen Anne, from 1702, rejected calls for a closer union between England and Ireland, such as were being heard anew from the Irish MP Robert Molesworth, formerly William of Orange's ambassador to Denmark. Molesworth had provided an influential account of a disordered state descending into tyranny in his *An account of Denmark as it was in the year 1692* (1694).

Molesworth and other worried Whig commonwealthmen, including his fellow member of the Irish parliament Henry Maxwell, were concerned not only with Ireland's trade, but with the possibility of enemies of liberty in England restoring absolutism by erecting a standing army staffed with Irish troops. As Maxwell put it, 'The constitution of free monarchies is such as cannot bear a constant standing force, which will sometime destroy it.' Subjecting Ireland was to 'make a present of our liberty to our future kings, as France, Spain and other sometime free monarchies have formerly done'. It was far better to develop Ireland economically, because 'with their poverty their resentment and despair will increase, and their poverty will make them fit instruments of slavery, to be made use of by succeeding kings'.[61]

Despite such voices, it was deemed too risky at the beginning of the eighteenth century for England to foster trade in Ireland, either by legislation freeing trade or by political union. In an ideal world devoid of war, such a policy might be conceivable. France, as always, was the problem. If England and Ireland were distinguished by their 'aptness for trade', the danger 'is from the French; and in truth no nation in the world can so well contest [trade] with England as they can'.[62] France was threatening to become a 'universal monarchy':[63] it was described as the 'common enemy of mankind' and 'hereditary enemy', devoted to the destruction of England, 'the bulwark of the Protestant religion and the only people who are capable of resisting [French] designs of universal monarchy'.[64] More particularly, in 1702 it was widely reported that by Louis XIV's 'seizure of the Spanish succession', the French king was closer 'towards the universal monarchy, than ever any other prince did since the days of Julius Caesar'.[65] England was 'struggling against the greatest foreign tyrant that ever assumed the Christian name'.[66] The jurist John Summers put it thus:

> Things are brought to the highest crisis that was ever seen in Europe. France plainly designs the Universal Monarchy. Tis war only that can determine whether she shall have it or no. If she prevail, our fate is manifest; we must come under the dominion of French Popery and tyranny.[67]

It was everywhere acknowledged that trade policy was a crucial element of the war. As one pamphlet had it, Louis XIV was scheming to use the wealth of the Spanish empire, 'the West-India bullion and mines' to achieve 'his idol of universal monarchy'. Such wealth was far more valuable than 'the dominions of Spain in Europe'. In consequence, it was vital 'to cut off the sinews of war' and 'oblige him to drop his sword', through a trade policy of closing the Spanish ports abroad.[68]

At the same time, there was a more general sense of impending doom and of economic decline across England. In the words of one anonymous pamphlet, the 'case of a nation' was 'like that of a private man', whose prudence and good husbandry would produce wealth, or whose extravagance would 'ruin his estate and beggar his family'. In the case of competition from foreign products, which destroyed English markets, it was self-ruin to allow it, 'when this trade drains away vast quantities of our treasure, and takes away the employment of our poor'. The advocates of free trade, the 'free trading merchants', had to accept that the Dutch, French, Venetians, Swedes, Danes and 'indeed all other trading nations, have made and do make restraining laws as the emergencies of their affairs require'.[69] England itself, through constant war and domestic upheaval over the previous sixty years, was 'exhausted, with long, and sharp wars, the debts of the nation are yet unpaid, our late mismanagements not rectified, and the criminals escape yet unpunished'. Old maxims, it was said, were useless, because the 'greatest part of Europe bows under [France]'.[70]

In such circumstances, the effects of alterations in the trading capacity of Ireland had to be assessed with the effects in mind for the relationship between France and England. It was perceived to be madness for the English to consider Ireland as anything other than 'one of our plantations', and entirely subservient to the interests of the mother country. Additional care was necessary because of the identity between French and Irish Catholics, and the perceived fact that 'Ireland can never be safe while the Irish overbalance the English' in population.[71] The politician and economic pamphleteer Charles Davenant characteristically summarised the controversy in an essay of 1699. Davenant accepted that Molyneux's view had merit. He concluded, however, that Molyneux's policy could not be contemplated in times of crisis and war. In particular, the parallel Molyneux drew between Ireland and Scotland was for Davenant entirely false:

> Ireland should judge of what is best for itself, this is just and fair; but in determinations that are to reach the whole, as namely what is most expedient for England and Ireland both, there, without all doubt, the supreme judgment ought to rest in the King, Lords, and Commons of England, by whose arms and treasure Ireland ever was, and must always be defended. Nor is this any claiming the same empire over Scotland, as Mr. Molyneux would suggest, for there is no parity of reason in the cases: Scotland to England (as Aragon to Spain) is a distinct

> state, governing itself by different laws, though under the same Prince, and is truly but a kingdom confederated with the realm of England, though subject to our King. The land thereof was not acquired to the present inhabitants by the arms of England . . . this puts them not in the degree of subordination we are treating of. They are not our descendants, and they are but politically our brethren; whereas the English-Irish, who are now chief lords of that soil, are naturally our offspring. Their inferior rule and jurisdictions are not disputed, but that supereminent dominion and supreme and uncontrollable regiment over themselves, which they pretend to, is neither safe for England to grant, nor for them to ask.[72]

Davenant was certain that William Petty and other political arithmeticians had proved that life was approximately a third cheaper in Ireland than in England. This meant that in the price of a product manufactured in Ireland, such as a wool garment, which was also produced in England, would be one third lower. Davenant held that if Irish woollens entered England, rents in England would fall and land prices would follow. The number of the poor would then increase and overall, 'the rivalship in trade of another country, would throw us into more disorders, than the most knowing man in England can readily describe'.[73] The only solution was to prevent Ireland from establishing woollen manufactures:

> No wise state, if it has the means of preventing the mischief, will leave its ruin in the power of another country. And if wars have been thought not only prudent, but just, which have been made to interrupt the too sudden growth of any neighbour nation, much more justifiable [*sic*] may a mother kingdom exercise the civil authority in relation to her own children; who from her had their being, and still have their protection, especially when her own safety is so much concerned. Nor can this be thought rigour; it is but a reasonable jealousy of state, and only severe wisdom, which governments should shew in all their councils; it is a preventing remedy which operates gently in the beginning of the disease, before there are many, and those inveterate humours to contend with. And if a timely stop be put to these exportations from Ireland, it will hurt but a very few, (which is never to be regarded, where the good of the whole public is in question) and even that few, without any great difficulty, may have their industry turned to safer objects.[74]

Davenant concluded that even the manufacture of linens ought to be forbidden in Ireland, because if they were supplied to the English, the

English would purchase fewer of such products from the very European powers who purchased English woollens. The only acceptable trade in Ireland was cattle, because the price of beef in England would be lowered, with positive effects upon population and costs.

A later historian, John Dalrymple, wrote that after Molyneux published his book, members of the English House of Commons vociferously complained about the effects of Irish production upon the English woollen industry: 'The jealousy of empire mingling itself with the jealousy of trade, the Commons presented two addresses to the King, one against the book of Mr Molineux, and the other for increasing the linen, but discouraging the woollen manufacture of Ireland.' The weak response of the Irish parliament created deep divisions between Ireland and England. From France, according to Dalrymple, it was reported that the 'intolerant' English treated the Irish and the Scots 'like slaves'.[75] Over the following decades, Ireland remained entirely dependent upon London, and the practice of considering the interests of England before Ireland's, whether in economics or in politics, was upheld.

V

The predicament of Ireland in the eighteenth century cannot be understood without reference to Scotland, described regularly in the later 1690s as a fellow victim of the English. At the time when English and Irish observers were debating sovereignty and trade, Scotland was seeking economic development through the creation of a national bank (1695), and a Company of Scotland Trading to Africa and the Indies (1696). The latter, inspired by William Paterson, engaged in the Darien adventure, the attempt to create a colony, New Caledonia, on the isthmus of Panama, with the ultimate aim of a land route linking the Pacific and Atlantic oceans. Paterson couched his proposal in cosmopolitan terms, promising a defence of the natives and the opening up of trade for the betterment of humanity. At the same time, it was evident that the country in control of the isthmus would be a great commercial empire, without having to undertake the normal route to empire through bloody war:

> Thus these doors of the seas and the keys of the universe would of course be capable of enabling their possessors to give laws to both oceans, and to become the arbitrators of the commercial world, without being liable to the fatigues, expenses, and dangers, or of contracting such guilt and blood, as Alexander and Caesar; since, as in theirs and

> all other empires that have been anything universal, the conquerors have at least been obliged to seek out their conquests from far; so the force and universal influence of those attractive magnets are such as can much more effectually bring empire home to their proprietors' doors.[76]

Five ships with twelve hundred settlers sailed in July 1698, reaching the isthmus early in November. Before the first ship sailed, doubts were expressed. Across Scotland opposition to the scheme had been voiced, often in the form of a more general attack upon the commercialisation of society. One observer in 1696 questioned whether 'the world might not have been happier by its continuance of confinement', avoiding the 'mercantile commerce' which 'has excited our lusts as well as fed them, and given provocation to vice'. Trade had, however, altered the world, being 'a nice a coy mistress, which you must not only industriously court to get possessed of, but sedulously pursue and tenderly cherish if you would preserve and secure it'.[77] Even war had been transformed, becoming dependent on wealth rather than upon valour:

> And the nature of war, being changed from what it was, when courage and bravery often decided a quarrel between states and kingdoms in a day, and seldom missed putting an end to a war, either by victory or accommodation, within the circle of one campaign; the success of it now is come to depend upon the largest purse, and not the bravest troops; and those who have most money, though not always the valuantest [*sic*: bravest] men, will have the better in the war, though they may sometimes have the worst in a battle: so that no poor nation can in the way that war is now managed, carry an offensive war against a wealthy.[78]

Trade was risky, inconstant, and tended to be dominated by the rich states, such as England, which had an interest in keeping states like Scotland 'weak and poor, and thereupon contemptible'.[79]

Against such arguments, it was stated that if a nation avoided trade it would always be weak and impoverished, since 'traffic is the spring and fountain of wealth, and . . . nations increase in riches in proportion to the kind and degrees of their manufacture, and the quality and extent of their commerce'.[80] The Darien project made sense, in consequence, as a means of increasing Scottish strength and riches. Indeed, the argument was made that Scotland would be left behind as a state, both impoverished and incapable of self-defence, if trading companies were not established:

> The world is now grown so prodigal, as that every country doth make use of foreign commodities, and these brought from all the corners of the earth; and dear or cheap have them they must, so it's the interest of every nation to purchase them at the easiest rates, and that must be by bringing them from their first ports directly home . . . The only way left unto us to better our condition, is for our nation and all ranks in it vigourously to ply trade, to exercise the same, and that companies at home, and plantations abroad, whereby we will be rendered more rich, and so better able to live like our neighbours of any about us. We may assure ourselves, if we grow not richer than we are, and do not more strenuously mind trade, we will grow in being condemned by all our neighbours, and it will not be in our princes power to hinder us to be trampled on at every turn.[81]

The English response to the possible establishment of a Scottish company was characterised by paranoid fear, with demands for severe penalties for investors.[82] The view was widespread that the Scots would 'undersell the English, and consequently draw the foreign trade from thence'.[83] One pamphlet, probably from 1696, concerned with the effects upon English sugar production, stated that the act creating the company had to be prevented, because 'already the Scotch are seeking to bribe and entice away our master-workmen, and had actually hired one, to whom the master was forced to advance his wages 10l. per annum to keep him'.[84] A different response was to suggest turning England into a free port, undercutting thereby the prices of Scottish exports and those of competing European states, because 'a free trade, for exportation of all manner of goods, will in few years make England the mart of Europe; and then shall land rise incredibly in its value, houses in their rents, the King grow glorious in the multitude of his people, and the merchants be able to keep pace, if not outdo our neighbours in trade'. In addition, free trade would 'bring the Jews and strangers out of the Netherlands, with their wealth and riches, and in a few years fill this nation with abundance of treasure'.[85]

In practice, the English took steps to prevent the Scottish company from raising funds. The settlers who arrived at Darien in 1698, and again in a second attempt in 1699, were beset by disaster, from disease and the lack of fresh water to the failure of crops, trade and defence. The Spanish, who claimed the land, laid siege to Port St Andrew in 1700, and the colony collapsed. The English gave no help to the settlers when they faced the wrath of Spain. After the project failed, on one side it was said that Paterson had always been a 'pedlar, tub-preacher, and at last whimsical projector'.[86] Another view held that the English were responsible, having prevented subscription, allowed their own East India Company to interfere, refused to trade with Darien and then rejected a relief effort 'which common humanity, and much more Christianity, obliges them to do to a Turk or a Jew in the like circumstances'.[87] Passions ran high, with accusations that jealousy and envy had motivated the English to 'invade the independency and sovereignty' of Scotland, reduce Scotland to a province and prevent the rightful exercise of liberties in trade.[88]

Lowland Scotland suffered terribly from the vast expenditure wasted in the Darien adventure, which led to a shortage of coin, and dreadful harvests after 1695 followed. In 1700 it was stated that 'trade and industry languish', a 'universal poverty' prevailed and 'our people wanting work and bread at home, are scattered over the world, and the nation is greatly dispersed'. Fighting for survival, merchants had become wolves, 'preying upon one another, or upon the nation in general, by importing such goods as are not only improfitable, but pernicious, and exporting of these subjects of manufactures and industry [which] . . . might make the nation populous and rich'.[89] In such circumstances, calls were made for a different relationship between England and Scotland. One pamphlet of 1700 was especially direct. The existing relationship 'of two distinct kingdoms under one sovereign' had proved to be 'oft times hurtful, especially to the weakest'. The solution was 'union of the two kingdoms, either entirely, or at least as to mutual trade amongst themselves'.[90] Since 'nothing can make us rich but trade', union was a logical step, because of England's vast market and demand for Scottish products such as linen and cattle.[91]

More sceptical voices demanded a turn away from foreign commerce, especially the export of wool, which was blamed for 'the starving of so many thousands during the late dearth, who died for want of food, and wanted food for want of work, and wanted work for want of wool'. In addition to the promotion of domestic consumption, measures were advised including 'a solid well digested sumptuary law, [to] prohibit the wearing, eating or drinking of these things which foster vanity and luxury'.[92] Closeness to England would also ensure that Scotland 'vanish in the crown of Great Britain'.[93] What was termed an 'incorporating union' was associated with 'extraordinary depopulation . . . desertion and desolation'.[94] For George Ridpath, an opponent of union, English policy was governed by 'a few clamorous selfish merchants and tradesmen, whose avarice the whole riches of the world is not able to satisfy'.[95] Andrew Fletcher of Saltoun had been involved with Paterson's Darien scheme, but was afterwards active in the Scottish parliament against union.[96] Fletcher was certain that if union with England occurred, Scotland would likely follow Wales in remaining 'poor, remote and barren', despite natural advantages, because trade tended to follow politics, moving centrifugally towards the seat of an empire.[97] Since trade was now sought by every nation, morality and justice were set aside. Reason of state dominated the politics of economic decision making at national levels. This was why the Scots ought to be pessimistic about union and more generally in their relations with England. Fletcher made this point in a remarkable reconstruction of a conversation between the parties, his *An Account of a Conversation concerning a right Regulation of Governments for the Common Good of Mankind*:

> I desired him to consider that Wales, the only country that ever had united with England, lying at a less distance from London, and consequently more commodiously to participate in the circulation of a great trade than we do, after three or four hundred years, is still the only place of that kingdom, which has no considerable commerce, though possessed of one of the best ports in the whole island; a sufficient demonstration that trade is not a necessary consequence of a union with England. I added, that trade is now become the golden ball, for which all nations of the world are contending, and the occasion of so great partialities, that not only every nation is endeavouring to possess the trade of the whole world, but every city to draw all to itself; and that the English are no less guilty of these partialities than any other trading nation.[98]

In Fletcher's scenario, a neutered Scotland would only be able to make its voice heard through rebellion and war against England. The dreadful fact was that wars 'are become universal, are now wholly managed by the force and power of money, and by that means most grievously oppress and afflict not only the places that are the theatres of action, but even the remotest village and most solitary cottage'.[99]

Fletcher's voice was overwhelmed by the ongoing Scottish crisis. By 1706, it was clear that 'no money or things of value can be purchased in the course of commerce, but where there is force to protect it'. Scotland, being 'without force to protect its commerce', needed 'the trade and protection of some powerful neighbour nation'. In short, union was the only hope for securing an extensive trade into the future.[100] As George Mackenzie, 1st Earl of Cromartie put it, division had always invited invasion in British history, since the time of the Romans; through union 'France will lose its best ally against England', and Scotland and England would become richer and stronger.[101] For Mackenzie, Scotland had been impoverished since the union of the crowns with regard to trade: 'there is no nation so much hurt in trade by England, as is Scotland; because we are under their head, but not of their politick body'.[102] Although economic historians have challenged such readings, emphasising especially the extent of English bribery and blackmail in the process of union, contemporaries recognised the extent to which Scottish prospects were parlous. Exchequer revenue in particular was insufficient to cover the basic functions of the state.[103] The Alien Act of 1705, passed by an English parliament in disagreement with that of Scotland about the Hanoverian succession, embargoed Scottish imports into England, including cattle, linen and coal; this threatened to devastate a Scotland which had experienced a run on the national bank in 1704. When the Union was agreed in 1707, after intensive debate about levels of taxation upon staples such as salt, the fourth article declared 'full freedom and intercourse of trade and navigation'. David Hume later underlined the worry on both sides of the border, drawing on Jean-Baptiste Dubos's *Les intérêts de L'Angleterre mal-entendus dans la guerre présente* (1704):

> Since the union has removed the barriers between Scotland and England, which of these nations gains from the other by this free commerce? Or if the former kingdom has received any increase of riches, can it reasonably be accounted for by anything but the increase of its art and industry? It was a common apprehension in England, before the union, as we learn from l'Abbé Dubos, that Scotland would soon drain them of their treasure, were an open trade allowed; and on the other side [of] the Tweed a contrary apprehension prevailed: With what justice in both, time has shown.[104]

Hume recognised and refuted the fundamental fear that the low price of labour in poor Scotland would undermine English trade, and lead to a flow of money and labour to the north. As he later wrote to his friend Henry Home, Lord Kames, who was acting as an intermediary between Hume and the Anglican political economist Josiah Tucker, the latter was right in emphasising the continued superiority of English manufactures despite competition from poorer countries:

> All the advantages which the author insists upon as belonging to a nation of extensive commerce, are undoubtedly real: great capital, extensive correspondence, skilful expedients of facilitating labour, dexterity, industry, &c., these circumstances give them an indisputed superiority over poor nations, who are ignorant and unexperienced.[105]

The economic effects of the Union up to 1740 have regularly been questioned in recent decades; but after that date, the linen, coal and tobacco trades soared, by which time too the Scottish universities were being praised as the best in Europe.[106] The point for contemporaries, however, was that although forced to adjust to English trading patterns, Scotland gained national security and financial stability, if at the price of political independence. As the agronomist James Anderson later put it, the Union marked an 'auspicious era', when 'the constitution of this country was secured upon the broad and stable base of universal liberty; when the laws became binding to the king upon the throne, and accessible to the beggar on the dunghill'. Property had been secured by the Union, he wrote, and (citing Micah 4:4) 'every man could sit under the shade of his own fig-tree, and eat the fruit of his own vine'.[107] Whether Scotland's economy had been transformed by union with England became a staple of Scottish and Irish debate. The controversy focused on whether rich countries maintained a perpetual advantage over poor countries, or whether, as Hume put it, 'we in Scotland possess also some advantages, which may enable us to share with them in wealth and industry'.[108]

VI

The debates of the 1690s and after made clear that reason-of-state arguments in politics were now dominant in the economic realm. States were competing with one another for markets, and it was irrational to allow rivals to take a portion of national wealth by giving them direct access to domestic markets. As one pamphleteer put it, commerce had become a field of conflict, and war was always to be anticipated: 'Does not every child know that riches beget pride, and that causes war?'[109] Robert Molesworth, in a preface to François Hotman's *Franco-Gallia* originally composed in 1705, lamented that having 'the example of those masters of the world, the Romans, before our eyes' had not led to the union of England, Scotland and Ireland. The Roman example and the example of England and Wales underlined the fact that, as Molesworth put it, 'both sides would incredibly gain by it [union], yet the rich and opulent country, to which such an addition is made, would be the greater gainer'.[110] In the aftermath of the Anglo-Scottish Union, arguments that the Scots had gained unfairly at Ireland's expense could easily be found. Jonathan Swift asked, 'Who ever yet a union saw / Of kingdoms without faith or law?' The result was anticipated as being 'Divided hearts, united states', and the loss of any sense of a common good. Swift predicted that 'tossing faction will o'erwhelm / Our crazy double-bottom'd realm'.[111] He described Scotland as 'poor and beggarly, and [getting] a sorry maintenance by pilfering wherever she goes'. Ireland, by contrast, had been ruined by the inconstancy of England.[112] Swift's verdict, that the recent history of Ireland was altogether tragic, was echoed throughout the eighteenth century. As he wrote to a friend, 'I reckon no man is thoroughly miserable unless he be condemned to live in Ireland.'[113]

The issue of England's crushing of Irish economic prospects was also prominent. The Declaratory Act of 1719 confirmed the right of the British parliament to pass legislation for Ireland. An attempt to create a national bank in Ireland was rejected by the parliament in Dublin in 1721, with accusations being levelled that it was a threat to liberty and land, being associated with luxury and the dominion of the moneyed interest.[114] Claims that the trade of Ireland was in decline became commonplace in commentaries, normally tracing the cause to the 'unnatural' effects of the laws imposed by England. Swift's voice again was prominent. Ireland illustrated the consequence of English corruption, and was taken up in the upsurge of Tory Country party and Commonwealth rhetoric in the 1720s and 1730s, especially directed against Robert Walpole and royal patronage.[115] Swift's pamphlet of 1720, *A Proposal for the Universal Use of Irish Manufacture*, 'to persuade the wretched people to wear their own Manufactures instead of those from England', was immediately prosecuted and condemned as a Jacobite tract. Such a response confirmed in Swift a feeling of 'how ill a taste for wit and sense prevails in the world, which politics and South-sea, and party, and opera's and masquerades have introduced'.[116] When William Wood, in 1722, was given permission to introduce a copper halfpenny coin into Ireland, purchasing the privilege from one of George I's mistresses, Swift, in his *Drapier's Letters*, ridiculed the debasement of the coinage as a product of English arrogance and brutality.[117] His *A Short View of the State of Ireland* (1727) then concluded that English prevention of Irish commerce meant that '[t]he conveniency of ports and havens, which nature hath bestowed so liberally on this kingdom, is of no more use to us, than a beautiful prospect to a man shut up in a dungeon'.[118] David Bindon, who had sided with Swift in the Wood's Hibernia halfpenny affair, wrote in 1729 that 'universal poverty . . . reigns among the common people of Ireland, and the numbers that daily quit the country, are such strong presages of yet greater calamities'[119] In 1733, Britain took yet another step to limit Irish trade, when the Molasses Act prohibited the import of sugar and derived products from the colonies. One of the effects of poverty was seen to be a general dishonesty among the population. Swift himself claimed to have abundant evidence of the effects of the crushing of trade in the corruption of national manners. This allowed him to express the paradox that Ireland, with natural resources to be among the richest countries in Europe, was actually the poorest:

> For, as to shopkeepers, I cannot deny that I have found some few honest men among them, taking the word honest in the largest and most charitable sense. But as to handicraftsmen, although I shall endeavour to believe it possible to find a fair dealer among their clans, yet I confess it has never been once my good fortune to employ one single workman, who did not cheat me at all times to the utmost of his power in the materials, the work, and the price. One universal maxim I have constantly observed among them, that they would rather gain a shilling by cheating you, than [gain] twenty in the honest way of dealing, although they were sure to lose your custom, as well as that of others, whom you might probably recommend to them. This, I must own, is the natural consequence of poverty and oppression. These wretched people catch at anything to save them a minute longer from drowning. Thus Ireland is the poorest of all civilized countries in Europe, with every natural advantage to make it one of the richest.[120]

In the midst of the jeremiad chorus, a counter-argument began to be formulated. Ireland's economic development was identified as a means of preventing the decline of English trade. History showed that commerce was a fickle mistress, and that commercial states always declined. As the indefatigable publicist John Browne put it,

> The Balance of Trade is as variable as the Balance of Power, and has as often shifted sides: there have been as many universal empires (if I may so call them) established upon the ocean as upon the land; but like those they have fallen to decay, and given place to others; for as industry begets trade and wealth, so whenever the minds of a people are unbent by excessive riches into indolence and luxury, and the price of their labour and navigation is thereby rendered dearer than that of their neighbours, they soon see their grandeur moulder away, and their slow acquired riches, depart with hasty strides to their rising successors.[121]

Ireland became attractive in such circumstances, because the opportunities for trade it presented, due to its natural resources and cheap labour, meant that developing Ireland could delay English decline. Irish wealth would naturally pass to England or allow English merchants to generate profits, in conditions where their own capacity for commerce was domestically limited because of the rise of labour costs and the accompanying spread of luxury:

> The Crown of England has annexed to it many dependencies, where labour is cheaper, the people hardier, easier to feed, and freer from taxes, than any of our neighbours, these like so many sponges (if I may be allowed the comparison) must be employed to suck up treasures from the ocean, in order to squeeze them out again into the grand receptacle of all the riches of her dependencies, Great Britain. These must, I saw, be employed to manage those branches of trade which we, by reason of an immense wealth, an increasing luxury, and an overbearing debt, are at present under a necessity to let strangers run away with.[122]

What Browne was suggesting was the opposite of the remedy for excessive luxury and commerce associated with the most popular book of the eighteenth century in western Europe, Fénelon's *Télémaque, fils d'Ulysse* (1699). *Télémaque* continued the fourth book of Homer's *Odyssey* by describing Telemachus's search for his father in the company of his tutor, Mentor. Fénelon outlined in his book a strategy to deal with states where luxury and war were rampant, through the imaginary example of Salentum. Salentum was easily identifiable as France at the end of the seventeenth century, suffering from the effects of Louis XIV's strategy for universal monarchy through empire, underpinned by state-supported trade promoted by his minister of finance between 1665 and 1683, Jean-Baptiste Colbert. Colbert's legacy, according to Fénelon, was a society founded on vanity, with domestic war between social groups lusting to satisfy fake needs, and international war to fill the coffers of a state in jeopardy because of the decline of neglected agriculture. Salentum experienced Fénelon's imagined solution for France, the abolition of luxury through the introduction of a sumptuary law and the forced movement of workers from the towns into the countryside, the latter by means of an agrarian law giving them land to farm. International trade in luxury goods was not abolished. It was, however, conducted in an isolated port city. Such drastic and draconian measures were necessary, according to Fénelon, in order to combat the attractiveness of neo-Colbertism, asserting that luxury supported 'the poor at the expense of the rich' and led to 'good taste, the perfection of the arts, and the politeness of a nation'.[123] Fénelon's grand claim was that such greatness and wealth would always be short-lived.

He believed that the transmission mechanism to poverty was likely to be war, but the gradual decline of competitiveness was identified as another. As the Irish banker Richard Cantillon put it in his *Essay on the Nature of Trade*, 'When a state has arrived at the highest point of wealth . . . it will inevitably fall into poverty by the ordinary course of things. The too great abundance of money, which so long as it lasts forms the power of states, throws them back imperceptibly but naturally into poverty . . . [because] the abundance of money raises the price of land and labour.'[124]

Browne's plan for Ireland was different. England, as a free monarchy where luxury had been allowed to grow, had to be left to decline. The ultimate collapse of the state could be delayed, however, by taking action to develop the trade of the areas of the kingdom or empire yet to experience commerce and luxury. Browne was followed by writers including Thomas Prior, Arthur Dobbs MP, George Berkeley and Samuel Madden. These men were members of the Dublin Society 'for improving husbandry, agriculture and other useful arts', founded in June 1731 at a meeting in Trinity College Dublin, who published a number of books and pamphlets dedicated to Irish economic improvement.[125] The pamphlets included demands by John Browne for public granaries, in order to address the ongoing dearth and perpetual risk of famine.[126] Arthur Dobbs advocated union between England and Ireland.[127]

Such arguments were too strong for many English neo-Colbertists. Bernard Mandeville, a Dutch physician living in London, had published in pamphlet form the poem *The Grumbling Hive, or Knaves Turn'd Honest* in 1705, turned it into a book in 1714, adding 'An inquiry into the original of moral virtue' and additional 'remarks', and again revised the book in 1723, making the title *The Fable of the Bees; or, Private Vices, Public Benefits*. Mandeville's *Fable* was influential, and in Ireland drew a vitriolic response from George Berkeley in his *Alciphron, or the Minute Philosopher* (1732). Mandeville held that 'bare virtue can't make nations live in splendour'. He ridiculed claims that luxury would lead to 'avarice and rapine', the corrupt sale of public offices and the loss of notions of the public good, and that it 'effeminates and enervates the people, by which the nations become an easy prey to the first invaders'. Governments ought instead to use pride and other negative passions to generate commerce. To this end, Mandeville advocated restrictions on competing trade from other states in addition to domestic bounties, in order to ensure that national commerce was protected. The national interest narrowly defined should always guide politicians:

> Every government ought to be thoroughly acquainted with, and steadfastly to pursue the interest of the country. Good politicians by dextrous management, laying heavy impositions on some goods, or totally prohibiting them, and lowering the duties on others, may always turn and divert the course of trade which way they please . . . But above all, they'll keep a watchful eye over the balance of trade in general, and never suffer that all the foreign commodities together, that are imported in one year, shall exceed in value what of their own growth or manufacture is in the same exported to others.[128]

Mandeville's assessment of national policy was embraced by numerous writers, and especially the legions of commentators who believed that England's commerce was either in decline, or soon likely to be in danger of collapse. Justifications for maintaining the restrictions upon Irish trade were acknowledged in consequence. If Irish industries began to grow, for example by allowing the export of wool, they would directly threaten 'the grand wheel of England's great machine of trade, that gives motion to every other branch': that is, wool exports.[129] The merchant Joshua Gee was one of the likely contributors to the popular twice-weekly journal *The British Merchant; or Commerce preserv'd: In Answer to The Mercator, or Commerce Retriev'd* in 1713–14, which employed John Cary's arguments in favour of the protection of English industries by preventing cheap foreign imports. Gee became famous for making the same claims in his *The Trade and Navigation of Great-Britain* (1729), which went through a number of editions over the following decades. For Gee, Colbert's example was crucial in the formulation of English policy. As he put it, '[T]he examples of Louis the Fourteenth so far opened the eyes of the princes of Europe, that most of them have put the same methods in practice, and the Emperor of Germany, Czar of Muscovy, and several other princes, see the way to make themselves more considerable, is to establish manufactures where their respective dominions produce materials for carrying them on.'[130]

Over the following decades counter-arguments in favour of removing restrictions upon Irish trade, on the grounds of anticipated benefits for the English economy, were equally commonplace.[131] The merchant Matthew Decker, writing in the 1740s, stated that 'the symptoms of our decay, the difficulties and discouragements our trade at present labours under' could be addressed if politicians 'abolish our monopolies, unite Ireland, and put all the subjects in these three kingdoms on the same footing in trade'. For Decker, 'the richer Ireland grows, the richer Britain must become'.[132] Equally, the Anglican clergyman Josiah Tucker advocated, in

1749, Anglo-Irish union and free trade across the entire kingdom.[133] At the same time, belief that English trade was in crisis, or that the growth of luxury had corrupted manners and weakened the state, proved the trump card in ensuring that relations with Ireland were not altered. John Brown's enormously successful *Estimate of Manners*, written at the beginning of the Seven Years' War in expectation of defeat, made the point that Britain had declined, and was both militarily and economically weak. The corruption of manners due to the growth of luxury was the cause. As Brown saw it, manners determined national behaviour, shaped laws and were more important than any other factor—a point Machiavelli had failed fully to understand:

> And here the penetrating Machiavel seems to have erred in his determinations on this point. He says, 'As good customs cannot subsist without good laws, so good laws cannot be executed without good Customs.' The latter part of the sentence is a great truth: The former part is a vulgar error. So long as the causes of corrupt manners are absent, good manners preserve themselves without laws, or without bad laws.[134]

All forms of commerce had to be scrutinised and controlled, with a view to preventing further luxury and corruption from further weakening Britain. Another voice questioning the value of commerce was the agriculturalist and translator John Mills, who warned that excessive trade always brought down both culture and empire:

> If a moderate trade preserves a people in the vigour of manhood, too vast a trade hastens on its old age. Cupidity, stimulated by fortunes made in trade, seizes the minds of all. Interest, the only idol of a trading nation, banishes virtue and talents. The desire of gold gives way to the thirst for gold . . . If the spirit and ardour of trade possess the mass of a nation; enlightened knowledge, virtue, and talents disappear. The love of riches and the desire of glory, have been, and will be, always incompatible. Do the annals of the world afford us a single instance of a rich people, plunged in luxury, or wholly intent upon trade, that ever distinguished themselves by their knoweldge or actions? Ancient Persia, the country most famous for its luxury and riches, did not produce one man, whom history has thought worth recording. The opulent city of Tyre contained only traders, and no great men. The Carthaginians were a barbarous, dastardly, cruel and perfidious people, contemners and persecutors of merit. The illustrious among the Alexandrians were all foreigners: their natives, absorbed in trade, knew nothing but

money. One astronomer excepted, the rich Marseilles did not see the name of any of her citizens transmitted to posterity . . . A single nation is an exception to this rule: but that nation owes this advantage to the singularity of its constitution, which mitigates the bad effects of a vast commerce, and which will not mitigate them long . . . too great a commerce diminishes agriculture, depopulates the country, and annihilates by degrees the class of husbandmen.[135]

VII

John Brown was proved wrong about the imminent collapse of Britain during the Seven Years' War. Yet the more general sense of the decline and fall of England, either by bankruptcy, invasion or domestic upheaval, became more dominant still in political argument after the Peace of Paris of 1763. Many in Ireland began in the 1740s either to join with English critics of government and demand reform, or to formulate strategies for Ireland should Britain in fact collapse as a polity. One prominent radical was the Dublin apothecary Charles Lucas, who ceaselessly attacked the board of aldermen who ran the city as a corrupt oligarchy. In 1743, Lucas's *A Remonstrance against Certain Infringements on the Rights and Liberties of the Commons and Citizens of Dublin* demanded the election of municipal officers by popular vote rather than back-room cabal.[136] For Lucas, the Irish were becoming slaves, and needed to look to history to inspire them to defend their liberty:

> [Let us] look around, and see all parts of the world utterly ruined and undone, wheresoever they have lost their liberty. Egypt, Greece, and Rome, in ancient history, best shew the difference between a state of Liberty and Slavery; Germany, Spain and France, in modern. The former, from whom, during their liberty, the rest of the world drew literature, arts, morals and policy, are now reduced to such a wretched state of slavery, and its attendants, ignorance and barbarism, as to be a scandal and reproach to human nature; and the latter, Spain and France, especially, who were not long since as free as we can boast, though they, with the recent Romans, still retain the title of Christians, are, notwithstanding, opprobrious to that divine appellation, nay even to human nature, having all the most horrible characteristics and badges of slavery; their lives and properties dependent on the lust or absolute will of the reigning tyrant, and their souls at the disposal of mercenary monks and priests.[137]

While attempting to gain election to parliament himself at the end of the 1740s, Lucas revived Molyneux's argument for the legislative independence of Ireland, and attacked the English for their treatment of the country in his *The Censor, or Citizen's Journal*.[138] This resulted in his condemnation by the lord lieutenant and flight to the Isle of Man and the continent, where he took a medical degree at Leiden, before returning in 1761 and obtaining a pardon. He was then elected as MP for Dublin. In the 1760s, he demanded regular elections, a national militia and legislative independence, particularly in the *Freeman's Journal*, published from 1763.[139] The journal was a joint enterprise with the playwright and poet Henry Brooke, a powerful advocate of the relaxation of the penal laws against Catholics. Brooke rested his view on the study of free states, 'the Commonwealths of Asia Minor, the Archipelago, the Grecian Continent, Italy, the Islands of the Mediterranean &c.', being places 'where the rights of nature, under forms of various institution, were asserted by liberty and guarded by law: where the assurance of property gave most reason for content.' Brooke could find in such states 'few instances of any people' who had been as loyal as Ireland's Catholic population.[140]

Tensions were already manifest between the crown and parliament before Lucas launched his assaults. The Irish parliament had traditionally been run by 'undertakers', the English and Scottish Protestant nobles who had received land in Ireland, and who were tied to the English crown by patronage.[141] Yet in 1753, the undertakers rebelled against the lord lieutenant, Lionel Cranfield Sackville, 1st Duke of Dorset, when the Irish House of Commons with its three hundred members rejected a bill granting the payment of surplus revenue towards the British national debt, on the grounds that the wording violated the 'sole and undoubted right' of the Commons to initiate financial legislation, a claim dating back to 1692. Henry Boyle MP led the opposition from his position as chancellor of the exchequer of Ireland; his resulting dismissal led to patriotic resistance among members of parliament, which lasted until 1755. Although Boyle was bought off in 1756, accepting a pension and the title of Earl of Shannon, new voices, joining that of Lucas, began to reassert Irish demands for self-rule and legislative reform.[142]

Henry Flood, the MP for Kilkenny County from 1759 and for Callan from 1761, in a series of parliamentary speeches demanded regular parliaments, a reduced civil list, an Irish militia and legislative independence. The first of these goals was partially achieved in 1768, when an act limited the term of any parliament to eight years. In 1769, Flood was in the vanguard of those who rejected a money bill sent from London, on the grounds that it did not originate in the Irish House of Commons. This led to the parliament being prorogued for fourteen months on command of the lord lieutenant George Townshend, 1st Marquess Townshend.[143] The extent of Irish opinion attacking British oppression of Ireland cannot be understated, and turned Flood into a popular hero. A multitude of prints had as their central motif Hibernia being oppressed and kept down by Britons, and more often than not by British ministers. A characteristic print is the anonymous 'Hibernia in distress' of 1772: this depicted a prostrate Hibernia with her harp broken, while a fund called 'Exchequer' is being plundered by Lord North, and while Sir George Macartney, as Irish chief secretary, has a conversation with Lord Townshend, as lord lieutenant, in which the latter says 'we must keep her down' and Macartney replies 'and exert ourselves [as] she will be too strong for us.' In the background a black man named Mungo demands that Lord North not forget his request for money, underlining the corruption of public funds: the figure of Mungo, derived from the contemporary opera *The Padlock* by Charles Dibdin and Isaac Bickerstaffe, which debuted at Drury Lane in 1768, represented Jeremiah Dyson, a lord of the treasury, whom the Irish-born politician Isaac Barré called 'Mungo' for his excessive servility towards ministers.[144]

In 1771, however, Flood again had a money bill rejected. Townshend was recalled, but the next lord lieutenant, Simon Harcourt, 1st Earl Harcourt blunted Flood's opposition by giving him a seat on the Privy Council. Leadership of the reform movement passed to the lawyer and MP Henry Grattan, who pushed for free trade, meaning that Irish goods be treated like all British products, and legislative independence for Ireland.[145]

The context of Grattan's movement was different. Times had changed in Ireland because of the North American crisis. In 1776, the British government put an embargo on Irish exports in order to secure supplies of provisions to the army and to the navy.[146] This had profound consequences, as the smuggling of goods to America fell away, and a depression in all markets brought demands for state action to relieve the condition of the poor. For the reform movement in Ireland, it was straightforward to relate Ireland's present economic predicament to longstanding English policy, and to call for radical surgery to allow Ireland to benefit from the privileges that came with membership of the British imperial or mercantile system.[147] For Edmund Burke, there was a 'dreadful schism in the British nation', and since 'we are not able to reunite the empire', it was necessary 'to give all possible vigour and soundness to those parts of it which are still content to be governed by our councils'. With regard to Ireland, he counselled 'moderation, prudence and equity', opening up

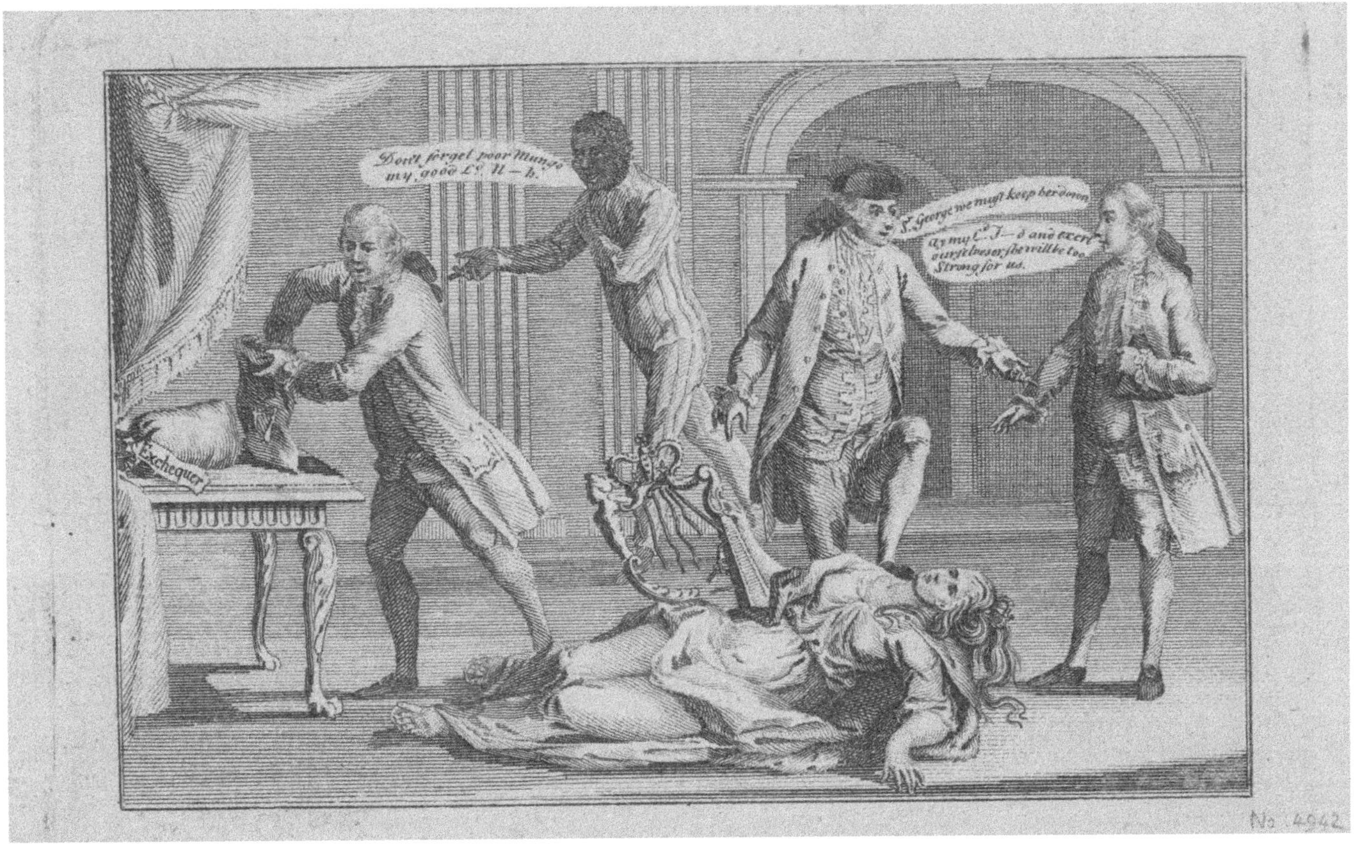

FIGURE 7.1. Anon., 'Hibernia in distress', 1772. British Museum Collection, no. 1855,0609.1934. Copyright © The Trustees of the British Museum

trade in the manner of that between England and Scotland, because Britain faced great dangers abroad, and a thriving Ireland would be of great benefit to all parties.[148] Another analysis of 1779 was typical in reporting that 'the present state of Ireland teems with every circumstance of national poverty'. Prices were falling, markets collapsing and large numbers of people being reduced to beggary 'for want to employment'. Ireland had suffered 'great and frequent distresses' throughout the century, and had now 'relapsed into its ancient state of imbecility', unable to raise revenues even to pay for its own defence. One reason was the reduction in demand for linens because of the loss of American exports during the war. The 'principal cause', however, was stated as being 'the discouragement of the woollen manufactures, by the English act of 1699'. Ireland, as late as 1692, had been flourishing in terms of its trade, 'the most improved and improving spot of ground in Europe', having survived being 'laid waste, and almost depopulated by civil war and religious fury'. The period after the English put an end to woollen exports, 'from the year 1699 to the death of queen Anne, is marked with the strongest circumstances of national distress and despondency'. Famine followed in 1728–29, 1740–41, 1757–59, 1765, 1770–71 and 1778–79, with thousands dying from 'absolute want'.[149] It was a 'melancholy truth' that English laws had damaged Ireland to a greater extent than civil war, with consequences unparalleled in modern history:

> [A] country will sooner recover from the miseries and devastation occasioned by war, invasion, rebellion, massacre, than from laws restraining the commerce, discouraging the manufactures, fettering the industry, and above all breaking the spirits of the people . . . Can the history of any other fruitful country on the globe, enjoying peace for fourscore years, and not visited by plague or pestilence, produce so many recorded instances of the poverty and wretchedness, and of the reiterated want and misery of the lower order of the people? There is no such example in ancient or modern story.[150]

The loss of manufacturing that was the product of English policy had led directly to the rising, from 1762, of the Whiteboys, who, appearing 'in those parts of the kingdom where manufactures are not established, . . . are a proof of the poverty and want of employment of the lower classes of the people'.[151]

John Hely-Hutchinson, an Irish MP, lawyer, member of the Privy Council and from 1774 provost of Trinity College Dublin, was the author of the tract. Hely-Hutchinson was a Patriot and had emerged in opposition circles at the same time as Flood. The fact that a figure presently involved in the government of Ireland was so openly calling for the abolition of restrictions was significant. In the early months of 1779, the movement for the non-importation of British goods was widely noticed. The lord lieutenant John Hobart, 1st Earl of Buckinghamshire, had already acknowledged the need for reform with the passing of the Catholic Relief Act of 1778, which allowed Catholics to purchase land and open schools. Buckinghamshire also arranged for short reports from prominent individuals on the likely effects of free trade on Irish revenue and the Irish and British economies. James Hewitt, 1st Viscount Lifford, the lord chancellor of Ireland, confirmed that the loss of clandestine trade in wool to North America had badly affected the country. The root cause of the problem, however, was the brutal restriction of Ireland's commerce by the English.[152] The solution had to be equality between the nations with regard to trade:

> As to the remedy for the present evils, I am afraid no adequate one will be found, till the people of both kingdoms shall be brought to that temper, that benignity of heart, that liberality of mind, and that equal and just sense of things, as shall dispose them to think of this great subject as citizens of the world, with an indifference whether a great manufacture of the empire be carried on in the county of York or in the county of Down, and as one people under one king, one constitution, with one and the same religion as the national one, and as bound to promote one end, the good and welfare of all.[153]

Another commentator, Edmund Sexton Perry, the speaker of the Irish House of Commons, asserted that 'the general cause of distress is undoubtedly the restraint upon the trade, and consequently upon the industry of the kingdom'. Ireland was almost entirely excluded from all direct commerce with British colonies in Asia, Africa and America, other than in foodstuffs. It was also 'under the severest penalties from sending to any part of the world any manufacture made of or mixed with wool'. In consequence Ireland was 'in effect cut off from all trade, at least what deserves the name of trade, with the rest of the world'. The exception was 'linens and provisions', and these trades were also restricted. The British were fools in assuming that Irish commerce would undercut British industry, because '[Britain] being the centre of power, all the riches of Ireland must ultimately flow to it'.[154] Another lawyer, Walter Hussey Burgh, emphasised the cost to Britain of supporting the defence of an increasingly impoverished Ireland, the choice being whether to allow Ireland to sustain itself, or for large amounts of money to be transferred from the mainland to the colony:

> It is now come to this. England must either support this kingdom or allow her the means of supporting herself. Her option is to give in trade or in money. Without one or the other I know not how the expenses of government can be supplied. In the one way she suffers a country of great extent and fertility to become a burden instead of a benefit. In the other, whatever wealth we may acquire will flow back upon herself. It is true she will have to encounter the jealousies of a few trading societies to enrich the empire. Those jealousies if local are unjust, if general they are groundless. If the question were put to me were what is for the benefit of Glasgow, what is for the benefit of Manchester? I should answer that monopolies however destructive of the general weal are beneficial to those who possess them. But when it is demanded, what is the most effectual measure for promoting the common strength, wealth and commerce of His Majesty's Subjects of both kingdoms, I answer—an equal and perfect freedom of trade, without which one of those kingdoms has neither strength, wealth nor commerce and without which she must become a burden on the other.[155]

The commissioners of revenue likewise concluded that 'a confined trade might suffice while the country was thinly inhabited', and when the 'poor and discontented with their condition would swarm to another country'; but North America, the 'asylum of the distressed' was now shut up, and trade had to be opened up to employ the poor in consequence.[156] When Frederick Howard, 5th Earl of Carlisle replaced Buckinghamshire as lord lieutenant in November 1780, the verdict that Ireland needed urgent relief from restrictions upon its trade was accepted. As Arthur Young put it, 'No policy was ever more absurd than the restricting system of England, which has been as prejudicial to herself as to Ireland.'[157] So grave had the situation become than the former lord lieutenant George Townshend wrote, 'I believe and hope that Ireland does not wish to be separated from England.'[158] His friend John Beresford was equally of the opinion that revolution in Ireland, following on the heels of the North Americans, was close: 'I cannot behold the situation in which the affairs of Ireland are brought without the greatest uneasiness and no small share of indignation. I see, on the one hand, the connections which subsist at present between the two countries in great danger of being dissolved.'[159]

VIII

When Irish trade was freed, and a measure of legislative independence granted, calm was not restored to Irish politics, however. Rather, the opposite. In speeches of June 1782, Henry Flood questioned whether the repeal of the Declaratory Act meant that British rule over Ireland had been renounced, or whether a 'final adjustment' was to be anticipated, which risked the reintroduction of British dominion. Flood depicted recent history as a transition from slavery to liberty. This was glorious, but the cause was the weakness of Britain during the American war. The question was whether a new dawn had indeed been created for Ireland. Without further guarantees from the British, Flood was sceptical, and demanded action by Irish MPs:

> [T]he national exertion began in the last year of Lord Buckingham's administration: it is now drawing to a period, and whether that shall be glorious or otherwise, depends on your wisdom. A short view of what we have done will be a guide to what we should do. Ireland had groaned for a century under an increasing usurpation. The American war broke out, and whilst we were called upon to shed our blood for Great Britain, we were insulted with the application of that principle to Ireland which had revolted America. Our feelings were exasperated by the application, and our trade was ruined by the war. We saw ourselves beggars in fact, and slaves in assertion. The merchants flew to a non-importation agreement, and the people flew to arms! Amidst this perturbation, Parliament assembled, and we amended our Address by the demand of a free trade, as we have lately amended our Address by the demand of a free constitution; that is, of an exclusive legislature, on which all freedom of trade must depend.[160]

Flood was concerned that Ireland had not been granted the right to formulate an economic strategy independent of that of Britain; rather, Ireland was expected to suffer taxes imposed by London, and be subject to economic laws formulated by British ministers. Under such conditions, the constitution of Ireland could not in fact be said to be free. On 14 June, Flood followed up his argument by stating that what had happened in Ireland was parallel to events in North America: 'A voice from America shouted to liberty, the echo of it caught your people as it passed along the Atlantic, and they renewed the voice till it reverberated here.' The ideal of independence, that he traced to Molyneux, Flood believed could now be achieved if the Irish parliament demanded that the British renounce the right to legislate for Ireland:

> The case of Ireland originally stated by the great Molyneaux, and burned at the Revolution by the Parliament of England, is not now afraid of the fire; it has risen from that phoenix urn, and with the flames of its cradle it illuminates our isle! What is the result? It is now in your power, and I trust it will be in your wisdom to do final justice to the rights and interests of your country.[161]

To underline the division from Britain, the speech of Willoughby Bertie, 4th Earl of Abingdon in the British House of Lords on 5 July 1782 was printed together with Flood's. Abingdon, who considered himself a friend to liberty, and especially at Geneva, argued in favour of the continued subservience of Irish to British law, and put forward a bill to repeal Irish free trade and assert British sovereignty over Ireland.[162] Significantly, Abingdon's speech was made the day after William Petty, Lord Shelburne became prime minister, following the unexpected death of Charles Watson-Wentworth, 2nd Marquess of Rockingham (at the age of fifty-two during an epidemic of influenza). Shelburne's ascent in London politics was to be of profound importance for the Geneva rebels.

CHAPTER EIGHT

Shelburne

WILLIAM PETTY, 2nd Earl of Shelburne and from 1784 1st Marquess of Lansdowne, was referred to as Lord Shelburne during his life, and by his many antagonists as 'Malagrida', after the notorious Portuguese Jesuit Gabriel Malagrida, who had described the Lisbon earthquake of 1755 as the judgement of God upon a sinful people, and who was later executed for purported involvement in a plot to assassinate King José I. Shelburne was likened to Malagrida in *The Public Advertiser* of 16 September 1767, and regularly thereafter, for calling himself a patriot while encouraging faction and opposition to George III, for associating with so-called republicans and levellers, for supporting John Wilkes's campaign for reinstatement as a member of parliament and for lacking any sense of humour.[1] For Shelburne's opponents, he was a dangerous Whig, a constitutional meddler, a friend to radicals and dissenters and likely to cause the collapse of the country if he ever gained power. In an anonymous etching dated 18 December 1782, for example, entitled 'The shell-born Jes-t', Shelburne appeared as Ignatius Loyola wearing a monk's habit, about to make a speech altogether uncertain in terms of argument, stating 'He wou'd & he wou'd not &c.' In the distance the sun, inscribed 'Poor Old England', is seen to be sinking below the horizon.

The point was that Shelburne had, in a speech of 13 December 1782, vacillated about the precise nature of the American independence he had been willing to accept in the provisional Paris treaty he had negotiated as prime minister. His opacity was deemed to be typical of such a crafty political operator. Shelburne was contradicting his own recent and fulsome condemnation of North American independence, having always followed Chatham in declaring he would 'as soon subscribe to transubstantiation as to sovereignty by right in the colonies'.[2] A contemporary

FIGURE 8.1. Anon., "The shell-born Jes-t", 18 December 1782. British Museum Collection, no. 1868,0808.4902. Copyright © The Trustees of the British Museum

anonymous portrait seemed apposite in identifying hypocrisy and deceit as Shelburne's key characteristics:

> He has the craft to appear a public enemy to luxury, yet yields to none in the vice he censors. Penurious by nature, he is extravagant by system . . . The whole stretch of his abilities exceeds not the compass of what is termed *intrigue*. He is in profession a Whig, a Tory in practice, pretends a regard for the people's rights, and is the unqualified champion for prerogative, in its most wide and dangerous operation.[3]

A major problem throughout Shelburne's career was the number of people who took against him.[4] Edmund Burke, who despised him, noted in a letter of 1768 that 'Shelburne continues in administration, though as adverse and as much disliked as ever'.[5] Charles James Fox, at a meeting of the City of Westminster in July 1782, declared that 'past experience has given me no cause for trusting him', citing as evidence Shelburne's *volte-face* over American independence and his failure when in office to introduce parliamentary reform.[6] Some of those he himself venerated were also offended by him. Shelburne regularly described Adam Smith as his great guide with regard to the nature of the contemporary world and its problems, Smith having revealed 'the difference between light and darkness'.[7] The phlegmatic Smith, however, apparently disliked Shelburne. David Hume, in a letter to Smith, noted that Shelburne had resigned from the ministry in 1763 because 'he found himself obnoxious on account of his share in the negotiation' for peace with France at the end of the Seven Years' War, and added: 'I see you [Smith] are much displeased with that nobleman but he always speaks of you with regard.'[8]

Entirely opposite responses prevailed among Shelburne's wide circle of friends and allies. In 1768, the author John Hawkesworth dedicated his *Telemachus*, a new translation of Fénelon's *Télémaque*, to Shelburne, stating that he had displayed 'early virtue and noble views', was a 'friend of man, jealous of public liberty' and altogether a 'citizen from whom . . . your country may expect yet more important service'.[9] Joseph Priestley, the dissenter and philosopher who served as Shelburne's librarian between 1772 and 1780, wrote, 'I conceive him to be, for ability and integrity together, the very first character in this kingdom.'[10] A poem written by 'Mr Heywood' included the lines 'What tho' Chatham be no more / Heroes still we have in store / For council form'd, or field / Still Shelburne, uncorrupt, remains.'[11] Shelburne was acknowledged by foreigners to be a true patriot.[12] Equally, his friendships were accepted as crossing religious and national boundaries:

> Men of learning find his doors open to receive them; the sciences find a warm and comfortable hospitality under his roof; not only Englishmen, but foreigners, acknowledge this truth, and Abbé Raynal, a real friend to human nature, gives Lord Shelburne a character that not only exalts the individual, but the country of which he is a Peer.[13]

Understanding the polarised perspectives upon Shelburne is important in the story of New Geneva. Getting a sense of what Shelburne saw himself to be doing, especially in terms of reform, is equally necessary. Shelburne perceived himself as a victim of a backward education, who discovered a new world, and wanted to promote a similar experience for as many others as possible. This means we have to start with his background and his self-perception.

Shelburne's grandfather on his father's side was the Irish earl Thomas Fitzmaurice, 21st Baron of Kerry, but he was named William Petty after his great-grandfather on his mother's side, the surveyor general of Ireland and advocate of Ireland's economic transformation. After a private education in Dublin, Shelburne abandoned Christ Church, Oxford to join the army in 1756, and fought at the battles of Minden (1759) and Kloster Kampen (1760) that prevented the French invasion of Hanover during the Seven Years' War. For his military valour, he was appointed aide-de-camp to George III. While still abroad, he was elected both to the British House of Commons, for Wycombe, and to the Irish House of Commons, for County Kerry. In 1761, however, the barony of Wycombe passed to Shelburne upon the death of his father, and his military friend the Irish-born Isaac Barré, deciding upon a political career, took Shelburne's seat in the House of Commons. With another associate, the barrister John Dunning, who was elected to Shelburne's other seat of Calne, Barré formed a supportive group in the Commons. Marriage to Sophia Carteret linked Shelburne to the Granville family, especially powerful in Wiltshire and in Cornwall, and a second marriage in the 1770s to Louisa Fitzpatrick linked him both to the earls of Ossory, with land in Bedfordshire, and to Holland House, since Louisa's sister Mary married Stephen, 2nd Lord Holland, the brother of Charles James Fox.[14] Shelburne briefly served in the government of George Grenville in 1763 as first lord of trade, but resigned because of a failure to include his then mentor, William Pitt the Elder, in the cabinet. Under Pitt himself he became secretary for the Southern Department between 1766 and 1768, and went into opposition against the government of Lord North until 1782, when Rockingham led the Whigs back into power, with Fox and Shelburne initially serving together as secretaries of state. One of the great tragedies of Shelburne's short-lived ministry, following the unexpected death of Rockingham, was the decision in July 1782 of Fox and the inheritor of Rockingham's estates, William Wentworth-Fitzwilliam, 4th Earl Fitzwilliam to split the Whig party and end support for Shelburne. This was also to have profound consequences for the Genevan rebels.

II

In an autobiographical account of his early life written in December 1800, Shelburne noted that he met, at Holyrood in Edinburgh, 'the last of the feudal lords, like my ancestors, in the person of [Archibald Douglas] the last Duke of Douglas'. The Highlander was armed, took offence at a perceived slight and was notable for being unable to read or write. Life under such lords Shelburne described as 'slavery and feudal habits'. He ascribed to the dominion of such men in society, and especially in Scotland and in Ireland, his father's tyrannical attitude to his own children and his own and his father's limitations as men. Shelburne was initially brought up under the care of his grandfather Thomas Fitzmaurice at Lixnaw House in Kerry. He admitted that he had 'not great chance at a liberal education'.[15] What he meant by this was that he considered himself to have been surrounded by ignorance, servility and barbarism, the culture that dominated Ireland and caused so many problems within the British polity:

> [I had] no great example before [me], no information in my way . . . good-breeding in my own family, which made part of the feudal system, but out of it nothing but those uncultivated, undisciplined manners and that vulgarity, which make all Irish society so justly odious all over Europe.[16]

Shelburne acknowledged that he was saved with regard to education only by his spirited and independent-minded aunt Lady Arabella Denny, having been placed for his further education with a 'narrow-minded' clergyman of Huguenot descent in Kerry, while his parents lived in England.[17] He again damned Irish culture, arguing that Irish backwardness economically could be traced to the lack of an aspiring middle-class:

> As to morals, whoever knows anything of Ireland knows how rare they are in any rank of life. In England they are much oftener to be met with in the middling classes, who are obliged to be active and diligent to make their own and their children's fortune, than among the higher classes, whose fortunes are made and have no motive for exertion except ambition, which may be one case in a hundred. In Ireland there was, at that time at least, no middling classes, and the manners of the better sort were, and are, justly proverbial.[18]

The contrast between the kinds of enlightenment to be found in an advanced commercial society and the feudal backwardness of provinces dominated by a selfish and largely ignorant landed elite was one of Shelburne's obsessions.

Shelburne concluded, in a further autobiographical fragment dated December 1801, that looking back his salvation was that he managed to 'unlearn the habits, manners and principles' that he had imbibed as a boy. He saw himself, once he had educated and enlightened himself, as having promoted 'the liberty of my native country' by 'solid acts' rather than 'vain words', and including the encouragement of 'education, morals, industry and agriculture'.[19] What he identified as his state of ignorance, however, began to be challenged only after he went to Christ Church, Oxford at sixteen. Here he studied 'a good deal of natural law and the law of nations, some history, part of Livy, and translated some of the Orations of Demosthenes with tolerable care'. He also 'read by myself a great deal of religion', found his own way in theology over two years of study and ultimately 'made up my own mind, and have never since had an anxious thought upon the subject'. The Anglican Shelburne left Oxford 'much struck with Machiavel's Discourses on Livy, Demosthenes, and by the law of nature more than the law of nations'. He attended William Blackstone's lectures on English law 'with great care, and profited considerably by them'. Blackstone had commenced the lectures in 1753, the year Shelburne arrived in Oxford.[20] Later in his life, in a speech in the House of Lords on 19 May 1775, Shelburne called religion and law 'the two great pillars of society', lamenting at the same time that religion was 'losing daily much of its influence' because 'a subtle metaphysical spirit of refinement had crept in' that made men treat 'religion and prejudice as synonymous'.[21] Despite such views he was at times accused of seeming 'to lean towards the Presbyterian system'.[22] Having been brought to Oxford 'full of prejudice', Shelburne said that while some of these views were augmented there and others ameliorated, he also gained 'little or no knowledge of the world'. This was remedied by the 'general panic' that he identified in politics, because of the loss of Minorca after Admiral Byng's defeat and the taking by the French general Montcalm of Fort Oswego in New York. These events inspired Shelburne to leave Oxford for the army, which in turn led to his remarkably rapid ascent in court and parliament.[23]

In his autobiographical fragment of 1800, Shelburne did not provide a straightforward history of virtue and corruption. His was not a story of radical Whiggery established and affronted by the malign forces of court and established church. Rather, Shelburne painted a picture of British political life in which almost every participant was actuated by self-interest, and where accident rather than design ensured the realisation of the public good. He claimed that his view of Britain was accurate because he had direct evidence of front-line politics, had enjoyed personal access to most of the major figures in London and had used rare historical documents that substantiated his own opinions. He derided those who associated Britain's success in the first half of the eighteenth century with the constitution established in 1688, the person of William III or the formation of the Whig party, and denounced as fantastical 'all that fine theory which Montesquieu and all the admirers of the English constitution suppose'.[24] William III, rather than being regarded as a great and virtuous man, was described as a monster, addicted to making war on France, destroying the Dutch Republic in the process and promoting dreadful favourites whose central quality was that they flattered his grotesque pride. Subsequent observers who felt positively about William III were mad: 'Nothing can be more false and absurd than the enthusiasm entertained for his character, on account of his supposed love of liberty.'[25]

Nor did the principles embodied in the Whig party provide an explanation for what Shelburne described as 'fifty years of unexampled prosperity' up to the accession of George III in 1760. He identified singular economic development, combined with the enjoyment of public order and civil liberty, as characterising the period following the end of war with France and the Peace of Utrecht in 1714:

> Commerce increased as rapidly as could be desired; property was secure under a steady administration of justice, subject to no changes of principles; and population increased as the course of nature rendered indispensable; liberty was untouched; the public morals were kept within due bounds; and order generally prevailed.[26]

But such benefits had little to do with either monarchs or politicians. Shelburne stated that the reign of Queen Anne was only marginally better than that of William and Mary, because politics were dominated by Sarah Churchill, Duchess of Marlborough, whose lust for power and avarice were unbounded. As he put it, making a point about women in politics that he repeated in other places, females were likely to be at least as lustful for power as men: 'like most women [Sarah Churchill] ran wild with the habits of power, having nobody to control her'.[27] While Shelburne praised Robert Walpole as an able minister, he derided the Whigs who followed him, in the persons of Henry Pelham and his brother Thomas Pelham-Holles, Duke of Newcastle. As Shelburne put it, the Pelhams 'had every talent for obtaining Ministry, none for governing the kingdom, except decency, integrity, and Whig principles'. Being motivated by 'all the allures of the Court', they ruled by 'cunning, plausibility, and the cultivation of mankind'.[28] The phrase 'cultivation of mankind' meant the use of bribery and patronage to maintain their places. Shelburne's conclusion was that political life had been governed by personal connections under the first two Hanoverian monarchs, and that self-interest rather than principle or party explained political behaviour:

> Sacheverel's trial gives a just notion of what is called the constitution, which degenerated in the reigns of George I and George II into a systematic false government; and is to be found described and detailed in the Walpole Papers, till there appeared with George III a new epoch.[29]

Direct involvement in eighteenth-century political life confirmed Shelburne in this opinion. He said that 'there are two classes of causes' that could be conceived in political actions. The first amounted to ideas for the public good, and as such were 'ostensible and plausible, calculated to meet the publick eye and mind'. The second was 'private and bye motives, which men scarcely dare to own to themselves'. Shelburne's conclusion was that 'few actions in life are there which cannot be traced to motives of the latter sort'.[30]

Shelburne actually had little faith in particular forms of government, believing rather that the character of a government was most likely to be shaped by the over-arching role of personalities in political history. As his comments upon Cromwell reveal, however, he did believe it was possible to formulate laws that embodied the public good. Limited government and the necessary abandonment of empire were two cardinal lessons he associated with the contemporary science of legislation. The latter he believed might be made universal, and imagined general moral principles 'as may embrace the Turk or the Gentoo [Hindu] equally with the Christian'. He defined the goal of an enlightened education as 'establishing certain fixed fundamental principles of law, commerce, morality and politics comprehensive enough to embrace all religions and all countries'.[31]

III

Shelburne's explanation for the stability of Britain and its economic success lay in accident and necessity. The key accident was the weakness of the first two Georges, who 'never imagined they would continue' because of the extent of the Jacobite threat. The Stuart Pretender to the throne enjoyed 'a very just right to the throne upon all Tory and monarchical principles and all old prejudices', and was supported by 'an immense body of property among the Tories, a considerable party among the Lords and Commons' and the Catholics in Ireland.[32] In addition, 'All Scotland was enthusiastically devoted to the exiled family, with a very few exceptions.'[33] Shelburne stated that he had direct evidence for Scottish support for Jacobitism, claiming that as late as 1756, when he had travelled through the country, men either 'sober or drunk' still favoured the return of the

Stuarts. It was Jacobitism that 'kept the reigning family in perpetual awe', and in desperation the first two Hanoverians 'threw themselves into the arms of the old Whigs, abjuring the rights and the manners of Royalty, in other words, telling the people "We are your slaves and blackamoors."'. There was, as he put it, 'a King and no King'.[34] Montesquieu's vaunted republic hidden beneath the form of a monarchy was actually a monarchy adopting republican policies by necessity.

Shelburne argued that the collapse of Jacobitism, continuing government by ministerial intrigue and corruption and, above all, the Seven Years' War and the personality of George III, combined to ruin Britain. War was the product of political insanity, in Shelburne's opinion. It was normally blundered into, badly executed and abjectly terminated. The War of the Austrian Succession, for example, he claimed was typical in being 'terminated by a peace, which paid no regard whatever to the commercial grievances which were the subject of so much clamour as to occasion the war'. Shelburne considered Britain's involvement to have been madness, because of the threat posed to the country's existence by rising Jacobitism domestically, and the war to have resulted in 'expense and incessant disgrace'.[35] He argued that the Seven Years' War was the product of accident, when conflict over the Anglo-French border in Canada led to British attacks upon French merchant ships: '[W]ar naturally makes itself, if there is no trouble taken to prevent it: and this I take to be the real cause of the war of 1755.'[36]

William Pitt the Elder (from 1766, 1st Earl of Chatham) took control of the country from 1757 by manipulating and bribing all parties into supporting him. Shelburne, emphasising his direct involvement in Pitt's administration, described the latter's strategy as having four elements: 'leaving the Duke of Newcastle the undisturbed enjoyment of the whole patronage of the Crown'; 'indulging Mr. [Henry] Fox's love of money [as paymaster general], which took full possession of him as soon as Mr. Pitt had shut the door on his ambition [to be prime minister]'; 'applying himself to gain the Court through the surest channel, Lady Yarmouth'; and 'determining to go every length to please the King in his ruling passion and that of the Hanover family, viz. German measures and personal avarice'.[37] Pitt's sole goal in practice had been, in Shelburne's view, to avoid blame for any disaster.

If one rogue elephant was the court, another was the public. The people as a body could never be trusted. Shelburne was no democrat, and he blamed popular passions and their articulation in the press for promoting war between states. Pitt, Britain's greatest statesman of the time, had acknowledged his own impotence before them: 'Lord Chatham told me that he could never be sure of the public passions, that all that he could do was to watch, and be the first to follow them.'[38] Shelburne found the populace to be inconstant and irrational. He confessed to being 'sorry to say upon an experience of forty years, that the public is incapable of embracing two objects at a time, or of extending their views beyond the object immediately before them'.[39]

If domestic corruption and war were the natural products of British politics, the ill state of Ireland was another. Shelburne was always concerned about his homeland, where he retained extensive landholdings. In his autobiographical fragment, he stated that Ireland was time after time the victim of stupid English strategy, inspired by the narrow interests of Westminster or the court. Ireland suffered under William III, Shelburne noted, and 'Parliament luckily stopped him from heaping on his Dutch favourites' forfeited Catholic lands. At the same time, William III missed a chance. Had he spread the land among the community of Huguenot refugees, 'he would have insured the tranquillity of Ireland for evermore, and promoted the wealth and industry of both Kingdoms'.[40] One of the people Shelburne hated was George Germain, 1st Viscount Sackville, 'who begun a career, every step of which was marked with infamy, by embroiling Ireland'. Sackville had been secretary to his own father Lionel Cranfield Sackville, 1st Duke of Dorset, who as lord lieutenant of Ireland between 1751 and 1755 had supported the Anglican archbishop of Armagh George Stone in a battle against the Irish parliament, leading to faction and a growing antagonism towards England; an opposition exemplified by the emergence of popular and patriotic politics associated with Charles Lucas.[41] Shelburne looked back positively to Cromwell, who had wished to 'make Ireland a field of experiment, and an example to England'.[42]

Cromwell was more generally a positive figure for Shelburne, having made laws and initiated strategies that continued to merit contemporary scrutiny. Shelburne considered that Cromwell 'has never had justice done him', and attacked in particular Hume's depiction of a hypocrite in his *History of England*, which could be contrasted with the historical record:

> [Cromwell] did set more things forward than all the kings who reigned during the century, King William included. England was never so much respected abroad; while at home, though Cromwell could not settle the Government, talents of every kind began to show themselves, which were immediately crushed or put to sleep at the Restoration. The best and most unexceptional regulations of different kinds are to be found

> in his ordinances and proclamations remaining to this day unexecuted; and during his life he not only planned but enforced and executed the greatest measures of which the country was then susceptible.[43]

Cromwell had recognised the distance between planning reform and putting it into practice, which was the great challenge of government. As Shelburne put it, it was possible to formulate laws for the public good, but 'the real difficulty remains in getting people to apply the principles which they have admitted, and of which they are now so fully convinced'. The problem was 'the mine composed of private interests and personal animosity'. An outstanding example of this was that 'Adam Smith's principles have remained unanswered for above thirty years, and yet when it is attempted to act upon any of them, what a clamour.' It was a universal truth that 'Men require to be bribed into doing good, or permitting it to be done.'[44]

This did not mean that Shelburne was a republican or leveller. Alongside Cromwell, the figure who was praised most in Shelburne's autobiographical fragment was Louis XIV, who had been 'a King in every sense of the word. He identified himself as few kings do with the public, with whom he was one and the same.' France emerged far greater from his rule, despite his 'over-devotion and religious prejudice'.[45] As we have seen, Shelburne had little or no faith in 'the people' as political agents, while acknowledging the necessary role they played, alongside a free press, in setting a limit to the power of monarchs.[46] As the century proceeded, he was increasingly concerned about the loss of what he termed 'natural subordination and affection', which he believed was generated by the paternal action of improving landlords in employing and caring for the poor in their communities. One of the points he made was that state action on a national level to help the poor would erode local responsibilities and disastrously turn this group into 'a separate interest in the state':

> I entirely agree with him [James Anderson, the Scottish agriculturalist] about the Poor Laws—They not only appear to me productive of all the inconvenience commonly apprehended and felt, but likewise are daily destroying all natural subordination and affection—The master manufacturer uninterested in the fate of the hands whom he employs becomes a mere negro driver—while the man of property loses that political influence, which it has been a fundamental principle of all constitutions to suppose attendant on property, by the poor being taught upon all occasions to look up to the King's Justices for relief and I shall not be surprised to see the poor make as separate an interest in the state as the clergy do.[47]

Such perspectives are significant. Shelburne was a Whig in terms of his major political relationships in parliament, his belief in civil liberty and concerns about the growing power of George III. He was far from being a radical Whig as traditionally conceived, however, despite a general support for parliamentary reform. Shelburne's radicalism was different. One of his main achievements was to articulate a new set of solutions to the grave problems he deemed to be particular to his own age. This emerges from his engagement with philosophers, physiocrats, dissenters and radicals.

IV

In part because of his personal sense that he had been inadequately educated, but also because of a zeal for finding solutions to the problems of society and, above all, because he was sure that Britain was in crisis, from the early 1760s Shelburne sought out the company of philosophers and reformers. He asked for their views, engaged in correspondence with them and in certain cases welcomed them to his residences at Bowood House in Wiltshire or Berkeley Square in London. During his life, he was convinced that figures as diverse as the physiocrats Anne-Robert-Jacques Turgot, Jean-Antoine-Nicolas de Condorcet and André Morellet, the dissenting ministers Richard Price, Joseph Priestley and Andrew Kippis and the Scottish philosophers Smith, Hume and Ferguson had all contributed to the development of a science of the statesmen or legislator formulating policies for the good of mankind. Shelburne cultivated such figures, and ultimately established a changing circle of philosophers, which later included Jeremy Bentham, Samuel Romilly and some of the Genevan rebels themselves. His ultimate goal was to enact reform. His personal genius, as he considered it, was to act as a statesman or legislator, and to overcome the issues that arose inevitably in putting reforms into practice. His long-standing engagement with advocates of the science of the statesman or legislator began with Hume and Smith.

Shelburne cultivated both Hume and Smith in the 1760s, from the first time that he became involved with John Stuart, 3rd Earl of Bute, and acted as a go-between from Bute to Henry Fox in the hope of establishing a ministry. Shelburne took from the Scots the argument that economic corruption in contemporary Britain was the greatest political vice. With Hume especially he agreed that contemporary Britain faced an acute crisis. As the philosopher put it in 1767, 'For of all our annual confusions, the present seems to be the most violent, and to threaten the most entire revolution, and the most important events.'[48] Shelburne became convinced that he had witnessed under the Hanoverians, and especially under George III, the development of a mercantile system or corrupt nexus between politicians and merchants who represented banks or trading companies, and who began to control politics for their own ends. Such practices were always in opposition to the public good. Adam Smith was of fundamental importance to Shelburne, because of his condemnation of the corrupt relationship between merchants and politicians. Shelburne clearly heard such arguments directly from Smith, but they were fully articulated in the *Wealth of Nations*, which Smith himself described as 'the very violent attack I . . . made upon the whole commercial system of Great Britain'.[49] Between the appearance of the book in 1776 and the early 1780s, Smith was especially concerned with fine-tuning his assault on government policy. In describing the changes which formed the third edition of the *Wealth of Nations* of 1783, he informed his friend William Strahan that they amounted to 'some new arguments against the corn bounty; against the herring buss bounty; a new concluding chapter upon the mercantile system; A short history and, I presume, a full exposition of the absurdity and hurtfulness of almost all our chartered trading companies'.[50] Shelburne considered himself to be Smith's disciple, in the sense that he was taking forward Smith's attack in parliament and the country. The particular problem he perceived himself to be addressing was that of combating the mercantile system. Smith had indicted it, but the even more difficult task was to dismantle it, and to prevent it from recurring in future generations.

By the later 1760s, Shelburne's closeness to other Scottish philosophers was also marked. He was perpetually searching for further resources with which to condemn London politics and policy, and to describe and to realise an alternative future. David Hume, in a letter to Hugh Blair, Presbyterian minister and professor of rhetoric at the University of Edinburgh (1760–83), which advised against the publication of Adam Ferguson's *Essay on the History of Civil Society*, noted that the text was now in 'General [Robert] Clerk & Lord Shelburne's hands'. Hume made the point that both men were 'not the most proper judges in the world; and if you do not interpose, they [Ferguson's *Essay*] will certainly be printed'.[51] In a letter of the following year, Clerk wrote to Ferguson that Shelburne was considering offering him the position of governor of West Florida, which had been ceded to Britain by Spain at the end of the Seven Years' War. Clerk advised Ferguson to remain as professor of moral philosophy at Edinburgh.[52] The impression Ferguson had upon readers such as Shelburne is instanced by a comment from the London literary hostess Elizabeth Montagu, to whom Shelburne had passed on Ferguson's work. She stated that she approved 'extremely of Mr Ferguson in the preference he gives to the magnanimous virtues, above the effeminate and luxurious arts of modern life; and wish he could infuse into us some of the Spartan spirit he admires so justly'. The tragedy was that Britons, she wrote, 'are in much more danger of becoming Sybarites than Lacedemonians [i.e., Spartans]'.[53]

Shelburne would have accepted Ferguson's assertion about the lack of fitness of the British for war because of the extent of selfishness and corruption. Turning Britons into Spartans, however, was the antithesis of Shelburne's aspiration. The basis of any reform, as he put it to Richard Price, was 'to cry down war throughout the whole world, which nothing can ever justify, and to prove the advantages of peace, and the right which all countries have to require it of their sovereigns'.[54] Shelburne's plan for peace entailed developing measures that would combat the causes of war, and link nations together to the extent that they would ideally no longer see any point in taking to arms, so irrational would war be recognised to be from an economic perspective. Economic perspectives had become important because, as Shelburne argued, the expansion of markets and the profits that could be generated from imperial endeavour increasingly caused nation states to go to war. As secretary for the Southern Department under Pitt, he attempted to combat wars motivated by a desire to subject a populace economically, and to profit from their ruin, which he perceived to be occurring across the British Empire. In 1758, he advised Francis Fauquier, lieutenant governor of the colony of Virginia, that he had received reports of violence against the native American tribes, including the Creeks in West Florida. The rationale behind threatening the tribes with military extirpation was clearly economic gain. Shelburne asserted that only peace led to production and the creation of wealth in the long term. This meant that existing treaties had to be respected, and peace maintained between the British settlers and the Native Americans:[55]

> His Majesty expects daily to hear, that the persons concerned in violating the Indian treaties, have been detected and brought to condign punishment. While the prosperity of the American colonies, especially their back settlers, depends so much on maintaining peace and friendship with the Indians, it is amazing, that such enormities can remain any time undiscovered: The provinces can never expect a lasting peace with the Indian tribes 'till they convince them they would rather protect than destroy them: The traders for selfish views, have but too much succeeded in inculcating into the minds of these poor people, that nothing will satisfy the colonies but their extirpation;

> and I fear that the inhabitants of Augusta and Bedford counties, in your province, have given too much room for their listening to such an insinuation.[56]

Over the following years, and in the light of the practices he had observed as secretary for the Southern Department, Shelburne came to the conclusion that one of the keys to dismantling the mercantile system was to reduce the role of government in economic affairs. He wanted to put an end to the close link between merchants and politicians, and sought to stop statesmen from perceiving commercial companies as branches of the state. Ultimately, he wanted to persuade politicians and monarchs to abandon empire, and to reject associations between glorious war and the acquisition of territory. His solution to the problem of the mercantile system was therefore distinctly anti-political. He made this point in the final section of his autobiography, reaffirming the influence of Adam Smith upon him, and that of another of his heroes, Benjamin Franklin. Like Franklin, Shelburne was convinced that a benevolent deity existed, which could be seen to be operating in the organisation of the economic realm. It was evident, for example, that 'Providence has so constituted the world, that very little government is necessary'. Shelburne gave the example of Franklin's intervention at the constitutional convention in Philadelphia, when the question of the right form of government was endlessly being debated. Franklin had arisen, 'to express his apprehension that if some plan was not speedily adopted, the people out of doors would learn a most dangerous secret, that things might go on very well without any positive form of government'. Shelburne then raised the question, 'How are all markets supplied?', and answered by stating that London had never been concerned about its food supply, having left the matter to merchants, and in consequence had never experienced famine. Equally, legislation to control the grain trade had led to 'mischief', while the Dutch, leaving their corn trade entirely free, '[have] never felt what scarcity was'. Shelburne advocated what he called 'negative government', which did not 'make conquests or . . . keep distant governments in dependence'.[57]

One of the major issues for Shelburne was how to move towards negative government. Hume did not believe it to be possible, seeing the party system and patronage as constitutive elements of the British polity in his essays 'That Politics May be Reduced to a Science', 'Of the Independency of Parliament', 'Whether the British Government inclines more to Absolute Monarchy or to a Republic' and 'Of Parties in General'. Smith, equally, accepted existence in a world of the second-best, where the transition to free trade was unlikely. As he memorably put it in the the *Wealth of Nations*, 'To expect, indeed, that the freedom of trade should ever be entirely restored in Great Britain, is as absurd as to expect that an Oceana or Utopia should ever be established in it.' The fact was that reform was opposed by 'the prejudices of the publick' and 'the private interests of many individuals'.[58] Shelburne never lost faith that genuine change was possible, and that a community could be constructed in which the kinds of political and economic behaviour that characterised contemporary life were things of the past. This led him to develop an extremely close relationship with radical Whigs, and especially the dissenting minister and philosopher Richard Price.

V

Price worked with Shelburne from the early 1770s to the end of his life in 1791. He was an Arian and Unitarian, a Commonwealthman, an advocate of elective monarchy and one who anticipated the end of days and the coming of a new millennium.[59] As he put it to Elizabeth Montagu, who arranged his first meeting with Shelburne in London, he was a 'plain man' and 'an utter stranger to the formalities of the world' who found solace in looking 'to that world where all the virtuous and worthy will meet and be happy together for ever' because the 'prospect of this is enough to dry up every tear, and to elevate us above this world of sin and tumult'.[60] In fact, Price was far from being an ordinary man and ignorant of the lives of the great. He had been born into a Glamorgan family with strong connections to the community of dissenters, served as family chaplain in the Stoke Newington household of the wealthy dissenter George Streatfield and became successively minister at Newington Green (1757), Poor Jewry Lane (1762) and Gravel-Pit Meeting Place in Hackney, from 1770 until 1791. Having published *A Review of the Principal Questions and Difficulties in Morals* (1758), and edited Thomas Bayes's manuscripts concerning probability, he was elected Fellow of the Royal Society in 1765, having been nominated by Benjamin Franklin. Price had met Franklin during the latter's first trip to Britain, between July 1757 and August 1762. Both men were members of the Club of Honest Whigs, which met every other Thursday for supper at St Paul's coffeehouse, and from 1772 at the London coffeehouse. The Club included dissenters like Priestley, James Burgh and Andrew Kippis, and even the Tory James Boswell, because of his support for Corsican independence. Price was also involved with the London merchant Samuel Vaughan, who, with Richard Oliver, James Townhend, John

Horne Tooke and John Sawbridge, had founded the Bill of Rights Society in the late 1760s, in order to support John Wilkes. In 1767, Marischal College, Aberdeen awarded Price the degree of doctor of divinity, and in the same year his *Four Dissertations* appeared, comprised of justifications of providence, prayer, miracles and reasons 'for expecting that virtuous men shall meet after death in a state of happiness'.[61]

Shelburne became close to Price because they were both convinced that Britain had declined since the seventeenth century, that virtue was everyday losing out in the war against corruption, and that the power of the throne was growing while the independence of parliament and its members receded. At the same time, the Anglican church maintained its dominion, violating the rights of heterodox protestants, while Britain suffered economic and population decline. Shelburne remained an Anglican Latitudinarian, although he shared Price's view of the need to relieve dissenting ministers and to reduce the power of the Church of England, supporting successive Relief acts in parliament in consequence.[62] Shelburne also supported parliamentary reform alongside Price and their friend Christopher Wyvill.[63] In letters that were reprinted by Wyvill, Shelburne declared in 1780 that a House of Commons assembled 'frequently and equally chosen' was 'the foundation stone of our government', and that a county-based militia was vital for the defence of liberty.[64] Shelburne sometimes employed the language of rights, of an ancient constitution and of liberties lost. This meant that he could appear to be a radical Whig in Price's mould, lacking only the religious heterodoxy. Shelburne did not, however, believe that parliamentary reform was the key to the salvation of Britain. Rather, bringing the people more directly into politics was intended to weaken the mercantile system by limiting the powers of patronage and the prevalence of placemen. Distributing seats according to population, and removing rotten boroughs, was intended to limit the power of a nobility that Shelburne regularly described as feudal. Regular elections would also increase the costs of bribery and election-rigging. There was a further reason for parliamentary reform: Shelburne was of the view that if a greater number of the people was involved in politics, they would be more likely to realise the limitations of empire-building, less likely to be corrupted and more willing to accept the rationality of peace and limited government, simply by virtue of their number and the lessening of parliamentary control by the court. In other words, the number of lives dedicated to political intrigue and personal gain that characterised Shelburne's own time would lessen drastically. This was why, in writing to Wyvill, Shelburne always emphasised the need for 'œconomical reform', the reduction in patronage and placemen, and the abandonment of 'exorbitant contracts' before he turned to the role of the people within the mixed constitution. Popular liberties were a means rather than an end.

Shelburne turned to Price not because of the latter's optimistic view of a world transformed by liberty and godliness, but rather because of his schemes for getting rid of the national debt, and for using the tax system to put an end to certain forms of corruption. These first appeared in his *Observations on Reversionary Payments*, originally published in 1771, with a second edition in 1772 and a third, enlarged, edition in 1773. This work undoubtedly drew Shelburne to Price, because it contained plans for paying the national debt, establishing annuities to cover the costs of ageing, and for combating the luxury and debauchery that Price associated with life in large towns. The latter he believed to be spreading to the countryside, leading to population decline in Britain and threatening the survival of the state. As he put it, 'corruptions and follies of the worst sort have, I am afraid, taken too deep root among us'.[65] In the third edition, Price suggested the establishment of a commission comprising the chief offices of the state and leading bankers, which would use public moneys to pay off the national debt gradually, and thereby prevent a national bankruptcy. He produced, in 1774, a 'A Sketch of Proposals for Discharging the Public Debts securing public Liberty, and preserving the State' for Shelburne. Shelburne praised Price fulsomely, but expressed a fear that if the committee for getting rid of the debt was conducted in secret, there was a risk of stockjobbing, because politicians and merchants were likely to take advantage of their position for personal gain. In the same letter, Shelburne praised North American policy with regard to the public revenues, stating that the Congress 'opens a new and important field for discussion, by separating regulations of trade from the considerations of a revenue'. One of Shelburne's core beliefs was that revenue-raising should not be a goal of trade policy; trade policy ought to foster trade and protect the public good, and nothing more. In Britain things were precisely the opposite, and Shelburne attacked the customs men who collected taxes 'at a great expense, and occasioning great corruption'. He also made a point about ambitious politicians and the likelihood of their enacting reforms if they were likely to benefit from corruption once in office. In short, anticipations of private gain by politicians would always encourage bad policy and prevent reform. Price's plan was unlikely to be adopted in consequence:

> As to a change of men, I don't myself know, whether it would not be better that the present should continue. The rage for ministry is so

> universal, and the consideration attached to it so much beyond the mark, that it requires a change of ideas to take place. Nor can it be expected that any man will be for lessening a power today, which tomorrow he expects to be in possession of. There is only one evil I foresee attending it, and that you'll say exists already in the minds of the people, who have long since lost all confidence in their representatives.[66]

Shelburne was forever attuned to the problem of putting policy into practice. Like Price, he believed that Britain's very existence as a state rested on a knife edge, so extensive was corruption and so damaged the political system. In another letter to Price, written early in 1775 in response to 'The Address to the King' by the Continental Congress of 26 October 1774, Shelburne noted, 'The times are dark, and in my idea, the most that can be done is to prevent bad opinions being lodg'd with the publick, and fresh injustice being done to the principles and intentions of our American brethren.'[67]

VI

By the mid-1770s, events in North America were beginning to be positively perceived by reformers like Shelburne and Price, from the perspective of their indictment of Britain. The North American rebellion proved that empires like Britain could not last, and that the mercantile system was self-destructive. In other words, it confirmed Price's and Shelburne's diagnoses of the ills of the domestic polity. It also raised the profile of advocates of reform, and boosted their self-confidence as would-be legislators, facing the near-impossible task of taking a state from corruption to virtue. The American lawyer Arthur Lee, a friend of John Wilkes, voiced such sentiments. Writing to Price about the dire state of Britain, he asserted that individuals like Shelburne were one perceptible source of salvation:

> If anyone can save a nation, so pressed within and threatened without, it is our friend Lord Shelburne. At least he is the only man of his rank, whom I have the honour of knowing, whose virtues and abilities seem equal to the arduous task of retrieving a public overwhelmed with so many evils, as that of England now is.

Lee did not underestimate the size of the task, so great were the evils of what he termed 'Scotch principles'. By these he meant not only the government of Lord North emulating the corruption associated with the 3rd Earl of Bute, but more broadly the Scottish manners that he associated in society with 'perfidy, slavery and ingratitude'. The task of reformation was so great as to 'require a People of more virtue than the world ever yet produced, or than human nature will admit of, to resist the contagion of Scotch principles'.[68] Shelburne at this time retained a hope that the rebels could be persuaded to return to membership of an altogether restructured empire. North America also increasingly served another function. Seeing the decisions of the Continental Congress, many of whose members they considered their reform-minded friends, Shelburne and Price argued that politics in North America revealed what could be done when a branch of the empire was set free from a corrupt mother-country. American examples began to become commonplace in letters and publications associated with Shelburne. A final point was that North America ultimately offered an asylum to the virtuous, a retreat for those who had been ground down by the baleful condition of Britain.

North America dominated Shelburne's speeches in the House of Lords in the second half of the 1770s. On 20 January, 1 February and 7 February 1775, Shelburne argued that attacks upon America by ministers were deluding and deceiving both parliament and the people. The North Americans were not 'traitors, vagabonds and rebels'. The battle was not between Britain as a country and enemies within, but was rather 'between administration on the one side, and all America on the other'. It was madness to follow a policy of 'coercing the Americans into a servile submission'. They were in fact Britons defending their established liberties. The innovators and persecutors were the ministers of a corrupt government, the true enemies of the British people and the British parliament, who were violating the division between the executive and the judiciary, had established the 'despotic system [which] has governed our councils' and plunged the empire into civil war.[69] In October 1775, Shelburne was vitriolic in his condemnation of American policy, inspired by ministerial despotism, and full of praise for the North Americans themselves, who had faced the 'lurking spirit of despotism':

> What secret grievance had compelled [the ministers] to heap errors on errors, grievance upon grievance, till they have shaken the constitution to its foundation, and brought the whole empire into danger and confusion. The Americans judge from facts. They have seen an uniform lurking spirit of despotism pervade every administration. It has prevailed over the wisest and most constitutional councils; it has precipitated us into the most pernicious of all wars; a war with our brothers, our

> friends, and our fellow subjects. It was this lurking spirit of despotism that produced the Stamp Act in 1765; that fettered the repeal of that act in 1766; that revived the principle of it in 1767; that has accumulated oppression upon oppression since, till it has openly established, by the Quebec bill, popery and arbitrary power over half America.[70]

In a speech of 31 October 1776, Shelburne declared the aim of the war to be 'professedly to enslave three millions of British-born subjects.'[71] The North Americans were people taking up arms in defence of their 'property, their privileges, their inalienable rights'. It was a mistake in consequence to describe them as rebels, because they were behaving exactly as the Whigs had behaved before the Glorious Revolution of 1688:

> If resisting a lawful authority, though perhaps not a rightful authority, be the essence of treason, the Whigs at the Revolution were rank rebels . . . King James II was their lawful King! It is true he endeavoured to trample, and in some instances did invade their rights.[72]

In the case of the English revolution, resistance had been undertaken against a legal power which had begun to perform illegal and arbitrary acts. The North American case was identical, being 'constitutional resistance to a power originally legal, but which, by an unconstitutional exercise of it, had degenerated into the most oppressive stages of an usurped arbitrary power'. Rather than attacking the North Americans as traitors, Shelburne recommended rather that contemporary Britons follow the example of the Romans, seeing the conflict as a battle within the imperial community, rather than condemning a legitimate part of the empire and all of its members:

> The Greeks and Romans had some wars of the king that is now carried on against America by this country. They never gave them the name of rebellions, nor acted against them as alien enemies. The latter, in one of a similar nature, called it the Social War. I call this the constitutional war. I say this war is fraught with innumerable mischiefs. Instead of exacting obedience, it declares nothing but a wish for separation; it mediates open destruction, not coercion. It goes not to the punishment of rebels, and the protection of the innocent. It is made contrary to every rule observed in commotions of this kind. Instead of being directed against individuals, who are the supposed authors of this rebellion, it is carried on as if against foreign enemies; war is made on the community at large.[73]

Shelburne's sense of the Americans was as of Britons whose rights had been violated, and who were straightforwardly asserting historic privileges to determine the level of taxation and the object of government revenue. He was clear that he would have done the same in related circumstances, and demanded redress:

> [The Americans were] in part, if not entirely, forced to take up arms in defence of their property, which has been attempted, by the acts of this legislature, to be wrested unjustly out of their hands. They have been taxed by the British Parliament for the purpose of raising a revenue. They have been thereby denied of the inalienable privilege of a British subject, that of voting away his own money, of judging the quantum, and the propriety of entirely withholding it, should he not approve of the uses or purposes to which it may be intended to be applied . . . the colonists are not in a state of rebellion, but are armed in support of their just, their inalienable constitutional rights, thus openly invaded and attacked.[74]

The policy of seeking to destroy North America economically was also condemned by Shelburne, on 16 March 1775, as self-defeating and expensive, as instanced by the bill to give a monopoly of the Newfoundland fishery to Quebec. Weakening the imperial economy, he warned, played into the hands of the French, who were always ready to take any action against Britain, even if their ministers professed peace.[75] On 26 October in the House of Lords, Shelburne asserted that 'the commerce of America is the vital stream of this great empire'.[76] Then in a speech of 15 December, he returned to the theme of madly damaging the trade of the colonies, arguing that the new policy of privileging trade with Nova Scotia violated the terms of 'that valuable and truly beneficial law, the act of navigation'. The latter was the key to the 'palladium of our commerce, that great source of all the advantages that we now happily enjoy, as the first commercial and trading nation in Europe; for the spirit and letter on which the whole of that law is founded are that no article or commodity shall be directly imported into the colonies from the place of their growth'.[77] Britain was taking action to support trade in corrupt places like Halifax, 'the gin shop of America', while allowing the infinitely more valuable trade with the colonies to be ruined. Shelburne was concerned about rumours of the use of mercenaries from Russia against the North Americans, and offers to Irish Roman Catholics to be paid to fight, in addition to letting 'the savages, of the back settlements, loose on the provincial subjects of Great Britain'. The fact that it was proving so difficult to raise troops domestically underlined the unpopularity of the war. Ministers did not appear to appreciate the danger of the 'wild and dangerous doctrine' of 'separating from America, and letting trade take its own course'. The point was that if the union was dissolved, Britain would be beggared economically, and 'If the cord is broken', Shelburne predicted, 'there will be an end to all hold[ers] of the funds.' It was a fact that '[t]he trade of America is mortgaged to our stockholders. It would be dishonest to touch it. The ministers ought to know this, and tremble at whatever hazarded the loss of our American commerce.'[78] Shelburne was pessimistic about Britain's prospects and horrified by the ministers' action in North America, because he was convinced that war was about to break out with France and with Spain. He argued, on 31 October 1776, that France was arming itself, and already had a naval fleet superior to that of Britain. Such concerns intensified in 1777, when he asserted that ministers were insane to take at face value French and Spanish promises of neutrality, because both states were already supplying the North American colonies extensively and had large numbers of troops of their own, in places such as Hispaniola, who could be called upon when war commenced. It was not too late to save the day, because the North Americans did not want to be independent. Letters published in the name of the Louis-Joseph de Montcalm, the French commander during the Seven Years' War, were reputed to have identified a desire for independence in New England, but Shelburne declared these to be a forgery.[79] Increasingly, however, the war was going badly, the navy and the army were being mismanaged, and Britain was pushing North America to become a set of small republics.[80]

In his speeches, Shelburne drew a direct parallel between Ireland and North America. Both colonies were 'subordinate to this country' but enjoyed 'rights, the free and unimpaired exercise of which should be preserved inviolate'. The most important and fundamental right was 'that of granting their own money'. The Irish had 'always exercised that right uninterrupted' and 'so has America till very lately'. The violation of this 'invaluable privilege' was the 'true grievance' that had inspired the rebellion. In 1775, Shelburne was confident that if Britain restored the status of the Americans to parity with that of the Irish, everything would 'soon return into its former channel'. North Americans, no longer taxed arbitrarily, would acknowledge once more the supremacy of parliament.[81] Proof of his position, Shelburne was certain, lay in Irish relations with Britain, because it was the case that however badly the war went, and however great the costs of fighting the Americans, 'Ireland should never be called on to contribute a shilling towards defraying the expense'. In Ireland, it was acknowledged that 'taking money without the consent of the people, was so fundamentally wrong' that 'the more we consider it, the more we must be convinced that we have no right to tax America'. Shelburne concluded that 'no subtlety of lawyers can subvert this truth; nothing could be more directly in point than the example of Ireland'.[82] Revenues generated by taxing profits from trade was acceptable to support the costs of a colonial establishment, and such measures 'interested the people in the protection of their trade, and it taught them to inspect into the application of their monies'. In North America, however, so great was the consumption of British goods that taxation would be a mistake; it was a maxim that 'if any position could be infallible, it was that a colony could not be an object of revenue while it consumed our manufactures'. Ireland, by contrast, ought to be a source of revenue because it did not consume British manufactures to any large extent. As Shelburne put it, 'the quota from the latter [Ireland] was not adequate to its abilities, though the proportion was unequally distributed; the rich were spared and the poor overburdened'. He recommended a parliamentary commission to examine the distribution of taxes in Ireland and the means to derive greater revenues from the colony. The tragedy was that in the case of America, the ministers of Britain were failing to act in accordance with justice and with liberty. Their behaviour was rather, in Shelburne's view, following the process identified by Sophocles in *Antigone* (vv. 620–23): *Quos Deus vult perdere, prius dementat* ('Those whom a god wishes to destroy he first drives mad').[83]

Again, following a parallel with Ireland, Shelburne held that Britain should retain 'the right of commercial control and regulation' over America, since 'the power of regulating the trade of the colonies was the very essence of the political connection subsisting between both countries'. The debt under which he said that the empire groaned was truly the debt of every person subject to the British crown. The Americans deserved redress for the offence of violating their rights, and a guarantee that they would enjoy henceforth the right to tax themselves through their own colonial legislative chambers. In other words, they would become exactly like the Irish. In October 1776, Shelburne declared that he had not changed his opinions, and that proof of these could be found in Price's work on events in America.[84] Price's book had appeared in February, with the title *Observations on the Nature of Civil Liberty, the Principles of Government and the Justice and Policy of the War with America*. Price sent the conclusion of the work to Shelburne, requesting that 'your Lordship be so good as to look over it, and to correct and alter it in any manner you think proper'. He particularly wanted a fuller account of Shelburne's plan for peace, noting that 'I am sensible that the account of your Lordship's plan wants to be filled up and amended'.[85] Shelburne's plan was based on his speeches to the Lords of 1775, condemning 'the specious language of the supremacy of the British legislature' and demanding for North Americans the right to raise their own revenues and administer their own government, while accepting trade policy and international relations determined from London. Price accepted from Shelburne 'all the alterations your Lordship has proposed', and added material concerning Nova Scotia that he had drawn upon in parliament.[86] The *Observations* appeared with a partial epigraph drawn from Virgil's *Aeneid*: 'What is this strange frenzy? Where are you headed now, alas, unhappy citizens? This is not the enemy and unhappy camps of Greeks that you are attacking. You are burning your own hopes.'[87]

The *Observations* included a summary of Shelburne's plan for peace, and argued that had it been adopted at the end of 1775, 'a pacification would have taken place, on terms highly advantageous to this kingdom'. The colonies would, Price argued, 'have consented to grant an annual supply', so that the national debt could have been partially paid off, 'some of our worst taxes might be taken off', and the price of manufactured products reduced as a result. Britain would have united, and 'our whole force would be free to meet at any time foreign danger'. With the end of the disturbances, 'the influence of the Crown would be reduced', 'our Parliament would become more independent' and the empire 'restored to a situation of permanent safety and prosperity'.[88] Instead, Britain was on the edge of a precipice, facing events that would end either in disaster or the improvement of the polity:

> An important revolution in the affairs of this kingdom seems to be approaching. If ruin is not to be our lot, all that has been lately done must be undone, and new measures adopted. At that period, an opportunity (never perhaps to be recovered, if lost) will offer itself for serving essentially *this country*, as well as *America*; by putting the national debt into *a fixed* course of payment; by subjecting to new regulations, the administration of the finances; and establishing measures for exterminating corruption and restoring the constitution.[89]

The outbreak of the Gordon riots confirmed Price and Shelburne in their diagnoses of the ills of Britain. On 2 June 1780, the Protestant Association of London, led by Lord George Gordon and fifty-thousand strong, marched on the House of Commons, and at night attacked the homes of Catholics in the Moorfields area, where numerous Irish immigrants lived, in addition to Newgate prison, the Bank of England and the Fleet prison.

The Protestants were enraged by the Papists Act of 1778, which in return for an oath of allegiance countered the penal laws upon Catholics, allowing them to open schools and to own and inherit land. Gordon had been successful in preventing the Act being incorporated into Scots law, and projected an image of Catholic soldiers, welcomed into the army because of events in North America, being employed to restore absolutism and the old faith. One anonymous commentator reported that the shocking events of the riots had divided the country in the manner of the religious disputes that had shattered England in the 1640s:

> [H]e who would thoroughly comprehend the danger of the late troubles, must travel back near a century and a half . . . to former troubles, which, though far more serious in their consequences, were, at the instant, much less alarming perhaps than those whereof we have been unhappy spectators.[90]

In speeches of 2 and 3 June 1780, Shelburne stated that 'the Ministers had themselves to thank for the present tumults', demanded reforms to the police of London, in part through the election of magistrates, and argued that having given in to similar disturbances in Scotland, the government had 'promised all that the zeal and enthusiasm of an enraged mob had prompted them to demand'.[91] Shelburne made clear his own fear of militant Catholicism, giving the example of his forcing a nobleman to shut down a seminary for Catholic education. In taking up arms against a mythical and imagined Catholic rebellion, however, Britain was dividing against itself, and in crisis. Shelburne was identified as one who, 'with other patriots', was 'constantly exposing the weakness of the British army and navy, and even representing them as much weaker than they in reality are', supplying 'melancholy pictures of the decayed trade and agriculture of England', leading to the aggravation of 'the discontents and divisions of its inhabitants' by predicting 'nothing less than national misery and ruin'.[92] Meanwhile a defence of Shelburne's support for Catholic liberties in Ireland, addressed to George Gordon, stated that 'all Europe begins to relax in severities which originated in superstition, and subsisted through the zeal of bigotry and ignorance':

> Remember my Lord [Gordon], that when an African negro sets his foot upon the English shore, he is then as free, to all intents and purposes, as the most respectable member of your Lordship's associations. How doubly barbarous is it then to attempt or wish to fetter those who have the good fortune of being born in such a country [as Ireland].[93]

VII

To Shelburne and to Price, debt and corruption were the great bugbears of the polity. In 1780, they collaborated with John Horne Tooke in a book that appeared anonymously under the title *Facts Addressed to the Landholders, Stockholders, Merchants, Farmers, Manufacturers, Tradesmen, Proprietors of Every Description, and Generally to All the Subjects of Great Britain and Ireland*, which went through at least seven editions during the year. The work commenced with the assertion that the independence of judges was one of the foundations of British liberty, and was a right won through long battle against the prerogative power of the crown:

> It was only by the death of one king and the expulsion of another, by a long train of cruel civil wars, and a deluge of the best blood in the country, that our ancestors could at length obtain from *prerogative*, that the judges (who only *declare the law*) should no longer be under the corrupt influence and power of the crown. And, though costly, they thought the purchase wisely made.[94]

The equivalent and contemporary battle for liberty was different. It was against the corruption of members of parliament 'through which the influence of the crown now threatens our ruin'. The text cited Bolingbroke's *Dissertation upon Parties*, which first appeared in *The Craftsman* in 1733, for a justification of the separation of parliament and the crown:

> What is now our struggle? That those who *make the laws* shall no longer be prostituted to infamous, and sordid gain: that the legislature itself may be rescued from temptations which flesh and blood cannot withstand. The violence of *prerogative* diverted the streams of justice, and turned the course of them from their natural and ordinary channel yet when the hand of violence was taken off, when the dam of prerogative was removed, the streams ran clear and purer than before. But the corruption of Parliament is not merely a turning of the course, it is a poisoning of the water at the fountain-head. 'The integrity of Parliament', it has been well observed, 'is the key-stone that keeps the whole together. If this be shaken, our constitution totters: if it be quite removed, our constitution falls into ruin.'[95]

It was declared that numerous current members of parliament could be considered as 'three or four hundred mercenaries' who had 'already effected against the prosperity and liberties of this country, what ten times as many thousands out of them would have attempted in vain'. Just as former generations had 'shut up, with all the bars and bolts of law' the prerogative power, it was vital in the present to 'close the avenue of corruption, through which the influence of the crown now threatens our final ruin'. The book was in consequence an explanation of the need for, and an explication of the means to 'a thorough and speedy reformation'.[96]

The latter-day Bolingbrokes were Charles Lennox, 3rd Duke of Richmond, and Shelburne himself. Richmond's and Shelburne's speeches against the power of the crown were especially critical from December 1779, attacking the civil list and extraordinary expenditure upon the army and the navy. The state was portrayed as close to being 'dashed to pieces' because of the decline of trade and national revenues, depopulation and the loss of confidence, the corruption of manners and the anticipation of 'a dreadful convulsion':

> Our trade is diminished; and together with it, private circulation and credit. Our manufacturers are taken off to the navy and army. Depopulation goes on with rapidity. The cash of the nation is scraped together for public loans; and, little being left for any other purpose, Industry is cramped, commerce starves, and land falls. Many persons, foreseeing danger, begin to hoard the coin. The Bank begins to find that it has issued as much paper as it can support. Most of the new taxes have proved deficient. Complaints of distress are general. The spirits of men are soured, and many disposed to break out into open resistance. These evils will increase whilst the war continues: and whether we are invaded or not, must at last terminate in a dreadful convulsion.[97]

A direct contrast needed to be drawn with France, where the administration of finance was characterised by openness and thrift. Shelburne, Price and Tooke stated that French reforms had succeeded in putting the monarchy on an altogether superior footing to Britain's, and that for Britain this was not simply an alarm bell but 'serious beyond consideration'. So extensive were the French reforms that normal rules of social hierarchy and office-holding had been abandoned, and a new system based upon merit was paying enormous dividends, exemplified by the posts held by the Genevan Protestant Jacques Necker in the treasury, and the naturalised Spaniard Antoine de Sartine as minister for the navy:

> If the monarch has wisely come forward to his people, the people in their turn have advanced towards his ministers. And perhaps the most striking feature (and not the least alarming circumstance) in the French nation at this moment, is; that the haughty noble has foregone

> his idle claim of birth, and the vain native renounced his national prejudice and religious bigotry; and the whole nation with universal joy and satisfaction behold *Le Petit-fils d'un Horloger, un Huguenot* (to lay everything in one word) *un Genevois*, at the head of their finance, and a Monsieur Sartine, *fils d'un Marchand de Drap*, directing the operations of war.[98]

Facts Addressed to the Landholders stated that French expenditure on the Seven Years' War had only been just over half that of Britain, and that French finances were so healthy that the current war was being paid for by retrenchment, and without recourse to additional taxes. The conclusion was that Britain was foolish to fight the French, and almost certain to be defeated.[99] Britain's public finances had become 'prey to rapacious money-lenders and an extravagant minister; who between them are wasting its treasure and completing its ruin'. Existing regulations could not be relied upon, and savings were vital, because 'the expenses of the nation are now so enormous'. At the same time, the corruption of parliament was so great that if George III decided, like Nero, to promote 'his horse to the office of First Lord of the Treasury, his neigh would be attended by as great a majority as that which now follows the heels of the present noble Lord in possession'. What was termed 'the corrupt influence of the crown' had risen 'to such a height' that either parliament needed to be purged of placemen or 'the nation is finally and irrecoverably undone'.[100] In the 1790s, the radical John Thelwall announced that he had become very interested in the text:

> I have been at considerable pains to procure a pamphlet, published in the year 1780, entitled, 'Facts,' (without any name, but which was, in reality, the joint production of Lord Shelburne, the late Dr. Price, and John Horne Tooke)—a pamphlet which, from the history it contains of the extent and progress of this corruption, is particularly worthy of your attention.[101]

Thelwall reported, however, that Shelburne had denied any connection to the text after it appeared, because of the sudden possibility that he would gain ministerial office.

Shelburne considered the need for economic reform to be as almost as great in Ireland as on the mainland. In the debates on America he had drawn a parallel with Ireland, and made the point that had the same policy been applied to this colony, similar levels of rebellion could have been anticipated. Shelburne had a longstanding interest in the country of his birth, where he was among the richest landowners.[102] He was not the archetypal absentee Protestant landlord of popular infamy. Rather, he visited the country on a regular basis, and was deeply interested in the improvement of his estates. Shelburne and his family were acknowledged improvers, interested in the productivity of their tenants and the yield of their land.[103] This was the verdict, during his travels across Ireland, of Arthur Young, who praised Shelburne's own penchant for improvement. Young noted that Shelburne had introduced a bailiff from Norfolk to manage his farm at Rathan at Lismore, in County Waterford, because of his knowledge of advanced farming methods.[104] Mention was also made of a planned new community at Kenmare Bay in Kerry, where Shelburne had proposed to give ten acres of land to enterprising tenants who would establish manufactures to take advantage of the international transport offered by the deep river.[105] The goal of the Kenmare project, being developed at the same time as New Geneva, was stated to be 'to establish trade, fix manufactures, open a harbour, build docks and ships, and change the face of a barbarous country'.[106] Young also praised Shelburne's brother, Thomas Fitzmaurice, who had followed their father in establishing cotton manufactures at Ballymote in Connacht:

> [T]he late Lord Shelburne, came to Ballymoat [*sic*], a wild uncultivated region, without industry or civility; and the people all Roman Catholics, without an atom of a manufacture, not even spinning. In order to change this stage of things, his Lordship contracted with people in the north, to bring protestant weavers and establish a manufactory, as the only means of making the change he wished.[107]

Young reported that Shelburne *père* had lost £5,000 in the attempt; and that his wife had established sixty looms. It was their son, however, who trained himself in the weaving process, established a factory of ninety looms, and personally supervised every aspect of the business, including moving Protestant weavers from the north of the island. This was all the more remarkable because Thomas Fitzmaurice had been advised 'by his friends, never to engage in so complex a business as a manufacture, in which he must of necessity become a merchant; also, engage in all the hazard, irksomeness, etc., of commerce, so totally different from his birth, education, ideas and pursuits'.[108]

That his family had experience of moving people within Ireland or from beyond Ireland, in order to develop manufactures, was important in convincing Shelburne of the potential presented by New Geneva. His fascination with the possibilities of water-based transport from Waterford must also have played a part in his persuading of the Genevans to move to the village of Passage East. At the same time, Shelburne had, historically, rarely been involved directly in Irish politics. He followed Chatham's line of argument, that Ireland ought to generate more revenue for the administration of the empire, and that in consequence the system of undertakers controlling the Irish parliament was in need of more direct ministerial governance. This had been why Chatham supported George Hervey, 2nd Earl of Bristol's appointment as viceroy in 1766–67, anticipating his gaining popular support among the Patriot opposition through a Septennial bill to set a limit the duration of parliaments, in addition to his constant residency in Ireland. Bristol was followed by George, 4th Viscount Townshend, who also attracted Patriot admiration by introducing the Octennial Act for parliaments, replacing the rule that elections occurred only at the accession of a new monarch (and adding a year to the provisions of the earlier Septennial bill so that there would be no overlap with British elections), as well as demanding that judges in Ireland be given tenure similar to that in England. Such strategies dovetailed with Patriots' arguments in favour of equal treatment for the two countries.[109] As secretary for the Southern Department, Shelburne had been concerned that Townshend's alterations to the constitution between Britain and Ireland might 'draw in question the nature of the connection between Great Britain and Ireland, which it has been always thought sound policy to avoid'.[110] Such commentary by Shelburne upon Irish politics was rare, in part because he despised both the undertaker system and the patronage of the crown, on the grounds that both led to jobbery.[111] Although he was well informed about goings-on, he avoided involvement, as far as possible. Another exception, however, was during the transition from the parliamentary rule of the undertakers, which Townshend called 'the crisis of Irish government', when his bill to augment the Irish army by three thousand men was initially defeated by the undertakers in parliament, only passing in 1769.[112] Townshend raised the costs of governing Ireland by increasing the numbers of placemen funded by the crown, just as expenditure on bounties was growing and the value of land decreasing with the decline of tillage, all of which inflated the Irish national debt. It was to contribute to servicing the debt that Townshend's successor Harcourt proposed a tax on the holdings of absentee landlords, many of whom were members of the London parliament. The opposition of the Rockingham Whigs, with Edmund Burke prominent among them, centred on the likely effect of the tax in reducing the value of landed property, in addition to sowing dissent between England and Ireland, and being likely to precede a more general tax on Irish land.[113] Shelburne reputedly thought the tax to be unjust.[114] He followed his mentor Chatham, however, who stated that the Irish House of Commons needed to be supreme in matters of revenue-raising, and that threats by the English to veto such measures risked turning Ireland into North America:

> I could not, as a peer of England, advise the King on principles of indirect, accidental English policy, to reject a tax on absentees, sent over here, as the genuine desire of the Commons of Ireland, acting in their proper and peculiar sphere, and exercising their inherent, exclusive right, by raising supplies in the manner they judge best. This great principle of the constitution is so fundamental, and, with me, so sacred and indispensable, that it outweighs all other considerations.[115]

Shelburne's concern about the state of Ireland, intensifying as time passed, was prompted, as his speeches reveal, by the parallel with North America, and the risk that events there would inspire the Irish too to rebel. The strategy he adopted was to encourage economic reform and cut expenditure in Britain and Ireland, to combat constitutional innovation and to ensure that popular disturbances were crushed. This was why, when Rockingham demanded action on Ireland in 1779, Shelburne declared against the movement of Volunteers, calling them 'an enraged mob':

> He was very sure that the bare knowledge of such a motion would do good in Ireland. The people, he knew, were loyal; and as to their being in arms, it was only an enraged mob, of whom there was not a man but would defend his country against the common enemy, should any attempt be made on it. As for the Associations, they could do no harm to Great Britain . . .'[116]

This (called by Martyn Powell 'a monumental gaffe') ensured that Shelburne was mistrusted by Irish Patriots and Volunteers up to his time as prime minister. On his appointment to the office, the Volunteers declared themselves against the proposed withdrawal of five thousand Irish troops for service in the British navy.[117]

When Lord North resigned as prime minister, on 20 March 1782, Ireland was in upheaval, with demands for legislative independence being expressed by Volunteers and Patriots, and with the Irish parliament due to reconvene on 16 April. Both of North's ministers in Ireland, the lord lieutenant Frederick Howard, 5th Earl of Carlisle and the Irish chief secretary William Eden, 1st Baron Auckland described their positions as 'a seat of thorns', with Carlisle seeing 'black clouds everywhere'.[118] William

Henry Cavendish Cavendish-Bentinck, 3rd Duke of Portland, was named the new lord lieutenant in the Rockingham ministry that replaced that of North, and in which Charles James Fox served as foreign secretary and Shelburne as home secretary. Portland attempted to negotiate with the Patriot leadership in Ireland, partly through Fox's links with James Caulfeild, 1st Earl of Charlemont, and proposed a negotiated 'final adjustment' of relations between England and Ireland.[119] The strength of feeling in Ireland, however, led Portland to accept that he was powerless before Grattan in the Commons and Charlemont in the Lords. Fox's offer of commissioners, of the kind that had been proposed at the time of the Scottish union, came to naught. Shelburne's advice to the new Irish chief secretary Richard Fitzpatrick, not to bow down to the Patriots, in mid-April, was recognised to be meaningless by the end of the month.[120] During the month of April, John Beresford had informed Shelburne's close friend Colonel Isaac Barré that 'things are become very serious here'.[121] Beresford followed up this warning in May, stating that '[t]he temper of the people at present is such that, if it be not managed with the greatest skill and nicety, there is no saying what the issue may be. The nature of mankind is prone to run from one extreme to the other, and it is in a peculiar manner the disposition of Ireland to be always in extremes.' Ireland had, in Beresford's view 'emerged from a state, if not of slavery, at least of obscurity, into a nation, has inspired the bulk of the people with ideas of their own consequence'. This had given the people formed into Volunteer companies 'an imaginary strength, which we suppose we possess from our armed associations, without allowing anything for the relative situations of the two countries'. Beresford warned Shelburne, through Barré, that Ireland remained in crisis because of misgovernment, and that the Duke of Portland, in giving up too much to the Patriots and the Volunteers, had weakened the bonds between colony and mother-country. Firm government was required:

> It was early foreseen that the spirit of the people would force a measure declaratory of our rights, as it is called, or, in other words, would no longer submit to the usurped right of your Parliament to make laws for us; and it was thought prudent, by a repeal of 6th George I, to quiet the minds of the people, and if that had been done, I am satisfied that everyone would have been contented, thinking that a great deal had been gained. But the measures which have been taken tend to raise the ideas and spirit of the people, and the leaving the country without any Government, I may say, for so long a period, has done infinite mischief.

> If you Ministers of England imagine that you can rule this country by the same modes that you do England, you are very much mistaken; what might answer very well with you will have a contrary effect here. You cannot govern this kingdom by popularity, it would annihilate the consequence of those persons who now guide the spirit of the people. If a Chief Governor was to be too popular, if all grievances were removed, the leaders of faction among the volunteers would be reduced to the level of their neighbours; and therefore Government here will find that they must take up the reins, and guide the State, even although they lose thereby a certain amount of popularity, and they may be certain that they will do so as soon as they exert themselves.[122]

By May 1782, Portland was informing Shelburne that 'the precise limits of the independence which is required' needed to be settled; Grattan, on 26 May, declared that he and his supporters would 'proceed as if refused', and was even contemplating the use of force.[123] By this time, Rockingham's cabinet had decided to yield to the Irish Patriots' demands for the repeal of the Declaratory Act and of Poyning's Law, and this had been ratified at Westminster in each House on 17 May, although accusations were made that dangerous 'distinct dominions' were being established.[124] Shelburne then informed Portland that the new relationship between England and Ireland had to be agreed upon, suggesting that in order to prevent 'future jealousy and discontent' the Irish might agree to 'share [Britain's] fate, likewise standing and falling with the British nation'. Shelburne hoped that this would entail giving the London government the right to supervise commercial policy, the Privy Councils the right to advise on legislation, a veto for the king and the standardisation of commercial regulation.[125] In a further letter, of 9 June, Shelburne confessed that the Patriots now had to accept British dominion, because the two kingdoms could only be one 'by Ireland now acknowledging the superintending power and supremacy to be where nature has placed it, in precise and unambiguous terms'.[126] In fact, Grattan was only willing to accept British dominion with regard to foreign policy, and not to trade policy too, and negotiations with Shelburne collapsed, the Patriots themselves becoming divided when Flood declared, against Grattan, that legislative independence had not been sufficient. The decrepit state of the relationship between politicians in Britain and in Ireland was underlined by two letters from Portland to Shelburne in June. In the first (6 June), Portland promised that an act would soon be passed by which 'the superintending power and supremacy of Great Britain, in all matters of state and general commerce, will be virtually and effectually acknowledged'; Ireland would even contribute to the costs of offensive or defensive war. Then on 22 June, Portland wrote, in 'disappointment and mortification', that so divided were the parties, and so lacking in trust and composure, that 'any attempt to conciliate the minds of this nation to any such measure as I intimated the hope of, would at this moment be delusive and impossible'.[127]

After Rockingham's unexpected death on 1 July that year, Shelburne focused on forming his own ministry. Few expected it to be successful. As the Irish Lord Charlemont put it, Shelburne's personality was not expected to maintain calm and cohesion, especially by contrast with Rockingham:

> The death of my beloved friend lord Rockingham had now brought about, as I ever imagined it must, a great change in the English ministry. Those discordant spirits, which had only been held together by the universal confidence in his character, now flew asunder. Such is the prevailing influence of virtue even in a depraved age, and among those who value her least. The [Whig] party was broken to pieces. Fox was displaced, and was followed by the Cavendishes, etc.; but such of the Whigs as were not his immediate adherents remaining attached to the royal party, Lord Shelburne was put at the head of the new administration, which with such a head promised but little stability.[128]

Charlemont was equally pessimistic about Shelburne's view of Irish independence, stating that 'There are two or three, I am told, in the cabinet by no means friendly to the emancipation of Ireland,—Lord Shelburne, and of course Dunning and Barré. However, if she is but firm and temperate, she may now obtain everything in spite of them.'[129] Shelburne, as noted in the previous chapter, made George Nugent-Temple-Grenville, later 1st Marquess of Buckingham (known as Earl Temple until 1784) lord lieutenant on 17 August 1782, and his brother William Wyndham Grenville, later 1st Baron Grenville, the new chief secretary. They were the sons of George Grenville, prime minister between 1763 and 1765, and Elizabeth Wyndham. Grenville was best known for the Stamp Act of 1765, which had brought down the wrath of the North American colonies, and for prosecuting John Wilkes. Earl Temple when in the House of Commons had opposed North American independence, but in the Lords, from 1779, he had been associated with Shelburne's demands for the reduction of public expenditure.

Ireland remained in crisis. Flood continued to battle for the British parliament to renounce formally the right to legislate for Ireland, and refuse British judges the right to hear appeals concerning decisions taken in Irish courts. The atmosphere was increasingly febrile. As the Irish peer the Earl of Mornington informed Grenville, relations between Britain and Ireland were tense, and recruitment to the navy was being refused on the grounds of Ireland's lack of independence:

> [T]he poison of Flood's insinuations has diffused itself through the country with more rapidity than even despondency could imagine. The people begin to think the repeal the sixth of George I an inadequate concession; they begin to lose their confidence in Grattan, the most upright and temperate demagogue that ever appeared in any country. Flood rises upon the ruins of Grattan's popularity and, to crown it all, several of the Volunteer Corps have ceased to recruit for the British navy. Lord Abingdon's bill and speech gave much offence.[130]

The young Earl Temple wanted to move away from the politics of opposition that he recognised continued to divide Ireland, including what he saw as the illegal campaigns of the Volunteers. He informed the Patriot leader Lord Charlemont that his aim as lord lieutenant was to 'reform [Ireland's] expenditure, and correct the abuses in her revenue, and finally to reduce that impolitic and unconstitutional influence which has been the bane and ruin of both countries'.[131] To this end, Temple rejected all groups within or beyond parliament that appeared before him in the guise of faction or party, and rejected demands for appointments as dangerously restoring 'that aristocracy which it cost this country so much to break'. At the same time, he was worried by Shelburne's response.

As Temple put it in a letter to his brother, 'Lord Shelburne does not see the situation of Ireland in the same alarming light with ourselves', because of his faith in the effects of international peace and economic reform. Peace would have positive effects, but 'Lord Shelburne is mistaken in thinking that the Volunteers will, by this event, be completely thrown upon their backs'.[132] In other words, Shelburne was failing to acknowledge the nature of the Irish crisis and the danger to British authority deriving from the extreme views and potential for deadly action of those in authority among the Patriots. Whigs such as Temple were straightforwardly afraid of Shelburne's long-term policy of economic reform and the maintenance of British dominion, not because it was bad policy, but because it could not deal with the crisis as it existed:

> We have seen enough of the country to know that it is impossible to reason upon probable events from the rule which commonly guides the conduct of mankind. The grievance is that the real Government of the

> country is in the hands of those who, for the most part, do not think consequently, and do not act from any fixed principle whatsoever.[133]

Shelburne seemed to be under the same delusion as Richard Price, who was in contact with the Volunteer companies, and encouraging them to embrace civil and political liberty and free trade, the sole measures necessary to address all of the problems of the colony:

> Ireland is peculiarly situated in two respects. A great majority of the inhabitants are Papists; and a distribution of property, more unequal than in England or America, subjects them more to aristocratic tyranny. I have hinted, as a remedy for the former inconvenience, the admission of Papists to equal rights; but there may be stronger objections to this than I am aware of . . . Trade and liberty, will, it is to be hoped, in time, diffuse more in Ireland, and produce a less unequal distribution of it.[134]

Temple thought that such reforms would come too late, and fail to deal with the day-to-day crisis in the relationship between Britain and Ireland. This was why he wrote to his brother Grenville that

> something of the kind [renunciation] is indispensable, and I think it will let us down as handsomely as we could hope for from a scene of real difficulty and will certainly give us a weight and strength in this country which we know will otherwise be equivocal. This, however, attended with our peace (if providentially we are to have one), materially alters the appearance of things.

Even with the peace Shelburne was establishing, Temple asserted that Ireland had to be considered in the negotiations; trade policies involving Ireland 'must proceed from the Parliament of Ireland'. A new world had come into being in which Irish policy, if it did not emanate from Irish councils, had to be seen to be justified within Ireland and by Irish politicians.[135]

This was why a panicked Earl Temple pushed Shelburne to accept what became the Irish Act of Appeals, or Renunciation Act, of 17 April 1783; he had to threaten to resign in order to obtain Shelburne's support, because Shelburne kept proposing commercial union as a solution to the problem of the growing demands of the Patriots, confirming Temple's view of Shelburne's strategy.[136] Shelburne's apparent shifting of position, and his refusal for so long to acquiesce in renunciation, made serving in his ministry a misery for Temple. As he put it, 'our tenure with such a premier is most unpleasant'.[137] He also reported to his brother wider concerns, including the extent of general dissatisfaction with Shelburne, and the likelihood of a new ministry led by Fox.[138] For Temple, difficulties in Ireland were so acute there was no alternative to immediate action on the part of the British government. It was the case that if a Renunciation bill was not passed, 'we [he and Grenville] cannot remain another hour in Ireland. And it would be equally clear that English Government would not long survive us.'[139] Ireland was on the verge of becoming independent, and of following the lead of the North American colonies. The English were unaware of the extent of the Irish crisis, in Temple's opinion. To his brother, he admitted that 'the state of Ireland is not truly understood in England', adding that 'Mr. Foster [the Irish MP] assured me that he never was more astonished than at the total ignorance which prevailed on that subject in England'.[140] Irish anger with the delay in granting legislative independence was so great that, as Temple reported, 'Flood is restless and angry and seems to put all on the issue of a bill of rights which his advocates still recommend, and upon which I say nothing but that I do not understand it'.[141]

At the same time, Temple felt that he was making headway in terms of the reformist policies he had initiated, which were gaining the trust of the people. In particular, when a bad harvest of corn and potatoes risked famine, Temple immediately forbade exports of such goods to England or to Scotland. Temple was said to work from nine in the morning until at least five or six in the afternoon, every day, on the problems of Ireland, and was given credit for his response to the food scarcity.[142] He also took steps to develop the Bank of Ireland created in 1781, sought to find solutions to an Ireland–Portugal trade dispute, and planned to reduce the civil list and numbers of placemen, having discovered that more than half of Irish sinecures went to men who lived on the mainland and had no connection to Ireland itself.[143] Acknowledging that Ireland needed new laws with regard to trade, he asked his brother to '[t]hrow out to Lord Shelburne the advantage to Ireland and to the East India Company by allowing the Company to freight immediately from India to Ireland'.[144] So necessary were such measures that Temple was sure that if he did resign, on the grounds of betrayal by Shelburne's administration, it would 'throw the kingdom into revolt'.[145] Temple's popularity was underscored during Rutland's viceroyalty, when the latter was hissed at the Theatre Royal in Smock Alley, Dublin, before the crowd got up a cheer for Temple, provoking Rutland's embarrassment; as the reporter put it, he suffered a spontaneous bout of 'Ague cheek'.[146]

Shelburne's policy with regard to Ireland was initially as intransigent as it had been with regard to the independence of North America; for a long time he would not budge. He argued against Temple and Grenville, through Thomas Townshend, that 'The intention of the government here [is] to keep conscientiously to the terms upon which the two countries agreed last year.' Even after the Renunciation Act was accepted, Shelburne continued to assert that Ireland needed more than anything else a new trading relationship with Britain. In a meeting of 15 December 1782, he raised the possibility of 'a sort of treaty, a commercial system between the two countries, and a proportionable contribution to be paid by Ireland for the general protection of the empire'.[147] In this, he was following not only Smith, but another of his former associates, the dean of Gloucester and political economist Josiah Tucker, who from the 1750s had been demanding 'that glorious revolution in the commercial system which we have happily obtained in the political'. It was only when this might occur that Britain could be said to have 'abolished all the remains of ancient despotic power and Gothic barbarity. For as long as these charters and exclusive companies remain, we bear about us the marks of our former slavery.'[148] Temple agreed that commercial reform had to be a central area of policy into the future:

> I agree fully with Lord Shelburne upon the necessity of a commercial settlement; much remains there to be done, and many questions are involved in the consideration. The Navigation Act will stand as a material barrier against the trade of Ireland with the British settlements, as she cannot export any part of their produce to England; a restriction the more extraordinary as it would be imagined that England would by the same Act equally be restrained from export of those articles to Ireland.[149]

Ireland had first to be pacified, however. Shelburne was convinced that the key to future politics was the dismemberment of the mercantile system that was causing war and commercial monopoly. He had little time to spare for Ireland or for Temple, because of his focus upon the negotiations at Paris, which included plans for a commercial treaty between Britain and France.[150] As his sometime secretary Benjamin Vaughan put it, it was the case that 'something beyond Peace was aimed at in the negotiations of 1782 and 1783, and was even supposed by both sides to have been obtained'.[151] With Benjamin Franklin and others, Shelburne discussed granting legislative autonomy to various parts of the British Empire, of creating free ports in Britain and in France and of establishing international peace in perpetuity. Destroying the mercantile system had to take priority. On the domestic front, Shelburne was especially concerned with the reduction of the civil list and of government expenditure.[152] As one associated with parliamentary reform, he was accused of making 'government itself the projector' and of 'new modelling the Government' with deadly consequences.[153] Internationally, Shelburne was reported to be 'moving heaven and earth to get a peace'.[154] This was the priority, as Richard Price emphasised in a letter, and was worth all of the personal sacrifices, because with peace Shelburne had saved the country. All that remained was to deal with debt and parliamentary corruption:

> My heart is now in a great measure at ease; and my resolution is to trouble myself as little for the future about politics as possible. I reckon it enough that I have lived to see two great events which I have been long wishing for; I mean, the salvation of my country by a peace, and a revolution in favour of the liberty of the world by the settlement with America. There remains still two events of the last consequence; and it is in the power of your Lordship and your friends to accomplish them both. I mean; the reduction of the public debts, and the reformation of the representation. Without the one, a convulsion must still come; and without the other, we cannot be called a free country.[155]

Ireland was significant as a state that had long been the victim of the mercantile system. Shelburne was interested in the New Geneva project because of his conviction that it would contribute to the realisation of the grand goal of moving to a world beyond corruption. That such a policy would only be effective in the long term was being made clear by the voices in Ireland attacking the ministry for raising five regiments of Fencibles to weaken the Volunteers, professing the loyalty of the companies of Volunteers and asserting the need for a further bill to confirm the independence of the Irish parliament.[156]

Shelburne's view that measures had to be taken to remove popular passions from politics, and to limit the capacity of the people to function as indepedent political agents, was shared by a number of contemporaries. The barrister Francis Dobbs, a sometime Volunteer and Patriot, declared in 1782 that Ireland had experienced 'a bloodless revolution', moving from tyranny to freedom, having won free trade and an independent parliament. Dobbs, a follower of Grattan and a critic of Flood, was convinced that the further pursuit of liberties and privileges had become unnecessary. The arrival of the Genevans was integral to this process of establishing a better future for Ireland:

> Let the Irish then, by their propriety of conduct, invite strangers to their land. They will bring their arts and wealth along with them. Their wealth will be dispersed, and what is better, their arts and industry will be diffused. I would rather see the promised colony from Geneva, which the Duke of Leinster has so gloriously invited, than twenty parchment renunciations, and twenty parchment bills of rights, that may be as easily broke through as the parchment that contains them. Let us get manufactures and people—let us become industrious, and thereby wealthy—and let us look forward to the only real strength of nations—men and money. This is the barrier I would raise to Irish Liberty.[157]

Dobbs described Ireland as existing 'almost in a state of nature' with 'her fields and her inhabitants' equally uncultivated, and where the production of linen alone was 'fully established'. Ireland as a country was superior to England in terms of natural resources, Dobbs held, but 'arts, industry and freedom' had 'raised England far above us', such that the English enjoyed 'peace and plenty in their looks', and were 'neat in their dress, and in their dwellings'. The Irish, by contrast, 'under light taxation, are meagre in their faces, filthy in their dress, and dwell in hovels'. This was a powerful rationale for the Genevan immigration.[158]

CHAPTER NINE

New Geneva

THE UNION LIGHT DRAGOONS of the City of Dublin had been established on 12 September 1780, under the leadership of Colonel Robert Cornwall, and wore a scarlet uniform with green facings.[1] They had responded positively to the meeting of the Ulster Volunteers at Dungannon on 15 February 1782, resolving with other Dublin corps, on 1 March, that as 'citizens and volunteers' they were seeking 'every constitutional mode of obtaining a redress of grievances'.[2] Meeting at Dublin on Monday 21 October 1782, the Dragoons were reported to have declared themselves to be resolved that 'Irishmen, armed in defence of their civil and religious liberties, ought to be attached to any country or body of people who have stood forward in support of so glorious a cause [as that of the Genevans]'.[3] A fuller version of this document was included in d'Ivernois's *Pièces relatives à l'asyle ouvert en Irlande aux Genevois opprimés*, which stated that the independent body of Dublin Volunteers, as reported by their secretary James Whilestone, had made this resolution, in addition to stating that the Genevans would be received 'among us as brothers and as friends'. The Union Light Dragoons had had Leinster's letter to d'Ivernois read out to them, and had similarly emphasised their entire support for the restoration of rights and liberties to the Genevans, and more generally for their 'glorious cause'.[4] D'Ivernois was reported to have accepted membership of the Dragoons and to have sported the uniform, alongside the watchmaker and merchant Ami Melly.[5] The Anglican pastor and tutor to the nobility William Coxe, who always had an eye on Geneva, wrote in 1789 that the New Geneva experiment saw 'the nobility and gentry of Ireland' seeming 'to vie with each other in countenancing the settlement'.[6] As noted above in chapter 6, both the Duke of Leinster and the Earl of Ely offered land to the former rebels. A similar level of support could evidently be found among the body of the people.

If the Genevans were from the first associated with the Volunteer movement, members of the governments in London and Dublin had very different ideas about their purpose. Shelburne undoubtedly had in mind combating France, and proving that Britain, whatever the views of the North American republicans, remained an asylum for liberty. In other words, New Geneva was indissolubly tied to the existing state of international relations. For others, New Geneva yielded a more positive image of Ireland. As the Catholic nobleman Robert Edward Petre, 9th Baron Petre put it, if the Gordon riots amounted to 'the black catalogue of the massacre, rapine and desolation . . . in the capital of the British empire, at the very threshold of their mild and beneficent sovereign', then a contrast could be drawn with Ireland. Ireland was not a papist enclave ready for rebellion, but rather 'a most comfortable and honourable asylum in the bosom of which, as the most promising nursery of toleration, happiness and freedom . . . oppressed Genevans have made choice for a place of refuge'.[7] The support of King George III for the project may well have been because it promised the promotion of forms of Protestantism, and of the morals associated with them that he admired. Jean-André Deluc, the author of the celebrated *Lettres physiques et morales, sur les montagnes et sur l'histoire de la terre et de l'homme* (1778), who was, as noted above, reader to Queen Charlotte at Windsor and a prominent member of the Georgian court, had been a leading defender of Calvinist mores at Geneva and a leader of the rebels in the city until he came to England in 1773. Many of the Genevan rebels were, as we have seen, his former political associates and friends. At the same time, however, there were rumours that Deluc, in part because of d'Ivernois's personal attacks upon him for failing to defend the *représentants*, was doing all he could to limit royal support for New Geneva.[8]

Once all parties had determined upon Ireland, a decision had to be made with regard to the location of New Geneva. Lord Temple took charge of this process. References to the project among his papers, and especially in letters to his brother and chief secretary William Wyndham Grenville, underline its significance for him. It was to Grenville that Temple reported in December 1782 that, the offer of land from the Duke of Leinster having been rescinded, he had decided instead to settle the Genevans on the Curragh of Kildare, inland and south-west of Dublin, because of its transport links and because of the availability of natural resources. Temple was at the time reforming the Bank of Ireland, which he expected to provide funds for the scheme:

> Mr. d'Ivernois is upon his return with his committee. The Duke of Leinster has abandoned them, and I have at last determined to settle them on the Curragh of Kildare, which from its vicinity to Dublin, to the Waterford river, to the Bog of Allen, and to Kilkenny coal seems the best spot. I fancy the Bank will lend the money.[9]

D'Ivernois was expected to return to Dublin before the end of 1782, and Temple informed his brother on 25 December that 'I am preparing for Mr. d'Ivernois, and have, I think, fixed for the Curragh of Kildare'.[10] Whether d'Ivernois rejected this location remains unknown, but he was involved with Temple throughout January, and particularly concerned that the home secretary, Thomas Townshend, might express British support for the government at Geneva that had replaced that of the *représentants* by force of arms. This was the first time that Temple complained about the exiles:

> D'Ivernois is very jealous for fear Townshend should write a civil letter wishing prosperity to the new Government of Geneva. Pray enquire about this. They are very unreasonable in their demands.[11]

By early February things had changed, and Waterford was being put forward as a better site for New Geneva. Temple had discussed with Grenville and with Shelburne the notion of establishing an educational institution within the new city, in part because of the expectation that professors of Geneva's Academy would be among the immigrants. This was to be kept secret, because of concern over the feelings of supporters of Trinity College Dublin, and the location of New Geneva at Waterford was to be shared only with Shelburne and Townshend:

> Tell Lord Shelburne that I am full of the idea, (which he must keep secret because of our University) of founding a Genevois College for education, in pursuance of the idea which we discussed together. Many circumstances decide me to wish to place them in the south; and I think we have nearly fixed our spot (near Waterford.) I wished to remove them from the northern republicans, and to place them where they might make an essential reform in the religion, industry, and manners of the south, who want it more. This you must dress in a wrote

> detail; but only mention the spot (which they eagerly press) to Lord Shelburne and to Townshend as a secret, which must be kept till the decision is finally prepared here to be submitted.[12]

The final decision was taken quickly. The Genevan commissioners 'gravely proposed that Ireland should lend' £100,000 for the new city, and were refused.[13] Their rationale was that the colony needed more than watchmakers, that skilled workers would flock to it if the conditions were right and that the result would be wealth for Ireland and 'general utility' for all.

Clavière underlined the extent to which the project had almost failed in a long letter, that must have circulated through *represéntant* circles throughout Geneva; we know this because it was transcribed in full by Ami-Aimé-Alexandre Dunant, a pastor at Céligny and *represéntant*, who kept a diary between 1782 and 1811. Clavière and his fellow commissioners had sought funds for the establishment of a jewellery and a watchmaking industry, falling back to the latter position when the British refused the higher level of investment requested.[14] The refusal of the larger sum was due to the fact that d'Ivernois, in his prior discussions with Temple and Shelburne, had suggested that the Genevans were already rich, and could cover many of the costs themselves.[15] Clavière made the same point: that the British had assumed they would arrive and immediately set Ireland working. On 3 March, the Genevan commissioners accepted the lower figure of £50,000, and Waterford as the location for New Geneva. Clavière was happy, calling Ireland 'a country preferable to all others', and Waterford ideal because of the grant of large amounts of land, 'given to us in full ownership, to dispose of in the manner that we deem most advantageous to New Geneva'. Waterford was superior to the land offered by the Duke of Leinster, because of the quality of the harbour and existing maritime trade.[16] The Waterford Union, at a meeting on 8 March 1783, affirmed their entire support for the project, and that the Genevans were opting rather for 'freedom in a foreign nation' than 'domestic slavery':

> Resolved unanimously, That from freemen armed, in defence of the essential rights of their country, every mark of respect is due to men who, whilst resistance was practicable, opposed the lawless attacks of despotism; and when, from inferiority of numbers, they found themselves unequal to the contest, relinquished a state whose rights they could no longer preserve. Resolved unanimously, That those free citizens of Geneva, who have sought an asylum in this nation, whose liberty has been newly restored to her by the public virtue of her armed

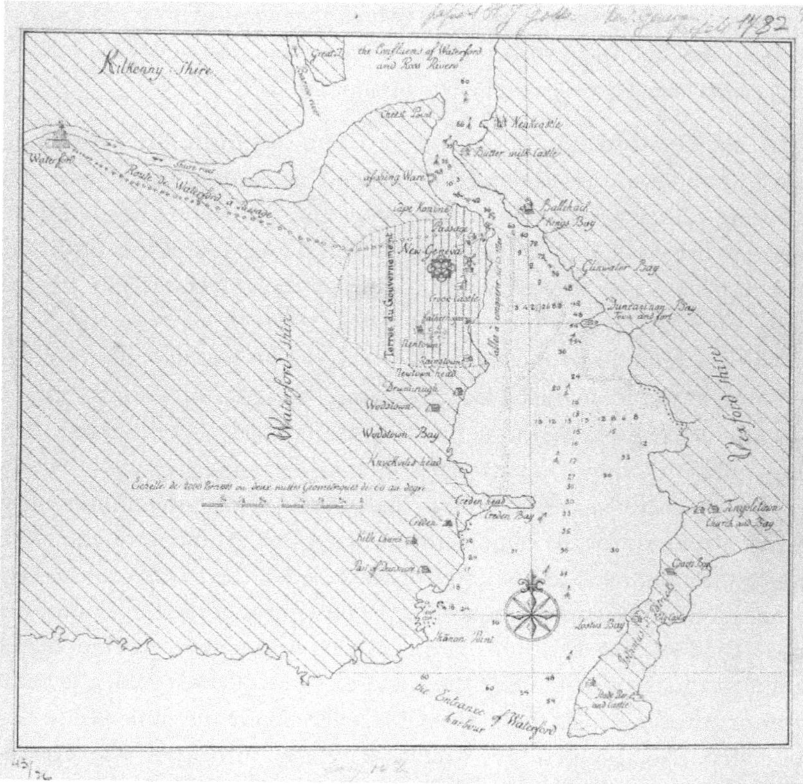

FIGURE 9.1. 'Map of New Geneva in Waterford'. Papiers H. A. Gosse, Département des manuscrits, Bibliothèque de Genève

> associations, demand our warmest exertions in support of their interests, and that we consider their cause and ours as one.[17]

It was public knowledge that Waterford was to be the location for New Geneva.

The Genevan commissioners Guillaume Ringler, Pastor Ésaïe Gasc, Ami Melly and Étienne Clavière were already in the city. On 14 February, having arrived in Dublin early that month, they dined with Temple, and with Du Roveray and d'Ivernois, at Dublin Castle. All of these men were naturalised as Irish subjects of George III, and promised an oath of fidelity to the crown: Ringler and Clavière on 5 February at Dublin, and Melly afterwards at Waterford.[18] Clavière signed himself 'Stephen' rather than Étienne in a letter he wrote at this time seeking to track down prints to encourage Genevan immigration that had gone missing in the customs house at Dover.[19] On travelling on to Waterford, Ringler, Gasc, Clavière and Melly were invited to dine with the officers of the Waterford Independent Company No. 1. As the lawyers within the party, d'Ivernois, Du Roveray and Grenus remained in Dublin to prepare the legal agreement with the British government.[20] The Waterford Company stated that they were so moved by the plight of the Genevans and 'so happy in the honourable distinction you have paid us, in choosing this kingdom for your asylum' that they entered the names of the Genevan commissioners on to the books of the Company.

Nine days later, on 17 March, a meeting of the Waterford Independent Light Company No. 2 was held, once more amidst scenes of ebullient support for the Genevans. The meeting resolved unanimously to do everything possible for the exiles:

> Resolved, that a people seeking refuge and protection in a Free Country, from the unjust and tyrannical attempts of a nation long famous for their boundless desire of enslaving mankind, deserve every encouragement and support from the sons of Freedom. Resolved, that we behold with the highest admiration the conduct of the Genevese, in relinquishing their native soil, when ruled by the iron hand of despotism, and preferring freedom in a foreign nation to domestic slavery; and we most heartily wish that this noble example may serve to evince, to the supporters of civil tyranny, the futility of attempting to enslave the minds of freemen, in whose breasts the flame of liberty glows superior to every interested consideration. Happy to see this nation become the protectress of distressed freedom, we shall receive the Genevese with open arms, and give them every assistance and support as fellow subjects and fellow citizens.[21]

The Genevan commissioners were appreciative of the support they were receiving at Waterford, replying on 19 March that

> Next to the approbation of their own consciences, nothing can yield greater satisfaction to the Genevans, who have in vain struggled to preserve the Independence, the Liberty, and the Laws of their country, than the marks of concern and esteem which they receive from the Volunteers of Ireland.[22]

At the same time, while they 'ardently wish[ed] to join their fate to that of a nation so respectable as yours', they asserted that they could not 'dissemble that it is to be feared that our countrymen will have the greatest obstacles to surmount, before it will be in their power personally to receive your fraternal offers of friendship'. Their stated goal was to become 'your countrymen'.

Negotiations between Temple, d'Ivernois and his commissioners, continued into the spring of 1783. This could have spelled disaster, because by 1 April Shelburne had fallen from power, being forced from office due to opposition to the peace with North America and the European powers that he had been negotiating in England and at Paris. Lord Grenville wrote to his friend William Pitt noting that, while peace was to welcomed, those who had supplied it were being condemned:

> I lament the state of the country, whilst I am ready to thank those who, not having contributed to the calamities of it, have had the courage and the perseverance to put a stop to them, at the risk of so much popular clamour and dissatisfaction.[23]

With the creation of the Fox-North coalition, between Charles James Fox and Frederick North (Lord North; from 1790 2nd Earl of Guilford), nominally under the leadership of William Cavendish-Bentinck, 3rd Duke of Portland, existing ministerial positions were thrown into turmoil. Antagonism towards Shelburne was rife, with commonplace portrayals of him as a madman and dreamer, who had brought down Britain through a shameful peace:

> Dr. Price, to serve the designs of Lord Shelburne, wrote several pamphlets to dishearten and degrade the nation; to prove by indirect indications, that none could retrieve the declining grandeur of this country, but men of trans-atlantic sentiments: experience has shown the vanity and presumption of the implication; the jesuitical temper and puny abilities of Lord Shelburne has proved, that his fantastic systems and idle theories, were but the wild creatures of a designing imagination, which, reduced into practice, bewildered and confused what was already sufficiently intricate and distracted.[24]

The initial good fortune of the Genevans was that Temple remained lord lieutenant until May, and only left Ireland on 5 June 1783. Temple continued to see Ireland as a place on the edge of a political precipice. In February, he had warned Thomas Townshend that the Irish army would have mutinied had he 'not proclaimed the same terms of discharge to them as appeared to have been given in England'. Like everything else in Ireland, in Temple's view, the army needed to be 'new modelled, and ought to follow the shape of the army in England'.[25] Just as he was welcoming the Genevans, in March, Temple received a delegation of weavers, who were suffering because of the collapse of their trade. Temple, it was said, 'received them with great politeness, and ordered one hundred pounds towards beginning a subscription for their relief', at the same time as he recommended the purchase of the products of Irish looms rather than foreign fabrics.[26] He was also fighting Scottish competition with the Irish herring industry, and requesting that ministers 'send me an order to take off the Cork embargo, now laid upon beef to France, Spain, Holland, and America', demanding it 'instantly, for it suspends all the trade of Ireland'.[27] This was one of the reasons why so many in Ireland petitioned for him to stay in office, including Travers Hartley at the Dublin Chamber of Commerce and James Cuffe in the Irish House of Commons. Many others across Ireland, but especially in Dublin, were vocal in their support of Temple:

> The Dublin volunteers, commanded by the Duke of Leinster, went in a body, with the Duke at their head, to the castle, with an address to his Excellency, requesting his continuance as chief governor. They were received in the most polite manner, as was also the corporation, which evinced its regard by means of the following declaration: 'The humble address of the Lord Mayor, Sheriffs, Commons, and Citizens of the city of Dublin, in Common-council assembled, presented, on the 11th day of March 1783, to the lord lieutenant. 'May it please your Excellency, We, the Lord Mayor, Sheriff's, Commons, and Citizens of the city of Dublin, in Common-council assembled, unanimously think it our indispensable duty at this time to approach your Excellency, with our sincere acknowledgments for your prudent and indefatigable regard to the honour and welfare of this country.[28]

John Beresford, also in the Irish Commons, noted the 'spontaneous and unsollicited' representations from Waterford, and announced that he had never known as diligent and dedicated a lord lieutenant.

Temple wrote to his brother a singularly candid letter, in which he blamed 'that old system of corruption' and 'faction' for 'the American war and all its circumstances', and predicted 'the total overthrow of our Constitution unless the property and weight of the nobility save it'. Temple's sense of the need for enlightened nobles like himself to hold fast meant that he did not leave office with Shelburne. He declared that he would not 'join an Opposition while the form of law or government continue to leave me a free man', that he did not 'look for Utopia in the hands of

Lord Shelburne or Lord North' and that the key in his view was to avoid extreme or foolish reform, his avowed intent being

> to support an Administration who will make head against the frenzy of reform; for I must freely own that I fear more from that reform than from the power of the Crown, which this convulsion in the empire will have truly weakened: upon this foundation I build my future . . . your object (like mine) is legal and real government; and I do not believe that the blessings of Mr. Fox's future administration will compensate with you the mischief which a successful popular opposition will bring forward.[29]

Temple ultimately refused to remain in office, because of the return of the Duke of Portland. Portland had, he believed, been a disaster as lord lieutenant in Ireland, by relying on the undertakers who had run the country into the ground and failed to address its many problems. Temple believed that by avoiding party lines, he had 'gained a solid and real strength in Ireland'. This had been 'certainly in the teeth of the party whom the Duke [of Portland] supported'. He was pessimistic, because Portland, he knew, was already intriguing with Lord Charlemont and Barry Yelverton, while Charles James Fox was doing the same with Grattan.[30] When he did resign, Temple was succeeded by lords lieutenant who also served for relatively short periods of time, and who were far less effective. Robert Henley, 2nd Earl of Northington followed Temple on 3 May 1783. Northington remained when William Pitt the Younger took office as prime minister on 19 December 1783, but was replaced on 11 February 1784 by Charles Manners, 4th Duke of Rutland.

Despite the turmoil at Westminster, agreement between the Genevan commissioners and their Irish counterparts was announced on 4 April 1783. Temple noted that a document had been determined upon by both sides, on the Irish side being the Earl of Tyrone, John Beresford, John Blaquiere, Henry Theophilus Clements, John Foster, Luke Gardiner, William Wyndham Grenville, James Cuffe, David La Touche, Andrew Caldwell, esq., Travers Hartley and Alexander Jaffray, and on the Genevan side Guillaume Ringler, Étienne Clavière, Jacques-Antoine Du Roveray, Ésaïe Gasc, Jacques Grenus and François d'Ivernois.[31] Temple's warrant referred to d'Ivernois's memorandum of September 1782, stating that the Genevans would 'bring with them their property, and . . . establish here those manufactures, which had rendered the citizens of that state so wealthy', and requesting 'the sum of fifty thousand pounds sterling, British money' which 'would be necessary to enable the first thousand emigrants to effect their purpose'. Of this money, 'a sum, not exceeding one half' was to be 'applied to defray the expences of their journey, and the carriage of their effects; and the remainder to be applied in the building, or providing houses for their reception'. This was declared to have been agreed upon by George III, who now confirmed the warrant for the settlement of the Genevans in accordance with 'principles truly interesting to justice and humanity'. The funds were to be set apart for the 'certain state officers and to certain of the nobility and gentry of this realm, together with the six commissioners now in this kingdom from the Genevans',

> to induce the said merchants, artists, and manufacturers, citizens, or inhabitants of Geneva, to settle in Ireland, under the conviction, that by their civil and religious principles, their industry, and their loyalty, they would materially contribute to the advantage of this kingdom.[32]

One of the problems with the document was that, while it specified that the funds were expected to be used, and granted the money 'in trust for the use of the Genevans settling in this country', the precise mechanism for expenditure was not described.

Temple asserted that a charter was to be drawn up specifying the laws of the colony with regard to politics and commercial life, but the warrant stated that the Genevans would be able to regulate their own internal concerns. They were to be naturalised, given land and supported in establishing manufactures. Further negotiation was advised with regard to the charter governing the Genevans, but it was accepted that a large dose of independence would be granted to the exiles, without violating existing law:

> To consider the rights, privileges, franchises, and immunities to be granted to the inhabitants of the said new intended town; and so soon as the general system shall have been submitted to, and approved of by us, then to prepare a draft of a charter, which will be referred to the consideration of his majesty's law servants for their opinion, and afterwards submitted to his majesty for his royal approbation, granting to the said citizens of the New Geneva, the establishment of magistrates, councils, or assemblies, with powers for regulating their internal concerns, in such manner as shall be most agreeable to the laws, under which they lived happily in their own country, and as shall be agreeable to the dispositions of the people, observing nevertheless, that, in no instance whatsoever, such municipal laws, or regulations, be repugnant to the laws of this kingdom.[33]

It was evident that d'Ivernois and Temple wanted to take forward the idea of moving the Genevan Academy to Waterford, as this became a key theme of the warrant:

> And whereas young persons of rank and fortune, from all parts of Europe, resorted to the city of Geneva, to profit from the system of education established there, under professors of eminence in useful and liberal studies and accomplishments; and whereas a school or academy, formed upon the same principles in this kingdom, would forward his Majesty's gracious dispositions for the encouragement of religion, virtue, and science, by improving the education and early habits of youth, and would remove the inducements to a foreign education; and being conducted with that attention to morality and virtue, which hath distinguished the establishments in that city, may attract foreigners to reside in this kingdom for the like purpose, we do farther pray and empower you to consider and digest a plan for a school and academy of education, to be established in the new colony, and to make a part of the constitution hereof, under such institution and regulations, and with such privileges as may best contribute to the ends hereby proposed.[34]

The importance of speedily realising George III's will was also emphasised in Temple's warrant. Already the Genevans were pressing the point that the colony would only be established if, in addition to resources being forthcoming, advantage was taken of the ill-will of the large body of *représentants* towards the government at Geneva:

> And we do pray and empower, that, after having given these subjects in general the fullest consideration, you do report unto us a particular detail of what shall be thought most fitting to be granted and ordered for the advantage and encouragement of the Genevans settling in this kingdom aforesaid, and for the welfare and prosperity of the new colony, that the necessary representations thereupon may be laid before his Majesty without loss of time; so that every facility may be given to the adoption of every measure calculated to give the said citizens of Geneva the fullest proofs of his majesty's royal protection and regard.[35]

It was reported on 24 April 1783, at Geneva by Ami Dunant, that letters were received from Clavière and Du Roveray to encourage the emigration. Clavière was altogether optimistic, 'exalting the advantages of a community in Ireland', but Du Roveray was more circumspect, underlining the need for the industrious, lacking wealth but with a taste for the sciences 'because the establishment of a university is desired', and especially tanners, fur-traders and masons. Against such views, a letter was mentioned from the watchmaker Léonard Bordier, who questioned the suitability of the climate, soil and buildings to be found in Waterford.[36]

With the fall of Shelburne and on account of the weakness of the Fox-North coalition—in part because of George III's detestation of Fox and every measure he proposed—Britain entered into a period of political uncertainty. Ireland went the same way, with concerns about the consequences of the peace, continued agitation for reform by the Volunteers and a dissolution of government that ultimately took place on 3 June 1783. Temple's departure and his replacement by Northington, in addition to Irish circumstances, caused Sackville Hamilton, acting as under-secretary to Northington, to reply to d'Ivernois only on 18 August 1783. Hamilton stated that he had prepared the documents necessary to put into practice the notions outlined in Temple's April warrant:

> I am commanded by my Lord Lieutenant to acquaint you, that he has signed a warrant to the proper officers to make out the draught of a commission, to be submitted to his Majesty for his royal signature, appointing the several noblemen and gentlemen who are to be entrusted with the settlement in this kingdom of the colony of Genevans as also the draft of a royal letter, granting the sum of £50,000 to those commissioners for that purpose. His Excellency has also given farther directions to the Prime Serjeant, Attorney, and Solicitor General, to prepare a draft of a grant of a charter of incorporation for the said colony, and draught of such bills to be laid before the Parliament at their next meeting, as shall be requisite for effecting the several purposes desired.[37]

Hamilton also asserted that Northington was as convinced of the merits of the scheme as his predecessor.

Resources were certainly forthcoming to facilitate the movement of the exiles. In October 1783, Lord North was said to have requested that the Admiralty send the brig *Lion* from the Downs to Ostend 'to carry the said Genevese from thence to Waterford'. Charles James Fox issued instructions that the Genevans should be granted 'every assistance and protection they may want'.[38] In the Irish House of Commons, the Patriot leader Henry Flood declared during a discussion of the need for a reduction of government expenditure that the Genevan colony had to be exempt, being a glorious example of virtuous men fighting against slavery, and therefore worthy of every support:

> [Discussion of retrenchment] should not have followed immediately the mention of the Genevan colony—a body of virtuous men, who, to avoid the most ignominious slavery, have sought an asylum in this country—it was not the proper place to use the word economy—there, it disgraces the virtuous and generous acts of men who have just recovered their own liberty; by placing it there, we may lose a great deal of honour, yet can save very little money.[39]

Between one hundred and two hundred and fifty exiles had by the winter of 1783 arrived from Geneva. The foundation stone of New Geneva was officially laid on 12 July 1784.[40]

II

John Angel wrote in 1781 that Ireland was ripe for economic development, having 'ornaments and natural advantages' in the form of 'the fertility of the soil, healthiness of the air, its many navigable rivers, large and safe harbours, the neighbourhood of the sea for the benefit of commerce, with all things necessary for the support and conveniences of life'. In addition, the country newly enjoyed the combination of laws well made and executed by Christian men of genuine merit:

> the blessings of an inviolable security of property, by mild and equitable laws, and a just and impartial distribution of justice, and where the constitution in church and state is established and revered, and where men of the greatest learning, piety and abilities, fill the most important stations.[41]

Another commentator wrote that 'Providence has done much for this country and man but little'.[42] Such circumstances could be turned to the advantage of Ireland, if the right form of development could be initiated. Waterford was in a perfect position in this regard, having harbours and navigable rivers, and a coast that made travel to England and to the continent straightforward, and having a long history of international trade. To the north of the county of Waterford lay those of Tipperary and of Kilkenny, separated by the river Suir; Waterford harbour was the boundary with the county of Wexford to the east, and to the west were the counties of Cork and again Tipperary. To the south, of course, was the Atlantic Ocean, and the proximity of St George's Channel and the Pembrokeshire coast meant that Wales and the mainland were remarkably close. That the rivers within County Waterford were navigable meant that travel within and beyond could be undertaken with ease.

Waterford was divided into the seven baronies of Coshmore and Coshbride, Decies-within-Drum, Decies-without-Drum, Gaultier, Glenahiry, Middle Third and Upperthird, and with the city of Waterford itself enjoying distinct liberties. Waterford was known historically for trade in cattle and in butter, for a cheese called 'Mullahawn', which was said to be so hard that only a hatchet could cut it, and for the production of salt, woad, fish and beer. The manufacture of linen had once employed large numbers of people, but had begun to fail. The manufacture of glass bottles had also declined, and that of fine glass, which was to make the city famous, was only initiated in 1783 by the Penrose family. Concerns about the effects of the American rebellion were voiced from 1775, when the people of Waterford presented a petition to the Irish House of Commons regarding the ban on the export of linen, a staple industry in the county, to the colonies. By 1778, the state of trade was so dire that resolutions were made at the summer assizes, blaming England for the state of affairs, and demanding that all members of community abjure foreign products in order to stimulate demand for local goods:

> Resolved, That we, our families, and all whom we can influence, shall, from this day, wear and make use of the manufactures of this country, and this country only, until such times as all partial restrictions on our trade, imposed by the illiberal and contracted policy of our sister kingdom, be removed: but if, in consequence of this our resolution, the manufacturers (whose interest we have more immediately under consideration) should act fraudulently, or combine to impose upon the public, we shall hold ourselves no longer bound to countenance and support them. Resolved, That we will not deal with any merchant or shopkeeper who shall, at any time hereafter, be detected in imposing any foreign manufacture as the manufacture of this country.[43]

The decline of trade in Waterford may well have been a reason for its choice as a location for New Geneva. It is likely that Beresford and other prominent figures from the county suggested it as a location in consequence. Waterford also enjoyed a long history of settlement by French Protestants. Two Waterford MPs, William Halsey and John Eyre, had been active in 1662 in supporting the act 'for encouraging Protestant strangers and others to inhabit Ireland', and in 1692, the two Waterford MPs Anthony Luxberry and Henry Nicholls support a similar act, passed in the same year.[44] This had led the Corporation of Waterford to provide funds, in March 1693, to support a large community of immigrants,

> [t]hat this city and liberties do provide habitations for fifty families of the French Protestants, to drive a trade of linen manufacture, they bringing with them a stock of money and materials for their subsistence till flax can be sown and produced on the lands adjacent; and that the freedom of the city be given to them gratis.[45]

A French church was also established at Waterford, in the choir of what had formerly been a Franciscan abbey, and the salary of the first minister, David Gervais, was paid for by the city. Many members of the French Protestant community became prominent in Waterford life over the following generations. An industry in the production of sailcloth was initiated, in conjunction with the famous Huguenot Lisburn linen merchant Louis Crommelin, author of an *Essay towards improving the hempen and flaxen manufactory in the kingdom of Ireland* (1705), and his associate John Latrobe. Subsidised by a series of government grants, this industry thrived into the 1740s, when it was patronised by the then lord lieutenant, Philip Dormer Stanhope, 4th Earl of Chesterfield. Chesterfield again encouraged Protestant emigration from mainland Europe, in the hope of stimulating Irish industry. His domestic chaplain was Richard Chenevix, whose father had moved to England after the revocation of the Edict of Nantes. Chenevix served as bishop of Waterford and Lismore between 1746 and his death in 1779, and was active in promoting members of Huguenot families within the Church of Ireland.

The particular location for New Geneva was selected to be in the parish of Crook, in the barony of Gaultier, six miles from Waterford, overlooking Waterford harbour, and comprising 1,831 acres. Crook had been the site of a castle belonging to the Knights of St John of Jerusalem until the Reformation, after which the lands had been granted by Elizabeth I to Protestant families.[46] New Geneva was to be erected between the small village of Passage and the headland of Crook, opposite Duncannon Fort, a star-shaped fortress erected in 1558 in order to combat Spanish invasion. The land, including the eleven acres selected for the town itself, was said to be owned by the crown, and therefore available as a royal grant, rather than requiring expenditure from the sum allocated by the state to establish New Geneva. The question of whether people needed to be paid for the land of New Geneva was to become contentious, but at the outset, it being presumed crown land, no difficulties were raised. The seriousness with which the project was approached was underlined by the allocation of an assay office to New Geneva, with a deputy assaymaster or assayer, in accordance with the provisions of the Acts of 23 & 24 Geo. III. c. 23, commencing on 1 June 1784. These Acts repealed the existing one with regard to the regulation of the manufacture or sale of silver or gold in Ireland. As a later account put it,

> The only standard of gold allowed by the Act 3 Geo. II. was that of 22 carat fine; this was altered by the 23 & 24 Geo. III. c. 23, whereby three standards are provided of 22, 20 and 18 carats fine, respectively. These standards were authorized by this Act to facilitate and encourage the manufacture of gold and silver wares and watch cases, &c., &c., in Ireland, and especially at New Geneva. This establishment and assay office did not continue to work over five or six years, and with this exception the Assay Office in Dublin has been, and is, the only one in Ireland, and has power and jurisdiction in all parts of Ireland. [47]

The prominent architect James Gandon provided a design for the town. Edward Stratford, 2nd Earl of Aldborough had proposed a plan of squares and gardens and buildings in a circular fashion, in the manner of so many walled towns of Europe. Gandon had different ideas. The first link with Gandon was through John Beresford, who had earlier, from November 1780, encouraged Gandon in secrecy to design a new custom house and docks, which he worked on from April 1781. Beresford and other commissioners for New Geneva were also 'Wide Streets' commissioners at Dublin, and their prior knowledge of Gandon ensured his commission. Gandon returned to Dublin in March 1782, and must have been on hand when the New Geneva plans were first agreed upon, as the work for Beresford in Dublin ultimately took ten years. He designed a new gaol and court house at Waterford for Beresford's brother, Lord Tyrone, between 1784 and 1787, and a crescent of five houses beside the new custom house in Dublin for Beresford's son John Claudius, between 1788 and 1793.[48] Gandon's plan for New Geneva survives. It included modest houses for watchmakers, a church at either end of the town and a grand quadrant, proposed to be half a mile in length. The very centre of the town was to be 'Temple Square', dedicated to the lord lieutenant, and including a statue of the great man carved by Edward Smyth.[49]

III

The process of building New Geneva was assigned to James Cuffe. Cuffe was the son of a landowner from County Mayo, and was elected MP for Mayo in 1769, a position his father had also held. Always seeking office,

Cuffe was appointed to the Barracks Board in 1772 and held this post until 1776, at which point he was made inspector of barracks, for which he was paid £600 per annum. He then became county governor of Mayo, a post which he held from 1779 to 1788, and on 17 September 1782 a member of the Privy Council. It was in the latter role that he had been informed about New Geneva, and must have put himself forward as one who could make a reality of the project. His appointment was to have profound ramifications.

Cuffe entered into an agreement with carpenters from Wicklow and from Dublin to commence the building of houses, and sent to Temple details of his agreement with them, and all of his plans, on 20 May 1783:

> Indented articles of agreement made and concluded upon the thirteenth day of March in the year of our Lord one thousand seven hundred and eighty-three. Between the Right Honourable James Cuffe of the City of Dublin one of His Majesty's most honourable Privy Council of the Kingdom of Ireland, Superintendant General appointed for the purpose of erecting the new intended town of Geneva in the County of Waterford on behalf of himself and the rest of the Commissioners appointed by His Majesty's Letters Patent for settling in this Kingdom a number of merchants' artists and manufacturers emigrants from Geneva of the one part and John Donnellan of Bray in the County of Wicklow carpenter and William Hendy of the City of Dublin carpenter of the other part. Whereas it is intended that certain dwelling houses and offices should be built and erected on the piece of ground marked out for the site of the said new town of Geneva on part of the Crown Lands near the town of Passage.[50]

Cuffe also enclosed descriptions of the properties, emphasising the quality of the planned works. The costs of two houses with two storeys were set at £392 and of two houses with one storey at £216. The initial promise was to have fifteen of the houses with double storeys completed before October 1783. A subsequent document from Cuffe stated that he expected thirty double-storey and ten single-storey houses to be completed by March 1784:

> Thirty of the double houses two storeys high with sheds, and ten of the double houses one storey high without sheds, as herein before described in one year from the date hereof—In consideration of to be paid for each of said houses of two storeys high, and for each of said houses of one storey high: with liberty of using any building materials trespass free, in said work, that is on the Crown Lands adjacent—money

> to be paid to the contractors from time to time, as the Superintendent General shall direct the Commiss(ione)^{rs} withholding a reasonable sum in their hands until the whole work is compleated pursuant to agreement.[51]

Temple anticipated swift results, and the end-date of March 1784 was agreed upon with all parties. The member of the Alcock family who held the leases on the crown lands set aside for New Geneva wrote to Temple in May 1783, via the under-secretary Sackville Hamilton, stating that he would 'hint to his Excellency that he is willing to surrender the Duncannon lease and will give a list of the tenants'. Temple had earlier contacted Henry Alcock, who happened to be MP for Waterford, on 9 March 1783. The profit from the existing lease over ten years was said to be £12,400. Temple accepted the calculation on 31 May.[52] The problem was that Cuffe and the Irish commissioners then appear to have done nothing at all in terms of making decisions or initiating the building work. One further issue was where the major buildings ought to be erected. An army engineer, Major James Ferrier, gave advice in July 1783 with regard to existing proposals, noting that the original site around the village of Passage included a Roman Catholic burial ground 'to which the Genevan Commissioners have a mark'd dislike and aversion'. On the grounds that there were problems with the lack of a water supply, with wind on high ground, and dry soil in certain places, and that he wanted to dispossess 'the smallest number possible of the inhabitants, whether of the useful labourers of the ground or the numerous fishermen in Passage of their potato gardens, without which they cannot subsist', Ferrier made a specific recommendation for 'the lands of Newtown east and west as at E.F. in the annexed sketch, including a small part of the Raheen and Crook Lands'.[53] Ferrier's sketch can be seen in the image below.

Cuffe again did nothing. In January 1784, Ferrier was writing to him making recommendations about where to procure clay bricks, and which suppliers to use; the recommendee was another of the Irish commissioners, Cornelius Bolton, as tended to be the case.[54] In the same month, Ferrier was acknowledging the complaints of the Genevans to the commissioner Alexander Alcock, but said that he did not know where to start building, because the commission had yet to inform him whether his own solution to the issue of the location had been accepted. Cuffe had not put Ferrier's letter of the previous July before the meetings of the commissioners, since he was on business in England and had not attended.[55] Alcock had cancelled a meeting of the commissioners in the same month: 'The

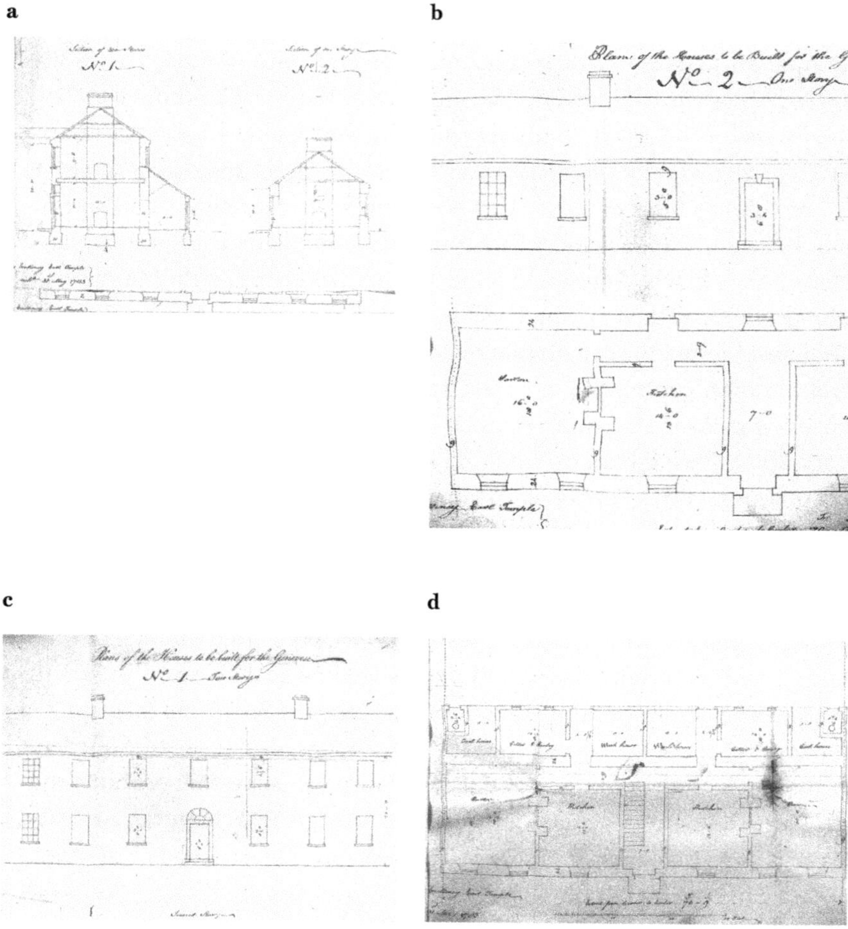

FIGURE 9.2, A–D. Floor plans and elevations of a pair of 'double houses' at New Geneva. Bolton Papers, National Library of Ireland

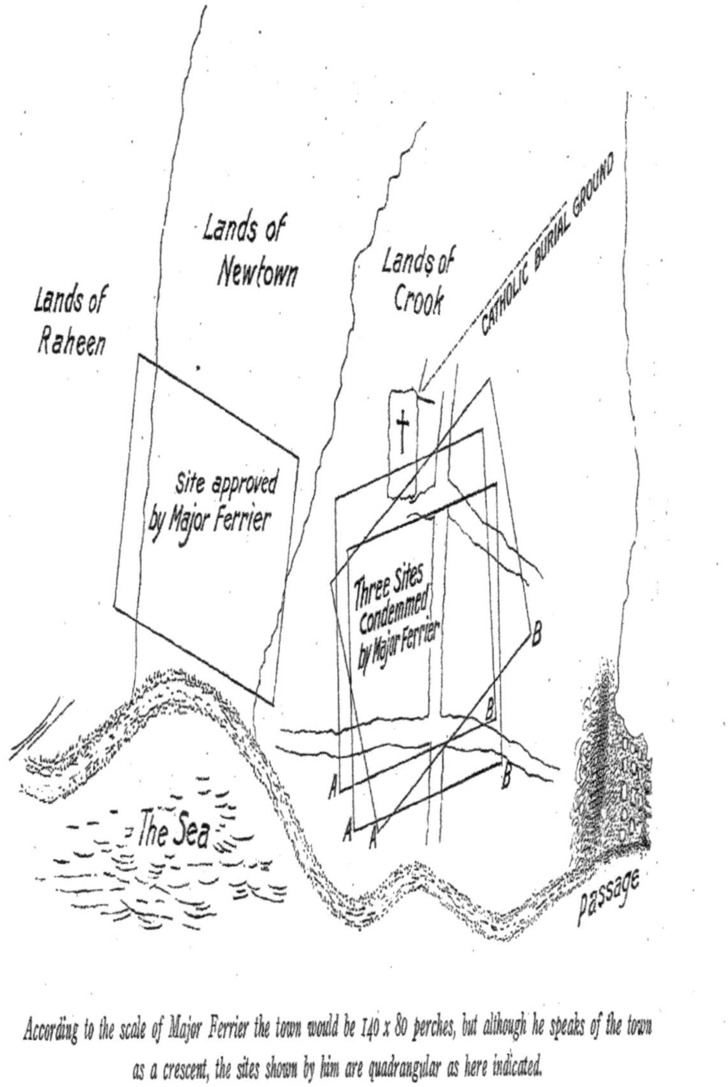

FIGURE 9.3. Major James Ferrier, sketch of the lands of Newtown east and west outside for New Geneva, letter to James Cuffe, 2 July 1783. Matthew Butler, 'New Geneva. Some correspondence relating to its foundation', *Journal of the Waterford and South-East of Ireland Archaeological Society*, XV (1912), 185–7

positive site of New Geneva not being fix'd I thought it unnecessary to call the Commissioners together not having any business to lay before them.'[56] It was only in March 1784, the date that the building was supposed to have been completed, that Ferrier's suggestion was accepted and it in fact began. Cuffe drew over £2,000 from the commissioners at the end of February. No doubt they were stirred into action after being pressed by the government, which had reaffirmed the support of George III for New Geneva on 27 February. A measure of activity tended to accompany demands from Cuffe for more funds, or for additional forms of support. In March 1784, Cuffe was writing to Temple stating that 'it will be absolutely necessary for me, in carrying on the business of a New Town for the Genevans, that I should be furnished with a covered waggon with proper harness from the ordnance stores'.[57]

IV

With the building of New Geneva delegated to Cuffe, the leading *représentants* dispersed. D'Ivernois appears largely to have lived in London, where a sizeable and influential community of expatriate Genevans could be found. Free from the austerity of the walled city, d'Ivernois embraced a bohemian lifestyle. This is implied by his correspondence with Isaac Du Roveray, the brother of his close friend Jacques-Antoine. A letter from Isaac Du Roveray dated 28 June 1783 reported that a young woman called Sally Taylor, who was evidently a domestic servant living at 13 Barking Alley on Tower Hill, had visited his lodgings at 3 George Lane, behind the Monument in London, several times, seeking contact with d'Ivernois, at the end of May. Taylor reported that she knew Du Roveray because he had taken d'Ivernois to 'Newman Street to see my cousin Durade', after which d'Ivernois had 'been constantly on her heels and that she could not have a moment of tranquility because of [him]'. She asserted 'that you [d'Ivernois] had been very rough with her and that you took with her liberties that displeased her a lot'. Du Roveray said that he had initially joked with Taylor, 'imagining that you had only taken liberties externally', but then realised 'that you had gone a little deeper than I imagined'.[58]

Taylor had already given birth to d'Ivernois's child. Du Roveray said that he was persuaded that d'Ivernois was 'an honest man, just and generous', and that he would want to pay for the mother and for the baby. Du Roveray promised that any sums supplied would be used 'in the most frugal way so that it costs you as little as possible'. He also offered to advance the funds himself, on the assumption that d'Ivernois lacked the resources, and said that he would keep the matter entirely secret, including from Jacques-Antoine Du Roveray, d'Ivernois's close friend. He finished by stating that 'this poor unfortunate woman is in the greatest misery' and that he included a letter from Taylor to d'Ivernois, which he had translated, because her English was so poor, being 'extremely badly written and misspelled':

> The distressing situation in which I find myself obliges me to write you these lines to inform you that I am in the greatest misery as a result of the connections we had together at n° 66 in Newman Street and my becoming pregnant and having given birth to a boy on the 18th of April (the poor child is your very portrait and likeness). This unfortunate circumstance has put me in the greatest distress, both of body and mind: ashamed of the state in which I live I kept it secret from everyone as long as it was possible for me to do. I was totally destitute of friends to whom I could make a confession of my circumstances, except for my sister and being reduced to the last extremity I saw myself finally forced to take [Du Roveray] into my confidence. My inclinations were always very far from bringing me to deal with any man, which you know because of the times that I rejected your advances, which I made to prevent the ruin of my honour. I hope, therefore, that your sentiments of humanity and Christian charity, as well as your sense of justice and of fairness, will lead you to send me something to supply the needs of our beloved child and of his afflicted mother.[59]

Taylor went on to state that the cost to her of nappies and a nanny, and of the time taken to wean the child, had altogether been seven guineas, part which she had been forced to borrow. Now she found herself 'without the strength and altogether destitute of means to procure for the necessities of life'. She asked, therefore, for 'a favorable hand in a situation so critical and so unfortunate'. She then declared that she would 'bear my unhappy lot without murmuring', if d'Ivernois offered support. If he failed to do so, however, 'reduced to the most dreadful despair', she would be forced to make her 'shame known to everyone and to declare under oath that you are the father of the child, before being obliged to give the boy over to the Parish'. This would 'ruin my reputation' and prevent her 'from ever going into service'. It would also likely lead to the death of the child and to public embarrassment for d'Ivernois. Du Roveray added a note to the letter, stating that he had emphasised the dreadful consequences for Sally Taylor if she publicly announced that d'Ivernois was the father.

D'Ivernois replied to Isaac Du Roveray denying paternity. This letter has been lost. Du Roveray then met Sally Taylor several times, and she provided a more detailed account of what had occurred. Du Roveray was convinced of Taylor's truthfulness. Her story, he said 'has always been the same'. D'Ivernois had started to go to the house where Sally Taylor worked soon after his arrival from Neuchâtel, in early August 1782. He had refused to accept Taylor's rejection of his advances, and had several times acted violently in order to force her to give in. Once she had done so, she remained reluctant, but his visits had continued until the middle of the month, at which time he must have left for Ireland. He had returned to see her in December, by which time she was aware that she was pregnant, and had attempted to inform d'Ivernois, but had never managed to be alone with him. It was only because she had been ill for so long during the pregnancy, because the child had been born a month early and because he was sickly, that she had turned to d'Ivernois for money, through Du Roveray. She was in dire straits, and Du Roveray was clearly impressed both by her honesty and by her fortitude.[60]

Isaac Du Roveray took the decision to reveal all to his brother Jacques-Antoine, on the grounds that the New Geneva project would be jeopardised if d'Ivernois was associated with a scandal, and because they did have enemies in London. In mentioning enemies, he must have meant supporters of the existing government at Geneva, which identified the rebels as dangerous anarchists. Du Roveray reported that both men had once again interviewed Sally Taylor, and again found her story believable and compelling. They reported to d'Ivernois that she owned a valuable watch given to her by d'Ivernois, and that she was about to go to the authorities and swear on oath that he was the father, and accepted that she was not seeking money for herself, but was in a terrible situation because of illness during the pregnancy and the ill-health of the child. The fact she had only contacted d'Ivernois after the birth confirmed their view that she was telling the truth. They warned him that the English did not take oaths lightly, and that if he ignored the situation things were likely to go from bad to worse. The baby was said to be very ill, having not grown since his premature birth. Jacques-Antoine Du Roveray had given Sally Taylor a guinea, in order to persuade her not to go to the authorities for a further month.[61] D'Ivernois then replied quickly, on 31 July. Once more he denied having had sex with Taylor, and promised that he too was willing to take an oath affirming that he was telling the truth. He also said that 'she is far from being an honest girl', that other men had had sex with her on their first visit to her, that he could not have been the father because of the dates and that they were all being played. He thanked the Du Roverays for keeping it all secret and for dealing with Taylor. Out of charity, he was willing to offer her a guinea, but asserted again that as an upright man dedicated to justice and law, he was innocent of every charge.[62] This was the last trace of Sally Taylor, in either d'Ivernois's papers or in history.

That d'Ivernois continued to enjoy himself while travelling between London and Dublin, is evident from further correspondence into the 1780s. He was evidently known to Anglo-Irish families such as the Sheridans, as he appears in the letters of Betsy Sheridan, the daughter of the actor Thomas Sheridan and the sister of the playwright Richard Brinsley Sheridan, calling upon the family in London, offering to take packages to Ireland, courting Sheridan herself, being called upon at his residence in Kensington and being faulted for his poor English.[63] In the later part of 1784, he was reported as living with the Hamilton family, undoubtedly the family of William Gerard Hamilton, alongside the American loyalist and judge William Smith, who became chief-justice in Canada; there were rumours of a scandal in Dublin involving d'Ivernois, which Betsy Sheridan played down.[64]

Of all of the Genevan exiles, Clavière was the most directly involved in New Geneva. Having arrived in London in January, and gone on to Dublin in February to be naturalised, he purchased a large property on Colbeck Street in Waterford.[65] By March he had decided to build up to fifty houses using his own funds, and also a church.[66] Something of Clavière's optimism about New Geneva can be discerned from a letter sent by his daughter Jeanne Vieusseux to her cousin and close friend:

> We have received news . . . which reports that they [d'Ivernois and Du Roveray] could not have been better received by [the British] ministers. The purity of gold is not said to present any difficulty. The Genevese are able to do in this respect whatever they want; moreover, they have been offered more land than they ever could have desired. It seems, as had been expected, that generosity is being emulated, and increases and increases among the English lords. This news is certain and you will rejoice. All this information is ignored at Geneva . . . it appears, according to all the signs, that Ireland will reunite all of us one day.[67]

In March, Clavière was reporting that the textile trade was worthy of investment, and that 'merchants will find resources here' and would be encouraged. This was especially the case regarding the production of cotton goods: he identified the production 'of cotton of all kinds', the value of which 'could easily be augmented by dyeing'. He also recommended the establishment of industries in tanning and paper-making. Writing to his friends at Geneva, he painted a picture that was highly optimistic:

> I hope that the eyes of our compatriots will turn more and more towards Ireland, and that they will display the necessary courage to break their ties with the corrupt and degraded Geneva, and make the journey [to Waterford]; if they fail to do so, can they be said to truly love freedom? Thus far, I do not see anything in the climate that should repel anyone, and those who criticise the project, do not know the circumstances, or want to discourage emigration. The working people [*Le Peuple laboureur*] [in Ireland] have no property, and cannot acquire it because of their misery, but the door is open to all positive improvements, and there is even an enthusiasm about the prospect of increasing public prosperity.[68]

To his friend the banker Théophile Cazenove, Clavière wrote that while the establishment of New Geneva was 'progressing slowly', there could be no doubt that Ireland was 'a free country, having its freedom guaranteed by a powerful people, located in a good country [and] with numberless natural resources'. He also said that he anticipated the creation of an outstanding educational institution. The question was whether the Genevans, who had lost their liberty, and had been impeded in every area of their lives, would embrace this new world. Clavière wondered whether the Genevan people were sufficiently courageous, or were 'different from what they perceive themselves to be'. The surest sign of the latter would be that they failed to join New Geneva.[69]

On 20 April, Clavière returned to Neuchâtel to see his family, travelling via the Genevan exile communities that were now establishing themselves in London, Brussels and even at Paris and Konstanz. At the same time, he had an eye upon Ireland. By July 1783, he was advising the acting Irish chancellor of the exchequer John Foster on the economic development of the country. The first part of a long letter underlined the value to Ireland of emigrants like the Genevans, 'who have established or are highly skilled in the arts, sciences and commerce'. Clavière complained at the same time that the benefits offered to the emigrants were not being realised: 'there is not yet a single provision which guarantees to the Genevan emigrants the fulfilment of the promises that were given to them by the government'. The mayor of Waterford was failing even in his duty of supplying temporary lodgings for emigrants who arrived from Geneva. Clavière reported that he had been reading John Holroyd, Lord Sheffield's *Observations on the commerce of the American states*, which had been published at Dublin and London in 1783, and which went through six editions by 1784. He found the book to be full of 'strong national prejudices', overestimating Britain's capacity to continue to dominate trade with its former colony. Britain's manufactures were being challenged across France and Germany, and the sole advantage enjoyed by Britain, in addition to linguistic connectedness, was really that as a free state, the North Americans would prefer to trade with it than with despots:

> The author seems to me to have strong national prejudices. The advantages which England can boast of are largely due to lack of intelligence among her neighbours: every day they become more enlightened. The American Revolution will hasten still further the progress of enlightenment [*le progrès des lumières*].[70]

Ireland could take advantage of the trading possibilities opened up by events in North America, because it was 'Europe's natural warehouse for commerce with other parts of the world, and especially with America'. Clavière told Foster to 'provide the room, the carpet, the cards', in order to make this a reality; in other words, to make Ireland attractive for merchants, by opening free ports and cutting duties, 'removing of all the things that keep [the merchant] at war with the Government'. The result would be that Ireland 'achieves the greatest prosperity'. The country needed to follow the example of the Dutch, also a warehouse nation, the difference being that Ireland enjoyed infinitely more natural advantages, especially in its superior ports. As Clavière put it, 'In a word, you must have at your country the Great Market [*Grand Marché*] where the products of Europe will be exchanged for those of the Indies.'

Such optimism about Ireland's prospects was coupled with frustration for Clavière, however, because he felt that the building of New Geneva was progressing too slowly, that the now near two hundred and fifty emigrants from old Geneva were not being welcomed or supported and that there was an increasing danger that the whole business would collapse.[71] In a revealing letter dated 26 July 1783, written at Waterford and sent to Foster, accompanying his 'Mémoire' on Irish trade, Clavière underlined his commitment to the economic development of his new country, but also gave something of an ultimatum. The Genevans had been promised new lives in a free state, but those who had travelled found no lodgings at New Geneva; rather, these people who had lost almost everything were being forced to pay inflated rents in Waterford. Ministers were not replying to letters written by Clavière, the people who had remained at Geneva were being oppressed by magistrates seeking to prevent the exodus and the chance of transforming Ireland was being lost. Clavière, as a rich investor, presented himself as offering far more than simply New Geneva. He was, however, frustrated and losing faith. His appeal to Foster was blunt and also desperate, underlining the suffering of the exiles and the dreadful effects upon families of the continued uncertainty about their future:

> Exiled forever from my country I have been forced to seek another, and as my family wishes to follow me, I must search for the one that will be the most advantageous for us. I had settled on Ireland [as that country], independently even of the fate of New Geneva. The meeting which I made here with a Swiss [gentleman], with whom I could have developed a [manufacturing] establishment of the kind most beneficial to this country [Ireland], had already led me to undertake work to this end. I was on the point of buying land in Wexford which would have been suitable. Some difficulties that have hindered the seller have delayed the conclusion of the sale. At present I have no courage, neither for action that would remove these obstacles, nor to seek other lands [to settle in]. I feel that I have presumed too much strength on my part; that in resolving to settle in Ireland, whatever the success of the colony, [I had] in my heart the hope that it would be established, that at least it would not have to wait for the government, & that such proceedings would attract to New Geneva a great number of my compatriots of all classes. This hope weakens me, shows me all that I have to fear from my sensibility: it is impossible for me to contemplate without fear the isolation of my family, and the distance we stand from our friends. We are too accustomed to the benefits brought by friendship, and of the society we habituated, so as often to become unhappy if we are alone in a country which is foreign to us.[72]

The supporters of New Geneva among the exiles were being accused, Clavière wrote, of painting 'a beautiful chimera' for Genevans who continued to love liberty and who wanted a homeland in Ireland. On account of the letting down of such people and the making of what were effectively false promises, because of the delays on the British side, Clavière admitted that he was being turned against Ireland: 'it would not be possible for me to seek useful occupations [*occupations utiles*] in a country which would have turned its back upon a Genevan colony after having called upon us to create one'. He begged Foster to 'scatter light in the darkness which perplexes us so greatly', such as would allow him to encourage his own family to move to Ireland in perpetuity. Support did not come quickly. In letters to the banker Alexander Jaffray at Dublin the following month (August 1783), Clavière stated that he was 'truly afflicted' by the kind of limbo in which the British government had left the exiles. In his view, the

Genevans had done all that they could. He informed Jaffray that he did not want to travel to Dublin in order to petition and complain: his charge was that such action would be pointless, because the impression was being given that 'the English ministers have resolved to do whatever they can to prevent immigration'. This transformation of British policy Clavière tied to the actions of French diplomats in London, whom he suspected had 'petitioned the English ministers so that the business dies by the slowness of the process, which is a sure-fire way to cause it to die'.[73]

V

The sudden pessimism of Clavière did not mean that he had given up on New Geneva. Rather the contrary; he was petitioning the Irish commissioners in order to get the message through that things were moving too slowly, and that the Genevans who were arriving were not receiving any support. The person who was embraced by the British government was Ami Melly. Melly had returned to Geneva towards the end of May in order, it was said, to collect his property and his family and to transport all of them to Ireland. In fact, he was undoubtedly an emissary of the Genevan commissioners, given the brief of encouraging other watchmakers to follow him to New Geneva. This was certainly the view of the government at Geneva, because as soon as Melly arrived back in the city, on the 24 May 1783, his house was surrounded by soldiers searching for papers concerned with the emigration. Melly was then imprisoned. On the same day his associate, named Agasse, was interrogated for two hours by members of the Council, and was accused of holding back Melly's letters of naturalisation, because they contained incriminating information. Agasse asserted that the documents had been lost, and then fled into Switzerland.[74] Melly was put on trial on 25 May, charged with seeking to persuade Genevan citizens to abandon the city for Ireland, thereby fostering emigration. On 7 June Melly declared that the tribunal was incompetent to judge him, because he was Irish. Irish gentlemen staying at Geneva confirmed that he was their compatriot. Melly's argument was that although he had not been banished from Geneva in 1782, he had refused to take the oath of loyalty demanded by the new regime, and believed that the edict of pacification allowed any person who desired to leave Geneva to do so.

From Bern, the British chargé d'affaires at Bern, Louis Braun, wrote to the Council of Twenty-Five to raise the question of the nature of the crime Melly had been accused of. Charles James Fox, now foreign secretary, followed this on 6 June with a letter to the syndics, which arrived at Geneva on the 16th, affirming Melly's status as a British subject, and complaining about his treatment by the authorities. Charles Stanhope, asserting his status at Geneva as a bourgeois, also denounced Melly's treatment, contending that as he was now British and he could not be treated as a domestic criminal; Stanhope then decided to renounce his status at Geneva, and asked to be removed from the civic roll. The Genevan magistrates throughout the process were working closely with Vergennes, and with authorities in Savoy, all of whom took action to suppress information about the case, and to prevent discussion in print, on the basis that it was seditious.[75] Vergennes reassured the magistrates that he would support them in any conflict with the British.[76] The syndics therefore confidently replied to Fox that Melly remained a citizen and was accused of undertaking actions that gravely threatened the prosperity of the state. Fox had shown two of Stanhope's letters to George III and informed the king that he had acted in order to save Melly's life. George III replied that it seemed to be more a matter of straightforward imprisonment, which Melly surely deserved, for 'attempting to get natives to expatriate'. George III had no sympathy, because Melly was violating the maxim that 'obedience from individuals is necessary, and that if every man is at liberty to choose for himself, society must be dissolved'. The king was, of course, no fan of Fox. Fox replied to the king that the government at Geneva 'had lately been settled by a foreign power', and in consequence emigration could be justified.[77] At the same time, Fox backed off from further confronting the magistrates at Geneva. It was said that Charles Saladin-Egerton, the Genevan government representative in London, who had married into the family of Elizabeth Egerton, was influencing the government and even the king.[78] Whatever the case, George III nevertheless did reaffirm his support for the Waterford experiment in February 1784, and this was one of the reasons for the spate of activity after this date.

Melly's trail recommenced on 19 June and continued until August, throughout which time he remained in prison. Some news did reach the papers. The *Journal politique de Bruxelles* announced that it had received a letter from a Genevan moving from the city to Ireland, which gave details of Melly's arrest, and the actions of the British. The paper noted that he had refused to take an oath in favour of the new regime, and had therefore already abandoned his privileges as a Genevan citizen. The edict of pacification was said to have given every bourgeois and citizen at Geneva the choice of taking the oath of loyalty, or becoming a foreigner. Melly having taken an oath at Waterford, his arrest at Geneva was declared to be 'not only an act of violence, but . . . in violation of the law of nations [*droit des nations*]'.[79] Melly was found guilty and sentenced on 8 August to a year of solitary confinement in prison, to be banished for five years afterwards and to have pay the costs of the trial. The punishment of Melly operated as a warning to other would-be emigrants. On the night of 16–17 August, however, he escaped from prison. He used his sheets to make a rope to get out of the window—the cell with bars on the windows was still being constructed—and then found a ladder to surmount the prison walls, and with help from friends entered a coach that was not stopped at the city gates. Taking the road to Neuchâtel, he returned with his family to London via Germany and Holland.[80]

Clavière took advantage of the situation by commissioning work in favour of Melly by Brissot de Warville. Brissot was in London, publishing a *Journal de Londres*, and setting up educational projects, none of which brought him the income he desired. He was also publishing, in several volumes, a philosophical commentary on European politics, which was especially concerned with miscarriages of justice, entitled *Correspondance sur ce qui intéresse le bonheur de l'homme et de la société*. In the second instalment of the second volume, Brissot published a lengthy analysis of Melly's situation, in a section concerned with criminal legislation, and entitled 'Genevois naturalisé Irlandois, jugé criminellement à Geneve: Question sur l'émigration examinée'. It was a fascinating piece of work, showing Clavière's involvement through the repetition of his own view of commerce, and sought to use Melly's case to justify the Genevan emigration. Brissot declared that Geneva had become a despotism like France, was in decline commercially and was violating domestic and international legal norms in its actions towards Melly. The intention behind the text was clearly to stimulate further the emigration, and Brissot provided a justification of New Geneva as an enterprise that was saving humanity from slavery and servility, and entirely in accordance with the principles of natural jurisprudence. Clavière must have been pleased, and the work may have been republished under a different title in other places.[81] Clavière would have rewarded Brissot with money, as he always did, but showed his faith in the young author more substantially by paying his debts, thereby saving him from bankruptcy, in September 1783, after he was imprisoned in the Bastille for libelling Marie Antoinette. Indeed, given that Brissot in his text on Melly refers to the trial in August 1783, the work may have been the price of Clavière's support, and have been written on Brissot's exit from the Bastille on 10 September. (Brissot had been in the prison since his arrest on 11 July.) This fact gave Brissot's language added venom, as he cursed the Genevan magistrates for turning their city into a French colony.

Brissot commenced his argument by justifying the emigration from Geneva. The revolutionaries of 1782 had not been the *représentants*, but rather the magistrates, who passed a radical new law code that transformed the state by removing all of the people's rights:

> The revolution carried out by force in the year 1782 in the small republic of Geneva, was consummated by illegally banishing the most virtuous citizens, which forced at the point of the sword a ridiculed General Council [to legitimise] a code which deprived the people of Geneva of all their rights. They had to emigrate because they could no longer resist.[82]

While 'several princes of Germany' and numerous other states had offered a refuge to the emigrants 'who had been persecuted by the spirit of aristocracy', the latter chose Ireland for their asylum, it being a 'deserted country' with 'excellent soil, navigable rivers, very advantageous ports'. Ireland had granted them land sufficient 'to build a city near a port', money for the costs of transport, a building for an academy or university and 'the privileges and rights they enjoyed in their old country'. The charter, Brissot claimed, had been finalised, and 'is about to receive parliamentary sanction'.[83] Brissot then went on to repeat what had been said about Melly in the *Journal politique de Bruxelles*, but in more detail, making the claim that abandoning a country, rather than being a crime, was in accordance with natural and political law (*le droit naturel et le droit politique*). Melly, as a foreigner, could only be judged through the law of the peoples (*droit des gens*), and he was in practice being treated as a slave or a serf. Given that he had been in the Bastille, the source of this information must have been Clavière or another commissioner. Brissot called the Genevan magistrates—always termed 'aristocrats' by Brissot—tyrants in the fashion of a Dionysius of Syracuse or a Tiberius. He likened their verdict, based on what were termed 'clear indicators' (*indices véhémens*) rather than direct evidence, to the *lettres de cachet* by which the French monarch could silence anyone who displeased him on a whim. The verdict had in fact been entirely political, a product of narrow 'ministerial reason of state' ('pour les tribunaux la raison d'état des ministres'). That reason of state—a doctrine that envisaged every state as being perpetually at war with every other—determined the law at Geneva was proven by the fact that a man named Prud'homme had been allowed to leave the city with two or three hundred workers for Lyon, because the French were in favour of the migration.[84]

The central argument of Brissot's text was that the Genevan people had been turned into slaves. Those whom he called 'jurisconsults', the jurists he associated with Germany, Poland and France, had largely ignored emigration while 'minutely classifying the [orders of] serfs, detailing the right of the lord over his vassal, and [rights] to the liberty of a man; but never have they spoken of the rights of the individual'. The juristic 'apostles of slavery and barbarism' taught that a serf could never be allowed to leave his homeland, or indeed his workshop. The English jurist Blackstone was as guilty as the continental jurists, for arguing that subject-hood could never be renounced without the permission of the prince. It was shocking, Brissot argued, that Blackstone was so 'cowardly and servile', given the English republican lineage that renounced slavery:

> [Blackstone is] . . . the compatriot of the Sidney, Milton, the contemporary of the historian of the House of the Stuart under the reign of Charles I [Edward Hyde, Earl of Clarendon], one of the most intrepid defenders of noble freedom. . . . Sir John Eliot, who died at the Tower [of London] a victim of despotism, wrote a book called *The Monarchy of Man*. It proves some of the principles I have laid down . . . Eliot [says] that kings must be subject to the laws. His work remains in manuscript, and is preserved at the British Museum.[85]

Following the English republicans of the seventeenth century, and Jean-Jacques Rousseau, Brissot held that it was 'the social contract, it is nature, which must be consulted in order to solve the problem of emigration'. For Brissot the purpose of life was happiness, and if a political association failed to satisfy an individual then it could be abandoned:

> What does the primitive pact of societies tell us? That man associates himself with man to be happy, that he submits to a leader to be so, that his duty goes hand in hand with his right, that the chief cannot break this pact without the subject becoming free on his side. It tells us that the individual may renounce his country when he is ill at ease, when the government, instead of protecting him, oppresses him, when the law has become the caprice of the prince.[86]

Men were born equal, without marks of slavery upon them, and in consequence the 'most sacred maxim' was *ubi bene, ibi patria* ('Where it is well with me, there is my country'). Such a maxim, which translated into a right to abandon countries marked by slavery and servility, had been used across history to justify emigration from Greece 'when the republican spirit was replaced by the tyrannical spirit', from Rome, as in the movement of Sartorius to Spain, or Cato of Utica's fleeing from Caesar's rule. In modern history, Brissot referred to the founding of Venice by immigrants, 'when Italy groaned under a foreign yoke', the movement of Presbyterians and Quakers to North America and above all the tale of the Huguenots who abandoned the tyranny of Louis XIV. The Genevan authorities were following Louis XIV in seeking to prevent emigration, as in 1699 the French government had sought to sequester and to condemn in perpetuity any person who abandoned the nation. It was Brissot's opinion that the city of Geneva itself was being turned into a gaol.[87]

Brissot then presented an argument that Clavière had used many times before: that wealth followed liberty, and that sovereigns who sought to promote the happiness of their subjects would be rewarded with thriving commerce and extensive revenues, while tyrants would be punished by impoverishment. Brissot gave the example of John Law, whose system had 'convulsed all France and then died a death'.[88] Trade, like people, could never properly be shackled, unless commerce was abandoned and the people were turned into slaves. Commerce and the arts were entirely cosmopolitan, having 'no other country but the universe':

> Let the sovereigns abjure, therefore, the fatal illusion with which they are cradled, that, by means of force they may retain industry, the arts, and commerce [in their country]. They act by force, and always with force. They were not aware that industry is a fragile plant in politics; if the breath [of life] even [slightly] shrinks it, this sheds the leaves and weakens the branches, what will happen? It will be dead. It is through freedom alone that commerce lives. Yes, leave to commerce the liberty to move where it wills; leave to your subjects the liberty to emigrate wherever they desire; allow your rivals the minimum resource of being able to poach your artists and manufacturers, being sure that they will return if the doors remain open to them, if you keep their arms free of chains, and you allow them to be as the fresh air . . . man is born the enemy of servitude . . . [in being free] he evinces a noble pride, his soul is elevated, and he benefits the country where he enjoys such beautiful rights.[89]

Geneva historically had only flourished, Brissot asserted, because of the ability of its citizens to trade across Europe. In preventing Melly from doing the same, the Genevan authorities were admitting that they were ruining the commerce of the city. In condemning him they were violating 'the law of nature, the social contract, the law of the peoples, and natural right, all in seeking to prevent a man from being free'. The emigration from Geneva would increase, Brissot stated, once Melly's story was heard. Melly's experience revealed to Genevans the dreadful nature of their existing situation and its inevitable future: a combination of economic decline and ongoing political terror.[90] Even in the final months of 1783, Clavière, through his mouthpiece Brissot, was appealing to the *représentants* at Geneva to follow him to Ireland.

VI

From the perspective of those who had ardently supported the Genevans from the British side, there were equally questions to be raised about the progress of New Geneva. As early as 7 March 1783, Temple was calling the new government of Fox, North and Portland 'this foul coalition'.[91] The Earl of Mornington informed Grenville that he was 'told the Geneva business does not proceed as rapidly as might be wished'. One of the reasons was that Ireland remained in crisis, with demands for parliamentary reform from the Volunteer companies escalating, and a broader sense of weakened government after the departure of Temple.[92] Mornington requested that Grenville send him 'Pitt's two pamphlets on parliamentary reform', because he had 'read Locke, and am quite of your opinion that he has been misapplied on that subject'.[93] The weakness of Lord Northington's administration in Ireland evidently resulted in the cause of the Genevans being almost entirely ignored. This changed when the Duke of Rutland became lord lieutenant in February 1784. William Pitt, the prime minister, stated to Rutland that one of the reasons for the neglect of the Genevans was that they were associated with Temple. This had alienated them from Northington, but they merited renewed support from the new administration in Ireland:

> I shall have a letter to write to you upon the subject of the Geneva emigrants, whom Lord Northington has affected to discountenance, because the scheme was Lord Temple's. I think they ought to have at present the support of Government, and that they will be of use to Ireland.[94]

Pitt's brother-in-law Charles Stanhope had a letter published in March 1784 stating that he was confident that the new ministry would give exactly this. No more 'doubts of success' should be allowed to inhibit potential immigrants. Stanhope announced that he would personally 'neglect no means of promoting the happiness and prosperity of the New Geneva'.[95]

Rutland, famous for his extravagant lifestyle, expenditure and consumption of claret, appointed Thomas Orde as his chief secretary. Orde had become MP for Aylesbury in 1780, served successfully on parliamentary committees and had worked as under-secretary to Shelburne at the Home Office under Rockingham, and then as secretary to the treasury under Shelburne himself. It was Shelburne who suggested Orde to Rutland, in part because of his capacity for work, and his mastery of detail. Rutland supported Shelburne's own ascent in 1784, when he became Marquess of Lansdowne. Significant figures in Irish politics such as Mornington were impressed by Rutland, who was said to have improved the governance of Ireland and 'rejected reform and Luke Gardiner's protecting duties'. This led to domestic turmoil throughout 1784, with the speaker John Foster burned in effigy and mobs at the Irish Commons threatening 'death and destruction to all the active members'.[96] Sedition was prosecuted, including newspapers critical of the government, and there were rumours of assassins being paid to murder prominent politicians. In circumstances of domestic crisis, New Geneva was gradually erected, and was expected to succeed as an establishment, as Mornington reported to Grenville, despite the ongoing disputes between the commissioners, which exasperated and exhausted the leading member of the Beresford family, Lord Tyrone:

> There have been some warm disputes at the Board of the Genevese Commissioners; Lord Tyrone has constantly attended and taken much pains in the business; which attendance, *he has desired me to inform you*, has been owing solely to his regard and respect to your Lordship, and that no other consideration should have induced him to undergo so much fatigue and anxiety. *Nota bene*. The emigrants, when settled, will have a considerable interest in the County of Waterford. Cuffe's salary has occasioned some contest, as I understand; he receives three pounds a day, as he says, by your Lordship's promise.[97]

Temple, watching Ireland from abroad, was increasingly concerned about what he called the 'ruinous system' of the government of Ireland, announcing that he 'tremble[d] for the meeting of Parliament under all these circumstances of indecision', and acknowledging that 'the storm has thickened to such a degree' that current relations between Britain and Ireland might not survive.[98] This view was seconded by Mornington, who admitted that 'I am more convinced every day that not only the peace of this country, but also the peace and eventually the existence of the empire depend upon the government of Ireland.' Mornington blamed Catholics who controlled newspapers and infected 'the minds of the middling and lower orders of the people' with the sentiment of rebellion.[99] Rutland and

Orde were first involved in the possibility of parliamentary reform in Ireland, which was favoured by Pitt; much of their time was then taken up with Pitt's scheme for a commercial settlement with Ireland. Orde failed in both projects: Pitt's plans for parliamentary reform and for the further commercial union between Britain and Ireland came to nothing. Orde did, however, put a great deal of energy into realising New Geneva. (Whereas Temple had himself negotiated directly with the Genevans, Rutland left the entire matter to Orde.) By the time that Orde arrived in Ireland, the project, like Ireland itself, was in crisis. The Genevans themselves had begun to question the commitment of the government, because of the experience of the first exiles. Having arrived in reasonably large numbers, some of those who had emigrated took the decision to abandon New Geneva because conditions were so poor. A sign of Genevan disaffection was the refusal of Gasc to act as minister for New Geneva;[100] this was reported within the community of *représentants* that stretched from London to Geneva, as evinced by a letter from David Chauvet to his friend the pastor Étienne-Salomon Reybaz:

> With regard to Ireland, I still do not know what to say about it, but I believe it goes badly, because too much time has passed, there is too much distance [between Geneva and Ireland], and the efforts of the British Government have been too slow . . . thirteen of those who had gone there have left in disgust, but there has been redoubled activity and zeal; we received yesterday the most satisfactory letters in this regard; if, then, the thing is wanting, it will be by the fault of the Genevans, and that is what I fear the most: I believe that the best thing is to be on guard against precipitateness, and to see things come to a certain point of maturation, before taking any part ourselves.[101]

On the other hand, a Genevan community had established itself at Waterford. The parents of the future Swiss general Guillaume-Henri Dufour were married there on 28 February 1784, and Bénédict Humbert, who in later life was a syndic at Geneva, remained in Ireland until later in 1784.[102] Jacques Grenus too was still at Waterford, and was present at a meeting of the commissioners on 10 February 1784, when he pressed to have the tenants removed from the lands where building was anticipated.[103]

That matters were so delayed that no building at all had taken place meant that March and April 1784 were the crisis times for New Geneva. Charles Stanhope, who had admitted to having been petitioned by the Genevan commissioners, made this clear to Orde in a letter of 18 April. Stanhope had been informed about the departures of some of the migrants. He wrote that in consequence, 'if something be not done, the whole will be left without the possibility of remedy'. What was needed was to accept the demand of d'Ivernois and Du Roveray for £10,000 'out of the £25,000 destined to the travelling expenses', to help to cover the costs faced by the Genevans in founding a watchmaking establishment. They had, he said, had problems selling property in old Geneva. Until circumstances for the first migrants were positive, the process would stall, risking the outcome that 'they must all go back to the continent'. Stanhope said that with regard to Orde himself, 'No person is more capable of feeling the advantage of this Esta[blishmen]t, or the necessity of encouraging the first Emigrants than yourself.' He also remained confident that the scheme could be made to succeed, predicting, 'It will grow, in 3 or 4 years to astonishing every one, who does not know the people of that country.'[104]

Orde knew exactly what Stanhope was talking about. He had received on 26 March a memorandum from Du Roveray and d'Ivernois which explained that the Genevans had set up a company dedicated to the manufacture of watches and jewellery at New Geneva, and that this company already had £30,000 in subscribed capital for shares. This had been on 10 October 1783. Then the first group of emigrants had arrived at New Geneva to find that no buildings had been erected, and that there appeared to be no prospect of the settlement existing, in the sense of giving people the opportunity to work there. In consequence, 'thirteen [emigrants] returned in disgust to Geneva'. Travel, with the end of the war, had now become cheap, because potential emigrants could go directly to Ireland through France. That meant that the costs of transporting them were much reduced. Du Roveray and d'Ivernois therefore proposed that the government lend the new company £10,000, with interest levied at four per cent. The Genevans would put in £5,000, and this would be sufficient to start the business initially at Waterford and ultimately at New Geneva. Action had to be taken, they said, by the spring, because so many potential emigrants had become despondent.[105] Orde then contacted the Irish commissioners, even before Stanhope's letter was received, to ask whether they felt a loan could be made.[106] The commissioners, characteristically, refused to give a verdict. Rutland therefore asked for a judgement from the attorney-general, John FitzGibbon. His verdict was negative, he being

> very clearly of Opinion that the Commission [responsible for the funds] are not authorised to *lend* any part of the sum granted by His Majesty to the Genevans, The Grant being expressly for the purpose of defraying and the expenses of transporting into this kingdom, and

> settling therein one thousand Genevan emigrants and an accession of national wealth is recited as an inducement to the Grant—which very plainly evinces that it was made under a supposition that the Genevan merchants who were to settle here had private capitals upon which they would be enabled to carry on trade and manufactures in this kingdom.[107]

FitzGibbon was a disastrous choice in terms of asking for a verdict. He was an advocate of Irish autonomy, resistant to foreign involvement and an enemy to Shelburne, having been angry that his close friend William Eden ceased to be secretary to the lord lieutenant when Rockingham came to power in 1782.[108] Avid in terms of his own capacity for office and preferment, FitzGibbon was related to John Beresford, and this may have been why he turned the Genevans down: the Irish involved in the project had other ideas about the use of the funds.[109]

Unaware of FitzGibbon's decision, and writing from their home in Dublin at 117 St Stephen's Green, Du Roveray and d'Ivernois continued to press Orde to release the funds in a letter of 18 April 1783. This made plain the crisis in the settlement, especially because of Orde's delay. The letter was a follow-up to a set of conversations with Orde, and the Genevans were evidently positively disposed towards the man, while being frustrated at his refusal to take action:

> The situation of most of the Genevans who are in Waterford is incapable of bearing a longer period of uncertainty. The experience that they have had up to the present time, without finding the means of carrying out their industry there, added to so many other losses that they have suffered arising out of the establishment that they came seeking in Ireland, is a burden to them [and] the effects are, to our eyes, becoming worse, in the most painful manner, as things drag on; it is the case that even if the determination of the government ought finally to be a result favourable to the request that we have made to you, there would be a strong fear that delay, should it last any longer, would be tantamount to giving them [the Genevans] a formal refusal.[110]

Du Roveray and d'Ivernois acknowledged Orde's situation, 'the full extent and the gravity of your preoccupations at the present time', and stated that they appreciated 'all the pains that you have taken through the effect of your good offices in establishing the Genevans'. At the same time, they asserted their duties 'towards our fellow citizens and even towards Ireland'.

With Clavière similarly petitioning Irish politicians, and Ami Melly being imprisoned at Geneva, the emigration stalled further, after Orde's and Rutland's refusal to release funds to the Genevan commissioners. In May 1784, d'Ivernois and Du Roveray issued a final letter to Orde, written on the 21st; although it has been lost, its contents can be gleaned from Orde's reply and the memorandum that accompanied it. The letter informed Orde and Rutland that on 2–3 May twelve Genevans had abandoned Waterford, and that on 7–8 May twenty-three others had followed them. In addition to sending the letter, Du Roveray and d'Ivernois formulated a new strategy, and sought to persuade Orde to embrace it by means of the accompanying memorandum. The rationale was that it was the only means to make something of New Geneva, because nothing to date had gone to plan. The memorandum outlined a history of the project, stating that since the 'change that has taken place in the government of Geneva in June 1782', which 'caused a great number of Genevans to resolve to leave their native land', several 'Princes and sovereign states on the continent' sought to create a new Geneva. D'Ivernois and his fellow *représentants* chose Ireland because of

> the freedom of the English Constitution, and the offers that Ireland made to them, whilst my Lord Shelburne was Prime Minister and My Lord Temple Viceroy [of Ireland] led them to prefer [Waterford] to all the other offers that were made to them.[111]

The original plan, Du Roveray and d'Ivernois asserted, had been to 'seize the moment' of 'initial despair' and facilitate the emigration of flourishing businesses into Ireland. Building the town as quickly as possible would be decisive, as Temple had recognised. Northington came close to wrecking everything, and little progress was made under Rutland. The key problem was that every measure planned by Temple and Shelburne with the Genevan commissioners had been delayed:

> My Lord Northington upon his arrival, revoked the orders to proceed with the introduction of formalities that he doubtless thought necessary, but the delays that resulted have had the most devastating effect in Geneva, and put an end to the measures that had been taken by the *représentants* and by some of the richest merchants to put together sufficient capital capable of sustaining and ensuring the prosperity of the manufacture of clocks at New Geneva. Since the Duke of Rutland was appointed Viceroy, contracts have been let to build eighty houses, but the foundations have not yet been laid. These lengthy delays, lasting

> two years, in a matter which should not have suffered any delay at all, have allowed the moment of the highest enthusiasm to pass.[112]

Those Genevans who did arrive at Waterford found matters so little advanced, in terms of housing and the capacity to undertake their trade, that they 'had accepted the sad necessity of returning home'. Things had been entirely different at Brussels, and families who left Geneva had now established a thriving community there, worth at least £10,000 sterling. The first version of New Geneva, based on watchmaking, was therefore dead. The second option had always been 'to attract to Ireland individuals who were highly respected for their talents, their knowledge and their wealth, who once established there, would not fail to attract others of their compatriots and the trade in which they were involved'. The creation of an academy was stated to be the surest option for establishing a flow of migrants into Waterford. The Academy, Du Roveray and d'Ivernois asserted, had been in the original plan for the city, and had 'been judged by the Viceroy and by the Commission nominated by My Lord Temple, as being of the greatest utility for Ireland', in addition to receiving 'the special approbation of His Majesty'. Once the academy was attracting students, rich Genevans would flock to it, and the wealth of the town could only be expected to increase. Du Roveray and d'Ivernois therefore requested 'the prompt and complete fulfilment of the solemn promises made to us and particularly, that the annual sum of £4244,13;8$^{St[erling]}$ which was promised for this academy [be released]'.[113]

Through the ever-committed Charles Stanhope, d'Ivernois passed to Orde a more detailed plan for the proposed academy at Waterford. Once more the justification relied upon a history of the project, underlining the support of Temple and the Irish Privy Council:

> On the 4th April 1783, My Lord Temple brought together a Commission at the head of which were several members of the Privy Council. The powers that the Viceroy gave to this Commission with regard to the establishment of an academy were promulgated as follows: And whereas young persons of rank and fortune from all parts of Europe resorted to the city of Geneva to profit from the system of education established there under professors of eminence in the useful and liberal studies and accomplishments; and whereas a school or academy formed upon the same principles in this kingdom and would forward His Majesty's dispositions for the encouragement of religion, virtue and science by improving the education and early habits of youth, and would remove the inducements to a foreign education; and being

> conducted with that attention to morality and virtue which hath distinguished the establishment in that city, may attract foreigners to reside in this kingdom for the like purpose; We do further pray and empower you to consider and digest a plan for a school and academy of education to be established in the new colony, and to make a part of the constitution thereof, under such institution and regulation, and with such privileges as may best contribute to the ends hereby proposed.[114]

The plan was for a higher and a lower school, with the latter having masters to teach reading, writing, arithmetic, English, French, Latin, Greek, drawing, mechanics, history and geography, dancing, fencing, the use of firearms and scripture. The higher lessons were to be taught by professors in ancient history and belles lettres, modern history and belles lettres, British history and belles lettres, mathematics, drawing, rational philosophy, natural philosophy, astonomy, civil law, English law, political and public law, business, agriculture, architecture, oriental languages (two professors) and a demonstrator in chemistry, in addition to the rector, his secretary and a librarian. The total annual salary for twenty-six masters was worked out as being £1,364 and that for twenty-two professors £3,070.[115]

It was stated that the plan for the academy had received the wholehearted support from the commissioners on both sides, and that the document agreeing to its creation had been signed 'in the Council Chamber on 7th May 1783 by Lord Tyrone, Sir John Blaquiere, J. T. Clement, J. Foster, Luke Gardiner, J. Cuffe, D. De La Touche, A. Caldwell, J. Hartley, A. Jaffray, and the Genevan Commissioners'. Although Temple made changes which reduced the planned annual expenditure by £500, it was sent by him to George III 'and received the Royal Assent in a letter from My Lord North to My Lord Northington'. Royal favour was then reaffirmed 'in a letter from My Lord Sydney (Thomas Townsend) to the Duke of Rutland on 22nd February 1784'. The original objective was agreed upon as being to create an establishment which would transform education in Ireland, for the rich and the poor, and attract foreign students, as a beacon of excellence:

> We think that it will contribute much instruction to the youth within this kingdom, particularly those whose parents are not in a position to meet the expenses necessary for the education of their children, and that, with regard to those who are better-off, it will be advantageous to them in that they will spend less than if they sent [their children]

> abroad to learn modern languages, and receive a good education. It seems better still to us, as it could lead to people in other countries to begin sending their children into this country and establish ties here. As a result, we are taking the liberty of recommending it to His Excellency in its entirety.[116]

D'Ivernois and Du Roveray did have a point. Orde had written to the Irish commissioners on 27 February 1784 to say that George III himself was pressing for action to be taken, mentioning the letter from Thomas Townsend (now Lord Sydney) to Rutland, and 'signifying His Majesty's Royal Pleasure that all expedition may be used in bringing forward every measure necessary to be taken for carrying to execution the plans approved of by His Majesty for establishing the Genevan emigrants in this kingdom agreeably to the benevolent design of His Majesty, and of the Parliament of Ireland'. Orde also mentioned that Rutland was keen to go forward with the Academy, and requested that the commissioners do exactly this:

> His Grace relies upon your taking the other parts of this business into your immediate consideration, among which is the plan proposed for establishing an academy in the intended new town, which establishment from the many men of eminence in the different branches of learning cultivated with success at Geneva, cannot fail of producing a considerable improvement upon the education of any country in which they may settle, and his Grace has no doubt that you will use your utmost endeavours to have it forwarded to its conclusion with every possible expedition.[117]

In addition to supporting his Genevan friends in Ireland, Stanhope caused to be published a letter he had written to 'un citoyen de Genève, sur l'état actuel de l'Etablissement des Genevois en Irlande'. It was dated 25 February 1784, and was intended to remind the Genevans that his brother-in-law, William Pitt, was now prime minister, that Thomas Townshend (Lord Sydney), as home secretary, was aware of the delays in establishing New Geneva and that both men had ordered the new Irish secretary to take any action necessary, following the explicit desire of George III, to turn New Geneva into a place where former republicans could thrive. The charter of incorporation, Stanhope said, was about to be made into law, and the Royal Navy stood ready to help Genevans who were willing to move to Ireland. In the circumstances, Stanhope's letter to Genevans still living in their old city represented the final throw of the dice.[118]

VII

Orde determined, in his reply to the mountain of evidence and the demands that had been laid at his door, to address the issues Du Roveray and d'Ivernois had raised head-on, and more especially the accusation that the Genevan emigration from New Geneva was entirely the fault of the Irish government. Orde's first point was that, from an administrative perspective, everything was on track with regard to the new city, and he wondered what the Genevans were complaining about, given that things took time, and the normal procedures had to be followed:

> His Grace is deeply concerned to find that such a resolution [the departure of the watchmakers from New Geneva] has been carried into execution, especially at a time when the Acts of the Legislature which were requisite to their establishment had passed both Houses of Parliament, when their new city was in forwardness and when they had received repeated proofs of the intentions of government that they should not suffer in the mean time by the want of proper accommodation, houses having actually been provided in Waterford in which all those who had arrived had been lodged, the expenses of their journey and voyage having been defrayed at the public charge.[119]

Orde went on to say that to complain of delays was incorrect, because he knew 'of none which did not arise from the necessity of regular parliamentary proceedings'. This was disingenuous. The timetable set out by Temple envisaged the first houses being erected within a matter of months, and the whole city laid out within a year. Orde had evidently decided to combat accusations of blame towards the British government and those involved on the Irish side, and to redirect it on to the Genevans themselves. In his view, the government had in fact done all that they had promised when the first charter was agreed upon:

> Lands have been set apart, to be distributed among the colonists to a very great value; That a Charter of Incorporation has been prepared to be executed whenever a sufficient number of Genevan manufacturers shall have arrived, which Charter will incorporate them with privileges, at least equal upon the whole to those enjoyed by any one corporation in this kingdom; that the standard of gold and silver has been altered by law in order to favour the Genevan manufacturers, and in short that every thing has been completed that could reasonably be expected from a prudent government.

Such points might have had some validity when considering the encouragement of domestic manufactures, or industries that were already established in a region, but the New Geneva experiment had been envisaged by Shelburne and by Temple, and by the Genevans themselves, as an enterprise of a different order of magnitude, and requiring, in consequence, more direct government involvement. Orde commended the actions of Du Roveray and d'Ivernois in support of New Geneva: 'The zeal and abilities with which you have conducted the interest of your fellow citizens cannot be exceeded.' At the same time, it was 'no less in justice due to government to declare that everything has been done to favour the emigrants that could be conceded with propriety'. If the government had gone further, 'it would have hazarded that very happiness in search of which you have offered yourselves to the friendly protection of a liberal nation'. The meaning of that sentence was unclear, but Orde was implying that the Genevans would have resisted greater involvement by the central administration, and have considered it a violation of their liberty. None of the Genevan commissioners ever did complain about an excess of government with regard to New Geneva, but always, rather, the opposite.

Orde had further bad news for Du Roveray and d'Ivernois with regard to the requests outlined in their letter of 21 May for additional inducements to be established in the charter of New Geneva, in order to encourage industry to locate to the city. Orde stated 'that your representation of the 21st, relative to the charter of the intended corporation has been considered', including by the law officers; this must have meant that FitzGibbon was once again involved. The demands of the Genevans were stated to be 'contrary to the present laws of the land'. This was because they requested the 'surrender of an undefined portion of the public revenues, granting exemptions from duties which would operate as a monopoly and extending privileges to the citizens of a New Geneva which do not belong to any of His Majesty's subjects'. The Genevans had requested exemption from paying the duty of tonnage and poundage on imported wine, the authority to levy duties on fishing boats, a 'grant of the great custom called bagnet', 'a power to every citizen and inhabitant to make and distil aqua vitæ' and exemption from customs and tolls. Orde reported that Rutland had considered the issue of opening an academy, and concluded that 'He cannot think this a fit time for the actual establishment of an academy even to the extent you propose.' Before any academy could be considered, the town had to be settled with 'a sufficient number of inhabitants', and their 'manufactures shall be fixed there to ensure that principal object' of the creation of New Geneva. The clear message was conveyed that once this was achieved, the answer to the question of the academy would be different.[120] Orde finished by passing on to Du Roveray and d'Ivernois advice from Rutland himself:

> [H]is Grace requests you to turn your attention [away] from those matters which cannot be granted, to the grants that have actually been made by the King and the Legislature, to the various instances of favour which have been shown to the promised emigration, and to the good faith which has been maintained by government through various administrations, and under circumstances of public affairs, which though they may have necessarily in some degree retarded the execution of the plan longer than you may have wished, have never turned the government aside from the completion of this great object.[121]

Rutland was evidently of the view that the building of New Geneva would now proceed, that the advantages of the place would become plain and that it was not too late to 'induce Genevan artists of genius and property to establish their manufacturies there, and introduce that industry and wealth into the kingdom, the hope of which first gave this country a desire of uniting the Genevans to them as fellow subjects'. Rutland's sudden optimism was seconded by John Foster in a conversation with Du Roveray, which the latter must have written up and sent back to Foster in the form of a memorandum, dated 18 May 1784. This insisted that the Irish government continued to support the project, that funds would be forthcoming to support the costs of emigrants wishing to move to Waterford and that all the buildings would be erected by the end of the year. Foster also promised additional funds of £10,000 towards a watchmaking factory, if evidence could be supplied that the Genevans themselves had already expended £5,000. Written proof of this offer, which had clearly been requested by Du Roveray, was said to be forthcoming from Orde.[122] In fact, despite Foster's assertions, Orde was the bringer of bad news rather than being willing to provide additional support.

The response of Du Roveray and d'Ivernois was then to send more justificatory material concerning the proposed academy, at the end of May and into June, as recounted above, in order to make clear their contrary view. The point was that with Genevans leaving Waterford, it was much more difficult to declare that the government was behind the project after all, and that things could now be carried to fruition. It was not a question of New Geneva going ahead without the academy, as Orde and Rutland implied. Rather, New Geneva had to become the academy, and if this was not accepted then the project was altogether dead. In May 1784, the

English translation of d'Ivernois's *Tableau historique et politique des révolutions de Genève*, first published in French in November 1782, appeared with the title *An Historical and Political View of the Constitution and Revolutions of Geneva in the eighteenth century*. The book had been translated by John Farell. Farell dedicated the work to David La Touche, one of the commissioners for New Geneva on the Irish side and of Huguenot descent, calling him 'one of the most zealous and enlightened promoters of that establishment'.[123] Notes that d'Ivernois had added for the English edition 'for the satisfaction of foreigners' were translated, including attacks on Bern for betraying the republican cause, and defences of Calvin as a republican legislator.[124]

The book reiterated arguments that the *représentants* had made commonplace before the revolution of 1782: that if '[Geneva] loses her liberty, industry will take its flight along with it', that an aristocracy had taken over the city and that traditional republican attacks on luxury, and defences of the rotation of offices, were vital if the city was to be saved.[125] What was most peculiar about the translation, however, was that it included the appeal to Louis XVI which had opened the original book, calling the French king a friend to moderate wealth, 'the *golden mean* earned by honest industry' and a defender of 'the simplicity of republican manners'. Louis was identified as 'a monarch who since the beginning of his reign has been an object of veneration to true republicans.' D'Ivernois's intention had been to appeal to the monarch at a time when there were rumours that Vergennes might fall from office. That it was not dedicated to George III, to Temple or to Rutland, and did not mention any of the Irish commissioners other than La Touche, underlined the extent to which relations had soured. In short, by the time d'Ivernois saw the translation, he anticipated the failure of the project which had taken up all of his time since June 1782. This was one of the reasons why the translation did not go beyond the original French volume, taking the story of the *représentants* only up to 1768.

In September 1784, Orde received an update on the progress of the building works. This stated that since the 'first stone' had been laid on 8 July 1784, Temple Square now consisted of 'thirty double houses', with 'half of the south side . . . ready for the roof by Monday the 13th [September]'. Substantial progress was stated to have been made, and the whole was to be ready by the following August:

> [T]he joists of the upper floor are now laid on a half of the north side, and it will be ready for the roof in three weeks from this date. The joists

> [are] also laying on part of the east side, half for which will be ready for the roof by the 15th of next month. The timber, the bricks and the stones to complete the whole are all laid in, and every part of the work going on in the very best manner and with such expedition as a will complete the present contract by the 1st of August next.[126]

Yet by this stage d'Ivernois had given up. His friend Betsy Sheridan wrote to her sister, 'With respect to the Genevese establishment I find it is totally at an end.' She reported that what d'Ivernois's future plans were 'is more than I can divine as he is very reserved on the subject'. He had informed Betsy, however, that he would not leave the country until he had seen her sister Alicia Sheridan LeFanu.[127] D'Ivernois was in Brussels in 1785, probably visiting the exiled community, which was thriving there. Meanwhile, Stanhope was trying to get him work as a tutor, including accompanying younger gentlemen on foreign travel. He ended up in the household of the banker Samson Gideon.[128]

Clavière, meanwhile, wrote to a friend at the end of 1784 that 'after the Irish adventure, I cannot think of a place that I could call my country'.[129] He had by this time moved to Paris, where he was involved in large-scale stock market speculation. It was reported among *représentants* that he had 'given himself too much to public affairs concerning finance'. It was noted too that he must have found it highly peculiar to have 'connections with the government of France'.[130] It was even said that Clavière had 'abandoned the cause of the *représentants*', although this was questioned as being unbelievable.[131] Expectations were high that things were changing at Paris after the fall of Vergennes. Clavière was one who responded, employing both Brissot and Honoré-Gabriel Riqueti de Mirabeau to support his monetary investments, by writing in favour of or against particular companies. Du Roveray too had abandoned New Geneva. He remained in Ireland, however, having, according to Otto Karmin, attempted to obtain a chair in public law at Trinity College Dublin. Du Roveray was granted a pension of £300 per year for the costs he had incurred since 1782.[132] At the same it was said that he had fallen into an apathy which was so deep as to be disconcerting to his friends.

The *représentants* had planned further works justifying what they had done and condemning the tyranny that they perceived to exist at Geneva. One possibility was that d'Ivernois would take his history up to and beyond 1782. It was clear by 1784, however, that d'Ivernois was either not capable or too busy with other projects, because it was widely reported that Honoré-Gabriel Riqueti de Mirabeau, who was already receiving funds from Clavière, would write the work. So despondent were the *représentants* that they had even given up on this by the end of 1785, describing Mirabeau as another party who could not be relied upon.[133] D'Ivernois resumed composition of his history once more in 1786, and was said to be working well, the promise being that he would identify the true culprits behind all the evils suffered by the city of Geneva.[134] The book was only published in 1789, as *Tableau historique et politique des deux révolutions de Genève*. Remarkably, d'Ivernois announced that America would have been the first choice of the exiles, and was only prevented from being so because the war had not ended and because 'Congress was under the influence of the same man [Vergennes] whose victims [the Genevans] had been'. Ireland had been chosen thanks to Shelburne, known to the Genevans as a friend both of Corsica and of North America, and whom Stanhope had vouched for as being 'attached to liberty on principle'. D'Ivernois also revealed that Stanhope had donated £5,000 of his own money to the project.[135]

D'Ivernois confirmed that Ireland had been chosen for having 'neither the high taxes that national pride has accumulated in the case of the English, nor an active industry that makes [taxes] so light'. Rather, all goods were low in price, and the industrious arts in their infancy. Patriotism was described as being powerful amongst the Irish, who, 'just as the Genevans had taken up arms to defend their independence, had armed themselves to recover their own'. They had 'just escaped as if by a miracle alarming convulsions', the hope being that a place of 'triumphant liberty would become an asylum to oppressed liberty'.[136] D'Ivernois was full of praise for the Irish response to the prospect of an exile community, and lauded especially Earl Temple and the Volunteer companies for their actions in support of the Genevans.[137] Disaster then came in the form of 'a ministerial revolution, entirely unexpected, which took from us, both in England and in Ireland, our two principal protectors [Temple and Shelburne]'. The successors in the relevant ministries were ignorant of the project, slow in taking action and obsessed with economy.

Answers had to be found, d'Ivernois acknowledged, to the question, why could not the Genevans have acted like the Phoenecians who founded Marseilles, 'with no more support than a passion for liberty', undertaking a series of difficult and ultimately glorious tasks in so doing? The point was that the world had changed. It was entirely different to arrange the emigration of 'a modern and manufacturing people' (*un peuple moderne et manufacturier*). Ancient republics 'little resemble those of today', in which 'the desire for profit and the love of consumption [*commodités*], carefully encouraged by the governments, necessarily weakens personalities and infinitely increases the difficulties [*énervent nécessairement les âmes & multiplient à l'infini les difficultés*] of a transplantation [of peoples]'.[138] Proof lay, d'Ivernois claimed, in the recent history of the Dutch Republic, where the 'persecuted class was precisely the wealthy [*la classe aisée*]'. With riches that could be moved across borders and the option of creating a new Utrecht in North America, they nevertheless failed to do so. It was the case that 'emigrations that were so frequent in antiquity, have become impracticable for moderns, and it is evident also that those who seek to dominate [republicans] are aware of this'.[139]

D'Ivernois emphasised the depression of many of the first emigrants to Ireland, who found nothing, and who realised that the failure to act quickly ruined the prospects for other potential emigrants, who lost their faith, and ended up dispersed across Europe or stuck in a Geneva marked by slavery. Two years had been wasted, and d'Ivernois blamed British ministers. By the time that Rutland was charged by 'the illustrious Pitt' to take action, Du Roveray and d'Ivernois had written to affirm, in October 1784, that it was too late.[140] Orde had made clear, in a letter of 13 October 1786, d'Ivernois took pains to make plain, that 'the failure of this enterprise is in no manner the fault of the Genevan commissioners'.[141] The tragedy for the would-be emigrants was that the Irish experiment, in raising hopes and then failing, meant that the *représentants*, in taking their eyes from Geneva itself, 'gave the Aristocracy all the time and security they required to develop and consolidate the new order of things'. Attacked by Cornuaud, the exiles experienced either 'a ruinous dispersion' or 'humiliating servitude'. The only places d'Ivernois praised as destinations for Genevan exiles were Brussels and Konstanz, where commerce, he said, had flourished in conditions of civil liberty.[142] Many of the Genevans, including those who had become Irish such as Melly, did indeed end up creating a community of watchmakers and jewellers, but this was at Konstanz, under the Holy Roman Emperor Joseph II. Gasc was the pastor for the community.[143] The community had over a hundred members at the end of 1785, and over three hundred by the end of 1786. The emperor granted the Genevans the right to live in accordance with their religion and laws, as long as the latter did not clash with existing legislation. Taxes were lowered substantially, in order to promote further the nascent industries. Although many members returned to Geneva after the revolution in the city of 1789, which restored the exiled to their former positions, the Genevan community at Konstanz continued to flourish at least until 1798.[144]

Orde now was meanwhile faced with the task of doing something with the New Geneva buildings. In 1785 he received an offer to turn the site into a settlement for manufacture of woollen textiles. In part the justification was to make use of the substantial funds that had been dedicated to the project, but which remained unspent:

> As the Parliament of Ireland did think fit some time ago to grant £50,000 for building of houses and creating a settlement for refugee watchmakers emigrating from Geneva; and that that project has failed but that the whole sum of £50,000 is not expended. It is therefore, that the following proposals are submitted to consideration, as what may turn to greater national benefit than watchmaking namely—That the buildings and works already erected and intended for forming the town and establishment for the use of the Genevan watchmakers may be assigned and appropriated to the establishing of a woollen manufacture And that so much of the £50,000 granted by Parliament for their support may be henceforth applied to the advancement of this said woollen manufacture.[145]

The proposal was not signed, but it may have been associated with James Cuffe or other Irish commissioners who were precisely aware of the expenditure on New Geneva to date. The description of a town devoted to industry promised to avoid 'narrow and selfish principles, favouring none but their own Members and Freemen, and excluding all others', but rather to be a place where 'strangers are as free as the natives to exercise their industry'. The result would be that 'emulation creates industry, and sobriety, which never fails to recompense those who diligently practise them'. Ireland would be following the great projects of the mainland, such 'inland navigations, turnpike roads, the paving of London, setting up of post chaises' and 'in Scotland, the joining of the two seas by uniting the Clyde and the Forth', all of which had avoided 'the interference and direction of governments'. But Orde rejected such offers. Rather, he passed the matter on to Cornelius Bolton, a local lawyer and long-time Irish commissioner, who worked out who owned what in terms of the land, and dealt with petitions from locals to be given leases on it from the crown.[146] As always seemed to be the case at New Geneva, things proceeded slowly. Orde was complaining to Rutland in August 1786 that he had presumed everything finished long before:

> New Geneva.—I thought these buildings had been finished long ago. I suppose Mr. Cuffe must view them and report, and advertisements

> must be prepared, stating the tenure, conditions, and other essential circumstances. These should be first privately communicated to Lord Tyrone and Mr. Bolton.[147]

It was at this point that Orde must have been persuaded by the Beresfords, and by Cuffe more especially, to turn New Geneva into a barracks.

VIII

What went wrong at New Geneva? Jean Théodore Rivier, who was about to marry into the Vieusseux and Clavière families, had predicted in 1783 that the emigration would come to nothing. He argued that Geneva had been dealt such a blow in 1782 that there was no longer what Rivier called 'republican blood' left, by which he meant the manners and morals capable of sustaining community life. With the defeat of the *représentants*, egotism was everywhere rampant:

> Your reflections on emigration would be very just, my dear friend, if you had a true idea of the mass of your fellow-citizens; you judge them all as thinking with the same purity and sincerity as your dear family; but I'm afraid you're wrong. The emigration will, I am sure, be very little, there is nothing decided for Ireland. The country is lost; it is impossible to have a new one; there is no longer much republican blood in the old Genevans, and you would be astonished to see how much selfishness wins and will win every day. For me, I would benefit eagerly and in time from the new republic if it were formed, since I am determined not to stay in Geneva, but I have very little faith, and it will be necessary in the end for each of us to go our own way, as where we can, and we will become selfish by necessity at least with regard to our homeland.[148]

In other words, Rivier ultimately blamed the Genevans themselves. This had been Orde's position in his final judgements on Du Roveray's and d'Ivernois's plans for an academy. It was also mentioned by Rutland when he was approached by Lord Aughrim, the son of Lord Athlone, who had the idea of taking advantage of the crisis in the United Provinces, where the forces of the stadholder were fighting patriotic republicans who were advocates of popular sovereignty. Rutland thought it would be a good idea to encourage industrious Dutch artisans to come to Ireland. His rationale was that they would be supporters of the stadholder, and therefore in favour of monarchy, rather than being wild republicans in the manner of the Genevans. With regard to the *représentants*, Lord Aughrim called them 'factious', advocates of 'unlimited notions of liberty' and incapable of accepting subordination of any form. These were exactly the descriptions that were launched at the *représentants* by their enemies, in the decades after 1764:

> It occurred to me if the Stadholder's affairs should become desperate, and if his friends should be obliged to seek a foreign asylum, that [if] Lord Athlone [could] induce a number of his countrymen to seek a retreat in Ireland, he would establish a solid claim on the liberality of the public. This would add weight to the Protestant interest, and bring a number of useful and industrious inhabitants who might be employed with effect in the infant fisheries of Ireland, and might settle under the protection of this Government. At the same time I should by no means recommend to put this country to any expence, should such a scheme at any time be deemed wise to be adopted. My idea only goes to afford a secure establishment to those who will venture at their own hazard. The country felt the burthen of a similar scheme in regard to the factious Genevois, about whom such animating expectations were formed, which terminated in delusion. The scheme I have described would be composed of persons who abandoned their country because they could not stem the torrent of a republican faction, who endeavoured to blot out the only resemblance of monarchy which existed in their constitution; whereas the other scheme was to introduce a body of men into Ireland whose notions of liberty were so unlimited, that they could not endure any form of government, any control, or any subordination whatever.[149]

The view was increasingly put forward that the Genevans themselves were incapable of forming any settlement, and especially any settlement in a constitutional monarchy, because they remained republicans, unruly and egalitarian in their attitudes to life. Jacques Mallet du Pan, the *natif* critic of the *représentants*, had asked in response to Brissot's justification of events in Ireland, 'Do you believe you can convert kings [to your views] with your democratic declamations?'[150] Francis Dobbs, looking back at the history of settlement, and having access to many of the documents that had been agreed upon to launch the scheme, also made mention of the republican manners of the Genevans as being incompatible with Irish mores. Dobbs added that New Geneva would always have failed, because Ireland remained an agricultural country, and was therefore unsuitable for artisans who had always lived in towns:

> The reciprocal advantages, which might have accrued to Ireland and the Genevese emigrants, from the proposed settlement, even had it taken place to the fullest extent, could never, it is presumed, have equalled, or been in any degree proportionable to the sanguine expectations some men had been led to form on this subject. It should be considered, first, that the Genevese are, for the most part, mechanics, and that therefore they must have been but ill-suited, from their former habits of life, to the toils of agriculture; next, that they were to be settled in a part of Ireland where their support must have arisen from their daily labours on the soil, and from their having but few wants of their own to gratify, more than from their ingenuity in forming and constructing a variety of ornamental articles, which the luxury and riches of populous and trading towns can only create a market for. Whether or no this measure of government had not in fact proved abortive as it did, it is very questionable whether it would ultimately have been productive of any real advantage to that kingdom.[151]

That the government had 'the most implicit and unqualified committment' Dobbs accepted, underlining what he called the 'levy' of 'the large sum of £50,000 upon a very distressed country', all 'to purchase the probable introduction of turbulent and democratic principles, with a thousand self-exiled martyrs to democracy, from the Antibazilican school of Geneva'. Another commentator of the following decades, the Catholic writer Theobald McKenna, stated that the government had been altogether mad to consider bringing wild republicans into Ireland. The consequences had since been made plain by Clavière's own extremist actions during the French Revolution:

> A few years fince there was a treaty on foot with Mr. Clavière (the late republican minister of the Convention) to lead into Ireland a number of men who had emigrated from Geneva, as too aristocratic. Nothing can better illustrate the delusion of the rulers of Ireland upon this subject, than the idea of correcting their own Roman Catholic royalists, by the mixture of a clan of republicans, too refractory for Geneva.[152]

The Genevans involved with New Geneva in part blamed Vergennes. References to enemies in London peppered the correspondence of the *représentants*. Vergennes certainly maintained his war against them. D'Ivernois's *Tableau historique* was forbidden at Paris and at Geneva, and an attempt was made to sequester every copy.[153] When Vergennes, known as 'the vizier' to the *représentants*, lost office, d'Ivernois, in a letter to Charles Stanhope, made the point that 'Geneva was a personal matter for the Comte de Vergennes'.[154]

Such opinions led the historian of Waterford Patrick Egan to describe the project as 'utter silliness'. He did, however, add a significant note, that New Geneva 'could be explained in no other form except we conclude that some object besides the ostensible one of doing good to the Kingdom of Ireland, actuated the Parliament'.[155] What did Egan mean? What had been wrong with those involved in New Geneva on the Irish side? C. T. Greville, a correspondent of Rutland's, argued that the nature of the link between Britain and Ireland was ultimately to blame. The granting of relative autonomy to the Irish parliament had, Greville argued, made life insecure in Ireland, and the forms of friendship and emulation that were vital to thriving trade were being lost in consequence. Ireland needed union with Britain to secure stability into the future, and this was why, however attractive the situation had seemed initially, projects like New Geneva had failed:

> Ireland is too great to be unconnected with us, and too near us to be dependent on a foreign state, and too little to be independent. The separation which has been made will require more than human wisdom to reconcile it with amity and generous emulation. The unsettled state of the country will deter men of property speculating and embarking their capitals in Ireland. Local advantages may on the map engage others as they did the Genevese, but on a view of Ireland, its government and component parts, those advantages appear counter-balanced; nothing but a union with Great Britain will give a permanent security to the landed property, life to manufactures, or draw into the country those advantages, which nature has granted to Ireland from its situation, favourable to commerce, to fisheries, and manufactures.[156]

Theobald McKenna, in addition to blaming the excessive republicanism of the Genevans, also pointed to the permanent crisis of Irish politics in the 1780s, and the foolishness of the expectation, espoused by Price and Shelburne, that commercial reform would bring industry to Ireland and address the problems of the people. For McKenna, the Irish were not free, and especially their Catholic majority. Therefore, Ireland could never be considered a free state or nation, and this meant that adventurers promising industry from whatever religious denomination would ultimately find the place unpalatable:

> The commercial restrictions were removed; these constituted, indeed, an evil of magnitude, of which the redress was highly beneficial . . . It

> was expected that our happy soil and commercial opportunities should attract strangers, who, pouring a sudden influx of capital, should rapidly enrich the kingdom. Foreigners wisely judged that the settlement of a country could not be secure, in which population [*sic*] was at variance with authority. Although very considerable encouragement was proposed, not even the Jews would accept the invitation. We quarrelled with the law of Poynings, but the law of Poynings had never made a pauper . . . The Parliament was not in consequence of this transaction more intimately blended with the Nation; or any improvement made in the connection, which might be supposed to subsist between them . . . Public spirit, and firmness, and dignity were yet to be supplied to Ireland, for she wanted a people.[157]

McKenna was turning the arguments of Shelburne and Price against them, accepting that commerce needed civil and political liberty, and underlining the lack of it in Ireland.

There was another factor at play in the early history of New Geneva. Egan, having made the point that there was something wrong with the parliament of Ireland, went on to give details of the use of the funds granted by the crown. This Egan took from the detailed transcriptions of Thomas Gimlette from the Waterford archives.[158] The commissioner Alexander Alcock received, 'for his interest in the lands of Knockroe, £12,796'. This figure was higher than the amount initially agreed with Temple, because it included interest for late payment. Hendy and Donnellan, the contractors for the building work, received £310. James Cuffe received £465 for supervising the building work; this would have been in addition to the salary he had taken of £3 per day. William Gibson, the architect, was paid £207. In total, Gimlette and Egan asserted, £23,336 was expended, and that remaining sum, £32,519, was refunded to the government. Egan made the point that the recipient of the vast sum of £12,796 'was of the same family as Henry Alcock who represented the city of Waterford this year, 1783'. The implication was that corruption on the Irish side had crippled the building of New Geneva. This goes against the view of at least one modern journalist, who claimed, without providing any evidence, that the fault lay with London, where politicians had been pressurised by merchants worried about competition from the Genevans in Ireland, and then shut down the project.[159] All of the British ministers who followed Temple and Shelburne were in fact preoccupied with other matters, and far less committed; much of the evidence that remains in archives points towards Irish figures putting a stop to the venture.

Such a view was corroborated in part by a long letter from Temple to Rutland, of April 1784. Rutland had clearly asked for Temple's view of New Geneva, and whether the Genevans were right to complain that the project had gone badly off course. Temple confirmed that this was the case, blaming Northington, and reaffirmed his own support for the proposed city:

> When I accepted the propositions made by Monsieur d'Ivernois on behalf of the Genevans, I clearly saw that much of the success of the measures depended upon the activity with which it was carried into execution. I had the mortification during the government of my successor to see the whole of that summer last, in which I had flattered myself that a considerable progress might have been made in the construction of the new Geneva & in his Excellency's speech from the Throne I found the attention of Parliament particularly directed to the economy of this establishment in a manner very pointed & which I could not help thinking highly invidious.[160]

Temple was sure that 'under your Grace's auspices this Measure will meet with every fair protection'. He also claimed that 'it is not too late to secure to Ireland that accession to the national wealth and the several advantages which were held out to meet in the original negotiation upon this subject', and added that he had been pleased that the 'gentlemen to whose abilities & integrity I had confided this important business . . . have so laudably taken on that first & essential object, an inquiry into the expenditure attending it'. Temple went on, however, to state that he had delegated the 'immediate execution of the buildings' to Cuffe. Rutland had evidently requested information from Temple about the terms of Cuffe's involvement. Temple confirmed that 'whilst he was actually employed in the survey or construction of these works . . . he should receive the same appointments, which had been deemed an adequate compensation to him when employed in the Barrack Department', emphasising that 'the allowance [could] only be made to him during his actual journeys to the new settlement or during his residence there on the public service'. With regard to the employment of Major James Ferrier in the building of New Geneva, Temple said that this was 'totally distinct from the Genevan Commission'. Above all, Ferrier could not be paid from the funds set aside for New Geneva:

> But I must again repeat that it was never in my contemplation to pay him [Ferrier] out of the grant of £50,000 which I always meant to keep

> sacred to the purposes for which it was originally granted, of constructing the new town & defraying the freight & journeys of the emigrants. I will only trespass further upon your Grace's patience to wish every success to this measure in which I feel peculiarly interested.

The implication was that Cuffe was drawing funds illegitimately, that others were being paid from the New Geneva funds who ought not to be being paid and that, in short, the funds overall were not being used for the purposes originally assigned. Certainly, the fact that the major funds expended on New Geneva tended to end up in the pockets of the Irish commissioners, including James Moore, the mayor of Waterford at the time, was suspicious. New Geneva undoubtedly fell prey to Irish corruption. The main business of the Irish commission seems to have been to respond to its own members in their requests for money, for work undertaken or work anticipated, lost leases or interest in the land in question.[161] Clavière, always perceptive, and who tended to see the writing on the wall before others, made a fascinating set of references to Cuffe in his letter to John Foster of the end of July 1783. He named Cuffe as one of the people failing to respond to his requests for clarification about the lack of progress on the building of New Geneva. Indeed, rather than reply to Clavière, Cuffe had left Waterford for Mayo. Clavière said that he had bluntly informed Cuffe that the quality of the building work was poor and that a lot of money was being wasted at New Geneva. Cuffe, he wrote, had 'taken such observations badly'. In the unresponsiveness of Cuffe, and in the seeming lack of interest of William Gibson and James Ferrier, Clavière perceived 'a hidden force [*une cause secrète*], whose nature I cannot understand, that acts against the establishment of the Genevans in Ireland'. The result was depression, because the Genevan commissioners were so devoted to the project and so invested in its success.[162]

The Irish commissioners would not allow d'Ivernois and Du Roveray funds for the academy, or to improve the lives of the first group of migrants. At the same time, and especially in Cuffe's case, they were taking money for themselves. The Genevans were naive initially, and then increasingly frustrated. Temple was equally foolish in delegating the creation of New Geneva to such figures. Shelburne might not have been as trusting, given his direct knowledge of local affairs, but he was initially otherwise engaged, and then altogether powerless. This explains references to arguments at the meetings between the two bodies of commissioners, Genevan and Irish. That New Geneva was turned into a barracks fits with this story. Cuffe, as already noted, had held office on the Barracks

Board from 1772 until 1776; he then became inspector of barracks, being paid £600 a year. He became a privy councillor on 17 September 1782, and first commissioner of barracks in January 1784, on £1,000 a year. Perhaps from the first Cuffe saw the New Geneva experiment as a means of self-advancement and enrichment.

Such a perspective was commonplace in public life in Britain and in Ireland. Temple himself asked, on his return to Britain from Ireland, why 'Lord Shelburne has the Garter, Lord Thurlow a pension, Lord Grantham the same, Townshend a peerage, as marks of the King's satisfaction', adding, 'would it be improper or impossible to state that I am returning (such as I am) without any feather?'[163] Cuffe's involvement explains the constant delay, the failure to build, the anger of the Genevans and the ultimate destiny of the site in the erection of a barracks. By the time he reported that he had laid the foundation stone of the city, the Genevans had abandoned Waterford. Cuffe would have been well aware that he was building a very expensive barracks. His 'feather', for his services to the government and to his Irish superiors, was to be made 1st Baron Tyrawley of Ballinrobe, on 22 November 1797. In 1802–03, however, when the levels of corruption at the Barracks Board were finally acknowledged, he was condemned and became a pariah figure.

CHAPTER TEN

Barracks and Prison

AT FIRST GLANCE, the transformation of New Geneva into a prison for United Irishmen can be seen to be a by-product of the very impulse that had inspired the Genevan republicans. Both the Genevan and the Irish radicals were seeking liberty in the face of a tyrannical oppressor, sought to rule themselves in free states, able to determine their own destinies by engagement with the will of the people and aspired to create worlds characterised by peace, toleration and prosperity. Each had taken up arms in defence of their liberties, and perceived the highest duty of a citizen to be self-sacrifice for the survival of the republic. Both parties were labelled by their enemies as anarchists and terrorists, and in the case of the United Irishmen also as agents of oppression. As one contemporary put it, '[Irish republicanism] originates in anarchy, proceeds in bloodshed, and ends in cruel and unrelenting despotism'.[1]

In each case, there was seemingly no limit to the wrath of a large power facing republicans seeking to create independent states either within or at its borders. The British response to republicans in their midst in the late 1790s was far more brutal than that of the French in 1782, one reason being the existence of a genuine republican alternative, being a direct challenge to the existence of the British state. Although Vergennes threatened to have the leaders of the *représentants* executed, and although there were rumours of assassination plots, the Genevans faced banishment, impoverishment and imprisonment rather than death. Such parallels can lead to the conclusion that Irish republicanism should be twinned with that espoused by the Genevans, to whom they may have been indebted, being part of the drive towards democratic revolution that marked the decades after 1776. To presume too close a connection, however, is a mistake. The Genevans were seeking to maintain what they saw to be the world of old

Europe, in all its variety and colour, and looked back to the republic of Geneva in its heyday as being independent, Protestant, commercial and venerated. Although they advocated popular sovereignty, for the Genevans free government was best envisaged as a walled town, in the senses both of a small community of the like-minded and of one where public mores could better be policed. They were intolerant of difference, and castigated the Francophile magistrates for destroying, in part by diversifying, the republican culture that had defined the city. At the same time, the Genevans were not republican exclusivists, and a world transformed into sister republics was as frightening to them as the prospect of the dominion of monarchical France. Europe, from the Genevan perspective, needed to be saved from the forces seeking to alter it.

The United Irishmen, by contrast, sought a new world. Some of them, in the fashion of Thomas Paine and many French fellow republicans of the 1790s, imagined a world without rank or hierarchy, where government would be limited in scope, and where the removal of ancient tyrannies would be sufficient, alongside republican education, to allow societies to live in peace in perpetuity. The first step to such a world, they increasingly recognised, following Paine in the second part of his *Rights of Man* (1792), was war to the death against the forces ranged against them, of aristocracy, monarchy and, in the Irish case, entrenched Protestant Ascendancy. Taking up arms to battle Britain's tyrants was a step associated with the Volunteers in the 1780s, but never embraced as a strategy by the Patriots themselves. The United Irishmen were different, accepting that military action would have to be taken, and organising themselves to such an end. The intention of creating a new republic based on an altogether transformed social system, founded upon equality, was more innovative still, marking out the republicanism that became so popular in the revolutionary decade. To show that there were two different kinds of republicanism operating in Ireland, one in the 1780s and the other in the 1790s, is the goal of this chapter. From the perspective of Ireland's rulers, if the forms of republicanism that emerged in the 1790s generated fear on an unprecedented scale, there was a direct link with the armed popular movements of the 1780s that perceived Ireland to be a newly liberated state, if one still loyal to Britain. That Ireland's rulers saw the Volunteer and Patriot movements as amounting to a military challenge to the state explained the acceptance of Cuffe's plan to make New Geneva into a barracks. The growth of a new kind of republicanism in France explained the formation of the prison, and the brutality that ultimately occurred within its walls.

II

The granting of legislative independence to Ireland, through the repeal of the Declaratory Act in 1782 and the Irish Appeals Act (Renunciation Act) of 1783, did little to counter the querulous sentiment that the Irish either remained unfree, with further steps needed to maintain the liberties so recently won, or that in the newly free state further legislation to embed reform was vital. The relaxing of the restrictions upon Irish trade in 1780 could as easily be said to have extended discontent within the country as to have led to pacification. The Acts of 1780 had allowed Ireland for the first time to export wool and other manufactured products, in addition to being able to trade with the colonies. They did not, however, deal with trade between Britain and Ireland. Economic problems that had arisen in Ireland since the commencement of the American war continued. During the conflict, emigration from Ireland was impeded, increasing numbers of the unemployed; the export of foodstuffs was forbidden, between 1776 and 1779; and the linen industry declined. The overlapping Volunteer and Patriot movements were as vociferous in the mid-1780 as they had been before legislative independence and a measure of free trade had been granted. Concerns about civil disorder and possible revolution severely limited the ability of British politicians to act on projects that were not a direct response to immediate difficulties. This was certainly the case with regard to New Geneva in the cases of Shelburne, Temple and Orde, all of whom lacked the time to help the exiles overcome the difficulties posed in practice by the Irish settlement. The problematic question of whether Ireland could enjoy civil liberty and political liberty, in the sense of legislative independence, in addition to free trade, bedevilled successive administrations in London and at Dublin Castle. There was a tension between legislative independence and membership of Britain's mercantile system on equal terms, because the latter entailed allowing London to dictate trade policy. The Irish had a choice to make between what was perceived to be commercial equality, and political liberty. British politicians who were notionally friends to liberty, such as Charles James Fox, argued strenuously that Ireland could not determine its own economic policy with regard to international trade, termed 'external legislation'.[2] Irish Patriots such as Henry Flood held that Ireland enjoyed control over all forms of legislation pertaining to the colony, being 'the new country, Ireland, in her emancipated and dignified state'.[3] This dilemma too contributed to the turning of New Geneva into a barracks, and then into a prison for republicans.

The subjects of complaints about the condition of Ireland in the mid-1780s ranged from economic problems to political corruption, with the latter concern centring on the incapacity of Irish politicians to act for the good of the nation, because their own interests were narrow, unrepresentative of the country as a whole or too dependent upon the monies that flowed from the mainland in return for obedience. Opposition grew towards those leaders of the Protestant Ascendancy deemed responsible for maintaining British rule; the very term 'Protestant Ascendancy' began to be used as a derogatory phrase to indicate the dominion of those who bled Ireland dry for their own gain and that of their clientele.[4] Patriot politicians and Volunteers focused on the deficiencies of the electoral system, voicing demands for an end to rotten boroughs, for greater representation of counties and large towns, for more frequent elections and a secret ballot and, in some cases, most radically of all, for the extension of the franchise to Catholics. The claim was made that if the system of representation in Ireland was not improved, the Irish themselves would remain slaves. Swift had famously made the point that if the English were corrupt, the Irish were 'slaves, and knaves, and fools; and all, but bishops and people in employment, beggars'.[5] The idea that Ireland was enslaved had been a staple of patriotic rhetoric in the 1750s.[6] In the 1780s, however, the argument that the Irish were among the most enslaved people on earth became both more commonplace and was more vehemently asserted, being tied to Henry Grattan's question, 'Shall the colonists of America be free, and the loyal people of Ireland slaves?'[7] Charles Lucas's claim was revived, that Irish elections were scenes of slavery, because the minds of electors were 'corrupted and vilified', being sold for money to the 'infamous bidder' and the 'shameful seducer'.[8] As the 'genius of England' was 'immersed in unrestrained luxury', having 'mistook wealth for virtue', the Irish could safely recover their rights, because they were 'undebauched by luxury'. Giving the people their rights was vital to combat 'the spirit of feudal subjection' which characterised 'the aristocratic spirit' of 'the landed interest', 'to be corrected only by the manners of the people, which, whatever be the form of government, should be strictly republican'.[9]

Such views inspired delegates from forty-five Volunteer corps to meet at Lisburn on 1 July 1783, where a decision was taken to develop plans for parliamentary reform. Proposals were then presented before 270 corps, gathered at another convention at Dungannon in September 1783. William Wenman Seward's *The Rights of the People Asserted* was among the most radical pamphlets to appear at this time, taking the form of a commentary upon the convention at Dungannon. Seward was a lawyer, an enemy of corruption and an advocate of the recovery of lost rights, suddenly possible because a free people was rediscovering its 'public spirit and virtue'. He was of the view that Ireland had long groaned 'under oppression and injustice; long were her rights trampled on and disregarded . . . long did a venal herd of prostituted sycophants, living on the spoils of their country, betray every public trust, and sacrifice her dearest rights'. Everything depended upon the imminent election of new members of parliament. Seward advised the would-be patriots to follow Machiavelli's advice in his *Discorsi*: regularly to restore constitutions to their first principles, returning thereby 'the British Constitution, that boast of former ages', to its 'primitive and justly admired foundation'. Seward's argument was that Ireland could lead the way in this process:

> If the people have made a virtuous and well directed choice in their new representatives, happy is their lot; The work of reformation will of course begin; and a Patriot Senate, backed by a Patriot Army, will restore independence to their country, and health to its sickly constitution. The freedom of Ireland thus asserted, what tool, what minion, dare oppose the voice of the people?[10]

Seward's analysis of the loss of liberty rested upon common arguments against the corruption of representatives by the patronage of the crown leading to parliaments of placemen. Britain as a whole had now 'drawn near to that period, at which the learned Montesquieu has predicted our downfall', because the constitution was 'miserably corrupted and decayed'. To prevent ruin, all 'placemen and pensioners' had to be excluded from 'the democratic part of our constitution'. The first step was Irish reform, because the 'prudence, spirit, and virtue of Hibernia's free-born sons' could repair 'this once glorious fabric'. Citing Locke, Molyneux, Francis Hutcheson, Rapin de Thoyras, Bolingbroke and Paine, Seward held that the aristocratic element of the constitution had extended itself in recent times, and the establishment of regular and free parliaments of independent members was the only remedy.[11] Related arguments emanated from the Catholic community, with the added claim that the representation of all freeholders, the independent men of property who could be trusted with law-making for the public good, both Protestant and Catholic, would bring a transformation of Ireland's economic prospects.[12]

Links were established by the Patriots and Volunteers in favour of parliamentary reform with English radicals, including Richard Price, John Cartwright and John Jebb. Price was especially despondent at the collapse of Shelburne's ministry, and at what he perceived to be the abandonment of principle in the formation of the Fox-North coalition. The dreadful fact, he wrote to Benjamin Franklin, was that the peace negotiated by Shelburne was being attacked, increasing the likelihood of future rebellion and war:

> You probably well know what a detestable coalition of parties has lately taken place among us. Never surely was there an instance of such profligate conduct. Mr Fox, the pretended friend of the country, united to Lord North, the destroyer of the country—the Rockingham party, a body of men who would be thought zealous Whigs, united to Tories and the friends of despotism to oppose and censure a peace which has saved the kingdom—I hope foreigners see this in its true light; as, merely, a struggle of ambitious and disappointed men to get into power. May the United States take care to guard against the danger and misery of such factions.[13]

Seeing a return to the forms of despotic politics that had ruined Britain and caused the war, Price counselled the Irish to follow the Americans and be 'unanimous and firm', because of the malign forces ranged against them:

> We are now governed by an odious coalition, formed between Whigs and the conductors of the late war, to gratify ambition and party rage by censuring the peace. These united parties are, in general, hostile to reformation; and this will make it more difficult for the people of Ireland to succeed in their views; but nothing can be difficult to a people determined to recover their rights.[14]

In an 'Address to the Associated Volunteers of Ireland' which accompanied the letter, Price was more optimistic. He asserted that the Irish needed to maintain the momentum for reform that had become possible because of events in North America. Writing as a 'citizen of the world and a warm friend to universal liberty', Price counselled the Irish Volunteers to push for what he termed 'a free and equal representation', in place of a parliament which was, in England at least, chosen 'by a few grandees and beggars'. Irish action he expected to be welcomed by English supporters of reform, including ministers; Price was writing just as Pitt entered office. Overall, he was confident of the success of the Volunteers:

> Is it not therefore almost certain, that the Volunteers and Patriots of Ireland will easily succeed in this understanding, if they set themselves to it with that glorious zeal which they have hitherto discovered, and by which they have exhibited to the world an example of public spirit

> and virtue scarcely ever before known, and which must render them the admiration of future ages?[15]

Jebb went further than Price in advocating the inclusion of Catholics in the civil polity and admired the 'fire of genuine patriotism' to be found in Ireland. He hoped, however, that a patriotic minister could unite all of Britain in the cause of extending popular liberties, rather than promoting reform in Ireland alone. He admitted that his favourite patriot, Charles James Fox, having joined the Portland ministry after Shelburne fell from power, was behaving more like Richlieu, 'the arbitrary minister . . . the subverter of the remaining liberties of France', than the person he ought to have been emulating, 'the immortal Sully, the friend of Henry [IV of France]—the friend of man'.[16] One pamphlet advocating an increase in the number of county MPs was dedicated to Shelburne, identified as an advocate of reform and the most virtuous of ministers, and as one who still enjoyed 'more of the esteem and confidence of the Irish nation . . . than any public character in Great Britain ever possessed'.[17]

When a national convention did meet, between the 10 and 29 November 1783, Lord Charlemont sat in the chair, but Henry Flood was indisputably the dominant figure. Indeed, Charlemont reportedly referred to Flood as a latter-day John Hampden—the great parliamentarian opponent of ship money during the reign of Charles I.[18] Flood had made his view of contemporary Ireland clear during a debate in the Irish Commons on 28 October 1783. His speech was in response to a motion by Sir Henry Cavendish to reduce the military establishment in Ireland, on the grounds of the state of national finances and the end of the war. Flood, in accordance with the views of the Rockingham Whigs and radicals on the mainland, asserted that England had declined and continued to be in a state of crisis, with politicians failing to listen to those dismissed as 'speculative men', who actually saw the grim prospects more clearly. Ireland, by contrast, had a brighter future:

> [Our Irish] retrenchments should reach establishments, and, not like England, plunge deeper each day in ruin. Ministry both here and in that kingdom, have often been warned of the consequence that must follow, but these warnings have been treated as the visions of speculative men. England, that great and mighty country now staggers under a load of debt, distress, and dismemberment; her expenses overwhelm her, and where is the man who will say, she shall be redeemed?[19]

It was over the issue of military retrenchment that Grattan almost fought a duel with Flood, only being prevented by the arrest of both men. In the debate, Grattan opposed the reduction of the military; Flood accused him of being 'the mendicant patriot, who was bought by his country for a sum of money, and sold his country for prompt payment'. Grattan replied that Flood had informed 'the nation that it is ruined by other men, while it is sold by you . . . I, therefore, tell you, in the face of your country, before all the world, and to your beard, you are not an honest man'.[20]

At the convention, Flood successfully pressed the delegates to embrace the enlargement of small boroughs, the residency of voters in their constituencies, triennial elections, the extension of the franchise to forty shilling leaseholders in addition to freeholders, as long as they were Protestant, and the removal from their seat for the duration of the parliament any pensioner or placeman of the crown.[21] Flood, having been entirely supported in the convention, then presented the proposals before the Irish Commons, on 29 November 1783, and was defeated. Barry Yelverton accused Flood of putting forward proposals that were illegitimate because they originated in an armed assembly. The government opposed Flood's bill on the same grounds, questioning the validity of 'an armed assembly, which was sitting in the metropolis to overawe parliament'.[22]

Flood replied to Yelverton that it was to the Volunteers that the liberties of commerce and of the constitution were owed:

> I have not introduced the Volunteers, but if they are aspersed, I will defend their character against all the world. By whom were the commerce and the constitution of this country recovered? By the Volunteers! Why did not the right honourable gentleman make a declaration against them when they lined our streets, when parliament passed through the ranks of those virtuous armed men to demand the rights of an insulted nation? Are they different men at this day, or is the right honourable gentleman different? He was then one of their body; he is now their accuser! He, who saw the streets lined, who rejoiced, who partook in their glory, is now their accuser! Are they less wise, less brave, less ardent in their country's cause, or has their admirable conduct made him their enemy? May they not say, we have not changed, but you have changed. The right honourable gentleman cannot bear to hear of volunteers; but I will ask him, and I will have a starling taught to hollow in his ear, who gave you the free trade? Who got you the free constitution? Who made you a nation? The Volunteers.[23]

Demands for parliamentary reform were taking place at a time of acute economic crisis. In the same month, November 1783, a mob marched to parliament demanding protective duties on the grounds that trade had declined so much that the people were starving. Foster and Grattan were threatened with violence and 'some great blow' was anticipated, especially because Catholics were also demanding their rights, and being repelled by Protestants among the Volunteer companies.[24] After petitions from Volunteers in numerous counties and towns, Flood reintroduced his bill in March 1784, only to lose once again on the 20th. Advocates of parliamentary reform continued to meet. In Dublin, in June 1784, a gathering of 'freemen', including James Napper Tandy and William Todd Jones, pressed once more for reform, including giving the vote to Catholics, although this group would still be prevented from acting as members of parliament. In Ulster, reformers such as Henry Joy and William Drennan also met to push for reform, but envisaged giving Catholic men the vote only if they owned property valued at £50 or more. Divisions began to emerge about the extent of reform deemed necessary, and the definition of the political nation that could be trusted not to seek to destroy the state itself.[25] Fears resurfaced of Catholics as a fifth column, likely to initiate a revolution and civil war that would be a prelude to invasion by France or Spain.[26] Westminster and Dublin Castle politicians continued to worry about the existence of movements profoundly unhappy with the state of Ireland, and dedicated to the further transformation of the country into what was perceived to be a truly free state. William Drennan was increasingly of this view, because the Irish remained 'slaves' despite notional free trade and independence, and because a corrupt aristocracy continued to control the state and to exploit the people. It was a mistake to follow apologists for the British constitution, among whom Drennan identified Montesquieu and Jean-Louis de Lolme. It was a fact that the vaunted British liberties existed only in the books of such men: 'the freedom of your present mutilated constitution is only to be found in the utopia of a fanciful French man, or the political reveries of a Genevan philosopher'.[27]

III

The fundamental problem facing those who dreamed of a free and transformed Ireland was the nature of the transition mechanism that might make it a reality, if reform strategies failed, as they appeared to have done with the rejection of Flood's electoral measures. One such route was to anticipate the collapse of Britain. If Britain became bankrupt, fell prey to civil war or was invaded by a foreign power, then Irish liberty might be secured. This was acknowledged at the same time to be unlikely, especially because of the linkage between the elites in Britain and in Ireland, many of whom could be expected to take up arms, and translate any domestic conflict to Ireland. From the Irish perspective, in the North American case it was accepted that liberty had been the product not simply of popular patriotism and rebellion against tyranny. The arms of the Americans had never been sufficient. Rather, it was France, with troops and with money, aided by the Spanish and the Dutch, who had made North America free. The step was not taken, in the 1780s, of approaching the French court for aid towards Ireland. The collapse of Britain seemed a surer route.

The British government was entirely aware of the situation in Ireland, and we have seen Orde's concern when in office with the possibility of armed rebellion. The response of William Pitt in the mid-1780s was to fall back upon Shelburne's argument, that economic reform in Ireland was the surest means to pacify those who were arguing that Britain could not be trusted to grant commercial liberties and legislative independence in perpetuity. Unsurprisingly, Pitt turned to John Beresford and John Foster in formulating proposals. Like Shelburne, he felt that Ireland might be transformed by being granted full membership of the British mercantile system, but demanded in return a contribution from Ireland towards the costs of defending the colony. Rutland warned Pitt that parliamentary reform in Ireland was dangerous, and was concerned both about supporters of Fox attacking the government and about the actions of Catholics in fomenting unrest, sometimes with the support of foreign powers:

> I have some time entertained suspicions that the lower classes of the people may have been wrought upon by French or American emissaries, from a general endeavour to mix the Roman Catholics with questions of parliamentary reform, and I have therefore on my part endeavoured to detach them as much as possible from mingling in those pursuits.[28]

Rutland ultimately advised a union within twenty years, because of the disaffection of the general populace and the existence of the armed Volunteers. He did, however, agree with Pitt with regard to trade policy:

> I hope the learned in trade may be able to strike out such regulations as may appease and conciliate the spirit of dissatisfaction and discontent which has obtained in this country, and at the same time not materially embarrass the commerce and manufactures of Great Britain.[29]

The latter issue proved a sticking point with Grattan and with Flood, but Pitt's ten commercial propositions were introduced into the Irish parliament by Orde on 7 February 1785 and presented again in full dress on 12 August, at which time the measure failed to obtain sufficient support to go beyond the stage of first reading. These commercial propositions of 1785 envisaged allowing goods from the colonies to be transported between Ireland and Britain without duties, and proposed the equalisation of duties on commerce directly undertaken between Britain and Ireland. In other words, Ireland was to gain full membership of Britain's mercantile system, on equal terms with England, Scotland or Wales. Commentators such as Hely-Hutchinson supported the proposals, reminding the Irish that the price of Scotland obtaining 'the protection of [England's] navigation laws and the benefits of her colony trade' had been 'the surrender of [Scotland's] sovereignty', while Ireland's, in the form of its parliament, would remain intact.[30] Pitt included a clause, against the advice of Orde, anticipating the economic benefits accruing to Ireland, to the effect that when Irish revenues reached a certain level, a contribution would be made to the costs of maintaining the British navy. This generated Irish opposition. Equally powerful voices against the bill emanated from English manufacturing interests concerned about Irish commerce undercutting them; these were led by Josiah Wedgewood, but Lord North, Charles James Fox, John Holroyd, Lord Sheffield and William Eden were also vociferous critics. The extent of concerns over the likely effects of Pitt's proposals was captured by an anonymous contemporary print, 'The Funeral of Trade, who died of a mortal stab receiv'd on the 13th of June 1785'. This showed Britannia with a broken shield, spinning-wheel and spear, kneeling at a pitiful fire in which shuttles and implements for wool production were burning. Warehouses devoid of goods on the London quays are also portrayed, with ships being dismantled, and men wearing aldermen's gowns—Dorothy George identified them as opponents of Pitt's bill, Sawbridge and Watkin Lewes, both MPs for the city of London—bearing the coffin of English trade to a black hole where a devil with Pitt's face stands with a pitchfork, declaring 'Bring all your Riches to my great Pitt'. 'Hibernia', by contrast, with an Irish harp and a whip, drives a British lion in front of her, carrying goods to Ireland. The message was that granting free trade to Ireland, in the sense of introducing Ireland into full membership of the mercantile system, would result in England's commercial ruin.

George Rose, Pitt's treasury secretary, held that whereas the earlier commercial freedoms granted to Ireland had been the product of necessity, 'without system, without concert', the revised structure proposed by the British government would create 'one common interest' between Britain and Ireland. Once enacted, it would ensure that 'all ground of future disputes, jealousies and animosities, will be prevented'.[31] John Foster, in the Irish Commons, asserted that the commercial propositions would

FIGURE 10.1. Anon., 'The Funeral of Trade, who died of a mortal stab receiv'd on the 13th of June 1785'. British Museum Collection, no. 1868,0808.5436. Copyright © The Trustees of the British Museum

bring 'wealth and security' to Ireland.[32] The acceptance of such hopes ensured that the bill passed in London, and the Irish Commons narrowly accepted a revised version of Pitt's propositions.[33] Opposition to them, however, remained clamorous, with Flood asserting that they amounted to a denial of Irish legislative independence, as their implication was that Ireland would always accept laws with regard to commerce and navigation from London. This was to reverse all the gains of the early 1780s. Pitt killed the bill in consequence.[34] This left Ireland in limbo, although Pitt did consider Irish interests both in the negotiation of the Eden-Rayneval commercial treaty between Britain and France and in the Navigation Act of 1786, which was passed in Ireland in 1787. With regard to the latter, Grattan, in a speech of 20 March 1787, summarised the situation of Irish trade, arguing that while protective duties might be a thing of the past, the 'equality of the re-export trade' did not exist, because English manufacturers were so worried about the capacity of the Irish to produce goods more cheaply, thereby undermining English markets:

> [English manufacturers] contemplated the low price of labour and of provisions in Ireland; they mistook the symptoms of poverty for the seeds of wealth; in your raggedness they saw riches in disguise; and in destitution itself they discovered a powerful rival to the capital, credit, and commerce of Great Britain.[35]

If the English were deemed to be jealous of Ireland's poverty, as Grattan put it, they were also resentful of Irish liberty, and the continued desire to coerce and dominate Ireland was held to explain Pitt's commercial policy. Pitt's propositions had been 'the result of a narrow mind, a sordid circumspection', so that his 'system of reciprocity clogged with a system of coercion; and thus fell the adjustment'. In other words, English commercial jealousy prevented more complete liberties from being granted to Ireland, and this meant that the Irish rejected them on the grounds of inadequacy. The old Navigation Act that continued to shape Britain's commerce, in refusing Ireland the capacity to formulate its own trade policy, and in preventing the free import and export of goods across the empire, remained in the interest of England rather than of Ireland, as Grattan explained:

> The Act of Navigation is an act of empire, not of commerce. Cromwell was no merchant; his mind was compass, power, and empire. The Navigation Act is a restriction on commerce in the benefit of shipping, a restriction on the sale of things imported and exported, confining the sale and purchase to vessels and ports of a certain description.

> The compensation Great Britain receives is in the carrying trade, and a doubt has arisen whether the benefits she receives from that trade, compensate for the restraint she imposes on the sale of the commodity; but as to Ireland, there can be no doubt at all. The Act of Navigation is clearly a restriction without the compensation . . . You [the Irish] do not desire the British market, but you wish to have the speculation of the British market, for the chance of your own. It is not another man's estate you desire, but a small channel through your neighbour's land, that you may water your own without fear of inundation. The English need not tremble: their estates in the plantations articled to render the produce to Great Britain, will not break these articles. Cork will not be the emporium of the empire. Old England will remain at the head of things. We only aspire that the little bark of this island may attendant sail, pursue the triumph, and perchance partake some vagrant breath of all those trade winds that waft the British empire along the tide of commerce.[36]

Domestic politics in Ireland were becoming ever more divided, with growing fears that the Volunteers were endangering the rule of law, and indirectly encouraging the Catholics to demand their own rights as a body.[37] Agrarian rebellions against unjust landlords promoting enclosure and excessive rents, or against tithes levied by the Church, and against other taxes, were rekindled in conditions of ongoing poverty, with the earlier Whiteboys and Heart of Oak Boys now termed 'Rightboys'; all this was met, in 1787, with an Act to Prevent Tumultuous Risings and Assemblies.[38] Sectarian tensions were also exacerbated, with Catholics pushing for an end to the penal laws. These were reduced in severity in 1793, with the passing of a Relief Act, which allowed Catholics to enter the law and Trinity College Dublin, to purchase freehold land and to vote if their property's rental value was forty shillings per year or above. The law did not allow Catholics to keep arms or ammunition, unless they had substantial freehold property or had some property and were willing to take the oath of allegiance to the crown. In such circumstances, opinion divided, with Protestant concern widespread that the Catholic population would now take power in Ireland, and also take their own wealth. Bands of Protestants called Peep o' Day Boys began to attack Catholics, justifying their actions on the grounds of needing to confiscate illegally held weapons. The response was the formation of a counter-organisation called the Defenders. Some Protestants advocated a union between Britain and Ireland, on the grounds of likely economic development and fear of a pro-French

Catholic majority population.[39] Others advocated the strengthening of loyalist forces in Ireland, an argument that gathered ever more force with the progress of the French Revolution. After the Milita bill was passed on 26 March 1793, requiring the constitution of regiments drawn from the population over the following months, often severe violence occurred; whether this was caused by the intensification of class or by religious antagonisms, opposition to the measures of government was becoming more extreme.[40]

IV

James Cuffe was involved in every aspect of the creation of the buildings at New Geneva, according to the details that survive. He was initially most concerned with the collection of rents on the land, with additional purchases of land deemed to have become a thoroughfare with all of the building work going on, and with claims upon the land by various parties who demanded money from the crown to compensate their loss.[41] When New Geneva was completed, in 1785, it certainly looked like a barracks rather than a town. A document has survived that gives a sense of the original structure.

At what point the buildings were turned into a barracks is unclear. One traveller visiting Waterford on 6 August 1794 described 'an elegant village regularly built . . . [with] buildings all two storey high forming a square, having a green of ten acres, within the houses, and the whole enclosed by a very high wall'. It was claimed that only three years before, in other words in 1791, the structure had become a barracks.[42] Orde himself made a final attempt to exploit New Geneva for the transformation of Irish political and moral culture, between 1785 and 1787. Since October 1783, John Hely-Hutchinson had been advocating the creation of major public schools modelled on those of England, the argument being that national knowledge of such subjects as languages and composition were so poor as to be affecting 'the knowledge, taste and manner of the people'.[43] He sent details of his scheme to Orde, who took matters further with outline plans in 1786, and the full version was presented to the Irish Commons in April 1787. Orde's vision was remarkably ambitious, detailing plans for the education of every rank in society, with different forms of instruction envisaged for what he called each 'division', from the peasantry upwards, and including proposals for the education of women. He presented the proposals as the necessary next step in the series of grand reforms that had transformed the country. As he put it, Ireland's 'constitution is settled; your

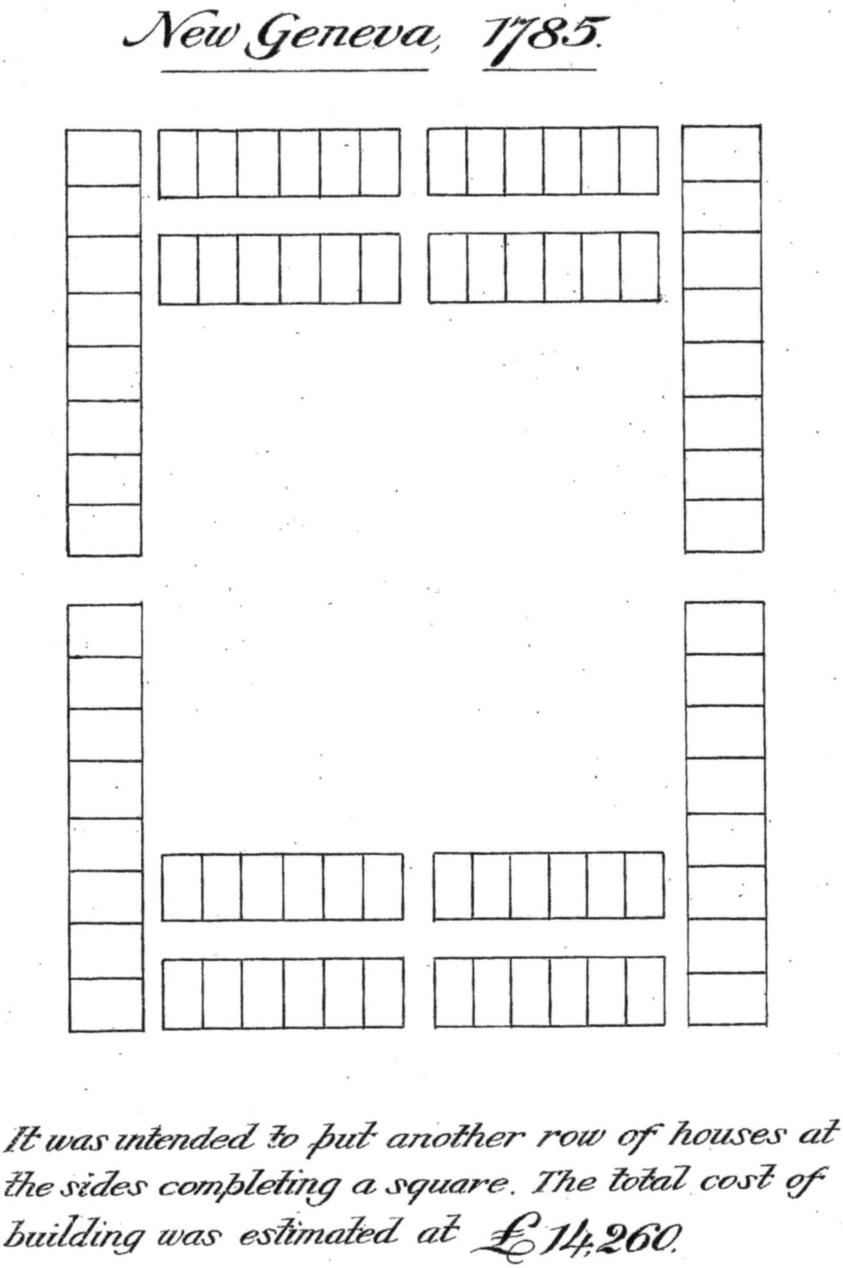

New Geneva, 1785.
It was intended to put another row of houses at the sides completing a square. The total cost of building was estimated at £14,260.

FIGURE 10.2. 'New Geneva 1785'. Matthew Butler, 'New Geneva. Some correspondence relating to its foundation', *Journal of the Waterford and South-East of Ireland Archaeological Society*, XVIII (1915), 113

commerce enlarged; your internal industry encouraged; your laws vindicated; various arts improved; culture spreading fertility and beautifying inanimate nature'. Now was the right time to 'cultivate your people'.[44] Orde advised the Irish to follow the Romans, who had instructed the entirety of their populace. It was evident that 'all ranks, all descriptions of society, are amended and ennobled by the lessons of virtue; and where morals are defective, the stain of vice corrupts and defiles the patrician still more than the peasant. Where has been the nation, to which learning has contributed no advantage?'[45] In the Irish case, it was vital to deal with the 'rude and disorderly multitude', accepting the need for force but also a need to 'make the wretches sensible that they compel the stroke, which reluctantly falls upon them'. To this end, the peasantry had to be seen as a 'rich metal in the mine', and capable of playing a role in making the state more stable and secure:

> Let them have instilled into their minds some little notion of the compact and the duties of society; make them comprehend in some degree the comforts as well as the restraints of civilization; the extent of their instruction may after all even thus be included in the simplest maxims of right and wrong. Remember always that rude as these materials may be, they are still the foundation for the superstructure of the state, and that by the simple process of a more graceful order and position, you may render that foundation not only more beautiful, but more secure and permanent.[46]

Orde described the existing educational provision as being patchy and poor. In its place, he envisaged a system for all children, including Catholics and dissenters, who, if they did well, would be rewarded with better food and dress, a hierarchical system of educational uniforms, as a mark of merit. The fear of losing such benefits would ensure that 'meritorious children' became part of an incentive-based process of increasing attainment: 'Pride and interest might thus conspire to create and support emulation, which would speedily produce other excellent effects.' Orde planned for a graduated process of learning, conveying skills associated with reading and grammar, writing and accounts, mathematics and navigation, husbandry and agriculture, mechanics, geometry and manufacture, drawing, foreign languages and geography. His plan was to promote knowledge of and numbers involved in seamanship, commerce and trades, manufactures, farming, surveying, architecture, languages, mathematics, geometry, drawing, husbandry and agriculture, thereby encouraging what he termed 'industry and ingenuity'. His ultimate goal was the creation of 'almost a new order of citizens [who] will be given to the state, in the superior exercise of the most useful occupations in husbandry, trade, manufacture, commerce and the arts'. Boys up to the age of sixteen were to be educated in a series of establishments, ranging from local schools to large academies, and a new university in Ulster.[47] Orde proposed that one of the large academies be created at New Geneva, on the basis that it would thus be located on the 'confines of two provinces, as to answer in a great degree for the convenience of both':

> The buildings raised at New Geneva, and at present without inhabitants, seem to invite a settlement of this kind to them. I would venture to recommend, that the commencement of this plan should be made there, if his Majesty will be graciously pleased to give his royal permission to convert the place and profits of the lands to this use.[48]

So serious was Orde about turning New Geneva into an educational establishment that he arranged for meetings to this end with Richard Brinsley Sheridan.[49] His plans proved controversial, however, in part because although he wanted both Catholics and dissenters to attend his schools, all children were to be educated in the doctrines of the established church, and teachers and tutors were expected to be members of the Church of Ireland. This angered both those concerned by the prospect of children born outside that church being educated, and those who would never allow their children to enter an educational system organised for its defence. As one Catholic pamphleteer wrote, 'nothing could be devised so favourable to the propagation of the Protestant religion':

> Upon the whole, we may pronounce his plan of education a barbarous penal law; such as Europe has not beheld for near a century past; the direct aim of which is to intercept the few vagrant rays of knowledge that enlighten the great body of the people of Ireland; and to extend still further the empire of patronage and of corruption. It would be too tedious a task to enter into a discussion of the various modes of restrictive intolerance practised by the present ministry.[50]

A similar response came from the Presbyterian minister William Campbell, sometime moderator of the Synod of Ulster, who wrote to Charlemont recommending that Orde return to the type of support he had earlier shown for the Genevans, who would not have accepted an educational system dominated by the established church:

> . . . It is said that the government intends to bring forward some plan of education. I hope it will not be Mr. Orde's. But is there any reason to

> hope that Presbyterians will be considered in it? Or are we to remain neglected? When Earl Temple was Lord Lieutenant, he thought highly of the Presbyterian mode of education, and recommended to commissioners for establishing 'Les Genevois,' that they would also establish a college under their care, and after the model of Geneva. Might not we, whose fathers were long fixed in this kingdom, have some claim to the like privilege?[51]

Orde's plans came to naught, not because of such opposition, but because of the unexpected death on 24 October 1787 of Rutland, at the age of thirty-three, from fever arising from a diseased liver. Orde resigned in the same month, and was replaced as chief secretary by Alleyne FitzHerbert under the returning lord lieutenant Earl Temple, now Marquess of Buckingham, who arrived on 16 December 1787. Although FitzHerbert introduced an inquiry into the state of education in Ireland in March 1788, his health was poor and he would have been ignorant of the background history to the New Geneva experiment. The result was that the empty buildings became a barracks, undoubtedly following the advice of the barrack-master James Cuffe. Ireland was in need of military barracks, because of the likelihood of unrest and violence.

V

Earl Temple in his returning role was concerned with the extent of popular unrest and poverty, especially in southern Ireland, and then became embroiled in the Regency crisis. Grattan, who was close to Temple, pushed for the amelioration of the taxes upon the poor, and especially tithes. As he put it, 'the White Boy should be hanged, but I think the tithe-farmer should be restrained'.[52] Due to divisions within the parliament, and continued fears about the growth of Catholic resistance, Grattan's reforms failed. After the Regency crisis, with John FitzGibbon (from 1795 Earl of Clare) as lord chancellor using bribes to secure parliamentary support for the lord lieutenant's party and against Catholic emancipation, Grattan concluded that corruption was so rife that Ireland had returned to being a land of slaves:

> [T]he canvass of the Ministry was everywhere, in the House of Commons, in the lobby, in the street, at the door of the parliamentary undertakers, rapped at and worn by the little caitiffs of Government, who offered amnesty to some, honours to others, and corruption to all; and where the word of the Viceroy was doubted, they offered their own.

> Accordingly we find a number of parliamentary provisions were created, and divers peerages sold with such effect, that the same Parliament who had voted the chief governor a criminal, did immediately after give that very Governor implicit support; and the subsequent Parliament did, under the same influence, on the Catholic question, on the pension question, on the place question, vote and unvote, and turn and change, according to the orders of Government, with a versatility that made an indignant public cry shame upon them! This policy was an attack on the moral as well as on the constitutional system, and guaranteed political slavery by moral prostitution; proposing that the gentlemen of Parliament should be systematically robbers, in order that the people should be systematically slaves: it was a condition on which no freedom, no government, no religion, no connection, no throne, could long rest . . . In a free country, the path of public treachery leads to the block; but in a nation governed like a province, to the helm![53]

In October 1789, Earl Temple was succeeded as lord lieutenant by John Fane, 10th Earl of Westmorland, who served until October 1794. Westmorland faced unremitting crisis in the form of an ever-deepening social and political division. Ongoing corruption and economic distress were blamed, as they had been across the century. Options for armed resistance multiplied, however, with the establishment of a new political model in the form of the French Republic on 22 September 1792, and the outbreak of war between Britain and revolutionary France on 1 February 1793. In the spring of that year the poet, former soldier and United Irishman Thomas Russell wrote, 'It has long been an hypothesis of mine . . . that this war would [be] long, bloody, general and almost the last with which Europe would be infested and that it would end in republicanism very generally. This I thought long before England engaged in the war.'[54] Edmund Burke had been concerned since 1790 that discontent across Ireland would be translated into sympathy for events in France, and in extreme cases direct imitation.[55] He was especially concerned about the susceptibility of the Catholics of Ireland, because the penal laws had 'divided the nation into two distinct bodies, without common interest, sympathy or connexion; one of which bodies was to possess *all* the franchises, *all* the property, *all* the education: The others were to be drawers of water and cutters of turf for them.'[56] Burke described the revolution in Ireland at the end of the seventeenth century as having been the opposite of glorious, because 'the establishment of the power of the smaller number, at the expense of the civil liberties and properties of the far greater part' made it 'not a revolution, but a conquest'.[57] The grave danger was that the Catholics would be tempted to follow the Jacobin assertion that political liberty ought and could be enjoyed by all. The granting of civil and political liberties to Catholics by removing the penal laws was therefore vital, because 'it would be healing; it would be satisfactory and protecting. The stigma would be removed.' For Burke this move would be central to avoiding what he termed 'the great danger of our time, that of setting up number against property'.[58] When reform was effected, granting partial equality to Catholics, Burke did not believe that it was sufficient, in part because the threat from revolutionary France was growing ever greater. Writing to Grattan in March 1793, he expressed concern about the 'mutinous spirit which is in the very constitution of the lower part of our compatriots of every description'.[59]

The unexpected subsequent French victories, which subdued the forces of the Holy Roman Empire, the Dutch Republic and Prussia, led Burke to call the Republic an original political entity, more frighteningly powerful than any in history to date, being 'a vast, tremendous, unformed spectre, in a far more terrific guise than any whichever yet have overpowered the imagination and subdued the fortitude of man'. The French Republic was 'that hideous phantom' which had 'overpowered those who could not believe it was possible she could at all exist'.[60] The shocking fact about it was that it violated normal rules of politics with regard to the relationship between commerce and power, but appeared at times militarily invincible:

> The poison of other states is the food of the new Republick. That bankruptcy, the very apprehension of which is one of the causes assigned for the fall of the monarchy, was the capital on which she opened her traffick with the world. The Republick of Regicide, with an annihilated revenue, with defaced manufactures, with a ruined commerce, with an uncultivated and half depopulated country, with a discontented, distressed, enslaved, and famished people, passing with a rapid, eccentric, incalculable course from the wildest anarchy to the sternest despotism, has actually conquered the finest parts of Europe, has distressed, disunited, deranged, and broke to pieces all the rest; and so subdued the minds of the rulers in every nation . . . At first the French force was too much despised. Now it is too much dreaded.[61]

Burke's final sentence indicated that he retained some faith that Britain would not be added to the list of states that had fallen before republican arms, and that the people would not welcome French invasion, as they had across Europe, as a form of liberation rather than servitude. Burke's close friend William Wentworth-Fitzwilliam, in a speech on 14 December 1795, agreed that the current war was 'of a nature different from all common wars', it being vital to combat a France that remained 'a pure democracy, containing the seeds of dissension and anarchy and affording no security for religion, property or order'.[62]

The grand opportunity for the United Irishmen was to anticipate popular revolution, supported by French invasion. The second part of Thomas Paine's *Rights of Man* (1792) became a manifesto, inundating Ireland in cheap editions, and justifying his call for republican revolution across the globe. Paine believed that if peace in the modern world was ever to be established, it was necessary to destroy the source of international war, the British state. Subscribing a hundred French livres to support an invading French army, Paine declared that if the peoples of earth were ever going to cease to be slaves, Britain had to be reconstituted:

> There will be no lasting peace for France, nor for the world, until the tyranny and corruption of the English Government be abolished, and England, like Italy, become a sister Republic. As to those men, whether in England, Scotland, or Ireland, who, like Robespierre in France, are covered with crimes, they, like him, have no other resource than in committing more; but the mass of the people are friends to liberty; tyranny and taxation oppress them, but they merit to be free.[63]

Britain was the loathsome enemy of revolution and the great protector of aristocracy and of monarchy; equally, Britain stood for the domination of other states by trade, and the crushing of native industries that competed with its own. Britain had to be defeated. As Paine well knew, Ireland in the 1790s was the preferred location for invasion, being accessible from French ports, and where oppression by the British was self-evident. French forces could invade Ireland's southern coast from bases at Brest or Lorient or from Spain, allied to France from 1796 to 1801 and 1804 to 1806, while the British navy had to arrive via the Scilly Isles.[64] Once the government collapsed, the people would join together, as they had done in France, to outlaw the nobility and to put an end to monarchy. Then would begin the era of republican peace, equality and fraternity between peoples. This was the origin of the process of events that culminated in the uprisings of 1798.[65]

Theobald Wolfe Tone arrived at Le Havre from North America on 2 February 1796. He was recommended to the French authorities by the American ambassador to Paris, James Monroe, and began to contribute to plans for invasion from April onwards. On 19 June, Tone was given the rank of *chef de brigade* (colonel) in the French army, and on 12 July, after meeting General Lazare Hoche, was promoted to adjutant general. Hoche was a republican hero, having defeated the Anglo-royalist invasion at Quiberon in July 1795. A brilliant strategist, he had rumours spread that the invasion force gathering at Brest was destined for Portugal. Confident of victory, he declared to his troops that once they arrived in Ireland, they could expect to find 'hospitality and fraternity', and that 'thousands of the inhabitants would swell their ranks.'[66] On 16 December 1796, Hoche and Admiral de Galles led a force of forty-three ships and fifteen thousand troops to Bantry Bay on the south west coast of Cork. Tone, leader of the United Irishmen, accompanied them. The invasion failed because Hoche's and de Galles's ship the *Fraternité* was separated from the main force by dense fog, and Admiral Bouvet refused to land without permission from his superior. On 23 December, a further gale forced twenty of the ships out to sea, and the invasion was abandoned. Tone, who had sailed on the *Indomptable*, was furious, because thirty-five ships had come sufficiently close to Irish soil on 22 December 'to toss a biscuit ashore'. He wrote in his journal that 'in all my life, rage never entered so deeply into my heart as when we turned our backs on the coast'.[67] Burke confessed to having trembled 'at the danger whilst I am rejoicing in the escape'.[68] Hoche was reputed to be planning larger-scale invasion, despite being appointed commander of the Army of the Rhine, but died within nine months of the failure, on 15 September 1797. A newspaper named *The Dublin Press* printed a eulogy, calling him a martyr to liberty and republican patriot:

WEEP! Gallia weep! in sorrow droop thy head.
Thy Hoche, thy hero, and thy friend is dead;
That man so truly great in freedom's cause,
That brave defender of his country's laws;
Who, from her fields the Pitt-leagued tyrants chased,
And all the hordes of slaves that laid them waste;
Made the crown'd robbers of his native soil,
Shake on their blood-stain'd thrones and quit their spoil.
Now pale and breathless, lo! the hero lies,
As envious fate had call'd him to the skies,
But still unconquered, tho' resigned his breath,
He springs immortal from the arms of death;
O! friend of man, upon thy honoured bier,
The good and brave shall drop a grateful tear;
Bright fame, thy virtues from oblivion save,

And snatch thy honours from the silent grave,
From age to age thy glorious deeds impart,
And make thy monument each Patriot's heart.[69]

Westmorland was succeeded as lord lieutenant by William Wentworth-Fitzwilliam, 4th Earl Fitzwilliam, who arrived in Ireland in January 1795. From the first, he was well informed. His close friend Burke advised him on his arrival that he felt 'an anxious awe' about Ireland because 'Everything is now critical; and certainly Ireland is not the least critical part of the Empire . . . You certainly go to a farm terribly havocked by the last tenants.'[70] Burke was of the view that the members of the Protestant Ascendancy in Ireland, by their brutality and dominion, were on the verge of destroying the state: 'their innumerable corruptions, frauds, oppressions, and follies are opening a back door for Jacobinism to rush in upon us and to take us in the rear'.[71] Burke called men such as John Beresford, first commissioner of the revenue, and John FitzGibbon, the lord chancellor, 'the Junto', and accused them of ruling Ireland by means of 'meditated and systematic corruption (private personal not politic corruption) of some; and the headlong violence and tyrannical spirit of others, totally destitute of wisdom'.[72] Ireland had become, in Burke's view, key to the future of Europe, because it could so easily fall prey to republican revolution, or see the kinds of reform that would amount to a genuine alternative to the French model. This was why the actions of the corrupt Protestant Ascendancy, in continuing to oppress the people, risked opening the door to the final victory of the French-style republicans over the inherited and glorious liberties of Europe's states:

> [Ireland] is no longer an obscure dependency of this Kingdom. What is done there vitally effects [*sic*] the whole System of Europe, whether you regard it offensively or defensively. Ireland is known in France; communications have been opened and more will be opened. Ireland will be a strong digue to keep out Jacobinism; or a broken bank to let it in. The Junto have weakened the old European System of Government there, and brought it into utter discredit.[73]

Fitzwilliam was entirely of Burke's opinion. He promised that he would ever seek to avoid the fate of Westmorland, who had been 'the sport and instrument of the same gang of Jobbers, that have been robbing and plundering in the most barefaced way for these 20 years back'.[74] For a time, Fitzwilliam gained popular support. He removed John Beresford and his associates from their offices in the revenue service, and also combated

FitzGibbon. Such actions, Fitzwilliam was convinced, led to his recall on 23 February 1795. Beresford and FitzGibbon had powerful supporters in London; this belief ultimately led to a duel being planned between Beresford and Fitzwilliam, prevented only by their arrest. The Reverend Thomas Hussey was convinced that because of Fitzwilliam's sacking, 'Ireland is now on the brink of civil war.'[75] Burke lamented the consequences of the removal of his friend from office: 'the whole System and its whole Spirit, will stand condemned by every man, who does not think one or two Jobbs and Jobbers of more importance than the very Being of Mankind'.[76] Writing to Grattan in March 1795, Burke argued that the twin evils of entrenched aristocracy and revolutionary Jacobinism were destroying contemporary politics: 'Nature is banished by the formalities of aristocracy, and the abominations of the rights of man; and no other than revolutionary tribunals exist on earth!'[77] By the summer of the year he saw Ireland as being likely to suffer rebellion and revolution.[78] As 1796 progressed, he wrote to his friend Hussey that, with regard to Ireland being in such a lamentable state, he'never could have less reason for regret in quitting the world than at this moment'.[79] When John Jeffreys Pratt, 1st Marquess of Camden replaced Fitzwilliam, popular opposition to government increased; in County Armagh conflict between Catholic Defenders and the Peep o'Day Boys resulted in the battle of the Diamond on 21 September 1795. Defenders and United Irishmen began to work together, now faced by the loyalist Orange Order, founded at Loughgall in the aftermath of the violence. Burke lamented the outbreak of sectarian violence on top of republican revolutionary sentiment, as he was certain it underlined 'the madness and folly, of driving men under the existing circumstances from any *positive* religion whatever into the irreligion of the times', because French-style republicanism amounted to 'sure concomitant principles of anarchy'.[80] Burke was dead by the time the combination of oppression and corruption paid dividends for the United Irishmen, with the outbreak of popular and organised resistance to British authority in the spring of 1798.

VI

Rebellion in the south of Ireland spread to County Wexford from Leinster in the third week of May 1798, in the midst of rumours that captured rebels were everywhere being massacred with their families by government forces. In a pitched battle at Oulart Hill on 27 May, over a hundred members of the loyalist North Cork Militia were killed and the town of Enniscorthy was captured. Two hundred men from the Donegal Militia under a Colonel Maxwell arrived at Wexford from New Geneva, and were involved in the defeat of the town on 30 May.[81] Many rebelled because they were afraid of the government, which they accused of putting numbers of people to death 'unarmed and unoffending, throughout the country'. Others feared militant anti-Catholic Protestants and the risk of 'being whipped, burned, and exterminated by the Orangemen'.[82] Some were convinced that the rebellion was the latest attempt by the Catholic church to regain control over Ireland. Richard Musgrave, an Irish MP, was certain that the rebellion had been orchestrated by the pope, following the seventeenth-century puritan William Prynne's analysis of the essentially subversive nature of Catholicism.[83] Castlereagh too identified the conflict as a return to the religious divisions that had scarred Europe in previous centuries, facilitated by the addition of Jacobinism to what he called 'Popish instruments':

> [I]t is perfectly a religious phrensy [*sic*]. The priests lead the rebels to battle: on their march, they kneel down and pray, and show the most desperate resolution in their attack . . . They put such Protestants as are reported to be Orangemen to death, saving others upon condition of their embracing the Catholic faith. It is a Jacobinical conspiracy throughout the kingdom, pursuing its object chiefly with Popish instruments; the heated bigotry of this sect being better suited to the purpose of the republican leaders than the cold, reasoning disaffection of the northern Presbyterians.[84]

For God-fearing Protestants, Catholicism was the religion of savages, and the people of Ireland had lived in a brutal and superstitious world until the English began to colonise and to civilise their country. The republican rebels were restoring barbarism in place of civilisation, and in so doing were destroying property and people, which proved to the opponents of Catholicism and republicanism the justice of the loyalist cause, increasingly perceived to be a defence at the same time of Protestantism itself. As one devout Wexford resident named Mrs Brownrigg recalled in a diary named 'A three weeks' terror', the horrific acts of Catholics against Protestants marked the conflict from the beginning:

> The rising began near Oulart, and let those gentlemen who even now expatiate on the excesses of the soldiery and the oppressed state of the people remember that there was not a single soldier from Gorey to Wexford, a distance of 21 miles, that there never had been any there, nor could any possible excuse of that kind be assigned for what ensued.

> One of their first steps was to attack Mr. Burrows' house and to murder him in the presence of his wife, children and a niece, whom I [have] since conversed with in Wexford. They also broke into Mr. D'Arcy's house at Ballynation, [and] offered to make him a Commander provided he wou'd turn Catholic. He said, 'No, he had lived a Protestant and wou'd die one.' He was immediately butchered.[85]

Brownrigg claimed that numerous priests were leaders among the rebels, asserting that the planning of the resistance had been going on for four years, and that it amounted to a religious war characterised by 'bigotry and the grossest superstition'. As Brownrigg put it, 'The rebel leaders said they fought for liberty, emancipation, and reform, their soldiers that they fought for religion, to punish the Protestants, and to save their own lives, as we were certainly to have massacred all of them on Whitsun Tuesday. This I was assured their Priests had preached to them.'[86]

The example of France inspired numerous Irish people again, on the grounds that when the people 'became members of a Republic, their condition would be bettered'.[87] Fired up with revolutionary ardour, and certain that a new state could be created in Ireland on the model of the French Republic, organised bodies of United Irishmen attacked British institutions in the hope that the Irish peasantry would flock to their cause, and that support would come from France once the rebellion had been initiated. A letter was found on the body of the priest Michael Murphy, who died at the battle of Arklow on 9 June 1798, to a friend named Houston, predicting that victory was near:

> Great events are ripening. In a few days we shall meet. The first fruits of your regeneration must be a tincture of poison and pike, in the metropolis, against hereticks. This is a tribunal for such opinions. Your talents must not be buried as a judge: Your sons must be steeled with fortitude against heresy, then we shall do; and you shall shine in a higher sphere. We shall have an army of brave republicans, one hundred thousand, with fourteen pieces of cannon, on Tuesday, before Dublin; your heart will beat high at the news. You will rise with a proportionable force.[88]

In the north, people took up arms in County Antrim and in County Down in early June. Their movement failed at Ballynahinch, only twelve miles from Belfast, when government forces routed the republicans. In the south, the rebels were largely confined to Wexford, and battle took place at Vinegar Hill on 21 June, where twenty thousand government troops defeated fifteen thousand republicans. The rebels were accused of murdering large numbers of Protestants and prisoners.[89] Many Protestants were themselves involved in the United Ireland cause; yet Catholics among the rebels were singled out. Father John Murphy, a Catholic priest who had been educated by the Dominicans in Seville in the 1780s, was prominent among the rebel leaders in Wexford, having fought at Oulart Hill, and led one of the columns that moved into Wicklow with the intention of taking Dublin, before falling back to Vinegar Hill. When he was captured in early July, after the fragmentation of rebel forces, he was flogged before being hung and decapitated, his head being put on public display and his body burned in a barrel of pitch.[90] Religious bigotry and hatred added to the excesses on both sides. Many viewed the conflict as essentially a religious war.

The response of the government was straightforwardly brutal. Informers were used to identify the enemies of the state. Sir Thomas FitzGerald, who commanded loyalist forces in Wexford, declared that 'in a time of terror and trepidation . . . by my strong measures, treason was soon discovered, traitors hunted down, and the rebellion quelled'.[91] This was FitzGerald's defence during a trial in which he was accused of the merciless whipping of an innocent merchant wrongly called a rebel by a government spy; the man was lashed so extensively both on the back and the buttocks that his flesh began to break apart. In 1801, a jury acquitted FitzGerald. Rebel leaders everywhere were hanged and beheaded, their heads put on spikes in prominent places as a warning to others, their corpses stripped, 'treated with the utmost brutality and indecency', and thrown into rivers or into the sea.[92]

In the minds of the loyalists there was not only a sense of the need to maintain the integrity of the state and to prevent foreign invasion. The belief that they were also defending Protestantism was pervasive. The added background was the recent history of the Terror at Paris, and the certainty that French invasion or an Irish Revolution would be followed by the massacre of innocents who committed the crime of not being terrorist revolutionaries. The destruction of property on a gargantuan scale would be the outcome. Society itself would dissolve into anarchy, as ranks and social hierarchies ceased to have any meaning. This was why those labelled traitors, republicans and revolutionaries, accused of fomenting terror and anarchy, were arrested in large numbers and condemned to death or to transportation. As advocates of treason against the British state, the prisoners were given little quarter. The United Irishmen were 'a band of systematic traitors'. Only 'the most unremitting coercion and the most vigorous resistance' could quell them.[93] Torture was openly practised upon any suspected of sympathy towards the rebellion. As Richard Musgrave put it,

> To disarm the disaffected was impossible, because their arms were concealed; and to discover all the traitors was equally so, because they were bound by oaths of secrecy, and the strongest sanctions of their religion, not to impeach their fellow traitors. But suppose the fullest information could have been obtained of the guilt of every individual, it would have been impracticable to arrest and commit the multitude.

Forced confession by whipping was introduced by 'some men of discernment and fortitude' who 'perceived that some new expedient must be adopted to prevent the subversion of government and the destruction of society'. Musgrave said that the use of torture had dissuaded the Catholic hordes from joining the rebellion, which he believed they entirely supported. It had also saved the lives of men of property and prevented the destruction of property itself: 'The massacre of many thousands of the most valuable members of society, and the loss of half a million of property, were prevented in the county of Tipperary by [torture].'[94]

A sense of the extent of the destruction after the rebellion had been crushed was given by Sir Jonah Barrington, the MP for Clogher and an Admiralty Court judge, who, after the capture of Wexford, 'traversed that county to see the ruins which had been occasioned by warfare'. He reported that wreckage and dilapidation abounded:

> Enniscorthy had been twice stormed, and was dilapidated and nearly burned. New Ross shewed most melancholy relics of the obstinate and bloody battle of full ten hours' duration, which had been fought in every street of it. The numerous pits crammed with dead bodies, on Vinegar Hill, seemed on some spots actually elastic as we stood upon them; whilst the walls of an old windmill on its summit appeared stained and splashed with the blood and brains of many victims who had been piked or shot against it by the rebels. The court house of Enniscorthy, wherein our troops had burned alive above eighty of the wounded rebels, and the barn of Scullabogue, where the rebels had retaliated by burning alive above one hundred and twenty Protestants, were terrific ruins! The town of Gorey was utterly destroyed, not a house being left perfect; and the bodies of the killed were lying half covered in sundry ditches in its vicinity.[95]

When New Geneva Barracks became a prison for United Irishmen and rebels of every stripe, tales of infamous brutality there too passed into folklore. Patrick Egan reported 'going among the peasantry of the neighbourhood' and meeting an ancient woman named Mary Muldoon.

Muldoon claimed that one man who had been conscripted into the ranks of the defending troops was himself killed in an accidental act of desertion. As Egan put it, 'the old lady helped us to listen with greater equanimity and steadiness of nerve by treating us to a "pinch" before she started' to speak. She then told the tale of 'a fine young man' who 'was drove into the barracks in '98, and made [to] join the sogers [soldiers]'. Not wanting to fight fellow Irishmen, the young man 'asked the officer, was there nothing to keep him but the high wall built all round'. The officer reported that 'if he got over that wall he'd give him his liberty.' The man 'made one spring, and up on the wall wud [with] him'. The officer then 'shot the poor boy on the wall, and many a day after his poor mother, a widow, came to see where his blood was spilt on the same wall, where it remains to the present day'. Another local whom Egan conversed with, named Tom Doolin, regaled him with a story of three rebels from County Kerry, who managed to escape New Geneva, before being chased and shot:

> 'Did you ever hear tell, sir, of the three Kerrymin?' We replied not, whereupon Tom, with both hands thrust into the pockets, his back against the Geneva wall, and his eyes twinkling at the placid waters of the bay, commenced. 'There wor [were] three Kerrymin arrested in the time of the rebellion, and brought hand-cuffed to this place. They called them at that time, I believe, 'croppies.' For seven days they were kept in, and the next mornin' they were all to be hung. The last night, what do you think, but one of the men jumped up and seized the gun the guard was carryin', took it from him, and threatened to blow his brains out if he'd stir a peg. This, of course, kept the fellow quiet, while the other two men made off. Then, you see, the fellow that tuk the gun was makin' off also, but the guard begged of him to give him the gun, or he'd be shot himself the next mornin'. The poor man took compassion upon him, and gave the sentry the gun, when wid [with] that he made off. He wasn't far gone, when our brave sentry went and told his story, and, I believe, half the regiment ran after the three Kerrymin and shot 'em on the spot.'[96]

The accusation was made by contemporaries that among the 'multitudes of young men, taken up in every direction . . . journeying to the Genevan Garrison, in numbers almost incredible' was a large body of innocent Catholics, taken as prisoners from among a potentially rebellious peasantry, and who were not 'guilty of anything, who were taken up, for following their lawful occupations . . . being convicted of hostility, from their religious opinions or dress'. The point was also made that so few survived the ordeals initiated at New Geneva that the history was already obscure in 1814: so many rebels had 'perished in the mines of Silesia, or in the garrison of Magdeburg', while the 'executioners have died on the French bayonet, or have yielded to the yellow fever in the West Indies'. It remained a fact that 'the sufferings which these men were exposed to, and the brutality of the keepers, exceed anything we read of in the history of the most cruel and wanton tyrants'.[97] After the Union of 1801, and the end of French-inspired republican rebellion, the prison was turned back into a barracks. A map of the place, dated 1818, gives a sense of order and functionality.

When the topographer Nicholas Carlisle made an entry for New Geneva in 1810, he noted, 'This village was erected in an elegant and regular manner by Government, a few years since, for the reception of expatriated citizens of Geneva. But they having relinquished the design of settling in Ireland, this place remains still uninhabited. It is governed by a Fort Major.'[98] Another traveller, James Fraser, writing at the end of the 1830s, noted the spot where an attempt had been made to 'locate a colony of Genevese', reporting that 'after spending fifty thousand pounds, the scheme being found impracticable, was abandoned'. A military barracks was then erected, Fraser said, but this too was given up, so that 'the building is now occupied as a farming village'.[99] André Vieusseux, in a history of Switzerland published in 1840, told a different story. Vieusseux, himself related to Clavière and others involved with New Geneva, stated that 'a deputation of the [Genevan] emigrants proceeded to Waterford in July, 1783, to superintend the building of the new town, which was called New Geneva'. According to Vieusseux, the buildings 'soon began to rise, and assume the appearance of a city'. Mysteriously, despite substantial expenditure, 'the whole scheme was suddenly abandoned, from causes which have never been entirely cleared up'. Vieusseux related that 'it was said that the Genevan emigrants demanded too many privileges in the articles of their charter, and that the corporation of Waterford became jealous, and wanted to extend its jurisdiction over the new colony'. Another factor was 'the recall of Earl Temple, from Ireland', who had been 'the principal patron'. The emigrants were said to have contacted the Duke of Rutland and 'signified their intention of relinquishing the project'. The buildings were initially unoccupied, and then became a barracks during the wars. The land was then sold, the houses were pulled down 'and few traces of the projected colony are now to be seen'.[100] One source used by Vieusseux was an anonymous but detailed account of New Geneva published in the

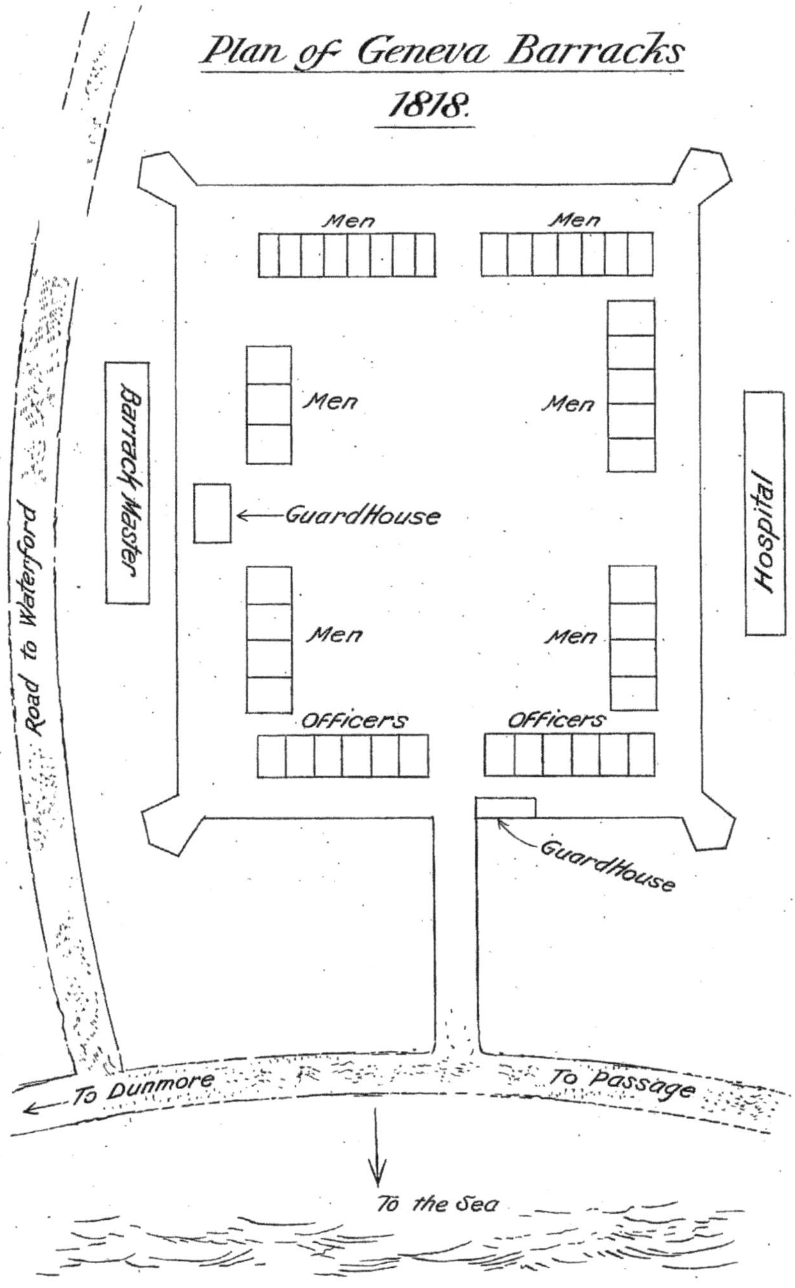

FIGURE 10.3. 'Plan of Geneva Barracks 1818'. Matthew Butler, 'New Geneva. Some correspondence relating to its foundation', *Journal of the Waterford and South-East of Ireland Archaeological Society*, XVIII (1915), 114

Dublin University Magazine in 1838, describing an air of tragedy around the site:

> The aspect of the place has something singularly sad and interested in it—as, at Nicaea, in Asia Minor, there are still the remains of a city now ruined and depopulated, reposing in solitary magnificence on the shore of a noble sheet of water, the walls that surrounded it still perfect, but the houses and all their inhabitants almost as completely obliterated as if they had been swallowed up in an earthquake. There is not a tree near it, to vary the desolate and naked appearance of the long, bare walls; and, though one inhabited house is still standing within the tottering gateway, its shattered windows and broken roof, if possible, increase the melancholy and ruined appearance of the place.

The sole inhabitant was said to be a 'tithe-defaulter', whose 'open resistance to the laws' formed a 'sad contrast' with the original intention of establishing an 'abode of the peaceful and industrious'. The author noted that the 'ruin has little to excite the curiosity of the antiquary', but was 'nevertheless connected with incidents as interesting as any to be found in the annals of Ireland'.[101]

James Sharp, a visitor in the 1850s, reported New Geneva to be 'now in ruins'.[102] The greatest nineteenth-century student of New Geneva, Patrick Egan, gave the verdict that the story of the emigration and the city was remarkable, but altogether fantastic and utopian. The ultimate turning of the place into a vile prison was an instance of 'what extremes the minority in a country will be led to, in the endeavour to suppress the voice of a nation, and to maintain a system of intolerance'. Egan, writing in the 1890s, claimed that the system of oppression of which New Geneva was an expression had 'happily died with those ages that are never to return'.[103] After it was decided that there was no longer a need for the buildings and the barracks, at some unspecified date, 'the barracks were levelled, and the materials sold'. This left, in Egan's words, a place 'as bare looking and desolate as a plot in the island of Atlantis after the deluge'.[104]

CONCLUSION

After Revolution

AS HAS BEEN POINTED OUT several times in this book, there was more than a hint of irony in the fact that members of the United Irishmen were put to death at New Geneva, and that this was one of the most significant outcomes of the Waterford experiment. The intention had never of course been to create a military base for soldiers. The buildings were made for republicans. Yet it was at the site of New Geneva that the British troops and loyalist volunteers employed dreadful violence against the United Irishmen. New Geneva Barracks passed into folklore because of the bloody treatment of the rebels. The British government, still at war with revolutionary France, used the example of what happened in 1798 to justify a 'Scottish solution' to the Irish problem: the Acts of Union of 1800, which created the Kingdom of Great Britain and Ireland from 1 January 1801.[1]

By the time of the Anglo-Irish union, French republicanism was on the defensive. The experience of France in the 1790s appeared for the first time to be explicable in historical terms. France had undergone a popular and democratic revolution that turned a monarchy into a republic. Like all republics created in this fashion, the result was civil and international war. Ultimately, like all large republics before it, the inability of republican politicians in France to maintain order led to the rise of a military figure or demagogue who could guarantee exactly this. The general or orator would ultimately turn himself into a king or an emperor. Those who had identified themselves as democratic republicans in the 1790s were forced to face down the accusation that they were terrorists and anarchists, on account of events at Paris when the Jacobins held sway. By 1800, they had to address the additional difficulty of being advocates of a failed republican experiment.

Bonaparte's *coup d'état* of 18 Brumaire, Year VIII of the French Republic (9 November 1799), when he put an end to the elected councils of the French Directory using military force, signalled a return to historical normality. Something of a sigh of relief accompanied the establishment of the Consulate. Rather than a new species of politics, so feared by Burke, the French Revolution became an explicable event. Like so many revolutions before it, and however frightening the new definition of the armed nation, the Revolution went through the stages of popular rebellion, demagogic leadership and civil and international war. Then it succumbed to a Caesar figure.[2] Liberty could be paired with discord. Restoring peace required authority figures. The Revolution was likened by one contemporary to a brain fever, moving through increasingly aggressive stages to a 'reign of Anarchy', when 'the frantic wretch' attacked everyone and everything. Such a fever demanded the medicine of 'armed despotism', by which the patient was prevented from doing further harm by removal of liberty. This explained the transition after the Directory from 'a proud Triumvirate to a perpetual Dictatorship, and from that to a sudden introduction of an Imperial Crown, and Sceptre of Iron'.[3] Bonaparte could be presented as a French tyrant of the traditional kind, seeking 'an unlimited empire on the wrecks of civilized society'.[4] Britain remained at war with France, with the brief exception of the Peace of Amiens between March 1802 and May 1803. Invasion scares were commonplace in the first decade of the new century.[5] In the case of Ireland, the British state had to show that the effects of union were altogether positive, and that the experience of Ireland would provide more evidence of Britain having become a cosmopolitan empire, rather than being a mercantile system; the latter, Jacques-Pierre Brissot explained in 1793, had led the British to wage 'a fratricidal war' against 'the liberty of all the peoples', which was 'a crime against humanity itself'.[6]

II

This book has related the complex story of an attempt to move a republic into a monarchy in the 1780s. It went on to tell the story of the attempt to turn part of a monarchy into a republic in the 1790s. It has explained the nature and failure of the Genevan rebellion, why the Genevan migration into Ireland was planned and why it was deemed to be of such importance to so many significant contemporaries. The book has also explained why the experiment failed, and why New Geneva became a place detested by republicans. Failure did not mean that the project ceased to matter. What happened in Waterford, it turns out, despite the end result seemingly being the erection of another barracks for British troops, had consequences for Europe, for the French Revolution and above all for ideas about empire, commerce and politics in Britain, especially after the union between Britain and Ireland in 1801. All in all, events at New Geneva confirmed for contemporaries that the grand reforms imagined by projectors and enthusiasts throughout the eighteenth century had come to naught. In order to restore the world to peace, and in order to define practical reform, there had to be an end to enlightenment.

Historians continue to link the French Revolution to modern ideas about democracy. Many still see it as having inaugurated our world, through an age of revolutions, commencing in Europe at Geneva in 1782 and continuing at Paris in 1789, all being inspired by the example of the earlier republican revolution in North America.[7] Alternatively, the age of revolutions can be seen as the product of 'the Enlightenment', when ideas about societal improvement and transformation, first sketched by visionaries in the final decades of the seventeenth century, were put into practice a hundred years later.[8] This book argues that both of these interpretations are mistaken. The key fact for contemporaries was that the kinds of social experiment developed during the Enlightenment era, such as at New Geneva, were acknowledged to have come to nothing. More significantly still, the French Revolution, at the close of the eighteenth century, looked more like a revolution explicable by reference to ancient history than an event that had altered everything in the present. French republicanism, which inspired the United Irishmen in the 1790s, had wreaked havoc on Europe, rather than establishing peace, prosperity and social harmony. Advocates of French forms of liberty were faced with the seemingly impossible task of arguing that they were not necessarily terrorists, anarchists, traitors and republican imperialists, or rebels whose hands would forever be stained with blood.

By contrast, there was much greater interest in the state that had appeared to be on the edge of dismemberment at the time of New Geneva. The British Empire was redefined and justified anew in the final decades of the eighteenth century.[9] It was widely described as a new kind of cosmopolitan empire, both more suited to commerce and more stable than any historical empire, more likely to establish perpetual peace, and more likely to favour economic development on a global scale.[10] When thinking about Britishness, we have to be aware that circumstances were transformed at the end of the century. National survival led to an entirely unanticipated sense of confidence about being British and about the nature of national identity. The eighteenth century was a century of crisis rather than of equipoise, in which very few expected existing society to be stable, or even able to be maintained at all.[11] No Enlightenment figure, from David Hume, Voltaire and Montesquieu to Rousseau, Smith and Kant, expected Britain to be able to sustain itself, let alone to become a constitutional model for others or a stable and successful empire. There were, of course, a large number of doubters, for whom Britain's demise had only been delayed. For others, the fact that the great hopes of the 1790s had been dashed, and that a state as corrupt and as mercenary as Britain had won through, was both depressing personally and devastating philosophically. Indeed, a bleak perspective upon the new century held that Britain was able to keep fighting France because it *was* a mercantile system. This argument had to be refuted by every advocate of reform. At the same time, the collapse of the grand hopes of the 1790s became the basic fact of politics. There were good reasons why Thomas Paine wrote so little in his final years, and died a drunk in New York. Similarly, the Abbé Sieyès, a major architect of the French Revolution and the indefatigable creator of constitutions throughout the 1790s, although he lived until 1836, wrote nothing during his long retirement.[12]

The radical argument of this book is that nineteenth-century intellectual life began with an acceptance of the *failure* of the French Revolution. Contemporaries, and especially former republicans such as Madame de Staël or Benjamin Constant, became increasingly interested in the perceived successes of the British state. More particularly, they became interested in Britain's purported capacity to maintain, to defend and to export both liberty and moderation. Sceptics continued to search for alternative means to a better world. These included, significantly, people such as Jeremy Bentham, who became republicans and democrats after the French Revolution, with full knowledge of the evils that had accompanied it.[13] At the end of the Enlightenment, the Britain that emerged from experiments like New Geneva, and from the brutal destruction of domestic republicans, set the terms for nineteenth-century political argument across most of Europe. Small-state republicans had found Europe in the final decades of the eighteenth century to be increasingly inhospitable. The nineteenth-century looked no better, with the outcome of the French Revolution confirming that the future favoured large states and monarchies, at least in Europe. Geneva itself, significantly, having been annexed by France in 1798, on becoming independent again in 1813 saw itself as a commercial version of Scotland when the decision was taken to unite with the larger Swiss confederation, which occurred in 1815. A significant figure who saw himself to be turning Geneva into a Scotland, by an incorporating union with a Switzerland modelled on Britain, was the now Sir Francis d'Ivernois. The major question was, had Britain won the Napoleonic wars because it was a corrupt commercial society with a rapacious politics to match? Alternatively, were there elements of virtue, moderation and public spiritedness, which Adam Smith had ignored in his depiction of the workings of the economy, that were the true source of Britain's strength? Ireland, as formerly, constituted a test case. For many, it remained Britain's Achilles' heel.

NOTES

Preface

1. Patrick Geoghegan, *The Irish Act of Union: A Study in High Politics, 1798–1801* (New York: St. Martin's Press, 2000); Michael Brown, Patrick M. Geoghegan and James Kelly (eds), *The Irish Act of Union, 1800: Bicentennial Essays* (Dublin: Irish Academic Press, 2003); Emma Vincent Macleod, *A War of Ideas: British Attitudes to the Wars against Revolutionary France, 1792–1802* (Aldershot: Ashgate, 1998).

2. On Protestantism and British identity, see Linda Colley, *Britons: Forging the Nation, 1707–1837* (London: Pimlico, 1992); Colin Kidd, 'North Britishness and the Nature of Eighteenth-Century British Patriotisms', *The Historical Journal*, 39 (1996), 361–82; J.C.D. Clark, *English Society, 1660–1832: Religion, Ideology and Politics during the Ancien Regime* (Cambridge: Cambridge University Press, 2000) and 'Protestantism, Nationalism and National Identity, 1660–1832', *The Historical Journal*, 43 (2000), 249–76; Tony Claydon, *Europe and the Making of England, 1660–1760* (Cambridge: Cambridge University Press, 2007).

3. R. F. Foster, *Modern Ireland, 1600–1972* (London: Allen Lane, 1988).

4. On eighteenth-century republicanism, see classically Caroline Robbins, *The Eighteenth Century Commonwealthman. Studies in the Transmission, Development and Circumstance of English Liberal Thought from the Restoration of Charles II until the War with the Thirteen Colonies* (Cambridge, MA: Harvard University Press, 1959); J.G.A. Pocock, *The Machiavellian Moment: Florentine Political Thought and the Atlantic Republican Tradition* (Princeton, NJ: Princeton University Press, 2016 [orig. 1975]) and *Barbarism and Religion, Vol. 3: The First Decline and Fall* (Cambridge: Cambridge University Press, 2005).

5. On the gap between republican and democratic ideas, see Bernard Manin, *The Principles of Representative Government* (Cambridge: Cambridge University Press, 1996); Biancamaria Fontana, *The Invention of the Modern Republic* (Cambridge: Cambridge University Press, 1994); John Dunn, *The Cunning of Unreason: Making Sense of Politics* (New York: Basic Books, 2000) and *Setting the People Free: The Story of Democracy* (London: Atlantic Books, 2005); Eric Nelson, *The Greek Tradition in Republican Thought* (Cambridge: Cambridge University Press, 2004). On justifications of democracy, see Rachel Hammersley, *French Revolutionaries and English Republicans: The Cordeliers Club, 1790–1794* (Woodbridge: Boydell & Brewer, 2005) and *The English Republican Tradition and Eighteenth-Century France* (Manchester: Manchester University Press, 2010); Joanna Innes and Mark Philp (eds), *Re-imagining Democracy in the Age of Revolutions: America, France, Britain, Ireland, 1750–1850* (Oxford: Oxford University Press, 2013); Manuela Albertone, 'Democratic Republicanism. Historical Reflections on the Idea of *Republic* in the 18th Century', *History of European Ideas*, 33 (2007), 108–30 and *National Identity and the Agrarian Republic. The Transatlantic Commerce of Ideas between America and France, 1750–1830* (Farnham: Ashgate, 2014).

6. Richard Whatmore, *Against War and Empire. Geneva, Britain and France in the Eighteenth Century* (New Haven, CT: Yale University Press, 2012); David Dickson, Dáire Keogh and Kevin Whelan (eds), *The United Irishmen: Republicanism, Radicalism and Rebellion* (Dublin: Lilliput Press, 1993); Ian McBride, *Eighteenth Century Ireland. The Isle of Slaves* (Dublin: Gill and Macmillan, 2009).

7. Paul W. Schroeder, *The Transformation of European Politics, 1763–1848* (Oxford: Oxford University Press, 1994); Isaac Nakhimovsky, *The Closed Commercial State: Perpetual Peace and Commercial Society from Rousseau to Fichte* (Princeton, NJ: Princeton University Press, 2011).

8. J.G.A. Pocock, 'Enthusiasm: The Antiself of Enlightenment', Huntington Library Quarterly, 60 (1997), 7–28; Lawrence E. Klein and Anthony L. La Vopa (eds), Enthusiasm and Enlightenment in Europe, 1650–1850 (San Marino, CA: Huntington Library, 1998).

Chapter 1. The Power of Place

1. Patrick M. Egan, 'The Genevese and the Settlement at New Geneva', in *History, guide & directory of county and city of Waterford* (Kilkenny: n. p., 1895), 211.

2. 'Where the Croppy Boy was Executed', *The Evening Herald* (Dublin), 1 February 1960, 6.

3. McBride, *Eighteenth Century Ireland*, 369–405.

4. On Drennan, see especially A.T.Q. Stewart, *A Deeper Silence: The Hidden Origins of the United Irishmen* (Belfast: Blackstaff Press, 1993), 129–42, 150–60; Ian McBride, 'William Drennan and the Dissenting Tradition', in Dickson, Keogh and Whelan (eds), *The United Irishmen: Republicanism, Radicalism and Rebellion*, 49–61.

5. William Drennan to Samuel McTier, 21 May 1791, in Jean Agnew (ed.), *The Drennan–McTier Letters, Volume 1, 1776–1793* (Dublin: Irish Manuscripts Commission, 1999), 357.

6. Theobald Wolfe Tone, *An Argument on Behalf of the Catholics of Ireland* (Belfast: Society of United Irishmen, 1791), 8–9. Mezentius was an Etruscan king noted for his savage cruelty, appearing in Virgil's *Aeneid*.

7. James Napper Tandy, meeting of the Society of United Irishmen of Dublin, 9 November 1791, in John Lawless, *The Belfast Politics Enlarged; being a compendium of the political history of Ireland, for the last forty years* (Belfast: D. Lyons, 1818), 272–3.

8. United Irishmen, 'Address from the Society of United Irishmen, in Dublin, to the Delegates for Promoting a Reform in Scotland', 23 November 1792. See further, James Robertson, *An Account of the Trial of Thomas Muir, Esq. Younger, Of Huntershill, Before the High Court of Justiciary, At Edinburgh, On the 30th and 31st Days of August, 1793, For Sedition* (Edinburgh: J. Robertson, 1793), 127.

9. Henry Dundas, 1st Viscount Melville, 'Report of Committee of Secrecy, 23 January 1799 to parliament on 15 March 1799', *Journals of the House of Commons, Volume 54* (London: HM Stationery Office, 1803), 330.

10. 'Copy of papers found upon Richard Fuller, for the seduction of the soldiery' and 'Copy of an address to the People of Ireland taken at division no. 2 of the United Irishmen, 10 March 1799, ibid., appendix 7 and 25, 353, 365.

11. On Paine's republicanism, see Gregory Claeys, *Thomas Paine: Social and Political Thought* (London: Unwin Hyman, 1989); 'The French Revolution Debate and British Political Thought', *History of Political Thought*, 11 (1990), 59–80; 'The Origins of the Rights of Labor: Republicanism, Commerce, and the Construction of Modern Social Theory in Britain, 1796–1805', *Journal of Modern History*, 66 (1994), 249–90; Richard Whatmore, '"A gigantic manliness": Paine's Republicanism in the 1790s', in Stefan Collini, Richard Whatmore and Brian Young (eds), *Economy, Polity and Society: British Intellectual History, 1750–1950* (Cambridge: Cambridge University Press, 2000), 135–57; Carine Lounissi, *La pensée politique de Thomas Paine en contexte: Théorie et pratique* (Paris: Honoré Champion, 2012); Mark Philp, *Reforming Ideas in Britain: Politics and Language in the Shadow of the French Revolution, 1789–1815* (Cambridge: Cambridge University Press, 2014); J.C.D. Clark, *Thomas Paine. Britain, America, and France in the Age of Enlightenment and Revolution* (Oxford: Oxford University Press, 2018).

12. Theobald McKenna, *Political essays relative to the affairs of Ireland: In 1791, 1792, and 1793; with Remarks on the Present State of That Country* (London: J. Debrett, 1794), 176.

13. Ibid., 184.

14. Ibid., 194.

15. Ibid., 197.

16. Ann Thomson, 'Thomas Paine and the United Irishmen', *Études irlandaises* (1991), 109–20. See also David Dickson, 'Paine and Ireland', in Dickson, Keogh and Whelan (eds), *The United Irishmen: Republicanism, Radicalism and Rebellion*, 135–50.

17. See, classically, Marianne Elliot, *Partners in Revolution: The United Irishmen and France* (Newhaven, CT: Yale University Press, 1980), 51–74 and *Wolfe Tone. Prophet of Irish Independence* (New Haven, CT and London: Yale University Press, 1989), 281–312; Liam Swords, *The Green Cockade. The Irish in the French Revolution 1789–1815* (Dublin: Glendale, 1989), 40–138.

18. Kevin Whelan, 'The Republic in the Village: The United Irishmen, the Enlightenment and Popular Culture', in *The Tree of Liberty. Radicalism, Catholicism and the Construction of Irish Identity 1760–1830* (Cork: Cork University Press, 1996), 59–98.

19. Thomas Russell (named as 'an United Irishman'), *A Letter to the People of Ireland, on the present situation of the country* (Belfast: Northern Star Office, 1796), 6.

20. Ibid., 15–21. On opposition to aristocracy, see J. R. Dinwiddy, *Radicalism and Reform in Britain, 1780–1850* (London: Hambledon Press, 1992); J.C.D. Clark, *The Language of Liberty, 1660–1832: Political Discourse and Social Dynamics in the Anglo-American World* (Cambridge: Cambridge University Press, 1994); Amanda Goodrich, *Debating England's Aristocracy in the 1790s: Pamphlets, Polemics and Political Ideas* (Woodbridge: Boydell & Brewer, 2005).

21. Translation of instructions to Brigadier-General Humbert, commanding the Secret Expedition entrusted to the Legion '*des Francs*', proclamation to the army of Ireland, *Journals of the House of Commons, Volume 54*, appendix 28, 367–9.

22. Ibid., 369.

23. Richard R. Madden, *The United Irishmen. Their Lives and Times* (Dublin: James Duffy, 1858), 2nd edn, 4 vols, I, 330.

24. 'Waterford, July 14 [1786]', *The Times* (London), 24 July 1786, 3 (issue 495).

25. Anon., 'Army in Ireland', *Oracle and Public Advertiser*, 10 August 1795.

26. Anon., 'Waterford, May 23 [1793]', *The Lady's magazine; or, Entertaining companion for the fair sex, appropriated solely to their use and amusement*, vol. 24, June 1793, 334.

27. 'Dublin, Sept. 1 [1792]', *The Times* (London), 7 September 1792, 3 (issue 2,406).

28. 'Ireland. Dublin, Sept. 26 [1793]', *The Times* (London), 3 October 1793, 3 (issue 2,796); 'Ireland. Dublin, Sept. 18 [1793]', *The Times* (London), 24 September 1793, 3 (issue 2,787). Richard Cannon, *Historical Record of the Fifty-Sixth, or the West Essex Regiment of Foot* (London: Parker, Furnivall & Parker, 1844), 22–3.

29. 'Dublin, Sept. 26 [1793]', *The Times* (London), 3 October 1793, 3 (issue 2,796).

30. 'A. J.', 'Reminiscences of the Irish Rebellion of 1798. Geneva Barracks, Waterford', *The Court Magazine and Belle Assemblée*, vol. 7, August 1835, 142.

31. Ibid.

32. 'Ireland', *Whitehall Evening Post* (London), 4–6 September 1798 (issue 8,075).

33. James Browne, *A History of the Highlands and of the Highland Clans . . . Volume 4* (London, Edinburgh and Dublin: A. Fullarton & Co., 1854), 375

34. 'A. J.', 'Reminiscences', 142.

35. 'Waterford, Oct. 13 [1798], *The Times* (London), 19 October 1798, 3 (issue 2,264).

36. 'Ireland. Dublin, Nov. 16 [1798]', *The Times* (London), 21 November 1798, 4 (issue 4,338); 'Ireland. Dublin, Nov. 27 [1798]', *The Times* (London), 3 December 1798, 4 (issue 4,347).

37. 'Waterford, Oct. 1 [1799]', *The Times* (London), 9 October 1799, 3 (issue 4,608).

38. 'Dublin, Sept. 27 [1799]', *The Times* (London), 2 October 1799, 2 (issue 4,602).

39. 'Dublin, April 30 [1799]', *The Times* (London), 6 May 1799, 3 (issue 4,476).

40. Egan, *History, guide & directory of county and city of Waterford*, 210–13, 560.

41. John Colfer, aged 85, resident of Passage East, Waterford, 'Croppies at Geneva Barracks', interviewed by Brigid Mason, The Schools' Collection (1934–1939), vol. 0652, 240–50, National Folklore Collection, University College Dublin: https://www.duchas.ie/en/cbes/4428156/4382339, accessed 27 May 2109.

42. Sabine Baring-Gould, *A Collection of ballads: chiefly printed in London by Catnach, J. Pitts and others, mostly between 1800 and 1870: but with a few of earlier date and with a few prose broadsides* (London: n. p., n. d.), 9 vols, II, 174.

43. Madden, *The United Irishmen*, I, 330–1. The origin of the tale is stated as [Walter] Cox's *Hibernian Magazine*, 1815, 52, which could not be found, but see the following note for a more likely source.

44. Anon., 'New Geneva and the Gallantry of British Officers', *Irish Magazine and Monthly Asylum for Neglected Biography*, October 1814, 473–4.

45. R. H. Foy, *Remembering All the Orrs. The Story of the Orr Families of Country Antrim and their Involvement in the 1798 Rebellion* (Belfast: Ulster Historical Foundation, 1999), 95–8.

46. Thomas Cloney, *A Personal Narrative of Those Transactions in the County Wexford, in which the Author was Engaged, During the Awful Period of 1798, Interspersed with Brief Notices of the Principal Actors in that Ill-fated, But Ever-memorable*

Struggle: With Reflections, Moral, Political and Historical (Dublin: James McMullen, 1832), 214–15.

47. Ibid., 127.

48. Ibid., 131–2.

49. Anon., *Bombay Courier*, vol. 8, 13 July 1799 (issue 355).

50. Earl Camden to Thomas Pelham, 6 June 1798, in Sir John Thomas Gilbert (ed.), *Documents relating to Ireland, 1795–1804: official account of secret service money. Governmental correspondence and papers. Notice of French soldiery at Killala. Statements by United Irishmen. Letters on legislative union with Great Britain, etc.* (Dublin: Joseph Dollard, 1893), 129.

51. Castlereagh to Thomas Pelham, 6 June 1798, in Gilbert, *Documents relating to Ireland, 1795–1804*, 130–1.

52. Ibid., 128.

53. Castlereagh to Thomas Pelham, 8 June 1798, in Gilbert, *Documents relating to Ireland, 1795–1804*, 130–1.

54. Camden to Thomas Pelham, 11 June 1798, in ibid., 132.

55. Castlereagh to Thomas Pelham, 13 June 1798, in ibid., 134.

56. Anon., 'Extract of a letter from Waterford, dated August 29 1798', in Robert Stewart, Viscount Castlereagh, *Memoirs and Correspondence of Viscount Castlereagh*, ed. Charles William Vane, Marquess of Londonderry (London: H. Colburn, 1848–53), 12 vols, I, 342–3.

57. Richard Hopkins Ryland, *The History, Topography and Antiquities of the County and City of Waterford: With an Account of the Present State of the Peasantry of that Part of the South of Ireland* (London: J. Murray, 1824), 101–2.

58. Anon., 'Extract of a letter from Waterford, Jan. 5', *The Hibernian Journal: or, Chronicle of Liberty*, vol. 29, 9 January 1799 (issue 4).

59. James Alexander, *Some Account of the First Apparent Symptoms of the Late Rebellion in the County of Kildare* (Dublin: John Jones, 1800), 127.

60. William Wickham to Castlereagh, 18 March 1799, 29 April 1799, 8 May 1799, in Stewart, Viscount Castlereagh, *Memoirs and Correspondence*, ed. Vane, II, 215, 292, 300.

61. 'Cork, August 1 [1799]', *The Times* (London), 10 October 1799, 3 (issue 4,609).

62. Anon., 'Memoirs of Edward Finn', *Irish Magazine and Monthly Asylum for Neglected Biography*, December 1811, 544–7.

63. 'A. J.', 'Reminiscences', 141–4.

64. 'The Reader', review of Rusden's *History of Australia*, *The Graphic* (London), 22 December 1883 (issue 734).

65. 'Dublin, May 8 [1799]', *The Times* (London), 14 May 1799, 3 (issue 4,483).

66. Anon., 'Cursory remarks on board *The Friendship*', *The Asiatic Journal and Monthly Register for British India and its Dependencies* (London: Black et al., 1819), vol. 8, 237–8.

67. Robert Jackson, *Remarks on the Constitution of the Medical Department of the British Army* (London: T. Cadell and W. Davies, 1803), 55.

68. Matthew Butler, 'New Geneva. Some correspondence relating to its foundation', *Journal of the Waterford and South-East of Ireland Archaeological Society*, XVIII (1915), 21–6, 108–12.

69. *The Times* (London), 14 July 1801, 2 (issue 5,158).

70. *The Dublin Evening Post*, 18 May 1799 (issue 7,612).

71. 'Extracts From The Papers Of The Late Major James Mill, H.p. 40th Regt., Selected By His Son, Capt. W. Macdonald Mill', *The United Service Magazine and Naval and Military Journal, 1870, part 1* (London: Hurst and Blackett, 1870), 493–4.

72. Ibid., 494.

73. Ibid., 494–6.

74. Charles James, *Collection of the charges, opinions, and sentences of general courts martial, as published by authority; from the year 1795 to the present time; intended to serve as an appendix to Tytler's treatise on military law, and forming a book of cases and references; with a copious index to which are added introductory observations respecting the power of the Crown over all officers belonging to the British Army, and persons officially connected with the receipt and distribution of military pay and allowances* (London: C. Roworth, 1820), 368–9.

75. *Freeman's Journal* (Dublin), 29 May 1821, 1.

76. Anon., 'New Geneva', *Dublin University Magazine*, October 1838, 407.

77. 'The Army', *The Scotsman* (Edinburgh), 18 September 1833, 5.

Chapter 2. The Waterford Experiment

1. Anon., 'Description of the State of Britain', *The Gentleman's Magazine and Historical Chronicle*, ed. Sylvanus Urban, May 1782, 253. The author developed the 'Descriptio Status Britanniae' that appeared in the March issue (120).

2. Adam Smith, *An Inquiry into the Nature and Causes of the Wealth of Nations*, vols 1 and 2, ed. R. H. Campbell and A. S. Skinner (Oxford: Oxford University Press, 1981), II, Book 4, ch. 8, 4.

3. Voltaire to Sir Everard Fawkener, 27 March 1752, in Voltaire [François-Marie Arouet], *Correspondence and Related Documents: XII: November 1750–March 1752, letters D4255–D4854*, ed. Theodore Besterman (Geneva, Banbury and Oxford: Institut et Musée Voltaire & Voltaire Foundation, 1971), 465–9 (Letter D4851).

4. Voltaire to Gaspard Le Compasseur de Créqui-Montfort de Courtivron, 12 July 1757, in Voltaire, *Correspondence and Related Documents: XVIII: April 1757–March 1758, letters D7223–D7704*, ed. Theodore Besterman (Geneva, Banbury and Oxford: Institut et Musée Voltaire & Voltaire Foundation, 1971), 96–7 (Letter D7310).

5. Voltaire, *Additions à l'Essai sur l'Histoire Générale, et sur l'Esprit & les Moeurs des Nations* (Amsterdam: n. p., 1764), 210–15, 407–12.

6. Johann Georg Zimmermann, *An Essay on National Pride. Translated from the German* (London: J. Wilkie, 1771), 140.

7. Francesco Guicciardini, *The history of Italy, from the year 1490, to 1532 . . .* (London: J. Towers, 1753–56), 20 vols, V, 330. I have modified the translation.

8. Edward Gibbon, *Miscellanea Gibboniana. Journal de mon voyage dans quelques endroits de la Suisse, 1755*, ed. Georges A. Bonnard, Gavin R. de Beer and Louis Junod (Lausanne: Librairie de l'Université, 1952), 12, 18, 33, 38, 41, 61, 64.

9. John Campbell, *The present state of Europe; explaining the interests, connections, political and commercial views of its several powers* (London: C. Hitch et al., 1761), 6th edn, 466.

10. Voltaire, *An Epistle of Voltaire, upon his arrival at his Estate near the Lake of Geneva, in March 1755* (London: J. Dodsley, 1755), 19–23.

11. William Coxe, *Sketches of the natural, civil, and political state of Swisserland: In a series of letters to William Melmoth, Esq.* (London: J. Dodsley, 1780), 2nd edn, 461.

12. Abraham Stanyan, *An Account of Switzerland: Written in the Year 1714* (London: Jacob Tonson, 1714), 191.

13. Anon. [John Lind], *Letters concerning the present state of Poland* (London: T. Payne, 1773), 2nd edn, 303–7.

14. James Boswell to Voltaire, 29 March 1767, in Voltaire, *Correspondence and Related Documents: XXXI: October 1766–March 1767, letters D13596–D14077*, ed. Theodore Besterman (Geneva, Banbury and Oxford: Institut et Musée Voltaire & Voltaire Foundation, 1974), 465–6 (Letter D14072).

15. Anon., *Junius: Including Letters by the Same Writer Under Other Signatures: To Which are Added his Confidential Correspondence With Mr. Wilkes . . .* (London: Rivington et al., 1814), 2nd edn, 3 vols, I, 411–12.

16. Quentin Skinner, *Liberty before Liberalism* (Cambridge: Cambridge University Press, 1998); 'A Third Concept of Liberty', *Proceedings of the British Academy*, 117 (2002), 237–68; 'A Genealogy of the Modern State', *Proceedings of the British Academy*, 162 (2009), 325–70; 'On the Liberty of the Ancients and the Moderns: A Reply to my Critics', *Journal of the History of Ideas*, 73 (2012), 127–46.

17. Édouard Chapuisat, *La prise d'armes de 1782 à Genève* (Geneva: A. Jullien, 1932); Jean-Daniel Candaux, 'La révolution genevoise de 1782: Un état de la question', in *Études sur le XVIIIe siècle*, vol. 7, *L'Europe et les révolutions (1770–1800)* (Brussels: Éditions de l'Université libre de Bruxelles, 1980), 77–90; Marc Neuenschwander, 'Les troubles de 1782 à Genève et le temps de l'émigration', *Bulletin de la société d'histoire et d'archéologie de Genève*, 19 (1989), 127–88; Whatmore, *Against War and Empire*; Janet Polasky *Revolutions without Borders. The Call to Liberty in the Atlantic World* (New Haven, CT and London: Yale University Press, 2015), 27–31.

18. Adam Ferguson, *An essay on the history of civil society* (Edinburgh and London: Millar, Caddel et al., 1767), 91.

19. Jennifer Powell McNutt, *Calvin Meets Voltaire. The Clergy of Geneva in the Age of Enlightenment, 1685–1798* (Farnham: Ashgate, 2013), 25–68.

20. Anon., *Les bigarures d'un citoyen de Genève: et ses conseils republicains dediés aux Américains; avec quantités d'anecdotes amusantes* (Philadelphia: General Congress [*sic*], 1776), 193.

21. Anon. [Jean-Robert Tronchin], *Notes d'un membre du Petit Conseil de Genève au sujet de la condamnation des ouvrages de Rousseau*, 18 June 1762, *CC*, XI, 295–7. See further, Helena Rosenblatt, *Rousseau and Geneva. From the First Discourse to the Social Contract, 1749–1762* (Cambridge: Cambridge University Press, 1997).

22. Jean-Louis Dupan to Abraham Freudenreich, 21 June 1762, *CC*, XI, 123.

23. Jean-Robert Tronchin, 'Conclusions du Procureur general sur deux Livres intitulés du Contrat social & de l'Education', 19 June 1762, *CC*, XI, 298–302.

24. Voltaire, *Sentiment des citoyens* ([Geneva]: n. p., [1765]), 6.

25. Rousseau to François-Henri d'Ivernois, 22 February 1765, *CC*, XXIV, 74.

26. Rousseau to François Henri d'Ivernois, 24 March 1768, *CC*, XXXV, 220–2.

27. Richard Whatmore, '"A lover of peace more than liberty." The Genevan

Response to Rousseau's Politics', in Avi Lifschitz (ed.), *Engaging with Rousseau: Reception and Interpretation from the Eighteenth Century to the Present* (Cambridge: Cambridge University Press, 2016), 1–16.

28. Jennifer Powell McNutt and Richard Whatmore, 'The Attempts to Transfer the Genevan Academy to Ireland and to America, 1782–1795', *The Historical Journal*, 56 (2013), 345–68.

29. Richard Whatmore, 'Saving Republics by Moving Republicans. Britain, Ireland and 'New Geneva' in the Age of Revolutions', *History. The Journal of the Historical Association*, 102 (2017), 386–413.

30. François d'Ivernois to John Stuart (Mount Stuart, 4th Earl of Bute from 1794), 11 June 1782, 6 July 1782 and 30 September 1782, 'Intelligence from Geneva 1779–1783', BdG, Ms. suppl. 32, fols 303, 372, 374.

31. *Whitehall Evening Post* (London), 29 April–1 May 1783 (issue 5,554).

32. The most detailed and accurate account of New Geneva can be found in Otto Karmin's *Sir Francis d'Ivernois 1757–1842. Sa vie, son oeuvre et son temps* (Geneva: Revue historique de la révolution française et de l'empire, 1920), 115–69. Other accounts include Hubert Butler, 'New Geneva in Waterford', *The Journal of the Royal Society of Antiquaries of Ireland*, 77 (1947), 150–5; J. Feldmann, *Die Genfer Emigranten von 1782/3* (Zurich: n. p., 1952); Peter Jupp, 'Genevese Exiles in County Waterford', *Journal of the Cork Historical and Archealogical Society*, 75 (1970), 29–35; Daniel Dowling, 'New Geneva', *Decies*, 29 (1985), 32–9; Federico Ferretti, 'On Uses of Utopian Maps: The Map of New Geneva in Waterford (1783) between Colonialism and Republicanism', *Journal of Research and Didactics in Geography* 1 (2017), 75–81.

33. Richard Whatmore, 'Geneva and Scotland: the Calvinist Legacy and After', *Intellectual History Review*, 26 (2016), 391–409.

34. Rousseau to Nicolas Bonaventure Duchesne, 23 May 1762, *CC*, X, 280–2.

35. John Shovlin, 'Toward a Reinterpretation of Revolutionary Anti-Nobilism: The Political Economy of Honor in the Old Regime', *Journal of Modern History* 72 (2000), 35–66 and *The Political Economy of Virtue: Luxury, Patriotism, and the Origins of the French Revolution* (Ithaca, NY: Cornell University Press, 2006); Ruth Scurr, *Fatal Purity: Robespierre and the French Revolution* (New York: Henry Holt, 2006); William Doyle, *Aristocracy and its Enemies in the Age of Revolution* (Oxford: Oxford University Press, 2009).

36. Emmanuel Joseph Sieyès, *Qu-est ce que le Tiers état?* ([Paris]: n. p., 1789), 3rd edn, 111. On Sieyès, see Pasquale Pasquino, *Sieyès et l'invention de la constitution en France* (Paris: Éditions Odile Jacob, 1998); Murray Forsyth, *Reason and Revolution: The Political Thought of the Abbé Sieyès* (Leicester: Leicester University Press, 1987); Michael Sonenscher, 'The Nation's Debt and the Birth of the Modern Republic: The French Fiscal Deficit and the Politics of the Revolution of 1789', *History of Political Thought*, 18 (1997): 64–103, 267–325.

37. Edmund Burke, *Reflections on the Revolution in France, And on the Proceedings in Certain Societies in London Relative to that Event* (London: J. Dodsley, 1790), 7th edn, 76–8, 105–7.

38. Edmund Burke to French Laurence, 12 May 1797, *CEB*, IX, 332–8.

39. Edmund Burke, *Two letters addressed to a member of the present Parliament:*

on the proposals for peace with the regicide directory of France (London: F. & C. Rivington, 1796), 7th edn, 7.

40. Edmund Burke to French Laurence, 12 May 1797, *CEB*, IX, 336.

41. Burke, *Two letters addressed to a member of the Present Parliament*, 9.

42. Gibbon to John Holroyd, Lord Sheffield, 27 October and 10 November 1792, in Edward Gibbon, *The Letters of Edward Gibbon*, ed. J. E. Norton (London: Cassell, 1956), 3 vols, III, 282–6, 290–2.

43. Marianne Elliott, *Partners in Revolution: The United Irishmen and France* (New Haven, CT: Yale University Press, 1982).

44. Gareth Stedman Jones, *An End to Poverty? A Historical Debate* (New York: Columbia University Press, 2004).

45. John Barrell, *Imagining the King's Death: Figurative Treason, Fantasies of Regicide, 1793–1796* (Oxford: Oxford University Press, 2000).

46. Günther Lottes, 'Radicalism, Revolution and Political Culture: An Anglo-French Comparison', in Mark Philp (ed.), *The French Revolution and British Popular Politics* (Cambridge: Cambridge University Press, 1991), 78–98; Frank O'Gorman, 'The Paine Burnings of 1792–1793', *Past & Present*, 193 (2006), 111–55.

47. John Barrell, *The Spirit of Despotism: Invasions of Privacy in the 1790s* (Oxford: Oxford University Press, 2006).

48. Michael Lobban, 'Treason, Sedition, and the Radical Movement in the Age of the French Revolution', *Liverpool Law Review*, 22 (2000), 205–34; John Barrell and John Mee (eds), *Trials for Treason and Sedition, 1792–1794*, Part 1: vols 1–5; Part 2: vols 5–8 (London: Pickering and Chatto, 2006–07).

49. William Hales, *MONSTROUS REPUBLIC: Or, french atrocities pourtrayed* (London: J. Wright, 1799), 5–6.

50. Jacques Mallet du Pan, *A short account of the invasion of Switzerland by the French, in a letter from M. Mallet du Pan to M. de M****** (London: J. Wright, 1798), 18–19.

51. Ibid., 28.

52. Thomas Brooke Clarke, *Misconceptions of Facts, and Mistatements of the Public Accounts, by the Right Hon. John Foster, Speaker of the Irish Parliament* (Dublin: J. Milliken, 1800), 41–5, 60.

53. Thomas Brooke Clarke, *The Political, Commercial, and Civil State of Ireland* (Dublin: J. Milliken, 1799), 48–59. See further, Richard Whatmore, 'Liberty, War and Empire. Overcoming the Rich State–Poor State Problem, 1789–1815', in Béla Kapossy, Isaac Nakhimovsky and Richard Whatmore (eds), *Commerce and Peace in the Enlightenment* (Cambridge: Cambridge University Press, 2017), 286–320.

Chapter 3. Religion and Enlightenment

1. Olivier Fatio and Nicole Fatio, *Pierre Fatio et la crise de 1707* (Geneva: Labor et Fides, 2007).

2. David Mallet to Alexander Pope, 1735, in Alexander Pope, *Correspondence of Alexander Pope: 1729–1735*, ed. George Sherburn (Oxford: Oxford University Press, 1956), 5 vols, III, 457–67.

3. Thomas Gray to Philip Gray, 25 October 1739, in Thomas Gray, *Correspondence of Thomas Gray: Volume 1: 1734–1755*, ed. Paget Toynbee and Leonard Whibley (Oxford: Oxford University Press, 1935), 123–5.

4. Paul Bairoch, 'Genève dans le contexte des villes suisses et européennes de 1500 à 1800', in Lilian Mottu-Weber and Dominique Zumkeller (eds), *Mélanges d'histoire économique offerts au professeur Anne-Marie Piuz* (Geneva: Istec, 1989), 17–33.

5. Anon. [John Campbell], *Travels and adventures of Edward Brown, Esq; formerly a merchant in London. Containing his observations on France and Italy; his voyage to the Levant* (London: A. Bettesworth et al., 1739), 58–62.

6. James Howell, letter of 5 December 1651, in James Howell, *Epistolæ Ho-Elianæ: familiar letters domestick and foreign, divided into four books: partly historical, political, philosophical* (London: D. Midwinter et al., 1737) 10th edn, 79–80.

7. Vendramino Bianchi, *An Account of Switzerland, and the Grisons: As Also of the Velesians, Geneva, the Forest-towns, and Their Other Allies, Containing the Geographical, and Present Political Estate of All Those Places* (London: J. Knapton, 1710), 138; Andrew Le Mercier, *A Geographical and Political Account of the Republick of Geneva: Containing an Exact Description of It's Scituation* [*sic*] (Boston: B. Green, 1735), 4; Martin Sherlock, *Letters from an English traveller Martin Sherlock, Esq. translated from the French original printed at Geneva. With notes* (London: J. Nichols, 1781), 102; Vincent Bernard de Tscharner, *Dictionnaire historique, politique et géographique de la Suisse* (Geneva: Barde et al., 1788), 2 vols, II, 63.

8. Mary Shelley to Fanny Imlay, 1 June 1816, in Mary Shelley, *History of a Six Weeks' Tour through a part of France, Switzerland, Germany, and Holland; with Letters Descriptive of a Sail Round the Lake of Geneva and of the Glaciers of Chamouni* (London: Hookam & Ollier, 1817), 100–4.

9. Corinne Walker, 'Les lois somptuaires ou le rêve d'un ordre social. Évolution et enjeux de la politique somptuaire à Genève (XVIe-XVIIIe siècles)', *Equinoxe*, 11 (1994), 111–29 and 'Les pratiques de la richesse. Riches Genevois au XVIIIe siècle', in Jacques Berchtold and Michel Porret (eds), *Être riche au siècle de Voltaire* (Geneva: Droz, 1996), 135–60.

10. For a survey of libertinism and crime, see Michel Porret, *Sur la scène du crime: Pratique pénale, enquête et expertises judiciaires à Genève (XVIIe-XIXe siècle)* (Montreal: Les Presses de l'Université de Montréal, 2008).

11. Charles Burney, *The Present State of music in France and Italy, or, the Journal of a tour through those countries, undertaken to collect materials for a general history of music, by Charles Burney* (London: T. Becket & Co., 1771), 52.

12. Vernet to Rousseau, 24 November 1758, *CC*, V, 239–41.

13. George Keate, *A Short Account of the Ancient History, Present Government, and Laws of the Republic of Geneva* (London: R. and J. Dodsley, 1761), 4–5.

14. Voltaire, *The civil war of Geneva: Or, the amours of Robert Covelle, an heroic poem, in five cantos. Translated from the French of M. de Voltaire, by T. Teres* (London: T. Durham et al., 1769), 5; Voltaire to Jacob Vernet, 14 September 1733, in Voltaire, *Correspondence and Related Documents: II: January 1730–April 1734, letters D370–D730*, ed. Theodore Besterman (Geneva, Banbury and Oxford: Institut et Musée Voltaire & Voltaire Foundation, 1969), 389–90 (Letter D653).

15. Voltaire to Jean Le Rond d'Alembert, 15 July 1762, in Voltaire, *Correspondence and Related Documents: XXIV: October 1761–May 1762, letters D10049–D10481*, ed. Theodore Besterman (Geneva, Banbury and Oxford: Institut et Musée Voltaire & Voltaire Foundation, 1972), 447–9 (Letter D.app.215).

16. Jacob Spon, *The history of the city and state of Geneva, from its first foundation to this present time: Faithfully collected from several manuscripts of Jacobus Gothofredus, Monsieur Chorier, and others* (London: Bernard White, 1687), 28.

17. Le Mercier, *Geographical and Political Account of the Republick of Geneva*, 16.

18. Joseph Planta, *The History of the Helvetic Confederacy* (London: John Stockdale, 1800), 2 vols, II, 174–9.

19. Maximilien Misson, *A new voyage to Italy: With curious observations on several other countries: as Germany; Switzerland; Savoy; Geneva; Flanders; and Holland* (London: C. Jephson et al., 1739), 5th edn, 2 vols, II, 657.

20. William Bromley, *Remarks in the grand tour of France and Italy: Perform'd by a person of quality, in the year, 1691* (London: John Nutt, 1705), 2nd edn, 246.

21. Abraham van Hoey, *Letters and negociations of M. van Hoey, ambassador from the States-General to His Most Christian Majesty* . . . (London: J. Nourse, 1743), 33–4; Richard Rolt, *An impartial representation of the conduct of the several powers of Europe, engaged in the late general war from 1739 to 1748* . . . (London: S. Birt, 1749–50), 4 vols, II, 92–3.

22. Jean Bodin, *Les six livres de la republique* (Paris: Jacques de Puy, 1576), 267–8.

23. Keate, *A Short Account*, 63.

24. Henri Fazy, *Les Constitutions de la République de Genève* (Geneva and Basle: H. Georg, 1890), 293–300.

25. Jean-Louis du Pan, *Édits de la République de Genève* (Geneva: Frères Detournes, 1735), 1–15.

26. Geoffrey Parker, *Global Crisis: War, Climate Change and Catastrophe in the Seventeenth Century* (New Haven, CT: Yale University Press, 2013).

27. Jean-Louis du Pan, *Edits de la République de Genève*, 2, 8.

28. Pierre Fatio, *Propositions des citoyens*, BdG, Gf 315/179 (20).

29. Jean-Pierre Bérenger, *Histoire de Genève depuis son origine jusqu'à nos jours* (Lausanne: n. p., 1772–73), 6 vols, III, 272–7.

30. Jacques-Pierre Brissot de Warville, *Philadelphien à Genève, ou Lettres d'un Américain sur la dernière revolution de Genève, sa Constitution nouvelle, l'émigration en Irlande, &c. Pouvant servir de tableau politique de Genève jusqu'en 1784* (Dublin: n. p., 1783), 15.

31. Jean Picot, *Histoire de Genève, depuis les temps les plus anciens, jusqu'à nos jours, accompagnée de détails sur les antiquités de la ville et de son territoire, sur les moeurs, les usages, le gouvernement, les lois, les monnoies, les progrès des sciences et des arts* (Geneva: Manget and Cherbuliez, 1811), 3 vols, III, 257–64.

32. Ibid., 253–5, 265–70, 275–6.

33. Albin Thourel, *Histoire de Genève depuis son origine jusqu'à nos jours* (Geneva: Collin, 1832–33), 3 vols, III, 101–3.

34. Anon., *Entretien politique entre quelques Suisses des treize cantons & des pays Alliés, sur L'état Présent Ouáse trouve le Corps Helvétique. Avec une carte curieuse & exacte de toute de la Suisse* (London: Samuel Harding, 1738), 50.

35. William Nicholls, *A supplement to the Commentary on The book of common-prayer* (London: James Holland and William Taylor, 1711), 11–12; Harro Höpfl, *The Christian Polity of John Calvin* (Cambridge: Cambridge University Press, 1985).

36. Nicholls, *A supplement to the Commentary*, 11–12.

37. Robert Fills, *The lawes and statutes of Geneva, as well concerning ecclesiastical discipline, as civil regiment: with certeine proclamations, duly executed, whereby God's religion is most purelie maintained, and their commonwealth quietly governed. Translated out of Frenche into Englische, by R. Fills. B.L* (London: R. Hall, 1562), 13–14, 23.

38. Robert M. Kingdom, 'Social Welfare in Calvin's Geneva', *American Historical Review*, 76 (1971), 50–69 and 'The Control of Morals in Calvin's Geneva', in L. P. Buck and J. W. Zophy (eds), *The Social History of Reformation* (Columbus, OH: Ohio State University Press, 1972), 3–16.

39. Andrew Le Mercier, *The church history of Geneva, in five books: As also a political and geographical account of that republick. By the Reverend, Mr. Andrew Le Mercier Pastor of the French church in Boston* (Boston, New-England: S. Gerrish, 1732), 218–19.

40. Anon., *Lettres genevoises: Contenant des détails peu connus sur les derniers troubles de la Republique de Geneve* ([Geneva]: n. p., 1782), 55.

41. Charles Borgeaud, *Histoire de l' Université de Genève, I. L'Academie de Calvin, 1559–1798* (Geneva: Georg & Co., 1900); Gillian Lewis, 'The Geneva Academy', in Andrew Pettegree, Alastair Duke and Gillian Lewis (eds), *Calvinism in Europe, 1540–1620* (Cambridge: Cambridge University Press, 1994), 35–63; Michael Heyd, *Between Orthodoxy and the Enlightenment. Jean-Robert Chouet and the Introduction of Cartesian Science in the Academy of Geneva* (The Hague: M. Nijoff, 1982), 227.

42. Keate, *A Short Account*, 129–32.

43. Timothy R. Phillips, 'The Dissolution of Francis Turretin's Vision of *Theologia*: Geneva at the End of the Seventeenth Century', in John B. Roney and Martin I. Klauber (eds), *The Identity of Geneva. The Christian Commonwealth, 1564–1864* (Westport, CT: Greenwood Press, 1998), 77–92.

44. Eugène de Budé, *Vie de J.-A. Turrettini, theólogien genevois 1671–1737* (Lausanne: G. Bridel, 1880); Martin I. Klauber, *Between Reformed Scholasticism and Pan-Protestantism: Jean-Alphonse Turretin (1671–1737) and Enlightened Orthodoxy at the Academy of Geneva* (Selingsgrove, PA: Susquehanna University Press, 1994). More broadly, see Maria-Cristina Pitassi, *De l'orthodoxie aux Lumières. Genève 1670–1737* (Geneva: Labor et Fides, 1992).

45. Martin I. Klauber, 'Reason, Revelation, and Cartesianism: Louis Tronchin and Enlightened Orthodoxy in Late Seventeenth-Century Geneva', *Church History*, 59 (1990), 326–39; Maria-Cristina Pitassi, 'From Exemplarity to Suspicion. The Genevan Church between the Late Seventeenth and Early Eighteenth Centuries', *History of European Ideas*, 37 (2011) 16–22.

46. Martin I. Klauber, 'The Context and Development of the Views of Jean-Alphonse Turrettini (1671–1737) on Religious Authority' (PhD thesis, University of Wisconsin-Madison, 1987); Ruth Rouse and Stephen C. Neill (eds), *A History of the Ecumenical Movement: 1517–1948* (Philadelphia: Westminster Press 1967). On Tillotson, see Jean Leclerc, 'A defence of Archbishop Tillotson and his writings', in Edward

Young, *The Life of the Most Reverend Father in God John Tillotson* (London: E. Curll et al., 1717).

47. Martin I. Klauber, 'The Drive Toward Protestant Union in Early Eighteenth-Century Geneva: Jean-Alphonse Turrettini on the "Fundamental Articles" of the Faith', *Church History*, 61 (1992), 334–49.

48. Jean Frédéric Ostervald, *A treatise concerning the causes of the present corruption of Christians, and the remedies thereof* (London: Richard Chiswell, 1702), 233–82; Samuel Werenfels, *Three discourses: one, A defence of private judgment; the second, Against the authority of the magistrate over conscience; the third, Some considerations concerning the reuniting of Protestants* . . . (London: James Knapton, 1718), 93–104.

49. Jean-Alphonse Turrettini, *An Oration of composing the differences among Protestants. Spoken at an Act of the University of Geneva, Jun. 1707* (London: William Taylor, 1709), 6–7; *A discourse concerning fundamental articles in religion. In which a method is laid down for the more effectual uniting of Protestants, and promoting a more general toleration amongst them* (London: A. Bell et al., 1720), 57–85.

50. Coxe, *Sketches of the natural, civil, and political state of Swisserland*, 393.

51. Jean d'Alembert, 'A Short Account of the Government of Geneva', in *Miscellaneous Pieces in Literature, History, and Philosophy* (London: C. Henderson, 1764), 70–3.

52. Jacob Vernet, *Lettres critiques d'un voyageur anglois sur l'Article Geneve du Dictionnaire Encyclopédique & sur la lettre de Mr. D'Alembert à Mr. Rousseau* (Utrecht: J. C. ten Bosch, 1761); Ronald Grimsley, *Jean d'Alembert (1717–83)* (Oxford: Oxford University Press, 1963), 56–77; Graham Gargett, *Voltaire and Protestantism* (Oxford: Voltaire Foundation, 1980), 135–55 and *Jacob Vernet, Geneva and the Philosophes* (Oxford: Voltaire Foundation, 1994), 144–65; Powell McNutt, *Calvin Meets Voltaire*, 169–75.

53. Henri-Marie Ducrotay de Blainville, *Travels through Holland, Germany, Switzerland: And Italy. Containing a particular description of the antient and present state of those countries* (London: J. Johnson & B. Davenport, 1767), 3 vols.

54. Stanyan, *An Account of Switzerland*), 175–6.

55. Anon., *Lettres genevoises*, 7.

56. Karl Ludwig, Freiherr von Pollnitz, *The memoirs of Charles-Lewis, Baron de Pollnitz. Being the observations he made in his late travels . . . In letters to his friend* (Dublin: G. Faulkner et al., 1738), 5 vols, V, 172.

57. Coxe, *Sketches of the natural, civil, and political state of Swisserland*, 387.

58. Keate, *A Short Account*, 104–7.

59. Johann Georg Keyssler, *Travels through Germany, Hungary, Bohemia, Switzerland, Italy, and Lorrain. Containing an accurate description of the present state and curiosities of those countries* (London: for the editor, 1758), 4 vols, I, 179.

60. Bianchi, *An Account of Switzerland and the Grisons*, 139.

61. Stanyan, *An Account of Switzerland*, 175.

62. Anne-Marie Piuz, Liliane Mottu-Weber et. al., *L'économie genevoise, de la Réforme à la fin de l'Ancien Régime XVIe et XVIIIe siècle* (Geneva: Société d'histoire et d'archéologie, 1990).

63. Herbert Lüthy, *La Banque protestante en France de la révocation de l'Édit de Nantes à la Révolution* (Paris: S. E. V. P. E. N., 1961), 2 vols, II, 47–58, 177–315; Helena Rosenblatt, '"Colonnes de la patrie" ou "froids égoïstes": Les capitalistes genevois vus de chez eux', *Revue suisse d'histoire*, 50 (2000), 304–24.

64. Stanyan, *An Account of Switzerland*, 175–6.

65. Jean-Louis de Lolme, *General Observations On The Power Of Individuals To Prescribe, By Testamentary Dispositions, The Particular Future Uses To Be Made Of Their Property* (London: Richardson, 1798), 2–4.

66. Thourel, *Histoire de Genève*, II, 474–5.

67. Marc Cramer, 'Les trente Demoiselles de Genève et les billets solidaires', *Revue suisse d'économie politique et de statistique*, 82 (1946), 109–38; Patrick O'Mara, 'Geneva in the Eighteenth Century: A Socio-Economic Study of the Bourgeois City-State During its Golden Age' (PhD thesis, University of California, Berkeley, 1954), 100–11.

68. John Lockman, *A history of the cruel sufferings of the Protestants, and others, by Popish persecutions, in various countries: Together with a view of the reformations from the Church of Rome* (London: J. Clarke et al., 1760), 148.

69. Jean-Frédéric Ostervald, *The grounds & principles of the Christian religion, explain'd in a catechetical discourse for the instruction of young people. Written in French by J. F. Ostervald, . . . Rendred into English by Mr. Hum. Wanley: and revis'd by Geo. Stanhope, D.D* (London: Joseph Downing, 1711), 2nd edn, 297–307.

70. Anon., 'Extrait d'une Histoire de Genève, par Mr. R. C** A Messieurs les Journalistes', *Journal Helvétique*, January 1755, 44.

71. Pierre-Jean Grosley, *New observations on Italy and its inhabitants. Written in French by two Swedish gentlemen. Translated into English by Thomas Nugent* (London: L. Davis & C. Reymers, 1769), 2 vols, II, 15.

72. Gilbert Burnet, *Voyage de Suisse, d'Italie, et de quelques endroits d'Allemagne & de France, fait és années 1685, & 1686* (Rotterdam: Abraham Acmer, 1688), 2nd edn, 435.

73. Joseph Addison, *Remarks on several parts of Italy, &c. In the years 1701, 1702, 1703* (London: J. Tonson, 1718), 2nd edn, 390.

74. O'Mara, 'Geneva in the Eighteenth Century', 163–84.

75. Anon., 'Reflexions Sur les Loix Somptuaires, par un Citoyen de Genève', *Journal Helvétique*, January 1769, 61–79.

76. Anon., 'A Mr. C[ramer]**. Sur l'Histoire de Genève & sur les Grands Homes que cette Ville a produite', *Journal Helvétique*, March 1755, 237–9; Ferdinando Galiani, *Dialogues sur le commerce des bleds* (London: n. p., 1770), 33–60.

77. Fabrice Brandli, *Le nain et le géant: La République de Genève et la France aux XVIIIe siècle: cultures politiques et diplomatie* (Rennes: Presses universitaires de Rennes, 2012).

78. *Discours fait par Monsieur De la Closure, Résident de France, Dans l'Audience qu'il a pris du Magnifique Conseil, le Samedi 21 Septembre 1737; Mémoire addressé par Monsieur De la Closure, Résident de la France, aupres de la Ville et République de Genève, au Magnifique Petit Conseil, Le Vendredi 4 Octobre 1737* ([Geneva]: n. p., 1737), 1.

79. Louise Seaward, 'The Small Republic and the Great Power: Censorship between Geneva and France in the Later Eighteenth Century', *The Library*, 18 (2017),

191–217. See also 'Censorship through Cooperation: The *Société typographique de Neuchâtel* (STN) and the French Government, 1769–89', *French History*, 28 (2014), 23–42.

80. Louis Henry de Rouvière, *Voyage du tour de la France* (1713), and Abraham Ruchat, *Les Délices de la Suisse* (1713), both in J.-D. Candaux (ed.), *Voyageurs européens à la découverte de Gèneve 1685–1792* (Geneva: Caisse d'Epargne de la République et Canton de Genève, 1966), 18, 28.

81. Keate, *A Short Account*, 101–2.

Chapter 4. Extremism

1. Pierre Guy de La Roche to Jean-Jacques Rousseau, between 6 November 1761 and 28 February 1762, *CC*, X, 123–34.

2. Béla Kapossy, *Iselin contra Rousseau: Sociable Patriotism and the History of Mankind* (Basle: Schwabe, 2006) and 'Republican Political Economy. Introduction: The Economic Society of Berne and the Reform of the Republican Household', *History of European Ideas*, 33 (2007), 377–89; Istvan Hont, *Politics in Commercial Society. Jean-Jacques Rousseau and Adam Smith*, ed. Béla Kapossy and Michael Sonenscher (Cambridge, MA: Harvard University Press, 2015).

3. Germaine de Staël, *Lettres sur les ouvrages et le caractère de J. J. Rousseau* (n. p., 1788), 2.

4. Alexis de Tocqueville, *The Old Regime and the Revolution*, trans. Alan S. Kahan (Chicago: University of Chicago Press, 2001), 2 vols, II, 57, cited in Jeremy Jennings, 'Rousseau and French Liberalism, 1789–1870', in Lifschitz (ed.), *Engaging with Rousseau*, 63.

5. R. R. Palmer, *The Age of the Democratic Revolution: A Political History of Europe and America, 1760–1800, Volume 1. The Challenge* (Princeton NJ: Princeton University Press, 1959), 111–40; Franco Venturi, *Settecento riformatore. La prima crisi dell'Antico Regime (1768–1776)* (Turin: Einaudi, 1979), 343–60.

6. J. L. Talmon, *The Origins of Totalitarian Democracy* (London: Secker & Warburg, 1960); Joan McDonald, *Rousseau and the French Revolution, 1762–1791* (London: Bloomsbury Academic, 1965); Norman Hampson, *Will and Circumstance: Montesquieu, Rousseau and the French Revolution* (Norman, OK: University of Oklahoma Press, 1983); James Swenson, *On Jean-Jacques Rousseau Considered as One of the First Authors of the Revolution* (Stanford, CA.: Stanford University Press, 2000); Carol Blum, *Rousseau and the Republic of Virtue. The Language of Politics in the French Revolution* (Ithaca, NY: Cornell University Press, 1986); Holger Ross Lauritsen and Mikkel Thorup (eds), *Rousseau and Revolution* (London: Continuum, 2011); Jonathan Israel, *Democratic Enlightenment: Philosophy, Revolution, and Human Rights 1750–1790* (Oxford: Oxford University Press, 2011), 641–7.

7. Achille Isnard, *Observations sur le principe qui a produit les révolutions de France, de Genève et d'Amérique dans le dix-huitième siècle* (Evreux: Malassis, 1789), 4. I am grateful to Gabriel Sabbagh for this reference.

8. Marie-Joseph Bardel, *Les Droits et les devoirs de l'homme, du citoyen et du chrétien. Par un prêtre de Savoie* (Paris: n. p., 1794), 1.

9. Voltaire to Jean-Jacques Gilbert, marquis de Fraigne, 25 January 1765, Louis Petit de Bachaumont, *Mémoires secrets pour servir à l'histoire de la république des lettres en France, depuis MDCCLXII jusqu'à nos jours* (London: J. Adamson, 1777), 18 vols, II, 162–3.

10. Augustin Barruel, *Mémoires pour servir à l'histoire du Jacobinisme* (Hamburg: P. Fauche, 1798), 2 vols, II, 100–60, 200–26.

11. Anon. [Jean-Robert Tronchin], *Notes d'un membre du Petit Conseil de Genève*, *CC*, XI, 295–7; Maurice Cranston, *The Solitary Self: Jean-Jacques Rousseau in Exile and Adversity* (Chicago: Chicago University Press, 1997), 2–8.

12. Maurice Cranston, *The Noble Savage: Jean-Jacques Rousseau, 1754–1762* (Chicago: University of Chicago Press, 1991), 340–58.

13. Théodore Tronchin to Jacob Vernes, 17 June 1762, *CC*, XI, 72–3.

14. Charles Bonnet to Albrecht von Haller, 15 June 1762, *CC*, XI, 85–8.

15. Jean-Louis Dupan to Abraham Freudenreich, 21 June 1762, *CC*, XI, 123.

16. Jean-Robert Tronchin, 'Conclusions du Procureur general sur deux Livres intitulés du Contrat social & de l'Education', 19 June, 1762, *CC*, XI, 298–301.

17. Paul-Claude Moultou to Rousseau, 19 May 1762, *CC*, X, 254–6.

18. Jacques-François Deluc, 'Projet de Réponse aux arrêtés des M. Conseils, tiré des Réflexions de divers Citoyens et Bourgeois sur cette matière', Archives d'État de Genève, Ms. Hist. 84 (13 February 1757), 70–1; Anon., *Représentations des citoyens et bourgeois de Genève au premier syndic de cette république; avec les réponses du Conseil à ces représentations* ([Geneva]: n. p., 1763), 61, 70.

19. Whatmore, *Against War and Empire*, 54–97.

20. Jacques-François Deluc, 'Représentations remises à M. le Procureur Général le 30 Décembre 1756', BdG, Ms. Cramer 81, 40–1.

21. D. G. Creighton, 'Rousseau and the Delucs in 1754', *Diderot Studies*, 19 (1978), 55–66.

22. Jacques-François Deluc to Rousseau, *CC*, III, 138–9.

23. Paul-Claude Moultou to Rousseau, 1 September 1762, *CC*, XIII, 3–4.

24. Paul-Claude Moultou to Rousseau, 22 September 1762, *CC*, XIII, 92–5.

25. Anon., *Représentations des citoyens et bourgeois de Genève*, 42–58.

26. Ibid., 16–17, 125.

27. Jean Cramer, 'Entretiens de Deluc père, 28 January 1763, *CC*, XV, 363–74.

28. Paul-Claude Moultou to Rousseau, 4 August 1762, *CC*, XII, 151–2.

29. Paul-Claude Moultou to Rousseau, 21 August 1762, *CC*, XII, 228–232.

30. Paul-Claude Moultou to Rousseau, 7 July 1762 *CC*, XI, 230–3.

31. Rousseau, *Confessions*, *OC*, I, 393; *Lettres écrites de la montagne*, *OC*, III, 830–1.

32. Anon., *Extraits du Registre du Consistoire*, 25 July 1754, and R. A. Leigh, 'Notes explicatives', *CC*, II, 322–4.

33. Jean-Jacques Rousseau, *Émile*, *OC*, IV, 610.

34. Jean-Jacques Rousseau, *Contrat social, ou Principes du droit politiques*, Book 4, ch. 8, 'De la religion civile' (Amsterdam: Marc Michel Rey, 1762), 311.

35. Jacob Vernet, 'Rapport sur deux ouvrages de M. Rousseau', 25 February 1763, *CC*, XV, 375–85.

36. Anon., *Réponse du Petit Conseil de Genève aux premières Représentations*, 25 June 1763, *CC*, XVI, 378–84.

37. Petit Conseil de Genève, *Réponse aux representations*, 14 October 1763, *CC*, XVIII, 253–56.

38. Paul-Claude Moultou to Rousseau, 19 February 1763, *CC*, XV, 208–9.

39. Francis de Crue, *L'Ami de Rousseau et des Necker. Paul Moultou à Paris en 1778* (Paris: Honoré Champion, 1926).

40. Paul-Claude Moultou to Rousseau, 10 November 1758, *CC*, V, 217–19.

41. Paul-Claude Moultou to Rousseau, late November to early December 1759, *CC*, VI, 210–14: '[V]ous avez vu plus loin que Montesquieux, que vous avez mieux prouvé dans ce peu de mots que les Monar[chies] ne peuvent se Soutenir que par des principes faux & corrupteurs, & qu'il ne peut y avoir de vertu que dans les petites Republiques, parce qu'elles forment moins ce qu'on appelle des Societés que des Associations d'hommes.'

42. Paul-Claude Moultou to François Coindet, March 1761, *CC*, VIII, 198–200.

43. Paul-Claude Moultou to Rousseau, 7 March 1761, *CC*, VIII, 225–30.

44. Paul-Claude Moultou to Rousseau, 13 June 1761, *CC*, IX, 18–21.

45. Paul-Claude Moultou to Rousseau, 3 February 1762, *CC*, X, 80–3: 'Non, on n'a rien écrit d'aussi fort, d'aussi lumineux, d'aussi vrai sur la Religion naturelle; & vous même, Monsieur, vous n'avez rien fait qui appròche de ce morceau.'

46. Paul-Claude Moultou to Rousseau, 15 March 1762, *CC*, X, 155–8: 'Vôtre religion Naturelle, n'est pas autre chose que le Christianisme bien entendu, toute la différence c'est que vous prouvez ce que l'Évangile nous enseigne par autorité. Vous ne differés donc du vrai Chrétien qu'en ce qu'il croit tenir du ciel même ce que vous reconoissez ne devoir qu'aux lumières de vôtre raison. Par consequent un Chrétien raisonable qui croiroit pourtant, touts les miracles de J.C. ne vous refuseroit pas le titre de Chrétien.'

47. Paul-Claude Moultou to Rousseau, 14 June 1762, *CC*, XI, 70–2.

48. Paul-Claude Moultou to Rousseau, 19 May 1762, *CC*, X, 254–56.

49. Paul-Claude Moultou to Élie Salomon François Reverdil, 8 June 1762, *CC*, XI, 50.

50. Paul-Claude Moultou to Rousseau, 5 June 1762, *CC*, XI, 29–31.

51. Paul-Claude Moultou to Rousseau, 16 June 1762, *CC*, XI, 88–91.

52. Paul-Claude Moultou to Rousseau, 18 June 1762, *CC*, XI, 108–11.

53. Paul-Claude Moultou to Rousseau, 23 May 1762, *CC*, XI, 137–9.

54. Paul-Claude Moultou to Rousseau, 22 May 1762, *CC*, XI, 128–31.

55. Paul-Claude Moultou to Léonhard Usteri: 17 July 1762, *CC*, XII, 48–50: 'Cette conduite est sans exemple . . . Que d'Alembert s'est trompé, nous somes pis que des intolerants, nous allons contre nos lumières, nous voulons a tout prix qu'on nous reproche encore le bucher de Servet, Je le voyais dans les flames qui consumaient des livres que le temps même ne detruira pas.'

56. Paul-Claude Moultou to Rousseau, 2 July 1762, *CC*, XI, 191–3.

57. Paul-Claude Moultou to Léonhard Usteri, 9 July 1762, *CC*, XI, 256–8.

58. Graham Gargett, 'Jacob Vernet, éditeur de Montesquieu: La première edition de "L'Esprit des lois"', *Revue d'histoire littéraire de la France*, 91 Année, 6 (1791), 890–900.

59. Paul-Claude Moultou to Rousseau, 13 October 1762, *CC*, XIII, 208–10; 9 November 1762, *CC*, XIV, 19–21. See also Paul-Claude Moultou to Jacob Vernes, 5 July 1763, *CC*, XVII, 18–21.

60. Paul-Claude Moultou to Rousseau, 19 March 1763, *CC*, XV, 296–9.

61. Paul-Claude Moultou to Rousseau, 23 March 1763, *CC*, XV, 316–18.

62. Paul-Claude Moultou to Rousseau, 30 March 1763, *CC*, XV, 346–8.

63. Paul-Claude Moultou to Rousseau, 26 April 1763, *CC*, XVI, 110–12.

64. Jean-Pierre Bérenger, *J. J. Rousseau justifié envers sa patrie* (London: n. p., 1775), 13.

65. Paul-Claude Moultou to abbé Pierre Quesnel, 20 May 1763, *CC*, XVI, 213–14.

66. Paul-Claude Moultou to Rousseau, 25 June 1763, *CC*, XVI, 338–40.

67. Marc Chappuis to Rousseau, 16 July 1762, *CC*, XII, 39–40.

68. Marc Chappuis to Rousseau, 18 May 1763, *CC*, XVI, 197–200.

69. Rousseau to Jacques-François Deluc, 28 May 1763, *CC*, XVI, 259–61.

70. Rousseau to Marc Chappuis, 26 May 1763, *CC*, XVI, 245–50.

71. *Journal encyclopédique ou universel* (Bouillon & Liège: Rousseau Toulouse), vol. 5, no. 1, 1 July 1763, 121–4.

72. Marc Chappuis to Rousseau, 25 June 1763, *CC*, XVI, 341–4.

73. Paul-Claude Moultou to Rousseau, 29 June 1763, *CC*, XVI, 357–60.

74. Rousseau to Paul-Claude Moultou, 7 July 1763, *CC*, XVII, 24–5.

75. Rousseau to Jacques-François Deluc, 7 July 1763, *CC*, XVII, 25–9.

76. Jean-Robert Tronchin, *Lettres écrites de la campagne* (Geneva: n. p., 1763), 49–52, 88–95.

77. Tronchin, *Lettres écrites de la campagne*, 11–12, 32–3, 113–15.

78. Paul-Claude Moultou to Rousseau, 27 July 1763, *CC*, XVII, 86–91; Jacob Vernes, *Lettres sur le Christianisme de Mr. J. J. Rousseau, addressées à Mr. I. L.* (Geneva: Étienne Blanc, 1763).

79. Paul-Claude Moultou to Rousseau, 29 October 1763, *CC*, XVIII, 79–81.

80. Paul-Claude Moultou to Léonhard Usteri: 30 November 1763, *CC*, XVIII, 170–3.

81. Paul-Claude Moultou to Élie-Salomon-François Reverdil, February 1764, *CC*, XIX, 153–66.

82. The *Règlement de la Médiation* stated: '*Article* 5. Toutes les matiéres qui Seront portées au Conseil Général ne pourront y être proposées que par les Syndics, petit & grand Conseil. *Article* 6. Il ne pourra rien être porté au Conseil des deux cent, qu'auparavant il n'ait eté traité & approuvé au Conseil des Vingt-cinq: Et il ne Sera rien porté au Conseil Général, qui n'ait auparavant traité & approuvé dans le Conseil des deux cent.'

83. Paul-Claude Moultou to Élie-Salomon-François Reverdil, February 1764, *CC*, XIX, 153–66.

84. Paul-Claude Moultou to Rousseau, 23 December 1764, *CC*, XXII, 277–9.

85. Paul-Claude Moultou to Rousseau, 30 January 1765, *CC*, XXIII, 233–6.

86. Hont, *Politics in Commercial Society*.

87. Rousseau to Nicolas Bonaventure Duchesne, 4 November 1764, *CC*, XXII, 12–13.

88. Rousseau to Jacques-François Deluc, 25 October 1763, *CC*, XVIII, 70; Jacques-François Deluc to Rousseau, 15 November 1763, *CC*, XVIII, 139–40; Rousseau to Marc Michel-Rey, 9 June 1764, *CC*, XX, 168–70; Rousseau to François-Henri d'Ivernois, 6 July 1764, *CC*, XX, 25–51. See further, Richard Whatmore, 'Rousseau and

the *représentants*: The Politics of the *Lettres écrites de la montagne*', *Modern Intellectual History*, 3 (2006), 1–29.

89. Jean-André Deluc to Rousseau, 15 December 1764, *CC*, XXII, 241.

90. François-Henri d'Ivernois to Rousseau, 21 December 1764, *CC*, XXII, 262.

91. Paul-Claude Moultou to Jakob Heinrich Meister, 25 1765, *CC*, XXIV, 113–14.

92. Rousseau, *OC*, III, 837–50.

93. François-Henri d'Ivernois to Rousseau, 5 January 1767, *CC*, XXXII, 21–2; Rousseau to François-Henri d'Ivernois, 7 February 1767, *CC*, XXXII, 116–17.

94. Rousseau to François-Henri d'Ivernois, 6 April 1767, *CC*, XXXIII, 11–12.

95. Rousseau to François-Henri d'Ivernois, 9 February 1768, *CC*, XXXV, 100–7; 23 February 1768, *CC*, XXXV, 141–3; 8 March 1768, *CC*, XXXV, 187–9.

96. Rousseau to François Henri d'Ivernois, 24 March 1768, *CC*, XXXV, 220–2.

97. Rousseau to Paul-Claude Moultou, 7 March 1768, *CC*, XXXV, 179–82.

98. Jean-Frédéric Chaillet to Rousseau, *c.* 20 March 1765, *CC*, XXIV, 260–5.

99. Vernet to abbé N.-C.-J. Trublet, 9 January 1765, *CC*, XXIII, 70–1.

100. Tronchin to Suzanne Necker, 18 February 1765, *CC*, XXIV, 41.

101. Étienne-Jean de Guimard des Rocheretz, baron de Montpéroux to César Gabriel de Choiseul, duc de Praslin, 22 December 1764, *CC*, XXII, 270–1.

102. Voltaire, *Sentiment des citoyens*, 6.

103. Voltaire, *A Letter from Mr. Voltaire to M. Jean-Jacques Rousseau* (London, 1766), 9, 11.

104. Voltaire to Charles-Augustin Ferriol, comte d'Argental, 23 December 1764, *CC*, XXII, 279–80.

105. Voltaire to Charles-Augustin Ferriol, comte d'Argental and Jeanne Grâce Bosc du Bouchet, comtesse d'Argental, 12 January 1765, in Voltaire, *Correspondence and Related Documents: XXVIII: July 1764–March 1765, letters D11971–D12514*, ed. Theodore Besterman (Geneva, Banbury and Oxford: Institut et Musée Voltaire & Voltaire Foundation, 1973), 316 (Letter D12309).

106. Peter Gay, *Voltaire's Politics: The Poet as Realist* (Princeton, NJ: Princeton University Press, 1959).

107. Manin, *Principles of Representative Government*; Richard Tuck, 'From Rousseau to Kant', in Béla Kapossy, Isaac Nakhimovsky, Sophus A. Reinert and Richard Whatmore (eds), *Markets, Morals, Politics. Jealousy of Trade and the History of Political Thought* (Cambridge, MA: Harvard University Press, 2018).

108. 'Declaration de Nos Magnifiques & Très Honorés Seigneurs, Sindics & Conseil', 12 February 1765, *CC*, XXIII, 369–72.

109. Pierre-Michel Hennin to César Gabriel de Choiseul, duc de Praslin, 6 January 1766, *CC*, XXVIII, 161–2; 1 February 1766, *CC*, XXVIII, 264–5.

110. Pierre-Michel Hennin to César Gabriel Choiseul, duc de Praslin, 8 January 1766, *CC*, XXVIII, 169.

111. Marc Chappuis to Rousseau, 20 February 1765, *CC*, XXIV, 54–9.

112. Charles Bonnet to Baron Albrecht von Haller, 22 July 1766, *CC*, XXX, 145.

113. Pierre de Buisson, chevalier de Beauteville to Étienne François de Choiseul-Stainville, duc de Choiseul, 30 May 1766, *CC*, XXIX, 229–35.

114. Pierre-Michel Hennin to Voltaire, 1 March 1766, in Voltaire, *Correspondence and Related Documents: XXX: January–September 1766, letters D13078–D13595*, ed.

Theodore Besterman (Geneva, Banbury and Oxford: Institut et Musée Voltaire & Voltaire Foundation, 1973), 114 (Letter D13191).

115. Voltaire to Pierre-Michel Hennin, (possible date) 12 July 1766, in ibid., 309 (Letter D13408).

116. Pierre de Buisson, chevalier de Beauteville to Rousseau, 9 May 1766, *CC*, XVIX, 180–1.

Chapter 5. Civil War

1. Étienne Clavière to Jacques Roux, 6 October 1766, BdG, Ms. fr. 2486.

2. Pierre de Buisson, chevalier de Beauteville to Étienne François de Choiseul-Stainville, duc de Choiseul, 26 June 1766, *CC*, XXX, 397–8.

3. Christopher Storrs, 'British Diplomacy in Switzerland (1689–1789) and Eighteenth Century Diplomatic Culture', *Études de lettres*, 3 (2010), 181–216.

4. Philip Stanhope to William Pitt, 2 February 1767, NA, 30/70/3/136; Philip Stanhope to William Pitt, 19 December 1766, NA, 30/70/3/135.

5. Pierre de Buisson, chevalier de Beauteville to Antoine Charles Esmangart de Bournonville, 2 July 1766, *CC*, XXX, 399–400.

6. Étienne François de Choiseul-Stainville, duc de Choiseul to Pierre de Buisson, chevalier de Beauteville, 26 November 1766, *CC*, XXXI, 359; Pierre de Buisson, chevalier de Beauteville to Étienne François de Choiseul-Stainville, duc de Choiseul, 5 December 1766, *CC*, XXXI, 360–1.

7. François d'Ivernois, *An historical and political view of the constitution and revolutions of Geneva, in the eighteenth century* (London: T. Cadell, 1784), 291.

8. Anon., *Lettre d'un citoyen de Genève à un autre citoyen. Le 15 Février 1768* (Geneva: n. p., 1768), 16.

9. Jean-Pierre Bérenger, *Le Natif, ou lettres de Theodore et d'Annette* (Geneva: n. p., 1767), 53–3.

10. Anon, *Exposé de la conduite des sindics et conseil de la république de Genève* ([Geneva]: n. p., 1767), 13.

11. Charles Bonnet to Antoine Charles Esmangart de Bournonville, 17 January 1767, *CC*, XXXII, 51.

12. Voltaire to Pierre-Michel Hennin, 30 November 1766, in Voltaire, *Correspondence and Related Documents: XXXI: October 1766–March 1767, letters D13596–D14077*, ed. Theodore Besterman (Geneva, Banbury and Oxford: Institut et Musée Voltaire & Voltaire Foundation, 1974), 113 (Letter D13702).

13. Rousseau, draft representation, written between 8 and 23 September 1763, *CC*, XVII, 318–21.

14. Rousseau to François-Henri d'Ivernois, 7 February 1767, *CC*, XXXII, 116–17; Rousseau to François-Henri d'Ivernois, 6 April 1767, *CC*, XXXIII, 11–12; Rousseau to François-Henri d'Ivernois, 9 February 1768, *CC*, XXXV, 100–7; Rousseau to François-Henri d'Ivernois, 23 February 1768, *CC*, XXXV, 141–3; Rousseau to François-Henri d'Ivernois, 8 March 1768, *CC*, XXXV, 187–9.

15. Rousseau to François-Henri d'Ivernois, 29 January 1768, *CC*, XXXV, 62–5.

16. Théodore Rivier-Rose, *La famille Rivier (1595 à nos jours)* (Lausanne: Imprimeries réunies, 1916), 95–116; André Gür, 'La négociation de l'Édit du 11 mars

1768, d'après le journal de Jean-André Deluc et la correspondance de Gédéon Turrettini', *Revue Suisse d'histoire*, 17 (1967), 216.

17. Théodore Rilliet, *Solution générale ou lettres à Monsieur Covelle le fils, citoyen de Genève, pour servir de réponse aux observations* (Lausanne: n. p., 1765), 30–48, 73–81.

18. Etienne Clavière to Théodore Rilliet and Jean-André Deluc, 21 July 1767, BdG, Ms. fr. 2486.

19. Jean-André Deluc to Jacques Necker, 1 May 1767, BdG, Ms. fr. 2465, fols 74–5.

20. Jean-André Deluc to Jacques-François Deluc, 25 July 1767, BdG, Ms. fr. 2475, fols 118–19; Etienne Clavière to Jacques Roux, 8 October 1766, BdG, Ms. Fr. 2486; Jean-André Deluc to F.-H. d'Ivernois, Rilliet and Clavière, 14 July 1767, BdG, Ms. fr. 2475, fols 101–3.

21. Étienne Clavière to Jacques Roux, 6 October 1766, BdG, Ms. fr. 2486.

22. Jean-André Deluc, 'Projet de conciliation pour la République de Genève', BdG, Ms. fr. 2475, fols 100–1.

23. Jean-Jacques de Chapeaurouge, *Edit du 11 Mars 1768* ([Geneva]: [1768]).

24. Étienne Clavière to Jean-André Deluc, 3 February 1773, BdG, Ms. fr. 2463, fol. 85; Clavière to Jean-André Deluc, 3 March 1773, BdG, Ms fr 2463, fol. 87.

25. Theodore S. Feldman, 'Deluc, Jean-André (1727–1817)', *ODNB*; Paul A. Tunbridge, 'Jean André Deluc, FRS, 1727–1817', *Notes and Records of the Royal Society*, 26 (1971), 15–33; Étienne Clavière to Jean-André Deluc, 21 December 1773, BdG, Ms. fr 2463, fols 92–3.

26. Jean-André Deluc to Jacques-François Deluc, 12 November 1768, BdG, Ms. fr. 2461, F1652, fols 3–30.

27. Jean-André Deluc to Jacques Vieusseux, 4 March 1777, BdG, Ms. fr. 2461 F1652, fols 33–47.

28. Ibid., fol. 36B.

29. André Gür, 'Quête de la richesse et critique des riches chez Étienne Clavière', in Berchtold and Porret (eds), *Être riche au siècle de Voltaire*, 97–115.

30. Étienne Clavière to Théodore Rilliet and Jean-André Deluc, 14 July 1767, BdG, Ms. fr. 2486.

31. Clavière to Jean-André Deluc, 3 February 1773, 3 March 1773, 25 June 1773, 10 September 1773 and 21 December 1773, BdG, Ms. fr. 2463, fols 85–112; Jean Bouchary, 'Étienne Clavière d'après sa correspondance financière et politique', in *Les manieurs d'argent à Paris à la fin du XVIIIe siècle* (Paris: M. Rivière, 1939–43), 3 vols, I, 13–20.

32. Gür, 'Quête de la richesse', 97–115.

33. Clavière to Jean-André Deluc, 6 March 1774, BdG, Ms. fr. 2463, fols 96–9.

34. Clavière to Jean-André Deluc, 17 April 1774, BdG, Ms. fr. 2463, fols 100–8.

35. James Hutton to William Petty, 2nd Earl of Shelburne, 6 February 1767, *CC*, XXXII, 282–3.

36. Jean-Paul Marat, *Nouvelle dénonciation de M. Marat, L'Ami du peuple, contre M. Necker, premier ministre des Finances, ou Supplément à la dénonciation d'un citoyen contre un agent de l'autorité* (Paris: Rozé, 1791), 6 and *Lettres de Marat aux Jacobins frères et amis, 19 avril 1793* (Paris: Société des Amis de la liberté, 1791), 7.

37. Jacques-Pierre Brissot to François d'Ivernois, 12 April 1782, BdG, Ms. suppl. 1010, fol. 12.

38. Jacques-Pierre Brissot de Warville, *Mémoires, 1754–1793*, ed. Cl. Perroud (Paris: Alphonse Picard, 1912), 2 vols, II, 28–9; I, 294–6. Further portraits of Clavière as 'un honnête et vertueux citoyen' can be found in J.-P. Brissot de Warville, *J.-P. Brissot, Correspondance et Papiers*, ed. Cl. Perroud (Paris: A. Picard & fils, 1911), p. 108; Étienne Clavière and Jacques-Pierre Brissot de Warville, *De la France et des États-Unis, ou De l'importance de la révolution de l'Amérique pour le bonheur de la France* (London: n. p., 1787), 28.

39. Jean Roget to Samuel Romilly, 1 February 1783, in Jean Roget, *Lettres de Jean Roget 1780–1783*, ed. F.-F. Roget (Geneva, Basle and Paris: Georg & Co. & Fischbacher, 1911), 297–301.

40. Ian Simpson Ross, *The Life of Adam Smith* (Oxford: Oxford University Press, 2010), 2nd edn, 129–31, 267.

41. Adam Smith to David Hume, 9 May 1775, in Adam Smith, *The Correspondence of Adam Smith*, ed. Ernest Campbell Mossner et al. (Oxford: Oxford University Press, 1987), 181–2.

42. Charles Du Bois-Melly, *Les moeurs génevoises de 1700 à 1760, d'après tous les documents officiels, pour servir d'introduction à l'histoire de la République et Seigneurie de Genève* (Geneva and Basle: H. Georg, 1892), 2nd edn, 331–7.

43. August Gottlieb Spangenberg, *The life of Nicholas Lewis, Count Zinzendorf, Bishop and Ordinary of the Church of the United (or Moravian) Brethren*, trans. Samuel Jackson (London: Samuel Holdsworth, 1838), 282–7, 474–5; Ami Bost, *History of the Bohemian and Moravian brethren* (London: Religious Tract Society, 1848), 3rd edn, 358–62.

44. Colin Podmore, *The Moravian Church in England, 1728–1760* (Oxford: Oxford University Press, 1998), 34–81.

45. James Hutton to Johannes de Watterville, 25 February 1767, in Daniel Benham, *Memoirs of James Hutton* (London: Hamilton Adams, 1856), 425–7.

46. Colin J. Podmore, 'Hutton, James (1715–1795)', *ODNB*.

47. *The memoirs of Charles-Lewis, baron de Pollnitz: Being the observations he made in his late travels from Prussia thro' Germany, Italy, France* (London: Daniel Swann, 1737), 200–1; Peter Adolph Winkopp, *Neuestes Staats-, Zeitungs-, Reise-, Post- und Handlungs-Lexikon oder geographisch-historisch-statistisches Handbuch von allen fünf Theilen Erbe* (Leipzig: Kleefeld, 1804), 121.

48. Édouard Chapuisat, 'Étienne Clavière', in *Figures et choses d'autrefois* (Paris and Geneva: Crès & Georg, 1920), 12–13.

49. Clavière to Jean-André Deluc, 6 March 1774, BdG, Ms. fr. 2463, fols 85–112.

50. Gür, 'Quête de la richesse', 97–115.

51. Étienne Clavière, *Reflexions politiques sur l'impôt proposé au Conseil Général* (26 December 1775), 14–16.

52. Étienne Clavière to Jean-André Deluc, 16–19 June 1774, BdG, Ms. fr 2463, fols 106–8.

53. See the 'Tableau des Constitutionnaires' described in Hippolyte Aubert, 'Les troubles de Genève en 1781 et 1782. Extrait des papiers de Perrinet des Franches conservés aux Archives Nationales de France', *Bulletin de la Societé d'Histoire at d'Archéologie de Genève*, 3 (1913), 420–1, n. 1.

54. Anon., *Très-humble et très-respectueuse Réquisition, Addressée au Mag. Petit*

Conseil par les membres Constitutionnaires du Magnifique Conseil des Deux-Cent. Remise par eux à Messieurs les Syndics le 9 Novembre 1780. Et appuyée par un grand nombre de Citoyens & Bourgeois ([Geneva]: n. p., 1780), 13–24, 40–2.

55. Anon. [Jean-Jacques Gautier], *Mémoire instructif sur les dissentions actuelles de la République de Genève* (Geneva: n. p., 1779], 70–1; Anon., *Réflexions Sur La Commission Conciliatrice Et sur les motifs qui l'ont fait réjetter* ([Geneva], n. p., [1780]), 3; Anon., *Très-humble et très-respectueuse déclaration, Remise à Messieurs les Syndics, au nom d'un très-grand nombre de Membres du Magnifique Conseil des Deux-Cent, le Dimanche soir 16 Janvier 1780* ([Geneva], n. p., [1780]); Anon., *À l'Auteur D'une Lettre prétendue écrite du Purgatoire* (Geneva: n. p., 1780), 4–7; Anon., *Très-humble et très-respectueuse Réquisition des membres Constitutionnaires du Magnifique Conseil des Deux-Cent, Addressée au Mag. Petit Conseil, Et remise à Messieurs les Syndics le 18 Mars 1780* (Geneva: n. p., 1780).

56. Anon., *Les Bigarrures, ou Récapitulation de plusieurs Brochures* ([Geneva]: n. p., [1780]), 16 November 1780 1–2.

57. Anon., *Le Code naturel, ou le rêve d'un bon citoyen* ([Geneva]: n. p., [1780]), 3, 9.

58. Anon., *Très-humble et très-respectueuse Réquisition, Addressée au Mag. Petit Conseil, par les membres du Magnifique Conseil des Deux-Cent et par les citoyens et bouregois Constitutionnaires. Remise à Messieurs les Syndics le 21 Novembre 1780* ([Geneva]: n. p., 1780), 3–7; *Très-humble et très-respectueuse Réquisition, Addressée au Mag. Petit Conseil, par les membres du Magnifique Conseil des Deux-Cent et par les citoyens et bouregois Constitutionnaires. Remise à Messieurs les Syndics le 7 Décembre 1780* ([Geneva]: n. p., 1780), 3–8.

59. Anon., *Seconde réponse aux deuxième, troisième & quatrième lettres d'un représentant qui cesse de paroître modéré* ([Geneva]: n. p., 1780), 18 December, 3–8.

60. Isaac Cornuaud, *Lettre d'un natif à un bourgeois de ses amis*, Geneva: n. p., 28 March 1777) and *Examen politico-patriotique des questions suivantes* (Geneva, 3 May 1777).

61. Anon. [Isaac Cornuaud], *Suite du natif patriote* ([Geneva]: n. p., 1780), 13 and *Lettre à l'Auteur des considérations sur l'état des natifs* (Geneva: n. p., 1780), 24–7; Isaac Cornuaud, *Mémoires de Isaac Cornuaud sur Genève et la Révolution de 1770 à 1795, publiés avec notice biographique, notes et table des noms par Mlle Émilie Cherbuliez* (Geneva: A. Jullien, 1912), 142–5, 174–6, 181, 189.

62. Anon. [Cornuaud], *Seconde adresse aux membres du comité des représentans* (Geneva: n. p., 1781), 3.

63. Anon. [Cornuaud], *Le Natif Interrogé, ou Confession morali-politique d'un patriote* (Geneva: n. p., 1781), 6–7, 26–32.

64. Cornuaud, *Mémoires de Isaac Cornuaud*, 155–158.

65. Jacques Mallet du Pan, *Idées soumises à l'examen de tous les conciliateurs, par un médiateur sans consequence* ([Geneva: n. p., 1780), 5, 10.

66. Ibid., 10–11.

67. Ibid., 12–15.

68. Ibid., 19–28.

69. Ibid., 29–30.

70. Ibid., 33–4, 47.

71. On Vergennes, see Munro Price, *Preserving the Monarchy: The Comte de Vergennes, 1774–1787* (Cambridge: Cambridge University Press, 1995).

72. Pierre-Michel Hennin to Charles Gravier, comte de Vergennes, 26 December 1774, in Voltaire, *Correspondence and Related Documents: XLI: June 1774–April 1775, letters D18968–D19448*, ed. Theodore Besterman (Banbury and Oxford: Institut et Musée Voltaire & Voltaire Foundation, 1975), 264–5 (Letter D19255).

73. Aubert, 'Les troubles de Genève en 1781 et 1782', 418–41, 418 n. 2.

74. François d'Ivernois, *Tableau historique et politique des deux dernières révolutions de Genève* (London: n. p., 1789), 2 vols, I, 108.

75. Cornuaud, *Mémoires de Isaac Cornuaud*, 234–40.

76. Anon., *Lettres genevoises*, 75–6; Voltaire to Pierre-Michel Hennin, 16 February 1770, in Voltaire, *Correspondence and Related Documents: XXXVI: February–December 1770, letters D16127–D16678*, ed. Theodore Besterman (Geneva, Banbury and Oxford: Institut et Musée Voltaire & Voltaire Foundation, 1975), 32–3 (Letter D16155); Pierre-Michel Hennin to Voltaire, 21 February 1770, in ibid., 49–50 (Letter D16175). See further, Albert Choisy, 'La prise d'armes de 1770 contre les natifs', *Étrennes genevoises* (1925), 47–77.

77. Voltaire, *Correspondence and Related Documents: XXXVI*, ed. Besterman: Pierre-Michel Hennin to César Gabriel de Choiseul, duc de Praslin, 25 May 1770, 484–5 (Letter D.app.325.III); Pierre-Michel Hennin to Voltaire, 16 February 1770, 29–30 (Letter D16151); Pierre-Michel Hennin to Voltaire, 17 June 1770, 259–60 (Letter D16421).

78. Jacques Mallet du Pan, *Compte rendu de la défense des Citoyens Bourgeois de Genève, addressé aux Commissaires des Citoyens Représentants* (Geneva: n. p., 1771); Cornuaud, *Mémoires de Isaac Cornuaud*, 113.

79. Jacques Mallet du Pan, *Memoirs and correspondence of Mallet du Pan, illustrative of the history of the French Revolution*, ed. André Sayous, (London: Richard Bentley, 1852), 2 vols, I, 18–20.

80. Étienne Clavière to Jean-André Deluc, 31 December 1775, BdG, Ms. fr 2463, fols 110–11.

81. Jean Gosse to Henri-Albert Gosse, 19 December 1779, in Danielle Plan, *Un Génevois d'autrefois: Henri-Albert Gosse (1753–1816) d'après des lettres et des documents inédits* (Paris and Geneva: Fischbaker and Kundig, 1909), 107–8.

82. Jean Roget to Samuel Romilly, January 1782, in Roget, *Lettres de Jean Roget*, ed. Roget, 124.

83. R. A. Leigh, *Unsolved Problems in the Bibliography of J-J. Rousseau* (Cambridge: Cambridge University Press, 1990), 114–46.

84. Jean Gosse to Henri-Albert Gosse, 12 May 1779, in Plan, *Un Génevois d'autrefois*, 71.

85. Jean Roget to Samuel Romilly, 23 January 1782, in Roget, *Lettres de Jean Roget*, ed. Roget, 136.

86. Étienne Clavière, 'Lettre à son excellence monsieur Le Comte de Vergennes, Du 21 Février 1780', *Pièces justificatives pour messieurs Du Roveray & Clavière* ([Geneva]: n. p., 1780), 5, 19, 48.

87. Cornuaud, *Mémoires de Isaac Cornuaud*, 323.

88. Clavière, 'Lettre à son excellence monsieur Le Comte de Vergennes', 51.

89. Ibid., 51–2.

90. Ibid., 52.

91. Ibid., 53.

92. Ibid., 54.

93. Marc-Théodore Bourrit to Clavière, 12 August 1781, in Chapuisat, 'Étienne Clavière', 24–6.

94. 'Lettre de M. de Vergennes à l. l. e. e. de Zurich, de Versailles le 25 juin, 1780', in *Révolution et troubles de Genève*, St Andrews Special Collections, fols 30–6.

95. Anon. [Cornuaud], *Réponse à Monsieur B., Secrétaire du Cercle de la Liberté des Représentans* (Geneva: n. p., 1781), 4.

96. Jean Roget to Samuel Romilly, 19 May 1780, in Roget, *Lettres de Jean Roget*, ed. Roget, 8.

97. Walker, 'Les pratiques de la richesse, 135–60.

98. Grégoire Favet, *Les syndics de Genève au XVIIIe siècle. Étude du personnel politique de la République* (Geneva: Droz, 1998).

99. Jean Roget to Samuel Romilly, 22 November 1780, in Roget, *Lettres de Jean Roget*, ed. Roget, 26.

100. Chapuisat, 'Étienne Clavière', in *Figures et choses*, 21–2.

101. Théodore Rilliet, *Lettres sur l'emprunt et l'impôt* ([Geneva]: n. p., 1779); Béla Kapossy, 'Genevan Creditors and English Liberty: The Example of Théodore Rilliet de Saussure', in Valérie Cossy, Béla Kapossy and Richard Whatmore (eds), *Genève, lieu d'Angleterre, 1725–1814* (Geneva: Slatkine, 2009), 169–84.

102. Étienne Clavière to Jean-André Deluc, 6 March 1774, BdG, Ms. fr. 2463, fols 96–9; Étienne Clavière to Jean-André Deluc, 17 April 1774, BdG, Ms. fr. 2463, fols 100–4.

103. Jacques-Antoine Du Roveray, *Très-humble et très-respectueuse représentation, remise aux seigneurs sindics et à monsieur le procureur-général, le 20 Octobre 1780, par les citoyens & bourgeois représentans* (Geneva: n. p., 1780), 1–6, 16, 20, 27, 30–1, 35, 44, 51.

104. Jacques-Antoine Du Roveray, *Remonstrance faite dans le Magnifique Petit Conseil, le 15 Novembre 1780, par monsieur le procureur-général, au sujet de la représentation remis aux seigneurs sindics & à lui . . . le 20 Octobre 1780* (Geneva: n. p., 1780), 8–11, 33–43, 48, 55.

105. Anon., *Très-humble et très-respectueuse Déclaration Des Citoyens & Bourgeois Représentans. Rémise aux Seigneurs Syndics, & à M. le Procureur-Général, le 23 Nov. 1780, par environ 1040 Citoyens ou Bourgeois* (Geneva: n. p., 1780), 4–7.

106. François d'Ivernois, *Lettre à son excellence le Comte de Vergennes* ([Geneva]: [1780]), 4; *Considérations d'un citoyen de Genève, Sur la Garantie, accordée, en 1738, à la République de Genève, par la France & les L. L. Cantons de Zurich & de Berne* ([Geneva]: [1780]), 20–1; *Lettre à Madame **** ([Geneva]: [1780]), 1–9; *Réflexions impartiales, Sur l'État actuel de la République de Geneve* ([Geneva]: [1780]), 34–7; *La Loi de la réélection* ([Geneva]: [1780]), 53–5.

107. Anon., *Le patriotism devoilé* ([Geneva]: n. p., 1780), 5, 22–5.

108. Jacques-Antoine Du Roveray, *Fameuse Remonstrance faite dans le Magnifique Petit Conseil de la République de Genève, le 11 Décembre 1780* (London: P. Elmsly & J. Sewel, 1781), 6–12.

109. Ibid., 13.

110. Ibid., 20–5.

111. Ibid., 28–34.

112. Ibid., 38–9.

113. Ibid., 41–5.

114. Anon., *Très-humble et très-respectueuse addresse de plusieurs Citoyens et Bourgeois au Mag. Petit Conseil, Remise aux Seigneurs Syndics le 11 Décembre 1780* ([Geneva]: n. p., [1780]), 12.

115. Vergennes to the Cantons of Zurich and of Bern, 24 December 1780, BdG, Ms. fr. 2476, 105–6; Vergennes to Gabard de Vaux, 30 December 1780, BdG, Ms. fr. 2476, 107; Extrait des Regîtres du Conseil du 17 Janvier 1781, BdG, Ms. fr. 2476, 110.

116. Jean Roget to Samuel Romilly, 13 January 1781 and 20 January 1781, in Roget, *Lettres de Jean Roget*, ed. Roget, 34–7, 39–44.

117. Frederick the Great to the Cantons of Zurich and of Bern, 30 January 1781, BdG, Ms. fr. 2476, 125.

118. Anon. [Ami Lullin], *Très-humble et très-respectueuse récquisition des membres Constitutionnaires du magnifique Conseil des Deux-Cent, addressée au Mag. Petit Conseil. Remise au Seigneur Premier-Syndic le 12 janvier 1781* ([Geneva]: n. p., 1781), 3–6.

119. Anon., *Note Remise le 13 Mai 1781 à Monsieur le Premier Syndic, par les Seigneurs représentans de Zurich et de Berne* ([Geneva]: n. p., 1781).

120. Alexandre Guillot, 'Du rôle politique de la Compagnie des Pasteurs de Genève dans les événements de 1781 et 1782', in *Étrennes religieuses*, new series (Geneva: Kündig, 1894), 231–78.

121. Cantons of Zurich and of Bern to Vergennes, 17 February 1781 and 31 March 1781, BdG, Ms. fr. 2476, 116, 134; Vergennes to the Cantons of Zurich and of Bern, 8 March 1780, BdG, Ms. fr. 2476, 123–4.

122. Vergennes, *Lettre de son excellence Monsieur le Comte de Vergennes, Ministre & Secretaire d'Etat au département des affaires étrangers. Aux Sindics et Conseil de la Ville & la République de Genève* (Versailles, [10 April] 1781), 1–2.

123. Perrinet des Franches to Marc Cramer, 22 April 1781, in Aubert, 'Les troubles de Genève en 1781 et 1782', 424–6.

124. Cornuaud to 1st syndic Barthélemy Rilliet, 1 March 1781, BdG, Ms. fr. 2476, 120–2.

125. Jean-André Deluc, *Mémoire remis le 21 Août 1781, a monsieur le Comte de Vergennes par J.-A. Deluc, comme étant le sommaire de ce qu'il avoit eu l'honneur d'exposer à son excellence dans des audiences précédentes. Journal de ce qui s'est passé d'intéressant à Genève à la fin de 1767 et au commencement de 1768, pour servir à l'histoire de l'Edit du 11e mars 1768* (Geneva: n. p., 1781), 5–11.

126. Anon. [Jean-André Deluc], *Journal de ce qui s'est passé d'intéressant à Genève à la fin de 1767 et au commencement de 1768, pour servir à l'histoire de l'Edit du 11e mars 1768.*

127. Isaac Cornuaud, *Examen du mémoire remis à S. E. M. le comte de Vergennes, le 21 août 1781, par M. J.-A. Deluc, ancien demagogue de la Bourgeoisie* (Geneva: [15 September] 1781) and *Mémoires de Isaac Cornuaud*, 318.

128. Jean Roget to Samuel Romilly, 3 October and 6 October 1781, in Roget, *Lettres de Jean Roget*, ed. Roget, 70–3; Cornuaud, *Mémoires de Isaac Cornuaud*, 295–8; Vergennes to the Cantons of Zurich and of Bern, 28 February 1781, BdG, Ms. fr. 2476, 117.

129. Jean Roget to Samuel Romilly, 1 December 1781, in Roget, *Lettres de Jean Roget*, ed. Roget, 98–104, 106; Jean Bénétruy, *L'Atelier de Mirabeau. Quatre proscrits genevois dans la tourmente révolutionnaire* (Geneva: Alex Jullien, 1962), 19.

130. Isaac Cornuaud, *Troisième adresse aux membres du Comité des Représentants* (Ferney: [15 November] 1781); *Cinquième adresse aux membres du Comité des Représentants* (Ferney: [15 January] 1781); *Septième adresse aux membres du Comité des Représentants* (Ferney: [17 February] 1782).

131. Perrinet des Franches to Marc Cramer, 9 September 1781, in Aubert, 'Les troubles de Genève en 1781 et 1782', 426–8 and the correspondence described in 427n.

132. Perrinet des Franches to Marc Cramer, 30 September 1781, in ibid., 428.

133. Marc Cramer to Perrinet des Franches, 9 October 1781, and Perrinet Des Franches to Marc Cramer, 4 November 1781, in ibid., 429, 432.

134. Anon. [Isaac Cornuaud and/or Joseph Des Arts], *Essai sur les considérations d'un patriote* (Geneva: n. p., 1781), 20–31.

135. Anon., *Très-humble et très-respectueuse déclaration, présentée au Mag. Petit-Conseil par les membres du Magnifique Conseil des Deux-Cent et des Citoyens et Bourgeois Constitutionnaires; addressée au Mag. Petit Conseil et remise à Messieurs les Syndics le 29 Octobre 1781* ([Geneva]: n. p., 1781), 39–43.

136. Anon., *Très-humble et très-respectueuse déclaration des membres du Magnifique Conseil des Deux-Cent et des Citoyens et Bourgeois Constitutionnaires; addressée au Mag. Petit Conseil et remise à Messieurs les Syndics le 26 Décembre 1781* ([Geneva]: n. p., 1781), 3–5.

137. Jean-Marie Roland de la Platière to Henri-Albert Gosse, 26 November 1781, in Plan, *Un Génevois d'autrefois*, 121.

138. Anon., *Très-humble et très-respectueuse représentation des Citoyens & Bourgeois représentans. Rémise aux Seigneurs Syndics, & à M. le Procureur-Général, le 24 Septembre 1781* (Geneva: n. p., 1781), 3–12.

139. Jacques-Antoine Du Roveray, *Très-humble et très-respectueuse représentation des citoyens et bourgeois représentans. Remise aux Seigneurs Sindics, & à Monsieur le Procureur Général, le 24 Octobre 1781* (Geneva: n. p., 1781).

140. Clavière to Henry Ziegler, 14 December 1781, Clavière to Diodati, 14 January 1782, Archives nationales (France), T//646/1.

141. Ibid.

142. François d'Ivernois, *Offrande à la liberté et à la paix; par un citoyen de Genève; ou idées de conciliation adressées à Mr. J. A. De Luc, en réfutation Du Mémoire qu'il remit le 21 Aoust 1781, à Monsieur le Comte de Vergennes* (Geneva: n. p., 1781), 19–26.

143. François-Joseph Rey and Jean-Pierre Raccaud, *Lettre d'un membre de la communauté de Fribourg en Suisse* ([Geneva]: n. p., 1781); Du Roveray's involvement in the composition of this pamphlet is unclear, but hundreds of copies were printed at Geneva through Du Roveray and Clavière. See 'Imprimeurs de Genève et Carouge au service des proscrits fribourgois (1781–1790)': Georges Andrey, 'Recherches sur la littérature politique relative aux troubles de Fribourg durant les années 1780'; Marc Neuenschwander, 'Solidaires et complices: Les gouvernements de Genève et de Fribourg à la poursuite des séditieux', both in Jean-Daniel Candaux et Bernard Lescaze (eds), *Cinq siècles d'imprimerie genevoise. Actes du Colloque international*

sur l'histoire de imprimerie et du livre à Genève, 27–30 avril 1978 (Geneva: Société d'histoire et d'archéologie, 1980–81), 2 vols, II, 115–56, 157–84.

144. Anon., *Très-humble et très-respectueuse représentation des Citoyens & Bourgeois représentans. Contenant les preuves de la légalité de l'edit de 1768. Tirées des faits, des Actes de tous les Conseils de la République, & des Déclarations même des négatifs. Rémise aux Seigneurs Syndics, & à M. le Procureur-Général, le 10 Décembre 1781* (Geneva: n. p., 1781), 16–27.

145. Jean-Pierre Bérénger, *Considérations sur l'édit du 10 février 1781* (Geneva: n. p., 1781), 6–16, 28–35, 54–60.

146. Chapuisat, *La prise d'armes*, 14.

Chapter 6. Revolution and Exodus

1. Anon., *Très-humble et très-respectueuse représentation des Citoyens & Bourgeois représentans, dans laquelle on réfute la partie de la Déclaration des Négatifs du 29e 8bre 1781, Qui traite de la prise d'armes & de l'Edit du mois de Février 1781. Suivie de notes essentielles sur la Souveraineté du Conseil Général. Rémise aux Seigneurs Syndics, et à M. le Procureur-Général, par la Généralité des Citoyens & Bourgeois Représentans, le 18e Mars 1782* (Geneva: n. p., 1782) 14–22, 44–8, 65, 75–81.

2. J.B.G. Galiffe, *D'un siècle à l'autre: Correspondances inédites entre gens connus et inconnus du XVIIIe et du XIXe siècle* (Geneva: Sandoz, 1877), 2 vols, I, 113–32.

3. Edouard Dufour, *Jacob Vernes, 1728–1791. Essai sur sa vie et sa controverse apologétique avec J.-J. Rousseau* (Geneva: W. Kündig, 1898), 13, 28.

4. Marguerite Maire, 'Le *Discours sur l'Histoire de Genève* de Jacob Vernes', *Revue suisse d'histoire*, 11 (1931), 1–43.

5. Jacob Vernes, *Catéchisme destiné particulièrement à l'usage des jeunes-gens* (Geneva: Du Villard, 1781), 112–13. See further, Maria-Cristina Pitassi, 'Le catéchisme de Jacob Vernes ou comment enseigner aux fidèles un "christianisme sage et raisonnable"', *Dix-huitième siècle*, 34 (2002), 213–23.

6. Anon., *Précis historique de la dernière révolution de Genève; Et en particulier de la Réforme que le Souverain de cette République a faite dans les Conseils Administrateurs* (Geneva: n. p., 1782), 11.

7. Clavière to François d'Ivernois, 9 October 1781, BdG, Ms. suppl. 1010, fol. 126.

8. Clavière to Théodore Bourrit, 4 February 1782, in Chapuisat, 'Étienne Clavière', 30–2.

9. Ibid.

10. Réné-Louis Brière to Georges-Pierre du Pan de Saussure, 12 April 1782, in Chapuisat, *La prise d'armes*, 212.

11. Clavière to Théodore Bourrit, 15 February 1782, in Chapuisat, 'Étienne Clavière', 32–6.

12. 'Registres de conseil', 18 January, 1777, 24 June, 1777, 2 November, 1781, in Théodore de Grenus, *Fragments biographiques et historiques extraits des Registres du Conseil d'État de la République de Genève* (Geneva: Cherbuliez, 1815), 360, 365.

13. Jacob Tronchin to Antoine Saladin de Crans, in Chapuisat, *La prise d'armes*, 13.

14. Charles Bonnet to Johann Heinrich Samuel Formey, 15 February 1765, 14 January 1767, in André Bandelier and Frédéric S. Eigeldinger (eds), *Lettres de Genève (1741–1793) à Jean Henri Samuel Formey* (Paris: Honoré Champion, 2010), 657–8, 713–14.

15. Charles Bonnet to Alexander Viktor Thormann, 9 January 1768, *CC*, XXXV, 21–2.

16. Charles Bonnet, 'Lettre au sujet de discours de M. J. J. Rousseau', in *Œuvres d'histoire naturelle et de philosophie* (Neuchâtel: Fauche, 1779–83), 8 vols, VIII, 336–67.

17. Jean-Jacques Burlamaqui, *Principes du droit politique* (Amsterdam: Zacharie Chatelain, 1751), 2 vols, I, 158–81.

18. Jean-Jacques Burlamaqui, *Principes du droit natural. Principes du droit politique* (Geneva: C. A. Philibert, 1763), 2 vols.

19. Jacob Vernet to Johann Heinrich Samuel Formey, 19 June 1767, 12 March 1769, in Bandelier and Eigeldinger (eds), *Lettres de Genève*, 733, 771.

20. Fabri d'Aire-la-Ville to Perrinet des Franches, 5 January 1782, in Aubert, 'Les troubles de Genève en 1781 et 1782', 423.

21. Perrinet des Franches to Marc Cramer, 6 December 1781, in ibid., 433.

22. Vasserot de Vincy-Turrettini to Perrinet des Franches, 7 December 1781, in ibid., 433–4

23. Chapuisat, *La prise d'armes*, 18, 22, 24, 30–1.

24. 'Registres de conseil', 9 April 1782, in de Grenus, *Fragments biographiques et historiques*, 366.

25. Marc Neuenschwander, 'Carrière et convictions', in Neuenschwander, Bernard Lescaze and Gabriel Mützenberg, *Un Genevois méconnu: Julien Dentand (1736–1817)* (Geneva: Bulletin de la Société d'histoire et d'archéologie de Genève, vol. 16, Book 2, 1977), 137–61.

26. Saconay to Perrinet des Franches, 12 April 1782 and the reply of 19 April 1782, in Aubert, 'Les troubles de Genève en 1781 et 1782', 435–6.

27. Chapuisat, 'Étienne Clavière', 44.

28. M. de Châtillon fils to Perrinet des Franches, 15 April 1782, in Aubert, 'Les troubles de Genève en 1781 et 1782', 440.

29. Chapuisat, *La prise d'armes*, 68–70.

30. Ibid., 52–3.

31. Ibid., 66.

32. Charles Gravier, comte de Vergennes *Lettre de son excellence Mr Le Comte de Vergennes, ministre des affaires étrangères aux syndics et conseil de la ville et république de Genève. A Versailles le 15 Avril 1782* (Geneva: n. p., 1782).

33. Chapuisat, *La prise d'armes*, 39–40, 43–6.

34. Guillot, 'Du rôle politique de la Compagnie des Pasteurs'.

35. Chapuisat, *La prise d'armes*, 49.

36. Henri-Albert Gosse to Jean-Marie Roland de la Platière, 16 March 1782, in Plan, *Un Génevois d'autrefois*, 123.

37. Charles Dardier, *Ésaïe Gasc, citoyen de Genève: sa politique et sa théologie, Genève—Constance—Montauban 1748–1813* (Paris: Sandoz & Fischbacher, 1876), 81.

38. Jean Roget to Samuel Romilly, 27 April 1782, in Roget, *Lettres de Jean Roget*, ed. Roget, 204.

39. Chapuisat, 'Étienne Clavière', 45–6.

40. Jacques Mallet du Pan, *Mémoires et correspondance de Mallet du Pan: pour servir à l'histoire de la Révolution française*, ed. Pierre-André Sayous (Paris: J. Cherbuliez, 1851), 2 vols, I, 72.

41. Thourel, *Histoire de Genève*, III, 285.

42. Henri-Albert Gosse to Jean-Marie Roland de la Platière, 3 May 1782, and Jean-Marie Roland de la Platière to Henri-Albert Gosse, 17 May 1782, in Plan, *Un Génevois d'autrefois*, 123–5.

43. For British diplomatic links with Europe more broadly, see Jennifer Mori, *The Culture of Diplomacy: Britain in Europe, c. 1750–1830* (Manchester: Manchester University Press, 2010).

44. Jean Roget to Samuel Romilly, 20 June 1782, in Roget, *Lettres de Jean Roget*, ed. Roget, 237.

45. Comte Isaac Pictet, 'Mémoire particulière pour My Lord Mountstuart', 4 December 1781, BdG, Ms. suppl. 32, fols 169–74.

46. D'Ivernois to Mount Stuart, 14 May 1782, BdG, Ms. suppl. 32, fols 351–2.

47. D'Ivernois to Charles James Fox, 14 May 1782, BdG, Ms. suppl. 32, fol. 353.

48. Jean Roget to Samuel Romilly, 10 August 1781, in Roget, *Lettres de Jean Roget*, ed. Roget, 64.

49. D'Ivernois to Mount Stuart, 4 June 1782, BdG, Ms. suppl. 32, fols 355–61.

50. D'Ivernois to Mount Stuart, 11 June 1782, BdG, Ms. suppl. 32, fols 362–3.

51. 'British and Foreign History', *The New annual register, or, General repository of history, politics, and littérature for the year 1782*, ed. Andrew Kippis (London: G. Robinson, 1783), 63–4.

52. D'Ivernois, *Tableau historique*, 254. Translations are from d'Ivernois, *An Historical and Political View of the Constitution and Revolutions of Geneva in the eighteenth century* (London: T. Cadell, 1784), 239.

53. Chapuisat, *La prise d'armes*, 75–80.

54. Anon., *Lettre adressée aux Magnifiques, puissans, et très-honorés seigneurs, les Seigneurs Bourguemaitre, Petit & Grand Conseils de la Ville & République de Zurich, et les Seigneurs Avoyer, Petit & Grand Conseils de la Ville & République de Berne, par les Citoyens & Bourgeois représentans de la ville & république de Genève. Suivie d'une addresse aux Seigneurs Syndics de la Ville & République de Genève, a eux rémise, le 9 Mai 1782* (Geneva: n. p., 1782), 28–38.

55. Anon., *Traduction d'une lettre du Louable Canton de Berne, Adressé aux Seigneurs Syndics* (Geneva: n. p., 1782), 4.

56. Chapuisat, *La prise d'armes*, 80–90.

57. Pierre Morren, *La vie lausannoise au 18 siècle: d'après Jean Henri Polier de Vernand, lieutenant Baillival* (Geneva: Labor et Fides, 1970), 240–7.

58. Anon. [,Isaac Cornuaud, Paul-Henri Mallet and Jean-Louis Micheli du Crest], *Rélation de la conjuration contre le gouvernement et le magistrat de Genève; qui a éclaté le 8 Avril 1782* (Geneva: n. p., 1782), 20–35.

59. Anon., *Très-humble et très-respectueuse déclaration des Citoyens & Bourgeois*

représentans. Rémise aux Seigneurs Syndics, & à M. le Procureur-Général, le 31 Mai 1782 (Geneva: n. p., 1782), 3–8.

60. Anon. [Isaac Cornuaud], *Pièces relatives aux troubles actuels de Genève* (Geneva: n. p., 1782), 30–45.

61. Pierre-Alexandre du Peyrou to Pierre Boin, 2 May 1782, BdG, Ms. suppl. 1010, fols 34–5.

62. Pierre-Alexandre du Peyrou to d'Ivernois, 16 May 1782, BdG, Ms. suppl. 1010, fol. 40.

63. D'Ivernois to Mount Stuart, 14 June 1782, BdG, Ms. suppl. 32, fol. 366.

64. D'Ivernois to Mount Stuart, 26 June 1782, BdG, Ms. suppl. 32, fol. 368; Dardier, *Ésaïe Gasc, citoyen de Genève*, 84.

65. Dardier, ibid., 82.

66. Chapuisat, *La prise d'armes*, 93–111.

67. 'Extract of a letter from *Neuchâtel* in Switzerland, July 16', *Parker's General Advertiser and Morning Intelligencer* (London), 5 August 1782.

68. Chapuisat, 'Étienne Clavière', 47.

69. Chapuisat, *La prise d'armes*, 111–15.

70. 'Court Exposé de ce qui s'est passé à Genève depuis l'Entrée des Troupes Le mardi 2nd Juillet 1782', 'Journal d'Ami Dunant', BdG, Ms. fr. 901, fol. 5r.

71. Dardier, *Ésaïe Gasc, citoyen de Genève*, 78.

72. Ibid., 85.

73. Chapuisat, *La prise d'armes*, 122–5.

74. Jacob de Chapeaurouge to Perrinet des Franches, 19 July 1782, in Aubert, 'Les troubles de Genève en 1781 et 1782', 440–1.

75. Guillaume-Joseph Saige to d'Ivernois, 17 June 1783, BdG, Ms. suppl. 1010, fol. 116.

76. Chapuisat, *La prise d'armes*, 130.

77. Anon., *Lettres genevoises*, 39, 72.

78. Marc Rigaud, *Lettres d'un constitutionnaire de Genève, sur les troubles de sa patrie, écrites à un ami à Paris; avec les pièces justificatives* (Neuchâtel: n. p., 1782), 34–5.

79. François-Xavier de Feller (ed.), *Journal historique et littéraire*, June 1782, 258.

80. Chapuisat, *La prise d'armes*, 134.

81. Anon., *Édit du 21 Novembre 1782. Extrait des registres du conseil des 5, 6, 11, 12, 13 & 14 Novembre 1782* ([Geneva]: n. p., 1782).

82. Chapuisat, *La prise d'arm*, 137–53.

83. 'Letter of the Mediating powers to the government of Geneva, 21st November 1782', in Jean-Louis Soulavie, *Historical and Political Memoirs of the Reign of Lewis XVI. From his marriage to his death* (London: G. & J. Robinson, 1802), 6 vols, V, 246–7; 'Extract of a letter from Geneva, November 29th', *The Morning Herald and Daily Advertiser* (London), 24 December 1782 (issue 672); Thourel, *Histoire de Genève*, III, 310.

84. Lullin de Chateauvieux to Hennin, 5 July 1782, cited in Karmin, *Sir Francis d'Ivernois*, 103 n. 2.

85. Dardier, *Ésaïe Gasc, citoyen de Genève*, 97–9.

86. 'Registres de conseil', 2 July, 30 October, 16–20 November, 25–26 November 1782, in de Grenus, *Fragments biographiques et historiques*, 366–8.

87. Anon. [Jacob Vernet], *Prière qui a été lue dans les Temples de la Ville de Genève, le Jeudi 21 Novembre 1782. Jour auquel l'Edit de Pacification avoit été accepté en Conseil-Général* (Geneva: Barthelemi-Chirol, 1782); Anon., *Collection des Édits Civils, Revus en 1713, Auxquels il n'a pas été dérogé par l'Edit de Pacification. Faite en exécution de l'Article VIII du Titre XVII de l'Edit de Pacification* (Geneva: Jean-Léonard Pellet, 1783).

88. Chapuisat, *La prise d'armes*, 221–3. A copy of the *Colporteur Genevois* exists in the French diplomatic archives, and the French government may well have collected it or sponsored its distribution: I owe this information to Louise Seaward.

89. 'Extract of a letter from *Neuchâtel*', *Parker's General Advertiser and Morning Intelligencer*, 5 August 1782.

90. Pierre-Alexandre du Peyrou to d'Ivernois, 26 May 1783, BdG, Ms. suppl. 1010, fols 49–50.

91. Marie-Jeanne Phlippon, Madame Roland, 'Voyage en Suisse', *Œuvres de M. J. PH. Roland, femme de l'ex-Ministre de l'Intérieur, . . . précédées d'un Discours préliminaire, par L.-A. Champagneux* (Paris: Bidault, An XIII [1800]), 3 vols, III, 288–9.

92. Ibid., 290–1.

93. D'Ivernois, *An Historical and Political View*, 111.

94. Ibid., 158n.

95. Jean Roget to Samuel Romilly, 29 June 1782, in Roget, *Lettres de Jean Roget*, ed. Roget, 252.

96. Henri-Albert Gosse to Jean Gosse, 2 July 1782 and 5 July 1782, and Jean Gosse to Henri-Albert Gosse, 3 July 1782, in Plan, *Un Génevois d'autrefois*, 128, 130–1.

97. Henri-Albert Gosse to Madame Roland, 24 June 1782, in ibid., 133–8.

98. Chapuisat, 'Étienne Clavière', 53.

99. Anon., 'Extract of a letter from Mannheim, October 1', *The Morning Chronicle and London Advertiser* (London), 21 October 1782 (issue 4,189).

100. Feldmann, *Die Genfer Emigranten*; Marc Neuenschwander, 'Les troubles de 1782 à Genève et le temps de l'émigration'. Mount Stuart was sent a copy of the Landgrave's invitation to the Genevans: BdG, Ms. suppl. 32, fols 329–30.

101. Mirabeau to Vergennes, 8 October 1782, cited in Karmin, *Sir Francis d'Ivernois*, 119.

102. D'Ivernois to Mount Stuart, 7 July 1782, BdG, Ms. suppl. 32, fols 370–1, cited in Karmin, *Sir Francis d'Ivernois*, 115–17.

103. Stanhope to Shelburne, 24 August 1782, BL, Bowood papers, Add. Ms. 88906/3/24 fols 4–6.

104. Brissot de Warville, *Philadelphien à Genève*, 150.

105. Ghita Stanhope and G. P Gooch, *The Life of Charles, Third Earl Stanhope* (London: Longmans, Green & Co., 1914), 1–19; Angela C. Bennett, 'The Stanhopes in Geneva: A study of an English Noble Family in Genevan Politics and Society, 1764–1774' (MA dissertation, University of Kent, 1992); G. M. Ditchfield, 'Stanhope, Charles, third Earl Stanhope (1753–1816)', *ODNB*.

106. Nicolas Chenevière, *Relation des réjouissances faites à Genève à l'occasion de*

Mylord Charles Stanhope, Vicomte de Mahon, Commandeur du Noble Exercise de l'Arc (Geneva: n. p., 1771), 6–48.

107. Charles Stanhope, 'Au Noble et Très Honoré Seigneur Commis, à Monsieur le Commandeur et à Messieurs les Officiers Conseillers et Chevaliers du Noble Exercice de l'Arc, à Genève, 10 May 1774', KCRO, Stanhope papers, U1590 C66 Document B, fol. 1.

108. Charles Stanhope, *Discours prononcé au Pré-l'Evêque le 9 août 1773* ([Geneva]: n. p., [1773]); Du Roveray to Stanhope, 15 October 1774, KCRO, Stanhope papers, U1590 C65.2 Document A, fol. 6.

109. Stanhope, *Discours prononcé au Pré-l'Evêque*, 5–6.

110. Stanhope to George-Louis Le Sage (the younger), 21 January 1776, KCRO, Stanhope papers, U1590 C62 Document B, fols 12–20.

111. Charles Stanhope, *Lettre de Milord M[ahon] à Mr . . . votre très fidèle combourgeois M . . .* (Chevening, [15 January] 1777). Émile Rivoire, in his definitive *Bibliographie historique de Genève au XVIIIème siècle* (Geneva: J. Jullien, 1897), 2 vols, entry 1,561, I, 246, states that the addressee was either a Mercier or Du Roveray. Stanhope's papers confirm that the recipient was Du Roveray (KCRO, Stanhope papers, U1590 C62–3 Document A, 'Copie d'une lettre à l'Avocat Du Roveray, Membre du Mag. Conseil des Deux Cent, du 15e Janvier 1777').

112. Stanhope, 'Copie d'une lettre à l'Avocat Du Roveray', KCRO, Stanhope papers, U1590 A2, A5–A6. The printed copy is Stanhope, *Lettre de Milord M[ahon]*, 7.

113. Stanhope, 'Copie d'une lettre à l'Avocat Du Roveray', KCRO, Stanhope papers, U1590 A17–A18; also A27–A28.

114. Stanhope, Speeches of 31 October 1780 and 5 January 1781, *The Parliamentary Register; or, History of the proceedings and debates of the House of Commons . . . during the first session of the fifteenth parliament of Great Britain, Vol. I* (London: J. Almon and J. Debrett, 1781), 13, 373.

115. Stanhope, Speeches of 6 May 1782 and 19–21 June 1782, *The Parliamentary Register; or, History of the proceedings and debates of the House of Commons . . . during the second session of the fifteenth parliament of Great Britain, Vol. VII* (London, J. Debrett, 1782), 112, 246, 257–9.

116. *The Remembrancer, or, Impartial repository of public events, for the year 1780* (London: J. Debrett, 1780), 302; *The Political magazine and parliamentary, naval, military, and literary journal, for July 1782* (London: 1782), 559.

117. Anon. [James Hartley], *History of the Westminster election* (London, 1784), 301.

118. Henry B. Wheatley (ed.), *The Historical and the Posthumous Memoirs of Sir Nathaniel William Wraxall, 1772–1784* (London: Bickers & son, 1884), 5 vols, III, 401.

119. Charles Stanhope, Speeches of Lord Mahon, 2 April 1781, 11 April 1781, *Journal of the House of Lords, Volume 36: 1779–1783* (London: 1767–1830), 136–7, 156–7; see also Jupp, 'Genevese Exiles in County Waterford', 32.

120. Charles Stanhope to Flournoy, 28 August 1782, in Karmin, *Sir Francis d'Ivernois*, 125 n. 36.

121. On the association of Stanhope with Shelburne in the early 1780s, see Anon., *The reformer: By an independent freeholder* (London: Fielding & Walker, 1780), 87; Anon. [Dennis O'Brien], *A defence of the Right Honorable the Earl of Shelburne: from*

the reproaches of his numerous enemies (London: J. Stockdale, 1784), 47; John Norris, *Shelburne and Reform* (London: Macmillan, 1963), 82–98; Derek Jarret, *The Begetters of Revolution: England's Involvement with France, 1759–1789* (London: Longman, 1973); Albert Goodwin, *The Friends of Liberty: The English Democratic Movement in the Age of the French Revolution* (Cambridge, MA: Harvard University Press, 1979), 101–5.

122. D'Ivernois to Shelburne, 28 July 1782, BL, Bowood papers, Add. Ms. 88906/3/14 fols 31–2.

123. D'Ivernois to Shelburne, 2 August 1782, BL, Bowood papers, Add. Ms. 88906/3/14 fols 33–5.

124. Stanhope to Shelburne, 24 August 1782, BL, Add. Bowood papers, Ms. 88906/3/24 fol. 3.

125. François d'Ivernois, 'Déclaration des Genevois remise aux Seigneurs Syndics, le mardi 2 Juillet, à deux heures après minuit, et par eux envoyée le même matin aux trois Généraux', in d'Ivernois, *Pièces relatives à l'asyle ouvert en Irlande aux Genevois opprimés* (n. p.: [1782]), 3.

126. François d'Ivernois, 'Mémoire addressé par M. l'Avocat d'Ivernois, le 27 Septembre 1782 à son excellence Mylord Temple, Vice-Roi d'Irlande', in d'Ivernois, *Pièces relatives à l'asyle ouvert en Irlande*, 3–4.

127. Ibid., 4–5.

128. Ibid., 6.

129. D'Ivernois, *Pièces relatives à l'asyle ouvert en Irlande*, 3.

130. Karmin, *Sir Francis d'Ivernois*, 141–4.

131. Earl Temple to unknown person, September 30 1782, Huntington Library, Stowe papers, STG Box 27 (21).

132. 'Extrait des Registres du Conseil Privé d'Irlande', in d'Ivernois, *Pièces relatives à l'asyle ouvert en Irlande*, 3.

133. Temple to d'Ivernois, 27 September 1782, in ibid., 8–9.

134. Ryland, *The History, Topography and Antiquities of the County and City of Waterford*, 169.

135. *The Morning Herald and Daily Advertiser* (London), 8 October 1782 (issue 606); *The Morning Chronicle and London Advertiser* (London), 16 October 1782 (issue 4,185).

136. Duke of Leinster to François d'Ivernois, Lord Ely to François d'Ivernois in 'Settlement of the Genevans in Ireland', *Whitehall Evening Post* (London), 29 April—1 May 1783 (issue 5,554), *The Morning Herald and Daily Advertiser* (London), 3 May 1783 (issue 784). Karmin dates Leinster's original letter as 30 September 1782 and Ely's as 3 October 1782: *Sir Francis d'Ivernois*, 124–125n, as confirmed by d'Ivernois's *Pièces relatives à l'asyle ouvert en Irlande aux Genevois opprimés.*

137. Ely to Shelburne, 4 April 1782, BL, Bowood papers, Add. Ms. 88906/3/9, fol. 50.

138. Leinster to d'Ivernois, 30 September 1782, in d'Ivernois, *Pièces relatives à l'asyle ouvert en Irlande*, 11.

139. Ely to d'Ivernois, 3 October 1782, in ibid., 10.

140. 'Journal d'Ami Dunant', BdG, Ms. fr. 901, fols 8–9.

141. Rivier-Rose, *La famille Rivier*, 258.

142. Karmin, *Sir Francis d'Ivernois*, 130–3.

143. *General Evening Post* (London) 23 April 1783–26 April 1783 (issue 7,673). See further, in *DIB*: James Kelly, 'Beresford, John' and 'de Blaquiere, Sir John'; James Quinn, 'Clements, Henry Theophilus'; James C. J. Woods, 'Caldwell, Andrew'; Desmond McCabe, 'Cuffe, James' and 'Hartley, Travers'; A.P.W. Malcolmson, 'Foster, John'; Jacqueline Hill, *From Patriots to Unionists: Dublin Civic Politics and Irish Protestant Patriotism, 1660–1840* (Oxford: Oxford University Press, 1997); Louis M. Cullen, *Princes and Pirates: the Dublin Chamber of Commerce, 1783–1983* (Dublin: Dublin Chamber of Commerce, 1983); A.P.W. Malcolmson, *John Foster and the Politics of the Anglo-Irish Ascendancy* (Oxford: Oxford University Press, 1978); G. O. Sayles, 'Contemporary Sketches of the Members of the Irish Parliament in 1782', *Proceedings of the Royal Irish Academy*, 56 C (1954), 227–86.

144. *London Evening Post* 15–17 October 1782 (issue 9,437).

145. Review of Brissot's 'Le Philadelphien à Genève', *The European Magazine, and London Review*, vol. 5 (June 1784), 436–9.

146. Review of Brissot's 'Le Philadelphien à Genève', *The English Review, or An Abstract of English and Foreign Literature*, vol. 4 (London: 1784), 129–33.

147. Thomas Robinson, second Baron Grantham (then secretary of state for the foreign department) to John Mount Stuart, 16 August 1782 (No 7, draft), Bedfordshire and Luton Archives and Record Service, L 29/561/15.

148. Samuel Romilly to Jean Roget, 25 October 1782, in Samuel Romilly, *Memoirs of the Life of Sir Samuel Romilly written by himself* (London: John Murray, 1840), 3 vols, I, 243–5.

149. Jean Roget to Samuel Romilly, 18 December 1782 in Roget, *Lettres de Jean Roget*, ed. Roget, 292–4.

150. Syndics and Council of Geneva to Thomas Townshend, 18 December 1782, NA, 95/8/12; Syndics and Council of Geneva to George III, 18 December 1782, NA, 95/8/12 f. 637.

151. Romilly, *Memoirs*, I, 2–3. See further, Olivier Reverdin, *Genève au temps de la révocation de l'Édit de Nantes, 1680–1705* (Geneva: Droz, 1985); Olivier Fatio, Michel Grandjean, Robert Martin-Achard, Liliane Mottu-Weber and Alfred Perrenoud (eds), *Genève au temps de la révocation de l'Édit de Nantes* (Geneva: Droz, 1986); Nathalie Rothstein, 'Huguenot Master Weavers: Exemplary Englishmen, 1700–c. 1750', in Randolph Vigne and Charles Littleton (eds), *From Strangers to Citizens. The Integration of Immigrant Communities in Britain, Ireland and Colonial America, 1550–1750* (Brighton and Portland, OR: Sussex Academic Press, 2001), 160–74; Susanne Lachenicht, 'Huguenot Immigrants and the Formation of National Identities', *The Historical Journal* 50 (2007), 309–31, and Lachenicht (ed.), *Religious Refugees in Europe, Asia and North America, 6th–21st Centuries* (Hamburg: Atlantic Cultural Studies, 2007).

152. John Angel, *A General History of Ireland, in Its Antient and Modern State* (Dublin: for the author, 1781), 2 vols, I, viii.

153. Nicholas Canny, *Making Ireland British, 1580–1650* (Oxford: Oxford University Press, 2001), 51–2, 132–4, 212–13, 247–50, 277–8, 289–90.

154. Nicholas Canny, *Kingdom and Colony. Ireland in the Atlantic World, 1560–1800* (Baltimore and London: Johns Hopkins University Press, 1988), 129.

155. John Bosher, 'Huguenot Merchants and the Protestant International in the Seventeenth Century', *William and Mary Quarterly*, 3rd series, 52 (1995), 77–102; Robin Gwynn, 'The Huguenots in Britain, the 'Protestant International' and the Defeat of Louis XIV', in Vigne and Littleton (eds), *From Strangers to Citizens*, 412–24; William O'Reilly, 'The Naturalisation Act of 1709 and the Settlement of Germans in Britain, Ireland and the Colonies', in ibid, 292–302; David E. Lambert, *The Protestant International and the Huguenot Migration to Virginia* (New York: Peter Lang, 2010).

156. François d'Ivernois to Mount Stuart, 30 September 1782, BdG, Ms. suppl. 32, fols 374–5.

157. Clavière to Cazenove, 29 May 1782, Clavière to Roman l'ainé, 29 November 1782, Archives nationales (France), T//646/1.

158. Jean Roget to Samuel Romilly, 19 October 1782, in Roget, *Lettres de Jean Roget*, ed. Roget, 277–8. D'Ivernois had in fact met Earl Temple on 27 September 1782.

159. Mirabeau to Vergennes, 4 October 1782, in (Honoré-Gabriel Riqueti, comte de) Mirabeau, *Mémoires biographiques, littéraires et politiques de Mirabeau, écrits par lui-même, par son père, son oncle et son fils adoptif*, ed. Lucas de Montigny (Brussels: 1834), 8 vols, V, 323–5. Jacques-Antoine Du Roveray's handwriting has been identified in the original manuscript of Mirabeau's letter: see Bénétruy, *L'Atelier de Mirabeau*, 42–3, and Karmin, *Sir Francis d'Ivernois*, 118.

160. Guillaume-Joseph Saige to d'Ivernois, 7 September 1783, BdG, Ms. suppl. 1010, fol. 123.

161. Guillaume-Joseph Saige to d'Ivernois, 17 June 1783, BdG, Ms. suppl. 1010, fols 121–2. For commercial links between Bordeaux and Ireland, see Louis Cullen, John Shovlin and Thomas Truxes (eds), *The Bordeaux-Dublin Letters, 1757: Correspondence of an Irish Community Abroad* (Oxford: Oxford University Press, 2013).

162. Brissot de Warville, *Philadelphien à Genève*, 146–9.

163. Ibid., 210–11.

164. Anon., 'Fragments of a letter from Geneva, of the 14th of November, 1782', *Parker's General Advertiser and Morning Intelligencer* (London), 8 January 1783 (issue 1,927).

Chapter 7. Ireland: Oppression and Opportunity

1. John Bergin, Eoin Magennis, Lesa Ní Mhunghaile and Patrick Walsh (eds), *New Perspectives on the Penal Laws* (Dublin: *Eighteenth-Century Ireland/Iris an dá chultúr*, special issue no. 1, 2011).

2. P.D.H. Smyth, 'The Volunteers and Parliament, 1779–1784', in Thomas Bartlett and David Hayton (eds), *Penal Era and Golden Age: Essays in Irish History, 1690–1800* (Belfast: Ulster Historical Foundation, 1979), 113–36; James Kelly, *Prelude to Union. Anglo-Irish Politics in the 1780s* (Cork: Cork University Press, 1992), 24–31; Martyn J. Powell, *Britain and Ireland in the Eighteenth-Century Crisis of Empire* (London: Palgrave, 2002), 166–77; Vincent Morley, *Irish Opinion and the American Revolution, 1760–1783* (Cambridge: Cambridge University Press, 2007), 285–334; Stephen Small, *Political Thought in Ireland, 1776—1798: Republicanism, Patriotism, and Radicalism* (Oxford: Oxford University Press, 2010), 83–112; Stephen O'Connor, 'The

Volunteeers, 1778–1793: Iconography and Identity' (PhD thesis, National University of Ireland, Maynooth, 2008), 109–40.

3. Henry Flood, *A Letter to the People of Ireland, on the Expediency and Necessity of the Present Associations in Ireland: In Favour of Our Own Manufactures, with Some Cursory Observations on the Effects of an Union* (Newry: Joseph Gordon, 1779), 3–6, 42. See further, James Kelly, *Henry Flood: Patriots and Politics in Eighteenth-Century Ireland* (Dublin: Four Courts Press, 1998).

4. James Crombie, *The Expedience and Utility of Volunteer Associations for National Defence and Security in the Present Critical Situation of Public Affairs Considered, in a Sermon, Preached before the United Companies of the Belfast Volunteers* (Belfast: James Magee, 1779).

5. Anon., *A View of the present state of Ireland: containing observations upon the following subjects, viz. its dependance, linen trade, provision trade, woolen manufactory, coals, fishery, agriculture . . . : intended for the consideration of Parliament, on the approaching enlargement of the trade of that kingdom: to which is added, A Sketch of some of the principal political characters in the Irish House of Commons* (London: R. Faulder, 1780), 86–7.

6. Benjamin Franklin to Lord Howe, 20 July 1776, in Benjamin Franklin and William B.Willcox, *The Papers of Benjamin Franklin, Volume 22: March 23, 1775, through October 27, 1776*, ed. William B. Willcox (New Haven, CT and London: Yale University Press, 1982), 518–21.

7. Thomas Allan to John Beresford, 27 November, 1779, in John Beresford, *The Correspondence of The Right Hon. John Beresford*, ed. William Beresford (London: Woodfall & Kinder, 1854), 2 vols, I, 97–8.

8. Kelly, *Prelude to Union*, 23 n. 48; Powell, *Britain and Ireland in the Eighteenth-Century Crisis of Empire*, 182–5.

9. Martyn J. Powell, 'Consumption: Commercial Demand and the Challenges to Regulatory Power in Eighteenth-Century Ireland', in Philip J. Stern and Carl Wennerlind (eds), *Mercantilism Reimagined. Political Economy in Early Modern Britain and Its Empire* (Oxford: Oxford University Press, 2013), 282–304; Patrick Walsh, 'The Fiscal State in Ireland, 1691–1769', *The Historical Journal*, 56 (2013), 629–56.

10. See the collection edited by Jane H. Ohlmeyer, *Political Thought in Seventeenth-Century Ireland. Kingdom or Colony* (Cambridge: Cambridge University Press, 2000)

11. Hervey Redmond, 2nd Viscount Mountmorres, *Plain Reasons for New-Modelling Poynings' Law: In Such a Manner As to Assert the Ancient Rights of the Two Houses of Parliament, Without Intrenching on the King's Prerogative* (Dublin: William Hallhead, 1780).

12. William Eden, *A Letter to the Earl of Carlisle: From William Eden, Esq. on the Representations of Ireland, Respecting a Free Trade* (Dublin: R. Marchbank, 1779), 8, 23.

13. William Eden to Lord North, 14 November 1781, in Beresford, *Correspondence*, ed. Beresford, I, 189.

14. Henry Grattan, 'Spoken on the 16 April 1782', in Henry Grattan, *Speeches of the Late Rt. Hon. Henry Grattan, in the Irish Parliament in 1780 and 1782* (London: Ridgway, 1821), 45–6.

15. Ibid., 49. See further, Gerard O'Brien, *Anglo-Irish Politics in the Age of Grattan and Pitt* (Dublin: Irish Academic Press, 1987).

16. Brendan Bradshaw, *The Irish Constitutional Revolution of the Sixteenth Century* (Cambridge: Cambridge University Press, 2008) and *'And So Began the Irish Nation': Nationality, National Consciousness and Nationalism in Pre-Modern Ireland* (London: Routledge, 2016).

17. S. J. Connolly, *Divided Kingdom: Ireland 1630–1800* (Oxford: Oxford University Press, 2008), 48.

18. Marianne Elliott, *When God Took Sides. Religion and Identity in Ireland—Unfinished History* (Oxford: Oxford University Press, 2009), 24–5.

19. Eamon Darcy, *The Irish Rebellion of 1641 and the Wars of the Three Kingdoms* (Woodbridge: Boydell & Brewer, Royal Historical Society Studies in History, 2013), 39.

20. 'Act for the Settlement of Ireland', 12 August 1652, in Estelle Epinoux, *Introduction to Irish History and Civilization: Texts and Documents on Ireland* (Limoges: Presses Universitaires de Limoges, 2007), 46.

21. S. J. Connolly, *Religion, Law and Power: The Making of Protestant Ireland 1660–1770* (Oxford: Oxford University Press, 1992), 12–17, 55–9, 147–9; *Divided Kingdom*, 5, 137–8, 156–7.

22. Richard Lawrence, *The Interest of Ireland in Its Trade and Wealth Stated: In Two Parts: First Part Observes and Discovers the Causes of Irelands Not More Increasing in Trade and Wealth from the First Conquest Till Now: Second Part Proposeth Expedients to Remedy All Its Mercanture Maladies by Which It Is Kept Poor and Low; Both Mix'd with Some Observations on the Politicks of Government Relating to the Incouragement of Trade and Increase of Wealth: with Some Reflections on Principles of Religion As It Relates to the Premisses* (Dublin: J. Ray and J. Howes: 1682).

23. D. W. Hayton, *Ruling Ireland 1685–1742: Politics, Politicians and Parties* (Woodbridge: Boydell & Brewer, 2004), esp. 35–105; L. M. Cullen, 'Catholics under the Penal Laws', *Eighteenth-Century Ireland*, 1 (1986), 23–36; T. P. Power and K. Whelan (eds), *Endurance and Emergence: Catholics in Ireland in the Eighteenth Century* (Dublin: Irish Academic Press, 1990); C. I. McGrath, 'Securing the Protestant Interest: The Origins and Purpose of the Penal Laws of 1695', *Irish Historical Studies*, 30 (1996–97), 25–46; Thomas Bartlett, *The Fall and Rise of the Irish Nation: The Catholic Question, 1690–1830* (Dublin: Gill and Macmillan, 1992).

24. James C. Beckett, *Protestant Dissent in Ireland, 1687–1780* (London: Faber & Faber, 1948).

25. Connolly, *Religion, Law and Power*; David Dickson, *New Foundations: Ireland, 1660–1800* (Dublin and Portland, OR: Irish Academic Press, 2000); Toby Barnard, *The Kingdom of Ireland, 1641–1760* (Basingstoke: Palgrave, 2004); Connolly, *Divided Kingdom*; McBride, *Eighteenth-Century Ireland.*

26. William King, archbishop of Dublin to Jonathan Swift, 27 February 1712, in Jonathan Swift, *The Correspondence of Jonathan Swift: 1690–1713*, ed. Harold Williams (Oxford: Oxford University Press, 1963), 5 vols, I, 289–91.

27. David Dickson, 'Famine and Economic Change in Eighteenth-Century Ireland', in Alvin Jackson (ed.), *The Oxford Handbook of Modern Irish History* (Oxford: Oxford University Press, 2014), 422–38.

28. Joseph Addison to Sidney Godolphin, 1st Earl of Godolphin, 11 July 1709, in Joseph Addison, *The Letters of Joseph Addison*, ed. Walter Graham (Oxford: Oxford University Press, 1941), 160–2 (Letter 191).

29. Joseph Addison to John Somers, 1st Baron Somers, 25 June 1709, in Addison, *Letters*, ed. Graham, 150–2 (Letter 183).

30. William King to Jonathan Swift, 18 September 1708, in Swift, *Correspondence*, ed. Williams, I, 96–8.

31. Anon., *The Popish pretenders to the forfeited estates in Ireland unmask'd, and lay'd open. Being an answer to a letter, desiring his friend to inquire into . . . who are like to be restored to their estates* (London: Booksellers of London and Westminster, 1702).

32. Anon., *Division Our Destruction: Or, a Short History of the French Faction in England* (London: John Nutt, 1702), 6.

33. Joseph Addison to Josiah Burchett, 27 March 1708, in Addison, *Letters*, ed. Graham, 101.

34. William Petty, 'The Political Anatomy of Ireland', in *Tracts; Chiefly relating to Ireland* (Dublin: Boulter Grierson, 1769), 354. See further, Ted McCormick, *William Petty: And the Ambitions of Political Arithmetic* (Oxford: Oxford University Press, 2009).

35. William Petty, *A Treatise of Taxes & Contributions: Shewing the Nature and Measures of Crown-Lands, Assessments, Customs, Poll-Moneys . . . &c.: with Several Intersperst Discourses and Digressions Concerning Warres, the Church, Universities, Rents & Purchases . . . &c.: the Same Being Frequently Applied to the Present State and Affairs of Ireland* (London: N. Brooke, 1662), 95.

36. Toby Barnard, *Improving Ireland?: Projectors, Prophets and Profiteers, 1641–1786* (Dublin: Four Courts Press, 2008); Andrew Sneddon, 'Legislating for Economic Development: Irish Fisheries as a Case Study in the Limitations of 'Improvement', in David Hayton, James Kelly and John Bergin (eds), *The Eighteenth-Century Composite State: Representative Institutions in Ireland and Europe, 1689–1800* (Basingstoke: Palgrave Macmillan, 2010), 136–59.

37. Petty, *A Treatise of Taxes & Contributions*, 99–100.

38. Ibid., 98–9.

39. Ibid., 101.

40. William Petty, *The French Politician Found Out, or Considerations on the Late Pretensions That France Claims to England and Ireland: And Her Designs and Plots in Order Thereunto* (London: Langley Curtiss, 1681), 12–13.

41. William Temple, 'An Essay upon the Advancement of Trade in Ireland', in William Temple, *The Works of Sir William Temple, Bart. Complete in Four Volumes. A New Edition* (London: Rivington et al., 1814), 4 vols, III, 9.

42. Locke's 1697 policy document (that his fellow members of the Board 'pitched upon' from several competing proposals on 24 August, and transmitted to the Lord Justices on the 31st of the same month) was published from the Board of Trade papers by H. R. Fox Bourne, *The Life of John Locke* (London: King, 1876), 2 vols, II, 363–72.

43. William Molyneaux to John Locke, 26 September 1696, in John Locke, *The Correspondence of John Locke*, ed. Edward S. de Beer (Oxford: Clarendon Press, 1976–89), 8 vols, V, 704.

44. Locke to William Molyneux, 22 February 1697, in Locke, *Correspondence*, ed. de Beer, VI, 7.

45. On Molyneaux, see Patrick Kelly, 'Recasting a Tradition: William Molyneux and the Sources of *The Case of Ireland . . . Stated* (1698)', in Ohlmeyer (ed.), *Political Thought in Seventeenth-Century Ireland*, 83–106.

46. William Molyneaux, *The Case of Ireland being Bound by Acts of Parliament in England, Stated* (London: J. Almon, 1770).

47. Ibid., 130.

48. Patrick Kelly, 'William Molyneux and the Spirit of Liberty in Eighteenth-Century Ireland', *Eighteenth-Century Ireland*, 3 (1988), 133–48; Jacqueline Hill, 'Ireland without Union: Molyneux and his Legacy', in John Robertson (ed.), *Union for Empire: Political Thought and the British Union of 1707* (Cambridge: Cambridge University Press, 271–96; Ian McBride, '*The Case of Ireland* in Context: William Molyneux and his Critics', *Proceedings of the Royal Irish Academy*, 118C (2018), 1–30.

49. Richard Cox, *Some Thoughts on the Bill Depending before the Right Honourable the House of Lords for Prohibiting the Exportation of the Woolen Manufactures of Ireland to Foreign Parts* (London: J. Darby and A. Bell, 1798), 9.

50. J. G. Simms, *William Molyneux of Dublin* (Dublin: Irish Academic Press, 1982), ed. P. H. Kelly, 111–12.

51. William Atwood, *The history and reasons of the dependency of Ireland upon the imperial crown of the kingdom of England: Rectifying Mr. Molineux's state of The case of Ireland's being bound by Acts of Parliament in England* (London: Daniel Brown, 1698), 204.

52. John Cary, *A Vindication of the Parliament of England: In Answer to a Book, Written by William Molyneux . . . Intituled, the Case of Irlands Being Bound by Acts of Parliament in England, Stated* (London: Freeman Collins, 1698), 96.

53. H. F. Kearney, 'The Political Background to English Mercantilism: 1695–1700', *Economic History Review*, 2nd series, 11 (1959), 484–96; Patrick Kelly, 'The Irish Woollen Export Prohibition Act of 1699: Kearney Re-visited', *Irish Economic and Social History*, 7 (1980), 22–43.

54. Anon., *The Irregular and Disorderly State of the Plantation-Trade Discuss'd and Humbly Offered to the Consideration of the Right Honourable the Lords and Commons in Parliament Assembled* ([London]: n. p., 1695), 1.

55. Anon., *An Answer to the Most Material Objections Made by the Linnen-drapers, against the Bill Which Restrains the Wearing East-India Wrought Silks, &c. in England: Humbly Submitted to the Consideration of the Most Honourable House of Lords* ([London]: n. p., [1699]), 3.

56. John Cary, *A Discourse Concerning the East-India-Trade, Shewing How It Is Unprofitable to the Kindome of England. Being Taken Out of an Essay on Trade* (London: E. Baldwin, 1699), 10.

57. John Cary, *A Discourse Concerning the Trade of Ireland and Scotland: As They Stand in Competition with the Trade of England* (London: n. p., 1696), 1–3.

58. Sir Francis Brewster, *New Essays on Trade, Wherein the present State of our Trade, it's [sic] Great Decay in the Chief Branches of it, and the Fatal Consequences thereof to the Nation . . . Under the Most Important Heads of Trade and Navigation* (London: H. Walwyn, 1702), 77–9.

59. Simon Clement, *The Interest of England, as it stands with relation to the trade of Ireland, considered; the Arguments against the Bill, for prohibiting the Exportation of Woollen Manufactures from Ireland to Forreign Parts, fairly discusst, and the reasonableness and necessity of Englands restraining her colonies in all matters of trade, that may be prejudicial to her own commerce, clearly demonstrated. With short remarques on a book, entituled, Some thoughts on the bill depending before the right honourable the House of Lords, for prohibiting the exportation of the woollen manufactures of Ireland to forreign parts* (London: John Atwood, 1698), 2–7.

60. 'William III, 1698–9: An Act for continueing severall Laws therein mentioned, and for explaining the Act intituled An Act to prevent the Exportation of Wooll out of the Kingdoms of Ireland and England into Forreigne Parts and for the Incouragement of the Woollen Manufactures in the Kingdom of England. [Chapter XIII. Rot. Parl. 11 Gul. III. p. 3. n. 4.]', in *Statutes of the Realm: Volume 7, 1695–1701*, ed. John Raithby (n. p.: Great Britain Record Commission, 1820), 600–2/*British History Online*, https://www.british-history.ac.uk/statutes-realm/vol7/pp607-608, accessed 27 May 2019.

61. Henry Maxwell, *An Essay Towards an Union of Ireland with England* (London: Timothy Goodwin, 1703), 19–22. See further, David W. Hayton, 'Henry Maxwell, M.P., Author of "An Essay upon an Union of Ireland with England (1703)"', *Eighteenth-Century Ireland/Iris an dá chultúr*, 22 (2007), 28–63. On Molesworth, see classically Robbins, *The Eighteenth-Century Commonwealthman*, 143–60. An excellent survey of the voluminous recent literature on the union issue since James Kelly's seminal article, 'The Origins of the Act of Union: An Examination of Unionist Opinion in Britain and Ireland, 1650–1800', *Irish Historical Studies*, 25 (1987), 236–63, is Charles Ivar McGrath, 'The "Union" Representation of 1703 in the Irish House of Commons: A Case of Mistaken Identity?', *Eighteenth-Century Ireland/Iris an dá chultúr*, 23 (2008), 11–35. See also Allan Macinnes, 'Union Failed, Union Accomplished: The Irish Union of 1703 and the Scottish Union of 1707', in Dáire Keogh and Kevin Whelan (eds), *Acts of Union: The Causes, Contexts, and Consequences of the Act of Union* (Dublin: Four Courts Press, 2001), 67–94; Jim Smyth, '"Like amphibious animals": Irish Patriots, Ancient Britons, 1691–1707', *The Historical Journal*, 36 (1993), 785–97.

62. Francis Brewster, *Essays on Trade and Navigation: In Five Parts* (London: John Cockeril, 1693), 1.

63. François P. de Lisola, *The Buckler of State and Justice against the Design Manifestly Discovered of the Universal Monarchy . . . the 2d Edition. to Which Is Added, a Free Conference Touching the Present State of England Both at Home and Abroad: in Order to the Designs of France. [translated from the French of François P. De Lisola.]* (London: Richard Royston, 1673).

64. Anon., *Private Debates in the House of Commons: In the Year 1677. in Relation to a War with France, and an Alliance with Holland, &c. . . . Together with Speeches by King Charles Ii, to the Lords and Commons. with a Discourse Showing the Absolute Necessity of a War with France on This Critical Juncture, in Order to Procure a Lasting Peace at Home* (London: J. Nutt, 1702), 16; Anon., *A Modest Defence of the Government: In a Dialogue between Kinglove, an Old Cavalier, and Meanwell, a Modern Tory. Written by a Sober Stander-By, Who Is Wholly Unconcern'd in the Ministry, or the Funds* (London: C.T., 1702), 23.

65. Anon., *The Dangers of Europe, from the Growing Power of France: With Some Free Thoughts on Remedies. and Particularly on the Cure of Our Divisions at Home: in Order to a Successful War [sic] Abroad against the French King and His Allies. by the Author Of, the Duke of Anjou's Succession Considered* (London: A. Baldwin, 1702), 3rd edn, 3.

66. Ibid., 59.

67. John Somers, 1st Baron Somers, *Jura Populi Anglicani: or the Subject's Right of Petitioning Set Forth. Occasioned by the Case of the Kentish Petitioners, Etc.* (London: n. p., 1701), 40.

68. Anon., *Dangers of Europe, from the Growing Power of France*, 61.

69. Anon., *An Answer to the Most Material Objections That Have Been Raised against Restraining the East-India Trade; with Five Queries* (n. p.: n. p., 1701), 1.

70. Anon., *A Debate between Three Ministers of State on the Present Affairs of England. in Relation to the Disposition of the Nation at Home, Our Alliances Abroad, and the Designs of France* (London: for the author, 1702), 7–9

71. Anon., *The Linnen and Woollen Manufactory Discoursed: With the Nature of Companies and Trade in General: and Particularly, That of the Companies for the Linnen Manufactory of England and Ireland. with Some Reflections How the Trade of Ireland Hath Formerly, and May Now, Affect England. Printed at the Request of a Peer of This Realm.* (London: Geo. Huddleston, 1698), 33, 41.

72. Charles Davenant, *An Essay Upon the Probable Methods of Making a People Gainers in the Ballance of Trade . . . by the Author of the Essay on Ways and Means* (London: James Knapton, 1699). Quotations are from Charles Davenant, *The Political and Commercial Works of That Celebrated Writer Charles D'avenant: Relating to the Trade and Revenue of England, the Plantation Trade, the East-India Trade and African Trade*, ed. Sir Charles Whitworth (London: R. Horsfield et al., 1771), 5 vols, II, 248.

73. Davenant, *Ballance of Trade, Works*, ed Whitworth, II, 253.

74. Ibid., 254–5.

75. John Dalrymple, *Memoirs Of Great Britain And Ireland: From The Dissolution Of The Last Parliament Of Charles II. till the Capture of the French and Spanish fleets at Vigo* (London: Strahan and Cadell, 1790), new edn, 3 vols, III, 183–4.

76. William Paterson, 'A Proposal to Plant a Colony in Darien; to protect the Indians against Spain; and to open the trade of South America to all nations' [1701], in Saxe Bannister (ed.), *The Writings of William Paterson: Founder of the Bank of England, and of the Darien Colony* (London: Judd & Glass, 1859), 3 vols, I, 159.

77. Anon., *Some Seasonable and Modest Thoughts Partly Occasioned By, and Partly Concerning the Scots East-India Company. Humbly offered to R. H. Esq. a Member of the present Parliament. By an unfeigned and hearty Lover of England* (Edinburgh: George Mosman, 1696), 3–4.

78. Ibid., 5.

79. Ibid., 26.

80. Robert Ferguson, *A Just and Modest Vindication of the Scots Design, for the Having Established a Colony at Darien: . . . with a Brief Display, How Much It Is Their Interest to apply themselves to Trade, and particularly to that which is Foreign* (n. p.: n. p., 1699), 15.

81. Anon., *A Letter from a Gentleman in the Country to His Friend at Edinburgh: Wherein It Is Clearly Proved That the Scottish African and Indian Company Is Exactly Calculated for the Interest of Scotland* (Edinburgh: George Mosman, 1696), 4–5.

82. Anon., *Some Remedies to Prevent the Mischiefs from the Late Act of Parliament Made in Scotland: In Relation to the East-India Trade* (London: n. p., [1695]), 1.

83. Anon., *Some Considerations Upon the Late Act of the Parliament of Scotland: For Constituting an Indian Company; in a Letter to a Friend* (London: n. p., 1695), 1.

84. Anon., *Some Considerations Concerning the Prejudice Which the Scotch Act Establishing a Company to Trade to the East and West-Indies, (with Large Priviledges, and on Easie Terms) May Bring to the English Sugar Plantations, and the Manufactury of Refining Sugar in England, and some means to prevent the same from Scotland and other Nations* (London: n. p., [1696]), 1.

85. Anon., *Some Arguments to Prove the Growing Greatness of the Northern Princes: And the Reason Thereof; with Many Other Remarks on Our Trade and Commerce, and an Effectual Remedy against the Scotch-Act* (London: n. p., [1695]), 1.

86. James Hodges, *A Defence of the Scots Abdicating Darien: Including an Answer to the Defence of the Scots Settlement There* (n. p.: n. p., 1700), epistle dedicatory.

87. George Ridpath, *An Enquiry into the Causes of the Miscarriage of the Scots Colony at Darien. or an Answer to a Libel Entituled a Defence of the Scots Abdicating Darien* (Glasgow: n. p., 1700), 2–5.

88. Walter Harris, *An Enquiry into the Caledonian Project: With a Defence of England's Procedure (in a Point of Equity) in Relation thereunto* (London: John Nutt, 1701), 60–1.

89. Anon., *Memorial Concerning the State of the Manufactures Before and Since the Year 1700, at Which Time the Laws Concerning Trade and Manufactures Were Revived and Increased: As Also, Some Remarks Upon the Arts Used for Eluding These Laws, Humbly Offered to His Grace, and the Honourable Estates of Parliament* (Edinburgh: n. p., 1704), 1.

90. Anon., *A serious advice to the African and Indian Company* ([Edinburgh]: n. p., [1700]), 1.

91. Anon. [John Buchan of Cairnbulg], *A Memorial Briefly Pointing at Some Advantages of the Union of the Two Kingdoms, Humbly Offered to the Consideration of the Commissioners Appointed for That End. (memorial Shewing the Advantages the Kingdom of Scotland May Have by the Undertaking . . . of Fishings for Export, Etc.)* (London: J. Nutt, 1702), 6.

92. Anon., *A Proposal for Remeeding* [*sic*] *Our Excessive Luxury* ([Edinburgh]: n. p., 1700), 2–3.

93. Anon. [George Mackenzie and John Nisbet], *A Letter Concerning the Union, with Sir George Mackenzie's Observations and Sir John Nisbet's Opinion Upon the Same Subject* ([Edinburgh]: n. p., 1706), 23.

94. James Hodges, *That Part of a Late Book Which Relates to a General Fast and Humiliation: Printed a Part. Nota. That the Book It Self Entitul'd the Rights and Interests of the Two British Monarchies* (Edinburgh: n. p., 1706), 30–1.

95. George Ridpath, *The Reducing of Scotland by Arms, and Annexing It to England As a Province, Considered. with an Historical Account of the Grievances the*

Scots Complain They Have Suffer'd in Their Religion, Liberty, and Trade, Since the Union of the Crowns, Etc. (London: Benjamin Bragg, 1705), 35.

96. John Robertson, 'Andrew Fletcher's Vision of Union', in Roger Mason (ed.), *Scotland and England, 1286–1815* (Edinburgh: John Donald, 1987), 203–25.

97. Andrew Fletcher, *An Account of a Conversation Concerning a Right Regulation of Governments: For the Common Good of Mankind, in a Letter to the Marquess of Montrose, the Earls of Rothes, Roxburgh, and Haddingtoun, from London the 1st of December, 1703* (London: A. Baldwin, 1704), in David Daiches (ed.), *Andrew Fletcher of Saltoun: Selected Political Writings and Speeches* (Edinburgh: Scottish Academic Press, 1979), 118–20.

98. Ibid., 120.

99. Ibid., 129.

100. William Seton of Pitmedden, Scottish Commissioner to the Scottish Parliament, 2 November 1706, cited in T. C. Smout, *Scottish Trade on the Eve of the Union* (Edinburgh: Oliver & Boyd, 1963), 274.

101. George Mackenzie, *A letter from E.C. to E.W. concerning the Union.* [by George Mackenzie, Earl of Cromarty, addressed to David Wemyss, Earl of Wemyss.] (Edinburgh[?]: n. p., [1706]), 3, 13.

102. George Mackenzie, *Parainesis pacifica: Or, A perswasive to the union of Britain* (Edinburgh: Andrew Symson, 1702), 9.

103. A. L. Murray, 'Administration and the Law', in T. I. Rae (ed.), *The Union of 1707: Its Impact on Scotland* (Glasgow: Blackie 1974), 30–57.

104. David Hume, 'Of the Balance of Trade', in *Essays, Moral, Political, and Literary*, ed. Eugene F. Miller (Indianapolis: Liberty Fund, 1987).

105. David Hume to Henry Home, Lord Kames, 4 March 1758, in David Hume, *The Letters of David Hume*, ed. J.Y.T. Greig (Oxford: Oxford University Press, 1932), 2 vols, I, 271.

106. C. A. Whatley, 'The Economic Causes and Consequences of the Union of 1707: A Survey', *The Scottish Historical Review*, 68 (1989), 150–81.

107. James Anderson, *Observations on the Means of Exciting a Spirit of National Industry: Chiefly Intended to Promote the Agriculture, Commerce, Manufactures, and Fisheries, of Scotland* (Edinburgh: T. Cadell and C. Elliot, 1777), ix.

108. David Hume to Henry Home, Lord Kames, 4 March 1758, in Hume, *Letters*, ed. Greig, I, 271.

109. Prince Butler, *Prince Butler's Queries Relating to the Bill for Settling the Trade to Africa in a Joynt-Stock Company, &c., As the Company Proposes* (London: n. p., 1699), 2.

110. François Hotman, *Franco-gallia: Or, an Account of the Ancient Free State of France and Most Other Arts of Europe Before the Loss of Their Liberties, Written Originally in Latin by the Famous Civilian Francis Hotoman in the Year 1574*, trans. Robert Molesworth (London: Queen's Head, 1721), translator's preface, xx.

111. Jonathan Swift, 'Verses said to be written on union' [1707], in Samuel Johnson (ed.), *The Works of the English Poets: With Prefaces, Biographical and Critical, by Samuel Johnson, Volume the Thirty Ninth* (London: J. Nicols, 1779), 37–8.

112. Jonathan Swift, 'The Story of the Injured Lady, written by Herself' [1707],

in *Jonathan Swift, Miscellanies by Dr Swift. The Eleventh Volume* (London: Hitch, David and Dodsley, 1749), 104.

113. Jonathan Swift to Ambrose Philips, 10 November 1709, in Swift, *Correspondence*, ed. Williams, I, 152–4.

114. Michael Ryder, 'The Bank of Ireland, 1721: Land, Credit and Dependency', *The Historical Journal*, 25 (1982), 557–82.

115. David Hayton, 'British Whig Ministers and the Irish question, 1714–25', in Stephen Taylor, Richard Connors and Clyve Jones (eds), *Hanoverian Britain and Empire: Essays in Memory of Philip Lawson* (Woodbridge: Boydell & Brewer, 1998), 37–64.

116. Jonathan Swift to Alexander Pope, 21 January 1721, in Pope, *Correspondence*, ed. Sherburn, II, 64–72. See further, Swift's *A Proposal for the Universal Use of Irish Manufacture: In Cloaths and Furniture of Houses, &c. Utterly Rejecting and Renouncing Every Thing Wearable That Comes from England* (Dublin: E. Waters, 1720).

117. Jonathan Swift, *Fraud Detected: Or, the Hibernian Patriot. Containing, All the Drapier's Letters to the People of Ireland, on Wood's Coinage, &c. Interspers'd with the Following Particulars, Viz. I. the Addresses of the Lords and Commons of Ireland, against Wood's Coin. Ii. His Majesty's Answer to the Said Addresses. Iii. the Report of His Majesty's Most Honourable Privy Council. Iv. Seasonable Advice to the Grand Jury. V. Extract of the Votes of the House of Commons of England, Upon Breaking a Grand Jury. Vi. Considerations on the Attempts, Made to Pass Wood's Coin. Vii. Reasons, Shewing the Necessity the People of Ireland Are Under, to Refuse Wood's Coinage. to Which Are Added, Prometheus. a Poem. Also a New Poem to the Drapier; and the Songs Sung at the Drapier's Club in Truck Street, Dublin, Never Before Printed. with a Preface, Explaining the Usefulness of the Whole* (Dublin: George Faulkner, 1725).

118. Jonathan Swift, *A Short View of the State of Ireland* (1727), in *Volume IV of the Author's Works, Containing, A Collection of Tracts Relating to Ireland* (Dublin: George Faulkner, 1735), 254.

119. David Bindon, *A Scheme for Supplying Industrious Men with Money to Carry on Their Trades: And for Better Providing for the Poor of Ireland* (Dublin: Thomas Hume, 1729), 5.

120. Jonathan Swift, 'Observations occassion'd by reading a paper, entitled, The Case of the Woollen Manufacturers of Dublin', in 'Miscellaneous Essays', *The Works of the Rev. Jonathan Swift*, ed. Thomas Sheridan and John Nicols (London: J. Johnson et al., 1801), 19 vols, XIX, 168.

121. John Browne, *A Collection of Tracts: Concerning the Present State of Ireland, with Respect to Its Riches, Revenue, Trade and Manufactures. Containing I. Seasonable Remarks on Trade. with Some Reflections on the Advantages That Might Accrue to Great Britain, by a Proper Regulation of the Trade of Ireland. II. an Essay on Trade in General; And, on That of Ireland in Particular. III. Considerations on Two Papers Lately Publish'd. the First Call'd Seasonable Remarks, &c. and the Other, an Essay on Trade in General, and That of Ireland in Particular. IV. An Appeal to the Reverend Dean Swift, by Way of Reply to the Observer on Seasonable Remarks. V. A Letter in Answer to a Paper, Intitl'd, an Appeal to the Reverend Dean Swift* (London: T. Woodward, 1729), 15.

122. Ibid., 22.

123. François Fénelon, *Telemachus*, ed. and trans. Patrick Riley (Cambridge: Cambridge University Press, 1994), 297.

124. Richard Cantillon, *Essai sur la nature du commerce en général. Edited with an English translation and other material by Henry Higgs* (London: Frank Cass & Co., 1959), 185.

125. James Livesey, 'The Dublin Society in Eighteenth-Century Irish Political Thought', *The Historical Journal*, 47 (2004), 615–40; Toby Barnard, 'The Dublin Society and other Improving Societies, 1731–85', in James Kelly and Martyn J. Powell (eds), *Clubs and Societies in Eighteenth-Century Ireland* (Dublin: Four Courts Press, 2010), 53–88.

126. John Browne, *Reflections Upon the Present Unhappy Circumstances of Ireland in a Letter to His Grace the Lord Archbishop of Cashel: With a Proposal for Publick Granaries, As the Principal Means Whereby to Retrieve Our Affairs* (Dublin: G. Faulkner, 1731).

127. Arthur Dobbs, *An Essay on the Trade and Improvement of Ireland. by Arthur Dobbs, Esq* (Dublin: J. Smith and W. Bruce, 1729), 69–72.

128. Bernard Mandeville, *The Fable of the Bees or Private Vices, Publick Benefits. With a Commentary Critical, Historical, and Explanatory by F. B. Kaye* (Indianapolis: Liberty Fund, 1988), 2 vols, I, 115–16.

129. Anon., *Remarks on the English Woollen Manufactury for Exportation And Necessity of Preventing the Irish Wool Being Run* (London: Geo. Grierson, 1730), 3.

130. Joshua Gee, *The Trade and Navigation of Great-Britain* (London: S. Buckley, 1730), preface.

131. Anon., *The Act for Permitting the Free Importation of Cattle from Ireland, Considered with a View to the Interests of Both Kingdoms* (London: J. Dodsley, 1760).

132. Matthew Decker, *An Essay on the Causes of the Decline of the Foreign Trade: Consequently of the Value of the Lands of Britain, and on the Means to Restore Both. Begun in the Year 1739* (Dublin: G. Faulkener, 1749), 2nd edn, v, 75, 157.

133. Josiah Tucker, *A Brief Essay on the Advantages and Disadvantages Which Respectively Attend France and Great Britain: With Regard to Trade, with Some Proposals for Removing the Principal Disadvantages of Great Britain* (London: for the author, 1749), 36–7.

134. John Brown, *An estimate of the manners and principles of the times* (London: Davis and Reymers, 1758), 2 vols, II, 22.

135. John Mills, *Essays Moral, Philosophical and Political* (London: S. Hooper, 1772), 211–15.

136. Charles Lucas, *A Remonstrance against Certain Infringements on the Rights and Liberties of the Commons and Citizens of Dublin: Humbly Addressed to the Right Honourable the Lord Mayor, the Recorder, the Board of Aldermen, the Sherifs, Commons, and Citizens of the Said City. by Charles Lucas, One of the Said Commons* (Dublin: n. p., 1743). On Lucas, see Morley, *Irish opinion and the American Revolution*, 40–4; Jim Smyth, ' Republicanism before the United Irishmen: The Case of Dr Charles Lucas', in D. George Boyce, Robert Eccleshall and Vincent Geoghegan (eds), *Political Discourse in Seventeenth- and Eighteenth-Century Ireland* (Basingstoke: Palgrave, 2001), 240–56.

137. Charles Lucas, *Divelina Libera: An Apology for the Civil Rights and Liberties of the Commons and Citizens of Dublin. Containing an Account of the Foundation and Constitution of This City* (Dublin: J. Esdall, 1744), 7–8.

138. Charles Lucas, *The Political Constitutions of Great-Britain and Ireland, Asserted and Vindicated: The Connection and Common Interest of Both Kingdoms, Demonstrated; and the Grievances, Which, Each, More Especially the Later, with It's Capital, Has Suffered, Under Oppressive and Tyrannical Governors, Usurping and Lawless Magistrates, Dependent and Iniquitous Judges, and Spurious and Corrupt Parlements, Set Forth in Several Addresses and Letters to the Free-Citizens of Dublin* (London: n. p., 1751), 2 vols.

139. Charles Lucas, *The Rights and Privileges of Parlements Asserted Upon Constitutional Principles: Against the Modern Anticonstitutional Clames of Chief Governors, to Take Notice Of, Animadvert Upon, and Protest against the Proceedings of Either House of Parlement: Humbly Addressed to His Excellency George, Lord Visc. Townshend* (Dublin: Tho. Ewing, 1770). On the associational context, see Martyn J. Powell, 'The Society of Free Citizens and Other Popular Political Clubs, 1749–89,' in Kelly and Powell (eds), *Clubs and Societies*, 243–63.

140. Henry Brooke, 'The Farmer's Case of the Roman Catholics of Ireland' [1760], in *Brookiana. Volume 1* (London: Richard Phillips, 1804), 208.

141. Patrick McNally, *Parties, Patriots and Undertakers: Parliamentary Politics in Early Hanoverian Ireland* (Dublin: Four Courts Press, 1997); Hayton, *Ruling Ireland*, 106–30, 209–36; Hill, *From Patriots to Unionists*; Powell, *Britain and Ireland in the Eighteenth-Century Crisis of Empire*, 48–81.

142. Kelly, *Prelude to Union*, 12–21.

143. Patrick Griffin, *The Townshend Moment: The Making of Empire and Revolution in the Eighteenth Century* (New Haven, CT: Yale University Press, 2017).

144. Jenna M. Gibbs, *Performing the Temple of Liberty. Slavery, Theater, and Popular Culture in London and Philadelphia, 1760–1850* (Baltimore: Johns Hopkins University Press, 2014), 59–66.

145. Powell, *Britain and Ireland in the Eighteenth-Century Crisis of Empire*, 158–221; James Livesey, 'Free Trade and Empire in the Anglo-Irish Commercial Propositions of 1785', *Journal of British Studies*, 52 (2013), 103–27.

146. Theresa M. O'Connor, 'The Embargo on the Export of Irish Provisions, 1776–9', *Irish Historical Studies*, 2 (1940), 3–11; Thomas M. Truxes, *Irish-American Trade, 1660–1783* (Cambridge: Cambridge University Press, 1988), 231–51.

147. James Stafford has recently completed a remarkable PhD thesis on this subject: 'Political Economy and the Reform of Empire in Ireland, 1776–1845' (University of Cambridge, 2016).

148. Edmund Burke, *Two Letters from Mr. Burke to Gentlemen in the City of Bristol, on the Bills Depending in Parliament relative to the Trade of Ireland* (London: J. Dodsley, 1778), 2nd edn, 4–13.

149. John Hely-Hutchinson, *The Commercial Restraints of Ireland Considered, in a Series of Letters to a Noble Lord. Containing an Historical Account of the Affairs of That Kingdom, so Far As They Relate to This Subject* (Dublin: W. Hallhead, 1779), vii, 4–8, 19–20, 30, 44–8, 76–7. See further, David Dickson, *Arctic Ireland: The Extraordinary Story of the Great Frost and Forgotten Famine of 1740–41* (Belfast: White Row

Press, 1997); James Kelly, 'Coping with Crisis: The Response to the Famine of 1740–1', *Eighteenth-Century Ireland/Iris an dá chultúr*, 27 (2012), 99–122.

150. Hely-Hutchinson, *The Commercial Restraints of Ireland Considered*, 31–2, 78–9.

151. Ibid., 69.

152. On this issue, see David Lammey, 'A Study of Anglo-Irish Relations between 1772 and 1782 with Particular Reference to the 'Free Trade' Movement'(PhD thesis, Queen's University, Belfast, 1984), and Lammey, 'The Free Trade Crisis: A Reappraisal,' in Gerard O'Brien (ed.), *Parliament, Politics, and People: Essays in Eighteenth-Century Irish History* (Dublin: Irish Academic Press, 1989), 69–92; Padhraig Higgins, *A Nation of Politicians: Gender, Patriotism, and Political Culture* (Madison, WI: University of Wisconsin Press, 2010), 202–33.

153. 'Opinion of Lord Lifford', 9 June 1779, in George O'Brien, 'The Irish Free Trade Agitation of 1779 (Part 1)', *The English Historical Review*, 38/152 (1923), 564–81, quote at 570; George O'Brien, 'The Irish Free Trade Agitation of 1779 (Part 2)', *The English Historical Review*, 39/153 (1924), 95–109.

154. 'Opinion of Edmund Sexton Pery', 12 June 1779, in O'Brien, 'Irish Free Trade Agitation (Part 1)', 571–2.

155. 'Opinion of Walter Hussey Burgh', 19 June 1779 in ibid., 575–6.

156. 'Opinion of the Commissioners of the Revenue', 26 June 1779, in ibid., 576–81.

157. Arthur Young, *A Tour In Ireland: With General Observations On The Present State Of That Kingdom, Made In The Years 1776, 1777 and 1778, and brought down to the end of 1779* (London: T. Cadell, 1780), 2 vols, II, 372.

158. George Townshend, 1st Marquess Townshend to John Beresford, 2 December 1779, in Beresford, *Correspondence*, ed. Beresford, I, 99.

159. John Beresford to John Robinson, March 14, 1780, in ibid., 128.

160. Henry Flood, speech of 11 June 1782, in Henry Flood, *The Celebrated Speeches of Colonel Henry Flood, on the Repeal of the Declatory Act of the 6th George Ist: As Delivered in the House of Commons of Ireland, on the 11th and 14th of June, 1782. Also, the Speech of Lord Abingdon, in the English House of Peers the 5th of July 1782, on Introducing His Bill for a Declaration of Right Over Every Part of the British Dependencies* (Dublin: C. Campbell, 1782), 11–12.

161. Henry Flood, speech of 14 June 1782, in ibid., 31.

162. Henry Grattan, *Memoirs of the Life and Times of the Rt. Hon. Henry Grattan* (London: Henry Colburn, 1839), 2 vols, II, 350; Morley, *Irish Opinion and the American Revolution*, 300–2.

Chapter 8. Shelburne

1. Anon., *Fugitive Political Essays, which Have Appeared in the Public Advertiser During the Last Winter, 1769 and 1770, Under the Several Names of Old Slyboots, Faction, Hortensius, a Lover of Consistency, & C* (London: Richardson and Urquhart, 1770), 89–93.

2. Chatham to Shelburne, December 1777, cited in Frank O'Gorman, 'Shelburne: A Chathamite in Opposition and in Government, 1760–82?', in Nigel Aston and Clarissa Campbell Orr (eds), *An Enlightenment Statesman in Whig Britain: Lord*

Shelburne in Context, 1737–1805 (Woodbridge: Boydell & Brewer, 2011), 137 n. 110; Shelburne replied on 23 December 1777, 'I am as entirely of your Lordship's opinion as to not subscribing to the independence of the colonies.' (ibid. n. 111).

3. Anon., 'Lord Shelburne', *London magazine, or, Gentleman's monthly intelligencer*, no. 51, 1782, 568.

4. Lawrence Klein, 'Sociability, Politeness, and Aristocratic Self-Formation in the Life and Career of the Second Earl of Shelburne', *The Historical Journal*, 55 (2012), 653–77.

5. Edmund Burke to Charles Watson-Wentworth, 2nd Marquess of Rockingham, 18 July 1768, *CEB*, II, 3.

6. 'Proceedings at a general meeting of the City of Westminster, held in Westminster Hall, on the 17th day of July, 1782', in Christopher Wyvill, *Political papers chiefly respecting the attempt of the County of York and other considerable districts, commenced in 1779, and continued during several subsequent years, to effect a reformation of the Parliament of Great-Britain* (York: W. Blanchard, 1794–1804), 6 vols, II, 163–9.

7. Shelburne to Dugald Stewart, 1795, in Dugald Stewart, *The Collected Works of Dugald Stewart*, ed. Sir William Hamilton (Edinburgh: Thomas Constable & Co., 1854–60), 11 vols, X, 95. See also, Shelburne to Morellet, 1802, in Edmond Fitzmaurice, *Life of William, Earl of Shelburne, First Marquess of Lansdowne, with extracts from his papers and correspondence* (London: Macmillan, 1912), revised 2nd edn, 2 vols, II, 430–1.

8. David Hume to Adam Smith, 13 September 1763, in Hume, *Letters*, ed. Greig, I, 394–7.

9. François Fénelon, *The adventures of Telemachus, the son of Ulysses. Translated from the French by John Hawkesworth* (London: W. Strahan, 1768), iii–iv.

10. Joseph Priestley to Richard Price, 21 July 1772, in Richard Price, *The Correspondence of Richard Price*, ed. D. O. Thomas and W. Bernard Peach (Durham, NC and Cardiff: Duke University Press and University of Wales Press, 1983–94), 3 vols, I, 132–5.

11. 'Song 765. A naval ode', *The Vocal Magazine; or, British Songster's Miscellany; containing all the English, Scotch and Irish songs, cantatas, glees, catches, airs, ballads* (London: J. Bew, 1778) (issue 6).

12. Antoine-Marie Cerisier, *Le destin de l'Amérique; ou, Dialogues pittoresques dans lesquels on developpe la cause des evenemens actuels, la politique et les interêts des puissances de l'Europe relativement à cette guerre et les suites qu' elle devrait avoir pour le bonheur de l'humanité* (London: J. Bew, 1782), 30.

13. Anon., *A Series of Letters addressed to the greatest politician in England: containing a description of several public characters; a defence of Sir George Savile; and of Lord Chatham's political sentiments, and his upright, spirited, and constitutional system, etc.* (London: Almon and Debrett, 1780), 62.

14. Nigel Aston, 'Petty and Fitzmaurice: Lord Shelburne and his Brother', in Aston and Campbell Orr (eds), *An Enlightenment Statesman in Whig Britain*, 29–50.

15. Fitzmaurice, *Life of William, Earl of Shelburne*, I, 5–7.

16. Ibid., 7–8

17. Clarissa Campbell Orr, 'Aunts, Wives, Courtiers: The Ladies of Bowood', in Aston and Campbell Orr (eds), *An Enlightenment Statesman in Whig Britain*, 51–78.

18. Fitzmaurice, *Life of William, Earl of Shelburne*, I, 9.

19. Ibid., 12.

20. William Blake Odgers, 'Sir William Blackstone', *Yale Law Journal* 28 (1919), 542–66; Wilfrid Prest, *William Blackstone: Law and Letters in the Eighteenth Century* (Oxford: Oxford University Press, 2008), 119–50.

21. Shelburne, speech of 19 May 1775, in *The Parliamentary Register; or, History of the proceedings and debates of the House of Commons [. . . of the House of Lords]; containing an account of the most interesting speeches and motions; accurate copies of the most remarkable letters and papers; of the most material evidence, petitions, &c. laid before, and offered to, the House, during the [first–sixth] session[s] of the Fourteenth Parliament of Great Britain* (London: J. Almon, 1775–80), 17 vols, II, 162.

22. Anon., 'Some Account of Lord Shelburne', *Hibernian magazine, or, Compendium of entertaining knowledge*, January 1780, 2.

23. Fitzmaurice, *Life of William, Earl of Shelburne*, I, 14–15.

24. Ibid., 16.

25. Ibid., 19. Shelburne did once declare in the House of Lords, on 26 October 1775, that 'I have more veneration for the character of King William than for any prince that ever swayed a sceptre', arguing against granting any British monarch the power to have a personal guard of foreign troops: *The Parliamentary Register . . . House of Lords*, V, 18.

26. Fitzmaurice, *Life of William, Earl of Shelburne*, I, 25–26.

27. Ibid., 20.

28. Ibid., 39.

29. Ibid., 24.

30. Ibid., 79.

31. Shelburne to Richard Price, 29 September 1786, in Price, *Correspondence*, ed. Thomas and Peach, III, 64.

32. Fitzmaurice, *Life of William, Earl of Shelburne*, I, 26.

33. Ibid., 38.

34. Ibid., 16–17.

35. Ibid., 41.

36. Ibid., 42.

37. Ibid., 69.

38. Ibid., 36.

39. Ibid., 80.

40. Ibid., 20.

41. Ibid., 44.

42. Ibid., 18.

43. Ibid., 17–18.

44. Ibid., 19.

45. Ibid., 17.

46. Ibid., 81.

47. Shelburne to Jeremy Bentham, 26 July 1781, in Jeremy Bentham, *The Correspondence of Jeremy Bentham, Volume 3: January 1781 to October 1788*, ed. Ian R. Christie (London: Athlone Press, 1971), 45–6.

48. David Hume to Tobias Smollett, 18 July 1767, in Hume, *Letters*, ed Greig, II, 151–2.

49. Adam Smith to Andreas Holt, 26 October 1780, in Smith, *Correspondence*, ed. Mossner et al., 249–53.

50. Adam Smith to William Strahan, 22 May 1783, in ibid., 266.

51. David Hume to Hugh Blair, 11 February 1766, in Hume, *Letters*, ed. Greig, II, 11–13.

52. Robert Clerk to Adam Ferguson, 10 October 1766, in Adam Ferguson, *The Correspondence of Adam Ferguson: 1745–1780*, ed. Vincenzo Merolle (London: Pickering & Chatto, 1995), 2 vols, I, 68.

53. Elizabeth Montagu to Henry Home, Lord Kames, 24 March 1767, in *Memoirs of the Life and Writings of the Honourable Henry Home of Kames: one of the Senators of the College of Justice, and one of the Lords Commissioners of Justiciary in Scotland; containing sketches of the progress of literature and general improvement in Scotland during the greater part of the Eighteenth century*, ed. Alexander Fraser Tytler of Woodhouselee (Edinburgh and London: William Creech, T. Cadell & W. Davies, 1807), 2 vols, II, 50–1.

54. Shelburne to Richard Price, 22 November 1786, in Price, *Correspondence*, ed. Thomas and Peach, III, 86–7.

55. On Shelburne's policy as derived from Bute's focus upon peace and security, see Rachel Banke, 'Bute's Empire: Reform, Reaction, and the Roots of Imperial Crisis', (PhD thesis, University of Notre Dame, IN, 2017).

56. Shelburne to Francis Fauquier, 19 February 1767, in Francis Fauquier, *The Official Papers of Francis Fauquier, Lieutenant Governor of Virginia, 1758–1768: 1764–1768* (vol. 3), ed. George Reese, *Virginia Historical Society Documents, Volume 16* (Charlottesville, VA: Published for the Virginia Historical Society by the University Press of Virginia, 1983), 1429–30.

57. Fitzmaurice, *Life of William, Earl of Shelburne*, I, 81.

58. Smith, *Wealth of Nations*, II, Book 4, ch. 2, 43.

59. Jack Fruchtman, Jr, *The Apocalyptic Politics of Richard Price and Joseph Priestley: A Study in Late Eighteenth-Century English Millennialism*, *Transactions of the American Philosophical Society*, 73, part 4 (Philadelphia: American Philosophical Society, 1983).

60. Richard Price to Elizabeth Montagu, 22 March 1771, in Price, *Correspondence*, ed. Thomas and Peach, I, 96–7.

61. Richard Price, *Four Dissertations* (London: A. Millar and T. Cadell, 1767).

62. G. M. Ditchfield, 'A Christian Whig: Lord Shelburne and the Latitudinarian Tradition', in Aston and Campbell Orr (eds), *An Enlightenment Statesman in Whig Britain*, 79–96, and 'The Subscription Issue in British Parliamentary Politics 1772–1779', *Parliamentary History*, 7 (1988), 45–80.

63. Wyvill, *Political papers chiefly respecting the attempt of the County of York*, I, 96, 107, 170, 190; II, 29–30, 156–7.

64. Shelburne to John Audry [chairman of the Wiltshire Committee], March 29 1780, in Wyvill, *Political papers chiefly respecting the attempt of the County of York*, IV, 131–6.

65. Richard Price, *Observations on Reversionary Payments: On Schemes for*

Providing Annuities for Widows, and for Persons in Old Age, on the Method of Calculating the Values of Assurances on Lives, and on the National Debt: to Which Are Added, Four Essays . . . Also, an Appendix, Containing a Complete Set of Tables (London: T. Cadell, 1772), 2nd edn, 365.

66. Shelburne to Richard Price, 26 December 1774, in Price, *Correspondence*, ed. Thomas and Peach, I, 178–80.

67. Shelburne to Richard Price, January 1775, in ibid., 185–6.

68. Arthur Lee to Richard Price, 20 April 1777, in ibid., 253–5.

69. Shelburne, speeches of 20 January, 1 February and 7 February 1775, *The Parliamentary Register . . . House of Lords*, II, 11–12, 25, 43–4, 48–50.

70. Shelburne, speech of 26 October 1775, ibid., V, 19.

71. Shelburne, speech of 31 October 1776, ibid., VII, 22.

72. Shelburne, speech of 31 October 1776, ibid., VII, 23–4.

73. Shelburne, speech of 20 December 1775, ibid., V, 165.

74. Shelburne, speech of 15 December 1775, ibid., V, 147.

75. Shelburne, speeches of 16 March 1775, ibid., II, 90–2.

76. Shelburne, speeches of 26 October 1775, ibid., V, 16.

77. Shelburne, speech of 15 December 1775, ibid., V, 149–50.

78. Shelburne, speech of 10 November, 1775, ibid., V, 69–72.

79. Shelburne, speech of 30 May, 1777, ibid., VII, 121–4.

80. Shelburne speech of 18 November 1777, ibid., X, 21–4.

81. Shelburne, speech of 15 November 1775, ibid., V, 96–7.

82. Shelburne, speech of 10 November 1775, ibid., V, 67.

83. Shelburne, speech of 10 November, 1775, ibid., V, 68–72.

84. Shelburne, speech of 31 October 1776, ibid., VII, 23–5.

85. Richard Price to Shelburne, 6 January, 1776, in Price, *Correspondence*, ed. Thomas and Peach, I, 237–8.

86. Price to Shelburne, 22 January 1776, in ibid., 238–40.

87. Virgil, *Aeneid*, 5: 667–74. Price's epigraph read: 'Quis furor iste novus? quo nunc, quo tenditis. Heu! misere cives? non Hostem inimicaque castra, Vestras Spes uritis'.

88. Richard Price, *Observations on the Nature of Civil Liberty, the Principles of Government and the Justice and Policy of the War with America* (London: T. Cadell, 1776), 104–9.

89. Price, *Observations on the Nature of Civil Liberty*, 109.

90. Anon., *Fanaticism and treason: or, a dispassionate history of the rise, progress, and suppression of the rebellious Insurrections in June 1780. By a real friend to religion and to Britain* (London: G. Kearsly, 1781), 2–3.

91. Shelburne, speeches of 2 June and 3 June 1780 in the House of Lords, *The Parliamentary History of England, from the earliest period to the year 1803. From which last-mentioned epoch it is continued downwards in the work entitled, 'The Parliamentary Debates.' Vol. XXI, comprising the period from the eleventh of February 1780, to the twenty-fifth of March 1781* (London: T. C. Hansard, 1814), 669–70, 677–82.

92. William Macintosh, *Travels in Europe, Asia and Africa; describing characters, customs, manners, laws, and productions of nature and art: containing various remarks on the political and commercial interests of Great Britain: and delineating,*

in particular, a new system for the government and improvement of the British settlements in the East Indies: Begun in the year 1777, and finished in 1781 (London: John Murray, 1782), 2 vols, I, 31–2.

93. Anon., *A serious answer to Lord George Gordon's letters to the Earl of Shelburne* (London: Hookham, 1782), 26.

94. Anon. [Shelburne, Richard Price and John Horne Tooke], *Facts Addressed to the Landholders, Stockholders, Merchants, Farmers, Manufacturers, Tradesmen, Proprietors of Every Description, and Generally to All the Subjects of Great Britain and Ireland* (London: 1780), 2nd edn, 3.

95. Ibid., 3–4.

96. Ibid., 4–5.

97. Ibid., 21.

98. Ibid., 27.

99. Shelburne's view of French financial wellbeing is precisely the opposite of the verdict of a recent historian, although his notion of the French threat to the entirety of the British Empire has been supported: Kenneth Margerison, 'Rogue Diplomacy: Sartine, Saint-Lubin and the French Attempt to Recover 'Lost India', 1776–80', *French History*, 30 (2016), 477–504.

100. [Shelburne, Price and Horne Tooke], *Facts Addressed to the Landholders*, 108, 114–15.

101. John Thelwall, 'The Connection between the CALAMITIES of the PRESENT REIGN, and the System of BOROUGH-MONGERING CORRUPTION', *The Tribune, a periodical publication, consisting chiefly of the political lectures of J. Thelwall, from the commencement of the second course in February, 1795, to the introduction of Mr. Pitt's Convention Act* (London: J. Thelwall, 1795), 3 vols, III, 6–7.

102. John Cannon, 'Petty [*formerly* Fitzmaurice], William, second earl of Shelburne and first marquess of Lansdowne (1737–1805), prime minister', *ODNB*.

103. Angel, *A General History of Ireland*, I, 169–70.

104. Young, *A Tour In Ireland*, I, 61.

105. Ibid., 439.

106. *The Morning Herald and Daily Advertiser* (London), 24 December 1782 (issue 672).

107. Young, *A Tour In Ireland*, I, 266.

108. Ibid., 267.

109. Griffin, *The Townshend Moment*, 165–216.

110. Martyn Powell, 'Shelburne and Ireland: Politician, Patriot, Absentee', in Aston and Campbell Orr (eds), *An Enlightenment Statesman in Whig Britain*, 141–60, at 144; Powell, *Britain and Ireland in the Eighteenth-Century Crisis of Empire*, 98–9.

111. Shelburne, 'Memorandum relative to my estates in Ireland', July and August 1770, cited in Powell, 'Shelburne and Ireland: Politician, Patriot, Absentee', 146 n. 23.

112. Powell, *Britain and Ireland in the Eighteenth-Century Crisis of Empire*, 100–6.

113. Thomas F. Moriarty, 'The Irish Absentee Tax Controversy of 1773: Study of Anglo-Irish Politics on the Eve of the American Revolution', *Proceedings of the American Philosophical Society*, 118 (1974), 370–408.

114. Ibid., 384 n. 21.

115. Chatham to Shelburne, 24 October 1773. Shelburne then reported Chatham's views, which were taken to be his own also, to Rockingham: Shelburne to Chatham, 31 October 1773: William Pitt, *Correspondence of William Pitt, Earl of Chatham*, ed. William Stanhope Taylor and John Henry Pringle (London: John Murray, 1840), 4 vols, IV, 300–5.

116. Shelburne, speech of 11 May 1779, *The Public Advertiser*, 12 May 1779. I am indebted to Martyn Powell for tracking down Shelburne's notorious assertion.

117. Powell, 'Shelburne and Ireland: Politician, Patriot, Absentee', 151 and n. 48.

118. Kelly, *Prelude to Union*, 35 and n. 11.

119. James Kelly, 'Caulfeild, James (1728–99), 1st Earl of Charlemont', *DIB*, II, 428–31.

120. Kelly, *Prelude to Union*, 36–9.

121. John Beresford to Isaac Barré, 7 April 1782, in Beresford, *Correspondence*, ed. Beresford, I, 193.

122. Beresford to Isaac Barré, 3 May 1782, in ibid., 198–9.

123. Kelly, *Prelude to Union*, 40–1 and n. 30.

124. Ibid., 42.

125. Ibid., 43–4.

126. Ibid., 44 and n. 39.

127. Portland to Shelburne, 6 June and 22 June 1782, in Anon., *Protestant Ascendancy and Catholic Emancipation Reconciled by a Legislative Union: With a View of the Transactions in 1782, Relative to the Independence of the Irish Parliament, and the Present Political State of Ireland, as Dependant on the Crown, and Connected with the Parliament of Great Britain* (London: J. Wright, 1800), 116–19.

128. James Caulfield, Lord Charlemont, *The Manuscripts and Correspondence of James, First Earl of Charlemont*, ed. John T. Gilbert (London: HMSO, 1891–94), 2 vols, I, 81.

129. Ibid., 400.

130. Richard Colley Wellesley, 1st Marquess Wellesley (known as the Earl of Mornington) to William Wyndham Grenville, 23 July 1782, in John Beville Fortescue, *The Manuscripts of J. B. Fortescue, esq., . . . preserved at Dropmore* (London: HMSO, 1892–1927), 10 vols, I, 164.

131. Peter Jupp, 'Earl Temple's Viceroyalty and the Renunciation Question, 1782–3', *Irish Historical Studies*, 17 (1971), 499–520, at 506.

132. Temple to Grenville, 1 December 1782, in Fortescue, *Manuscripts of J. B. Fortescue*, I, 166.

133. Ibid., 167.

134. Richard Price to Lieutenant-Colonel William Sharman, 7 August 1783, in Price, *Correspondence*, ed. Thomas and Peach, II, 188–91.

135. Temple to Grenville, 1 December 1782, in Fortescue, *Manuscripts of J. B. Fortescue*, I, 166–7.

136. Kelly, *Prelude to Union*, 51–4; Jupp, 'Earl Temple's Viceroyalty'.

137. Temple to Grenville, 25 December 1782, in Fortescue, *Manuscripts of J. B. Fortescue*, I, 173.

138. Temple to Grenville, 15 January, 1783, in ibid., 182.

139. Temple to Grenville, 4 December 1782, in ibid., 168.

140. Ibid., 169.

141. Temple to Grenville, 15 January, 1783, in ibid., 182–3.

142. Caulfield, *Manuscripts and Correspondence*, ed. Gilbert, I, 157.

143. Temple to Grenville, 14 and 21 December 1782, in Fortescue, *Manuscripts of J. B. Fortescue*, I, 170–2; James Kelly, 'The Irish Trade Dispute with Portugal 1780–87', *Studia Hibernica*, 25 (1990), 7–48; Temple to Grenville, 25 December 1782 and 5 February 1783, in Fortescue, *Manuscripts of J. B. Fortescue*, I, 174, 188.

144. Temple to Grenville, 2 February 1783, in ibid., 187.

145. Temple to Grenville, 15 January, 1783, in ibid., 181.

146. There are a number of newspaper reports hostile to Rutland and supportive of Temple, with the most antagonistic towards Rutland being a report in the *Volunteers Journal or Irish Herald*, 12 July 1784, 3. On opposition in the theatre, see Helen Burke, *Riotous Performances: The Struggle for Hegemony in the Irish Theater, 1712–1784* (Notre Dame, IN: Notre Dame University Press, 2003). I owe these references to Martyn Powell.

147. Kelly, *Prelude to Union*, 52.

148. Josiah Tucker, *The elements of commerce, and theory of taxes* (n. p.: n. p., 1755), 88–9.

149. Temple to Grenville, 13 January 1783, in Fortescue, *Manuscripts of J. B. Fortescue*, I, 179.

150. Richard Whatmore, 'Shelburne and Perpetual Peace: Small States, Commerce and International Relations within the Bowood Circle', in Aston and Campbell Orr (eds), *An Enlightenment Statesman in Whig Britain*, 249–73.

151. Benjamin Vaughan to John Quincy Adams, 24 August 1828, cited in Craig C. Murphy, *Benjamin Vaughan (1751–1835): The Life of an Anglo-American Intellectual* (PhD thesis, Columbia University, 1989), 74. Vaughan later dedicated his anonymously published *New and old principles of trade compared; or a treatise on the principles of commerce between nations* (London: J. Johnson, 1786) to Shelburne: 'To the most honourable the Marquis of Lansdown, this treatise is inscribed as a sincere and respectful tribute, due to the liberality of his lordship's public principles, and the importance of his public services.'

152. Norris, *Shelburne and Reform*, 171–239.

153. Eden to Lord Loughborough, 6 August 1782, William Eden, *The journal and correspondence of William, Lord of Auckland* (London: Richard Bentley, 1861), 2 vols, I, 20–1.

154. Caulfield, *Manuscripts and Correspondence*, ed. Gilbert, I, 422.

155. Richard Price to Shelburne, 20 January 1783, in Price, *Correspondence*, ed. Thomas and Peach, II, 166–70.

156. Anon. [Charles Coote, 1st Earl of Bellomont], *A Letter to the Earl of Shelburne, &c. &c. &c. from a noble Earl of the Kingdom of Ireland* [i.e., Coote] *upon the subject of final explanation respecting the legislative rights of Ireland* (London: G. Robinson and J. Robinson, 1783), 2nd edn, 3–9, 23–6.

157. Francis Dobbs, *A history of Irish affairs, from the 12th of October, 1779, to the*

15th September, 1782, the day of Lord Temple's arrival (Dublin: M. Mills, 1782), 150–1. On Dobbs, see David Lammey, 'Dobbs, Francis (1750–1811), politician and barrister', *ODNB*.

158. Dobbs, *History of Irish affairs*, 150.

Chapter 9. New Geneva

1. Thomas MacNevin, *The History of the Volunteers of 1782* (Dublin: R. Martin & Co., 1845), 4th edn, 236.

2. Charles Henry Wilson, *A Compleat Collection of the Resolutions of the Volunteers, Grand Juries, & C of Ireland, which Followed the Celebrated Resolves of the First Dungannon Diet: To which is Prefixed a Train of Historical Facts Relative to the Kingdom, from the Invasion of Henry II. Down, with the History of Volunteering, &c.* (Dublin: Joseph Hill, 1782), 2 vols, I, 12.

3. *The Remembrancer, or, Impartial repository of public events, for the year 1782, part 2* (London: J. Debrett, 1782), 370–1.

4. François d'Ivernois, 'Traduction de l'arrêté du Corps indépendant des Voltonaires de Dublin' and 'Traduction de l'arrêté des Dragons légers de la Cité de Dublin', *Pièces relatives à l'asyle ouvert en Irlande*, 12.

5. Karmin, *Sir Francis d'Ivernois*, 136.

6. William Coxe, *Travels in Switzerland* (London, 1789), 2 vols, II, 385.

7. Robert Edward Petre, *Reflections on the policy and justice of an immediate and general emancipation of the Catholics of Great Britain and Ireland* (London: E. Booker, 1804), 31, 40.

8. Étienne Clavière to Jean-André Deluc, 21 December 1773, BdG, Ms. fr. 2463, fols 92–3; Clarissa Campbell Orr, 'The Late Hanoverian Court and the Christian Enlightenment', in Michael Schaich (ed.), *Monarchy and Religion. The Transformation of Royal Culture in Eighteenth-Century Europe* (Oxford: Oxford University Press, 2007); Jean Roget to Samuel Romilly, 18 December 1782, in Roget, *Lettres de Jean Roget*, ed. Roget, 292.

9. Temple to Grenville, 21 December 1782, in Fortescue, *Manuscripts of J. B. Fortescue*, I, 172.

10. Temple to Grenville, 25 December 1782, in ibid., 174.

11. Temple to Grenville, 17 January, 1783, in ibid., 183.

12. Temple to Grenville, 9 February, 1783, ibid., 191.

13. Temple to Grenville, 2 March, 1783, ibid., 199.

14. Clavière to Jean-François Sautter-Martin, 3 March 1783, transcribed in the 'Journal d'Ami Dunant', BdG, Ms. fr. 901, fol. 39r. Reference is made to the letter in Karmin, *Sir Francis d'Ivernois*, 134–5, n. 32.

15. Temple to Thomas Townshend, 2 October 1783, cited in Karmin, *Sir Francis d'Ivernois*, 134 n. 29: 'the hopes which the sieur d'Ivernois holds out of raising amongst themselves the money which must be borrowed for their transportation and other expenses'.

16. Clavière to Jean-François Sautter-Martin, 3 March 1783, transcribed in the 'Journal d'Ami Dunant', BdG, Ms. fr. 901, fols 39–40.

17. 'At a full meeting of the Waterford Union, on Sunday 8th of March 1783', *The*

Remembrancer, or, Impartial repository of public events, for the year 1783, part 1 (London: J. Debrett, 1783), 321.

18. Chapuisat, 'Étienne Clavière', 55–6; Karmin, *Sir Francis d'Ivernois*, 136.

19. Clavière to [James?] Bernard, 3 April 1783, PRONI, T2627/6/1/16.

20. Karmin, *Sir Francis d'Ivernois*, 136.

21. 'At a Meeting of the Independent Light Company, No. 2, of the City of Waterford, on Monday the 17th of March 1783', *The Remembrancer . . . for the year 1783, part 1*, 322.

22. 'To the Gentlemen Volunteers of the Waterford Union, and the Company, No. 1', 19 March 1783', ibid.

23. Grenville to William Pitt, 12 February 1783, in Fortescue, *Manuscripts of J. B. Fortescue*, I, 194.

24. John King, *Thoughts on the Difficulties and Distresses in which the Peace of 1783 has involved the People of England* (London: J. Fielding et al., 1783), 16.

25. Temple to Grenville, 15 February 1783, in Fortescue, *Manuscripts of J. B. Fortescue*, I, 195.

26. Alexander Stephens, 'The Marquis of Buckingham', in *Public Characters of 1803–1804* (London: Richard Philips, 1804), 172.

27. Temple to Grenville, 2 March 1783, in Fortescue, *Manuscripts of J. B. Fortescue*, I, 199.

28. Stephens, 'Marquis of Buckingham', 173–80.

29. Temple to Grenville, 11 February 1783, in Fortescue, *Manuscripts of J. B. Fortescue*, I, 192–3.

30. Temple to Grenville, 1 March 1783, in ibid., 198.

31. William Wenman Seward, *Collectanea politica; or The political transactions of Ireland* (Dublin: Alex Stuart, 1801), 3 vols, I, 328.

32. Ibid., 329.

33. Ibid., 330.

34. Ibid., 331.

35. Ibid., 331–2.

36. 'Journal d'Ami Dunant', BdG, Ms. fr. 901, fol. 48r.

37. Sackville Hamilton to d'Ivernois, 18 August 1783, in Seward, *Collectanea politica*, I, 332–333.

38. *The London Chronicle*, 4 October 1783–7 October 1783 (issue 4,202).

39. Henry Flood, speech of 28 October 1783 in the Irish House of Commons, in Warden Flood, *Memoirs of the life and correspondence of the Right Hon. Henry Flood, M.P., colonel of the volunteers: containing reminiscences of the Irish commons, and an account of the grand national convention of 1783* (Dublin: John Cumming, 1838), 197.

40. Karmin, *Sir Francis d'Ivernois*, 155.

41. Angel, *A General History of Ireland*, I, vii–viii.

42. Ryland, *The History, Topography and Antiquities of the County and City of Waterford*, 1.

43. Ibid., 97–8.

44. Thomas Gimlette, 'The French Settlers in Ireland: No. 7. The Settlement in Waterford', *Ulster Journal of Archaeology*, 1st series, 4 (1856), 198–221. See further, Grace Lawless Lee, *The Huguenot Settlements in Ireland* (London: Longmans, 1936).

45. Gimlette, 'The French Settlers in Ireland, 201.

46. Samuel Lewis, *A Topographical Dictionary of Ireland: Comprising the Several Counties; Cities; Boroughs; Corporate, Market and Post Towns; Parishes; and Villages* . . . (London: for the author, 1837), 2 vols, I, 435.

47. William Chaffers, *Hall Marks on Gold and Silver plate, illustrated with the tables of annual date letters employed in the assay offices of England, Scotland & Ireland, a fac-simile of a copper-plate of markers' marks at Goldsmith's Hall* (London: J. Davy & sons, 1862), 54–7.

48. James Gandon and T. J. Mulvany (eds), *The Life of James Gandon* (1846); Frederick O'Dwyer, 'Gandon, James (1742–1823)', *ODNB*.

49. Edward McParland, *James Gandon: Vitruvius Hibernicus* (1985), 175–7.

50. 'Estimate of the houses for the Genevese, 20 May 1783', NLI, Bolton papers, Ms. 15910, (1–2), fol. 6.

51. Ibid., fol. 24.

52. Matthew Butler, 'New Geneva. Some correspondence relating to its foundation', *Journal of the Waterford and South-East of Ireland Archaeological Society*, XV (1912), 181–94.

53. Major James Ferrier to Cuffe, 2 July 1783, in Butler, ibid., 185–7.

54. Major James Ferrier to Cuffe, 21 January 1784, in Butler, ibid., 191–2.

55. Major James Ferrier to Alexander Alcock, 31 January 1784, in Butler, ibid., 193–4.

56. Alexander Alcock to Henry George Quinn, 31 January 1784, in Matthew Butler, 'New Geneva. Some correspondence relating to its foundation', *Journal of the Waterford and South-East of Ireland Archaeological Society*, XVI (1913), 1–17, at 1.

57. James Cuffe to the Lord Lieutenant, 24 March 1784, NLI, Bolton papers, Ms. 15910, (1–2), fol. 32.

58. Isaac Du Roveray to d'Ivernois, 28 June 1783, BdG, Ms. suppl. 1010, fols 51–2.

59. Isaac Du Roveray, 'Traduction d'une lettre de Sally Taylor à Monsieur d'Ivernois', BdG, Ms. suppl. 1010, fols 53–4.

60. Isaac Du Roveray to d'Ivernois, 24 July 1783, BdG, Ms. suppl. 1010, fols 54–6.

61. Isaac Du Roveray to d'Ivernois, undated, BdG, Ms. suppl. 1010, fols 57–8.

62. D'Ivernois to Isaac Du Roveray, 31 July 1783, BdG, Ms. suppl. 1010, fols 58–9.

63. Betsy Sheridan to Alicia LeFanu, 30 September 1784, in Betsy Sheridan, *Betsy Sheridan's Journal: Letters from Sheridan's Sister, 1784–1786 and 1788–1790*, ed. William LeFanu (Oxford: Oxford University Press, 1986), 23–33.

64. Betsy Sheridan to Alicia LeFanu, 18 October 1784, in ibid., 33–5.

65. Gimlette, 'The French Settlers in Ireland', 217–18.

66. Chapuisat, 'Étienne Clavière', 55–6.

67. Jeanne Vieusseux to Susette Vieusseux, 13 January 1783, in Rivier-Rose, *La famille Rivier*, 258; Jean-Marc Rivier, *Étienne Clavière (1735–1793). Un révolutionnaire, ami des Noirs* (Paris: Panormitis, 2006), 39.

68. Clavière to Jean-François Sautter-Martin, 3 March 1783, transcribed in the 'Journal d'Ami Dunant', BdG, Ms. fr. 901, fols 40–2.

69. Clavière to Théophile Cazenove, end of April 1783, in Bouchary, 'Étienne Clavière d'après sa correspondance', 29.

70. Étienne Clavière, 'Mémoire' submitted to Foster, July 1783, PRONI, Foster

papers, D262/8535. I am indebted to William Stafford for directing me to these manuscripts.

71. Karmin, *Sir Francis D'Ivernois*, 154.

72. Clavière to Foster, 26 July 1783, PRONI, Foster papers, D262/8535.

73. Clavière to Alexander Jaffray at Dublin, 6 August 1783, in Bouchary, 'Étienne Clavière d'après sa correspondance', 31.

74. 'Journal d'Ami Dunant', BdG, Ms. fr. 901, fols 51^r, 54^r.

75. Neuenschwander, 'Genève et Fribourg à la poursuite des séditieux', concerning Melly at 176–7.

76. Karmin, *Sir Francis d'Ivernois*, 146–7 and n. 29.

77. Fox to George III, 9 June 1783; George III to Fox, 10 June 1783; Fox to George III, 11 June 1783, in George III, *The Correspondence of King George the Third from 1760 to December 1783*, ed. Sir John Fortescue (London, Macmillan, 1927–28), 6 vols, VI, 392–3.

78. Hubert Butler, 'New Geneva in Waterford', *The Journal of the Royal Society of Antiquaries of Ireland*, 77 (1947), 154. Butler's source may have been a comment confirming Fox's contact with Saladin Egerton in the 'Journal d'Ami Dunant', BdG, Ms. fr. 901, fol. 51^v, stating that two copies of letters informing the British government about the pacification of Geneva had been lost, but would be responded to if they were sent again.

79. Anon., 'Angleterre', *Journal politique de Bruxelles*, 7 July 1783, 120.

80. Karmin, *Sir Francis d'Ivernois*, 150–1; 'Journal d'Ami Dunant', BdG, Ms. fr. 901, fols 58–9.

81. Joseph-Marie Quérard, in his *La France littéraire ou Dictionnaire bibliographique des savants, historiens et gens de lettres de la France, ainsi que des littérateurs étrangers qui ont écrit en français, plus particulièrement pendant les XVIIIe et XIXe siècles. Tome sixième* (Paris: Didot Frères, 1834), 29, made note of a *Dissertation apologétique et justificative, en faveur de M. Ami Melly, ci-devant citoyen de Genève et membre du CC*, being 'extraite du "Journal de Londres", no. 2 volume II, intitulé: 'Correspondance sur ce qui intéresse le bonheur de l'homme et de la société'. The work was said to have been published 'A la nouvelle Genève (Irlande), 1784'. No copy of this work appears to have survived, and I suspect that it was a republication in pamphlet form of Brissot's work on Melly. Brissot had a tendency to publish the same work in different places. The same work on Melly appeared as 'Législation criminelle. Genevois naturalisé Irlandois, jugé criminellement à Geneve: Question sur l'émigration examinée', in Brissot's *Bibliothèque philosophique du législateur, du politique, du jurisconsulte* (Berlin: n. p., 1785), 10 vols, X, 3–37. This was a shortened version, missing the final six paragraphs that had been published in the *Correspondance* of 1783, because they referred to New Geneva as a going concern.

82. Jacques-Pierre Brissot de Warville, 'Genevois naturalisé Irlandois, jugé criminellement à Geneve: Question sur l'émigration examinée', *Correspondance sur ce qui intéresse le bonheur de l'homme et de la société*, no. 2 volume 2 (London: E. Cox, 1783), 193.

83. Ibid., 94.

84. Ibid., 94–101, 123n.

85. Ibid., 103–4n. Brissot was referring to a work only published in the nineteenth

century: *The Monarchy of Man by Sir John Eliot (1590–1632). Now for the First Time Printed, from the Author's Manuscript in Harleian Collection*, ed. Alexander B. Grosart (London: Chiswick Press, 1879).

86. Brissot de Warville, 'Genevois naturalisé Irlandois, jugé criminellement à Geneve', 105.

87. Ibid., 106–8, 114.

88. Ibid., 119.

89. Ibid., 119–20.

90. Ibid., 122–4.

91. Temple to Grenville, 7 March 1783, in Fortescue, *Manuscripts of J. B. Fortescue*, I, 201.

92. Earl of Mornington to Grenville, 15 September 1783, in ibid., 220–1.

93. Earl of Mornington to Grenville, 28 September 1783, in ibid., 222.

94. Chatham to Rutland, 17 February 1784, in John Henry Manners, 5th Duke of Rutland, *The Manuscripts of His Grace the Duke of Rutland . . . preserved at Belvoir Castle* (London: HMSO, 1888–1905), 4 vols, III, 75.

95. Charles Stanhope, 'Letter addressed by Lord Mahon to a citizen of Geneva: Downing-Street, Feb. 24', *The Morning Chronicle and London Advertiser*, 13 March 1784 (issue 4,625).

96. Earl of Mornington to Temple, 10 April 1784, in Fortescue, *Manuscripts of J. B. Fortescue*, I, 227–8.

97. Ibid., 229.

98. Temple to Grenville, [1–7] September 1784, in ibid., 233.

99. Earl of Mornington to Grenville, 3 October 1784, in ibid., 238–9.

100. Karmin, *Sir Francis d'Ivernois*, 154.

101. David Chauvet to Reybaz, 14 March 1784, BdG, Ms. fr. 916, fol. 87.

102. Karmin, *Sir Francis d'Ivernois*, 155 and n. 15.

103. Butler, 'New Geneva. Some correspondence', *Journal of the Waterford and South-East of Ireland Archaeological Society*, XVI, 2.

104. Charles Stanhope to Thomas Orde, 18 April 1784, NLI, Bolton papers, Ms. 15914 (2), fols 33–4.

105. Du Roveray and d'Ivernois to Rutland (received 26 March 1784), in Butler, 'New Geneva. Some correspondence', *Journal of the Waterford and South-East of Ireland Archaeological Society*, XVI, 9–15.

106. Orde to the Commissioners appointed for settling the Genevan Emigrants, 27 March 1784, in Butler, 'New Geneva. Some correspondence relating to its foundation', *Journal of the Waterford and South-East of Ireland Archaeological Society*, XVI, 86–92, at 91.

107. John FitzGibbon to Rutland, 31 March 1783, NLI, Bolton papers, Ms. 15914 (1), fols 36–7.

108. On FitzGibbon, see Ann Kavanaugh, 'FitzGibbon, John, first earl of Clare (1748–1802), lord chancellor of Ireland', *ODNB*, and Ann C. Kavanaugh, *John FitzGibbon, Earl of Clare: Protestant Reaction and English Authority in Late Eighteenth-Century Ireland* (Dublin: Irish Academic Press, 1997).

109. FitzGibbon informed the then lord lieutenant Carlyle, on 27 May 1782, that his criticisms of the Irish Commons had not been shared 'with any man in Ireland . . .

except Beresford': John FitzGibbon, D. A. Fleming and A.P.W. Malcomson, *'A Volley of Execrations'. The Letters and Papers of John FitzGibbon, Earl of Clare 1772–1802* (Dublin: Irish Manuscripts Commission, 2005), 7.

110. Du Roveray and d'Ivernois to Orde, 18 April 1783, NLI, Bolton papers, Ms. 15913 (1), 40–1.

111. Du Roveray and d'Ivernois to Orde, undated [May 1784], 'Mémoire sur l'Etablissement des Genevois en Irlande', NLI, Bolton papers, Ms. 15914(3), fol. 59.

112. Ibid., fols 59–61.

113. Ibid., fols 60–1.

114. 'Additional Memorial from Mons. d'Ivernois delivered to me by Lord Mahon', 11 June 1784 Ms. 15914(3).

115. Ibid.

116. Ibid.

117. Orde to Commissioners for settling in Ireland a Colony of Emigrants from Geneva, 27 February 1784, in Butler, 'New Geneva. Some correspondence', *Journal of the Waterford and South-East of Ireland Archaeological Society*, XVI, 6–7.

118. Charles Stanhope, *Lettre à un citoyen de Genève, sur l'état actuel de l'Etablissement des Genevois en Irelande* (n. p.: n. p., [25 February 1784]).

119. Orde to Du Roveray and d'Ivernois, 28 May 1784, NLI, Ms. 15914(1), fol. 47.

120. Ibid., fols 47–51.

121. Ibid., fols 51–2.

122. 'Extrait de ce que Monsieur Foster a dit le Mardi matin 18 May 1784 à M. Du Roveray', PRONI, D262/8535.

123. D'Ivernois, *An Historical and Political View*, iv.

124. Ibid., 3n, 48n.

125. D'Ivernois, *Tableau historique*, vi–vii, xviii–xix, xxxiv, 396; *An Historical and Political View*, vii–viii, xviii, 10, 370.

126. William Gibson, 'State of the Works now carrying on at New Geneva 8th Sep. 1784', NLI, Bolton papers, Ms. 15915(1), fol. 68.

127. Betsy Sheridan to Alicia LeFanu, 30 September 1784, in Sheridan, *Betsy Sheridan's Journal*, ed. LeFanu, 32–3.

128. Charles Stanhope to d'Ivernois, 19 July 1785, BdG, Ms. suppl. 1010, fols 127–8.

129. Clavière to Jean Bérenger, 30 December 1784, in Chapuisat, 'Etienne Clavière', 57.

130. David Chauvet to Reybaz, 11 March 1785, BdG, Ms. fr. 916 fol. 88.

131. David Chauvet to Reybaz, 29 December, 1786, BdG, Ms. fr. 916 fols 96–7.

132. Karmin, *Sir Francis d'Ivernois*, 155–6.

133. David Chauvet to Reybaz, 20 May, 1785, Ms. fr. 916 fol. 93.

134. David Chauvet to Reybaz, 29 December, 1786, BdG, Ms. fr. 916 fol. 97.

135. D'Ivernois, *Tableau historique*, 188–9.

136. Ibid., 189–91.

137. Ibid., 195–6.

138. Ibid., 198–9.

139. Ibid., 199n.

140. Ibid., 200–4.

141. Ibid., 204.

142. Ibid., 205–6.

143. Dardier, *Ésaïe Gasc, citoyen de Genève*, 105–8.

144. Louis Dufour-Vernes, *L'ancienne Genève 1535–1798. Fragments historiques* (Geneva: Librairie Kündig, 1909), 103–19.

145. Anon., 'Scheme for disposing of the Buildings erected for the Genevese Emigrants', 24 September 1785, NLI, Ms. 15916(3) fols 74–6.

146. Bolton to Orde, 12 January 1786, and Orde to Bolton, 7 February 1786, NLI, Ms. 15916(3) fols 78–9, 81–2.

147. Thomas Orde, Memoranda, 10 August 1786, in Manners, *Manuscripts of His Grace the Duke of Rutland*, III, 332.

148. Jean Théodore Rivier, then fiancé of Susette Vieusseux, to Jeanne Vieusseux, undated [1783], Rivier-Rose, *La famille Rivier*, 123.

149. Rutland to Lord Sydney, 8 November 1786, in Manners, *Manuscripts of His Grace the Duke of Rutland*, III, 355.

150. Anon. [Jacques Mallet du Pan], *Supplément nécessaire à un écrit, intitulé: Le Philadelphien à Genève, &c. Sous Dublin 1783. Ou lettre à l'auteur anonyme de cette brochure* (n. p.: n. p., 1783), 34.

151. Francis Dobbs, *An historical review of the state of Ireland from the invasion of that country under Henry II. to its union with Great Britain on the first of January 1801* (London: T. Egerton, 1803), 2 vols, II, 27.

152. McKenna, *Political essays relative to the affairs of Ireland*, lx, n.

153. Karmin, *Sir Francis d'Ivernois*, 110–11, 141–51; Bénétruy, *L'Atelier de Mirabeau*, 28–9.

154. D'Ivernois to Charles Stanhope, 20 November 1784, KCRO, Stanhope papers, U1590 C65.3 Document C, fols 1–3.

155. Egan, *History, guide & directory of county and city of Waterford*, 209.

156. C. T. Greville to Rutland, 3 December 1784, in Manners, *Manuscripts of His Grace the Duke of Rutland*, III, 155.

157. McKenna, *Political essays relative to the affairs of Ireland*, xl–xli.

158. Gimlette, 'The French Settlers in Ireland' 216–17.

159. Robert Phelan, 'The New Geneva', *The Munster Express*, 22 January 1999.

160. Temple to Rutland, 30 April 1784, NLI, Bolton papers, Ms. 15913(2), 42–5.

161. Matthew Butler, 'New Geneva. Some correspondence relating to its foundation' *Journal of the Waterford and South-East of Ireland Archaeological Society*, XVI (1913), 1–17, 86–92; XVII (1914), 164–9; XVIII (1915), 21–6, 108–12.

162. Clavière to Foster, 26 July 1783, PRONI, Foster papers, D262/8535.

163. Temple to Grenville, 23 March 1783, in Fortescue, *Manuscripts of J. B. Fortescue*, I, 205.

Chapter 10. Barracks and Prison

1. Standish O'Grady, 19 September 1803, speech at the trial of Robert Emmet, in Madden, *The United Irishmen*, III 438. For a similar example, see the novel by James M'Henry, *O'Halloran; or, the Insurgent Chief. A tale of the United Irishmen* (Belfast: John Henderson, 1847), 424.

2. Martyn J. Powell, 'Charles James Fox and Ireland', *Irish Historical Studies*, 33 (2002), 169–90.

3. Henry Flood, speech of 28 October 1783 in the Irish House of Commons, in Flood, *Memoirs of the life and correspondence*, 196.

4. Anon. [James Mason], *Thoughts on the Protestant Ascendancy in Ireland* (London: J. Harding and J. Archer, 1805), 78.

5. Swift to Francis Grant, 3 April 1734, in Swift, *Correspondence*, ed. Williams, IV, 228–31.

6. Anon., *Remarks on the examiner and examination of the critical review of the liberties of British subjects, &c: With a further account of the P-rl-ry and M-l-y persecutions of the subjects of L-d in general, of the loyal citizens of D-n in particular, which attended the late proscription of Charles Lucas, now an exile for the cause of truth, and the constitution of his country. By the author of The critical review, &c.* (London: H. Carpenter, 1750), 5–13.

7. Henry Grattan's speech of 16 April 1782 in the Irish House of Commons, *The Scots Magazine, Volume 44* (1782), 192.

8. Charles Lucas, *Seasonable advice to the electors of members of Parlement at the ensuing general election. Addressed to the free and independent electors of the kingdom of Ireland in general, to those of Dublin in particular, upon the present critical conjuncture of affairs. Part II* (Dublin: Thomas Ewing, 1768), 10.

9. Anon., *Letter to henry flood, esq. on the present state of representation in Ireland* (Belfast: Henry and Robert Joy, 1783), 21–4.

10. Anon. [William Wenman Seward], *The rights of the people asserted, and the necessity of a more equal representation in parliament stated and proved. Wherein the resolutions of the volunteer delegates at Dungannon, Sept. 8, 1783, are particularly considered* (Dublin: P. Byrne and J. Hill, 1783), 3–9.

11. Ibid., 21–4, 27–9, 34, 41–9, 55–7.

12. John Keogh, *Thoughts on Equal Representation; with Hints for Improving the Manufactures and Employment of the Poor of Ireland* (Dublin: T. Heery, 1784).

13. Richard Price to Benjamin Franklin, 10 March 1783, in Price, *Correspondence*, ed. Thomas and Peach, II, 176–7.

14. Richard Price to Lieutenant-Colonel William Sharman, 7 August 1783, in ibid., 188–91.

15. Richard Price, 'Address to the Associated Volunteers of Ireland', in ibid., 191–2.

16. John Jebb, *Letters addressed to the volunteers of Ireland, on the subject of a parliamentary reform* (London: J. Stockdale, 1783), 17–18.

17. Anon., *Arguments to prove the interposition of the people to be constitutional and strictly legal: in which the necessity of a more equal representation of the people in Parliament is also proved: and a simple, unobjectionable mode of equalizing the representation is suggested* (Dublin: P. Byrne, 1783), 3–4.

18. Flood, *Memoirs of the life and correspondence*, 192.

19. Henry Flood, speech of 28 October 1783 in the Irish House of Commons, in ibid., 197.

20. Flood, *Memoirs of the life and correspondence*, 203, 207.

21. Ibid., 247–8.

22. Earl of Mornington to Grenville, 30 November 1783, in Fortescue, *Manuscripts of J. B. Fortescue*, I, 225.

23. Flood, *Memoirs of the life and correspondence*, 259, 261.

24. Earl of Mornington to Grenville, 23 November 1783, in Fortescue, *Manuscripts of J. B. Fortescue*, I, 223–4. See further, Higgins, *A Nation of Politicians*, 215–33.

25. Francis Dobbs, *Thoughts on the Conduct and Continuation of the Volunteers of Ireland* (Dublin: James Williams, 1783); Anon., *A Reform of the Irish House of Commons, Considered* (Dublin: Henry Watts, 1783).

26. Anon. [Patrick Duigenan], *The Alarm: or, An Address to the Nobility, Gentry and Clergy of the Church of Ireland, as by Law Established* (Dublin: Henry Watts, 1783).

27. William Drennan, *Letters of Orellana, an Irish Helot: to the Seven Northern Counties not represented in the National Assembly of Delegates, held at Dublin, in October, 1784, for obtaining a more equal representation of the People in the Parliament of Ireland. Originally published in the Belfast Newsletter* (Dublin: Chambers & T. Heery, 1785), 9.

28. Rutland to Pitt, Dublin Castle, 24 July 1784, in [William Pitt and Charles Manners], *Correspondence between the Right Hon. William Pitt and Charles, Duke of Rutland, Lord Lieutenant of Ireland. 1781–1787* (London: A. Spottiswoode, 1842), 22–4.

29. Rutland to Pitt, 16 June 1784, in ibid., 14–18. See also Pitt to Rutland, 4 December 1784, 46–7.

30. Anon. [John Hely-Hutchinson], *A letter from the secretary of state to the mayor of Cork, on the subject of the bill presented by Mr. Orde on the 15th August 1785, for effectuating the intercourse and commerce between Great Britain and Ireland* (Dublin: P. Byrne, 1785), 16.

31. George Rose, *The proposed system of trade with Ireland explained* (London: John Nichols, 1785), 8, 57.

32. William Woodfall, *An impartial sketch of the debate in the House of Commons of Ireland: on a motion made on Friday, August 12, 1785, by the Right Honourable Thomas Orde, secretary to His Grace Charles Manners, Duke of Rutland, Lord Lieutenant, for leave to bring in a Bill for effectuating the intercourse and commerce* (Dublin: Luke White, 1785), 194 [electronic resource].

33. R. B. McDowell, *Ireland in the Age of Imperialism and Revolution 1760–1801* (Oxford: Oxford University Press, 1979) 311–38; Paul Kelly, 'British and Irish Politics in 1785', *The English Historical Review*, 90 (1975), 536–63; Malcolmson, *John Foster*, 51–2.

34. John Ehrman, *The Younger Pitt: The Years of Acclaim* (London: Constable, 1969), 194–221.

35. Speech of Grattan, 20 March 1787, in Henry Grattan, *Memoirs of the Life and Times of the Rt. Hon. Henry Grattan, Volume 3* (London: H. Colburn, 1841), 290.

36. Ibid., 290–1.

37. Anon., *A Series of Letters Addressed to the Volunteers of Ireland* (Dublin: n. p., 1785).

38. James S. Donnelly and James J. Donnelly, 'The Rightboy Movement 1785–8', *Studia Hibernica*, 17/18 (1977–78), 120–202; Jim Smyth, *Men of No Property: Irish Radicals and Popular Politics in the Late Eighteenth Century* (London: Macmillan, 1992), 33–51.

39. Anon., *The utility of an union between Great Britain and Ireland, considered, by a friend to both countries* (London: J. Stockdale, 1788).

40. Thomas Bartlett, 'An End to Moral Economy: The Irish Militia Disturbances of 1793', *Past & Present* 99 (1983), 41–64; Ivan F. Nelson, 'The First Chapter of 1798?: Restoring a Military Perspective to the Irish Militia Riots of 1793', *Irish Historical Studies*, 33 (2003), 369–86.

41. Butler, 'New Geneva. Some correspondence' *Journal of the Waterford and South-East of Ireland Archaeological Society*, XVIII, 108–12.

42. Anon., 'A Journey through part of the Province of Munster. In a Letter to a Friend in Milford', *Walker's Hibernian Magazine, or Compendium of entertaining knowledge*, October 1794, 356–7.

43. Hely-Hutchinson to Orde, December 1785, cited in Donald H. Akenson, *The Irish Education Experiment: The National System of Education in the Nineteenth Century* (London: Routledge & Kegan Paul, 1970), 60. For the story of Orde's plan and its reception, see pp. 61–9, and James Kelly, 'The Context and Course of Thomas Orde's Plan of Education of 1787', *The Irish Journal of Education*, 20 (1986), 3–26.

44. Thomas Orde, *Mr Orde's plan of an improved system of education in Ireland; submitted to the House of Commons, April, 12, 1787; with the debate which arose thereon. Reported by John Giffard, Esq.* (Dublin: W. Porter, 1787), 20.

45. Ibid., 15–17.

46. Ibid., 14.

47. Ibid., 23–54.

48. Ibid., 52, 54.

49. Alicia LeFanu (ed.), *Memoirs of the life and writings of Mrs. Frances Sheridan: mother of the late Right Hon. Richard Brinsley Sheridan and author of 'Sidney Biddulph', 'Nourjahad', and 'The discovery'*... (London: G. and W. B. Whittaker, 1824), 365–6.

50. Anon. [Charles Brennan], *The unbiased Irishman: an answer to the publication on the state of the established church by Dr. Woodward, with strictures on the violation of the articles of Limerick, &c., to which is prefixed a review of the system for managing the affairs of Ireland from the commencement of the Pittite administration to the present day* (Dublin: H. Fitzpatrick, 1808 [orig. 1787]), 109.

51. William Campbell to the Earl of Charlemont, 9 February 1788, in Timothy Corcoran, *State Policy in Irish Education, A.D. 1536 to 1816, Exemplified in Documents Collected for Lectures to Postgraduate Classes* (Dublin: Fallon Brothers; New York: Longmans, Green & Co., 1916), 120.

52. Speech of Grattan, 14 February 1788, in Grattan, *Memoirs of the life and times ... Volume 3*, 322.

53. Grattan, comment of 1789, in ibid., 388–9, 392.

54. Thomas Russell, *Journals and Memoirs of Thomas Russell, 1791–5*, ed. C. J. Woods (Dublin: Irish Academic Press, 1991), 75.

55. For a classic overview, see Richard Bourke, *Empire and Revolution: The Political Life of Edmund Burke* (Princeton, NJ: Princeton University Press, 2015), 676–739, 866–917.

56. Edmund Burke, *A Letter from The Right Hon. Edmund Burke, M.P., in the Kingdom of Great Britain, to Sir Hercules Langrishe: Bart. M.P. on the subject of Roman Catholics of Ireland, and the propriety of admitting them to the elective*

franchise, consistently with the principles of the constitution as established at the Revolution (London: J. Debrett, 1792), 8–9.

57. Ibid., 40–1.

58. Ibid., 82.

59. Edmund Burke to Henry Grattan, 8 March 1793, *CEB*, VII, 360–1.

60. Burke, *Two letters addressed to a member of the present Parliament*, 6–7.

61. Ibid., 7–8.

62. E. A. Smith, *Whig Principles and Party Politics. Earl Fitzwilliam and the Whig Party, 1748–1833* (Manchester: Manchester University Press, 1975), 221.

63. Thomas Paine, 'To the Council of 500', in *Miscellaneous Letters & Essays, on Various Subjects* (London: R. Carlile, 1819), 8.

64. K. P. Ferguson, 'The Army in Ireland from the Restoration to the Act of Union' (PhD thesis, Trinity College Dublin, 1980); J. E. Cookson, *The British Armed Nation, 1793–1815* (Oxford: Oxford University Press, 1997), 40–62.

65. James Gordon, *History of the Rebellion in Ireland: In the Year 1789* (Dublin: J. D. Dewick, 1803), 4–14.

66. Lazare Hoche, 'À l'armée française destinée á opérer la révolution d'Irelande', in Édouard Guillon, *La France & l'Irlande pendant la révolution, Hoche et Humbert: d'après les documents inédits des archives de France et d'Irlande* (Paris: A. Colin, 1888), 467.

67. Theobald Wolfe Tone, *The Life of Theobald Wolfe Tone . . . Written by himself, and continued by his son . . .*, ed. W. T. W. Tone (Washington: Gales & Seaton, 1826), 2 vols, II, 256.

68. Edmund Burke to William Windham, 5 January 1797, *CEB*, IX, 223.

69. T. Crofton Croker, *Popular Songs, Illustrative of the French Invasions of Ireland* (London: The Percy Society, 1847), 32.

70. Edmund Burke to Earl Fitzwilliam, 9 September 1794, *CEB*, VII, 9.

71. Edmund Burke to William Windham, 16 October 1794, *CEB*, VIII, 33–4.

72. Ibid..

73. Edmund Burke to William Windham, 16 October 1794, *CEB*, VIII, 42.

74. Fitzwilliam to Burke, 21 October 1794, *CEB*, VIII, 58.

75. Thomas Hussey to Edmund Burke, 27 February 1795, *CEB*, VIII, 162.

76. Edmund Burke to William Elliot, 24 February 1795, *CEB*, VIII, 158.

77. Edmund Burke to Henry Grattan, 20 March 1795, *CEB*, VIII, 206.

78. Bourke, *Empire and Revolution*, 880–1.

79. Edmund Burke to Revd. Thomas Hussey, after 9 December 1796, *CEB*, IX, 161.

80. Edmund Burke, 'Letter on the Affairs of Ireland, written in the year 1797', in Edmund Burke, *The Writings and Speeches of Edmund Burke*, Volume 9, ed. R. B. McDowell and William B. Todd (Oxford: Oxford University Press, 1991), 680.

81. 'An Extract from Mr. Taylor's Account of the Rebellion in the County of Wexford', *Methodist Magazine*, June 1804, 275–8.

82. Edward Hay, *History of the Insurrection of the County of Wexford, A. D. 1798* (Dublin: J. Stockdale, 1803), 87.

83. Richard Musgrave, *A Concise Account of the Material Events and Atrocities Which Occurred in the Present Rebellion* (Cork: A Edwards, 1799), 30–5; Anon.,

'Richard Musgrave, Bart.', *The Annual Biography and Obituary for the Year 1820*, vol. 4 (London: n. p., 1820), 35–64.

84. Lord Castlereagh to Mr. Wickham, Dublin Castle, 12 June 1798, Stewart, Viscount Castlereagh, *Memoirs and Correspondence*, ed. Vane, I, 219.

85. H.F.B. Wheeler and A. M. Broadley, *The War in Wexford; An Account of the Rebellion in the South of Ireland in 1798, told from Original Documents* (London: John Lane, 1910), 164–5.

86. Ibid., 181–2.

87. Anon., *An Account of the Late Insurrection of Ireland; in which is laid open the secret correspondence between the United Irish and the French Government* (London: n. p., 1799), 22.

88. Wheeler and Broadley, *The War in Wexford*, 227.

89. Edward Baines, *History of the Wars of the French Revolution: From the Breaking Out of the War in 1792, to the Restoration of a General Peace in 1815; Comprehending the Civil History of Great Britain and France During the Period* (London: Longman, Hurst, Rees et al., 1817), 2 vols, I, 230–4.

90. Kevin Whelan, 'The Role of the Catholic Priest in the 1798 Rebellion in County Wexford', in Kevin Whelan and William Nolan (eds), *Wexford: History and Society* (Dublin: Geography Publications, 1987), 296–315; Ruán O'Donnell, 'Murphy, John (1753–1798)', *ODNB*.

91. Anon., *A Report of an Interesting Case Wherein Mr Francis Doyle, of Carrick-on-Suir, Merchant and Cloth Manufacturer, was plaintiff, and Sir Thomas Judkin Fitzgerald, High-Sheriff of the County of Tipperary in the Year 1798, was defendant* (Dublin: H. Fitzpatrick, 1801), 33.

92. Hay, *History of the Insurrection of the County of Wexford*, 250–1; Nicholas Furlong, 'Grogan, Cornelius (1738–1798)', *ODNB*; Ruán O'Donnell, 'Harvey, Beauchamp Bagenal (1762–1798)', *ODNB*.

93. Anon., review of Alexander Knox, *Essays on the Political Circumstances of Ireland* (1799), in *The Anti-Jacobin Review and Magazine for March 1799* (London: J. Plymsell, 1799) 2 vols, II, 234.

94. Richard Musgrave, 'Observations on whipping and free-quarter', *Memoirs of the Different Rebellions in Ireland, from the Arrival of the English* (London and Dublin: R. Marchbank, 1802), 3rd edn, 2 vols, II, 479.

95. Sir Jonah Barrington, *Personal Sketches and Recollections of His Own Times* (New York: Redfield, 1854), 5th edn, 146.

96. Egan, *History, guide & directory of county and city of Waterford*, 209.

97. Anon., 'New Geneva and the Gallantry of British Officers', 473.

98. Nicholas Carlisle, 'GENEVA, *or*, NEW GENEVA, in the Barony of Gualtiere, Co. of WATERFORD', *A topographical dictionary of Ireland; exhibiting the names of the several cities, towns, parishes and villages, with the barony, county, and province, to which they respectively belong . . .* (London: William Miller, 1810).

99. James Fraser, *Guide through Ireland. Descriptive of its scenery, towns, seats, antiquities, etc. with various statistical tables* (Dublin: William Curry, 1838), 68.

100. André Vieusseux, *The History of Switzerland: From the Irruption of the Barbarians to the Present Day* (London: Society for the Diffusion of Useful Knowledge, 1840), 205.

101. Anon., 'New Geneva', *Dublin University Magazine*, October 1838, 402.

102. James A. Sharp, *A new gazetteer, or, Topographical dictionary of the British Islands and narrow seas: comprising concise descriptions of about sixty thousand places, seats, natural features, and objects of note* (London: Longman, Brown, Green and Longmans, 1852), 2 vols, II, 295.

103. Egan, *History, guide & directory of county and city of Waterford*, 210–13, 560.

104. Ibid., 209.

Conclusion. After Revolution

1. Colin Kidd, *Union and Unionisms: Political Thought in Scotland, 1500–2000* (Cambridge: Cambridge University Press, 2006).

2. Gustav von Schlablendorf, *Bonaparte and the French People under his Consulate, translated from the German* (London: Tipper & Richards, 1804), preface.

3. Anon. [Felix Freeman], *A View of the Present State of France; With a Retrospect of the Past; Wherein the True Interests of the Continental Powers, and the Blessings of our Constitution, are clearly demonstrated* (Edinburgh: Oliver & Co., 1807), 4–9.

4. William Cobbett, *A collection of facts and observations: relative to the peace with Bonaparte, chiefly extracted from the Porcupine, and including Mr. Cobbett's letters to Lord Hawkesbury* (London: Cobbett and Morgan, 1801), 11.

5. Mark Philp (ed.), *The British Response to the Threat of Invasion, 1797–1815* (Aldershot: Ashgate, 2006).

6. Jacques-Pierre Brissot de Warville, 'Rapport sur les hostilités du Roi d'Angleterre, et du Stadhouder des Provinces-Unies, et sur la nécessité de déclarer que la République Françoise est en guerre avec eux; présenté le première Février 1793 à la Convention, Par J.-P. Brissot, au nom du Comité du défense générale', in *Brissot, député du département de l'Eure et Loire, à ses commettans, précédé d'autres Pièces intéressantes de Brissot* (London: R. Edwards et al., 1794), 62–7.

7. R. R. Palmer, *The Age of the Democratic Revolution: A Political History of Europe and America, 1760–1800: Volume 1: The Challenge* and *Volume 2: The Struggle* (Princeton, NJ: Princeton University Press, 1959, 1964).

8. Jonathan Israel, *A Revolution of the Mind: Radical Enlightenment and the Intellectual Origins of Modern Democracy* (Princeton, NJ: Princeton University Press, 2010); *Democratic Enlightenment: Philosophy, Revolution, and Human Rights, 1750–1790* (New York: Oxford University Press, 2011).

9. Murray Forsyth, 'The Old European States-System: Gentz versus Hauterive', *The Historical Journal*, 23 (1980), 521–38; Emma Rothschild, 'Language and Empire, c. 1800', *Historical Research*, 78 (2005), 208–29; Marc Belissa, *Repenser l'ordre européen (1795–1802): De la société des rois aux droits des nations* (Paris: Kimé, 2006); Isaac Nakhimovsky, 'The "Ignominious Fall of the European Commonwealth": Gentz, Hauterive, and the Armed Neutrality of 1800', in Koen Stapelbroek, *Trade and War: The Neutrality of Commerce in the Interstate System* (Helsinki: Collegium, 2011), 177–90, available at http://www.helsinki.fi/collegium/journal/volumes/volume_10/index.htm, accessed 27 May 2109.

10. Friedrich Gentz, *A vindication of Europe and Great Britain from*

misrepresentation and aspersion; extracted and translated from Mr. Gentz's answer to Mr. Hauterive (London: 1803).

11. Frank O'Gorman, *The Long Eighteenth Century: British Political and Social History 1688–1832* (London: Arnold, 1997); Roy Porter, *English Society in the Eighteenth Century* (London: Penguin, 1982); Dror Wahman, *The Making of the Modern Self: Identity and Culture in Eighteenth-Century England* (New Haven, CT: Yale University Press, 2004). The sense of perpetual crisis is conveyed in J.G.A. Pocock's 'The Varieties of Whiggism from Exclusion to Reform: A History of Ideology and Discourse', in Pocock, *Virtue, Commerce, and History: Essays on Political Thought and History, Chiefly in the Eighteenth Century* (Cambridge: Cambridge University Press, 1985), 215–310.

12. Paul Bastid, *Sieyès et sa pensée* (Paris: Hachette, 1939); Michael Sonenscher, *Sans-Culottes: An Eighteenth-Century Emblem in the French Revolution* (Princeton, NJ: Princeton University Press, 2008).

13. Philip Schofield, *Utility and Democracy: The Political Thought of Jeremy Bentham* (Oxford: Oxford University Press, 2006).

Manuscript Sources

Archives d'État de Genève, Ms. Hist. 61, 70–1, 84.
Archives nationales (France), T//646/1.
Bedfordshire and Luton Archives and Record Service, L 29/561/15.
Bibliothèque de Genève (BdG)
Ms. Cramer 81, fols 40–1
Ms. fr. 901, fols 5r, 8–9, 39, 39r, 40, 41, 42, 48r, 51r, 51v, 54r, 58, 59
Ms. fr. 916 fols 87, 88, 93, 96, 97
Ms. fr. 2461, F1652, fols, 3–30, 33–47
Ms. fr. 2461, fol. 36B
Ms. fr 2463, fols 85–112
Ms. fr. 2465, fols 74–5
Ms. fr. 2475, fols 100–3, 118–19
Ms. fr. 2476, 105–7, 110, 116, 117, 120–5, 134
Ms. fr. 2486
Ms. suppl. 32, fols 169–74, 303, 329–30, 351–3, 355–63, 366, 368, 370–2, 374–5
Ms. suppl. 1010, fols 12, 34–5, 40, 49–59, 116, 121–3, 126–8
Gf 315/179 (20).
British Library (BL), Bowood papers
Add. Ms. 88906/3/9, fol. 50.
Add. Ms. 88906/3/14 fols 31–5
Add. Ms. 88906/3/24 fol. 3–6.
Huntington Library, Stowe papers, STG Box 27 (21).
Kent County Record Office (KCRO), Stanhope papers, U1590 A2, A5–6, A17–18, A27–8, C62–3, C65–6.
National Archives (NA)
Foreign Office, 95/8/12
Public Record Office, 30/70/3/135, 30/70/3/136.
National Library of Ireland (NLI), Bolton papers
Ms. 15910, (1–2), fol. 6, 24, 32
Ms. 15913 (1–2), fols 40–5
Ms. 15914 (1–3), fols 33–4, 36–7, 47–52, 59–61
Ms. 15915(1), fol. 68
Ms. 15916(3) fols 74–6, 78–9, 81–2.
Public Record Office of Northern Ireland (PRONI), Foster papers, D262/8535, T2627/6/1/16.
St Andrews Special Collections, *Révolution et troubles de Genève*, fols 30–6.

Online Resources

The Schools' Collection (1934–1939), vol. 0652, 240–50, National Folklore Collection, University College Dublin, https://www.duchas.ie/en/cbes/4428156/4382339.

Stapelbroek, Koen, *Trade and War: The Neutrality of Commerce in the Interstate System* (Helsinki: Collegium, 2011): http://www.helsinki.fi/collegium/journal/volumes/volume_10/index.htm.

Statutes of the Realm: Volume 7, 1695–1701, ed. John Raithby (s.l: Great Britain Record Commission, 1820): *British History Online*, https://www.british-history.ac.uk/statutes-realm/vol7/pp607-608.

Printed Primary Sources

'A. J.', 'Reminiscences of the Irish Rebellion of 1798. Geneva Barracks, Waterford', *The Court Magazine and Belle Assemblée*, vol. 7, August 1835

Addison, Joseph, *Remarks on several parts of Italy, &c. In the years 1701, 1702, 1703* (London: J. Tonson, 1718), 2nd edn.

Addison, Joseph, *The Letters of Joseph Addison*, ed. Walter Graham (Oxford: Oxford University Press, 1941).

Alembert, Jean-Baptiste le Rond d', 'A Short Account of the Government of Geneva', in *Miscellaneous Pieces in Literature, History, and Philosophy* (London: C. Henderson, 1765).

Alexander, James, *Some Account of the First Apparent Symptoms of the Late Rebellion in the County of Kildare* (Dublin: John Jones, 1800).

Anderson, James, *Observations on the Means of Exciting a Spirit of National Industry: Chiefly Intended to Promote the Agriculture, Commerce, Manufactures, and Fisheries, of Scotland* (Edinburgh, T. Cadell and C. Elliot, 1777).

Angel, John, *A General History of Ireland, in Its Antient and Modern State* (Dublin: for the author, 1781).

Anon., *Some Arguments to Prove the Growing Greatness of the Northern Princes: And the Reason Thereof; with Many Other Remarks on Our Trade and Commerce, and an Effectual Remedy against the Scotch-Act* (London: n. p., [1695]).

Anon., *Some Considerations Upon the Late Act of the Parliament of Scotland: For Constituting an Indian Company; in a Letter to a Friend* (London: n. p., 1695).

Anon., *Some Remedies to Prevent the Mischiefs from the Late Act of Parliament Made in Scotland: In Relation to the East-India Trade* (London: n. p., [1695]).

Anon., *The Irregular and Disorderly State of the Plantation-Trade Discuss'd and Humbly Offered to the Consideration of the Right Honourable the Lords and Commons in Parliament Assembled* ([London]: n. p., 1695).

Anon., *A Letter from a Gentleman in the Country to His Friend at Edinburgh: Wherein It Is Clearly Proved That the Scottish African and Indian Company Is Exactly Calculated for the Interest of Scotland* (Edinburgh: George Mosman, 1696).

Anon., *Some considerations concerning the prejudice which the Scotch act establishing a company to trade to the East and West-Indies, (with large priviledges, and on easie terms) may bring to the English sugar plantations, and the manufactury of refining sugar in England, and some means to prevent the same from Scotland and other nations* (London: n. p., [1696]).

Anon., *Some Seasonable and Modest Thoughts Partly Occasioned By, and Partly Concerning the Scots East-India Company. Humbly offered to R. H. Esq. a Member of the present Parliament. By an unfeigned and hearty Lover of England* (Edinburgh: George Mosman, 1696).

Anon., *The Linnen and Woollen Manufactory Discoursed: With the Nature of Companies and Trade in General: and Particularly, That of the Companies for the Linnen Manufactory of England and Ireland. with Some Reflections How the Trade of Ireland Hath Formerly, and May Now, Affect England. Printed at the Request of a Peer of This Realm* (London: Geo. Huddleston, 1698).

Anon., *An Answer to the Most Material Objections Made by the Linnen-drapers, against the Bill Which Restrains the Wearing East-India Wrought Silks, &c. in England: Humbly Submitted to the Consideration of the Most Honourable House of Lords* ([London]: n. p., [1699]).

Anon., *A Proposal for Remeeding [sic] Our Excessive Luxury* ([Edinburgh]: n. p., 1700).

Anon., *A Serious advice to the African and Indian Company* ([Edinburgh]: n. p., [1700]).

Anon., *An Answer to the Most Material Objections That Have Been Raised against Restraining the East-India Trade; with Five Queries* (n. p.: n. p., 1701).

Anon., *A Debate between Three Ministers of State on the Present Affairs of England. in Relation to the Disposition of the Nation at Home, Our Alliances Abroad, and the Designs of France* (London: for the author, 1702).

Anon., *A Modest Defence of the Government: In a Dialogue between Kinglove, an Old Cavalier, and Meanwell, a Modern Tory. Written by a Sober Stander-By, Who Is Wholly Unconcern'd in the Ministry, or the Funds* (London: C.T., 1702).

Anon., *Division Our Destruction: Or, a Short History of the French Faction in England* (London: John Nutt, 1702).

Anon., *Private Debates in the House of Commons: In the Year 1677. in Relation to a War with France, and an Alliance with Holland, &c. . . . Together with Speeches by King Charles Ii, to the Lords and Commons. with a Discourse Showing the Absolute Necessity of a War with France on This Critical Juncture, in Order to Procure a Lasting Peace at Home* (London: J. Nutt, 1702).

Anon., *The Dangers of Europe, from the Growing Power of France: With Some Free Thoughts on Remedies. and Particularly on the Cure of Our Divisions at Home: in Order to a Successful War [sic] Abroad against the French King and His Allies. by the Author Of, the Duke of Anjou's Succession Considered* (London: A. Baldwin, 1702), 3rd edn.

Anon., *The Popish pretenders to the forfeited estates in Ireland unmask'd, and lay'd open: Being an answer to a letter from a member of Parliament desiring his friend to inquire into the character and circumstances of some persons, who (by the Act relating to Forfeitures,) have been, or are likely to be restored to their estates* (London: Booksellers of London and Westminster, 1702).

Anon., *Memorial Concerning the State of the Manufactures Before and Since the Year 1700, at Which Time the Laws Concerning Trade and Manufactures Were Revived and Increased: As Also, Some Remarks Upon the Arts Used for Eluding These Laws, Humbly Offered to His Grace, and the Honourable Estates of Parliament* (Edinburgh: n. p., 1704).

Anon., *Remarks on the English Woollen Manufactury for Exportation And Necessity of Preventing the Irish Wool Being Run* (London: Geo. Grierson, 1730).

Anon., *Entretien politique entre quelques Suisses des treize cantons & des pays Alliés, sur L'état Présent Ouáse trouve le Corps Helvétique. Avec une carte curieuse & exacte de toute de la Suisse* (London: Samuel Harding, 1738).

Anon., *Remarks on the examiner and examination of the critical review of the liberties of British subjects, &c: With a further account of the P-rl-ry and M-l-y persecutions of the subjects of L-d in general, of the loyal citizens of D-n in particular, which attended the late proscription of Charles Lucas, now an exile for the cause of truth, and the constitution of his country. By the author of The critical review, &c.* (London: H. Carpenter, 1750).

Anon., 'Extrait d'une Histoire de Genève, par Mr. R. C** A Messieurs les Journalistes', *Journal Helvétique*, January 1755.

Anon., *The Act for Permitting the Free Importation of Cattle from Ireland, Considered with a View to the Interests of Both Kingdoms* (London: J. Dodsley, 1760).

Anon., *Représentations des citoyens et bourgeois de Genève au premier syndic de cette république; avec les réponses du Conseil à ces representations* ([Geneva]: n. p., 1763).

Anon, *Exposé de la conduite des sindics et conseil de la république de Genève* ([Geneva]: n. p., 1767).

Anon., *Lettre d'un citoyen de Genève à un autre citoyen. Le 15 Février 1768* (Geneva: n. p., 1768).

Anon., 'Reflexions Sur les Loix Somptuaires, par un Citoyen de Genève', *Journal Helvétique*, January 1769.

Anon., *Fugitive Political Essays, which Have Appeared in the Public Advertiser During the Last Winter, 1769 and 1770, Under the Several Names of Old Slyboots, Faction, Hortensius, a Lover of Consistency, & C* (London: Richardson and Urquhart, 1770).

Anon., *Les bigarures d'un citoyen de Genève: et ses conseils republicains dediés aux Américains; avec quantités d'anecdotes amusantes* (Philadelphia: General Congress [*sic*], 1776).

Anon., *À l'Auteur D'une Lettre prétendue écrite du Purgatoire* (Geneva: n. p., 1780).

Anon., *A Series of Letters addressed to the greatest politician in England: containing a description of several public characters ; a defence of Sir George Savile ; and of Lord Chatham's political sentiments, and his upright, spirited, and constitutional system, etc.* (London: Almon and Debrett, 1780).

Anon., *A view of the present state of Ireland: Containing observations upon the following subjects, viz. its dependance, linen trade, provision trade, woolen manufactory, coals, fishery, agriculture, of emigration, import trade of the city of Dublin, effect of the present mode of raising the revenue, on the health and happiness of the people, the revenue, a national bank, and an absentee tax : intended for the consideration of Parliament, on the approaching enlargement of the trade of that kingdom : to which is added, A sketch of some of the principal political characters in the Irish House of Commons* (London: R. Faulder, 1780).

Anon., *Le Code naturel, ou le rêve d'un bon citoyen* ([Geneva]: n. p., [1780]).

Anon., *Les bigarrures ou récapitulation de plusieurs brochures* ([Geneva]: n. p., [1780]).

Anon., *Réflexions Sur La Commission Conciliatrice Et sur les motifs qui l'ont fait réjetter* ([Geneva], n. p., [1780]).

Anon., *Seconde réponse aux deuxième, troisième et quatrième lettres d'un représentant qui cesse de paroître modéré* ([Geneva]: n. p., 1780).

Anon., *The reformer: By an independent freeholder* (London: Fielding & Walker, 1780).

Anon., *Très-humble et très-respectueuse addresse de plusieurs Citoyens et Bourgeois au Mag. Petit Conseil, Remise aux Seigneurs Syndics le 11 Décembre 1780* ([Geneva], n. p., [1780]).

Anon., *Très-humble et très-respectueuse Déclaration Des Citoyens & Bourgeois Représentans. Rémise aux Seigneurs Syndics, & à M. le Procureur-Général, le 23 Nov. 1780, par environ 1040 Citoyens ou Bourgeois* (Geneva: n. p., 1780).

Anon., *Très-humble et très-respectueuse déclaration, Remise à Messieurs les Syndics, au nom d'un très-grand nombre de Membres du Magnifique Conseil des Deux-Cent, le Dimanche soir 16 Janvier 1780* ([Geneva], n. p., [1780]).

Anon., *Très-humble et très-respectueuse Réquisition, Addressée au Mag. Petit Conseil par les membres Constitutionnaires du Magnifique Conseil des Deux-Cent. Remise par eux à Messieurs les Syndics le 9 Novembre 1780. Et appuyée par un grand nombre de Citoyens & Bourgeois* ([Geneva]: n. p., 1780).

Anon., *Très-humble et très-respectueuse Réquisition, Addressée au Mag. Petit Conseil, par les membres du Magnifique Conseil des Deux-Cent et par les citoyens et bouregois Constitutionnaires. Remise à Messieurs les Syndics le 21 Novembre 1780* ([Geneva]: n. p., 1780).

Anon., *Très-humble et très-respectueuse Réquisition, Addressée au Mag. Petit Conseil, par les membres du Magnifique Conseil des Deux-Cent et par les citoyens et bouregois Constitutionnaires. Remise à Messieurs les Syndics le 7 Décembre 1780* ([Geneva]: n. p., 1780).

Anon., *Très-humble et très-respectueuse Réquisition des membres Constitutionnaires du Magnifique Conseil des Deux-Cent, Addressée au Mag. Petit Conseil, Et remise à Messieurs les Syndics le 18 Mars 1780* (Geneva: n. p., 1780).

Anon., *Fanaticism and treason: or, a dispassionate history of the rise, progress, and suppression, of the rebellious insurrections in June, 1780. By a real friend to religion and to Britain* (London: G. Kearsly, 1781).

Anon., *Note Remise le 13 Mai 1781 à Monsieur le Premier Syndic, par les Seigneurs représentans de Zurich et de Berne* ([Geneva]: n. p., 1781).

Anon., *Très-humble et très-respectueuse déclaration des membres du Magnifique Conseil des Deux-Cent et des Citoyens et Bourgeois Constitutionnaires; addressée au Mag. Petit Conseil et remise à Messieurs les Syndics le 26 Décembre 1781* ([Geneva]: n. p., 1781).

Anon., *Très-humble et très-respectueuse déclaration, présentée au Mag. Petit-Conseil par les membres du Magnifique Conseil des Deux-Cent et des Citoyens et Bourgeois Constitutionnaires; addressée au Mag. Petit Conseil et remise à Messieurs les Syndics le 29 Octobre 1781* ([Geneva]: n. p., 1781).

Anon., *Très-humble et très-respectueuse représentation des Citoyens & Bourgeois représentans. Contenant les preuves de la légalité de l'edit de 1768. Tirées des faits, des Actes de tous les Conseils de la République, & des Déclarations même des négatifs. Rémise aux Seigneurs Syndics, & à M. le Procureur-Général, le 10 Décembre 1781* (Geneva: n. p., 1781).

Anon., *Très-humble et très-respectueuse représentation des Citoyens & Bourgeois représentans. Rémise aux Seigneurs Syndics, & à M. le Procureur-Général, le 24 Septembre 1781* (Geneva: n. p., 1781).

Anon., *A serious answer to Lord George Gordon's letters to the Earl of Shelburne: In which an attempt is made, by fair and ingenuous argument, to give ample satisfaction to His Lordship's doubts, and to relieve him, if possible, from any inquietude for the salvation of the state: considered either in a moral, political, or religious view* (London: Hookham, 1782).

Anon., *Édit du 21 Novembre 1782. Extrait des registres du conseil des 5, 6, 11, 12, 13 & 14 Novembre 1782* ([Geneva?]: n. p., 1782).

Anon., *Lettre adressée aux Magnifiques, puissans, et très-honorés seigneurs, les Seigneurs Bourguemaitre, Petit & Grand Conseils de la Ville & République de Zurich, et les Seigneurs Avoyer, Petit & Grand Conseils de la Ville & République de Berne, par les Citoyens & Bourgeois représentans de la ville & république de Genève. Suivie d'une addresse aux Seigneurs Syndics de la Ville & République de Genève, a eux rémise, le 9 Mai 1782* (Geneva: n. p., 1782).

Anon., *Lettres genevoises: Contenant des details peu connus sur les derniers troubles de la Republique de Geneve* ([Geneva]: n. p., 1782).

Anon., *Précis historique de la dernière Révolution de Genève; Et en particulier de la Réforme que le Souverain de cette République a faite dans les Conseils Administrateurs* (Geneva: n. p., 1782).

Anon., *Traduction d'une lettre du Louable Canton de Berne, Adressé aux Seigneurs Syndics* (Geneva: n. p., 1782).

Anon., *Très-humble et très-respectueuse déclaration des Citoyens & Bourgeois représentans. Rémise aux Seigneurs Syndics, & à M. le Procureur-Général, le 31 Mai 1782* (Geneva: n. p., 1782).

Anon., *Très-humble et très-respectueuse représentation des Citoyens & Bourgeois représentans, dans laquelle on réfute la partie de la Déclaration des Négatifs du 29e 8bre 1781, Qui traite de la prise d'armes & de l'Edit du mois de Février 1781. Suivie de notes essentielles sur la Souveraineté du Conseil Général. Rémise aux Seigneurs Syndics, et à M. le Procureur-Général, par la Généralité des Citoyens & Bourgeois Représentans, le 18e Mars 1782* (Geneva: n. p., 1782).

Anon., *A Reform of the Irish House of Commons, Considered* (Dublin: Henry Watts, 1783).

Anon., 'Angleterre', *Journal politique de Bruxelles*, 7 July 1783.

Anon., *Arguments to prove the interposition of the people to be constitutional and strictly legal: in which the necessity of a more equal representation of the people in Parliament is also proved: and a simple, unobjectionable mode of equalizing the representation is suggested* (Dublin: P. Byrne, 1783).

Anon., *Collection des Édits Civils, Revus en 1713, Auxquels il n'a pas été dérogé par l'Edit de Pacification. Faite en exécution de l'Article VIII du Titre XVII de l'Edit de Pacification* (Geneva: Jean-Léonard Pellet, 1783).

Anon., *Letter to henry flood, esq. on the present state of representation in Ireland* (Belfast: Henry and Robert Joy, 1783).

Anon., *A Series of Letters Addressed to the Volunteers of Ireland* (Dublin: n. p., 1785).

Anon., *The utility of an union between Great Britain and Ireland, considered, by a friend to both countries* (London: J. Stockdale, 1788).

Anon., 'A Journey through part of the Province of Munster. In a Letter to a Friend in Milford', *Walker's Hibernian Magazine, or Compendium of entertaining knowledge*, October 1794, 356–7.

Anon., *An Account of the Late Insurrection of Ireland; in which is laid open the secret correspondence between the United Irish and the French Government* (London: n. p., 1799).

Anon., review of Alexander Knox, *Essays on the Political Circumstances of Ireland* (1799), in *The Anti-Jacobin Review and Magazine for March 1799* (London: J. Plymsell, 1799), 2 vols.

Anon., *Protestant Ascendancy and Catholic Emancipation Reconciled by a Legislative Union: With a View of the Transactions in 1782, Relative to the Independence of the Irish Parliament, and the Present Political State of Ireland, as Dependant on the Crown, and Connected with the Parliament of Great Britain* (London: J. Wright, 1800).

Anon., *A Report of an Interesting Case Wherein Mr Francis Doyle, of Carrick-on-Suir, Merchant and Cloth Manufacturer, was plaintiff, and Sir Thomas Judkin Fitzgerald, High-Sheriff of the County of Tipperary in the Year 1798, was defendant* (Dublin: H. Fitzpatrick, 1801).

Anon., *Junius: Including Letters by the Same Writer Under Other Signatures: To Which are Added his Confidential Correspondence With Mr. Wilkes . . .* (London: Rivington et al., 1814), 2nd edn, 3 vols.

Anon., 'Richard Musgrave, Bart.', *The Annual Biography and Obituary for the Year 1820*, vol. 4 (London: n. p., 1820).

Anon., 'New Geneva', *Dublin University Magazine*, October 1838, 402.

Anon. [John Buchan of Cairnbulg], *A Memorial Briefly Pointing at Some Advantages of the Union of the Two Kingdoms, Humbly Offered to the Consideration of the Commissioners Appointed for That End. (memorial Shewing the Advantages the Kingdom of Scotland May Have by the Undertaking . . . of Fishings for Export, Etc.)* (London: J. Nutt, 1702).

Anon. [Charles Brennan], *The unbiased Irishman: an answer to the publication on the state of the established church by Dr. Woodward, with strictures on the violation of the articles of Limerick, &c., to which is prefixed a review of the system for managing the affairs of Ireland from the commencement of the Pittite administration to the present day* (Dublin: H. Fitzpatrick, 1808 [orig. 1787]).

Anon. [John Campbell], *Travels and adventures of Edward Brown, Esq; formerly a merchant in London. Containing his observations on France and Italy; his voyage to the Levant* (London: A. Bettesworth et al., 1739).

Anon. [Charles Coote, 1st Earl of Bellomont], *A Letter to the Earl of Shelburne, &c. &c. &c. from a noble Earl of the Kingdom of Ireland* [i.e., Coote] *upon the subject of final explanation respecting the legislative rights of Ireland* (London: G. Robinson and J. Robinson, 1783), 2nd edn.

Anon. [Isaac Cornuaud] *Lettre à l'Auteur des considérations sur l'état des natifs* (Geneva: n. p., 1780).

Anon. [Isaac Cornuaud], *Suite du natif patriote* ([Geneva]: n. p., 1780).
Anon. [Isaac Cornuaud], *Le Natif Interrogé, ou Confession morali-politique d'un patriote* (Geneva: n. p., 1781).
Anon. [Isaac Cornuaud], *Réponse à Monsieur B., Secretaire du Cercle de la Liberté des Représentans* (Geneva: n. p., 1781).
Anon. [Isaac Cornuaud], *Second adresse aux membres du comité des représentans* (Geneva: n. p., 1781).
Anon. [Isaac Cornuaud and/or Joseph Des Arts], *Essai sur les considérations d'un patriote* (Geneva: n. p., 1781).
Anon. [Isaac Cornuaud], *Pièces relatives aux troubles actuels de Genève* (Geneva: n. p., 1782).
Anon. [Isaac Cornuaud, Paul-Henri Mallet and Jean-Louis Micheli du Crest], *Rélation de la conjuration contre le gouvernement et le magistrat de Genève; qui a éclaté le 8 Avril 1782* (Geneva: n. p. 1782).
Anon. [Jean-André Deluc], *Journal de ce qui s'est passé d'intéressant à Genève à la fin de 1767 et au commencement de 1768, pour servir à l'histoire de l'Edit du 11e mars 1768.*
Anon. [Patrick Duigenan], *The Alarm: or, An Address to the Nobility, Gentry and Clergy of the Church of Ireland, as by Law Established* (Dublin: Henry Watts, 1783).
Anon. [Felix Freeman], *A View of the Present State of France; With a Retrospect of the Past; Wherein the True Interests of the Continental Powers, and the Blessings of our Constitution, are clearly demonstrated* (Edinburgh: Oliver & Co., 1807).
Anon. [Jean-Jacques Gautier], *Mémoire instructif sur les dissentions actuelles de la République de Genève* (Geneva: n. p., 1779]).
Anon. [James Hartley], *History of the Westminster election* (London: 1784).
Anon. [John Hely-Hutchinson], *A letter from the secretary of state to the mayor of Cork, on the subject of the bill presented by Mr. Orde on the 15th August 1785, for effectuating the intercourse and commerce between Great Britain and Ireland* (Dublin: P. Byrne, 1785).
Anon. [John Lind], *Letters concerning the present state of Poland* (London: T. Payne, 1773), 2nd edn.
Anon. [Ami Lullin], *Très-humble et très-respectueuse récquisition des membres Constitutionnaires du magnifique Conseil des Deux-Cent, addressée au Mag. Petit Conseil. Remise au Seigneur Premier-Syndic le 12 janvier 1781* ([Geneva]: n. p., 1781).
Anon. [George Mackenzie and John Nisbet], *A Letter Concerning the Union, with Sir George Mackenzie's Observations and Sir John Nisbet's Opinion Upon the Same Subject* ([Edinburgh]: n. p., 1706).
Anon. [Jacques Mallet du Pan], *Supplément nécessaire à un écrit intitulé: Le Philadelphien à Genève: Sous Dublin 1783 : ou Lettre à l'auteur anonyme de cette brochure* (n. p.: n. p., 1783).
Anon. [James Mason], *Thoughts on the Protestant Ascendancy in Ireland* (London: J. Harding and J. Archer, 1805).
Anon. [Dennis O'Brien], *A defence of the Right Honorable the Earl of Shelburne: from the reproaches of his numerous enemies* (London: J: Stockdale, 1784).
Anon. [William Wenman Seward], *The rights of the people asserted, and the necessity of a more equal representation in parliament stated and proved. Wherein the*

resolutions of the volunteer delegates at Dungannon, Sept. 8, 1783, are particularly considered (Dublin: P. Byrne and J. Hill, 1783).

Anon. [Shelburne, Richard Price and John Horne Tooke], *Facts Addressed to the Landholders, Stockholders, Merchants, Farmers, Manufacturers, Tradesmen, Proprietors of Every Description, and Generally to All the Subjects of Great Britain and Ireland* (London: 1780), 2nd edn.

Anon. [Jacob Vernet], *Prière qui a été lue dans les Temples de la Ville de Genève, le Jeudi 21 Novembre 1782. Jour auquel l'Edit de Pacification avoit été accepté en Conseil-Général* (Geneva: Barthelemi-Chirol, 1782).

Atwood, William, *The history and reasons of the dependency of Ireland upon the imperial crown of the kingdom of England: Rectifying Mr. Molineux's state of The case of Ireland's being bound by acts of Parliament in England* (London: Daniel Brown, 1698).

Bachaumont, Louis Petit de, *Mémoires secrets pour servir à l'histoire de la république des lettres en France, depuis MDCCLXII jusqu'à nos jours* (London: J. Adamson, 1777).

Baines, Edward, *History of the Wars of the French Revolution: From the Breaking Out of the War in 1792, to the Restoration of a General Peace in 1815; Comprehending the Civil History of Great Britain and France During the Period* (London: Longman, Hurst, Rees et al., 1817), 2 vols.

Bandelier, André and Frédéric S. Eigeldinger (eds), *Lettres de Genève (1741–1793) à Jean Henri Samuel Formey* (Paris: Honoré Champion, 2010).

Bardel, Marie-Joseph, *Les Droits et les devoirs de l'homme, du citoyen et du chrétien: Par un prêtre de Savoie* (Paris: n. p., 1794).

Baring-Gould, Sabine, *A Collection of ballads: chiefly printed in London by Catnach, J. Pitts and others, mostly between 1800 and 1870: but with a few of earlier date and with a few prose broadsides* (London: n. p., n. d.), 9 vols.

Barrington, Sir Jonah, *Personal Sketches and Recollections of His Own Times* (New York: Redfield, 1854), 5th edn.

Barruel, Augustin, *Mémoires pour servir à l'histoire du Jacobinisme* (Hamburg: P. Fauche, 1798), 2 vols.

Benham, Daniel, *Memoirs of James Hutton, comprising the Annals of his Life and Connection with the United Brethren* (London: Hamilton, Adams & Co., 1856).

Bentham, Jeremy, *The Correspondence of Jeremy Bentham, Volume 3: January 1781 to October 1788*, ed. Ian R. Christie (London: Athlone Press, 1971).

Bérenger, Jean-Pierre, *Le Natif, ou lettres de Théodore et d'Annette* (Geneva, 1767).

Bérenger, Jean-Pierre, *Histoire de Genève depuis son origine jusqu'à nos jours* (Lausanne: 1772–73), 6 vols.

Bérenger, Jean-Pierre, *J. J. Rousseau justifié envers sa patrie* (London: n. p., 1775).

Bérenger, Jean-Pierre, *Considérations sur l'édit du 10 février 1781* (Geneva: n. p., 1781).

Beresford, John, *The Correspondence of The Right Hon. John Beresford*, ed. William Beresford (London: Woodfall & Kinder, 1854), 2 vols.

Bianchi, Vendramino, *An Account of Switzerland, and the Grisons: As Also of the Velesians, Geneva, the Forest-towns, and Their Other Allies, Containing the Geographical, and Present Political Estate of All Those Places* (London: J. Knapton, 1710).

Bindon, David, *A Scheme for Supplying Industrious Men with Money to Carry on Their Trades: And for Better Providing for the Poor of Ireland* (Dublin: Thomas Hume, 1729).

Blainville, Henri-Marie Ducrotay de, *Travels through Holland, Germany, Switzerland: And Italy. Containing a particular description of the antient and present state of those countries* (London: J. Johnson & B. Davenport, 1767), 3 vols.

Bodin, Jean, *Les six livres de la republique* (Paris: Jacques de Puy, 1576).

Bonnet, Charles, 'Lettre au sujet de discours de M. J. J. Rousseau', in *Œuvres d'histoire naturelle et de philosophie* (Neuchâtel: Fauche, 1779–1783), 8 vols.

Brewster, Francis, *Essays on Trade and Navigation: In Five Parts* (London: John Cockeril, 1693).

Brewster, Francis, *New Essays on Trade, Wherein the present State of our Trade, it's* [*sic*] *Great Decay in the Chief Branches of it, and the Fatal Consequences thereof to the Nation . . . Under the Most Important Heads of Trade and Navigation* (London: H. Walwyn, 1702).

Brissot de Warville, Jacques-Pierre, 'Genevois naturalisé Irlandois, jugé criminellement à Geneve: Question sur l'émigration examinée', *Correspondance sur ce qui intéresse le bonheur de l'homme et de la société*, no. 2 volume II, (London: E. Cox, 1783)

Brissot de Warville, Jacques-Pierre, *Philadelphien à Genève, ou Lettres d'un Américain sur la dernière revolution de Genève, sa Constitution nouvelle, l'émigration en Irlande, &c. Pouvant servir de tableau politique de Genève jusqu'en 1784* (Dublin: n. p., 1783).

Brissot de Warville, Jacques-Pierre, *Bibliothèque philosophique du législateur, du politique, du jurisconsulte* (Berlin: n. p., 1785), 10 vols.

Brissot de Warville, Jacques-Pierre, 'Rapport sur les hostilités du Roi d'Angleterre, et du Stadhouder des Provinces-Unies, et sur la nécessité de déclarer que la République Françoise est en guerre avec eux; présenté le première Février 1793 à la Convention, Par J.-P. Brissot, au nom du Comité du défense générale', in *Brissot, député du département de l'Eure et Loire, à ses commettans, précédé d'autres Pièces intéressantes de Brissot* (London: R. Edwards et al., 1794).

Brissot de Warville, J.-P., *J.-P. Brissot, Correspondance et Papiers*, ed. Cl. Perroud (Paris: A. Picard & fils, 1911).

Brissot de Warville, Jacques-Pierre, *Mémoires, 1754–1793*, ed. Cl. Perroud (Paris: Alphonse Picard, 1912), 2 vols.

Bromley, William, *Remarks in the grand tour of France and Italy: Perform'd by a person of quality, in the year, 1691* (London: John Nutt, 1705), 2nd edn.

Brooke, Henry, 'The Farmer's Case of the Roman Catholics of Ireland' [1760], in *Brookiana. Volume 1* (London: Richard Phillips, 1804).

Browne, John, *A Collection of Tracts: Concerning the Present State of Ireland, with Respect to Its Riches, Revenue, Trade and Manufactures. Containing I. Seasonable Remarks on Trade. with Some Reflections on the Advantages That Might Accrue to Great Britain, by a Proper Regulation of the Trade of Ireland. II. an Essay on Trade in General; And, on That of Ireland in Particular. III. Considerations on Two Papers Lately Publish'd. the First Call'd Seasonable Remarks, &c. and the Other, an Essay on Trade in General, and That of Ireland in Particular. IV. An Appeal to the Reverend Dean Swift, by Way of Reply to the Observer on Seasonable Remarks. V. A Letter in Answer to a Paper, Intitl'd, an Appeal to the Reverend Dean Swift* (London: T. Woodward, 1729).

Browne, John, *Reflections Upon the Present Unhappy Circumstances of Ireland in a Letter to His Grace the Lord Archbishop of Cashel: With a Proposal for Publick*

Granaries, As the Principal Means Whereby to Retrieve Our Affairs (Dublin: G. Faulkner, 1731).

Brown, John, *An estimate of the manners and principles of the times* (London: Davis and Reymers, 1758), 2 vols.

Burke, Edmund, *Two Letters from Mr. Burke to Gentlemen in the City of Bristol, on the Bills Depending in Parliament relative to the Trade of Ireland* (London: J. Dodsley, 1778), 2nd edn.

Burke, Edmund, *Reflections on the Revolution in France, And on the Proceedings in Certain Societies in London Relative to that Event* (London: J. Dodsley, 1790), 7th edn.

Burke, Edmund, *A Letter from The Right Hon. Edmund Burke, M.P., in the Kingdom of Great Britain, to Sir Hercules Langrishe: Bart. M.P. on the subject of Roman Catholics of Ireland, and the propriety of admitting them to the elective franchise, consistently with the principles of the constitution as established at the Revolution* (London: J. Debrett, 1792).

Burke, Edmund, *Two letters addressed to a member of the Present Parliament: on the proposals for peace with the regicide directory of France* (London: F. & C. Rivington, 1796), 7th edn.

Burke, Edmund, *The Correspondence of Edmund Burke*, ed. Thomas W. Copeland et al. (Chicago: Chicago University Press, 1958–78), 10 vols [*CEB*].

Burke, Edmund, *The Writings and Speeches of Edmund Burke, Vol. 9*, ed. R. B. McDowell and William B. Todd (Oxford, Oxford University Press, 1991).

Burlamaqui, Jean-Jacques, *Principes du droit politique* (Amsterdam: Zacharie Chatelain, 1751), 2 vols.

Burlamaqui, Jean-Jacques, *Principes du droit natural. Principes du droit politique* (Geneva: C. A. Philibert, 1763), 2 vols.

Burnet, Gilbert, *Voyage de Suisse, d'Italie, et de quelques endroits d'Allemagne & de France, fait és années 1685, & 1686* (Rotterdam: Abraham Acmer, 1688), 2nd edn.

Burney, Charles, *The Present State of music in France and Italy, or, the Journal of a tour through those countries, undertaken to collect materials for a general history of music, by Charles Burney* (London: T. Becket & Co., 1771).

Butler, Prince, *Prince Butler's Queries Relating to the Bill for Settling the Trade to Africa in a Joynt-Stock Company, &c., As the Company Proposes* (London: s.n., 1699).

Campbell, John, *The present state of Europe; explaining the interests, connections, political and commercial views of its several powers, comprehending also, a clear and concise history of each country* (London: C. Hitch et al., 1761), 6th edn.

Cantillon, Richard, *Essai sur la nature du commerce en général. Edited with an English translation and other material by Henry Higgs* (London: Frank Cass & Co., 1959).

Carlisle, Nicholas, 'GENEVA, *or*, NEW GENEVA, in the Barony of Gualtiere, Co. of WATERFORD', *A topographical dictionary of Ireland; exhibiting the names of the several cities, towns, parishes and villages, with the barony, county, and province, to which they respectively belong . . .* (London: William Miller, 1810).

Cary, John, *A Discourse Concerning the Trade of Ireland and Scotland: As They Stand in Competition with the Trade of England* (London: n. p., 1696).

Cary, John, *A Vindication of the Parliament of England: In Answer to a Book, Written by William Molyneux . . . Intituled, the Case of Irlands Being Bound by Acts of Parliament in England, Stated* (London: Freeman Collins, 1698).

Cary, John, *A Discourse Concerning the East-India-Trade: A Discourse Concerning the East-India-Trade, Shewing How It Is Unprofitable to the Kindome of England. Being Taken Out of an Essay on Trade* (London: E. Baldwin, 1699).

Caulfield, James, Lord Charlemont, *The Manuscripts and Correspondence of James, First Earl of Charlemont*, ed. John T. Gilbert (London: HMSO, 1891–94), 2 vols.

Cerisier, Antoine-Marie, *Le destin de l'Amerique; ou, Dialogues pittoresques dans lesquels on developpe la cause des evenemens actuels, la politique et les interêts des puissances de l'Europe relativement à cette guerre et les suites qu' elle devrait avoir pour le bonheur de l'humanité* (London: J. Bew, 1782).

Chapeaurouge, Jean-Jacques de, *Edit du 11 Mars 1768* ([Geneva], n. p. [1768]).

Chenevière, Nicolas, *Relation des réjouissances faites à Genève à l'occasion de Mylord Charles Stanhope, Vicomte de Mahon, Commandeur du Noble Exercise de l'Arc* (Geneva: n. p., 1771).

Clarke, Thomas Brooke, *The Political, Commercial, and Civil State of Ireland* (Dublin: J. Milliken, 1799).

Clarke, Thomas Brooke, *Misconceptions of Facts, and Mistatements of the Public Accounts, by the Right Hon. John Foster, Speaker of the Irish Parliament* (Dublin: J. Milliken, 1800).

Clavière, Étienne, *Reflexions politiques sur l'impôt proposé au Conseil Général* (26 December 1775).

Clavière, Étienne, 'Lettre à son excellence monsieur Le Comte de Vergennes, Du 21 Février 1780', in *Pièces justificatives pour messieurs Du Roveray & Claviere* ([Geneva]: 1780).

Clavière, Étienne and Jacques-Pierre Brissot de Warville, *De la France et des États-Unis, ou De l'importance de la révolution de l'Amérique pour le bonheur de la France* (London: n. p., 1787).

Clement, Simon, *The Interest of England, as it stands with relation to the trade of Ireland, considered; the Arguments against the Bill, for prohibiting the Exportation of Woollen Manufactures from Ireland to Forreign Parts, fairly discusst, and the reasonableness and necessity of Englands restraining her colonies in all matters of trade, that may be prejudicial to her own commerce, clearly demonstrated. With short remarques on a book, entituled, Some thoughts on the bill depending before the right honourable the House of Lords, for prohibiting the exportation of the woollen manufactures of Ireland to forreign parts* (London: John Atwood, 1698).

Cloney, Thomas, *A Personal Narrative of Those Transactions in the County Wexford, in which the Author was Engaged, During the Awful Period of 1798, Interspersed with Brief Notices of the Principal Actors in that Ill-fated, But Ever-memorable Struggle: With Reflections, Moral, Political and Historical* (Dublin: James McMullen, 1832).

Cobbett, William, *A collection of facts and observations: relative to the peace with Bonaparte, chiefly extracted from the Porcupine, and including Mr. Cobbett's letters to Lord Hawkesbury* (London: Cobbett and Morgan, 1801).

Cornuaud, Isaac, *Lettre d'un natif à un bourgeois de ses amis* ([Geneva]: n. p., 28 March 1777)

Cornuaud, Isaac, *Examen politico-patriotique des questions suivantes* (Geneva: n. p., 3 May 1777).

Cornuaud, Isaac, *Cinquième adresse aux membres du Comité des Représentants* (Ferney: n. p., [15 January] 1781).
Cornuaud, Isaac, *Examen du mémoire remis à S. E. M. le comte de Vergennes, le 21 août 1781, par M. J.-A. Deluc, ancien demagogue de la Bourgeoisie* (Geneva: n. p., [15 September] 1781).
Cornuaud, Isaac, *Troisième adresse aux membres du Comité des Représentants* (Ferney: n. p., [15 November] 1781).
Cornuaud, Isaac, *Septième adresse aux membres du Comité des Représentants* (Ferney: n. p., [17 February] 1782).
Cornuaud, Isaac, *Mémoires de Isaac Cornuaud sur Genève et la Révolution de 1770 à 1795, publiés avec notice biographique, notes et table des noms par Mlle Émilie Cherbuliez* (Geneva: A. Jullien, 1912).
Cox, Richard, *Some Thoughts on the Bill Depending before the Right Honourable the House of Lords for Prohibiting the Exportation of the Woolen Manufactures of Ireland to Foreign Parts* (London: J. Darby and A. Bell, 1798).
Coxe, William, *Sketches of the natural, civil, and political state of Swisserland: In a series of letters to William Melmouth, Esq.* (London: J. Dodsley, 1780), 2nd edn.
Coxe, William, *Travels in Switzerland* (London, 1789), 2 vols.
Crombie, James, *The Expedience and Utility of Volunteer Associations for National Defence and Security in the Present Critical Situation of Public Affairs Considered, in a Sermon, Preached before the United Companies of the Belfast Volunteers* (Belfast: James Magee, 1779).
Croker, T. Crofton, *Popular Songs, Illustrative of the French Invasions of Ireland* (London: The Percy Society, 1847).
D'Alembert, Jean, 'A Short Account of the Government of Geneva', in *Miscellaneous Pieces in Literature, History, and Philosophy* (London: C. Henderson, 1764).
Dalrymple, John, *Memoirs Of Great Britain And Ireland: From The Dissolution Of The Last Parliament Of Charles II. till the Capture of the French and Spanish fleets at Vigo* (London: Strahan and Cadell, 1790), new edn., 3 vols.
Davenant, Charles, *An Essay Upon the Probable Methods of Making a People Gainers in the Ballance of Trade . . . by the Author of the Essay on Ways and Means* (London: James Knapton, 1699).
Davenant, Charles, *The Political and Commercial Works of That Celebrated Writer Charles D'avenant: Relating to the Trade and Revenue of England, the Plantation Trade, the East-India Trade and African Trade*, ed. Sir Charles Whitworth (London: R. Horsfield et al., 1771), 5 vols.
Decker, Matthew, *An Essay on the Causes of the Decline of the Foreign Trade: Consequently of the Value of the Lands of Britain, and on the Means to Restore Both. Begun in the Year 1739* (Dublin: G. Faulkener, 1749), 2nd edn.
Deluc, Jean-André, *Mémoire remis le 21 Août 1781, a monsieur le Comte de Vergennes par J.-A. Deluc, comme étant le sommaire de ce qu'il avoit eu l'honneur d'exposer à son excellence dans des audiences précédentes* (Geneva: 1781).
Dobbs, Arthur, *An Essay on the Trade and Improvement of Ireland. by Arthur Dobbs, Esq* (Dublin: J. Smith and W. Bruce, 1729).
Dobbs, Francis, *A history of Irish affairs, from the 12th of October, 1779 to the 15th of September, 1782, the day of Lord Temple's arrival.* (Dublin: M. Mills, 1782).

Dobbs, Francis *Thoughts on the Conduct and Continuation of the Volunteers of Ireland* (Dublin: James Williams, 1783).

Dobbs, Francis, *An Historical Review of the State of Ireland from the Invasion of that Country under Henry II. to its Union with Great Britain on the First of January 1801* (London: T. Egerton, 1803), 2 vols.

Drennan, William, *Letters of Orellana, an Irish Helot, to the Seven Northern Counties not represented in the National Assembly of Delegates, held at Dublin, October, 1784, for obtaining a more equal representation of the People in the Parliament of Ireland. Originally published in the Belfast Newsletter* (Dublin: J. Chambers & T. Heary, 1785)

Drennan, William, *The Drennan-McTier Letters Volume 1, 1776–1793* (Dublin: Irish Manuscripts Commission 1999).

Dundas, Henry, 1st Viscount Melville, 'Report of Committee of Secrecy, 23 January 1799 to parliament on 15 March 1799', *Journals of the House of Commons, Volume 54* (London: House of Commons, 1803).

Eden, William, *A Letter to the Earl of Carlisle: From William Eden, Esq. on the Representations of Ireland, Respecting a Free Trade* (Dublin: R. Marchbank, 1779).

Eden, William, *The journal and correspondence of William, lord of Auckland* (London: Richard Bentley, 1861), 2 vols.

Eliot, John, *The Monarchy of Man by Sir John Eliot (1590–1632). Now for the First Time Printed, from the Author's Manuscript in Harleian Collection*, ed. Alexander B. Grosart (London: Chiswick Press, 1879).

Fauquier, Francis, *The Official Papers of Francis Fauquier, Lieutenant Governor of Virginia, 1758–1768: 1764–1768* (vol. 3), ed. George Reese. *Virginia Historical Society Documents, Volume 16* (Charlottesville, VA: Published for the Virginia Historical Society by the University Press of Virginia, 1983).

Fills, Robert, *The lawes and statutes of Geneva, as well concerning ecclesiastical discipline, as civil regiment: with certeine proclamations, duly executed, whereby God's religion is most purelie maintained, and their commonwealth quietly governed. Translated out of Frenche into Englische, by R. Fills. B.L.* (London: R. Hall, 1562).

Fénelon, François, *The adventures of Telemachus, the son of Ulysses: Translated from the French by John Hawkesworth* (London: W. Strahan, 1768).

Fénelon, François, *Telemachus*, ed. and trans. Patrick Riley (Cambridge: Cambridge University Press, 1994).

Ferguson, Robert, *A Just and Modest Vindication of the Scots Design, for the Having Established a Colony at Darien: . . . with a Brief Display, How Much It Is Their Interest to apply themselves to Trade, and particularly to that which is Foreign* (n. p.: n. p., 1699).

Ferguson, Adam, *An essay on the history of civil society* (Edinburgh and London: Millar, Caddel et al., 1767).

Ferguson, Adam, *The Correspondence of Adam Ferguson: 1745–1780*, ed. Vincenzo Merolle (London: Pickering & Chatto, 1995), 2 vols.

FitzGibbon, John, D. A. Fleming and A.P.W. Malcomson, *'A Volley of Execrations'. The Letters and Papers of John FitzGibbon, Earl of Clare 1772–1802* (Dublin: Irish Manuscripts Commission, 2005).

Fitzmaurice, Edmond, *Life of William, Earl of Shelburne, First Marquess of Lansdowne, with extracts from his papers and correspondence* (London: Macmillan, 1912), revised 2nd edn, 2 vols.

Fletcher, Andrew, *An Account of a Conversation Concerning a Right Regulation of Governments: For the Common Good of Mankind, in a Letter to the Marquess of Montrose, the Earls of Rothes, Roxburgh, and Haddingtoun, from London the 1st of December, 1703* (London: A. Baldwin, 1704), in David Daiches (ed.), *Andrew Fletcher of Saltoun: Selected Political Writings and Speeches* (Edinburgh: Scottish Academic Press, 1979).

Flood, Henry, *A Letter to the People of Ireland, on the Expediency and Necessity of the Present Associations in Ireland: In Favour of Our Own Manufactures, with Some Cursory Observations on the Effects of an Union* (Newry: Joseph Gordon, 1779).

Flood, Henry, *The Celebrated Speeches of Colonel Henry Flood, on the Repeal of the Declatory Act of the 6th George Ist: As Delivered in the House of Commons of Ireland, on the 11th and 14th of June, 1782. Also, the Speech of Lord Abingdon, in the English House of Peers the 5th of July 1782, on Introducing His Bill for a Declaration of Right Over Every Part of the British Dependencies* (Dublin: C. Campbell, 1782).

Flood, Warden, *Memoirs of the life and correspondence of the Right Hon. Henry Flood, M.P., colonel of the volunteers: containing reminiscences of the Irish commons, and an account of the grand national convention of 1783* (Dublin: John Cumming, 1838).

Fortescue, John Beville, *The Manuscripts of J. B. Fortescue . . . preserved at Dropmore* (London: HMSO, 1892–1927), 10 vols.

Franklin, Benjamin and William B. Willcox, *The Papers of Benjamin Franklin, Volume 22: March 23, 1775, through October 27, 1776*, ed. William B. Willcox (New Haven, CT and London: Yale University Press, 1982).

Fraser, James, *Guide through Ireland. Descriptive of its scenery, towns, seats, antiquities, etc. with various statistical tables* (Dublin: William Curry, 1838).

Galiani, Ferdinando, *Dialogues sur le commerce des bleds* (London: n. p., 1770).

Gandon, James, and T. J. Mulvany (eds), *The Life of James Gandon* (Dublin: Hodges and Smith, 1846).

Gee, Joshua, *The Trade and Navigation of Great-Britain* (London: S. Buckley, 1730).

George III, King of Great Britain, 1738–1820, *The Correspondence of King George the Third from 1760 to December 1783*, ed. Sir John Fortescue (London: Macmillan, 1927–28), 6 vols.

Gentz, Friedrich, *A vindication of Europe and Great Britain from misrepresentation and aspersion; extracted and translated from Mr. Gentz's answer to Mr. Hauterive* (London: 1803).

Gibbon, Edward, *Miscellanea Gibboniana. Journal de mon voyage dans quelques endroits de la Suisse, 1755*, ed. Georges A. Bonnard, Gavin R. de Beer and Louis Junod (Lausanne: Librairie de l'Université, 1952).

Gibbon, Edward, *The Letters of Edward Gibbon*, ed. J. E. Norton (London: Cassell, 1956), 3 vols.

Gilbert, John Thomas (ed.), *Documents relating to Ireland, 1795–1804: official account of secret service money. Governmental correspondence and papers. Notice of French soldiery at Killala. Statements by United Irishmen. Letters on legislative union with Great Britain, etc.* (Dublin: Joseph Dollard, 1893).

Gordon, James, *History of the Rebellion in Ireland: In the Year 1789* (Dublin: J. D. Dewick, 1803).

Grattan, Henry, *Speeches of the Late Rt. Hon. Henry Grattan, in the Irish Parliament in 1780 and 1782* (London: Ridgway, 1821).

Grattan, Henry, *Memoirs of the Life and Times of the Rt. Hon. Henry Grattan* (London: Henry Colburn, 1839), 2 vols.

Grattan, Henry, *Memoirs of the Life and Times of the Rt. Hon. Henry Grattan, Volume 3* (London: H. Colburn, 1841).

Gray, Thomas, *Correspondence of Thomas Gray: Volume I: 1734–1755*, ed. Paget Toynbee and Leonard Whibley (Oxford: Oxford University Press, 1935).

Grenus, Théodore de, *Fragments biographiques et historiques extraits des Registres du Conseil d'État de la République de Genève* (Geneva: Cherbuliez, 1815).

Grosley, Pierre-Jean, *New observations on Italy and its inhabitants. Written in French by two Swedish gentlemen. Translated into English by Thomas Nugent, L.L.D. and fellow of the Society of Antiquaries* (London: L. Davis & C. Reymers, 1769), 2 vols.

Guicciardini, Francesco, *The history of Italy, from the year 1490, to 1532: Written in Italian by Francesco Guicciardini, a nobleman of Florence. In Twenty books. Translated into English by the Chevalier Austin Parke Goddard, knight of the military order of St. Stephen* (London: J. Towers, 1753–56), 20 vols.

Hales, William, *MONSTROUS REPUBLIC: Or, french atrocities pourtrayed* (London: J. Wright, 1799).

Harris, Walter, *An Enquiry into the Caledonian Project: With a Defence of England's Procedure (in a Point of Equity) in Relation thereunto* (London: John Nutt, 1701).

Hay, Edward, *History of the Insurrection of the County of Wexford, A. D. 1798* (Dublin: J. Stockdale, 1803).

Hely-Hutchinson, John, *The Commercial Restraints of Ireland Considered, in a Series of Letters to a Noble Lord. Containing an Historical Account of the Affairs of That Kingdom, so Far As They Relate to This Subject* (Dublin: W. Hallhead, 1779).

Hoche, Lazare, 'À l'armée française destinée á opérer la révolution d'Irelande', in Édouard Guillon, *La France & l'Irlande pendant la révolution, Hoche et Humbert: d'après les documents inédits des archives de France et d'Irlande* (Paris: A. Colin, 1888).

Hodges, James, *A Defence of the Scots Abdicating Darien: Including an Answer to the Defence of the Scots Settlement There* (n. p.: n. p., 1700).

Hodges, James, *That Part of a Late Book Which Relates to a General Fast and Humiliation: Printed a Part. Nota. That the Book It Self Entitul'd the Rights and Interests of the Two British Monarchies* (Edinburgh: n. p., 1706).

Hoey, Abraham van, *Letters and negociations of M. van Hoey, ambassador from the States-General to His Most Christian Majesty. Containing an exact representation of the present state of the court of France, with the Characters of the King and his principal Ministers; Also Several curious Particulars relating to the Life and Ministry of the late Cardinal De Fleury ; with many Pieces of secret but authentic History, in respect to the Commencement and Continuance of the present War, and the Intrigues that have been carried on in order to prevent their High Mightinesses from affording any Effectual Succours to the Queen of Hungary: Together with Some memorable Anecdotes as to the past and present Conduct of Great Britain* (London: J. Nourse, 1743).

Home, Henry, *Memoirs of the Life and Writings of the Honourable Henry Home of Kames: one of the Senators of the College of Justice, and one of the Lords Commissioners of Justiciary in Scotland; containing sketches of the progress of literature and general improvement in Scotland during the greater part of the Eighteenth century*, ed., Alexander Fraser Tytler of Woodhouselee (Edinburgh and London: William Creech, T. Cadell & W. Davies, 1807), 2 vols.

Hotman, François, *Franco-gallia: Or, an Account of the Ancient Free State of France and Most Other Arts of Europe Before the Loss of Their Liberties, Written Originally in Latin by the Famous Civilian Francis Hotoman in the Year 1574*, trans. Robert Molesworth (London: Queen's Head, 1721).

Howell, James, *Epistolæ Ho-Elianæ: familiar letters domestick and foreign, divided into four books: partly historical, political, philosophical* (London: D. Midwinter et al., 1737) 10th edn.

Hume, David, *The Letters of David Hume*, ed. J.Y.T. Greig (Oxford: Oxford University Press, 1932), 2 vols.

Hume, David, 'Of the Balance of Trade', in *Essays, Moral, Political, and Literary*, ed. Eugene F. Miller (Indianapolis, IN: Liberty Fund, 1987).

Isnard, Achille-Nicholas, *Observations sur le principe qui a produit les révolutions de France, de Genève et d'Amérique dans le dix-huitième siècle* (Evreux: Malassis, 1789).

Ivernois, François d', *Considérations d'un citoyen de Genève, Sur la Garantie, accordée, en 1738, à la République de Genève, par la France & les L. L. Cantons de Zurich & de Berne* ([Geneva]: n. p., [1780]).

Ivernois, François d', *La Loi de la réélection* ([Geneva]: n. p., [1780]).

Ivernois, François d', *Lettre à Madame **** ([Geneva]: n. p., [1780]).

Ivernois, François d', *Lettre à son excellence le Comte de Vergennes* ([Geneva]: [1780]).

Ivernois, François d', *Réflexions impartiales, Sur l'Etat actuel de la République de Geneve* ([Geneva]: n. p., [1780]).

Ivernois, François d', *Offrande à la liberté et à la paix; par un citoyen de Genève; ou idées de conciliation adressées à Mr. J. A. De Luc, en réfutation Du Mémoire qu'il remit le 21 Aoust 1781, à Monsieur le Comte de Vergennes* (Geneva: n. p., [1781]).

Ivernois, François d', 'Déclaration des Genevois remise aux Seigneurs Syndics, le mardi 2 Juillet, à deux heures après minuit, et par eux envoyée le même matin aux trois Généraux', in d'Ivernois, *Pièces relatives à l'asyle ouvert en Irlande aux Genevois opprimés.*

Ivernois, François d', 'Extrait des Registres du Conseil Privé d'Irlande' in d'Ivernois, *Pièces relatives à l'asyle ouvert en Irlande aux Genevois opprimés.*

Ivernois, François d', 'Mémoire addressé par M. l'Avocat d'Ivernois, le 27 Septembre 1782 à son excellence Mylord Temple, Vice-Roi d'Irelande', in d'Ivernois, *Pièces relatives à l'asyle ouvert en Irlande aux Genevois opprimés.*

Ivernois, François d', *Pièces relatives à l'asyle ouvert en Irlande aux Genevois opprimés* (n. p.: n. p., [1782]).

Ivernois, François d', *Tableau historique et politique des révolutions de Genève dans le dix-huitième siècle dédié à sa majesté très-chrétienne Louis XVI* (Geneva: 1782).

Ivernois, François d', Temple to d'Ivernois, 27 September 1782, in d'Ivernois, *Pièces relatives à l'asyle ouvert en Irlande aux Genevois opprimés.*

Ivernois, François d', 'Traduction de l'arrêté du Corps indépendant des Voltonaires de Dublin' and 'Traduction de l'arrêté des Dragons légers de la Cité de Dublin', in d'Ivernois, *Pièces relatives à l'asyle ouvert en Irlande aux Genevois opprimés.*

Ivernois, François d', *An historical and political view of the constitution and revolutions of Geneva in the eighteenth century* (London: T. Cadell, 1784).

Ivernois, François d', *Tableau historique et politique des deux dernières révolutions de Genève* (London: n. p., 1789), 2 vols.

Jackson, Robert, *Remarks on the Constitution of the Medical Department of the British Army* (London: T. Cadell and W. Davies, 1803).

James, Charles, *Collection of the charges, opinions, and sentences of general courts martial, as published by authority: from the year 1795 to the present time: intended to serve as an appendix to Tytler's treatise on military law, and forming a book of cases and references: with a copious index: to which are added introductory observations respecting the power of the Crown over all officers belonging to the British army, and persons officially connected with the receipt and distribution of military pay and allowances* (London: C. Roworth, 1820).

Jebb, John, *Letters addressed to the volunteers of Ireland, on the subject of a parliamentary reform* (London: J. Stockdale, 1783).

Journal of the House of Lords, Volume 36: 1779–1783 (London: 1767–1830).

Journals of the House of Commons, Volume 54 (London: HM Stationery Office, 1803).

Keate, George, *A Short Account of the Ancient History, Present Government, and Laws of the Republic of Geneva* (London: R. and J. Dodsley, 1761).

Keogh, John, *Thoughts on Equal Representation; with Hints for Improving the Manufactures and Employment of the Poor of Ireland* (Dublin: T. Heery, 1784).

Keyssler, Johann Georg, *Travels through Germany: Hungary, Bohemia, Switzerland, Italy, and Lorrain. Containing an accurate description of the present state and curiosities of those countries. . . . By John George Keysler, F.R.S. To which is prefixed, the life of the author, by Mr. Godfrey Schutze . . . Translated from the Hanover edition of the German* (London: for the editor, 1758), 4 vols.

King, John, *Thoughts on the Difficulties and Distresses in which the Peace of 1783 has involved the People of England* (London: J. Fielding et al., 1783).

Lawrence, Richard, *The Interest of Ireland in Its Trade and Wealth Stated: In Two Parts: First Part Observes and Discovers the Causes of Irelands Not More Increasing in Trade and Wealth from the First Conquest Till Now: Second Part Proposeth Expedients to Remedy All Its Mercanture Maladies by Which It Is Kept Poor and Low; Both Mix'd with Some Observations on the Politicks of Government Relating to the Incouragement of Trade and Increase of Wealth: with Some Reflections on Principles of Religion As It Relates to the Premisses* (Dublin: J. Ray and J. Howes: 1682).

Le Mercier, Andrew, *Geographical and Political Account of the Republick of Geneva: Containing an Exact Description of It's Scituation* [*sic*] (Boston: B. Green, 1735).

Le Mercier, Andrew, *The church history of Geneva, in five books: As also a political and geographical account of that republick. By the Reverend, Mr. Andrew Le Mercier Pastor of the French church in Boston* (Boston, New-England: S. Gerrish, 1732)

Leclerc, Jean, 'A defence of Archbishop Tillotson and his writings', in Edward Young, *The Life of the Most Reverend Father in God John Tillotson* (London: E. Curll et al., 1717).

LeFanu. Alicia (ed.), *Memoirs of the life and writings of Mrs. Frances Sheridan: mother of the late Right Hon. Richard Brinsley Sheridan and author of 'Sidney Biddulph', 'Nourjahad', and 'The discovery'* (London: G. and W. B. Whittaker, 1824).

Lewis, Samuel, *A Topographical Dictionary of Ireland: Comprising the Several Counties; Cities; Boroughs; Corporate, Market and Post Towns; Parishes; and Villages . . .* (London: for the author, 1837), 2 vols.

Lisola, François P. de, *The Buckler of State and Justice against the Design Manifestly Discovered of the Universal Monarchy . . . the 2d Edition. to Which Is Added, a Free Conference Touching the Present State of England Both at Home and Abroad: in Order to the Designs of France. [translated from the French of François P. De Lisola.]* (London: Richard Royston, 1673).

Locke, John, *The Correspondence of John Locke*, ed. Edward S. de Beer (Oxford: Clarendon Press, 1976–89), 8 vols.

Lockman, John, *A history of the cruel sufferings of the Protestants, and others, by Popish persecutions, in various countries: Together with a view of the reformations from the Church of Rome* (London: J. Clarke et al, 1760).

Lolme, Jean Louis de, *General Observations On The Power Of Individuals To Prescribe, By Testamentary Dispositions, The Particular Future Uses To Be Made Of Their Property* (London: Richardson, 1798).

Lucas, Charles, *A Remonstrance against Certain Infringements on the Rights and Liberties of the Commons and Citizens of Dublin: Humbly Addressed to the Right Honourable the Lord Mayor, the Recorder, the Board of Aldermen, the Sherifs, Commons, and Citizens of the Said City. by Charles Lucas, One of the Said Commons* (Dublin: n. p., 1743).

Lucas, Charles, *Divelina Libera: An Apology for the Civil Rights and Liberties of the Commons and Citizens of Dublin. Containing an Account of the Foundation and Constitution of This City* (Dublin: J. Esdall, 1744).

Lucas, Charles, *The Political Constitutions of Great-Britain and Ireland, Asserted and Vindicated: The Connection and Common Interest of Both Kingdoms, Demonstrated; and the Grievances, Which, Each, More Especially the Later, with It's Capital, Has Suffered, Under Oppressive and Tyrannical Governors, Usurping and Lawless Magistrates, Dependent and Iniquitous Judges, and Spurious and Corrupt Parlements, Set Forth in Several Addresses and Letters to the Free-Citizens of Dublin* (London: n. p., 1751), 2 vols.

Lucas, Charles, *Seasonable advice to the electors of members of Parlement at the ensuing general election. Addressed to the free and independent electors of the kingdom of Ireland in general, to those of Dublin in particular, upon the present critical conjuncture of affairs. Part II* (Dublin: Thomas Ewing, 1768).

Lucas, Charles, *The Rights and Privileges of Parlements Asserted Upon Constitutional Principles: Against the Modern Anticonstitutional Clames of Chief Governors, to Take Notice Of, Animadvert Upon, and Protest against the Proceedings of Either House of Parlement: Humbly Addressed to His Excellency George, Lord Visc. Townshend* (Dublin: Tho. Ewing, 1770).

Macintosh, William, *Travels in Europe, Asia and Africa; describing characters, customs, manners, laws, and productions of nature and art: containing various remarks on the political and commercial interests of Great Britain: and delineating, in particular, a new system for the government and improvement of the British settlements in the East Indies: begun in the year 1777, and finished in 1781* (London: John Murray, 1782), 2 vols.

Mackenzie, George, *Parainesis pacifica: Or, a perswasive to the union of Britain* (Edinburgh: Andrew Symson, 1702).

Mackenzie, George, *A letter from E.C. to E.W. concerning the Union* [by George Mackenzie, Earl of Cromarty, addressed to David Wemyss, Earl of Wemyss.] (Edinburgh[?]: n. p., 1706).

Mallet du Pan, Jacques, *Compte rendu de la défense des Citoyens Bourgeois de Genève, addressé aux Commissaires des Citoyens Représentants* (Geneva: 1771).

Mallet du Pan, Jacques, *Idées soumises à l'examen de tous les conciliateurs, par un médiateur sans consequence* ([Geneva: n. p., 1780]).

Mallet du Pan, Jacques, *A Short Account of the Invasion of Switzerland by the French, in a Letter from M. Mallet du Pan to M. de M****** (London: J. Wright, 1798).

Mallet du Pan, Jacques, *Mémoires et correspondance de Mallet du Pan: pour servir à l'histoire de la Révolution française*, ed. Pierre-André Sayous (Paris: J. Cherbuliez, 1851), 2 vols.

Mallet du Pan, Jacques, *Memoirs and correspondence of Mallet du Pan, illustrative of the history of the French Revolution*, ed. André Sayous (London: Richard Bentley, 1852), 2 vols.

Mandeville, Bernard, *The Fable of the Bees or Private Vices, Publick Benefits. With a Commentary Critical, Historical, and Explanatory by F. B. Kaye* (Indianapolis: Liberty Fund, 1988), 2 vols.

Manners, John Henry, 5th Duke of Rutland, *The Manuscripts of His Grace the Duke of Rutland . . . preserved at Belvoir Castle* (London: HMSO, 1888–1905), 4 vols.

Marat, Jean-Paul, *Lettres de Marat aux Jacobins frères et amis, 19 avril 1793* (Paris: Société des Amis de la liberté, 1791).

Marat, Jean-Paul, *Nouvelle dénonciation de M. Marat, L'Ami du peuple, contre M. Necker, premier ministre des Finances, ou Supplément à la dénonciation d'un citoyen contre un agent de l'autorité* (Paris: Rozé, 1791).

Maxwell, Henry, *An Essay Towards an Union of Ireland with England* (London: Timothy Goodwin, 1703).

McKenna, Theobald, *Political essays relative to the affairs of Ireland: In 1791, 1792, and 1793; with remarks on the present state of that country* (London: J. Debrett, 1794).

Mills, John, *Essays Moral, Philosophical and Political* (London: S. Hooper, 1772).

Mirabeau, Honoré-Gabriel de Riqueti, comte de, *Mémoires biographiques, littéraires et politiques de Mirabeau, écrits par lui-même, par son père, son oncle et son fils adoptif*, ed. Lucas de Montigny (Brussels: 1834), 8 vols.

Misson, Maximilien, *A new voyage to Italy: With curious observations on several other countries; as, Germany; Switzerland; Savoy; Geneva; Flanders; and Holland* (London: C. Jephson et al., 1739), 5th edn, 2 vols.

Molyneaux, William, *The Case of Ireland being Bound by Acts of Parliament in England, Stated* (London: J. Almon, 1770).

Musgrave, Richard, *A Concise Account of the Material Events and Atrocities Which Occurred in the Present Rebellion* (Cork: A Edwards, 1799).

Musgrave, Richard, 'Observations on whipping and free-quarter', in *Memoirs of the Different Rebellions in Ireland, from the Arrival of the English* (London and Dublin: R. Marchbank, 1802), 3rd edn, 2 vols.

Nicholls, William, *A supplement to the Commentary on The book of common-prayer* (London: James Holland and William Taylor, 1711).

Orde, Thomas, *Mr Orde's plan of an improved system of education in Ireland; submitted to the House of Commons, April, 12, 1787; with the debate which arose thereon. Reported by John Giffard, Esq.* (Dublin: W. Porter, 1787).

Ostervald, Jean Frédéric, *A treatise concerning the causes of the present corruption of Christians, and the remedies thereof* (London: Richard Chiswell, 1702).

Ostervald, Jean-Frédéric, *The grounds & principles of the Christian religion, explain'd in a catechetical discourse for the instruction of young people. Written in French by J. F. Ostervald, . . . Rendred into English by Mr. Hum. Wanley: and revis'd by Geo. Stanhope, D.D* (London: Joseph Downing, 1711), 2nd edn.

Paine, Thomas, *Miscellaneous Letters & Essays, on Various Subjects* (London: R. Carlile, 1819).

Pan, Jean-Louis du, *Édits de la République de Genève* (Geneva: Frères Detournes, 1735).

Paterson, William, 'A Proposal to Plant a Colony in Darien; to protect the Indians against Spain; and to open the trade of South America to all nations' [1701], in Saxe Bannister (ed.), *The Writings of William Paterson: Founder of the Bank of England, and of the Darien Colony*, vol. 1 (London: Judd & Glass, 1859).

Petre, Robert Edward, *Reflections on the policy and justice of an immediate and general emancipation of the Catholics of Great Britain and Ireland* (London: E. Booker, 1804).

Petty, William, *A Treatise of Taxes & Contributions: Shewing the Nature and Measures of Crown-Lands, Assessments, Customs, Poll-Moneys . . . &c.: with Several Intersperst Discourses and Digressions Concerning Warres, the Church, Universities, Rents & Purchases . . . &c.: the Same Being Frequently Applied to the Present State and Affairs of Ireland* (London: N. Brooke, 1662).

Petty, William, 'The Political Anatomy of Ireland', in *Tracts; Chiefly relating to Ireland* (Dublin: Boulter Grierson, 1769).

Petty, William, *The French Politician Found Out, or Considerations on the Late Pretensions That France Claims to England and Ireland: And Her Designs and Plots in Order Thereunto* (London: Langley Curtiss, 1681).

Picot, Jean, *Histoire de Genève, depuis les temps les plus anciens, jusqu'à nos jours, accompagnée de détails sur les antiquités de la ville et de son territoire, sur les moeurs, les usages, le gouvernement, les lois, les monnoies, les progrès des sciences et des arts* (Geneva: Manget and Cherbuliez, 1811), 3 vols.

Pitt, William, *Correspondence of William Pitt, Earl of Chatham. Volume 4*, ed. William Stanhope Taylor and John Henry Pringle (London: John Murray, 1840).

[Pitt, William and Charles Manners], *Correspondence between the Right Hon. William Pitt and Charles, Duke of Rutland, Lord Lieutenant of Ireland. 1781–1787* (London: A. Spottiswoode, 1842).

Planta, Joseph, *The History of the Helvetic Confederacy* (London: John Stockdale, 1800), 2 vols.

Pollnitz, Karl Ludwig, Freiherr von, *The Memoirs of Charles-Lewis, Baron de Pollnitz: Being the Observations he made in his Late Travels from Prussia thro' Germany, Italy, France* (London: Daniel Swann, 1737).

Pollnitz, Karl Ludwig, Freiherr von, *The Memoirs of Charles-Lewis, Baron de Pollnitz. Being the Observations he Made in his Late Travels . . . In Letters to his Friend* (Dublin: G. Faulkner et al., 1738), 5 vols.

Pope, Alexander, *Correspondence of Alexander Pope: 1719–1728*, ed. George Sherburn (Oxford: Oxford University Press, 1956), 5 vols.

Price, Richard, *Four Dissertations* (London: A. Millar and T. Cadell, 1767).

Price, Richard, *Observations on Reversionary Payments: On Schemes for Providing Annuities for Widows, and for Persons in Old Age, on the Method of Calculating the Values of Assurances on Lives, and on the National Debt: to Which Are Added, Four Essays . . . Also, an Appendix, Containing a Complete Set of Tables* (London: T. Cadell, 1772), 2nd edn.

Price, Richard, *Observations on the Nature of Civil Liberty, the Principles of Government and the Justice and Policy of the War with America* (London: T. Cadell, 1776).

Price, Richard, *The Correspondence of Richard Price*, ed. D. O. Thomas and W. Bernard Peach (Durham, NC and Cardiff: Duke University Press and University of Wales Press, 1983–94), 3 vols.

Quérard, Joseph-Marie, *La France littéraire ou Dictionnaire bibliographique des savants, historiens et gens de lettres de la France, ainsi que des littérateurs étrangers qui ont écrit en français, plus particulièrement pendant les XVIIIe et XIXe siècles. Tome sixième* (Paris: Didot Frères, 1834).

Redmond, Hervey, 2nd Viscount Mountmorres, *Plain Reasons for New-Modelling Poynings' Law: In Such a Manner As to Assert the Ancient Rights of the Two Houses of Parliament, Without Intrenching on the King's Prerogative* (Dublin: William Hallhead, 1780).

Rey, François-Joseph and Jean-Pierre Raccaud, *Lettre d'un membre de la communauté de Fribourg en Suisse* ([Geneva]: 1781).

Ridpath, George, *An Enquiry into the Causes of the Miscarriage of the Scots Colony at Darien. or an Answer to a Libel Entituled a Defence of the Scots Abdicating Darien* (Glasgow: n. p., 1700).

Ridpath, George, *The Reducing of Scotland by Arms, and Annexing It to England As a Province, Considered. with an Historical Account of the Grievances the Scots Complain They Have Suffer'd in Their Religion, Liberty, and Trade, Since the Union of the Crowns, Etc.* (London: Benjamin Bragg, 1705).

Rigaud, Marc, *Lettres d'un constitutionnaire de Genève, sur les troubles de sa patrie, écrites à un ami à Paris ; avec les pièces justificatives* (Neuchâtel: n. p., 1782).

Rilliet, Théodore, *Solution générale ou lettres à Monsieur Covelle le fils, citoyen de Genève, pour servir de réponse aux observations* (Lausanne: n. p., 1765).

Rilliet, Théodore, *Lettres sur l'emprunt et l'impôt* ([Geneva]: n. p., 1779).

Robertson, James, *An Account of the Trial of Thomas Muir, Esq. Younger, Of Huntershill, Before the High Court of Justiciary, At Edinburgh, On the 30th and 31st Days of August, 1793, For Sedition* (Edinburgh: J. Robertson, 1793).

Roget, Jean, *Lettres de Jean Roget 1780–1783*, ed. F.-F. Roget (Geneva, Basle and Paris: Georg & Co. and Fischbacher, 1911).

Roland, Marie-Jeanne Phlippon, Madame, 'Voyage en Suisse', *Œuvres de M. J. PH. Roland, femme de l'ex-Ministre de l'Intérieur, . . . précédées d'un Discours préliminaire*, par L.-A. Champagneux (Paris: Bidault, An XIII [1800]), 3 vols.

Rolt, Richard, *An impartial representation of the conduct of the several powers of Europe, engaged in the late general war: Including a particular account of all the military and naval operations; from the commencement of hostilities between the crowns of Great Britain and Spain, in 1739: to the conclusion of the general treaty of pacification at Aix la Chapelle, 1748* (London: S. Birt, 1749–50), 4 vols.

Romilly, Samuel, *Memoirs of the Life of Sir Samuel Romilly written by himself* (London: John Murray, 1840), 3 vols.

Rose, George, *The proposed system of trade with Ireland explained* (London: John Nichols, 1785).

Rousseau, Jean-Jacques, *Correspondance complète de Jean-Jacques Rousseau*, ed. R. A. Leigh et al. (Oxford: The Voltaire Foundation at the Taylor Insititute, 1965–98), 52 vols [*CC*].

Rousseau, Jean-Jacques, *Œuvres complètes*, ed. Bernard Gagnebin and Marcel Raymond in collaboration with Pierre Burgelin, Henri Gouhier, John S. Spink, Roger de Vilmorin and Charles Wirz (Paris: Gallimard, 1959–95), 5 vols [*OC*].

Rousseau, Jean-Jacques, *Contrat social, ou Principes du droit politiques*, (Amsterdam: Marc Michel Rey, 1762).

Rouvière, Louis Henry de, *Voyage du tour de la France* (1713), in J.-D. Candaux (ed.), *Voyageurs européens à la découverte de Gèneve 1685–1792* (Geneva: Caisse d'Epargne de la République et Canton de Genève, 1966).

Roveray, Jacques-Antoine Du, *Très-humble et Très-respectueuse représentation, remise aux seigneurs sindics et à monsieur le procureur-général, le 20 Octobre 1780, par les citoyens & bourgeois représentans* (Geneva: n. p., 1780).

Roveray, Jacques-Antoine Du, *Remonstrance faite dans le Magnifique Petit Conseil, le 15 Novembre 1780, par monsieur le procureur général, au sujet de la représentation remis aux seigneurs sindics & à lui . . . le 20 Octobre 1780* (Geneva: n. p., 1780).

Roveray, Jacques-Antoine Du, *Fameuse Remonstrance faite dans le magnifique Petit Conseil de la République de Genève, le 11 Décembre 1780* (London: P. Elmsly & J. Sewel, 1781).

Ruchat, Abraham, *Les Délices de la Suisse* (1713), in J.-D. Candaux (ed.), *Voyageurs européens à la découverte de Gèneve 1685–1792* (Geneva: Caisse d'Epargne de la République et Canton de Genève, 1966).

Russell, Thomas, *A Letter to the People of Ireland, on the present situation of the country* (Belfast: Northern Star Office, 1796).

Russell, Thomas, *Journals and Memoirs of Thomas Russell, 1791–5*, ed. C. J. Woods (Dublin: Irish Academic Press, 1991

Schlablendorf, Gustav von, *Bonaparte and the French People under his Consulate, Translated from the German* (London: Tipper & Richards, 1804).

Seward, William Wenman, *Collectanea politica; or The political transactions of Ireland* (Dublin: Alex Stuart, 1801), 3 vols.

Shelley, Mary, *History of a Six Weeks' Tour through a part of France, Switzerland, Germany, and Holland; with Letters Descriptive of a Sail Round the Lake of Geneva and of the Glaciers of Chamouni* (London: Hookam & Ollier, 1817).

Sherlock, Martin, *Letters from an English traveller Martin Sherlock, Esq. translated from the French original printed at Geneva. With notes* (London: J. Nichols, 1781).

Sheridan, Betsy, *Betsy Sheridan's Journal: Letters from Sheridan's Sister, 1784–1786 and 1788–1790*, ed. William LeFanu (Oxford: Oxford University Press, 1986).

Sieyès, Emmanuel Joseph, *Qu-est ce que le Tiers état?* ([Paris]: n. p., 1789), 3rd edn.

Smith, Adam, *An Inquiry Into the Nature and Causes of the Wealth of Nations*, Vols 1 and 2, ed. R. H. Campbell and A. S. Skinner (Oxford: Oxford University Press, 1981).

Smith, Adam, *The Correspondence of Adam Smith*, ed. Ernest Campbell Mossner et al. (Oxford: Oxford University Press, 1987).

Somers, John, 1st Baron Somers, *Jura Populi Anglicani: or the Subject's Right of Petitioning Set Forth. Occasioned by the Case of the Kentish Petitioners, Etc.* (London: n. p., 1701).

Soulavie, Jean-Louis, *Historical and Political Memoirs of the Reign of Lewis XVI. From his marriage to his death* (London: G. & J. Robinson, 1802), 6 vols.

Spon, Jacob, *Histoire de la ville et de l'estat de Geneve* (Geneva: Fabri and Barrillot, 1730), 2 vols.

Spon, Jacob, *The history of the city and state of Geneva, from its first foundation to this present time: Faithfully collected from several manuscripts of Jacobus Gothofredus, Monsieur Chorier, and others* (London: Bernard White, 1687).

Staël, Germaine de, *Lettres sur les ouvrages et le caractère de J. J. Rousseau* (n. p.: n. p., 1788).

Stanhope, Charles, *Discours prononcé au Pré-l'Evêque le 9 août 1773* ([Geneva]: n. p., [1773]).

Stanhope, Charles, *Lettre de Milord M[ahon] à Mr . . . votre très fidèle combourgeois M . . .* (Chevening, [15 January] 1777).

Stanhope, Charles, 'Letter addressed by Lord Mahon to a citizen of Geneva: Downing-Street, Feb. 24', *The Morning Chronicle and London Advertiser*, 13 March 1784.

Stanyan, Abraham *An Account of Switzerland: Written in the Year 1714* (London: Jacob Tonson, 1714).

Stephens, Alexander, 'The Marquis of Buckingham', in *Public Characters of 1803–1804* (London: Richard Philips, 1804).

Stewart, Dugald, *The Collected Works of Dugald Stewart*, ed. Sir William Hamilton (Edinburgh: Thomas Constable & Co., 1854–1860), 11 vols.

Stewart, Robert, Viscount Castlereagh, *Memoirs and Correspondence of Viscount Castlereagh*, ed. Charles William Vane, Marquess of Londonderry (London: H. Colburn, 1848–53), 12 vols.

Swift, Jonathan, *A Proposal for the Universal Use of Irish Manufacture: In Cloaths and Furniture of Houses, &c. Utterly Rejecting and Renouncing Every Thing Wearable That Comes from England* (Dublin: E. Waters, 1720).

Swift, Jonathan. *Fraud Detected: Or, the Hibernian Patriot. Containing, All the Drapier's Letters to the People of Ireland, on Wood's Coinage, &c. Interspers'd with the Following Particulars, Viz. I. the Addresses of the Lords and Commons of Ireland, against Wood's Coin. Ii. His Majesty's Answer to the Said Addresses. Iii. the Report of His Majesty's Most Honourable Privy Council. Iv. Seasonable Advice to the Grand Jury. V. Extract of the Votes of the House of Commons of England, Upon Breaking a Grand*

Jury. Vi. Considerations on the Attempts, Made to Pass Wood's Coin. Vii. Reasons, Shewing the Necessity the People of Ireland Are Under, to Refuse Wood's Coinage. to Which Are Added, Prometheus. a Poem. Also a New Poem to the Drapier; and the Songs Sung at the Drapier's Club in Truck Street, Dublin, Never Before Printed. with a Preface, Explaining the Usefulness of the Whole (Dublin: George Faulkner, 1725).

Swift, Jonathan, *A Short View of the State of Ireland* (1727), in *Volume IV of the Author's Works, Containing, A Collection of Tracts Relating to Ireland* (Dublin: George Faulkner, 1735).

Swift, Jonathan, 'The Story of the Injured Lady, written by Herself' [1707], in *Jonathan Swift, Miscellanies by Dr Swift. The Eleventh Volume* (London: Hitch, David and Dodsley, 1749).

Swift, Jonathan, 'Verses said to be written on union' [1707], in Samuel Johnson (ed.), *Jonathan Swift, The Works of the English Poets: With Prefaces, Biographical and Critical, by Samuel Johnson, Volume the Thirty Ninth* (London: J. Nicols, 1779).

Swift, Jonathan, 'Observations occassion'd by reading a paper, entitled, The Case of the Woollen Manufacturers of Dublin', in 'Miscellaneous Essays', *The Works of the Rev. Jonathan Swift*, ed. Thomas Sheridan and John Nicols (London: J. Johnson et al., 1801), 19 vols.

Swift, Jonathan, *The Correspondence of Jonathan Swift: 1690–1713*, ed. Harold Williams (Oxford: Oxford University Press, 1963), 5 vols.

Temple, William, 'An Essay upon the Advancement of Trade in Ireland', in *The Works of Sir William Temple, Bart. Complete in Four Volumes. A New Edition* (London: Rivington et al., 1814), 4 vols.

The Parliamentary History of England, from the earliest period to the year 1803. From which last-mentioned epoch it is continued downwards in the work entitled, 'The Parliamentary Debates.' Vol. XXI, comprising the period from the eleventh of February 1780, to the twenty-fifth of March 1781 (London: T. C. Hansard, 1814).

The Parliamentary Register; or, History of the proceedings and debates of the House of Commons . . . during the first session of the fifteenth parliament of Great Britain, Vol. I (London: J. Almon and J. Debrett, 1781).

The Parliamentary Register; or, History of the proceedings and debates of the House of Commons . . . during the second session of the fifteenth parliament of Great Britain, Vol. VII (London, J. Debrett, 1782).

The Parliamentary Register; or, History of the proceedings and debates of the House of Commons [. . . of the House of Lords]; containing an account of the most interesting speeches and motions; accurate copies of the most remarkable letters and papers; of the most material evidence, petitions, &c. laid before, and offered to, the House, during the [first–sixth] session[s] of the Fourteenth Parliament of Great Britain (London: J. Almon, 1775–80), 17 vols.

Thelwall, John, 'The Connection between the Calamities of the Present Reign, and the System of Borough-Mongering Corruption', *The Tribune, a periodical publication, consisting chiefly of the political lectures of J. Thelwall, from the commencement of the second course in February, 1795, to the introduction of Mr. Pitt's Convention Act.* (London: J. Thelwall, 1795), vol. 3.

Tocqueville, Alexis de, *The Old Regime and the Revolution*, trans. Alan S. Kahan (Chicago: University of Chicago Press, 2001), 2 vols.

Tone, Theobald Wolfe, *An Argument on Behalf of the Catholics of Ireland* (Belfast: Society of United Irishmen, 1791).

Tone, Theobald Wolfe, *The Life of Theobald Wolfe Tone . . . Written by himself, and continued by his son . . .*, ed. W. T. W. Tone (Washington: Gales & Seaton, 1826), 2 vols.

Tscharner, Vincent Bernard de, *Dictionnaire historique, politique et géographique de la Suisse* (Geneva: Barde et al., 1788), 2 vols.

Tucker, Josiah, *A Brief Essay on the Advantages and Disadvantages Which Respectively Attend France and Great Britain: With Regard to Trade, with Some Proposals for Removing the Principal Disadvantages of Great Britain* (London: for the author, 1749).

Tucker, Josiah, *The elements of commerce, and theory of taxes* (n. p.: n. p., 1755).

Turrettini, Jean-Alphonse, *An Oration of Composing the Differences among Protestants. Spoken at an Act of the University of Geneva, Jun. 1707* (London: William Taylor, 1709).

Turrettini, Jean-Alphonse, *A discourse concerning fundamental articles in religion. In which a method is laid down for the more effectual uniting of Protestants, and promoting a more general toleration amongst them* (London: A. Bell et al., 1720).

United Irishmen, 'Address from the Society of United Irishmen, in Dublin, to the Delegates for Promoting a Reform in Scotland', 23 November 1792.

Vaughan, Benjamin, *New and old principles of trade compared; or a treatise on the principles of commerce between nations* (London: J. Johnson, 1786).

Vergennes, Charles Gravier, comte de, *Lettre de son excellence Monsieur le Comte de Vergennes, Ministre & Secretaire d'Etat au département des affaires étrangers. Aux Sindics et Conseil de la Ville & la République de Genève* (Versailles, [10 April] 1781).

Vergennes, Charles Gravier comte de, *Lettre de son excellence Mr Le Comte de Vergennes, ministre des affaires étrangères aux syndics et conseil de la ville et république de Genève. A Versailles le 15 Avril 1782* (Geneva: n. p., 1782).

Vernes, Jacob, *Lettres sur le Christianisme de Mr. J. J. Rousseau, addressées à Mr. I. L.* (Geneva: Etienne Blanc, 1763).

Vernes, Jacob, *Catéchisme destiné particulièrement à l'usage des jeunes-gens* (Geneva: Du Villard, 1781).

Vernet, Jacob, *Lettres critiques d'un voyageur anglois sur l'Article Geneve du Dictionnaire Encyclopédique & sur la lettre de Mr. D'Alembert à Mr. Rousseau* (Utrecht, 1761).

Vieusseux, André, *The History of Switzerland: From the Irruption of the Barbarians to the Present Day* (London: Society for the Diffusion of Useful Knowledge, 1840).

Voltaire [François-Marie Arouet], *An Epistle of Voltaire, upon his arrival at his Estate near the Lake of Geneva, in March 1755* (London: J. Dodsley, 1755).

Voltaire, *Additions à l'Essai sur l'Histoire Générale, et sur l'Esprit & les Moeurs des Nations* (Amsterdam: n. p., 1764).

Voltaire, *Le Sentiment des citoyens* ([Geneva]: n. p., [1765]).

Voltaire, *A Letter from Mr. Voltaire to M. Jean-Jacques Rousseau* (London, 1766).

Voltaire, *The Civil War of Geneva: Or, the Amours of Robert Covelle, an Heroic Poem, in Five Cantos. Translated from the French of M. de Voltaire, by T. Teres.* (London: T. Durham et al., 1769).

Voltaire, *Correspondence and Related Documents*, ed. Theodore Besterman, vols 85–135 in *The Complete Works of Voltaire* (Geneva, Banbury and Oxford: Institut et Musée Voltaire & Voltaire Foundation, 1968–77).

Werenfels, Samuel, *Three discourses: one, A defence of private judgment; the second, Against the authority of the magistrate over conscience; the third, Some considerations concerning the reuniting of Protestants: The two first translated from the Latin, the third from the French, of Dr. Samuel Werenfels Professor of Divinity in the University of Bale, in Switzerland. With a prefatory epistle to the Reverend Dr. Tenison; giving an account of the occasion of translating them, and their use in the Bishop of Bangor's controversy* (London: James Knapton, 1718).

Wilson, Charles Henry, *A Compleat Collection of the Resolutions of the Volunteers, Grand Juries, & C of Ireland, which Followed the Celebrated Resolves of the First Dungannon Diet: To which is Prefixed a Train of Historical Facts Relative to the Kingdom, from the Invasion of Henry II. Down, with the History of Volunteering, &c.* (Dublin: Joseph Hill, 1782), 2 vols.

Winkopp, Peter Adolph, *Neuestes Staats-, Zeitungs-, Reise-, Post- und Handlungs-Lexikon oder geographisch-historisch-statistisches Handbuch von allen fünf Theilen Erbe* (Leipzig: Kleefeld, 1804).

Woodfall, William, *An impartial sketch of the debate in the House of Commons of Ireland: on a motion made on Friday, August 12, 1785, by the Right Honourable Thomas Orde, secretary to His Grace Charles Manners, Duke of Rutland, Lord Lieutenant, for leave to bring in a Bill for effectuating the intercourse and commerce* (Dublin: Luke White, 1785).

Wyvill, Christopher, *Political papers chiefly respecting the attempt of the County of York and other considerable districts, commenced in 1779, and continued during several subsequent years, to effect a reformation of the Parliament of Great-Britain* (York: W. Blanchard, 1794–1804), 6 vols.

Young, Arthur, *A Tour In Ireland: With General Observations On The Present State Of That Kingdom, Made In The Years 1776, 1777 and 1778, and brought down to the end of 1779* (London: T. Cadell, 1780), 2 vols.

Zimmermann, Johann Georg, *An Essay on National Pride. Translated from the German* (London: J. Wilkie, 1771).

Newspapers and Magazines

The Asiatic Journal and Monthly Register for British India and its Dependencies (London: Black et al., 1819), vol. 8.

Bombay Courier, vol. 8, 13 July 1799 (issue 355).

The Court Magazine and Belle Assemblée, vol. 7, August 1835.

The Dublin Evening Post, 18 May 1799 (issue 7,612).

Dublin University Magazine, October 1838.

The English Review, or An Abstract of English and Foreign Literature, vol. 4 (London: 1784)

The European Magazine, and London Review, vol. 5, June 1784.

The Evening Herald (Dublin), 1 February 1960.

Freeman's Journal (Dublin), 29 May 1821.

General Evening Post (London), 23–26 April 1783 (issue 7,673).

The Gentleman's Magazine and Historical Chronicle, ed. Sylvanus Urban, March, May 1782.

The Graphic (London), 22 December 1883 (issue 734).

The Hibernian Journal: or, Chronicle of Liberty, vol. 29, 9 January 1799 (issue 4).

Hibernian Magazine, or, Compendium of entertaining knowledge, January 1780; October 1794.

Irish Magazine and Monthly Asylum for Neglected Biography, December 1811; October 1814.

Journal encyclopédique ou universel (Bouillon and Liège: Rousseau Toulouse), vol. 5, no. 1, 1 July 1763.

Journal Helvétique, January 1755; March 1755; January 1769.

Journal historique et littéraire, ed. François-Xavier de Feller, June 1782.

The Lady's magazine; or, Entertaining companion for the fair sex, appropriated solely to their use and amusement, vol. 24, June 1793.

The London Chronicle, 4–7 October 1783 (issue 4,202).

London Evening Post, 15–17 October 1782 (issue 9,437).

London magazine, or, Gentleman's monthly intelligencer, no. 51, 1782.

Methodist Magazine, June 1804.

The Morning Chronicle and London Advertiser, 16 October 1782 (issue 4,185); 21 October 1782 (issue 4,189); 13 March 1784 (issue 4,625).

The Morning Herald and Daily Advertiser (London), 8 October 1782 (issue 606); 24 December 1782 (issue 672); 3 May 1783 (issue 784).

The New Annual Register, or, General repository of history, politics, and littérature for the year 1782, ed. Andrew Kippis (London: G. Robinson, 1783).

Oracle and Public Advertiser, 10 August 1795.

Parker's General Advertiser and Morning Intelligencer (London), 5 August (no issue no.); 8 January 1783 (issue 1,927).

Public Advertiser, 12 May 1779.

The Political magazine and parliamentary, naval, military, and literary journal, for July 1782 (London: 1782).

The Remembrancer, or, Impartial repository of public events, 1780; 1782, part 2; 1783, part 1 (London: J. Debrett, 1780–83).

The Scots Magazine, Volume 44 (1782).

The Scotsman (Edinburgh), 18 September 1833.

The Times (London), 24 July 1786, 3 (issue 495); 7 September 1792, 3 (issue 2,406); 24 September 1793, 3 (issue 2,787); 3 October 1793, 3 (issue 2,796); 19 October 1798, 3 (issue 2,264); 21 November 1798, 4 (issue 4,338); 3 December 1798, 4 (issue 4,347); 6 May 1799, 3 (issue 4,476); 14 May 1799, 3 (issue 4,483); 2 October 1799, 2 (issue 4,602); 9 October 1799, 3 (issue 4,608); 10 October 1799, 3 (issue 4,609); 14 July 1801, 2 (issue 5,158).

The United Service Magazine and Naval and Military Journal, 1870, part 1 (London: Hurst and Blackett, 1870).

The Vocal Magazine; or, British Songster's Miscellany; containing all the English, Scotch and Irish songs, cantatas, glees, catches, airs, ballads (London: J. Bew, 1778) (issue 6).

Volunteers Journal or Irish Herald, 12 July 1784.
Whitehall Evening Post (London), 29 April–1 May 1783 (issue 5,554); 4–6 September 1798 (issue 8,075).

Secondary Sources

Albertone, Manuela, 'Democratic Republicanism. Historical Reflections on the Idea of *Republic* in the 18th Century', *History of European Ideas*, 33 (2007), 108–30.

Albertone, Manuela, *National Identity and the Agrarian Republic. The Transatlantic Commerce of Ideas between America and France, 1750–1830* (Farnham: Ashgate, 2014).

Akenson, Donald H., *The Irish Education Experiment: The National System of Education in the Nineteenth Century* (London: Routledge & Kegan Paul, 1970).

Andrey, Georges 'Recherches sur la littérature politique relative aux troubles de Fribourg durant les années 1780' ('Imprimeurs de Genève et Carouge au service des gouvernements de Genève et de Fribourg à la poursuite des séditieux'), in Jean-Daniel Candaux and Bernard Lescaze (eds), *Cinq siècles d'imprimerie genevoise. Actes du Colloque international sur l'histoire de imprimerie et du livre à Genève, 27–30 avril 1978* (Geneva: Société d'histoire et d'archéologie, 1980–81), 2 vols, II, 115–56.

Aston, Nigel, 'Petty and Fitzmaurice: Lord Shelburne and his Brother', in Aston and Campbell Orr (eds), *An Enlightenment Statesman in Whig Britain* (2011), 29–50.

Aston, Nigel and Clarissa Campbell Orr (eds), *An Enlightenment Statesman in Whig Britain: Lord Shelburne in Context, 1737–1805* (Woodbridge: Boydell & Brewer, 2011).

Aubert, Hippolyte, 'Les troubles de Genève en 1781 et 1782. Extrait des papiers de Perrinet des Franches conservés aux Archives Nationales de France, *Bulletin de la Societé d'Histoire at d'Archéologie de Genève*, 3 (1913), 418–40.

Bairoch, Paul 'Genève dans le contexte des villes suisses et européennes de 1500 à 1800', in Lilian Mottu-Weber and Dominique Zumkeller (eds), *Mélanges d'histoire économique offerts au professeur Anne-Marie Piuz* (Geneva: Istec, 1989).

Barnard, Toby, *The Kingdom of Ireland, 1641–1760* (Basingstoke: Palgrave, 2004).

Barnard, Toby, *Improving Ireland?: Projectors, Prophets and Profiteers, 1641–1786* (Dublin: Four Courts Press, 2008).

Barnard, Toby, 'The Dublin Society and other Improving Societies, 1731–85', in James Kelly and Martyn J. Powell (eds), *Clubs and Societies in Eighteenth-Century Ireland* (Dublin: Four Courts Press, 2010), 53–88.

Barrell, John, *Imagining the King's Death: Figurative Treason, Fantasies of Regicide, 1793–1796* (Oxford: Oxford University Press, 2000).

Barrell, John, *The Spirit of Despotism: Invasions of Privacy in the 1790s* (Oxford: Oxford University Press, 2006).

Barrell, John, and John Mee (eds), *Trials for Treason and Sedition, 1792–1794*, (London: Pickering & Chatto, 2006–07), 8 vols.

Bartlett, Thomas 'An End to Moral Economy: The Irish Militia Disturbances of 1793', *Past & Present* 99 (1983), 41–64.

Bartlett, Thomas, *The Fall and Rise of the Irish Nation: The Catholic Question, 1690–1830* (Dublin: Gill and Macmillan, 1992).

Bastid, Paul, *Sieyès et sa pensée* (Paris: Hachette, 1939).

Beckett, James C., *Protestant Dissent in Ireland, 1687–1780* (London: Faber & Faber, 1948).

Belissa, Marc, *Repenser l'ordre européen (1795–1802): De la société des rois aux droits des nations* (Paris: Kimé, 2006).

Bénétruy, Jean, *L'Atelier de Mirabeau. Quatre proscrits genevois dans la tourmente révolutionnaire* (Geneva: Alex Jullien, 1962).

Bergin, John, Eoin Magennis, Lesa Ní Mhunghaile and Patrick Walsh (eds), *New Perspectives on the Penal Laws* (Dublin: *Eighteenth-Century Ireland/Iris an dá chultúr*, special issue no. 1, 2011).

Blum, Carol, *Rousseau and the Republic of Virtue. The Language of Politics in the French Revolution* (Ithaca, NY: Cornell University Press, 1986).

Bois-Melly, Charles Du, *Les moeurs génevoises de 1700 à 1760, d'après tous les documents officiels, pour servir d'introduction à l'histoire de la République et Seigneurie de Genève* (Geneva and Basle: H. Georg, 1892), 2nd edn.

Borgeaud, Charles, *Histoire de l'Université de Genève, 1. L'Academie de Calvin, 1559–1798* (Geneva: Georg & Co., 1900).

Bosher, John, 'Huguenot Merchants and the Protestant International in the Seventeenth Century', *William and Mary Quarterly*, 3rd series, 52 (1995), 77–102.

Bost, Ami, *History of the Bohemian and Moravian Brethren* (London: Religious Tract Society, 1848), 3rd edn.

Bouchary, Jean, 'Étienne Clavière d'après sa correspondance financière et politique', *Les manieurs d'argent à Paris à la fin du XVIIIe siècle* (Paris: M. Rivière, 1939–43), 3 vols.

Bourke, Richard, *Empire and Revolution: The Political Life of Edmund Burke* (Princeton, NJ: Princeton University Press, 2015).

Bradshaw, Brendan, *The Irish Constitutional Revolution of the Sixteenth Century* (Cambridge: Cambridge University Press, 2008).

Bradshaw, Brendan, *'And So Began the Irish Nation': Nationality, National Consciousness and Nationalism in Pre-Modern Ireland* (London: Routledge, 2016).

Brandli, Fabrice, *Le nain et le géant: La République de Genève et la France aux XVIIIe siècle: Cultures politiques et diplomatie* (Rennes: Presses universitaires de Rennes, 2012).

Brown, Michael, Patrick M. Geoghegan and James Kelly (eds), *The Irish Act of Union, 1800: Bicentennial Essays* (Dublin: Irish Academic Press, 2003)

Browne, James, *A History of the Highlands and of the Highland Clans . . . Volume 4* (London, Edinburgh and Dublin: A. Fullarton & Co., 1854).

Budé, Eugène de, *Vie de J.-A. Turrettini, theólogien genevois 1671–1737* (Lausanne: G. Bridel, 1880).

Burke, Helen, *Riotous Performances: The Struggle for Hegemony in the Irish Theater, 1712–1784* (Notre Dame, IN: Notre Dame University Press, 2003).

Butler, Hubert, 'New Geneva in Waterford', *The Journal of the Royal Society of Antiquaries of Ireland*, 77 (1947), 150–5.

Butler, Matthew, 'New Geneva. Some correspondence relating to its foundation', *Journal of the Waterford and South-East of Ireland Archaeological Society*, 15–18 (1912–15).

Candaux, Jean-Daniel, 'La révolution genevoise de 1782: Un état de la question', in *Études sur le XVIIIe siècle*, vol. 7, *L'Europe et les révolutions (1770–1800)*, (Brussels: Éditions de l'Université libre de Bruxelles, 1980), 77–90.

Cannon, John, 'Petty [*formerly* Fitzmaurice], William, second earl of Shelburne and first marquess of Lansdowne (1737–1805), prime minister', *ODNB*.

Cannon, Richard, *Historical Record of the Fifty-Sixth, or the West Essex Regiment of Foot* (London: Parker, Furnivall & Parker, 1844).

Canny, Nicholas, *Kingdom and Colony. Ireland in the Atlantic World, 1560–1800* (Baltimore and London: Johns Hopkins University Press, 1988).

Canny, Nicholas, *Making Ireland British, 1580–1650* (Oxford: Oxford University Press, 2001).

Chaffers, William, *Hall Marks on Gold and Silver Plate, illustrated with the tables of annual date letters employed in the assay offices of England, Scotland & Ireland, a fac-simile of a copper-plate of markers' marks at Goldsmith's Hall* (London: J. Davy & sons, 1862).

Chapuisat, Édouard, 'Étienne Clavière', in *Figures et choses d'autrefois* (Paris and Geneva: Crès & Georg, 1920).

Chapuisat, Édouard, *La prise d'armes de 1782 à Genève* (Geneva: A. Jullien, 1932).

Choisy, Albert, 'La prise d'armes de 1770 contre les natifs', *Étrennes genevoises*, (1925), 47–77.

Claeys, Gregory, *Thomas Paine: Social and Political Thought* (London: Unwin Hyman, 1989).

Claeys, Gregory, 'The French Revolution Debate and British Political Thought', *History of Political Thought*, 11 (1990), 59–80.

Claeys, Gregory, 'The Origins of the Rights of Labor: Republicanism, Commerce, and the Construction of Modern Social Theory in Britain, 1796–1805', *Journal of Modern History*, 66 (1994), 249–90.

Clark, J.C.D., *The Language of Liberty 1660–1832: Political Discourse and Social Dynamics in the Anglo-American World* (Cambridge: Cambridge University Press, 1994).

Clark, J.C.D., *English Society, 1660–1832: Religion, Ideology and Politics during the Ancien Regime* (Cambridge: Cambridge University Press, 2000).

Clark, J.C.D., 'Protestantism, Nationalism and National Identity, 1660–1832', *The Historical Journal*, 43 (2000), 249–76.

Clark, J.C.D., *Thomas Paine. Britain, America, and France in the Age of Enlightenment and Revolution* (Oxford: Oxford University Press, 2018).

Claydon, Tony, *Europe and the Making of England, 1660–1760* (Cambridge: Cambridge University Press, 2007).

Colley, Linda, *Britons: Forging the Nation, 1707–1837* (London: Pimlico, 1992).

Connolly, S. J., *Religion, Law and Power: The Making of Protestant Ireland, 1660–1760* (Oxford: Oxford University Press, 1995).

Connolly, S. J., *Divided Kingdom: Ireland 1630–1800* (Oxford: Oxford University Press, 2008).

Cookson, J. E., *The British Armed Nation, 1793–1815* (Oxford: Oxford University Press, 1997).

Corcoran, Timothy, *State Policy in Irish Education,* A.D. *1536 to 1816, Exemplified in Documents Collected for Lectures to Postgraduate Classes* (Dublin: Fallon Brothers; New York: Longmans, Green & Co., 1916).

Cramer, Marc, 'Les trente Demoiselles de Genève et les billets solidaires', *Revue suisse d'économie politique et de statistique*, 82 (1946) 109–38.

Cranston, Maurice, *The Noble Savage: Jean-Jacques Rousseau, 1754–1762* (Chicago: University of Chicago Press, 1991).

Cranston, Maurice, *The Solitary Self: Jean-Jacques Rousseau in Exile and Adversity* (Chicago: Chicago University Press, 1997).

Creighton, D. G., 'Rousseau and the Delucs in 1754', *Diderot Studies*, 19 (1978), 55–66.

Crue, Francis de, *L'Ami de Rousseau et des Necker. Paul Moultou à Paris en 1778* (Paris: Honoré Champion, 1926).

Cullen, Louis M., *Princes and Pirates: The Dublin Chamber of Commerce, 1783–1983* (Dublin: Dublin Chamber of Commerce, 1983).

Cullen, Louis M. 'Catholics under the Penal Laws', *Eighteenth-Century Ireland*, 1 (1986), 23–36.

Cullen, Louis M., John Shovlin and Thomas Truxes (eds), *The Bordeaux-Dublin Letters, 1757: Correspondence of an Irish Community Abroad* (Oxford: Oxford University Press, 2013).

Darcy, Eamon, *The Irish Rebellion of 1641 and the Wars of the Three Kingdoms* (Woodbridge: Boydell & Brewer, Royal Historical Society Studies in History, 2013).

Dardier, Charles, *Ésaïe Gasc, citoyen de Genève: sa politique et sa théologie, Genève—Constance—Montauban 1748–1813* (Paris: Sandoz & Fischbacher, 1876).

Dickson, David, 'Paine and Ireland', in Dickson, Keogh and Whelan (eds), *The United Irishmen: Republicanism, Radicalism and Rebellion*, 135–50.

Dickson, David, *Arctic Ireland: The Extraordinary Story of the Great Frost and Forgotten Famine of 1740–41* (Belfast: White Row Press, 1997).

Dickson, David, *New Foundations: Ireland, 1660–1800* (Dublin and Portland, OR: Irish Academic Press, 2000).

Dickson, David, 'Famine and Economic Change in Eighteenth-Century Ireland', in Alvin Jackson (ed), *The Oxford Handbook of Modern Irish History* (Oxford: Oxford University Press, 2014), 422–38.

Dickson, David, Dáire Keogh and Kevin Whelan (eds), *The United Irishmen: Republicanism, Radicalism and Rebellion* (Lilliput Press: Dublin, 1993).

Dinwiddy, J. R., *Radicalism and Reform in Britain, 1780–1850* (London: Hambledon Press, 1992).

Ditchfield, G. M., 'Stanhope, Charles, third Earl Stanhope (1753–1816)', *ODNB*.

Ditchfield, G. M., 'The Subscription Issue in British Parliamentary Politics 1772–1779', *Parliamentary History*, 7 (1988), 45–80.

Ditchfield, G. M., 'A Christian Whig: Lord Shelburne and the Latitudinarian Tradition', in Aston and Campbell Orr, (eds), *An Enlightenment Statesman in Whig Britain*, 79–96.

Donnelly, James S. and James J. Donnelly, 'The Rightboy Movement 1785–8', *Studia Hibernica*, 17/18 (1977–78), 120–202.

Dowling, Daniel 'New Geneva', *Decies*, 29 (1985), 32–9.

Doyle, William, *Aristocracy and its Enemies in the Age of Revolution* (Oxford: Oxford University Press, 2009).

Dunn, John, *The Cunning of Unreason: Making Sense of Politics* (New York: Basic Books, 2000).

Dunn, John, *Setting the People Free: The Story of Democracy* (London: Atlantic Books, 2005).

Dufour, Edouard, *Jacob Vernes, 1728–1791. Essai sur sa vie et sa controverse apologétique avec J.-J. Rousseau* (Geneva: W. Kündig, 1898).

Dufour-Vernes, Louis, *L'ancienne Genève 1535–1798. Fragments historiques* (Geneva: Librairie Kündig, 1909).

Egan, Patrick M., *History, guide & directory of county and city of Waterford* (Kilkenny: n. p., 1895).

Ehrman, John *The Younger Pitt: The Years of Acclaim* (London: Constable, 1969).

Elliot, Marianne, *Partners in Revolution: The United Irishmen and France* (, CT: Yale University Press, 1980).

Elliot, Marianne, *Wolfe Tone. Prophet of Irish Independence* (New Haven, CT and London: Yale University Press, 1989).

Elliott, Marianne, *When God Took Sides. Religion and Identity in Ireland—Unfinished History* (Oxford: Oxford University Press, 2009).

Epinoux, Estelle, *Introduction to Irish History and Civilization: Texts and Documents on Ireland* (Limoges: Presses Universitaires de Limoges, 2007).

Fatio, Olivier and Nicole Fatio, *Pierre Fatio et la crise de 1707* (Geneva: Labor et Fides, 2007).

Fatio, Olivier, Michel Grandjean, Robert Martin-Achard, Liliane Mottu-Weber and Alfred Perrenoud (eds), *Genève au temps de la révocation de 'l'Édit de Nantes* (Geneva: Droz, 1986).

Favet, Grégoire, *Les syndics de Genève au XVIIIe siècle. Étude du personnel politique de la République* (Geneva: Droz, 1998).

Fazy, Henri, *Les Constitutions de la République de Genève* (Geneva and Basle: H. Georg, 1890).

Feldman, Theodore S., 'Deluc, Jean-André (1727–1817)', *ODNB*.

Feldmann, J., *Die Genfer Emigranten von 1782/3* (Zurich: n. p., 1952).

Ferretti, Federico 'On Uses of Utopian Maps: The Map of New Geneva in Waterford (1783) between Colonialism and 'Republicanism', *Journal of Research and Didactics in Geography* 1 (2017), 75–81.

Fontana, Biancamaria, *The Invention of the Modern Republic* (Cambridge: Cambridge University Press, 1994).

Foster, R. F., *Modern Ireland, 1600–1972* (London: Allen Lane, 1988).

Forsyth, Murray, 'The Old European States-System: Gentz versus Hauterive', *The Historical Journal*, 23 (1980), 521–38.

Forsyth, Murray, *Reason and Revolution: The Political Thought of the Abbé Sieyès* (Leicester: Leicester University Press, 1987).

Foy, R. H., *Remembering All the Orrs. The story of the Orr families of Country Antrim and their Involvement in the 1798 Rebellion* (Belfast: Ulster Historical Foundation, 1999).

Fox Bourne, H. R., *The Life of John Locke* (London: H. S. King, 1876), 2 vols.

Fruchtman, Jr, Jack, *The Apocalyptic Politics of Richard Price and Joseph Priestley: A Study in Late Eighteenth-Century English Millennialism, Transactions of the American Philosophical Society*, 73, part 4 (Philadelphia: American Philosophical Society, 1983).

Furlong, Nicholas, 'Grogan, Cornelius (1738–1798)', *ODNB*.

Galiffe, J.B.G., *D'un siècle à l'autre: Correspondances inédites entre gens connus et inconnus du XVIIIe et du XIXe siècle* (Geneva: Sandoz, 1877), 2 vols.

Gargett, Graham, *Voltaire and Protestantism* (Oxford: Oxford University Press, 1980).

Gargett, Graham, 'Jacob Vernet, éditeur de Montesquieu: La première edition de "l'Esprit des lois"', *Revue 'd'histoire littéraire de la France*, 91 Année, 6 (1991), 890–900.

Gargett, Graham, *Jacob Vernet, Geneva and the Philosophes* (Oxford: Voltaire Foundation, 1994).

Gay, Peter, *Voltaire's Politics: The Poet as Realist* (Princeton, NJ: Princeton University Press, 1959).

Geoghegan, Patrick *The Irish Act of Union: A Study in High Politics, 1798–1801* (New York: St. Martin's Press, 2000).

Gibbs, Jenna M., *Performing the Temple of Liberty. Slavery, Theater, and Popular Culture in London and Philadelphia, 1760–1850* (Baltimore: Johns Hopkins University Press, 2014).

Gimlette, Thomas, 'The French Settlers in Ireland: No. 7. The Settlement in Waterford', *Ulster Journal of Archaeology*, 1st series, 4 (1856), 198–221.

Goodrich, Amanda, *Debating England's Aristocracy in the 1790s: Pamphlets, Polemics and Political Ideas* (Woodbridge: Boydell & Brewer, 2005).

Goodwin, Albert, *The Friends of Liberty: The English Democratic Movement in the Age of the French Revolution* (Cambridge, MA: Harvard University Press, 1979).

Griffin, Patrick, *The Townshend Moment: The Making of Empire and Revolution in the Eighteenth Century* (New Haven, CT: Yale University Press, 2017).

Grimsley, Ronald, *Jean 'd'Alembert (1717–83)* (Oxford: Oxford University Press, 1963).

Guillot, Alexandre, 'Du rôle politique de la Compagnie des Pasteurs de Genève dans les événements de 1781 et 1782', in *Étrennes religieuses*, new series (Geneva: Kündig, 1894), 231–78.

Gür, André, 'La négociation de l'Édit du 11 mars 1768, d'après le journal de Jean-André Deluc et la correspondance de Gédéon Turrettini', *Revue Suisse d'histoire*, 17 (1967), 166–217.

Gür, André, 'Quête de la richesse et critique des riches chez Étienne Clavière', in Jacques Berchtold and Michel Porret (eds), *Être riche au siècle de Voltaire* (Geneva: Droz, 1996).

Gwynn, Robin, 'The Huguenots in Britain, the "Protestant International" and the Defeat of Louis XIV', in Randolph Vigne and Charles Littleton (eds), *From Strangers to Citizens. The Integration of Immigrant Communities in Britain, Ireland and Colonial America 1550–1750* (Brighton and Portland, OR: Sussex Academic Press, 2001), 412–24.

Hammersley, Rachel, *French Revolutionaries and English Republicans: The Cordeliers Club, 1790–1794* (Woodbridge: Boydell & Brewer, 2005).

Hammersley, Rachel, *The English Republican Tradition and Eighteenth-Century France* (Manchester: Manchester University Press, 2010).

Hampson, Norman, *Will and Circumstance: Montesquieu, Rousseau and the French Revolution* (Norman, OK: University of Oklahoma Press, 1983).

Hayton, David W., 'British Whig Ministers and the Irish question, 1714–25', in Stephen Taylor, Richard Connors and Clyve Jones (eds), *Hanoverian Britain and Empire: Essays in Memory of Philip Lawson* (Woodbridge: Boydell & Brewer, 1998).

Hayton, David W., *Ruling Ireland 1685–1742: Politics, Politicians and Parties* (Woodbridge: Boydell & Brewer, 2004).

Hayton, David W. 'Henry Maxwell, M.P., Author of "An Essay upon an Union of Ireland with England (1703)"', *Eighteenth-Century Ireland/Iris an dá chultúr*, 22 (2007), 28–63.

Heyd, Michael, *Between Orthodoxy and the Enlightenment. Jean-Robert Chouet and the Introduction of Cartesian Science in the Academy of Geneva* (The Hague: M. Nijoff, 1982).

Higgins, Padhraig, *A Nation of Politicians: Gender, Patriotism, and Political Culture* (Madison, WI: University of Wisconsin Press, 2010).

Hill, Jacqueline, 'Ireland without Union: Molyneux and his Legacy', in John Robertson (ed.), *Union for Empire: Political Thought and the British Union of 1707* (Cambridge: Cambridge University Press, 1995).

Hill, Jacqueline, *From Patriots to Unionists: Dublin Civic Politics and Irish Protestant Patriotism, 1660–1840* (Oxford: Oxford University Press, 1997).

Hont, Istvan, *Politics in Commercial Society. Jean-Jacques Rousseau and Adam Smith*, ed. Béla Kapossy and Michael Sonenscher (Cambridge, MA: Harvard University Press, 2015).

Höpfl, Harro, *The Christian Polity of John Calvin* (Cambridge: Cambridge University Press, 1985).

Innes, Joanna and Mark Philp (eds), *Re-imagining Democracy in the Age of Revolutions: America, France, Britain, Ireland, 1750–1850* (Oxford: Oxford University Press, 2013).

Israel, Jonathan, *A Revolution of the Mind: Radical Enlightenment and the Intellectual Origins of Modern Democracy* (Princeton, NJ: Princeton University Press, 2010).

Israel, Jonathan, *Democratic Enlightenment: Philosophy, Revolution, and Human Rights 1750–1790* (Oxford: Oxford University Press, 2011).

Jarret, Derek, *The Begetters of Revolution: England's Involvement with France, 1759–1789* (London: Longman, 1973).

Jupp, Peter 'Genevese Exiles in County Waterford', *Journal of the Cork Historical and Archealogical Society*, 75 (1970), 29–35.

Jupp, Peter, 'Earl Temple's Viceroyalty and the Renunciation Question, 1782–3', *Irish Historical Studies*, 17 (1971).

Kapossy, Béla, *Iselin contra Rousseau: Sociable Patriotism and the History of Mankind* (Basle: Schwabe, 2006).

Kapossy, Béla, 'Republican Political Economy. Introduction: The Economic Society of Berne and the Reform of the Republican Household', *History of European Ideas*, 33 (2007), 377–89.

Kapossy, Béla, 'Genevan Creditors and English Liberty: The Example of Théodore Rilliet de Saussure', in Valérie Cossy, Béla Kapossy and Richard Whatmore (eds), *Genève, Lieu d'Angleterre, 1725–1814* (Geneva: Slatkine, 2009).

Karmin, Otto, *Sir Francis d'Ivernois 1757–1842. Sa vie, son oeuvre et son temps* (Geneva: Revue historique de la révolution française et de l'empire, 1920).

Kavanaugh, Ann C., 'FitzGibbon, John, first earl of Clare (1748–1802), lord chancellor of Ireland', *ONDB*.

Kavanaugh, Ann C., *John FitzGibbon, Earl of Clare: Protestant Reaction and English Authority in Late Eighteenth-Century Ireland* (Dublin: Irish Academic Press, 1997).

Kearney, H. F., 'The Political Background to English Mercantilism: 1695–1700', *Economic History Review*, 2nd series, 11 (1959), 484–96.

Kelly, James, 'The Context and Course of Thomas Orde's Plan of Education of 1787', *The Irish Journal of Education*, 20 (1986), 3–26.

Kelly, James, 'The Origins of the Act of Union: An Examination of Unionist Opinion in Britain and Ireland, 1650–1800', *Irish Historical Studies*, 25 (1987), 236–63.

Kelly, James, 'The Irish Trade Dispute with Portugal 1780–87', *Studia Hibernica*, 25 (1990), 7–48.

Kelly, James, *Prelude to Union. Anglo-Irish Politics in the 1780s* (Cork: Cork University Press, 1992).

Kelly, James, *Henry Flood: Patriots and Politics in Eighteenth-Century Ireland* (Dublin: Four Courts Press, 1998).

Kelly, James, 'Coping with Crisis: The Response to the Famine of 1740–1', *Eighteenth-Century Ireland/Iris an dá chultúr*, 27 (2012), 99–122.

Kelly, James, 'Beresford, John' and 'de Blaquiere, Sir John', *DIB*.

Kelly, James and James Quinn, 'Clements, Henry Theophilus', *DIB*.

Kelly, Patrick, 'The Irish Woollen Export Prohibition Act of 1699: Kearney Re-visited', *Irish Economic and Social History*, 7 (1980), 22–43.

Kelly, Patrick, 'William Molyneux and the Spirit of Liberty in Eighteenth-Century Ireland', *Eighteenth-Century Ireland*, 3 (1988), 133–48.

Kelly, Patrick, 'Recasting a Tradition: William Molyneux and the Sources of *The Case of Ireland . . . Stated* (1698)', in Ohlmeyer (ed.), *Political Thought in Seventeenth-Century Ireland*, 83–106.

Kelly, Paul 'British and Irish Politics in 1785', *The English Historical Review*, 90 (1975), 536–63.

Kidd, Colin, 'North Britishness and the Nature of Eighteenth-Century British Patriotisms', *The Historical Journal*, 39 (1996), 361–82.

Kidd, Colin, *Union and Unionisms: Political Thought in Scotland, 1500–2000* (Cambridge: Cambridge University Press, 2006).

Kingdom, Robert M., 'Social Welfare in Calvin's Geneva', *American Historical Review*, 76 (1971), 50–69.

Kingdom, Robert M.,'The Control of Morals in Calvin's Geneva', in L. P. Buck and J. W. Zophy (eds), *The Social History of Reformation* (Columbus, OH: Ohio State University Press, 1972).

Klauber, Martin I., 'Reason, Revelation, and Cartesianism: Louis Tronchin and Enlightened Orthodoxy in Late Seventeenth-Century Geneva', *Church History*, 59 (1990), 326–39.

Klauber, Martin I. 'The Drive Toward Protestant Union in Early Eighteenth-Century Geneva: Jean-Alphonse Turrettini on the "Fundamental Articles" of the Faith', *Church History*, 61 (1992), 334–49.

Klauber, Martin I., *Between Reformed Scholasticism and Pan-Protestantism: Jean-Alphonse Turretin (1671–1737) and Enlightened Orthodoxy at the Academy of Geneva* (Selingsgrove, PA: Susquehanna University Press, 1994).

Klein, Lawrence, 'Sociability, Politeness, and Aristocratic Self-Formation in the Life and Career of the Second Earl of Shelburne', *The Historical Journal*, 55 (2012), 653–77.

Klein, Lawrence E. and Anthony L. La Vopa (eds), *Enthusiasm and Enlightenment in Europe, 1650–1850* (San Marino, CA: Huntington Library, 1998).

Lachenicht, Susanne, 'Huguenot Immigrants and the Formation of National Identities', *The Historical Journal* 50 (2007), 309–31.

Lachenicht, Susanne (ed.), *Religious Refugees in Europe, Asia and North America, 6th–21st Centuries* (Hamburg: Atlantic Cultural Studies, 2007).

Lambert, David E., *The Protestant International and the Huguenot Migration to Virginia* (New York: Peter Lang, 2010).

Lammey, David, 'The Free Trade Crisis: A Reappraisal', in Gerard O'Brien (ed.), *Parliament, Politics, and People: Essays in Eighteenth-Century Irish History* (Dublin: Irish Academic Press, 1989).

Lammey, David, 'Dobbs, Francis (1750–1811), politician and barrister', *ODNB*.

Lauritsen, Holger Ross and Mikkel Thorup (eds), *Rousseau and Revolution* (London: Continuum, 2011).

Lawless, John, *The Belfast Politics Enlarged; being a Compendium of the Political History of Ireland, for the last Forty Years* (Belfast: D. Lyons, 1818).

Lawless Lee, Grace, *The Huguenot Settlements in Ireland* (London: Longmans, 1936).

Leigh, R. A., *Unsolved Problems in the Bibliography of J-J. Rousseau* (Cambridge: Cambridge University Press, 1990).

Lewis, Gillian, 'The Geneva Academy', in Andrew Pettegree, Alastair Duke and Gillian Lewis (eds), *Calvinism in Europe, 1540–1620* (Cambridge: Cambridge University Press, 1994).

Lifschitz, Avi, *Engaging with Rousseau. Reaction and Interpetation from the Eighteenth Century to the Present* (Cambridge: Cambridge University Press, 2016).

Livesey, James, 'The Dublin Society in Eighteenth-Century Irish Political Thought', *The Historical Journal*, 47 (2004), 615–40.

Livesey, James, 'Free Trade and Empire in the Anglo-Irish Commercial Propositions of 1785', *Journal of British Studies*, 52 (2013), 103–27.

Lobban, Michael, 'Treason, Sedition, and the Radical Movement in the Age of the French Revolution', *Liverpool Law Review*, 22 (2000), 205–34.

Lottes, Günther, 'Radicalism, Revolution and Political Culture: An Anglo-French Comparison', in Mark Philp (ed.), *The French Revolution and British Popular Politics* (Cambridge: Cambridge University Press, 1991).

Lounissi, Carine, *La pensée politique de Thomas Paine en contexte: Théorie et pratique* (Paris: Honoré Champion, 2012).

Lüthy, Herbert, *La Banque protestante en France de la révocation de l'Édit de Nantes à la Révolution* (Paris, S. E. V. P. E. N., 1961), 2 vols.

MacInnes, Allan, 'Union Failed, Union Accomplished: The Irish Union of 1703 and the Scottish Union of 1707', in Dáire Keogh and Kevin Whelan (eds), *Acts of Union: The Causes, Contexts, and Consequences of the Act of Union* (Dublin: Four Courts Press, 2001).

Macleod, Emma Vincent, *A War of Ideas: British Attitudes to the Wars against Revolutionary France, 1792–1802* (Aldershot: Ashgate, 1998).

MacNevin, Thomas, *The History of the Volunteers of 1782* (Dublin: R. Martin & Co., 1845), 4th edn.

Madden, Richard R., *The United Irishmen. Their Lives and Times* (Dublin: James Duffy, 1858), 2nd edn, 4 vols.

Maire, Marguerite, 'Le '*Discours sur l'Histoire de Genève*' de Jacob Vernes', *Revue suisse d'histoire*, 11 (1931), 1–43.

Malcolmson, A.P.W., *John Foster: The Politics of the Anglo-Irish Ascendancy* (Oxford: Oxford University Press, 1978).

Malcolmson, A.P.W., 'Foster, John', *DIB*.

Manin, Bernard, *The Principles of Representative Government* (Cambridge: Cambridge University Press, 1995).

Margerison, Kenneth, 'Rogue Diplomacy: Sartine, Saint-Lubin and the French Attempt to Recover "Lost India", 1776–80', *French History*, 30 (2016), 477–504.

McBride, Ian, 'William Drennan and the Dissenting Tradition', in Dickson, Keogh and Whelan (eds), *The United Irishmen: Republicanism, Radicalism and Rebellion*, 49–61.

McBride, Ian, *Eighteenth Century Ireland. The Isle of Slaves* (Dublin: Gill and Macmillan, 2009).

McBride, Ian, '*The Case of Ireland* in Context: William Molyneux and his Critics', *Proceedings of the Royal Irish Academy*, 118C (2018), 1–30.

McCabe, Desmond, 'Cuffe, James' and 'Hartley, Travers', *DIB*.

McCormick, Ted, *William Petty: And the Ambitions of Political Arithmetic* (Oxford: Oxford University Press, 2009).

McDonald, Joan, *Rousseau and the French Revolution, 1762–1791* (London: Bloomsbury Academic, 1965).

McDowell, R. B., *Ireland in the Age of Imperialism and Revolution 1760–1801* (Oxford: Oxford University Press, 1979).

McGrath, Charles Ivar, 'Securing the Protestant Interest: The Origins and Purpose of the Penal Laws of 1695', *Irish Historical Studies*, 30 (1996–97), 25–46.

McGrath, Charles Ivar, 'The "Union" Representation of 1703 in the Irish House of Commons: A Case of Mistaken Identity?', *Eighteenth-Century Ireland/Iris an dá chultúr*, 23 (2008), 11–35.

McNally, Patrick, *Parties, Patriots and Undertakers: Parliamentary Politics in Early Hanoverian Ireland* (Dublin: Four Courts Press, 1997).

McNutt, Jennifer Powell, *Calvin Meets Voltaire. The Clergy of Geneva in the Age of Enlightenment, 1685–1798* (Farnham: Ashgate, 2013).

McNutt, Jennifer Powell and Richard Whatmore, 'The Attempts to Transfer the Genevan Academy to Ireland and to America, 1782–1795', *The Historical Journal*, 56 (2013), 345–68.

McParland, Edward, *James Gandon: Vitruvius Hibernicus* (London: A. Zwemmer, 1985).

M'Henry, James, *O'Halloran; or, the Insurgent Chief. A tale of the United Irishmen* (Belfast: John Henderson, 1847).

Mori, Jennifer, *The Culture of Diplomacy: Britain in Europe, c. 1750–1830* (Manchester: Manchester University Press, 2010).

Moriarty, Thomas F., 'The Irish Absentee Tax Controversy of 1773: Study of Anglo-Irish Politics on the Eve of the American Revolution', *Proceedings of the American Philosophical Society*, 118 (1974), 370–408.

Morley, Vincent, *Irish Opinion and the American Revolution, 1760–1783* (Cambridge: Cambridge University Press, 2007).

Morren, Pierre, *La vie lausannoise au 18 siècle: D'après Jean Henri Polier de Vernand, lieutenant Baillival* (Geneva: Labor et Fides, 1970).

Murray, A. L., 'Administration and the Law', in T. I. Rae (ed.), *The Union of 1707: Its Impact on Scotland* (Glasgow: Blackie, 1974), 30–57.

Nakhimovsky, Isaac, *The Closed Commercial State: Perpetual Peace and Commercial Society from Rousseau to Fichte* (Princeton, NJ: Princeton University Press, 2011).

Nakhimovsky, Isaac, 'The "Ignominious Fall of the European Commonwealth": Gentz, Hauterive, and the Armed Neutrality of 1800', in Koen Stapelbroek (ed.), *Trade and War: The Neutrality of Commerce in the Interstate System* (Helsinki: Collegium, 2011), 177–90.

Nelson, Eric, *The Greek Tradition in Republican Thought* (Cambridge: Cambridge University Press, 2004).

Nelson, Ivan F., 'The First Chapter of 1798?: Restoring a Military Perspective to the Irish Militia Riots of 1793', *Irish Historical Studies*, 33 (2003), 369–86.

Neuenschwander, Marc, 'Carrière et convictions', in Marc Neuenschwander, Bernard Lescaze and Gabriel Mützenberg, *Un Genevois méconnu: Julien Dentand (1736–1817)* (Geneva: Bulletin de la Société d'histoire et d'archéologie de Genève, vol. 16, Book 2, 1977), 137–61.

Neuenschwander, Marc, 'Solidaires et complices: Les gouvernements de Genève et Fribourg à la poursuite des séditieux' ('Imprimeurs de Genève et Carouge au service des gouvernements de Genève et de Fribourg à la poursuite des séditieux'), in Jean-Daniel Candaux and Bernard Lescaze (eds), *Cinq siècles d'imprimerie genevoise. Actes du Colloque international sur l'histoire de l'imprimerie et du livre à Genève, 27–30 avril 1978* (Geneva: Société d'histoire et d'archéologie, 1980–81), 2 vols, II, 157–84.

Neuenschwander, Marc, 'Les troubles de 1782 à Genève et le temps de l'émigration', *Bulletin de la société d'histoire et d'archéologie de Genève*, 19 (1989), 127–88.

Norris, John, *Shelburne and Reform* (New York: St Martin's Press, 1963).

O'Brien, George, 'The Irish Free Trade Agitation of 1779 (Part I),' *The English Historical Review*, 38 (1923), 564–81.

O'Brien, George, 'The Irish Free Trade Agitation of 1779 (Part II)', *The English Historical Review*, 39 (1924), 95–109.

O'Brien, Gerard, *Anglo-Irish Politics in the Age of Grattan and Pitt* (Dublin: Irish Academic Press, 1987).

O'Connor, Theresa M., 'The Embargo on the Export of Irish Provisions, 1776–9', *Irish Historical Studies*, 2 (1940), 3–11.

O'Donnell, Ruán, 'Murphy, John (1753–1798)' and 'Harvey, Beauchamp Bagenal (1762–1798)', *ODNB*.

O'Dwyer, Frederick, 'Gandon, James (1742–1823)', *ODNB*.

O'Gorman, Frank, *The Long Eighteenth Century: British Political and Social History 1688–1832* (London: Arnold, 1997).

O'Gorman, Frank, 'The Paine Burnings of 1792–1793', *Past & Present*, 193 (2006), 111–55.

O'Gorman, Frank, 'Shelburne: A Chathamite in Opposition and in Government 1760–82?', in Aston and Campbell Orr (eds), *An Enlightenment Statesman in Whig Britain*, 117–40.

O'Reilly, William, 'The Naturalisation Act of 1709 and the Settlement of Germans in Britain, Ireland and the Colonies', in Randolph Vigne and Charles Littleton (eds), *From Strangers to Citizens: the Integration of Immigrant Communities in Britain, Ireland, and colonial America, 1550–1750* (Brighton and Portland, OR: Sussex Academic Press, 2001), 292–302.

Odgers, William Blake, 'Sir William Blackstone', *Yale Law Journal* 28 (1919), 542–66.

Ohlmeyer, Jane H. (ed.), *Political Thought in Seventeenth-Century Ireland. Kingdom or Colony* (Cambridge: Cambridge University Press, 2000).

Orr, Clarissa Campbell, 'The Late Hanoverian Court and the Christian Enlightenment', in Michael Schaich (ed.), *Monarchy and Religion. The Transformation of Royal Culture in Eighteenth-Century Europe* (Oxford: Oxford University Press, 2007).

Orr, Clarissa Campbell, 'Aunts, Wives, Courtiers: The Ladies of Bowood', in Aston and Campbell Orr (eds), *An Enlightenment Statesman in Whig Britain*, 51–78.

Palmer, R. R., *The Age of the Democratic Revolution Age of the Democratic Revolution: A Political History of Europe and America, 1760–1800* (Princeton NJ: Princeton University Press, 1959) 2 vols.

Parker, Geoffrey, *Global Crisis: War, Climate Change and Catastrophe in the Seventeenth Century* (New Haven, CT: Yale University Press, 2013).

Pasquino, Pasquale, *Sieyès et l'invention de la constitution en France* (Paris, Éditions Odile Jacob, 1998).

Phelan, Robert, 'The New Geneva', *Munster Express*, 22 January 1999.

Phillips, Timothy R., 'The Dissolution of Francis Turretin's Vision of Theologia: Geneva at the End of the Seventeenth Century', in John B. Roney and Martin I. Klauber (eds), *The Identity of Geneva. The Christian Commonwealth, 1564–1864* (Westport, CT: Greenwood Press, 1998), 77–92.

Philp, Mark (ed.), *The British Response to the Threat of Invasion, 1797–1815* (Aldershot: Ashgate, 2006).

Philp, Mark, *Reforming Ideas in Britain: Politics and Language in the Shadow of the French Revolution, 1789–1815* (Cambridge: Cambridge University Press, 2014).

Pitassi, Maria-Cristina, *De l'orthodoxie aux Lumières. Genève 1670–1737* (Geneva: Labor et Fides, 1992).

Pitassi, Maria-Cristina, 'Le catéchisme de Jacob Vernes, ou comment enseigner aux fidèles un "christianisme sage et raisonnable"', *Dix-huitième siècle*, 34 (2002), 213–23.

Pitassi, Maria-Cristina, 'From Exemplarity to Suspicion. The Genevan Church between the Late Seventeenth and Early Eighteenth Centuries', *History of European Ideas*, 37 (2011), 16–22.

Piuz, Anne-Marie, Liliane Mottu-Weber et. al., *L'économie genevoise, de la Réforme à la fin de l'Ancien Régime XVIe et XVIIIe siècle* (Geneva: Georg: Société d'histoire et d'archéologie, 1990).

Plan, Danielle, *Un Génevois d'autrefois: Henri-Albert Gosse (1753–1816) d'après des lettres et des documents inédits* (Paris and Geneva: Fischbaker & Kundig, 1909).

Pocock. J.G.A., 'The Varieties of Whiggism from Exclusion to Reform: A History of Ideology and Discourse', in *Virtue, Commerce, and History: Essays on Political Thought and History, Chiefly in the Eighteenth Century* (Cambridge: Cambridge University Press, 1985), 215–310.

Pocock, J.G.A., 'Enthusiasm: The Antiself of Enlightenment', *Huntington Library Quarterly*, 60 (1997), 7–28.

Pocock, J.G.A., *Barbarism and Religion, Vol. 3: The First Decline and Fall* (Cambridge: Cambridge University Press, 2005).

Pocock, J.G.A., *The Machiavellian Moment: Florentine Political Thought and the Atlantic Republican Tradition* (Princeton, NJ: Princeton University Press, 2016 [orig. 1975]).

Podmore, Colin, *The Moravian Church in England, 1728–1760* (Oxford: Oxford University Press, 1998).

Podmore, Colin J., 'Hutton, James (1715–1795)', *ODNB*.

Polasky, Janet, *Revolutions without Borders. The Call to Liberty in the Atlantic World* (New Haven, CT and London: Yale University Press, 2015).

Porret, Michel, *Sur la scène du crime: Pratique pénale, enquête et expertises judiciaires à Genève (XVIIe–XIXe siècle)* (Montreal: Les Presses de l'Université de Montréal, 2008).

Porter, Roy, *English Society in the Eighteenth Century* (London: Penguin, 1982).

Powell, Martyn J., *Britain and Ireland in the Eighteenth-Century Crisis of Empire* (London: Palgrave, 2002).

Powell, Martyn J., 'Charles James Fox and Ireland', *Irish Historical Studies*, 33 (2002), 169–90.

Powell, Martyn J., 'The Society of Free Citizens and Other Popular Political Clubs, 1749–89', in James Kelly and Martyn J. Powell (eds), *Clubs and Societies in Eighteenth-Century Ireland* (Dublin: Four Courts Press, 2010), 243–63.

Powell, Martyn J., 'Shelburne and Ireland: Politician, Patriot, Absentee', in Aston and Campbell Orr (eds), *An Enlightenment Statesman in Whig Britain*, 141–59.

Powell, Martyn J., 'Consumption: Commercial Demand and the Challenges to Regulatory Power in Eighteenth-Century Ireland', in Philip J. Stern and Carl Wennerlind (eds), *Mercantilism Reimagined. Political Economy in Early Modern Britain and Its Empire* (Oxford: Oxford University Press, 2013), 282–304.

Power, T. P., and K. Whelan (eds), *Endurance and Emergence: Catholics in Ireland in the Eighteenth Century* (Dublin: Irish Academic Press, 1990).

Prest, Wilfrid, *Blackstone: Law and Letters in the Eighteenth Century* (Oxford: Oxford University Press, 2008).

Price, Munro, *Preserving the Monarchy: The Comte de Vergennes, 1774–1787* (Cambridge: Cambridge University Press, 1995).

Reverdin, Olivier, *Genève au temps de la révocation de 'l'Édit de Nantes 1680–1705* (Geneva: Droz, 1985).

Rivier, Jean-Marc, *Étienne Clavière (1735–1793). Un révolutionnaire, ami des Noirs* (Paris: Panormitis, 2006).

Rivier-Rose, Théodore, *La famille Rivier (1595 à nos jours)* (Lausanne: Imprimeries réunies, 1916).

Rivoire, Émile, *Bibliographie historique de Genève au XVIIIème siècle* (Geneva: J. Julien, 1897), 2 vols.

Robbins, Caroline, *The Eighteenth-Century Commonwealthman: Studies in the Transmission, Development, and Circumstance of English Liberal Thought from the Restoration of Charles II Until the War with the Thirteen Colonies* (Cambridge, MA: Harvard University Press, 1959).

Robertson, John, 'Andrew Fletcher's Vision of Union', in Roger Mason (ed.), *Scotland and England, 1286–1815* (Edinburgh: John Donald, 1987).

Rosenblatt, Helena, *Rousseau and Geneva. From the First Discourse to the Social Contract, 1749–1762* (Cambridge: Cambridge University Press, 1997).

Rosenblatt, Helena, '"Colonnes de la patrie" ou "froids égoïstes": Les capitalistes genevois vus de chez eux', *Revue suisse d'histoire*, 50 (2000), 304–24.

Ross, Ian Simpson, *The Life of Adam Smith* (Oxford: Oxford University Press, 2010), 2nd edn.

Rothschild, Emma, 'Language and Empire, c. 1800', *Historical Research*, 78 (2005), 208–29.

Rothstein, Nathalie, 'Huguenot Master Weavers: Exemplary Englishmen, 1700–c. 1750', in Randolph Vigne and Charles Littleton (eds), *From Strangers to Citizens. The Integration of Immigrant Communities in Britain, Ireland and Colonial America, 1550–1750* (Brighton and Portland, OR: Sussex Academic Press, 2001), 160–74.

Rouse, Ruth and Stephen C. Neill (eds), *A History of the Ecumenical Movement: 1517–1948* (Philadelphia, 1967).

Ryder, Michael, 'The Bank of Ireland, 1721: Land, Credit and Dependency', *The Historical Journal*, 25 (1982), 557–82.

Ryland, Richard Hopkins, *The History, Topography and Antiquities of the County and City of Waterford: With an Account of the Present State of the Peasantry of that Part of the South of Ireland* (London: J. Murray, 1824).

Sayles, G. O., 'Contemporary Sketches of the Members of the Irish Parliament in 1782', *Proceedings of the Royal Irish Academy*, 56C (1954), 227–86.

Schofield, Philip, *Utility and Democracy: The Political Thought of Jeremy Bentham* (Oxford: Oxford University Press, 2006).

Schroeder, Paul W., *The Transformation of European Politics, 1763–1848* (Oxford: Oxford University Press, 1994).

Scurr, Ruth, *Fatal Purity: Robespierre and the French Revolution* (New York: Henry Holt, 2006).

Seaward, Louise, 'Censorship through Cooperation: The *Société typographique de Neuchâtel* (STN) and the French Government, 1769–89', *French History*, 28 (2014), 23–42.

Seaward, Louise, 'The Small Republic and the Great Power: Censorship between Geneva and France in the Later Eighteenth Century', *The Library*, 18 (2017), 191–217.

Sharp, James A., *A new gazetteer, or, Topographical dictionary of the British Islands and narrow seas: comprising concise descriptions of about sixty thousand places, seats, natural features, and objects of note* (London: Longman, Brown, Green and Longmans, 1852), 2 vols.

Shovlin, John, 'Toward a Reinterpretation of Revolutionary Anti-Nobilism: The Political Economy of Honor in the Old Regime', *Journal of Modern History*, 72 (2000), 35–66.

Shovlin, John, *The Political Economy of Virtue: Luxury, Patriotism, and the Origins of the French Revolution* (Ithaca, NY: Cornell University Press, 2006).

Simms, J. G., *William Molyneux of Dublin* (Dublin: Irish Academic Press, 1982).

Skinner, Quentin, *Liberty before Liberalism* (Cambridge: Cambridge University Press, 1998).

Skinner, Quentin, 'A Third Concept of Liberty', *Proceedings of the British Academy*, 117 (2002), 237–68.

Skinner, Quentin, 'A Genealogy of the Modern 'State', *Proceedings of the British Academy*, 162 (2009), 325–70.

Skinner, Quentin, 'On the Liberty of the Ancients and the Moderns: A Reply to my Critics', *Journal of the History of Ideas*, 73 (2012), 127–46.

Small, Stephen, *Political Thought in Ireland, 1776—1798: Republicanism, Patriotism, and Radicalism* (Oxford: Oxford University Press, 2010).

Smith, E. A., *Whig Principles and Party Politics. Earl Fitzwilliam and the Whig Party, 1748–1833* (Manchester: Manchester University Press, 1975).

Smout, T. C., *Scottish Trade on the Eve of the Union* (Edinburgh: Oliver & Boyd, 1963).

Smyth, Jim *Men of No Property: Irish Radicals and Popular Politics in the Late Eighteenth Century* (London: Macmillan, 1992).

Smyth, Jim, '"Like amphibious animals": Irish Patriots, Ancient Britons, 1691–1707', *The Historical Journal*, 36 (1993), 785–97.

Smyth, Jim, ' Republicanism before the United Irishmen: The Case of Dr Charles Lucas', in D. George Boyce, Robert Eccleshall and Vincent Geoghegan (eds), *Political Discourse in Seventeenth- and Eighteenth-Century Ireland* (Basingstoke: Palgrave, 2001), 240–56.

Smyth, P.D.H., 'The Volunteers and Parliament, 1779–1784', in Thomas Bartlett and David Hayton (eds), *Penal Era and Golden Age: Essays in Irish History, 1690–1800* (Belfast: Ulster Historical Foundation, 1979), 113–36.

Sneddon, Andrew, 'Legislating for Economic Development: Irish Fisheries as a Case Study in the Limitations of "Improvement"', in David Hayton, James Kelly and John Bergin (eds), The *Eighteenth-Century Composite State: Representative Institutions in Ireland and Europe, 1689–1800* (Basingstoke: Palgrave Macmillan, 2010).

Sonenscher, Michael 'The Nation's Debt and the Birth of the Modern Republic: The French Fiscal Deficit and the Politics of the Revolution of 1789', *History of Political Thought*, 18 (1997), 63–103, 267–325.

Sonenscher, Michael, *Sans-Culottes: An Eighteenth-Century Emblem in the French Revolution* (Princeton, NJ: Princeton University Press, 2008).

Spangenberg, August Gottlieb, *The life of Nicholas Lewis, Count Zinzendorf, Bishop and Ordinary of the Church of the United (or Moravian) Brethren*, trans. Samuel Jackson (London: Samuel Holdsworth, 1838).

Stanhope, Ghita, and G. P Gooch, *The Life of Charles, Third Earl Stanhope* (London: Longmans, Green & Co., 1914).

Stedman Jones, Gareth, *An End to Poverty? A Historical Debate* (New York: Columbia University Press, 2004).

Stewart, A.T.Q., *A Deeper Silence, The Hidden Origins of the United Irishmen* (Belfast: Blackstaff Press, 1993).

Storrs, Christopher, 'British Diplomacy in Switzerland (1689–1789) and Eighteenth Century Diplomatic Culture', *Études de lettres*, 3 (2010), 181–216.

Swenson, James, *On Jean-Jacques Rousseau Considered as One of the First Authors of the Revolution* (Stanford, CA: Stanford University Press, 2000).

Swords, Liam, *The Green Cockade. The Irish in the French Revolution 1789–1815* (Dublin: Glendale, 1989).

Talmon, J. L., *The Origins of Totalitarian Democracy* (London: Secker & Warburg, 1960).

Thomson, Ann, 'Thomas Paine and the United Irishmen', *Études irlandaises* (1991), 109–120.

Thourel, Albin, *Histoire de Genève depuis son origine jusqu'à nos jours* (Geneva: Collin, 1832–33), 3 vols.

Truxes, Thomas M., *Irish-American Trade 1660–1783* (Cambridge: Cambridge University Press, 1988).

Tuck, Richard, 'From Rousseau to Kant', in Béla Kapossy, Isaac Nakhimovsky, Sophus A. Reinert and Richard Whatmore (eds), *Markets, Morals, Politics. Jealousy of Trade and the History of Political Thought* (Cambridge, MA, Harvard University Press, 2018).

Tunbridge, Paul A., 'Jean André Deluc, FRS, 1727–1817', *Notes and Records of the Royal Society*, 26 (1971).

Venturi, Franco, *Settecento riformatore. La prima crisi dell'Antico Regime (1768–1776)* (Turin: Einaudi, 1979).

Wahman, Dror, *The Making of the Modern Self: Identity and Culture in Eighteenth-Century England* (New Haven, CT: Yale University Press, 2004).

Walker, Corinne, 'Les lois somptuaires ou le rêve d'un ordre social. Évolution et enjeux de la politique somptuaire à Genève (XVIe-XVIIIe siècles)', *Equinoxe*, 11 (1994), 111–29.

Walker, Corinne, 'Les pratiques de la richesse. Riches Genevois au XVIII', in J. Berchtold and M. Porret (eds), *Être riche au siècle de Voltaire* (Geneva: Droz, 1996), 135–60.

Whatley, C. A., 'The Economic Causes and Consequences of the Union of 1707: A Survey', *The Scottish Historical Review*, 68 (1989), 150–81.

Whatmore, Richard '"A gigantic manliness": Paine's Republicanism in the 1790s', in Stefan Collini, Richard Whatmore and Brian Young (eds), *Economy, Polity and Society: British Intellectual History, 1750–1950* (Cambridge: Cambridge University Press, 2000).

Whatmore, Richard, 'Shelburne and Perpetual Peace: Small States, Commerce and International Relations within the Bowood Circle', in Aston & Campbell Orr (eds), *An Enlightenment Statesman in Whig Britain*, 249–73.

Whatmore, Richard, *Against War and Empire. Geneva, Britain and France in the Eighteenth Century* (New Haven, CT: Yale University Press, 2012).

Whatmore, Richard, '"A lover of peace more than liberty". The Genevan Response to Rousseau's Politics', in Avi Lifshitz (ed.), *Engaging with Rousseau: Reception and Interpretation from the Eighteenth Century to the Present* (Cambridge: Cambridge University Press, 2016).

Whatmore, Richard, 'Geneva and Scotland: The Calvinist Legacy and After', *Intellectual History Review*, 26 (2016), 391–409.

Whatmore, Richard, 'Liberty, War and Empire. Overcoming the Rich State–Poor State Problem, 1789–1815', in Béla Kapossy, Isaac Nakhimovsky and Richard Whatmore (eds), *Commerce and Peace in the Enlightenment* (Cambridge: Cambridge University Press, 2017).

Whatmore, Richard, 'Saving Republics by Moving Republicans. Britain, Ireland and "New Geneva" in the Age of Revolutions', *History. The Journal of the Historical Association*, 102 (2017), 386–413.

Wheatley, Henry B. (ed.), *The Historical and the Posthumous Memoirs of Sir Nathaniel William Wraxall, 1772–1784* (London: Bickers & son, 1884), 5 vols.

Wheeler H.F.B. and A. M. Broadley, *The War in Wexford; An Account of the Rebellion in the South of Ireland in 1798 Told from Original Documents* (London: John Lane, 1910).

Whelan, Kevin, 'The Role of the Catholic Priest in the 1798 Rebellion in County Wexford', in Kevin Whelan and William Nolan (eds), *Wexford: History and Society* (Dublin: Geography Publications, 1987), 296–315.

Whelan, Kevin, 'The Republic in the Village: The United Irishmen, the Enlightenment and Popular Culture', in *The Tree of Liberty. Radicalism, Catholicism and the Construction of Irish Identity 1760–1830* (Cork: Cork University Press, 1996), 59–98.

Woods, James C. J., 'Caldwell, Andrew', *DIB*.

Unpublished Dissertations and PhD Theses

Banke, Rachel, 'Bute's Empire: Reform, Reaction, and the Roots of Imperial Crisis', PhD thesis, University of Notre Dame, 2017

Bennett, Angela C., 'The Stanhopes in Geneva: A Study of an English Noble Family in Genevan Politics and Society, 1764–1774', MA dissertation, University of Kent, 1992.

Ferguson, K. P., 'The Army in Ireland from the Restoration to the Act of Union', PhD thesis, Trinity College Dublin, 1980.

Klauber, Martin I., 'The Context and Development of the Views of Jean-Alphonse Turrettini (1671–1737) on Religious Authority', PhD thesis, University of Wisconsin, 1987.

Lammey, David, 'A Study of Anglo-Irish Relations between 1772 and 1782 with Particular Reference to the "Free Trade" Movement', PhD thesis, Queen's University Belfast, 1984.

Murphy, Craig C., 'Benjamin Vaughan (1751–1835): The Life of an Anglo-American Intellectual', PhD thesis, Columbia University, 1989.

O'Connor, Stephen, 'The Volunteers 1778–1793: Iconography and Identity', PhD thesis, National University of Ireland, Maynooth, 2008.

O'Mara, Patrick, 'Geneva in the Eighteenth Century: A Socio-Economic Study of the Bourgeois City-State During its Golden Age,' PhD thesis, University of California, Berkeley, 1954.

Stafford, James, 'Political Economy and the Reform of Empire in Ireland, 1776–1845', PhD thesis, University of Cambridge, 2016.

INDEX

A NOTE ON THE TYPE

THIS BOOK has been composed in Miller, a Scotch Roman typeface designed by Matthew Carter and first released by Font Bureau in 1997. It resembles Monticello, the typeface developed for The Papers of Thomas Jefferson in the 1940s by C. H. Griffith and P. J. Conkwright and reinterpreted in digital form by Carter in 2003.

Pleasant Jefferson ("P. J.") Conkwright (1905–1986) was Typographer at Princeton University Press from 1939 to 1970. He was an acclaimed book designer and AIGA Medalist.

The ornament used throughout this book was designed by Pierre Simon Fournier (1712–1768) and was a favorite of Conkwright's, used in his design of the *Princeton University Library Chronicle*.

Lightning Source UK Ltd.
Milton Keynes UK
UKHW011057121121
393837UK00002B/9

9 780691 206646